SAŠA ŽIKOVIĆ

MARKET RISK IN TRANSITION COUNTRIES – VALUE AT RISK APPROACH

Saša Žiković

MARKET RISK IN TRANSITION COUNTRIES – VALUE AT RISK APPROACH

efri

FACULTY OF ECONOMICS UNIVERSITY OF RIJEKA
RIJEKA, 2010.

Published 2010

Faculty of Economics University of Rijeka
I. Filipovica 4, 51000 Rijeka
Croatia

Solutio Ltd,
Pehlin 74/1, 51000 Rijeka
Croatia

Email (for orders and customer service enquiries): solutio@ri.t-com.hr

This publication is designed to provide accurate and authoritative information in regard to the subject matter covered. It is sold on the understanding that the Publisher is not engaged in rending professional services. If professional advice or other expert assistance is required, the services of a competent professional should be sought.

National Library Cataloging-in-Publication Data

Žiković, Saša
Market Risk in Transition Countries – Value at Risk Approach / Saša Žiković.
394 p. 24 cm.
Includes bibliographical references and index.

ISBN: 978-953-6148-87-5 (Faculty of Economics University of Rijeka)
ISBN: 978-953-7332-05-1 (Solutio Ltd)
I. Risk management
II. Transition countries

120405062

Typeset in 11/12pt Times

TABLE OF CONTENTS

Preface
Acknowledgments

PREFACE

Financial markets offer the ideal testing ground for new statistical ideas. The fact that there is a large number of participants, with divergent anticipations and interests, simultaneously present in these markets, leads to unpredictable behaviour. In the last decade, financial institutions have greatly increased their holdings of trading assets, such as equities, bonds, interest rate and equity derivatives, foreign exchange and commodity positions. Their motive in this has been to make trading profits and to hedge exposures elsewhere in their portfolios. The increase in the relative importance of market risk in bank portfolios has obliged regulators to reconsider the system of capital requirements agreed in the 1988 Basle Capital Accord. The common framework for treating risk laid down by the 1988 Accord was designed primarily for limiting credit risk and had clear drawbacks in its treatment of market risk. These problems led the European Commission and the Basle Supervisors' Committee to study alternative ways of treating trading book positions. The European Commission's Capital Adequacy Directive (CAD), agreed on in 1993 and introduced at the beginning of 1996, established EU minimum capital requirements for the trading books of banks and securities firms. The Basle Committee proposals were summarized in a paper issued in January 1996 entitled "Overview of the Amendment of the Capital Accord to Incorporate Market Risks".

One of the most significant advances in the past two decades in the field of measuring and managing market risk has been the development and the ever-growing use of Value at Risk (VaR) methodology for measuring risks. VaR methodology was specifically developed for measuring and managing risk of portfolios across the entire financial institution. VaR represents a method of assessing risk using standard statistics, commonly used in technical fields. VaR measures the worst expected loss over a given horizon under normal market conditions at a given confidence level. Due to the Basel Committee's approval for using internally developed VaR models for measuring market risk in 1996, a large number of different approaches to calculating VaR figures have been developed. The three main approaches to calculating VaR estimates are: the Parametric, the Nonparametric and the Semi-parametric (hybrid) approach. Each of these approaches has its own advantages and disadvantages, and none of them is superior to others in all the circumstances and markets.

The main advantage of VaR as a risk measure is that it is very simple and can be used to summarize the risks of individual positions, and/or the risk of a large internationally diversified portfolio. Although there is an abundance of articles and books regarding VaR and market risk measurement and management, all of the existing models are developed and tested on mature, developed and liquid markets. Theoretical investigation and quantitative testing of VaR models in other, less developed or developing financial market is, at best, scarce. This is exactly the area that this book aims to fill. Since most of the transition countries are all exposed to very similar processes of strong inflow of foreign direct and portfolio investments, and offer possibilities of huge profits for investors, these countries represent a very interesting opportunity for foreign and domestic banks, investment funds, insurance companies and other institutional investors. Banks and investment funds when investing in these financial markets employ the same risk measurement models for measuring market risk and forming of provision as they do in the developed markets.

When using VaR models, which are created and suited for developed and liquid markets, in these, developing markets some important questions arise: *Do the VaR models, developed and tested in the developed and liquid financial markets, apply to the volatile and shallow financial markets of transition countries? Do the commonly used VaR models adequately capture market risk of these markets or do they only give a false sense of security?*

Employing VaR models in forming bank's provisions that are not suited to developing markets can have serious consequences and can result in big losses in portfolio that could pass undetected by the employed risk measurement models, leaving thus the financial institutions unprepared. Banks could also be penalized by the regulators, via higher scaling factor when forming their market risk provisions, due to the use of a faulty risk measurement model.

This book provides a cutting-edge overview of VaR estimation. Given the size and rate of growth of VaR literature, it is virtually impossible to cover this field completely and comprehensively. Within the focus of this book, i.e. measuring market risk, the coverage of the literature provided in this book is fairly extensive, but can only provide, a rather subjective view of the main highlights of the risk literature.

The book is intended for two main audiences. The first group consists of practicioners in risk measurement and management; people developing, testing (backtesting) and using VaR measurement. The second, consists of students in MBA, MA, MSc and professional programmes in the field of quantitative finance, risk measurement and related subject, where this book can be used as a textbook. The understanding of this book requires basic knowledge of statistics (especially distribution functions and regression analysis), mathematics, finance (especially financial engineering and derivatives theory) and computing. I presume the reader is familiar with the assumptions underlying the use of ordinary least squares, concepts of correlation and covariance. It is presumed that the reader is familiar with the use of t-tests and F-tests in a regression framework. The terms such as mean square error, significance level and unbiased estimate are used without explaining their meaning. Most academics and practicioners should have no trouble with the text, but students should first master basic econometrics and finance. To reexamine and test the findings from this book it is necessary to have access to software packages, such as MATLAB, GAUSS, STATA, SAS, RATS or EVIEWS.

It is my hope that this research will give banks and other investors operating in the financial markets of transition countries an inside view into the true nature of risk in these markets and help them in developing in-house VaR models. With the selection of a correct VaR model in forming of capital requirements, financial institutions can be protected from unexpected market losses. Futhermore they can save considerable amounts of money by forming lower market risk provisions than required under the Basel standardized approach, when the market allows it. It is my desire that this book and research into market risk measurement and modelling will inspire further research of this and other related fields.

The book is divided in two parts - the chapters discussing the nature of risk, regulatory framework behind risk measurement and management as well as risk measurement methods and approaches, and the empirical investigation on the implementation and performance of VaR models in the turbulent and illiquid stock markets of transition countries.

The book is composed of six chapters. The first chapter of the book serves as an introduction to the nature and theory of financial risk. The basic notions in risk management are presented as well as the explanation and description of the basic forms of risks encountered in banking. The second chapter presents the development of current Basel rules for measuring and managing market risk in banks. It also presents the two available approaches of calculating provisions for market risk. The main advantages and disadvantages of both the standardized and internal approach are analysed and discussed. This part of the book concludes with an overview of risk measurement and management importance, characteristics and practices in the banking sector of transition countries. The third chapter deals with the Value at Risk (VaR) as a method of calculating capital charge for market risk. The definition, historical development and the rationale behind Value at Risk are presented. Possible opportunities for using Value at Risk method beyond market risk measurement are also presented and discussed. The third chapter concludes with the presentation of the main advantages and disadvantages of Value at Risk as a method of measuring market risk. In the fourth chapter, the theoretical basis for the understanding and development of Value at Risk models is presented. This chapter begins with the explanation of time series models used in financial engineering and risk management. Special attention is given to generalized autoregressive heteroskedasticity (GARCH) models. The fourth chapter continues with the theoretical explanation and rationale of parametric and nonparametric models to calculating VaR. In the last part of this chapter a family of semi parametric VaR models is presented. In this part of the book the author develops a new semi parametric VaR model, called Hybrid Historical simulation (HHS). Fifth chapter deals with backtesting of the VaR forecasts and introduces the best-known and newest methods of backtesting and evaluating VaR estimates. Advantages and disadvantages of each backtesting procedure are presented and discussed in detail. Chapter six represents an empirical analysis of selected VaR models presented and discussed in this book. The summary of empirical research into VaR is presented. Characteristics of analysed stock indexes from transition countries are presented and obtained results are discussed. Data, methodology, as well as VaR and volatility forecasting models used in the testing of stock indexes are explained in detail. The sixth chapter concludes with the actual backtesting across different criteria of the selected VaR models as well as the new VaR model presented in Chapter 4.

ACKNOWLEDGMENTS

Many people have contributed to this book over the years. I first encountered the VaR during my M.Sc. study at the Faculty of Economics in Ljubljana, Slovenia. Probably the greatest help and inspiration in my research of risk was Kevin Dowd's book "Measuring Market Risk" and Barry Schachter's website www.gloriamundi.org. I am very gratefull to my mentors: prof. Ivan Ribnikar and prof. Marko Košak for their support and help while writing my PhD thesis. I would also like to thank prof. Antun Jurman for whom I worked as an assistant on a number of courses.

My view of the subjects covered in this book would not have been the same without my friends from KD Bank and Abank Vipa; Dejan Divjak and Polona Černilec.

I am gratefull to my great friend prof. Mario Pečarić, prof. Zdenko Prohaska and prof. Helena Blažić who encouraged me to write this book.

Special gratitude goes to my friend and investment wizard Boris Sorgo. I would also like to thank Tanja for her support and understanding. I am thankful to my grandmother Margareta Bujan for her wisdom and support. Most of all, I am gratefull to my mother Sonja Bujan for her encouragement, faith and love.

1   INTRODUCTION

"Randomness stems from our incomplete knowledge of reality, from the lack of information which forbids a perfect prediction of the future: randomness arises from complexity, from the fact that causes are diverse, that tiny perturbations may result in large effects. For over a century now, Science has abandoned Laplace's deterministic vision, and has fully accepted the task of deciphering randomness and inventing adequate tools for its description. The surprise is that, after all, randomness has many facets and that there are many levels to uncertainty, but, above all, that a new form of predictability appears, which is no longer deterministic but statistical."

(Bouchaud, Potters, 2001)

Over the past 20 years, many corporations have found it less costly to raise money from the public (by issuing bonds) than to borrow directly from banks. Banks have found themselves competing more and more fiercely, reducing their profit margins, and lending in larger sizes, longer maturities, and to customers of lower credit quality. Customers, on their part, are demanding more sophisticated and complicated ways to finance their activities, to hedge their financial risks, and to invest their liquid assets. In some cases, they are simply looking for ways to reduce their risk exposure. In other instances, they are willing to assume additional risk, if they are properly compensated for it, in order to enhance the yield of their portfolio.

Banks are, therefore, increasingly engaged in what might be called "risk shifting" activities. These activities demand increasing expertise and know-how in controlling and pricing the risks that banks manage in the financial market. As the banking industry has evolved, the managerial emphasis has shifted away from considerations of profit and maturity intermediation (usually measured in terms of the spread between the interest paid on loans and the cost of funding) toward risk intermediation. Risk intermediation implies a consideration of both the profits and the risks associated with banking activities. It is no longer sufficient to charge a high interest rate on a loan; the relevant question is whether the interest charged compensates the bank appropriately for the risk that it has assumed. The change in emphasis from simplistic profit-oriented management to risk/return management can also be seen in non-bank corporations. Many major corporations are now engaged in active risk management. Of course, risk was always a major consideration in deciding whether to take advantage of investment opportunities. However, rejecting projects because they seem to be risky can lead companies to reject investment opportunities that in fact offer excellent returns. The real problem is how to quantify risk and price it appropriately.

1.1   Role of risk measurement and management in modern banking

Financial institutions are specialists in risk management. Their primary expertise stems from their ability to both measure and manage risk exposure on their own behalf and on behalf of their clients - either through the evolution of financial market products to shift risks or through the absorption of their clients' risk onto their own balance sheets. Because financial institutions are risk intermediaries, they maintain an inventory of risk that must be measured carefully so as to ensure that the risk exposure does not threaten the intermediary's solvency. Thus, accurate measurement of risk is an essential first step for proper risk management, and financial intermediaries, because of the nature of their business, tend to be leading developers of new risk measurement techniques. In the past, many of models for measuring risks were internal models, developed in-house by financial institutions. In the banking industry there has been a significant widening of the focus, from the traditional qualitative risk assessment toward a quantitative measurement of risks, due to evolving risk practices and central bank regulation. Risk measurement requires capturing both the source of the risk and the magnitude of potential adverse effect on profitability, where profitability refers to both accounting and mark-to-market measures. Risk can be broadly defined as hazard, a chance of bad consequences, loss or exposure to mischance. Risk can also be defined as any event or action that may adversely affect an organisation's ability to achieve its objectives and execute it strategies, or the quantifiable likelihood of loss or less-than-expected returns (McNeil, Frey, Embrechts, 2005, p.1). Financial risk can be defined as a probability of occurrence of unwanted financial results and consequences. Bessis (2002) defines risk as uncertainties resulting in adverse variations of profitability or in losses (Bessis, 2002, p. 11). In the field of finance it is usual to distinguish between market, credit, liquidity, operational and legal risks. All these risks could generate losses that would be more or less prejudicial for an institution or for a single investor. Moreover, even if these definitions of risk given by (McNeil, Frey, Embrechts, 2005) and Bessis (2002) are very close to the definition of uncertainty it is necessary to distinguish between these two concepts. Uncertainty corresponds to a situation where the decisions of every economic agent depend on exogenous factors whose states could not be predicted with certainty (Meyfredi, 2004, p. 1). Only when uncertainty could be quantified, i.e. when it is possible to assign a probability distribution, it is possible to speak about risk. Finally, dealing with risk requires answers to two questions: How much can a bank lose? and What is the probability that this loss will occur? Risk constitutes an important field of research that has been of increasing interest in the last ten years. There are at least two reasons for handling risk. Firstly, there is a necessity for the decision-maker to act with full knowledge of the facts. Secondly, risk must be limited and also managed. A bad assessment could lead to bankruptcy or even to a systemic crisis. Recent history is full of outstanding examples: the stock market crash of '87, Barings Bank, Orange County, Daiwa and LTCM are some typical cases.

1.2   Financial risks in banking

1.2.1   Types of financial risks

Firms are exposed to various types of risk, which can broadly be classified into business and nonbusiness risks. Business risks are those that the corporation willingly assumes to create a competitive advantage and add value for shareholders. Business, or operating, risk pertains to the product market in which a firm operates and includes technological innovations, product design and marketing. Operating leverage, involving the degree of fixed versus variable costs, is also largely a choice variable. Judicious exposure to business risk is a core competency of all business activity. Business activities also include exposure to macroeconomic risks, which result from economic cycles, or fluctuations in incomes and monetary policies.

Other risks, over which firms have no control, can be grouped into nonbusiness risks. These include strategic risks, which result from fundamental shifts in the economy or political environment. These risks are difficult to hedge, except by diversifying across business lines and countries. Finally, financial risks can be defined as those that relate to possible losses in financial markets, such as losses due to interest rate movements or defaults on financial obligations. Exposure to financial risks can be optimised carefully so that firms can concentrate on what they do best - manage exposure to business risks (Jorion, 2001, p. 4).

In contrast to industrial corporations, the primary function of financial institutions is to manage financial risks actively. The purpose of financial institutions is to assume, intermediate, or advise on financial risks. These institutions realize that they must measure sources of risk as precisely as possible in order to control and properly price risks. Understanding risk means that financial managers can consciously plan for the consequences of adverse outcomes and, by so doing, be better prepared for the inevitable uncertainty.

Due to the growing variety and complexity of financial risks in modern banking industry, a large number of classifications and types of financial risks can be found in literature. One of the widely used classifications of financial risks is presented in figure 1.

Figure 1– Schematic presentation, by categories, of risk exposure in a bank

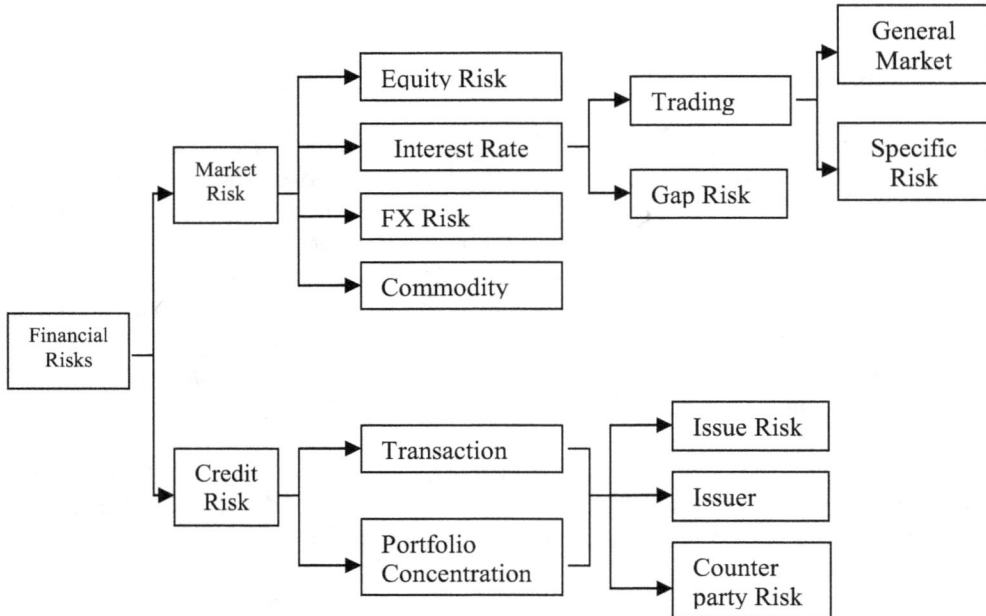

Source: Crouhy Michael, Galai Dan, Mark Robert: Risk Management. New York: McGraw-Hill, 2001. p. 39.

This, often used, classification is somewhat simplistic since every financial institution is exposed to numerous other risks. In the reminder of this chapter the most important risks in financial industry (Jorion, 2001, p. 15, Saunders, Cornett, 2003, p.138, McNeil, Frey, Embrechts, 2005, p. 2-3) will be explained in greater detail:

- credit risk,
- market risk (position risk, interest rate risk, foreign exchange risk, commodity risk),
- operational risk,
- liquidity risk,
- country risk,
- performance risk,
- solvency risk and
- model risk.

1.2.2   Credit risk

Credit risk is the first of all risks in terms of importance for a bank. Default risk, a major source of loss, is the risk that customers default, meaning that they fail to comply with their obligations to service debt. Default triggers a total or partial loss of any amount lent to the counterparty. Credit risk is also the risk of a decline in the credit standing of an obligor of the issuer of a bond or stock (McNeil, Frey, Embrechts, 2005, p. 326). Such deterioration does not imply default, but it does imply that the probability of default increases. In the market universe, a deterioration of the credit standing of a borrower does materialize into a loss because it triggers an upward move of the required market yield to compensate the higher risk and triggers a value decline. Issuer risk designates the obligors' credit risk, to make it distinct from the specific risk of a particular issue, among several of the same issuer, depending on the nature of the instrument and its credit mitigants (seniority level and guarantees).

Credit risk is critical since the default of a small number of important customers can generate large losses, potentially leading to insolvency of the bank. There are various default events, such as: delay in payment obligations, restructuring of debt obligations due to a major deterioration of the credit standing of the borrower and bankruptcies. Simple delinquencies, or payment delays, do not turn out as plain defaults, with a durable inability of lenders to face debt obligations. Many are resolved within a short period. Restructuring is very close to default because it results from the view that the borrower will not be able to pay his obligations unless its funding structure changes. Plain defaults imply that the non-payment will be permanent (Jorion, 2001, p. 16). Bankruptcies, possibly liquidation of the firm or merging with an acquiring firm, are possible outcomes. They all trigger significant losses. Default means any situation other than a simple delinquency. Credit risk is difficult to quantify on an ex ante basis, since it is necessary to assess the likelihood of a default event and of the recoveries under default, which are context-dependent. In addition, banking portfolios benefit from diversification effects, which are much more difficult to capture because of the scarcity of data on interdependencies between default events of different borrowers.

Financial markets value the credit risk of issuers and borrowers through pricing. Unlike loans, the credit risk of traded debts is also indicated by the specialized agencies' ratings (the most famous ones are: Moody's, Standard & Poor's (S&P), Fitch etc.), assessing the quality of public debt issues, or through changes of the value of their stocks. Credit risk is also visible through credit spreads, the add-ons to the risk-free rate defining the required market risk yield on debts. The capability of trading market assets mitigates the credit risk since there is no need to hold these securities until the deterioration of credit risk materializes into effective losses. If the credit standing of the obligor declines, it is still possible to sell these instruments in the market at a lower value. The loss due to credit risk depends on the value of these instruments and their liquidity. If the default is unexpected, the loss is the difference between the pre- and post-default prices. The faculty of trading the assets limits the loss if sale occurs before default and the selling price depends on the market liquidity. Therefore, there is a clear interaction between credit risk and market risk. For over-the-counter instruments, such as derivatives (e.g. swaps and options), whose development has been spectacular in the recent period, sale is not readily feasible and the bank faces the risk of losing the value of such instruments when it is positive. Since this value varies constantly with the market parameters, credit risk changes with market movements during the entire residual life of the instrument.

Even though procedures for dealing with credit risk have existed since banks started lending, credit risk measurement raises several issues (Bessis, 2002, p. 14). The major credit risk components are exposure, likelihood of default, or of a deterioration of the credit standing, and the recoveries percentage under default. Scarcity of data makes the assessment of these components a real challenge for practitioners.

Ratings are traditional measures of the credit quality of debt. Some major features of ratings systems are (Bessis, 2002, p. 14-15):

- Ratings are ordinal or relative measures of risk rather than cardinal or absolute measures, such as default probability.
- External ratings of rating agencies apply to debt issues rather than issuers because various debt issues from the same issuer have different risks depending on seniority level and guarantees. Detailed rating scales of agencies have 20 levels, ignoring the near default rating levels.
- By contrast, an issuer's rating characterizes only the default probability of the issuer.
- Banks use internal rating scales because most of their borrowers do not have publicly rated debt issues. Internal rating scales of banks are customized to banks' requirements, and usually characterize both borrower's risk and facility's risk.
- There are various types of ratings. Ratings characterize sovereign risk, the risk of country debt and the risk of the local currency. Ratings are also either short-term or long-term. There are various types of country-related ratings: sovereign ratings of government sponsored borrowers; ratings of currencies; ratings of foreign currencies held locally; ratings of transfer risk, the risk of being unable to transfer cash out of the country.
- Because ratings are ordinal measures of credit risk, they are not sufficient to value credit risk.

Ratings apply only to individual debts of borrowers, and they do not address the bank's portfolio risk, which benefits from diversification effects. Portfolio models show that portfolio risk varies across banks depending on the number of borrowers, the discrepancies in size between exposures and the extent of diversification among types of borrowers, industries and countries. The portfolio credit risk is critical in terms of potential losses and, therefore, for finding out how much capital is required to absorb such losses. Modelling default probability directly with credit risk models remained a major challenge, not addressed until recent years. A second challenge of credit risk measurement is capturing portfolio effects. Due to the scarcity of data in the case of credit risk, quantifying the diversification effect is a formidable challenge. It requires assessing the joint likelihood of default for any pair of borrowers, which gets higher if their individual risks correlate. Given its importance for banks, it is not surprising that banks, regulators and model designers made a lot of effort to better identify the relevant inputs for valuing credit risk and model diversification effects with portfolio models.

Under the Basel II framework the Basel Committee permits banks a choice between two broad methodologies for calculating their capital requirements for credit risk. One alternative is to measure credit risk in a standardised manner, supported by external credit assessments. The alternative methodology, which is subject to the explicit approval of the bank's supervisor, allows banks to use their internal rating systems for credit risk.

Banks that have received supervisory approval to use the Internal Ratings-Based (IRB) approach may rely on their own internal estimates of risk components in determining the capital requirement for a given exposure. The risk components include measures of the probability of default (PD), loss given default (LGD), the exposure at default (EAD), and effective maturity (M). In some cases, banks may be required to use a supervisory value as opposed to an internal estimate for one or more of the risk components. The IRB approach is based on measures of unexpected losses (UL) and expected losses (EL). The risk-weight functions produce capital requirements for the UL portion (Basel Committee on Banking Supervision, 2004a, p. 48).

1.2.3 Market risk

Market risk is the risk of adverse deviations of the mark-to-market value of the trading portfolio, due to market movements, during the period required to liquidate the transactions (Bessis, 2002, p. 18). Market risk can also be defined as a result of changing market prices of securities in capital markets. The term market risk refers to a broad category of financial risks. Interest rate risk, foreign exchange risk, position risk and commodity risk are all considered as market risk. On the other hand, many authors (e.g. Hull, White, 1998b, Marrison, 2002, Dowd, 2002, Bessis, 2002) under the term market risk consider only the risk of price changes of securities, currencies or commodities (position risk) and deal with interest rate risk separately, because of its importance. Following the same methodology, author in this book considers market risk in the narrower sense of the word, as the risk of price changes of a bank portfolio.

Market risk can take two forms (Jorion, 2001, p.15-16): relative market risk – risk measured relative to a specific benchmark index resulting in a tracking error (deviation from the benchmark index) and absolute risk – risk measured in a chosen currency, reflecting the volatility of total returns. Market risk arises from movement in the underlying risk factors of a particular security, such as: equity prices, interest rates, exchange rates and commodity prices. A single factor or a combination of these risk factors affects the value of the bank's portfolio. Market risk exposure of a bank's portfolio is determined by both the volatility of the underlying risk factors as well as the sensitivity of the bank's portfolio to movements of these risk factors.

Market risk can also be classified into directional and nondirectional risks. Directional risks involve exposures to the direction of movements in financial variables. These exposures are measured by linear approximations such as beta for exposure to stock market movements, duration for exposures to interest rate, and delta for exposure of options to the underlying asset price. Nondirectional risks involve the remaining risks, which consist of nonlinear exposures and exposures to hedge positions or to volatilities. Second order or quadratic exposures are measured by convexity when dealing with interest rates and gamma when dealing with options. Basis risk is created from unanticipated movements in relative prices of assets in a hedged position, such as futures or interest rate swaps. Volatility risk measures exposure to movements in the actual or implied volatility.

The period of liquidation is critical to assess adverse deviations. If it gets longer, so do the deviations from the current market value. Earnings for the market portfolio are profit and loss arising from transactions. The return between two dates is the variation of the market value. Any decline in value results in a market loss. The potential worst-case loss is higher when the holding period gets longer because market volatility tends to increase over longer horizons. However, it is possible to liquidate tradable instruments or to hedge their future changes of value at any time. This is the rationale for limiting market risk to the liquidation period. In general, the liquidation period varies with the type of instruments. It could be short (1 day) for foreign exchange or much longer for exotic derivatives. The Basel Committee provides rules to set the liquidation period. Committee uses as reference a 10-day liquidation period and imposes a multiple over banks' internal measures of market value potential losses. Liquidation involves asset and market liquidity risks. Price volatility is not the same in high-liquidity and poor-liquidity situations. When liquidity is high, the adverse deviations of prices are much lower than in a poor-liquidity environment, within a given horizon. Pure market risk, generated by changes of market parameters, differs from market liquidity risk. The liquidity issue becomes critical in developing markets such as those of transition countries, because prices in developing markets often diverge considerably from a theoretical fair value.

Market risk does not refer to market losses due to causes other than market movements, loosely defined as inclusive of liquidity risk. Any deficiency in the monitoring of the market portfolio might result in market values deviating by any magnitude until liquidation finally occurs. In the meantime, the potential deviations can exceed by far any deviation that could occur within a short liquidation period. But this risk is considered to be an operational risk, not a market risk.

In order to define the potential adverse deviation, a methodology is required to identify what could be a maximum adverse deviation of the portfolio market value. Controlling market risk means keeping the variations of the value of a given portfolio within given boundary values through actions on limits, which are upper bounds imposed on risks, and hedging for isolating the portfolio from the uncontrollable market movements.

1.2.4   Operational risk

Deregulation and globalisation of financial services, together with the growing sophistication of financial technology, are making the activities of banks and thus their risk profiles (i.e. the level of risk across a firm's activities and/or risk categories) more complex. Developing banking practices suggest that risks other than credit, interest rate and market risk can be substantial. Examples of these new and growing risks faced by banks include (Basel Committee on Banking Supervision, 2003, p. 1):

- If not properly controlled, the greater use of more highly automated technology has the potential to transform risks from manual processing errors to system failure risks, as greater reliance is placed on globally integrated systems;
- Growth of e-commerce brings with it potential risks (e.g., internal and external fraud and system security issues) that are not yet fully understood;
- Large-scale acquisitions, mergers, de-mergers and consolidations test the viability of new or newly integrated systems;
- The emergence of banks acting as large-volume service providers creates the need for continual maintenance of high-grade internal controls and back-up systems;
- Banks may engage in risk mitigation techniques (e.g., collateral, credit derivatives, netting arrangements and asset securitisations) to optimise their exposure to market risk and credit risk, which in turn may produce other forms of risk (e.g. legal risk) and
- Growing use of outsourcing arrangements and the participation in clearing and settlement systems can mitigate some risks but can also present significant risks to banks.

The diverse set of these risks can be grouped under the heading of operational risk, which the Basel Committee defines as the risk of loss resulting from inadequate or failed internal processes, people and systems or from external events. The definition includes legal risk but excludes strategic and reputation risk.

Operational risk events that can result in substantial losses for a bank include (Basel Committee on Banking Supervision, 2003, p. 2):

- Internal fraud (e.g. intentional misreporting of positions, employee theft, and insider trading on an employee's own account).
- External fraud (e.g. robbery, forgery, cheque kiting and damage from computer hacking).
- Employment practices and workplace safety (e.g. workers compensation claims, violation of employee health and safety rules, organised labour activities, discrimination claims and general liability).
- Clients, products and business practice (e.g. fiduciary breaches, misuse of confidential customer information, improper trading activities on the bank's account, money laundering and sale of unauthorised products).

- Damage to physical assets (e.g. terrorism, vandalism, earthquakes, fires and floods).
- Business disruption and system failures (e.g. hardware and software failures, telecommunication problems and utility outages).
- Execution, delivery and process management (e.g. data entry errors, collateral management failures, incomplete legal documentation, unapproved access given to client accounts, non-client counterparty misperformance, and vendor disputes).

Management of specific operational risks is not a new practice; it has always been important for banks to try to prevent fraud, maintain the integrity of internal controls, reduce errors in transaction processing, etc (Basel Committee on Banking Supervision, 2003, p. 2-3). Relatively new is the view of operational risk management as a comprehensive practice comparable to the management of credit and market risk in principle, if not always in form. In the past, banks relied almost exclusively upon internal control mechanisms within business lines, supplemented by the audit function, to manage operational risk. While these remain important, recently there has been an emergence of specific structures and processes aimed at managing operational risk. In this regard, an increasing number of organisations have concluded that an operational risk management programme provides for bank safety and soundness, and are therefore making progress in addressing operational risk as a distinct class of risk similar to their treatment of credit and market risk.

In developing sound practices, the Basel Committee has drawn upon its existing work on the management of other significant banking risks, such as credit risk, interest rate risk and liquidity risk (Basel Committee on Banking Supervision, 2003, p. 3). Nevertheless, it is clear that operational risk differs from other banking risks in that it is typically not directly taken in return for an expected reward, but exists in the natural course of corporate activity, and that this affects the risk management process. Under Basel II capital accord framework there are three general methods for calculating operational risk capital requirements (Basel Committee on Banking Supervision, 2004, p. 137):

1) Basic Indicator Approach;
2) Standardised Approach and
3) Advanced Measurement Approach.

Internationally active banks and banks with significant operational risk exposures are expected to use an approach that is more sophisticated than the Basic Indicator Approach and that is appropriate for the risk profile of the institution. A bank is permitted to use the Basic Indicator or Standardised Approach for some parts of its operations and an Advanced Measurement Approach for others provided certain minimum criteria are met (Basel Committee on Banking Supervision, 2004, p. 137). Banks using the Basic Indicator Approach must hold capital for operational risk equal to the average over the previous three years of a fixed percentage of positive annual gross income. Figures for any year in which annual gross income is negative or zero should be excluded from both the numerator and denominator when calculating the average (Basel Committee on Banking Supervision, 2004, p. 137).

In the Standardised Approach, banks' activities are divided into eight business lines: corporate finance, trading & sales, retail banking, commercial banking, payment & settlement, agency services, asset management, and retail brokerage. Within each business line, gross income is a broad indicator that serves as a proxy for the scale of business operations and thus the likely scale of operational risk exposure within each of these business lines. The capital charge for each business line is calculated by multiplying gross income by a factor (beta) assigned to that business line. Beta serves as a proxy for the industry-wide relationship between the operational risk loss experience for a given business line and the aggregate level of gross income for that business line. In the Standardised Approach gross income is measured for each business line, not the whole institution, i.e. in corporate finance, the indicator is the gross income generated in the corporate finance business line. The total capital charge is calculated as the three-year average of the simple summation of the regulatory capital charges across each of the business lines in each year. In any given year, negative capital charges (resulting from negative gross income) in any business line may offset positive capital charges in other business lines without limit. However, where the aggregate capital charge across all business lines within a given year is negative, then the input to the numerator for that year is zero. (Basel Committee on Banking Supervision, 2004, p. 139-140).

Under the Advanced Measurement Approach, the regulatory capital requirement equals the risk measure generated by the bank's internal operational risk measurement system using the quantitative and qualitative criteria for the Advanced Measurement Approach. The board of directors and senior management of each subsidiary are responsible for conducting their own assessment of the subsidiary's operational risks and controls and ensuring the subsidiary is adequately capitalised in respect of those risks (Basel Committee on Banking Supervision, 2004, p. 140-141).

1.2.5   Liquidity risk

Liquidity, or the ability to fund increases in assets and meet obligations as they come due, is crucial to the ongoing viability of any banking organisation. Therefore, managing liquidity is among the most important activities conducted by banks. Sound liquidity management can reduce the probability of serious problems. Indeed, the importance of liquidity transcends the individual bank, since a liquidity shortfall at a single institution can have system-wide repercussions. For this reason, the analysis of liquidity requires bank management not only to measure the liquidity position of the bank on an ongoing basis but also to examine how funding requirements are likely to evolve under various scenarios, including adverse conditions. In its work on the supervision of liquidity, the Basel Committee has focused on developing a greater understanding of the way in which banks manage their liquidity on a global, consolidated basis (Basel Committee on Banking Supervision, 2000, p. 1). Recent technological and financial innovations have provided banks with new ways of funding their activities and managing their liquidity. In addition, a declining ability to rely on core deposits, increased reliance on wholesale funds, and recent turmoil in financial markets globally have changed the way banks view liquidity. All of these changes have also resulted in new challenges for banks.

Banks' management should set limits to ensure adequate liquidity and supervisors should review these limits. Limits could be set, for example, on the following (Basel Committee on Banking Supervision, 2000, p. 5):

- The cumulative cashflow mismatches (i.e. the cumulative net funding requirement as a percentage of total liabilities) over particular periods – next day, next five days, next month. These mismatches should be calculated by taking a conservative view of marketability of liquid assets, with a discount to cover price volatility and any drop in price in the event of a forced sale, and should include likely outflows as a result of drawdown of commitments etc.
- Liquid assets as a percentage of short term liabilities. Again, there should be a discount to reflect price volatility. The assets included in this category should only be those that are highly liquid – i.e. only those in which there is judged to be a ready market even in periods of stress.

Since a bank's future liquidity position will be affected by factors that cannot always be forecast with precision, assumptions need to be reviewed frequently to determine their continuing validity, especially given the rapidity of change in banking markets. The total number of major assumptions to be made, however, is fairly limited and consists of four broad categories: assets, liabilities, off-balance-sheet activities, and other (Basel Committee on Banking Supervision, 2000, p. 9).

1.2.5.1 Assets

Assumptions about a bank's future stock of assets include their potential marketability and use as collateral which could increase cash inflows, the extent to which assets will be originated and sold through asset securitisation programs, and the extent to which maturing assets will be renewed, and new assets acquired. In some countries, supervisors have observed a trend of relying more heavily on a stock of liquid assets (a liquidity warehouse) in order to offset greater uncertainty about liability holder behaviour. Determining the level of a bank's potential assets involves answering three questions (Basel Committee on Banking Supervision, 2000, p. 9):

- what proportion of maturing assets will a bank be able and willing to roll over or renew?
- what is the expected level of new loan requests that will be approved?
- what is the expected level of drawdowns of commitments to lend that a bank will need to fund?

These commitments may take the form of: committed commercial lines without material adverse change (MAC) clauses and covenants, which a bank may not be legally able to turn away even if the borrower's financial condition has deteriorated; committed commercial lines with MAC clauses which some customers could draw down in crisis scenarios; and other commercial and consumer credit lines.

In estimating its normal funding needs, some banks use historical patterns of roll-overs, draw-downs and new requests for loans; others conduct a statistical analysis taking account of seasonal and other effects believed to determine loan demand (e.g., for consumer loans). Alternatively, a bank may make judgmental business projections, or undertake a customer-by-customer assessment for its larger customers and apply historical relationships to the remainder. Drawdowns and new loan requests represent a potential drain of funds for a bank. Nevertheless, a bank has some leeway to control these items depending on current conditions. For example, during adverse conditions, a bank might decide to risk damaging some business relationships by refusing to approve new loan requests that it would approve under normal conditions, or it might refuse to honour lending commitments that are not binding. The growth of secondary markets for various asset classes has broadened a bank's opportunities to sell or securitise more assets with greater speed. Under normal circumstances, these assets can be quickly and easily converted to cash at reasonable cost and many banks include such assets in their analysis of available sources of funds. However, over reliance on the securitisation and sale of assets, such as loans, as a means of providing liquidity raises concerns about a bank's true ability to match cash flows received from the sale of assets with funding needs. In determining the marketability of assets, they can be segregated into four categories by their degree of relative liquidity (Basel Committee on Banking Supervision, 2000, p. 10):

- the most liquid category includes components such as cash and government securities which are eligible as collateral in central banks' routine open market operations; these assets may be used to either obtain liquidity from the central bank or may be sold or repoed, or otherwise used as collateral in the market;
- a second category is other marketable securities, for example equities, and interbank loans which may be saleable but which may lose liquidity under adverse conditions;
- a less liquid category comprises a bank's saleable loan portfolio. The task here is to develop assumptions about a reasonable schedule for the disposal of a bank's assets. Some assets, while marketable, may be viewed as unsaleable within the time frame of the liquidity analysis;
- the least liquid category includes essentially unmarketable assets such as loans not capable of being readily sold, bank premises and investments in subsidiaries, as well as, possibly, severely troubled credits;
- assets pledged to third parties are deducted from each category.

The view underlying the classification process is that different banks could assign the same asset to different categories on the maturity ladder because of differences in their internal asset-liability management. For example, a loan categorised by one bank as a moderately liquid asset - saleable only late in the liquidity analysis time-frame - may be considered a candidate for fairly quick and certain liquidation at a bank that operates in a market where loans are frequently transferred, that routinely includes loan-sale clauses in all loan documentation and that has developed a network of customers with whom it has concluded loan-purchase agreements. In categorising assets, a bank would also have to decide how an asset's liquidity would be affected under different scenarios. Some assets that are very liquid during times of normal business conditions may be less so under adverse conditions. This asymmetry of liquidity is increasingly an issue as markets for higher credit risk instruments and structured financial transactions have expanded. Consequently, a bank may place an asset in different categories depending on the type of scenario it is forecasting.

1.2.5.2   Liabilities

Analysing the liability side of the balance sheet for sources of funding requires a bank to understand the characteristics of their fund providers and funding instruments. To evaluate the cash flows arising from a bank's liabilities, a bank would first examine the behaviour of its liabilities under normal business conditions. This would include establishing (Basel Committee on Banking Supervision, 2000, p. 11):

- the normal level of roll-overs of deposits and other liabilities;
- the effective maturity of deposits with non-contractual maturities, such as demand deposits and many types of savings accounts;
- the normal growth in new deposit accounts.

As in assessing roll-overs and new requests for loans, a bank could use several possible techniques to establish the effective maturities of its liabilities, such as using historical patterns of deposit behaviour. For sight deposits, whether of individuals or businesses, many banks conduct a statistical analysis that takes account of seasonal factors, interest rate sensitivities, and other macroeconomic factors. For some large wholesale depositors, a bank may undertake a customer-by-customer assessment of the probability of roll-over. The difficulty of establishing such estimates of liability behaviour has increased with the growing competition of investment alternatives to deposits.

In examining the cash flows arising from a bank's liabilities under abnormal circumstances (bank-specific or general market problems), a bank would examine four basic questions (Basel Committee on Banking Supervision, 2000, p. 11):

- which sources of funding are likely to stay with the bank under any circumstance, and can these be increased?
- which sources of funding can be expected to run off gradually if problems arise, and at what rate? Is deposit pricing a means of controlling the rate of runoff?

- which maturing liabilities or liabilities with non-contractual maturities can be expected to run off immediately at the first sign of problems? Are there liabilities with early withdrawal options that are likely to be exercised?
- does the bank have back-up facilities that it can draw down and under what circumstances?

The first two categories represent cash-flow developments that tend to reduce the cash outflows projected directly from contractual maturities. In addition to the liabilities identified above, bank's capital and term liabilities not maturing within the horizon of the liquidity analysis provide a liquidity buffer. Long-term liabilities are a particularly important form of liquidity buffer. The liabilities that make up the first category may be thought to stay with a bank, even under "worst-case" scenario. Some core deposits generally stay with a bank because, in some countries, retail and small business depositors may rely on the public-sector safety net to shield them from loss, or because the cost of switching banks, especially for some business services such as transactions accounts, may be prohibitive in the short run.

The second category, liabilities that are likely to stay with a bank during periods of mild difficulties and to run off relatively slowly in a crisis, may include such liabilities as core deposits that are not already included in the first category. In addition to core deposits, in some countries, some level of particular types of interbank funding may remain with a bank during such periods. A bank's own liability roll-over experience as well as the experiences of other troubled institutions should help in developing a timetable for these cash flows.

The third category comprises the remainder of the maturing liabilities, including some without contractual maturities, such as wholesale deposits. Under each scenario, this approach adopts a conservative stance and assumes that these remaining liabilities are repaid at the earliest possible maturity, especially in crisis scenarios, because such money may flow to government securities and other safe havens. Factors such as diversification and relationship building are seen as especially important in evaluating the extent of liability runoff and a bank's capacity to replace funds. Nevertheless, when market problems exist, some high-quality institutions may find that they receive larger-than-usual wholesale deposit inflows, even as funding inflows dry up for other market participants. However, banks should be wary of relying on this as a source of funding, as customers may equally decide to favour holding cash or transferring their assets outside the domestic banking system. Some banks, for example smaller banks in regional markets, may also have credit lines that they can draw down to offset cash outflows. While these sorts of facility are somewhat rare among larger banks, the possible use of such lines could be addressed with a bank's liability assumptions. Where such facilities are subject to material adverse change clauses, then they may be of limited value, especially in a bank specific crisis.

1.2.5.3   Off-balance-sheet activities

A bank should also examine the potential for substantial cash flows from its off-balance- sheet activities. The contingent nature of most off-balance-sheet instruments adds to the complexity of managing off-balance-sheet cash flows. In particular, during stressful situations, off-balance-sheet commitments can have a significant drain on liquidity. Contingent liabilities, such as letters of credit and financial guarantees, represent potentially significant drain of funds for a bank, but are usually not dependent on a bank's condition. A bank may be able to ascertain a "normal" level of cash outflows under routine conditions, and then estimate the scope for an increase in these flows during periods of stress. However, a general market crisis may trigger a substantial increase in the amount of drawdowns of letters of credit because of an increase in defaults and bankruptcies in the market. Other potential sources of cash outflows include swaps, written over-the-counter options, other interest rate and forward foreign exchange rate contracts, margin calls, and early termination agreements. Since over-the-counter derivative and foreign exchange products are principal-to-principal contracts, counterparties are likely to be sensitive to the credit rating of the bank and may ask for early cash-out collateral in the event of a decline in the bank's credit rating or creditworthiness.

1.2.5.4   Other assumptions

Looking solely at instruments may ignore some factors that could significantly impact a bank's cash flows. Besides the liquidity needs arising from their own business activities, banks also require funds to support other operations. For example, many large banks provide correspondent banking services for foreign banks or provide access to payment systems for smaller domestic banks and other financial institutions. Where banks provide clearing services to correspondent banks, especially for trading activities, the value of their payment traffic will often be sufficiently large to affect the overall liquidity position of the payment bank. Banks should ask these customers to forecast their payment traffic so that the bank can plan its overall liquidity needs, although an element of unpredictability will remain. In the case of payment inflows, the correspondent is dependent on the sender making the payment as expected. If these plans are revised, there may be a delay before it, in turn, gives information to the payment bank. In the case of payment outflows, the bank may have some element of control over the scheduling of a payment during the day, although certain payments may have to be made before intra-day deadlines. The bank will, however, remain vulnerable to cancellation or delay of a payment by its customer, or an unexpected need to make a payment.

1.2.6   Country Risk

Country risk is the risk of economic or political changes in a foreign country; for example, lack of currency reserves will cause delays in loan payments to creditor banks, exchange control by monetary authorities, or even repudiation of debt (Fitch,

2000, p. 113). There are many risks related to local crises, including (Bessis, 2002, p.15-16):

- Sovereign risk, which is the risk of default of sovereign issuers, such as central banks or government sponsored banks. The risk of default often refers to that of debt restructuring for countries.
- A deterioration of the economic conditions. This might lead to a deterioration of the credit standing of local obligors, beyond what it should be under normal conditions. Indeed, firms' default frequencies increase when economic conditions deteriorate.
- A deterioration of the value of the local foreign currency in terms of the bank's base currency.
- The impossibility of transferring funds from the country, either because there are legal restrictions imposed locally or because the currency is not convertible any more. Convertibility or transfer risks are common and restrictive definitions of country risks.
- A market crisis triggering large losses for those holding exposures in the local markets.

A common practice stipulates that country risk is a floor for the risk of a local borrower, or equivalently, that the country rating caps local borrowers' ratings. In general, country ratings serve as benchmarks for corporate and banking entities. The rationale is that, if transfers become impossible, the risk materializes for all companies in the country. There are debates around such rules, since the intrinsic credit standing of a borrower is not necessarily lower than on that of the country.

1.2.7   Performance Risk

Performance risk exists when the transaction risk depends more on how the borrower performs for specific projects or operations than on its overall credit standing. Performance risk appears notably when dealing with commodities (Bessis, 2002, p.16). As long as delivery of commodities occurs, what the borrower does has little importance. Performance risk is transactional because it relates to a specific transaction. Moreover, commodities shift from one owner to another during transportation. The lender is at risk with each one of them sequentially. Risk remains more transaction-related than related to the various owners because the commodity value backs the transaction. Sometimes, oil is a major export, which becomes even more strategic in the event of an economic crisis, making the financing of the commodity immune to country risk. In fact, a country risk increase has the paradoxical effect of decreasing the risk of the transaction because exports improve the country credit standing.

1.2.8   Solvency risk

Solvency risk is the risk of being unable to absorb losses, generated by all types of risks, with the available capital. It differs from bankruptcy risk resulting from defaulting on debt obligations and inability to raise funds for meeting such obligations. Solvency risk is equivalent to the default risk of the bank.

Solvency is a joint outcome of available capital and of all risks. The basic principle of capital adequacy, promoted by regulators, is to define what level of capital allows a bank to sustain the potential losses arising from all current risks and complying with an acceptable solvency level. The capital adequacy principle follows the major orientations of risk management. The implementation of this principle requires (Bessis, 2002, p. 20):

- Valuing all risks to make them comparable to the capital base of a bank.
- Adjusting capital to a level matching the valuation of risks, which implies defining a tolerance level for the risk that losses exceed this amount, a risk that should remain very low to be acceptable.

Meeting these specifications drives the regulators' philosophy and prudent rules. The value at risk concept addresses these issues directly by providing potential loss values for various confidence levels.

1.2.9   Model risk

Models are formal frameworks that enable the users to determine the values of outputs (e.g., asset prices, hedge ratios, VaR, etc.) based on postulates about the factors that determine those outputs. There are three main types of models, and the most important are fundamental models, which are formal systems tying outputs to inputs based on assumptions about dynamic processes, interrelationships between variables, etc. (Jorion, 2001, p.19). Some examples are the Black-Scholes option pricing model, which links the option price to the underlying price, the strike price, etc., parametric VaR models based on assumptions of some predetermined distribution of asset price. The second class of models are descriptive models, which are more superficial, but often insightful and easier to work with. They can be regard as short cuts to fundamental models. An example is a bond price model based on assumptions about yield movements - a model that sidesteps the complexities of the term structure by focusing instead on simplified 'stories' about yields. Both fundamental and descriptive models attempt to explain cause and effect - for instance, to explain bond prices in terms of the term structure or bond yields. The third class of models are statistical models that attempt to capture the regression or statistical best fit between variables, with the emphasis on the correlation between them rather than any causal connection.

A model is only a representation of something, and should never be mistaken for what it represents. In the words of Emanuel Derman (Dowd, 2002, p. 217):

"... even the finest model is only a model of the phenomena, and not the real thing. A model is just a toy, though occasionally a very good one, in which case people call it a theory. A good scientific toy can't do everything, and shouldn't even try to be totally realistic. It should represent as naturally as possible the most essential variables of the system, and the relationships between them, and allow the investigation of cause and effect. A good toy doesn't reproduce every feature of the real object; instead, it illustrates for its intended audience the qualities of the original object most important to them. A child's toy train makes noises and flashes lights; an adult's might contain a working miniature steam engine. Similarly, good models should aim to do only a few important things well."

The best way to understand how models can go wrong is to understand how they are constructed. To understand a financial model, it is necessary to (Dowd, 2002, p. 218):

- Understand the securities involved, and the markets in which they are traded.
- Isolate the most important variables, and separate out the causal (exogenous) variables from the caused (endogenous) variables.
- Decide which exogenous variables are deterministic and which are stochastic or random, determine the way how the exogenous variables are to be modelled, and how the exogenous variables affect the endogenous ones.
- Decide which variables are measurable, and which are not; decide how the former are measured, and consider whether and how the non-measurable variables can be proxied or implicitly solved from other variables.
- Consider how the model can be solved, and look for the simplest possible solutions. It is wise to consider the possible benefits and drawbacks of using approximations instead of exact solutions.
- Program the model, taking account of programming considerations, computational time, and so on.
- Test and backtest the model.
- Implement the model, and evaluate its performance.

A model, by definition, is a highly simplified structure, and it is unrealistic to expect a perfect representation of observed data. Some degree of error is to be expected, and this can be thought of as a risk of error - a form of model risk. However, not all output errors are due to model inadequacy (e.g., simulation methods generally produce errors due to sampling variation) and models that are theoretically flawed or inappropriate can sometimes produce very good results (e.g., simple options pricing models often perform well even when some of the assumptions are known to be invalid)[1]. The main outputs of financial models are prices (e.g., option prices for option pricing models, etc.), Greek hedge ratios (i.e., option deltas, gammas, etc.) or

---

[1] For example, see e.g. Nelson, Foster, 1992, Härdle, Hlavka, Stahl, 2006.

risk measures such as VaR. But whatever the output, model risk in financial models always boils down to pricing error. This is self-evident when the output is itself a price, but is equally true for the other outputs as well. If the goal is to estimate VaR, it is necessary to estimate the value or price of the portfolio at the end of the holding period as an intermediate step.

Model risk is not a particularly big issue when dealing with simple instruments. Model risk can be a much greater problem for complex positions because lack of transparency, unobserved variables (e.g., such as volatilities), interactions between risk factors, calibration issues, numerical approximations, and so on all make pricing more difficult. Model risk can arise from many different sources, and one of the most important is incorrect model specification. This can manifest itself in several ways (Dowd, 2002, p. 219-220):

- Stochastic processes might be misspecified.
- Missing risk factors.
- Misspecified relationships among variables.

2 BASEL COMMITTEE AND ITS' ROLE IN MARKET RISK AWARENESS

A market-based financial system relies on the existence of prudential, organizational and protective regulations, in order to preserve the safety and soundness of the financial system, to ensure its smooth functioning, and to provide adequate protection to users of financial services[2]. The particular business characteristics of banks have important implications regarding the need for their regulation. The need for bank regulation, given the objective of maintaining confidence in the financial system, arises from the fact that banks are uniquely vulnerable to contagious (systemic) illiquidity and insolvency collapse, and their failures can cause severe negative social externalities. This inherent vulnerability comes from the liquid nature of banks' liabilities and the illiquid nature of their assets, as well as the fact that banks' assets are worth less in liquidation than on a going-concern basis. In order to prevent bank runs, authorities provide protection to depositors through either formal deposit insurance schemes or informal support operations. Because the prospect of such protection tends to undermine market discipline by making depositors less careful where they place their money (moral hazard), thus permitting risky banks to take advantage of this safety net by choosing lower capital ratios than they would otherwise do, regulators seek to constrain risk-taking in order to limit the claims on the deposit insurance fund and/or the taxpayer[3]. The limited ability to price through risk-related premiums, or ration through limited coverage, the benefits of the safety net, turn the government effectively into the largest uninsured creditor of banks, forcing it to resort to the use of regulatory capital requirements.

2.1 Regulatory objectives

The fulfilment of prudential regulatory objective is subject to the following constraints (Constantinos, 1996, p. 5):
- it must not discriminate between institutions providing the same functions, that is it should maintain a level playing field (competitive neutrality);
- it must not distort portfolio choices by imposing substantial compliance costs, and thus reduce the risk-transfer efficiency of the banking system. There is therefore a trade-off between the cost of imposing capital requirements and the costs of default. Given this trade-off, the optimal capital structure of a financial institution from a social viewpoint inevitably exposes society to some risk. Under the present piecemeal approach to capital standards, a more limited condition to the above is that the standard has risk weights consistent with the individual positions' contributions to the risk component for which the standard is being applied.

---

[2] For a detailed discussion on these issues see Vitas, 1991.
[3] See Buser, Chen, Kane, 1981 for the notion of capital regulation as an implicit premium for deposit insurance.

Finally, the international harmonization of rules is another important objective nowadays, in order to prevent regulatory arbitrage and to reduce compliance costs. The techniques of bank regulation that have evolved reflect these regulatory objectives. Due to their inherently illiquid nature, banks typically have access to a lender of last resort facility, which is also related to the banks' important role in the payments system and in the transmission mechanism of monetary policy. In addition, there are other, implicit or explicit, measures of the regulatory safety net that protect the safety and soundness of banks. On the need to maintain solvency in difficult economic times, as well as to prevent moral hazard behaviour arising from the existence of the safety net, it is the function of bank capital to provide a permanent cushion against unexpected losses, enabling individual banks, as well as the whole financial system, to survive. The concept of capital adequacy relates the risk exposure of a bank to the amount of capital, with minimum capital standards being the minimum permissible amount of capital in a bank. Risk-based capital standards seek to replace depositor pressures to limit bank risk-taking with regulator-required increases in capitalization as a bank's operations become riskier. In this regulatory definition of capital, bank supervisory authorities must define the balance sheet instruments that comprise the capital resources of a bank, in order to determine compliance with the minimum capital standards. Historically, measures of capital standards were based on various leverage ratios, usually expressing the amount of capital as a percentage of the bank's total assets. The growth of off-balance sheet activity and the existence of widely divergent classes of assets and instruments, which can greatly influence bank overall risk exposure, has rendered the use of total assets an increasingly imperfect proxy for the relative risks of an institution. Modern capital regimes often classify regulatory capital into two Tiers: Tier 1 - "core" capital, incorporating the highest elements (for example, equity and disclosed reserves); and Tier 2 - "secondary" or "supplemental" capital, incorporating elements that have the capacity to absorb unexpected losses but are less permanent in nature - for example, various debt instruments such as subordinated debt[4].

In their traditional banking business - lending financed by deposits from customers - the main sources of risk for banks, as well as their regulation, were credit risk in their loan books and internal control systems. Credit risk requirement was accounted for in the Basel Committee's 1988 Basle Capital Accord, which provided for the first time minimum credit risk-based capital standards. Besides the credit risk banks may also be exposed to securities market risk because, for example, they have lent to investment firms and they hold securities as collateral, because they engage in trading business off their own balance sheets, or because they have securities of subsidiaries or affiliates. Whereas, though, the first of these exposures can be dealt with, at least in principle, through regulatory limits on large exposures, the other two exposures inextricably link the bank's solvency to its securities operations. In effect, therefore, the bank's capital stands behind its securities unit. Attempts to incorporate

---

[4] For a discussion on the role and concept of capital in financial institutions see e.g. Berger, Herring, Szegö (1995).

market risk into the framework of risk-based capital standards were largely based on the deregulation of interest rates, the dismantling of capital controls, and the relaxation of banks' authorized range of activities. These developments have permitted the rapid growth in securities, foreign exchange, and derivatives trading by banks. Whereas exchange traded derivatives are extensively regulated by government agencies, it is the unregulated nature of OTC derivatives trading, as well as its fast growth, that has and it is still does cause concern for the regulators. Because trading-book exposures are taken with a view to resale or short-term profit, rather than to holding until maturity, the assets are treated as short-term and valued on a mark-to-market basis - the current price at which they could be sold in the market. Though it is widely agreed that the risks for end users or dealers involved in derivative activities are not new, derivatives business has two special attributes which distinguish it from more conventional financial activity: increased complexity and rapid risk transformation. The result is reduced transparency of financial markets and an inability to correctly assess the risks of a financial institution. The concerns here are that firstly, trading desk activities may lead to rapid changes in bank capital because of the potential volatility of the trading portfolio's value; and secondly, the failure of large banks involved in derivatives may have systemic implications. In effect, the heavy social costs associated with bank failures are carried over into the securities markets. Globalisation, by increasing the potential for transmission of cross-border financial contagion, has expanded those risks. This has been a primary motivation for the explicit introduction of market risk into risk-based capital adequacy standards.

2.2 Capital adequacy regulation in banks prior to 1996 Basel Committee's Amendments to the capital accord to incorporate market risk

On June 26, 1974, German central bank - Deutche Bundesbank forced the troubled Bank Herstatt into liquidation. That day, a number of banks had released payment of DEM to Herstatt in Frankfurt in exchange for USD that was to be delivered in New York. Because of time-zone differences, Herstatt ceased operations between the times of the respective payments. The counterparty banks did not receive their USD payments. Responding to the cross-jurisdictional implications of the Herstatt debacle, the G-10 countries formed a standing committee under the auspices of the Bank for International Settlements (BIS)[5]. This committee is now known as Basle Committee on Banking Supervision. The committee comprises representatives from central banks and regulatory authorities. Over time, the focus of the committee has evolved, embracing initiatives designed to (Holton, 2002, p.11):

---

[5] The BIS is an international organization that fosters international monetary and financial cooperation and serves as a bank for central banks. It was originally formed by the Hague Agreements of 20 January 1930, which had a primary purpose of facilitating Germany's payment of reparations following World War I. Today, BIS is a focal point for research and cooperation in international banking regulation.

- define roles of regulators in cross-jurisdictional situations;
- ensure that international banks or bank holding companies do not escape comprehensive supervision by some "home" regulatory authority;
- promote uniform capital requirements so banks from different countries may compete with one another on a "level playing field."

While the Basle Committee's recommendations lack force of law, G-10 countries are implicitly bound to implement its recommendations as national laws. In 1988, the Basle Committee published a set of minimal capital requirements for banks. These were adopted by the G-10 countries, and have come to be known as the 1988 Basle Accord. The 1988 Basle Accord differed from the SEC's Uniform Net Capital Rule (UNCR)[6] in two fundamental respects:

- It was international, whereas the UNCR applied only to US firms.
- It applied to banks whereas the UNCR applied to securities firms.

Historically, minimum capital requirements have served fundamentally different purposes for banks and securities firms. Banks were primarily exposed to credit risk. They held illiquid portfolios of loans supported by deposits. Loans could be liquidated rapidly only at "fire sale" prices. This placed banks at risk of "runs." If depositors feared a bank might fail, they would withdraw their deposits. Forced to liquidate its loan portfolio, the bank would succumb to staggering losses on those sales. Deposit insurance and lender-of-last-resort provisions eliminated the risk of bank runs, but they introduced a new problem. Depositors no longer had an incentive to consider a bank's financial viability before depositing funds. Without

---

[6] Securities and Exchange Commission (SEC) is the primary regulator of US securities markets. In 1975, the SEC updated its capital requirements, implementing a Uniform Net Capital Rule (UNCR) that would apply to all securities firms trading non-exempt securities. As with the SEC's earlier capital requirement, haircuts were applied to proprietary securities positions as a safeguard against market losses that might arise during the time it would take to liquidate such positions. Financial assets were divided into 12 categories such as government debt, corporate debt, convertible securities, preferred stock, etc. Some of these were further broken down into subcategories primarily according to maturity. To reflect hedging effects, long and short positions were netted within subcategories, but only limited netting was permitted within or across categories. An additional haircut was applied to any concentrated position in a single asset. Haircut percentages ranged from 0% for short-term treasuries to, in some cases, 30% for equities. Even higher haircuts applied to illiquid securities. The percentages were apparently based upon the haircuts banks were applying to securities held as collateral. In 1980, extraordinary volatility in interest rates prompted the SEC to update the haircut percentages to reflect the increased risk. This time, the SEC based percentages on a statistical analysis of historical security returns. The goal was to establish haircuts sufficient to cover, with 95% confidence, the losses that might be incurred during the time it would take to liquidate a troubled securities firm - a period the SEC assumed to be 30 days. Although it was presented in the archaic terminology of "haircuts", the SEC's new system was a rudimentary VaR measure. In effect, the SEC was requiring securities firms to calculate one-month 95% VaR and hold extra capital equal to the indicated value (Holton, 2002, p.9).

such marketplace discipline, regulators were forced to intervene. One solution was to impose minimum capital requirements on banks. Because of the high cost of liquidating a bank, such requirements were generally based upon the value of a bank as a going concern.

The primary purpose of capital requirements for securities firms was to protect clients who might have funds or securities on deposit with a firm. Securities firms were primarily exposed to market risk. They held liquid portfolios of marketable securities supported by secured financing such as repos. A troubled firm's portfolio could be unwound quickly at market prices. For this reason, capital requirements were based upon the liquidation value of a firm. In a nutshell, banks entailed systemic risk and needed long-term capital in the form of equity or long-term subordinated debt. Securities firms could operate with more transient capital, including short-term subordinated debt and were not perceived as posing systemic risk. The 1988 Basle accord focused upon a bank's viability as a going concern. It set minimum requirements for long-term capital based upon a formulaic assessment of a bank's credit risks. It did not specifically address market risk. The SEC's UNCR focused on a securities firm's liquid capital with haircuts for market risk. Because banks and securities firms are so different, it is appropriate to apply separate minimum capital requirements to each. This was feasible in the United States and Japan, which both maintained a statutory separation of banking and securities activities. The United Kingdom enforced no statutory separation of banking and securities industries, but distinguished between them as a matter of custom. The Bank of England supervised banks. Securities markets were traditionally self-regulating, but the sweeping 1986 Financial Services Act, informally called the "Big Bang" changed this. It established the Securities and Investment Board (SIB) to regulate securities markets. The SIB delegated much of its authority to self-regulating organizations (SROs), granting responsibility for wholesale securities markets primarily to the Securities and Futures Authority (SFA). If a British based firm engaged in both banking and securities activities, both the Bank of England and the SFA would provide oversight, with one playing the role of lead regulator. In 1992, the SFA adopted financial rules for securities firms, which included capital requirements for credit and market risks. These specified a crude VaR measure for determining market risk capital requirements for equity, fixed income, foreign exchange and commodities positions. By the 1990's, concepts from portfolio theory were widely used by institutional equity investors. London had traditionally emphasized equity financing to a greater extent than other financial centres, and this emphasis appears to have influenced the SFA in designing its VaR measure. While crude from a theorist's standpoint, the measure incorporated concepts from portfolio theory, including the CAPM distinction between systematic and specific risk. The measure did not employ covariances, but summing risks under square root signs and applying various scaling factors seems to have accomplished the same purpose. Because of its pedigree, the SFA's VaR measure came to be called the "portfolio approach" to calculating capital requirement. As fate would have it, the SFA's initiative would soon be overtaken by events within the European Union (Holton, 2002, p.12-13). As opposed to United Kingdom and USA, Germany on the other hand was traditionally oriented toward universal banking, which made no distinction between banks and securities firms. Under German law, securities firms were banks, and a single regulatory authority oversaw banks. France and the Scandinavian countries had similar regimes. Accordingly, Europe supported two alternative models for financial regulation:

- Continental, or German model of universal banking, and
- Anglo-Saxon, or British model of generally separate banking and securities activities.

The European Union (EU) had a goal of implementing a common market by 1993. As the nations of Europe moved towards integrating their economies, the two models of financial regulation came into conflict. New EU laws needed either to choose between or somehow blend the two approaches. The issue was settled by the 1989 Second Banking Coordination Directive and the 1993 Investment Services Directive. These granted European nations broad latitude in establishing their own legal and regulatory framework for financial services. Financial firms were granted a "single passport" to operate throughout the EU subject to the regulations of their home country. A bank domiciled in a EU country that permitted universal banking could conduct universal banking in another EU country that prohibited it. With France and Germany committed to universal banking, the single passport model effectively opened all of Europe to universal banking. It also permitted Britain to maintain a separate regulatory framework for its non-bank securities firms.

Since the securities operations of Germany's universal banks would be competing with Britain's non-bank securities firms, there was a desire to harmonize capital requirements for the two. The solution implemented with the 1993 Capital Adequacy Directive (CAD) was to regulate functions instead of institutions. The CAD established uniform capital standards applicable to both universal banks' securities operations and non-bank securities firms. A universal bank would identify a portion of its balance sheet as comprising a trading book. Capital for the trading book would be held in accordance with the CAD while capital for the remainder of the bank's balance sheet would be held in accordance with the 1988 Basle Accord, as implemented by Europe's 1989 Solvency Ratio Directive[7]. Bank capital was conservatively defined according to the 1989 Own Funds Directive, but local regulators had discretion to apply more liberal rules for capital supporting the trading book. A bank's trading book would include equities and fixed income securities held for dealing or proprietary trading. It would also include equity and fixed income OTC derivatives, repos, certain forms of securities lending and exposures due to unsettled transactions. Foreign exchange exposures were not included in the trading book, but were addressed organization-wide under a separate provision of the CAD. A minimum capital requirement for the market risk of a trading book was based upon a crude VaR measure intended to loosely reflect a 10-day 95% VaR metric. This entailed separate general risk and specific risk

---

[7] The CAD and 1988 Basle Accord only set minimum requirements. National authorities were free to set higher requirements.

computations, with the results summed. The measure has come to be known as the "building-block" approach. General risk represented risk from broad market moves. Positions were divided into categories, one for equities and 13 for various maturities of fixed income instruments. Market values were multiplied by category-specific risk weights, 8% for equities and maturity-specific percentages for fixed income instruments. Weighted positions were netted within categories, and limited netting was permitted across fixed income categories. Specific risk represented risk associated with individual instruments. Positions were divided into four categories, one for equities and three covering central government, qualifying and other fixed income instruments. Risk weights were (Holton, 2002, p. 14):

- 2% for equities,
- 0% for central government instruments,
- 0.25%, 1% or 1.6% for qualifying instruments, depending upon maturity, and
- 8% for other instruments.

Results were summed without netting, either within or across categories. By netting positions in its general risk calculation, the CAD recognized hedging effects to a greater extent than the SEC's UNCR. Like the UNCR, it recognizes no diversification benefits. In this regard, both the CAD and UNCR were less sophisticated than the SFA's portfolio approach (Holton, 2002, p. 16).

2.3 Measurement and management of market risk in financial institutions under 1996 market risk Amendments and "Basel II" capital adequacy accord

With banks increasing activity in capital markets, in the early 1990s, the Basle Committee decided to update its 1988 accord to include bank capital requirements for market risk. This would also have implications for non-bank securities firms. As indicated earlier, capital requirements for banks and securities firms served different purposes. Bank capital requirements had existed to address systemic risks of banking. Securities capital requirements had originally existed to protect clients who left funds or securities on deposit with a securities firm. Regulations requiring segregation of investor assets as well as account insurance had largely addressed this risk. Increasingly, capital requirements for securities firms were being justified on two new grounds (Holton, 2002, p. 15):

- Although securities firms did not pose the same systemic risks as banks, it was argued that bank securities operations and non-bank securities firms should face the same capital requirements. The goal of CAD was to create a competitive level playing field through the harmonization between the two.
- Some securities firms were active in the OTC derivatives markets. Unlike traditional securities, many OTC derivatives were illiquid and posed significant credit risk for one or both counterparties. This was compounded by their high leverage that could inflict staggering market losses on unwary

firms. Fears were mounting that the failure of one derivatives dealer could cause credit losses at other dealers. For the first time, non-bank securities firms were posing systemic risks.

Any capital requirements the Basle Committee adopted for banks' market risk would be incorporated into future updates of Europe's CAD and thereby apply to Britain's non-bank securities firms. If the same framework were extended to non-bank securities firms outside Europe, then market risk capital requirements for banks and securities firms would be harmonized globally. In 1991, the Basle Committee entered discussions with the International Organization of Securities Commissioners (IOSCO)[8] to jointly develop such a framework. The two organizations formed a technical committee, and work commenced in January 1992. At that time, European regulators were completing work on the CAD, and many wanted the Basle-IOSCO initiative to adopt a similar building-block VaR measure. US regulators were hesitant to abandon the VaR measure of the UNCR, which has come to be called the "comprehensive" approach. The SFA's portfolio approach was a third alternative (Shirreff, 1992). Of the three VaR measures, the portfolio approach was theoretically most sophisticated, followed by the building-block approach and finally the comprehensive approach. The technical committee soon rejected the portfolio approach as too complicated. Lead by European regulators, the committee gravitated towards the building-block measure, but US regulators resisted (Dimson, Marsh, 1995). Richard Breeden was chairman of the SEC and chairman of the technical committee. Ultimately, he balked at discarding the SEC's comprehensive approach. An analysis by the SEC indicated that the building block measure might reduce capital requirements for US securities firms by 70% or more. Permitting such a reduction, simply to harmonize banking and securities regulations, seemed imprudent. The Basle-IOSCO initiative had failed. In the US, banking and securities capital requirements remained distinct for the time being.

In April 1993, following the failure of its joint initiative with IOSCO, the Basle committee released a package of proposed amendments to the 1988 Basel accord. This included a document proposing minimum capital requirements for banks' market risk. The proposal generally conformed to Europe's CAD. Banks would be required to identify a trading book and hold capital for trading book market risks and organization-wide foreign exchange exposures. Capital charges for the trading book would be based upon a building-block VaR measure loosely consistent with a 10-day 95% VaR metric. Like the CAD measure, this partially recognized hedging effects but ignored diversification effects. The committee received numerous comments on the proposal. Commentators perceived the building-block VaR measure as a step backwards. Many banks were already using proprietary VaR measures. A 1993 survey conducted for the Group of 30 (1994) by Price Waterhouse found that, among 80 responding derivatives dealers, 30% were using VaR to

---

[8] IOSCO was founded in 1974 to promote the development of Latin American securities markets. In 1983, its focus was expanded to encompass securities markets around the world.

support market risk limits. Another 10% planned to do so. Most of these modelled diversification effects, and some recognized portfolio non-linearities. Commentators wondered if, by embracing a crude VaR measure, regulators might stifle innovation in risk measurement technology. In April 1995, the Basel committee released a revised proposal. The 1995 proposal introduced capital charges to be applied to the current market value of open positions (including derivative positions) in interest rate-related instruments and equities in banks' trading books, and to banks' total currency and commodities positions. The extension to market risk provides two alternative techniques for assessing capital charges. The building-block measure - which was now called the standardized approach was changed modestly from the 1993 proposal and allows measurement of the four risks: interest rate, equity position, foreign exchange and commodity risks, using sets of forfeits. Risk weightings remained unchanged, so it may reasonably be interpreted as still reflecting a 10-day 95% VaR metric. Extra capital charges were added in an attempt to recognize non-linear exposures. Under the standardized approach, there are specific forfeits and rules for defining to which base they apply, allowing some offsetting effects within portfolios of traded instruments. Offsetting effects reduce the base for calculating the capital charge by using a net exposure rather than gross exposures. Full netting effects apply only to positions subject to an identical underlying risk or, equivalently, a zero basis risk. For instance, it is possible to offset opposite positions in the same stocks or the same interest rates.

The second method allows banks to use risk measures derived from their own internal risk management models. Use of a proprietary VaR models requires approval of national central banks. A bank would have to have an independent risk management function and satisfy the regulator that it was following acceptable risk management practices. Regulator – central bank would also need to check if the proprietary VaR measure was sound. Proprietary measures would need to support a 10-day 99% VaR metric and be able to address the non-linear exposures of options. Diversification effects could be recognized within broad asset categories - fixed income, equity, foreign exchange and commodities - but not across asset categories. Market risk capital requirements were set equal to the greater of (Basel Committee on Banking Supervision, 1996a, p.2):

- previous day's VaR, or
- average VaR over the previous sixty days, multiplied by three.

The April 1995 proposal allowed banks to use new Tier 3 capital, essentially made up of short-term subordinated debt to meet their market risks. Tier 3 capital is subject to a number of conditions, such as being limited to market risk capital and being subject to a "lock-in clause", stipulating that no such capital can be repaid if that payment results in a bank's overall capital being lower than a minimum capital requirement. The Basle Committee's new proposal was incorporated into an Amendment to the 1988 accord, which was adopted in 1996. The Amendment went into effect in 1998. In November 2005 Basel Committee published an updated version of Amendments to the Capital Accord to incorporate market risks, which is practically identical to 1996 version of the Amendments, differing only in the treatment of specific risk, which was brought in line with Basel 2 capital accord.

According to 2005 version of Amendments to the capital accord to incorporate market risk a trading book consists of positions in financial instruments and commodities held either with trading intent[9] or in order to hedge other elements of the trading book. To be eligible for trading book capital treatment, financial instruments must either be free of any restrictive covenants on their tradability or able to be hedged completely. In addition, positions should be frequently and accurately valued, and the portfolio should be actively managed.

A financial instrument is any contract that gives rise to both a financial asset[10] of one entity and a financial liability[11] or equity instrument of another entity. Financial instruments include both primary financial instruments (or cash instruments) and derivative financial instruments. Banks must have clearly defined policies and procedures for determining which exposures to include in, and to exclude from, the trading book for purposes of calculating their regulatory capital, to ensure compliance with the criteria for trading book set forth in the Amendments and taking into account the bank's risk management capabilities and practices. Compliance with these policies and procedures must be fully documented and subject to periodic internal audit. These policies and procedures should, at a minimum, address a set of key points for overall management of a firm's trading book (Basel Committee on Banking Supervision, 2005, p. 55-57):

- The activities the bank considers to be trading and as constituting part of the trading book for regulatory capital purposes;
- The extent to which an exposure can be marked-to-market daily by reference to an active, liquid two-way market;
- For exposures that are marked-to-model, the extent to which the bank can:
    - identify the material risks of the exposure;
    - hedge the material risks of the exposure and the extent to which hedging instruments would have an active, liquid two-way market;
    - derive reliable estimates for the key assumptions and parameters used in the model.
- The extent to which the bank can and is required to generate valuations for the exposure that can be validated externally in a consistent manner;
- The extent to which legal restrictions or other operational requirements would impede the bank's ability to effect an immediate liquidation of the exposure;

---

[9] Positions held with trading intent are those held intentionally for short-term resale and/or with the intent of benefiting from actual or expected short-term price movements or to lock in arbitrage profits, and may include for example; proprietary positions, positions arising from client servicing (e.g. matched principal broking) and market making.

[10] A financial asset is any asset that is cash, the right to receive cash or another financial asset; or the contractual right to exchange financial assets on potentially favourable terms, or an equity instrument.

[11] A financial liability is the contractual obligation to deliver cash or another financial asset or to exchange financial liabilities under conditions that are potentially unfavourable.

- The extent to which the bank is required to, and can, actively risk manage the exposure within its trading operations; and
- The extent to which the bank may transfer risk or exposures between the banking and the trading books and criteria for such transfers.

The basic requirements for positions eligible to receive trading book capital treatment are the following (Basel Committee on Banking Supervision, 2005, p.56):
- Clearly documented trading strategy for the position/instrument or portfolios, approved by senior management (which would include expected holding horizon).
- Clearly defined policies and procedures for the active management of the position, which must include:
    - positions are managed on a trading desk;
    - position limits are set and monitored for appropriateness;
    - dealers have the autonomy to enter into/manage the position within agreed limits and according to the agreed strategy;
    - positions are marked to market at least daily and when marking to model the parameters must be assessed on a daily basis;
    - positions are reported to senior management as an integral part of the institution's risk management process; and
    - positions are actively monitored with reference to market information sources (assessment should be made of the market liquidity or the ability to hedge positions or the portfolio risk profiles). This would include assessing the quality and availability of market inputs to the valuation process, level of market turnover, sizes of positions traded in the market, etc.
- Clearly defined policy and procedures to monitor the positions against the bank's trading strategy including the monitoring of turnover and stale positions in the bank's trading book.

Positions in the bank's own eligible regulatory capital instruments are deducted from capital. Positions in other banks', securities firms', and other financial entities' eligible regulatory capital instruments, as well as intangible assets, will receive the same treatment as that set down by the national supervisor for such assets held in the banking book, which in many cases is deduction from capital. Where a bank demonstrates that it is an active market maker then a national supervisor may establish a dealer exception for holdings of other banks', securities firms', and other financial entities' capital instruments in the trading book. In order to qualify for the dealer exception, the bank must have adequate systems and controls surrounding the trading of financial institutions' eligible regulatory capital instruments.

2.3.1 The building-blocks approach to measuring capital charge for market risk

The Basle Standardized Measure (BSM) is one of the two approaches prescribed by the Basle Committee in its market risk standard. Like the CAD, the general approach is based on the building-blocks approach, whereby the capital charge calculated for each position is the sum of two components: a specific risk requirement and a general risk requirement. The capital charges thus calculated are intended to substitute for the credit risk weightings which have been applied to trading book items (debt and equity securities and derivatives) in deriving capital adequacy ratios. The investment book is the subject to the provision of the Basel II Capital Accord. The capital charge for each risk category (interest rate, FX, equities and commodities) is first calculated separately and than simply added together to obtain the bank's overall market risk capital charge.

2.3.1.1 Interest Rate Instruments

The interest rate capital charge under the standardized approach represents a sum of two components of market risk, each of which is separately calculated. Specific risk charge applies to the net open position for each particular instrument. General market risk refers to the general movement of interest rates in the market and for the purpose of calculating capital charge, long and short positions in different securities can be partially offset, which is not the case when calculating specific risk capital charge. The capital charge for the specific risk is designed to protect the bank from adverse movements in the price of a security that is due to the change in the creditworthiness of its issuer. For this reason, offsetting is allowed only between matched positions in the security issued by the same issuer. Because the change in the creditworthiness of the issuer may have a different impact on the value of a different securities that were issued by the same issuer, two securities can not be even partially offset when they differ in: maturity, coupon, call features etc (Basel Committee on Banking Supervision, 2005, p.7). The capital charge applies whether the bank has a net long or a net short position in a particular security. Specific risk charges for various types of bank's debt positions are presented in table 1.

Table 1 - Specific risk charges for bank's debt positions

Debt category*	Maturity	Capital charge(%)
Government	Any	0,00
Qualifying	6 month or less	0,25
	6 – 24 months	1,00
	over 24 months	1,60
Other	Any	8,00

*Weighting factors apply to the market values of the debt instrument not its notional amount
Source: Basel Committee on Banking Supervision: Amendments to the Capital Accord to incorporate market risks. Bank for International settlements, Nov 2005. p. 8.

The government category in table 1 includes all debt instruments issued by OECD central governments and non-OECD central governments provided that established prerequisites are satisfied. The qualifying category includes debt instruments issued by OECD public sector entities and investment-grade rated instruments. In measuring general market risk banks may choose between two methods of calculation: maturity ladder or duration ladder. The duration ladder method present a better alternative but in its concept is very similar to maturity ladder method. Duration method uses a series of duration bands that are divided into duration zones. Duration bands and zones are set to take into account the differences in price sensitivities and interest rate volatilities across different duration periods. Calculating required capital consists of two steps:

- The first step consists of allocating the marked to market value of a particular instrument to a corresponding duration band. Fixed rate instruments are allocated according to the residual duration, floating rate instruments are allocated according to the remaining duration until their next repricing date.
- The second step consists of risk weighing instruments in each duration band according to the predescribed sensitivities.

2.3.1.2   Equity

As with debt securities, the minimum capital standard for equities is expressed in terms of two separately calculated charges for the specific risk of holding a long or short position in an individual equity and for the general market risk of holding a long or short position in the market as a whole. Specific risk is defined as the bank's gross equity positions (i.e. the sum of all long equity positions and of all short equity positions) and general market risk as the difference between the sum of the longs and the sum of the shorts (i.e. the overall net position in an equity market). The long or short position in the market must be calculated on a market-by-market basis, i.e. a separate calculation has to be carried out for each national market in which the bank holds equities. The capital charge for specific risk is 8%, unless the portfolio is both liquid and well-diversified, in which case the charge will be 4%. Given the different characteristics of national markets in terms of marketability and concentration, national authorities will have discretion to determine the criteria for liquid and diversified portfolios. The general market risk charge is set at 8% (Basel Committee on Banking Supervision, 2005, p.19). Matched positions in each identical equity or stock index in each market may be fully offset, resulting in a single net short or long position to which the specific and general market risk charges will apply. For example, a future in a given equity may be offset against an opposite cash position in the same equity (Basel Committee on Banking Supervision, 2005, p.20). Besides general market risk, a further capital charge of 2% is applied to the net long or short position in an index contract comprising a diversified portfolio of equities. This capital charge is intended to cover factors such as execution risk. National supervisory authorities have to take care to ensure that this 2% risk weight applies only to well-diversified indices and not, for example, to sectoral indices (Basel Committee on Banking Supervision, 2005, p.20).

2.3.1.3 Foreign exchange

Two processes are needed to calculate the capital requirement for foreign exchange risk. The first is to measure the exposure in a single currency position. The second is to measure the risks inherent in a bank's mix of long and short positions in different currencies. Gold is dealt with as a foreign exchange position rather than a commodity because its volatility is more in line with foreign currencies and banks manage it in a similar manner to foreign currencies. The bank's net open position in each currency should be calculated by summing (Basel Committee on Banking Supervision, 2005, p.23):

- the net spot position (i.e. all asset items less all liability items, including accrued interest, denominated in the currency in question);
- the net forward position (i.e. all amounts to be received less all amounts to be paid under forward foreign exchange transactions, including currency futures and the principal on currency swaps not included in the spot position);
- guarantees (and similar instruments) that are certain to be called and are likely to be irrecoverable;
- net future income/expenses not yet accrued but already fully hedged (at the discretion of the reporting bank);
- depending on particular accounting conventions in different countries, any other item representing a profit or loss in foreign currencies;
- the net delta-based equivalent of the total book of foreign currency options.

Positions in composite currencies need to be separately reported but, for measuring banks' open positions, may be either treated as a currency in their own right or split into their component parts on a consistent basis. Under the standardized approach, the nominal amount (or net present value) of the net position in each foreign currency and in gold is converted at spot rates into the reporting currency. The capital charge is equal 8% of the overall net open position. The overall net open position is measured by aggregating (Basel Committee on Banking Supervision, 2005, p.25):

- the sum of the net short positions or the sum of the net long positions, whichever is the greater; plus
- the net position (short or long) in gold, regardless of sign.

A bank doing negligible business in foreign currency and which does not take foreign exchange positions for its own account may, at the discretion of its national authority, be exempted from capital requirements on these positions provided that (Basel Committee on Banking Supervision, 2005, p.25):

- its foreign currency business, defined as the greater of the sum of its gross long positions and the sum of its gross short positions in all foreign currencies, does not exceed 100% of eligible capital; and
- its overall net open position as defined above does not exceed 2% of its eligible capital.

2.3.1.4   Commodities

A commodity is defined as a physical product, which is or can be traded on a secondary market, e.g. agricultural products, minerals (including oil) and precious metals excluding gold, which is treated as a foreign currency (Basel Committee on Banking Supervision, 2005, p.26).   The price risk in commodities is often more complex and volatile than that associated with currencies and interest rates. Commodity markets may also be less liquid than those for interest rates, equity and currencies and, as a result, changes in supply and demand can have a more dramatic effect on price and volatility. Banks need also to guard against the risk that arises when the short position falls due before the long position. Owing to a shortage of liquidity in some markets it might be difficult to close the short position and the bank might be squeezed by the market. These market characteristics can make price transparency and the effective hedging of commodities risk more difficult. For spot or physical trading, the directional risk arising from a change in the spot price is the most important risk. However, banks using portfolio strategies involving forward and derivative contracts are exposed to a variety of additional risks, which may well be larger than the risk of a change in spot prices. These include (Basel Committee on Banking Supervision, 2005, p.26):
- basis risk (the risk that the relationship between the prices of similar commodities alters through time);
- interest rate risk (the risk of a change in the cost of carry for forward positions and options);
- forward gap risk (the risk that the forward price may change for reasons other than a change in interest rates);

In addition banks may face credit counterparty risk on over-the-counter derivatives, but this is captured by the Basel II Capital Framework. The funding of commodities positions may well open a bank to interest rate or foreign exchange exposure and if that is so the relevant positions should be included in the measures of interest rate and foreign exchange risks. There are two options for measuring commodities position risk under the standardized approach. These are the very simple framework and a measurement system which captures forward gap and interest rate risk separately by basing the methodology on seven time-bands. Both the simplified approach and the maturity ladder approach are appropriate only for banks which, in relative terms, conduct only a limited amount of commodities business. Major traders would be expected over time to adopt an internal model approach. For the simplified approach and the maturity ladder approach, long and short positions in each commodity may be reported on a net basis for the purposes of calculating open positions. However, positions in different commodities will as a general rule not be offsettable in this fashion. Nevertheless, national authorities have the discretion to permit netting between different sub-categories[12] of the same commodity in cases where the subcategories are deliverable against each other. They can also be considered as offsettable if they are close substitutes against each other and a

---

[12] Commodities can be grouped into clans, families, sub-groups and individual commodities.

minimum correlation of 0.9 between the price movements can be clearly established over a minimum period of one year. However, a bank wishing to base its calculation of capital charges for commodities on correlations has to satisfy the relevant supervisory authority of the accuracy of the method, which has been chosen, and obtain its prior approval. Where banks use the models approach they can offset long and short positions in different commodities to a degree that is determined by empirical correlations, in the same way as a limited degree of offsetting is allowed, for instance, between interest rates in different currencies.

In calculating the capital charges under maturity ladder approach banks first have to express each commodity position (spot plus forward) in terms of the standard unit of measurement (barrels, kilos, grams etc.). The net position in each commodity is then converted at current spot rates into the national currency. Secondly, in order to capture forward gap and interest rate risk within a time-band (which, together, are sometimes referred to as curvature/spread risk), matched long and short positions in each time-band carry a capital charge. The methodology is rather similar to that used for interest rate related instruments. Positions in the separate commodities (expressed in terms of the standard unit of measurement) are first entered into a maturity ladder while physical stocks are allocated to the first time-band. A separate maturity ladder is used for each commodity. For each time-band, the sum of short and long positions which are matched is multiplied first by the spot price for the commodity, and then by the appropriate spread rate for that band. The residual net positions from nearer time-bands may then be carried forward to offset exposures in time-bands that are further out. However, recognising that such hedging of positions among different time-bands is imprecise, a surcharge equal to 0.6% of the net position carried forward is added in respect of each time-band that the net position is carried forward. The capital charge for each matched amount created by carrying net positions forward is calculated as described. At the end of this process a bank will have either only long or only short positions, to which a capital charge of 15% applies (Basel Committee on Banking Supervision, 2005, p.28). Under the simplified approach calculating the capital charge for directional risk, the same procedure will be adopted as in the maturity ladder approach. Once again, all commodity derivatives and off-balance-sheet positions, which are affected by changes in commodity prices, should be included. The capital charge equals 15% of the net position, long or short, in each commodity. In order to protect the bank against basis risk, interest rate risk and forward gap risk, the capital charge for each commodity is subject to an additional capital charge equivalent to 3% of the bank's gross positions, long plus short, in that particular commodity. In valuing the gross positions in commodity derivatives for this purpose, banks should use the current spot price.

Both the BSM and the CAD are minimum standards, leaving national authorities considerable latitude to apply additional requirements generally or to specific institutions. There are only a small number of divergences between the CAD and the BSM, the main ones being (Hall, 1995).

- with regards to the scope of coverage, the BSM is drawn up from a banking perspective, that is, it is only for banks (including bank holding groups) doing securities business. The CAD, in contrast, is targeted primarily at investment firms and then by extension at banks undertaking securities business. Moreover, the CAD is much more comprehensive - for example, it contains provisions relating to underwriting exposures and settlement risks which are not covered under the BSM;
- with regards to regulatory capital, the BSM, despite having a more lenient lock-in clause, is more restrictive on the use of short-term Tier 3 (subordinated loan) capital, as a percentage of original Tier 1 capital (own funds);
- with regards to gross equity positions, a more stringent approach to specific risk is adopted under the BSM, which does not allow the capital requirement (set at 8%, or 4% for highly liquid and well-diversified portfolios) to be lowered to 2%, as permitted under the CAD;
- with regards to foreign exchange risk, the BSM is more demanding, under its basic approach, in the capital charge it sets for an institution's net open foreign exchange position.

The combination of the Basle II capital accord for credit and Amendments for market risks means that banks have to satisfy the following overall minimum capital requirements:
- the credit risk requirements from the application of the 2004 Basle 2 capital accord to the banking book - that is, excluding debt and equity securities in the trading book and all positions in commodities, but including the credit counterparty risk on all OTC derivatives in both trading and banking books;
- the capital charge for market risk as a result of the application of market risk-based requirements, whether using the BSM or the internal model.

2.3.2 Internal model approach to measuring capital charge for market risk

As a result of the public criticism of the building-blocks approach proposals, the Basle Committee has, in its final market risk standard decision, agreed to include the Internal model approach as an alternative approach to the building-blocks approach. The market risk standard covers the trading account of internationally active banks only. After a two-year implementation period, on the first of January 1998 the standard was adopted on a voluntary basis depending on the decision by the country's regulatory authorities. The assumptions underlying the Internal model approach are that banks are in a better position than regulators to devise models that accurately measure risk exposure over a holding period of concern to regulators, and that the regulatory authority can verify that each bank's model is providing such an accurate measure. In effect, the regulators relied on a bank's existing risk-management model to determine levels of risk capital to be held. At the heart of this approach lies the VaR methodology that will be described in greater detail in Chapter 5. The use of an internal model is conditional upon the explicit approval of the bank's supervisory authority. Home and host country supervisory authorities of banks that carry out material trading activities in multiple jurisdictions have to work co-operatively to ensure an efficient approval process. The supervisory authority will only give its approval if at a minimum (Basel Committee on Banking Supervision, 2005, p.35):

- it is satisfied that the bank's risk management system is conceptually sound and is implemented with integrity;
- the bank has in the supervisory authority's view sufficient numbers of staff skilled in the use of sophisticated models not only in the trading area but also in the risk control, audit, and if necessary, back office areas;
- the bank's models have in the supervisory authority's judgement a proven track record of reasonable accuracy in measuring risk;
- the bank regularly conducts stress tests.

Supervisory authorities have the right to insist on a period of initial monitoring and live testing of a bank's internal model before their final decision on use of such models for supervisory capital purposes.

Setting capital adequacy standards under Internal model approach is a three-stage process. Firstly, the regulators set the quantitative standards (risk parameters) for capital calculation. Quantitative standards were placed in an attempt to make consistent estimates across institutions. This was done in response to important differences in model practice, identified when the Basle Committee compiled and distributed a test portfolio to fifteen banks in the major G-10 countries in order to get their VaR estimates. Moreover, the standards aim to address some overall measurement shortcomings. Quantitative standards are the following (Basel Committee on Banking Supervision, 2005, p.40-41):

- model must cover all material risks in the trading book and must have a minimum number of thirteen risk factors (maturity bands). Moreover, it must be able to account for the non-linear pricing characteristics of option instruments;
- a 99% one-sided confidence interval, in order to account for adverse movements only. This amounts to a risk estimate of three standard deviations away from the mean of a normal distribution of portfolio value changes;
- ten trading-day holding period. This has been imposed to extend the period sufficiently to be of interest to regulators, and can be justified by appealing to concerns about illiquidity and the inability to wind down positions during extreme market movements;
- a minimum of one year as the observation period for historical data to be used in calculating volatility, to be updated at least once a quarter. This is intended to resolve problems of differential volatilities and correlations arising from the choice of the size of the sample period;
- all correlations are allowed, both within and across different asset classes (risk categories), to be estimated with equally-weighted daily data;

- since there is no economic model for determining how to extrapolate daily VaRs to the ten trading-day holding period, regulatory capital requirement is scaled up by the square root of time. Options exposures, which have nonlinear payoffs as a function of time, must be measured directly by considering the variance of two-week price movements. This can be done through nonlinear approximation methods involving higher-order risk factor sensitivities (gamma risk), volatility changes (vega risk), and spread risk;
- bank's capital charge is based on the larger of the bank's previous day VaR estimate, and the average of its risk estimates over the prior sixty business days subject to a multiplication factor. This minimum scaling factor is included as a measure of the regulators' conservatism regarding the model's capital estimates. The proposed minimum value is 3, making the implied holding period equivalent to 90 days of unhedged exposure. The multiplier can be increased if the supervisor is not satisfied with the accuracy of the estimates;
- an additional capital charge for the specific (idiosyncratic) risk of trading book debt and equity positions is levied. This is equal to one-half of the specific risk capital charge as calculated under the building-blocks approach;
- for verifying risk estimates, a one-day backtesting methodology is proposed to be used quarterly, based on the frequency of realized daily losses exceeding the model's predicted losses at the 1% critical values. Banks are required to add to the multiplication factor a "plus factor" directly related to the ex-post performance of the model.

Secondly, regulators must validate the VaR statistical models and processes which banks use to measure risk using the following qualitative standards (Basel Committee on Banking Supervision, 2005, p.36-37):

- there must exist senior management oversight and active involvement in the process;
- model must be fully integrated into the daily risk management process;
- risk management must be independent of the business line - that is, it must belong to an autonomous risk control unit;
- controls over inputs, data, model changes, and systems must be strong;
- modelling system and the risk management process should be subject to an adequate, independent validation by the bank or a third party. This can be based on either, or both, the adequacy of the VaR estimates - for example, through backtesting and stress tests - and the documentation of the bank's policies and procedures.

Finally, the bank must estimate overall VaR capital requirements on a daily basis. Stress testing simulations have to be periodically used in order to address concerns about the complexity and opaqueness of derivative instruments risks. There are also rules regarding banks that temporarily use a combination of the building-blocks approach and the Internal model approach. The Basle Committee, despite setting no timetable, is keen to ensure that a bank which has developed one or more models will not be able to revert to measuring the risk using the building-blocks approach, unless the supervisor withdraws approval for the model.

The scaling factor has been largely criticized as an unnecessary regulatory adjustment that undercuts the benefits of basing a capital charge on bank's internal measuring system (Hendricks, Hirtle, 1997, p.4). Because the main advantage of using an internal measuring system for calculating capital charge is that it provides a more accurate measure of individual bank's risk exposure than does the standardized approach, multiplication by a scaling factor is seen as a return to the standardized approach. Usually, in the developed markets, the internal measure will result in much lower capital charges for market risk (Crouhy, Galai, Mark, 2001, Jorion, 2001). Setting the minimum scaling factor to 3 is seen by many as being overly conservative and could in fact deter the banks from developing their own internal models, at least for the purpose of calculating the capital charge for its' market risk. Regulators argue that the purpose of the scaling factor is to secure the desired degree of coverage for the market risk capital charge. The market risk charge is intended to secure the bank from adverse movements in the financial markets and the subsequent fall of value in the bank's portfolio. But even a correctly measured 99% - 10 day holding period VaR does not provide the sufficient coverage in many cases. A perfectly calculated VaR figure would still mean that the bank is expected to lose an amount greater than its' reserves one ten-day period in a hundred, which means that such an extreme event is expected to occur once every four years. Occurrence of such losses, so frequently cannot be tolerated by the regulators, especially because there exists a real threat that such a loss could occur for multiple banks simultaneously (Hendricks, Hirtle, 1997, p.4). The extreme losses could occur simultaneously because banks use similar forecasting models and similar trading strategies. Such a scenario could result in a "domino effect" on the grand scale. It can be argued that in comparison to the other solutions, such as setting an even higher confidence level or a longer holding period, the scaling factor provides a simple solution that is easy to implement. Higher confidence levels than 99% are very difficult to calculate and even harder to backtest since such events happen so rarely. The use of scaling factor by the regulators can also be justified by the very nature of VaR models. Each of the approaches used for calculating VaR figures has its' own disadvantages and faults that can result in erroneous VaR forecasts. VaR models based on historical simulation are subject to the threat that historical observation period they are using does not entail extreme market events and for that reason they can be unsuitable for VaR estimates in case of sudden market crashes or regime shifts. Monte Carlo based VaR figures same as the parametric approach suffer from assuming that the distribution of the returns in the market is known, and these models usually assume that the distribution of returns is normal or lognormal. Normal distribution is adequate for forecasting the central part of a distribution, but not its' tail parts. Parametric VaR models, including Monte Carlo methods, suffer from another drawback, and that is the assumption that the correlation between individual securities is constant. It has been empirically proven that in times of financial crisis correlation coefficients converge to 1, thus nullifying the diversification effect (see Campbell, Koedijk, Kofman, 2002).

For additional protection when using the internal model approach, market risk capital charge incorporates another feature intended to reward the satisfactory measuring models and punish the ones that are systematically underestimating the risk exposure of the bank's portfolio. This additional requirement is called the backtesting requirement. Backtesting is a simple process of testing the accuracy of VaR models. A very simple statistical test also known as the Kupiec test is used to count the number of times during the year that the trading losses exceeded the VaR estimate (Basel Committee on Banking Supervision, 1996b).

Bank using a model that experiences more exceptions then allowed, is subject to a higher scaling factor. Imposing the higher scaling factor for banks using models that experience five or more exceptions during the last 250 business days is based on a simple statistical technique using binomial distribution, that calculates the probability that an accurate VaR model would generate a certain number of exceptions during a year. The backtesting is set in such a way to minimize the risk of an accurate model being dismissed as faulty and the setting of higher scaling factor for the bank that has an accurate internal measurement model in place. The number of exception experienced during a year using a 99% confidence level and the accompanying scaling factors are presented in table 2.

Table 2 - Number of exception experienced during a year and the accompanying scaling factors

Number of exceptions in 250 trading days	Scaling factor	Cumulative* probability (%)
0 - 4	3,00	10,78
5	3,40	4,12
6	3,50	1,37
7	3,65	0,40
8	3,75	0,11
9	3,85	0,03
10 and more	4,00	< 0,01

*Cumulative probability indicates the probability that an accurate model generates more than the number of exceptions reported in the first column. Probabilities are calculated using a binomial distribution with a sample size of 250 days. For the purpose of backtesting, an accurate model will produce more than five exceptions over a 250-day period 4,12 % of the time.
Source: Basel Committee on Banking Supervision: Supervisory framework for the use of "backtesting" in conjunction with the internal models approach to market risk capital requirements. Bank for International settlements, Jan. 1996, p. 15.

Banks that cannot meet all the requirements needed for the implementation of internal model approach are allowed to use the combination of the standard model and internal model. The combining of approaches is not allowed within the individual risk category, but among different categories of risk. Once calculated the capital charge for the specific risk obtained through the standardized approach is simply added to the general market risk capital charge obtained by the internal model. If a combination of approaches is used, total capital charge is obtained as a simple sum of the two, and in that way, it ignores any diversification effects that are present in the portfolio.

2.3.3   Advantages and disadvantages of standardized and internal model approach to measuring capital charge for market risk

Internal models approach is clearly superior to standardized approach. Some in their criticism of standardized approach go so far, like Jorion (2001, p. 67), as to claim that the standardized approach is so inefficient that it requires as much as seven times more capital than a 10-day VaR, and that even with a multiplicative factor of three, banks will be able to cut their capital charges in half by adopting the internal models approach. Unfortunately, the real life situation is not so black and white, especially when applied to the developing financial markets. The truth is that both the standardised approach and the internal models approach have their own advantages and disadvantages, but the advantages of internal models approach outweigh its disadvantages, as opposed to the standardized approach. A number of criticisms can be brought up against the building-blocks approach, as it has been encapsulated in the CAD and the Basel's standardized approach. Firstly, splitting a bank's business into a trading and a non-trading component, and applying separate and distinct definitions of capital to each, appears to make little prudential sense (Constantinos, 1996, p. 15-16):

- Requiring the firm to hold different amounts of capital if it has holdings in a particular security in both its trading and banking books is not consistent with the stated aim of regulation as being neutral between different transactions. Moreover, the trading book concept is open to regulatory arbitrage in the form of switches between the banking and trading books. Given the existence of incentives because of the differential capital rules, banks can be motivated to present their longer-term investments as trading assets. The implication is that for most large borrowers of investment grade status, securities market financing, especially securitization, becomes relatively cheaper to conventional bank borrowing. To the extent that the process is due to arbitrary differences in the regulatory treatment of different types of debt issued by the same borrower, important inefficiencies and distortions are introduced. Also, many banks prefer to avoid the marking-to-market that comes with a switch to a trading book because of the fluctuations it causes to their earnings. Therefore, there are limits to the benefits of this type of regulatory arbitrage;
- Artificially carving up the bank's business in two parts is not efficient in a portfolio sense since it ignores the possibility of transactions undertaken in the trading book which incidentally offset (hedge against) the exposures in the banking book. Hedging instruments falling within the trading book would continue to be subject to the credit risk-based capital requirements;

- While the trading book segregates assets used for trading purposes, as well as the regulatory capital used to back such assets, it does not segregate non-capital liabilities. This means that a mixed securities and banking business - for example, a universal bank - is free to use its deposit base to fund its securities trading book. The problem here is that, since bank deposits generally enjoy deposit protection, deposit rates do not incorporate a risk premium that adequately reflects the risks a bank incurs. In a sense, banks' activities are being subsidized if banks are permitted to use protected deposits to fund their trading book. This in turn provides incentives for excessive risk taking (moral hazard) within the trading book. These difficulties could be avoided or at least alleviated if there existed funding rules that prevented or limited the use of deposits to support a bank's trading book and instead required funding in the form of outside risk money, the cost of which would depend on the perceived risk characteristics of the institution concerned. For such a funding rule to be effective, however, it would be necessary to have banks' securities activities conducted through separately incorporated entities;
- Separation of risk-bearing from risk-taking is one reason why banks are subject to such extensive and conservative regulation on the asset side. Moreover, deposit funding of securities business gives EU banks an important competitive advantage over investment firms.

The mandatory "lock-in provision" applicable to short-term subordinated debt does not provide the protection that is intended. A bank forced to invoke this clause in respect of its trading book, in effect defaulting, would immediately become suspect in the eyes of the marketplace, thereby risking a deposit run. Accordingly, a bank would feel compelled to make good any capital shortfall arising on its trading book so as to prevent the triggering of the lock-in. The presence of short-term subordinated debt to back the trading book therefore increases the solvency risk for the bank, because such debt cannot in practice be used to absorb losses on the trading book. On the other hand, a parent bank that provides "inside" subordinated debt to its securities subsidiary would have to hold bank capital against this exposure. There is therefore little purpose in segregating a bank's securities assets for capital adequacy purposes if the risks in this part of the business cannot be segregated from the bank. Secondly, splitting market risk into specific and general risk provides an effective basis for allowing the offsetting of long and short positions. However, by splitting market risk in this way, the implication is that the two elements are independent (that is, uncorrelated). If that is true, then mathematically total market risk should therefore be the square root of the sum of the squares of the two components, rather than their simple addition. In adopting the latter approach, it can only be presumed that the Commission considered it to be a sufficient approximation for total market risk. Moreover, complaints have also been directed at various rules within those two categories (Constantinos, 1996, p. 17):

- CAD rules treat all equities equally, recognizing no qualitative distinctions such as the identity or credit rating of the issuer, and the market on which the equity is quoted or traded;

- CAD and BSM capital provisions for foreign exchange, large exposures (especially underwriting), and derivative transactions, are seen as being excessively high;
- neither the CAD nor the BSM indicate specific levels of capital to be maintained against interest rate risk on the banking book, perhaps in the belief that the existing credit risk framework is effective in capturing those risks;
- positions of the same sign in different securities or maturities are not assigned any diversification benefits.

These criticisms are the inevitable result of the adoption of a set of rule-of-thumbs that crudely assigns risk charges to specific instruments. Risk is treated as though it can be evaluated separately by security type and maturity, in contrast to modern portfolio theory. The result is that:

- firms hold too much capital because some of the benefits of diversification and hedging are ignored;
- effective risk management is not encouraged since it is not aligned to industry's best practice, that of sophisticated in-house risk measurement and management models;
- it will be difficult to adapt the proposal to new products, because of its static nature.

Finally, another controversial issue with respect to the CAD is the desirability and feasibility of a level playing field between banks and investment firms in EU countries. The reason is the different views taken by regulators for the two types of financial institutions, focusing more on solvency and systemic risk for banks, and liquidity and customer protection for securities firms. Bearing in mind all the stated critiques of the standardized approach it should be stressed that much depends on the manner in which these provisions are implemented by the national authorities, as well as on the institutional framework, particularly differences in accounting practices. Accounting practices that can have the greatest influence on the size of capital requirements and deserve significant consideration are (Constantinos, 1996, p. 18):

- extent to which assets and liabilities can be offset against each other;
- rules governing hedge accounting; the valuation of securities positions;
- methodologies employed in marking derivatives to market;
- application of net present value accounting techniques to value and report financial instruments.

One important advantage of the building-blocks approach that is readily apparent, based on the experience of the 1988 Basle Accord and given the similarity in the methodology to Standardized approach from Basel II Accord, is the willingness of many countries to implement regulations, such as this one, that are relatively simple to follow. However, it is fair to say that the building-blocks approach is not a very efficient approach to measure, and defend against, market risk. The "one size fits all" approach does not reflect the diversity of portfolios and strategies that exist, nor does it keep up with changing circumstances. Moreover, though the opportunity for gaming the rules by financial institutions is present in all types of regulations, the building-blocks approach is particularly vulnerable because of its crudeness. The fundamental problem is that the procedure for measuring market risk is crude and it is at variance with industry best practice in risk measurement, the use of sophisticated in-house models.

The main advantages of the internal models approach, as proposed by the Basle Committee, over the building-blocks approach are the following:
- it does not generate excessive capital requirements for a widely diversified book in the way that the simple building-blocks approach does, unfortunately this assumption is highly questionable in the developing capital market (Soczo, 2001);
- it encourages sophisticated risk management by allowing the use of the same internal VaR model used for daily operations, and by rewarding continuous improvement (by way of lower capital requirements) in the way that models are built and risks are measured. By contrast, the CAD rules state that European banks are allowed to submit their VaR figures only if they are higher than the figures that would apply to them using the old building-blocks approach. This is rarely the case, implying that the incentive to improve risk measurement systems is not there;
- supervisory task may be simplified compared to the building-blocks approach, since the regulator only has to set the risk parameters and validate each bank's risk assessment methodology. This argument is not universally acceptable though because of the problems that validation poses;
- it allows regulatory risk measures to evolve at the same time as risk measurement techniques used in banks' VaR models.

However, there are also some problems with the internal models approach. Some of the assumptions on which the approach is based have been challenged on various grounds. Firstly, the regulators may find it extremely difficult to evaluate and verify the accuracy of sophisticated risk management models - a question of regulatory transparency and capacity. Since there is no standard regulatory benchmark model, an ex ante approach to validation is not possible. However, ex post verification through the comparison of the bank's prior risk estimate and the portfolio's subsequent performance is unappealing. The reason is the low statistical power of such tests: is the violation a rare occurrence of a low probability event that exceeds the size of an accurately estimated tail probability, or is the bank's estimate of the probability of the event biased? Basel Committee tries to resolve this problem through the use of a large sample (one year of daily data or 250 observation points) and probability analysis. Specifically, it estimated the probability that the prediction of an accurate model would be wrongly classified as an exception at the 99% confidence level, and set a maximum number of exceptions per year of backtesting, beyond which a plus factor is activated. Secondly, extrapolation from single-day potential losses to longer periods does not adequately measure risk exposures[13]. On

---

[13] Implications of this assumption are explained in detail in Chapter 4.1.2.5.

the one hand, the process assumes a static portfolio position. In reality, a trading desk would be constantly adjusting its portfolio to reflect changing market conditions - the so-called endogeneity of trading risk. Over longer periods than daily, therefore, it is unrealistic to assume a fixed portfolio composition, especially during periods of significant asset price volatility, unless there has been such a severe market movement that it is impossible to liquidate existing positions (the so-called price gapping), or enter into others. On the other hand, there are two more problems with extrapolation, both of them purely statistical. One is that the true short-run distribution of primitive asset returns - those into which all positions are converted as units of measurement - is in practice not normal. The other is that the returns on primitive assets may not time-aggregate in a uniform fashion across different asset categories. Both compromise the accuracy of long horizon risk estimates derived from one-day estimates. Moreover, option nonlinearities, if not adequately captured, invalidate the linear measure of trading risk exposure implicit in short-horizon risk measurement models due to curvature. It should be noted, however, that the criticisms of non-normality and curvature are not shortcomings of the models themselves but of the attempt to scale-up from linear, one-day VaRs to a 10-day horizon. These weaknesses were recognized by the Basle Committee, which allowed them in order to limit the industry burden. At the same time, however, the Basle Committee has encouraged the switch by firms to a 10-day full revaluation of their portfolio positions in market shock model simulations.

Thirdly, the various constraints imposed on banks' internal models may create perverse incentives for banks in two ways (Constantinos, 1996, p. 26):

- they may lead, in the extreme, to a second set of models maintained only for regulatory risk-based capital determination. This would allow banks to adjust the constrained models in order to minimize their capital requirements. By micromanaging modelling, the internal model approach invites gaming by the bank, in the same way that the building-blocks approach does;
- choice of model parameters may be too conservative for the bank and internally inconsistent. For example, the arbitrary choice of a large minimal multiplier number 3, which came about as a compromise figure by regulators in different countries, as well as the choice of a 60 business day moving average of daily VaR calculations and the imposition of an artificial floor on specific risk charges may impose unduly burdensome capital requirements on most banks. In favour of this argument speaks the research by the International Swaps and Derivatives Association (ISDA) Task Force, which has shown that the core parameters of the capital set-aside alone provide enough capital cover of profit and loss movements for the 1987 stock market crash, the 1990 Gulf War, the 1992 ERM crisis, and the 1994 bond market decline. Moreover, the proposed ten-day holding period assumption compromises the performance of meaningful backtesting. It will then be natural for banks to respond by reducing their effective capital costs. This can be done through the increase in their multiperiod risk relative to their daily VaRs - for instance by increasing the use of option securities with nonlinear payoff - thereby gaming the regulations once again. Alternatively, they can simply choose to forego the development of their own

internal models in favour of the building-blocks approach. This is a very serious concern that is also confirmed in work done by members of the London investment Banking Association (LIBA) and ISDA.

Fourthly, the VaR concept itself focuses solely on the probability of losses greater than a specified amount but totally ignores how large those losses are expected to be when they occur[14]. Although the fixed VaR multiplier can be thought of as providing an additional layer of prudence, designed to account for the extent of maximum losses, as well as for possible market illiquidity and for leptokurtotic distributions of financial returns, the multiplier only addresses the average-loss distribution. This might not be so bad in the sense that the regulators now clearly delineate a situation of extreme financial stress, beyond which they can be expected to intervene. However, the system is open to gaming since banks can invest in projects that trade slightly higher expected returns for larger, though no more likely, potential losses. Fifth, adjustments for conservatism are reflected in many of the Internal model approach quantitative constraints, even though not all VaR measurement shortcomings err on the non-conservative side. This does not lead to a transparent risk measurement. Banks have argued that, if regulators want to add conservatism, they should do it with other means - the multiplication factor, the plus factor, or the confidence interval - but not by artificially building in assumptions, which are not the best estimate of the model. Finally, if the regulators are concerned with the calculation of VaR on a liquidation basis as opposed to a going concern basis, VaR can no longer be used with confidence to measure potential loss in the event of having to liquidate positions. The reason is that the liquidation horizon for any position cannot be arbitrarily set, as assumed under the conventional VaR measure, but depends on the costs of liquidation (Constantinos, 1996, p. 28).

2.4 Characteristics of risk measurement and management in transition markets

On May 1, 2004, ten new Member States - eight CEE countries, Malta and Cyprus joined the EU. This enlargement raised the EU population by 74 million inhabitants to 454 million. The large number of countries and the size of the population involved (20% of the EU-15) made it EU's biggest enlargement ever. In early November 2003, the European Commission published its Monitoring Report on the implementation of the acceding countries' commitments (made in the accession negotiations) regarding the acquis communautaire. The report notes that the acceding countries made considerable progress in adopting the EU's acquis communautaire. However, it also lists a number of issues that still have to be resolved by the new Member States. Poland has to ensure the independence of its central bank and accelerate the harmonization of the legal framework for the

---

[14] A preferred measure of maximum loss over a holding period is the expected tail loss (ETL) / expected shortfall (ES) (see e.g. Yamai, Yoshiba, 2002a, 2002b, Acerbi, Tasche, 2001, 2002, Acerbi, Nordio, Sirtori, 2001, Tasche, 2002).

financial sector. The same holds for the insurance sector of Latvia, Lithuania, Slovakia and Czech Republic as well as for investment services and securities markets in Estonia, Latvia, Lithuania and Cyprus. Further, the report states that independence of financial market supervision has to be strengthened in all of the European transition states. In addition, Latvia will have to further liberalize capital movements and Lithuania will have to introduce appropriate payment systems. Republic of Croatia started its accession negotiations on 03.10.2005 and is hopping to become a full EU member by 2012. Although still not a member, and lagging behind the EU new member states in a number of areas and requirements that it still needs to fulfil, when looking at undertaken reforms, legal framework and development of financial, and especially banking sector, Croatia is equal to the EU new member states. Croatian banking sector has been practically completely privatised by the late '90's, with only a negligible part of banking sector still being owned by domestic shareholders and state. Banks from EU member countries, predominately Italy and Austria at present hold 91,3% of banks' assets in Croatia (Croatian National Bank, 2005, 106 p.).

The financial markets of European transition countries, but especially CEEC have been liberalized and there are an increasing number of foreign financial institutions now operating in them. All segments of the financial sector have undergone a process of consolidation, and just a few companies now control most of the total financial assets in majority of the countries. Similarities in their economic histories and experiences, as well as comparable methods applied to building the market economies, lead to creation of similar structures and institutions. Similarities are especially pronounced in the financial sector. In all of the transition countries, there is a clear domination of banks as financial intermediaries (in terms of asset size); their share in total assets of financial institutions exceeds eighty percent (in Slovakia and Croatia even over ninety percent) (National Bank of Slovakia, 2005, Croatian National Bank, 2005). A limited role of the equity market and great importance of public debt financing needs undermine the role of intermediaries active on the market, mainly investment funds and brokerage houses. In some countries, there are a large number of institutions licensed, but assets under their management are disproportionably low (Golajewska, Wyczański, 2002, 8 p.). The depth of the financial markets is highly diversified across the countries, as measured by total assets to GDP ratio. It ranges from as low as 66 percent (Poland, Hungary), to well above 100 percent (Czech Republic), which is comparable to the level in developed countries (Golajewska, Wyczański, 2002, 9-10 p.). In most countries banking sector is relatively strongly concentrated, as a result of traditionally dominant role of savings banks in planned economies, as well as due to the recent mergers and acquisitions within banking sectors (partly stemming from mergers of strategic investors abroad, mainly from Italy and Austria). Role and size of the stock exchange in most countries is still relatively low as a source of capital, which is shown by the low ratio of stock market capitalization to GDP. Another important indicator of development of financial market is the presence and importance of IPOs (initial public offerings) and SPOs (secondary public offerings), which are rare in European transition countries. As a consequence, the banking sector plays the most important role in financial intermediation. Thus, robustness and stability of banks seem to be crucial for further growth of the countries in question, mobilizing savings and utilizing them for financing investment projects. Foreign participation in banking sector in most European transition countries is high; the highest proportion is in Croatia, Czech Republic, Hungary and Poland; similar strategy of greater openness to foreign capital in banking is also implemented in Slovakia. Interestingly, despite the warnings and pressure from institutions promoting the liberalization process, foreign ownership is very low in Slovenia and its financial system is none the less sound and stable. Another common feature of European transition countries is the lack of empirical research about the impact of changes in banking regulation on their national banking sectors and economies. Furthermore, in the European Union not even all the members of the EU-15 countries have systematically conducted research on the consequences and impact of regulation changes on their banking sectors. Transition countries are even further behind in these issues. These states are all significantly lagging behind the most developed EU countries in many fields but especially in matters of: financial legislation, market discipline, insider trading, disclosure of information (financial and other), embezzlement, fraud and knowledge of financial instruments and markets as well as the associated risks.

The past 10 to 15 years have been associated with significant changes in the reliance on risk management in a number of transition markets. In the past, the extension of credit in many economies reflected government guidelines or existing banking relationships. Institutional conditions played a large role; many banks were state-owned or were subject to government guidelines. There was no culture of risk management, the government, other banks, or the profitable segments of the corporate networks (which were often relied upon to provide guarantees to their weaker partners) would provide support in case of financial difficulty. Supervisory oversight was formal and focused on compliance with rules rather than risk mitigation. The system was not transparent, and market discipline was absent or ineffective. The high costs of this system (financial crises, persistent losses among public banks) have led to significant changes. On the other hand, this system achieved some beneficial results, such as capital projects of great importance for local communities and state, that would not have been build in a strictly market (profit) driven economy. State-owned banks have been privatised in many countries. Competition has been encouraged by liberalising entry, notably by foreign banks. There has been more reliance on market discipline, requiring greater transparency in governance and accounting. Prudential oversight has shifted towards ensuring that financial institutions are run in a way that is conducive to financial stability, as opposed to ensuring compliance with rules. To varying degrees, these changes have increased the accountability of bank managers and their incentives to improve risk management. In the past 10 years, risk management units have been established in banks in transition market economies or their role has been strengthened, and boards of directors of these banks now explicitly consider risk management issues. Ongoing technical improvements include changes in the approach to valuation, including marking to market or fair value assessments, and the quantification of various risks, including the use of VaR calculations and stress testing, focused on market risks and to some extent on credit risks; pricing and allocation of credit, as well as provisioning and the allocation of capital on the basis of risk assessment. There has been a shift towards marking to market and fair value accounting that in many cases is broadly consistent with international or accounting standards of developed countries. Implementation appears to be well advanced in some emerging markets while lagging in others. Many countries are taking steps to implement international accounting standards for fair value accounting (IAS 39). Transparent accounting is a prerequisite for effective risk management and the exercise of market discipline. In addition, it creates the right incentives for bank managers. For example, a number of CEEC markets have kept non-performing loans on their books for extended periods without recognising the losses. The implementation of IAS 39 requires banks to recognise these losses, creating a strong incentive to dispose of such loans.

Notwithstanding these advantages, the growing adoption of fair value accounting raises a number of issues that have no simple answer. For example, how does the designated use of a financial instrument affect its measurement (e.g. a loan which is a hedged item in a fair value hedge and a loan which is not; debt securities held to maturity, held for sale and trading securities; a derivative instrument which is a hedging instrument in a cash flow hedge and a derivative which is not). How does one deal with measurement differences of instruments that differ in their legal form, but are similar in their economic substance (for example: loans and debt securities that are not traded). Another important question is how to obtain reasonable fair value for instruments that are priced in illiquid and shallow markets of transition economies, and how relevant are unrealised valuation changes, especially those that are not intended to be realised for a long while. Such valuation changes mean bank financial statements can become more volatile. This could raise regulatory capital requirements, and possibly lead to procyclicality. Views on how to address this last issue vary considerably, with some opting for deferred recognition of valuation changes and others stressing the importance of immediate recognition. The Committee of EU Banking Supervisors had introduced prudential filters that help limit the impact of IAS introduction on regulatory capital and presumably attenuate any procyclical impact at the macro level. On the other hand some central banks, such as the Czech National Bank, argue that the financial statement volatility contains important information. Czech National Bank points out that movements in the yield curve introduce volatility into the profit and loss statement only if a bank is not hedging its interest rate risk; it is appropriate to show this profit and loss volatility by fair value accounting. Under old accounting practices, this volatility was hidden. To understand the importance of market risk in modern banking in the transition countries it is important to determine the amount of securities that banks in these countries hold on their balance sheets. It is surprising that ECB or the BIS do not publish these figures, thus it is necessary to find these from national banking statistics. Because it is impossible to consistently determine across all countries which securities are held by the banks in banking book, and which in the trading book, both books are considered. In the following table 3 and figure 2 the sum of debt securities, shares and derivatives from both books is presented to give a feel of the importance of securities in banks' total assets. In table 3 the gross share of securities and their average values during the five-year period, in assets of consolidated balance sheet of commercial banks in transition countries [15] is presented. For the purpose of comparison the data for three mature economies - EU member states, Austria, Germany and France is also presented.

Table 3 – Gross share of securities in assets of consolidated balance sheet of commercial banks in national economies, in the period 2001- 2005.

Year	Pol	Slov	Cze	Hun	Slo	Cro	Est	Latv	Lith	Avg
2001	16.8%	27.0%	27.8%	19.3%	28.1%	18.4%	15.8%	N/A	10.6%	20.5%
2002	16.3%	35.0%	26.0%	18.0%	34.0%	18.2%	17.3%	N/A	11.8%	22.1%
2003	16.4%	36.4%	26.4%	19.0%	34.2%	12.9%	9.4%	4.9%	10.0%	18.8%
2004	16.2%	32.5%	26.6%	16.3%	28.9%	12.1%	8.0%	3.9%	7.2%	16.9%
2005	14.5%	23.6%	28.3%	14.4%	28.0%	12.9%	6.9%	2.9%	5.4%	15.2%
Avg	16.0%	30.9%	27.0%	17.4%	30.6%	14.9%	11.5%	3.9%	9.0%	18.7%

Year	Austria	Germany	France	Avg
2001	13,1%	18,5%	39,1%	23,6%
2002	12,2%	18,0%	37,7%	22,7%
2003	15,7%	18,5%	41,2%	25,1%
2004	17,0%	19,9%	42,2%	26,4%
2005	17,9%	20,7%	43,9%	27,5%
Avg	15,2%	19,1%	40,8%	25,1%

Source: National central banks

---

[15] Excluding Malta and Cyprus for which no information about the detailed composition of consolidated balance sheets is available.

Figure 2 – Gross share of securities in assets of consolidated balance sheet of commercial banks in transition countries (excluding Malta and Cyprus), in the period 2001- 2005.

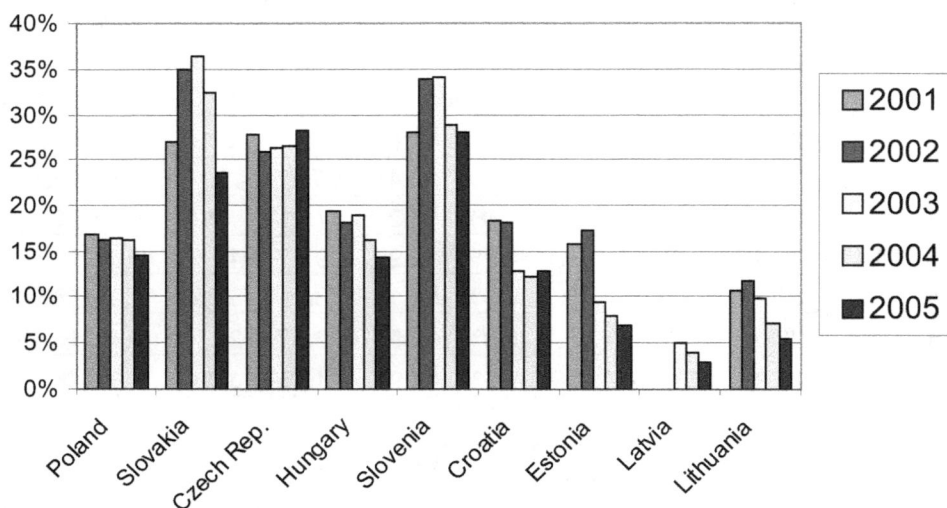

Source: Table 3

The data from table 3 shows that in the transition countries (excluding Malta and Cyprus) there is a clear trend of decreasing the gross share of assets held in securities. In the transition countries in 2001 securities formed 20,5% of total banking assets, and this share fell to 15,2% in 2005. The country with the lowest share of securities in total banking assets (excluding Latvia, for which data for 2001 and 2002 is not available) is Lithuania, where in period 2001-2005, securities on average formed only 9,0% of total banking assets. In the same period the country with the highest share of securities in total banking assets was Slovakia with on average 30,9%. On the other hand, in the developed European countries there is a clear trend of growth in the gross share of securities in total banking assets. The average value of securities in total assets for Austria, Germany and France grew from 23,6% in 2001 to 27,5% in 2005. In this group of countries, the country with the lowest share of securities in total banking assets was Austria, where in period 2001-2005, securities on average formed 15,2% of total banking assets, but with a clear upward trend. In the same period the country with the highest share of securities in total banking assets was France with on average 40,8%. The opposite trends between the European transition countries and EU old member states can be, at least partially, explained by the cleaning of banks' balance sheets in transition countries from state issued securities and sale of stakes in the companies that banks in transition countries obtained as collateral for bad loans during the privatisation and restructuring process. After this process is brought to the end it can be expected that European transition countries will follow the same trend that is present in the developed EU member states. Given the level of securities in total banking assets in both the developed and transition economies it is clear that market risk management has a very important role in modern banking in Europe, and its importance is expected to grow.

Although there is no study of risk management development in the banking sector of transition countries, surveys of the central banks of these countries and major rating agencies can be used to asses the situation regarding the measurement and management of market risk in these countries. One of the most insightful studies is the one conducted in 2004 by Deloitte. The Deloitte 2004 survey is based on responses from 162 organizations from all sectors of the financial services industry that varied in size from local institutions to global leaders. Out of total 162 organizations that participated in Deloitte study, Europe was represented by 41 participants, some of which were from European transition countries. Integrated financial institutions provided the greatest number of participants with commercial banks just behind, investment banks and other were third, and retail banks fourth. The survey presents a comprehensive look at global risk management practices across financial institutions. It addresses a range of key risk management issues facing these firms including: risk governance, regulatory and economic capital, enterprise risk management, credit risk management, market risk, asset/liability management, operational risk management and risk systems and technology. The most interesting findings for Europe as a region are (Deloitte, 2004, p. 6-7):

- 46% of respondents cited the board of directors as having overall responsibility for risk management – the second highest total among the regions, highest Asia Pacific, South America lowest.
- Region with the second highest proportion of respondents with a Chief Risk Officer (CRO) – 88%, highest South America lowest Asia Pacific.
- 12% of respondents indicated the CRO reported to the Chief Financial Officer (CFO) - highest proportion of all regions.
- 21% of firms indicated that their Enterprise Risk Management (ERM) and Sarbanes-Oxley (or equivalent) programs were managed separately.
- Europe had the largest proportion of firms that calculate economic capital - 80%. For comparison in the North America 69% of companies calculate economic capital, and in the South America only 51%.

The Deloitte 2004 survey shows that the development of more sophisticated capital calculation methodologies continues, due to both business and regulatory drivers – primarily Basel II capital accord. Many of the market risk analyses commonly used build upon the seminal developments in VaR methodology of the late '90s. Many firms are continuing their developments in this area by researching new econometric models and adding coverage of additional products. Study participants reported an increased frequency of updating model volatility parameters, suggesting a more systematized and developed infrastructure. The frequency of stress testing also showed an increase, which indicates a greater attention and requirement for current market risk analyses. Asset/liability management also continues to build upon core analytics and methods in place. Professionals in this area frequently report a number of practical challenges that they continue to address. Integration of various books, both on- and off-balance sheet positions continues to pose challenges for some. In addition, the proportion planning to implement simulation-based analyses increased.

The overall responsibility for managing risk has been elevated in many institutions to the board of directors or a board level risk management committee, making it a focal point of governance strategy. It is clear that responsibility for risk management lies with the board of directors, thus suggesting an increasing trend toward vesting responsibility at the highest level in the organization. There is a clear distinction between the more advanced EU countries and new member states, where risk management is still not treated with attention it requires and risk management function is treated more as pro forma, only to satisfy the regulator. It is safe to say that risk management culture has not yet been fully embraced in transition countries.

The composite view of financial institutions indicated a variety of organizational approaches to risk oversight. The current landscape reflects a continued preference for centralized risk management functions or a combination of centralized and decentralized functions. Of those that employ a decentralized approach to risk management, most of them were organized by risk type, then by business unit and by region or geographic location. The preference for one organizational form of risk management over another varies geographically, with European firms indicating a clear preference for the centralized approach and firms in North America and Asia-Pacific showing preference for a more decentralised approach. Part of this result can be explained by the relative size of the firms within each region, as larger firms tend to favour a mix of centralized and decentralized approaches whereas smaller firms tend toward the centralized model. As would be expected, financial institutions in transition countries, under the influence of their parent companies from EU-15 states, have adopted a strictly centralised approach to risk management. Although transition countries were not included in Deloitte 2002 survey in is interesting to note that the inclusion of transition countries in 2004 survey did not distort the overall picture and trends. The number of organizations with a Chief Risk Officer (CRO) in the EU member states continues to increase when compared to Deloitte study from 2002. For organizations employing a CRO, there is a noticeable trend in elevated reporting lines as 33% of respondents from EU indicated that the CRO reported to the Chief Executive Officer (CEO), 30% to the board of directors, and 12% to a board level risk committee. The role played by the CRO continues to vary greatly in each institution, with the position including a mixed roster of responsibilities. While the majority of respondents indicated that they had a CRO or equivalent position, there was a range of key responsibilities attributed to the role. Each institution's risk appetite and culture influences the job description of the CRO, and therefore it is not unusual to have some variation in the distribution of duties among the respondents.

The results of 2004 survey are consistent with those from 2002 in terms of primary responsibilities assigned to the CRO or independent risk oversight function:
- Risk analytics and reporting (85% considered primary responsibility).
- Developing controls, policies and monitoring compliance (79%).
- Monitoring of risk exposure versus limits (74%).
- Independent verification of risk methodologies (70%).

Deloitte 2004 survey results pertaining to market risk suggest that most respondents currently use the Standard Approach to measuring their regulatory capital, and the simulation VaR is the least represented, as can be seen from figure 3.

Figure 3 - Current and planned approaches to calculating market risk regulatory capital

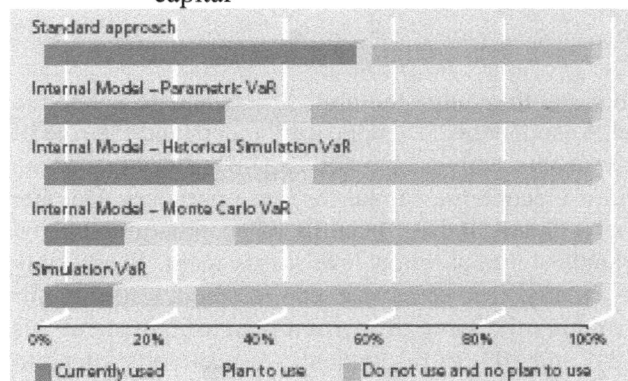

Source: Deloitte: 2004 Global risk management survey, 2004, p. 15.

Given the relative maturity of the market risk measurement area, a significant number of respondents already have internal capabilities for measuring market risk on a VaR basis (primarily through the most basic parametric VaR or a simulated historical VaR measure), or are planning to develop these capabilities. Although some respondents currently feel they have the capability of using a pure simulated VaR approach or are planning to use this sophisticated approach, the clear majority of respondents (72%) do not intend to use these means of market risk measurement. This is a very disappointing finding because it shows that a part of financial institutions have not yet adopted even the most simple and rudimentary risk measurement models.

The question whether this can be attributed to lack of interest by firm's management, lack of skilled and educated employees, or something else, is still unanswered. Several financial institutions have implemented internal economic capital models of varying sophistication and granularity over the last decade. Deloitte 2004 survey results suggest that the sophistication and level of use of these economic capital methodologies vary considerably across respondents as shown in figure 4.

Figure 4 - Uses of economic capital measurements

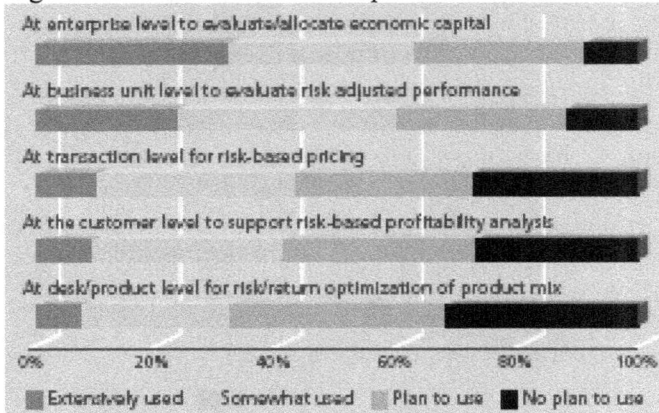

Source: Deloitte: 2004 Global risk management survey, 2004, p. 16.

For the most part, respondents believe they have the ability to calculate economic capital at an enterprise-wide level. Respondents also appear to understand the role of enterprise-wide economic capital results and its use for capital allocation, as an overwhelming 91% use or plan to use economic capital for these purposes. Deloitte results also show that firms seem to understand the benefits of an economic capital model that can support more granular or transaction level assessment. While only one third of the respondents currently use economic capital model results for product-based decision making, roughly the same proportion plan to implement this ability in the future. Similarly, 32% and 30% of respondents, respectively, intend to use economic capital based results for customer level and transaction level profitability/pricing. Another interesting aspect of economic capital framework is the types of risks that are included. As figure 5 shows, almost all respondents who calculate economic capital include credit and market risks within their frameworks.

Figure 5 - Types of risks included in economic capital framework

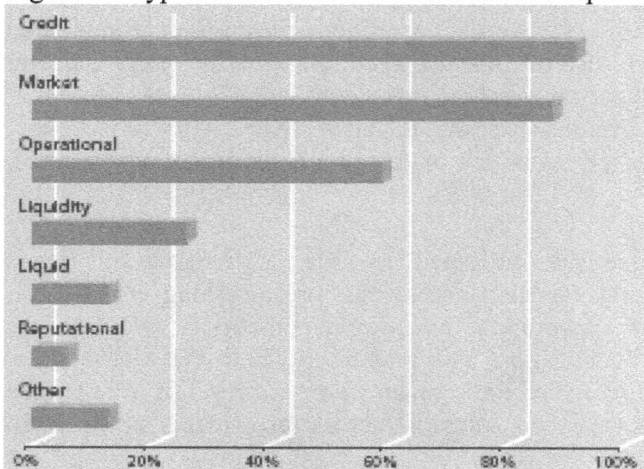

Source: Deloitte: 2004 Global risk management survey, 2004, p. 16.

The presented results are consistent with the Risk management survey conducted by PricewaterhouseCoopers in November 2002, which are presented in table 4.

Table 4 - Enterprise risk management programme priority for year 2002 (2001 ranking is given in parentheses)

1	Credit (1)
2	Market (2)
3	Operational (3)
4	Treasury/Liquidity Planning (4)
5	Changing Regulations (5)
6	Insurance/Business Continuity (6)
7	Rogue Trader/Fraud (8)
8	E-business Security (7)
9	Sovereign/Political (10)
10	Key Pearson Retention (9)
11	Restatement of Financial Results (11)
12	Pension Surplus (12)

Source: PricewaterhouseCoopers: Risk management survey, 2002, p. 5.

These results aligns well with the emphasis being currently placed on these risk types by the Basel II Framework as well as the more advanced risk measurement techniques available for these risks.

Market risk management methodology and techniques are fairly well developed within limited number of financial institutions. The trend of increasing sophistication in market risk management frameworks is present across the banking landscape. With a few notable exceptions, there is continued development and implementation of these methodologies, as they are applied to new asset classes, new market and industry sectors, and to new players within the banking industry.

Consistent with many institutions' initial modelling of plain vanilla instruments within VaR analytics, it comes as no surprise that fixed income and foreign-currency are the assets most broadly covered among survey participants (figure 6).

Figure 6 - Market risk VaR coverage

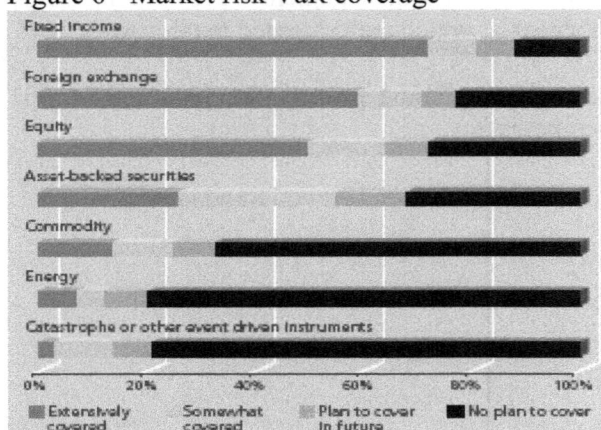

Source: Deloitte: 2004 Global risk management survey, 2004, p. 25.

This finding is consistent with the last Deloitte's survey results from 2002, although the transition countries were not included in 2002 survey. 2004 survey findings reveal substantial variation among asset classes with respect to the coverage of more structured products. This may be due, at least partially, to the fact that not all survey members actively trade these products globally. Asset backed securities and equities products are covered by over half the participants. Coverage of asset backed securities products within VaR portfolios recorded the largest increase, relative to all other asset classes (from 48% to 55%, relative to 2002 survey results). Less than a quarter of the companies currently cover commodities, energy, and catastrophe instruments within their VaR portfolios.

Incorporation of event risk into VaR calculations generally increased from 2002 to 2004. As it visible from figure 7, deterministic stress testing scenarios (65%) remain the most popular and widely used method.

Figure 7 - Methods for incorporating event risk into VaR analytics

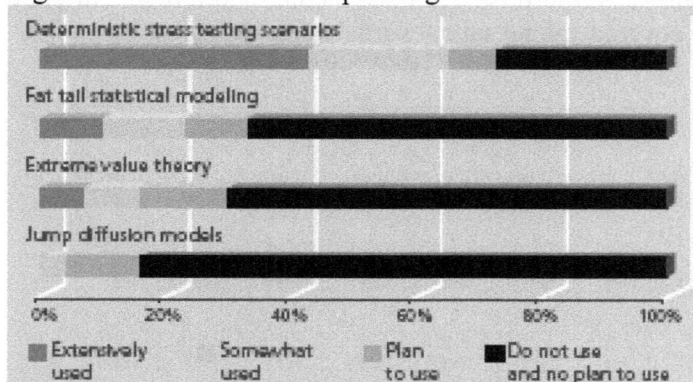

Source: Deloitte: 2004 Global risk management survey, 2004, p. 26.

A greater number of 2004 survey participants are using Extreme Value Theory (doubling from 8% to 16%) and fat-tailed statistical models (from 16% to 23%), however responses indicating future plans to incorporate these methods were less than half of what they were in the 2002 survey. This decline may be due to a variety of reasons such as a shift in the population from planning to actual implementation, potential loss of interest in these methods or reluctance to initiate new projects at this time. The drop in institutions planning to use jump diffusion models may in part be due to institutions downsizing their trading activity in energy and commodity markets, where these models are currently more commonly used. This interpretation would be consistent with observations made on asset coverage within VaR models. Participants seem to be updating their models on a more frequent basis since the 2002 survey. Firms updating volatility data sets on a weekly basis increased from 10% to 15%. Firms with monthly updates have increased by 13% to 29%. Annual updates (8%) of market volatility models are now conducted by the smallest percentage of participants. The results of the earlier surveys and other industry surveys have indicated that the use of stress testing continues to be quite common among practitioners. Concerning the use of stress test analysis, as shown in figure 8 the majority of respondents reported that they use it for reporting to senior management (80%), and for gaining an understanding of the firm's risk profile (68%).

In transition countries incorporation of event risk into VaR analytics is practically non-existent. Use of stress testing is not wide spread, and is used almost exclusively for reporting to the regulator, and not for asset allocation.

Figure 8 - Use of stress testing results

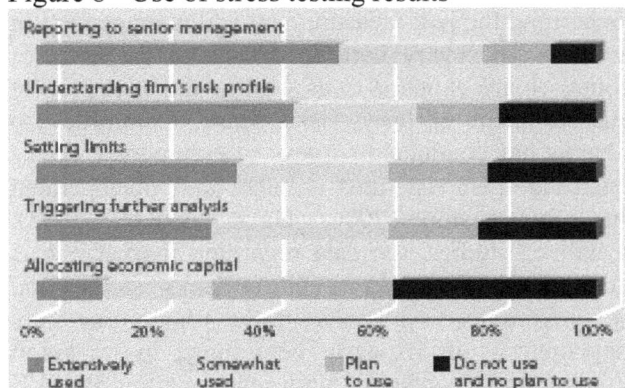

Source: Deloitte: 2004 Global risk management survey, 2004, p. 26.

These results may be due to the more intuitive nature of stress test analysis rather than the somewhat more statistical Value-at-Risk measure. In addition, the proportion of respondents using stress test analysis to set limits and as a trigger for further analysis remains high (63% for both). A finding regarding potential trends is that the proportion of respondents planning to use stress tests to allocate economic capital increased from 23% to 33% since the 2002 survey. One notable difference from 2002 survey was the stress testing frequency results shown in figure 9.

Figure 9 - Frequency of stress testing for different books

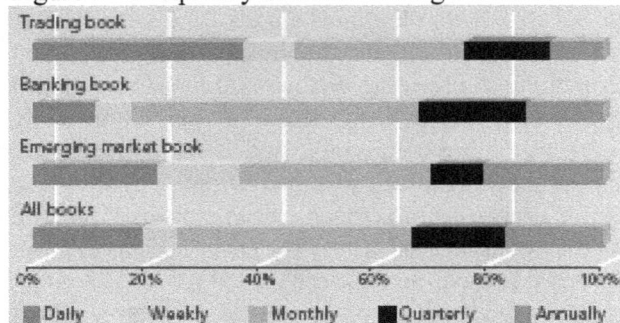

Source: Deloitte: 2004 Global risk management survey, 2004, p. 26.

Whereas the most frequently chosen response was previously to conduct stress testing on an annual basis, 2004 responses indicate that monthly stress testing is the most frequently chosen response (the trading book is the lone exception with 37% of respondents stress testing this book on a daily basis and 30% performing these procedures monthly). Stress testing of the emerging market book showed the greatest increase in frequency as the number of respondents who stress test this book on a daily basis has increased from 6% to 22%. This overall migration to higher stress testing frequency is also demonstrated in the increase in daily responses across all books (from 2% to 19%).

Due to the lack of information concerning the risk measurement and management in banks operating in transition countries it is very hard to determine the level of market risk the banks in these countries are exposed to as well as the adequacy of the methods they use in the measurement of these risks. Basel Committee in cooperation with several central banks has conducted surveys of commercial banks operating in these countries, regarding their risk measurement and management (Basel Committee on Banking Supervision, 2006, Galac, Dukić, 2005). Unfortunately, even in these specialised studies, the data regarding market risk is very scarce. From the available data that is disclosed in central banks' studies and interviews with the risk managers from leading banks in the region one may conclude that market risk management is in its early beginnings in transition countries. Most of the survey participants are concerned with implementing Basel II capital accord, especially procedures for measurement of operational and market risks. In August of 2006 BIS published a study "The banking system in emerging economies: how much progress has been made?" covering risk management practices in emerging economies. The study is very indicative of the current situation, since it also includes some of the transition countries. Especially interesting is the paper by Ramon Moreno "The changing nature of risks facing banks" where a survey of central banks regarding risk management practices in their countries is analysed. In this study a number of questionnaire respondents noted that the growth in bank trading books has increased exposure to market risk in a number of economies; such risk was generally not considered significant and was not analysed ten years ago. However, exposure to market risk is in many cases still quite small. To illustrate the range of exposures, in Korea marketable securities grew 21% in 2004, to reach over 14% of total assets. In Mexico, about 75% of the total risk of financial institutions, as measured by VaR, can now be traced to market risk (from positions that are sensitive to interest rate fluctuations); ten years ago the main source of risk was credit risk (Moreno, 2006, p. 71-72). In the Czech Republic, capital requirements for market risks (trading book, including capital requirements for the credit risk of the trading book) have almost doubled over the last five years; however, they still comprise less than one tenth of the capital requirements for the banking book (credit risk). In Poland, the direct market risk to banks is considered small. In Poland's case this is because banks tend to have closed positions in foreign currencies, and floating interest rates apply to both long-term deposits and loans. Risk on the trading book from fluctuations in interest rates is particularly important in some countries where government securities form a significant part of banks' assets (Moreno, 2006, p.72). In a number of countries, these holdings have been a large source of trading profits when interest rates were falling but have resulted in losses when rates rose. Stress tests revealed that banking systems' exposure to this type of risk is also significant in other emerging markets, whether due to holdings of government or private securities. In contrast to past episodes in which currency depreciation was the main concern, there could be risks in possible currency appreciation in countries where foreign currency holdings are significant as is the case in all of the transition countries.

All of the transition countries adopted the directives for measuring market risk and backtesting internal models published by Basel Committee for Banking Supervision in Amendments from 1996 (updated in 2005). Survey conducted by Croatian National Bank (Galac, Dukić, 2005) showed the same characteristics as those in transition countries. Based on the overall results it can be concluded that:

1) There are huge differences within national economies regarding the level of knowledge about risk management and Basel II standards for measuring and managing risks. Foreign owned banks are better versed in this subject compared to domestic banks that are significantly lagging.

2) Significant differences can be seen in the actual preparation for the full implementation of Basel guidelines. Foreign owned banks – under the pressure from their parent companies have started adopting the internal models for measurement of financial risks provided by their parent companies. Smaller, domestic banks rely on the standardized approach prescribed by the Basel Committee and national central banks.

3) The largest banks are preparing for the adoption of the most advanced – internal models of measuring all financial risks, probably because of already developed methodology for implementing risk measurement and management systems.

Conducted surveys reveal that most of the middle and smaller size banks do not even have a risk management department. It is worrisome that even larger banks have understaffed risk management departments and lack managers in charge of every aspect of financial risk. Besides the problem of understaffed risk management department, another serious problem is the dubious quality and lack of knowledge and skill of current employees. As expected, only the largest banks provided data concerning market risk measurement. Most of these banks calculate the daily and monthly VaR figures, and only a smaller part of these banks already use VaR forecasts to set limits to trading desks. Even in these banks VaR is not calculated for all market risks, usually it is only FX and equity risk. For most banks, using VaR estimates to calculate economic capital and capital requirements is in the medium term plans. Despite the positive attitude of the banks towards VaR as a measure of risk, when considering the number of banks that actually calculate VaR and those that plan to use it as means to calculating capital requirement, this seams more like a reflection of the bank management's desire than the actual plan. While the extent to which more market-oriented or sophisticated risk management tools have been adopted varies considerably, the good news is that the use of such tools now appears to be a more common part of banking practice in emerging markets, at least for bigger banks. Risk management techniques used by the banks in the emerging economies are illustrated in figure 10.

Figure 10 - Risk management techniques used by the banks in the emerging economies

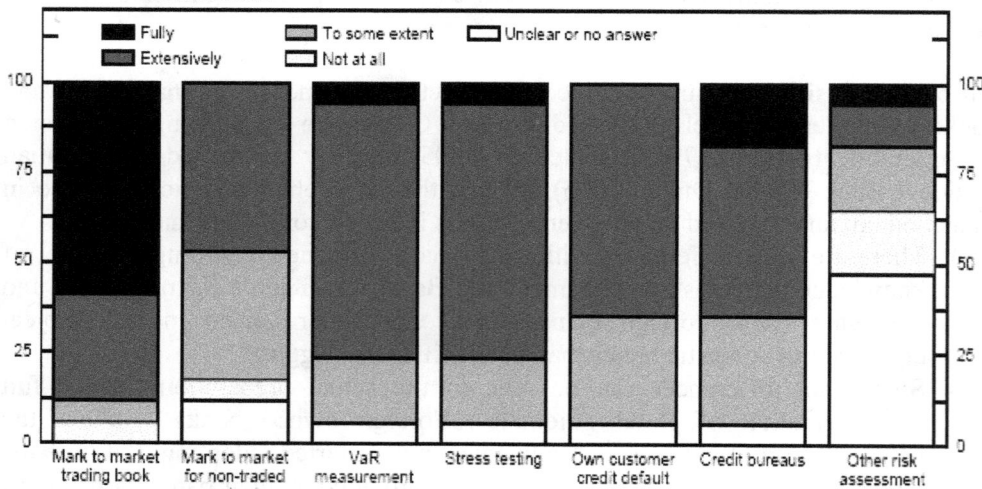

Respondents comprise Chile, China, Colombia, the Czech Republic, Hong Kong SAR, Hungary, Indonesia, Korea, Malaysia, Mexico, the Philippines, Poland, Russia, Saudi Arabia, Singapore, Thailand and Turkey.

Source: Moreno Ramon: The changing nature of risks facing banks. in "The banking system in emerging economies: how much progress has been made?". BIS papers No. 28, Aug 2006. 75 p.

In about 40% of responding countries there has been full or extensive adoption of marking to market, VaR (typically of market risks), stress testing, and reliance on credit default information or credit bureaus.

An interesting indicator of the establishment of VaR as a risk measurement standard and the preparedness of the banks to fully implement Basel II capital accord is the fact that only a small fraction of the banks have gained approval from the national regulator to use the internal approach to calculate capital requirements.

It is clear that banks in transition markets are adopting more advanced techniques for risk assessment, such as VaR, stress testing and credit scoring. Underlying this have been sustained efforts by financial institutions in many emerging market economies to introduce functional risk management groups as well as large improvements in IT infrastructure needed to handle up-to-date valuation and risk measurement requirements. In a number of economies, risk assessment is now used as the basis for daily transactions, and to improve such risk management practices, as limits to different positions. Three problematic areas in implementing more sophisticated risk assessment techniques may be highlighted:

Data issues. Modern techniques of risk management, reflected in the methodological approach of 1996 market risk Amendments and Basel II, involve the estimation of model parameters from longer time series. Banks often lack sufficient data on historical prices and rates. Foreign banks get around the problem by relying on data from their home country operations, but these data might not be entirely applicable to the transition countries.

Expertise. Banks also lack suitable techniques for designing and calibrating models to evaluate alternative scenarios. Measures of VaR or market risk are sometimes not standardised, and it is difficult to verify the economic validity of estimated values.

The human resources and infrastructure (IT and other) costs of implementing advanced techniques of risk assessment can be very large.

The reason for not implementing more sophisticated, market specific VaR models can often be attributed to plain overconfidence of parent companies in their VaR models without testing them in transition markets. Such overconfidence could result in serious losses for banks' portfolios that might go undetected by used VaR models until it is too late. The critiques on choice of model parameters discussed earlier are even more pronounced in transition countries where the volatility of the financial instruments is far greater than in developed markets. A study by Soczo (2001) has shown than in Hungarian capital market the banks would be required to hold as much as three times greater capital requirements for market risk when calculated by an internal model as opposed to the basic building-block approach (Soczo, 2001, p. 65-66).

3 MEASURING MARKET RISK VIA VALUE-AT-RISK (VAR) METHODOLOGY

Recent financial disasters in financial, non-financial firms and governmental agencies stress the need for various forms of risk management. Financial misadventures are hardly a new phenomenon, but the rapidity with which economic entities can get into trouble is. Banks and similar financial institutions need to meet forthcoming regulatory requirements for risk measurement and capital. However, it is a serious error to think that meeting regulatory requirements is the sole or even the most important reason for establishing a sound, scientific risk management system. Managers need reliable risk measures to direct capital to activities with the best risk/reward ratios. They need estimates of the size of potential losses to stay within limits imposed by readily available liquidity, by creditors, customers, and regulators. They need mechanisms to monitor positions and create incentives for prudent risk-taking by divisions and individuals. Risk management is the process by which managers satisfy these needs by identifying key risks, obtaining consistent, understandable risk measures, choosing which risks to reduce and which to increase and by what means, and establishing procedures to monitor the resulting risk position.

3.1 Approaches to measuring market risk

There are significant differences in the internal and external views of what is a satisfactory market risk measure. Internally, bank managers need a measure that allows active, efficient management of the bank's risk position. Bank regulators want to be sure a bank's potential for catastrophic net worth loss is accurately measured and that the bank's capital is sufficient to survive such a loss. Both managers and regulators want up-to-date measures of risk. For banks active in trading, this may mean selective intraday risk measurement as well as a daily measurement of the total risk of the bank. Intraday measures that are relevant for asset allocation and hedging decisions are measures of the marginal effect of a trade on total bank risk and not the stand-alone riskiness of the trade. Regulators, on the other hand, are concerned with the overall riskiness of a bank and are less concerned with the risk of individual portfolio components. Nonetheless, given the ability of a sophisticated manager to "window dress" a bank's position on short notice, regulators might also like to monitor the intraday total risk. As a practical matter, they probably must be satisfied with a daily measure of total bank risk.

The need for a total risk measure implies that risk measurement cannot be decentralized. For parametric measures of risk, such as standard deviation, this follows from the theory of portfolio selection (Markowitz, 1952) and the well-known fact that the risk of a portfolio is not, in general, the sum of the component risks. More generally, imperfect correlation among portfolio components implies that simulations of portfolio risk must be driven by the portfolio return distribution, which will not be invariant to changes in portfolio composition. Finally, given costly regulatory capital requirements, choices among alternative assets require managers to consider risk/return or risk/cost trade-offs where risk is measured as the change in portfolio risk resulting from a given change in portfolio composition. The appropriate risk scaling measure depends on the type of change being made. For example, the pertinent choice criterion for pure hedging transactions might be to maximize the marginal risk reduction to transaction cost ratio over the available instruments while the choice among proprietary transactions would involve minimizing marginal risk per unit of excess return. Risk measurement is costly and time consuming. Consequently, bank managers compromise between measurement precision on the one hand and the cost and timeliness of reporting on the other. This trade-off will have a profound effect on the risk measurement method a bank will adopt. Bank regulators have their own problem with the cost of accurate risk measurement, which is probably one reason they have chosen to monitor, and stress test bank risk measurement systems rather than undertaking their own risk measurements.

Bank regulators have a singular risk measurement goal. They want to know, to a high degree of precision, the maximum loss a bank is likely to experience over a given horizon. They then can set the bank's required capital (i.e. its economic net worth) to be greater than the estimated maximum loss and be almost sure that the bank will not fail over that horizon. In other words, regulators should focus on the extreme tail of the bank's return distribution and on the size of that tail in adverse circumstances. Bank managers have a more complex set of risk information needs. In addition to shared concerns over sustainable losses, they must consider risk/return trade-offs. That calls for a different risk measure than the "tail" statistic, a different horizon, and a focus on more usual market conditions. Furthermore, even when concerned with the level of sustainable losses, the bank manager may want to monitor on the basis of a probability of loss that can be observed with some frequency (e.g. over a month rather than over a year) (Pyle, 1997, p. 6-7).

There are four common approaches to measuring market risk (Marrison, 2002, p. 88):
   1) Sensitivity analysis
   2) Stress testing
   3) Scenario testing
   4) Value at Risk (VaR)

3.1.1.1 Sensitivity analysis

Sensitivity analysis is a useful measure to quickly show how changes in the portfolio's value depend on the bank's position. Position is a general term used to describe the composition of the assets and liabilities in the portfolio. Sensitivity analysis is a description of how much of a portfolio's value (V) is expected to change if there is a small change in one of the market-risk factors (f). The market-risk factors are market variables from which the value of all other instruments can be derived. The main risk factors are: interest rates, credit spreads, equity prices, exchange rates, implied volatility, commodity prices and forward prices for each of these factors. There are three distinct but equivalent ways of thinking about sensitivity: it is the relative change, the first derivative, or the best linear approximation (Marrison, 2002, p. 88).

The relative change is the change in value of the portfolio when a risk factor changes by a small amount (ε), divided by the change in the risk factor (Marrison, 2002, p. 89):

$$Sensitivity = \frac{V(f+\varepsilon) - V(f)}{\varepsilon} \qquad (3.1)$$

The first derivative is the calculus extreme of the relative change when ε tends to zero:

$$Sensitivity = \left[\frac{V(f+\varepsilon) - V(f)}{\varepsilon}\right]_{\varepsilon \to 0} = \frac{\partial V}{\partial f} \qquad (3.2)$$

The linear approximation is the sensitivity that best satisfies the following equation:

$$V(f + \varepsilon) = V(f) + \varepsilon \times Sensitivity \qquad (3.3)$$

The sensitivity to equity prices of a portfolio containing equity from a single issuer is simply the number of equities being held (N) multiplied by the change in the value of a share (S):

$$\begin{aligned} V &= N \times S \\ \frac{\delta V}{\delta S} &= N \times \frac{\partial S}{\partial S} \\ \delta V &= N \delta S \end{aligned} \qquad (3.4)$$

Extending the logic, in a portfolio composed of various equities the sensitivity with respect to each company's share price should be calculated, but this creates too much data to be analysed easily. A commonly used alternative is to look at how the value of the portfolio changes with a general market change. This analysis has three steps. The first is to describe each equity's value in terms of its beta, i.e., the extent to which its price tends to change when the general market changes. This is found from the historical covariance between the stock price and market price. The equity's value, at current market level (M_0), is then described as being the current value (S_0), plus beta times the market change, plus a random idiosyncratic change (ε) (Marrison, 2002, p. 90):

$$S = S_0[1 + \beta m + \varepsilon] \qquad \text{where} \quad m = \frac{M - M_0}{M_0} \qquad (3.5)$$

The second step is to differentiate the equation for value with respect to the market level.

$$\frac{\partial S}{\partial m} = S_0 \beta \qquad\qquad (3.6)$$

The final step is to sum the sensitivity to the market for all the equities in the portfolio.

$$\frac{\partial V_p}{\partial m} = \sum_{k=1}^{p} N_k S_{k,0} \beta_k \qquad\qquad (3.7)$$

where P is the total number of different equities in the portfolio, and V_p is the value of the portfolio.

Equation 3.7 gives the expected change in the value of the portfolio if the general market changes. For example, if the market falls by p%, the portfolio is expected to lose (Marrison, 2002, p. 91):

$$\delta V = \frac{\partial V_p}{\partial m} \times \delta m = p\% \times \left(\sum_{k=1}^{p} N_k S_{k,0} \beta_k \right) \qquad (3.8)$$

The sensitivity analyses give decent approximations for the change in the value of the portfolio when the change in the market-risk factors is small. However, if the change in a risk factor is large (e.g., in a crisis), the linear sensitivity will not give a good estimate to the change in the value of a portfolio.

3.1.1.2   Stress testing

In stress testing, large changes are made in the risk factors, and full, nonlinear pricing is used to revalue the portfolio and estimate the loss. The purpose of stress testing is to provide a clear, objective measure of risk that is easily understood by everyone. This approach has the additional advantage of not requiring a distributional assumption for the risk calculation. For stress testing, a standard set of changes in the risk factors is set, and the subsequent change in portfolio value is calculated. For example, a typical stress statement would be "If interest rates move up by 2%, the company is expected to lose €12 million; if they move by 4%, it would lose €23 million". Typically, the movements are standardized in order to communicate them easily throughout the organization. For example, the changes in all equity values may be set at -20%, -10%, and +10% and +20% (McNeil, Frey,

Embrechts, 2005, p.36). Deciding which factors should be moved together to analyze the results more easily is called "blocking." One example of blocking is to move all transition country's exchange rates at the same time rather than having one result for each currency. However, one downside of exchange-rate blocking is that the gains from one currency would perfectly offset losses from another. Therefore, there is no indication of the loss that would occur if the rates moved differently. Usual steps required to construct a stress test are (Marrison, 2002, p. 93):

1. Determining the complete set of market factors that could affect the value of the portfolio.
2. Deciding which factors should be blocked together or moved independently; e.g., a Croatian bank would probably block together all its exposures to Asian currencies because they would be a small part of the portfolio, and analyzing them individually would distract management from the main sources of risk.
3. Deciding what approximate change is a reasonable test for each factor. Four or six times the standard deviation of daily movements for each factor would be reasonable.
4. Applying the price movements.
5. Revaluating all positions affected by the risk factor. For example, a change in FX will affect FX spots, forwards, swap options, and the value of the holdings of foreign equities. Using full, nonlinear pricing models to revalue the portfolio. For example, changes in option values should be calculated using a full option pricing model and not just the Greeks.
6. Reporting the change in present value.

It should be clear that stress testing can provide regulators with the desired lower tail estimates, but is of limited use in day-to-day risk management. Even for the regulators, reliance on a given scenario carries the risk of establishing a last line of defence against a catastrophic event. While stress testing is generally helpful, there are three main drawbacks (Marrison, 2002, p. 95):

1. The test can yield a lot of data without directly indicating which result represents the most significant problem.
2. The chosen moves in the risk factors are not tightly related to a probability of movement.
3. The test makes the simple assumption that the correlation between the movements in different risk factors is zero or one; i.e., they move independently or in lockstep. This can mask potentially serious losses that could occur if one rate moved slightly differently from another rate. For example, a Croatian bank is holding an FX forward in which it is paying Croatian kunas and receiving pounds sterling and a swap in which it will receive the same amount of Croatian kunas and pay euros. If sterling and the euro were blocked together, when different rates were tested, any estimated loss on one trade would be offset by gains on the other, and it would appear that the overall portfolio had no risk. However, if the sterling and euro rates were to move separately, there could be considerable losses.

3.1.1.3   Scenario testing

Scenario testing is one approach to avoid some drawbacks of stress testing. Stress testing and scenario testing are similar in that both use specified changes in the market-risk factors and reprice the portfolio with full, nonlinear pricing models. However, in stress testing, the changes in risk factors are very uniform and objective. In scenario testing, the changes are tailored and subjectively chosen. In scenario testing, informed opinion is used to create a limited set of worst-case scenarios. Each scenario corresponds to a specific type of market crisis, such as equities market crashes, a default by a major bond issuer, or the raising of oil prices. Typically, 5 to 10 "worst-case" scenarios are chosen. The scenarios are typically derived from one of three sources: previous crises, the bank's current portfolio, and the opinion of bank's experts such as the head trader, bank economists, and the risk management group. In using previous crises, the risk management group looks at historical data from many markets and asks: what if those events were to happen here and now? For example, if a 20% one-day drop in the U.S. market happened in 1987, one scenario could be that the same happens for all the euro markets (Marrison, 2002, p. 95). In basing the scenarios on the current portfolio, the bank's experts look at the current state of the portfolio and ask: what event would be most damaging to us given this portfolio? Basing the scenarios on the bank's expert opinion allows the bank's staff to test their greatest worries given their knowledge of the current economy and market. Once each scenario has been chosen, it is then necessary to estimate how all of the risk factors would change in that scenario. For example, a crash in the Croatian equities market would affect Croatian interest rates, neighboring equity markets, exchange rates, and all the other factors. By moving all the risk factors, the scenario implicitly includes all the correlations between risk factors. Meaningful scenario analysis is dependent on having valuation models that are accurate over a wide range of input parameters, a characteristic that is shared to a considerable extent by VaR models. Research on capital asset pricing (Sharpe, 1964), option pricing (Black, Scholes, 1973, Merton, 1973), and term structure modelling (Vasicek, 1977) has provided the basic tools for valuation models, but unfortunately they are still far from being perfect.

Usual steps required to create and use a scenario analysis are (Marrison, 2002, p. 96):
1. Choosing 5-10 scenarios that would upset the markets in which the bank trades. Estimating the changes in each risk factor based on the crisis scenarios the bank has identified. This estimation can be based on expert opinion and/or historical data from previous crises.
2. Revaluating the portfolio under the given scenario using full, nonlinear pricing models.
3. Testing the portfolio each day to see how much could be lost under each scenario.
4. Reviewing and updating the scenarios quarterly, or more often if events dictate.

While scenario analysis is generally helpful, there are four major drawbacks (Marrison, 2002, p. 96):
1. Its proper implementation is time-consuming.
2. Only a limited number of scenarios can be tested.
3. The values chosen are very subjective.
4. There is the potential for conflict of interest, as the person taking the risk and making the trade is often the expert who is asked to provide the worst-case scenario.

3.1.1.4   Value at Risk (VaR)

One of the most important developments in risk management over the past few years has been the implementation of a new class of risk measures that are specifically designed to measure and aggregate diverse risky positions across an entire institution using a common conceptual framework. Although these measures come under any one of many different institution-specific guises (e.g. Bankers Trust's Capital at Risk (CaR), J.P. Morgan's Value at Risk (VaR) and Daily Earnings at Risk (DEaR), other institutions' Dollars at Risk (DaR) and Money at Risk (MaR)), they all have as their foundation a common definition comprising three elements: VaR is generically defined as the maximum possible loss for a given position or portfolio within a known confidence interval over a specific time horizon (Alexander, 2000, p. 61).

Graphical representation of VaR concept can be seen in figure 11.

Figure 11 - Value at Risk

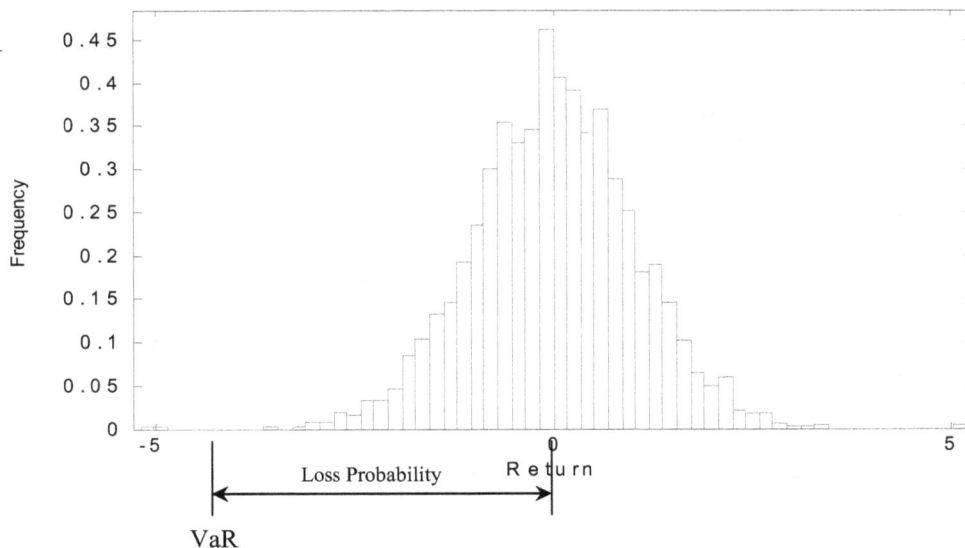

Probably the most broadly accepted definition of VaR is given by Linsmeier and Pearson (2000, p. 48):

"Value at risk is a single, summary, statistical measure of possible portfolio losses. Specifically, value at risk is a measure of losses due to "normal" market movements. Losses greater than the value at risk are suffered only with a specified small probability. Subject to the simplifying assumptions used in its calculation, value at risk aggregates all of the risks in a portfolio into a single number suitable for use in the boardroom, reporting to regulators, or disclosure in an annual report. It is simply a way to describe the magnitude of the likely losses on the portfolio".

3.2   Development of Value-at-Risk methodology

Early VaR measures developed along two parallel lines. One was portfolio theory, and the other was capital adequacy computation. Markowitz (1999) and Holton (2002) have documented the history of VaR measures in the context of portfolio theory.

The origins of portfolio theory can be traced to non-mathematical discussions of portfolio construction. Papers by authors such as Hardy from 1923 and Hicks from 1935 discussed intuitively the merits of diversification. Leavens in his paper from 1945 offered a quantitative example, which may be the first VaR measure ever published. Writing for a non-technical audience, Leavens did not explicitly identify a VaR metric, but he mentioned repeatedly the "spread between probable losses and gains" (Holton, 2002, 2 p.)

Markowitz (1952) and Roy (1952) independently published VaR measures that were surprisingly similar. Each was working to develop a means of selecting portfolios that would, in some sense, optimise reward for a given level of risk. For this purpose, each proposed VaR measures that incorporated covariances between risk factors in order to reflect hedging and diversification effects. While the two measures were mathematically similar, they supported different VaR metrics. Markowitz (1952) used a variance of simple return metric. Roy (1952) used a metric of shortfall risk that represents an upper bound on the probability of the portfolio's gross return being less than some specified "catastrophic return."

Both Markowitz (1952) and Roy (1952) did not explore in depth the issue of how probabilistic assumptions might be specified. Roy's VaR measure required a mean vector and covariance matrix for risk factors that were conditioned on their past values. Markowitz's VaR measure required only a covariance matrix for risk factors.

Markowitz (1952) and Roy (1952) intended their VaR measures for practical portfolio optimisation work. Markowitz was aware of this problem and proposed a more tractable VaR measure that employed a diagonal covariance matrix. William Sharpe described this VaR measure in his paper from 1963. The measure was in different form, but helped motivate Sharpe's (1964) Capital Asset Pricing Model (CAPM).

Because of the limited availability of processing power, VaR measures from this period were largely theoretical, and were published primarily in the context of the emerging portfolio theory. This encompassed the work of Tobin (1958), Sharpe (1964), Lintner (1965) and Mossin (1966). The VaR measures they employed were best suited for equity portfolios. There were few alternative asset categories, and applying VaR to these would have raised a number of modelling issues. For example, applying VaR to either debt instruments or futures contracts entails modelling term structures. Also, debt instruments raise issues of credit spreads. Futures that were traded at the time were primarily for agricultural products, which raise seasonality issues.

Lietaer in his paper from 1971 described a practical VaR measure for foreign exchange risk. He wrote during the waning days of fixed exchange rates when risk manifested itself as currency devaluations. Since World War II, most currencies had devalued at some point; many had done so several times. Governments were secretive about planned devaluations, so corporations maintained ongoing hedges. Lietaer proposed a sophisticated procedure for optimising such hedges. It incorporated a VaR measure with a variance of market value VaR metric. It assumed devaluations occurred randomly, with the conditional magnitude of a devaluation being normally distributed. Computations were simplified using a modification of Sharpe's (1963) model. Lietaer's work may be the first instance of the Monte Carlo method being employed in a VaR measure (Holton, 2002, 4 p.).

The 1970s and 1980s wrought sweeping changes for markets and technology. For VaR, these had the combined effect of:
- expanding the universe of assets to which VaR might be applied;
- changing how organizations took risk; and
- providing the means to apply VaR in these new contexts.

Perhaps the greatest consequence of the financial innovations of the 1970s and 1980s was the proliferation of leverage. Prior to 1970, avenues for compounding risk were limited. With the proliferation of new instruments, opportunities for leverage abounded. Not only new instruments, but new forms of transactions also offered leverage. Commodity leasing, securities lending, repos and short sales are leveraged transactions. All of these either did not exist or had limited use prior to 1970. Within organizations, leveraging decisions became decentralized. Portfolio managers, traders, product managers and even salespeople acquired the tools of leverage. As leverage proliferated, trading organizations sought new ways to manage risk taking. In turn, this motivated a need for new measures of risk. The traditional risk metrics of financial accounting were ineffective, especially when applied to derivatives. Exposure metrics such as duration, convexity, delta, gamma, and vega were widely adopted, but were primarily of tactical value. Supervising trading activities within a company became almost impossible, with each trading desk adopting risk metrics suitable for its own transactions. Even when two desks adopted similar metrics, there was no means of measuring their aggregate risks. Organizations increasingly needed a single risk metric that could be applied consistently across asset categories.

By 1990, a single processor could easily perform the most complex analyses proposed by Markowitz (1952). The age of the mainframe was waning. Personal computers were ascendant. Financial firms were embracing technology and were using it for such tasks as Monte Carlo pricing of complex derivatives. Another important development was the rapid growth of a financial data industry. Reuters, Telerate, Bloomberg and more specialized firms started compiling databases of historical prices. These would provide the raw data needed to specify probabilistic assumptions used by VaR measures.

As the 1970s turned to the 1980s, markets were becoming more volatile. Firms were becoming more leveraged, and the need for financial risk measures, such as VaR, was growing. The resources to implement VaR were becoming available, but VaR remained primarily a theoretical tool of portfolio theory. Firms needed some way to measure market risk across disparate asset categories, but did not recognized how VaR might fill this need. US regulators were laying the groundwork for them to do so.

By 1993, a fair number of financial firms were employing proprietary VaR measures to assess market risk, allocate capital or monitor market risk limits. The measures took various forms. The most common approach generally followed Markowitz (1952). A portfolio's value would be modelled as a linear polynomial of certain risk factors. A covariance matrix would be constructed for the risk factors, and from this, the standard deviation of portfolio value would be calculated. If portfolio value were assumed normal, a quantile of loss could be calculated. Thomas Wilson was working as a project manager for McKinsey & Co. Wilson's 1993' paper represents the first published attempt to reflect leptokurtosis and heteroskedasticity in the practical VaR measures used on trading floors (Holton, 2002, 17 p.). It is also the first detailed description of a VaR measure for use in a trading environment. The author's casual assumption that readers are familiar with the use of VaR measures on trading floors is indicative of how widespread such use had already become. Without acknowledging his doing so, Wilson also touched on a philosophical issue of some practical importance. He suggested that the covariance matrix for risk factors actually exists, but that a user may have limited knowledge as to its values. This objective interpretation of the underlying probabilities runs counter to Markowitz's (1952) subjective approach, which suggests that the covariance matrix does not actually exist, but is constructed by the user to reflect his own perceptions.

In 1990's, risk management was novel. Many financial firms lacked an independent risk management function. This concept was practically unheard of in non-financial firms. As unease about derivatives and leverage spread, this started to change. The term "risk management" was not new. It had long been used to describe techniques for addressing property and casualty contingencies. Holton (2002) traces such usage to the 1960s and 1970s when organizations were exploring alternatives to insurance, including:

- risk reduction through safety, quality control and hazard education, and
- alternative risk financing, including self-insurance and captive insurance.

Such techniques, together with traditional insurance, were collectively referred to as risk management. More recently, derivative dealers were promoting risk management as the use of derivatives to hedge or customize market-risk exposures. For this reason, derivative instruments were sometimes called risk management products. The new risk management that evolved during the 1990's is different from either of the earlier forms. It tends to view derivatives as a problem as much as a solution. It focuses on reporting, oversight and segregation of duties within organizations. In the summer of 1992, Paul Volker, chairman of the Group of 30[16] approached Dennis Weatherstone, chairman of JP Morgan, and asked him to lead a study of derivatives industry practices. Weatherstone formed an international steering committee and a working group of senior managers from derivatives dealers, end users and related legal, accounting and academic circles. They produced a 68-page report, which the Group of 30 published in July 1993 entitled "Derivatives: Practices and Principles", which has come to be known as the G-30 Report (Holton, 2002, 18 p). It describes then-current derivatives use by dealers and end-users. The heart of the study was a set of 20 recommendations to help dealers and end-users manage their derivatives activities. Topics included (Holton, 2002, 19 p):

- the role of boards and senior management,
- the implementation of independent risk management functions
- the various risks that derivatives transactions entail.

With regard to the market risk faced by derivatives dealers, the report recommended that portfolios be marked-to-market daily, and that risk be assessed with both VaR and stress testing. While the G-30 Report focused on derivatives, most of its recommendations were applicable to the risks associated with other traded instruments. For this reason, the report largely came to define the new risk management of the 1990's. The report is also interesting, as it may be the first published document to use the word "value-at-risk."

During the late 1980's, JP Morgan developed a firm-wide VaR system. This system modelled several hundred risk factors. A covariance matrix was updated quarterly from historical data. Each day, trading units would report by e-mail their positions' deltas with respect to each of the risk factors. These were aggregated to express the combined portfolio's value as a linear polynomial of the risk factors. From this, the standard deviation of portfolio value was calculated. Various VaR metrics were employed. One of these was one-day 95% USD VaR, which was calculated using an assumption that the portfolio's value was normally distributed. With this VaR measure, JP Morgan replaced a cumbersome system of notional market risk limits

---

[16] Founded in 1978, the Group of 30 is a non-profit organization of senior executives, regulators and academics. Through meetings and publications, it seeks to deepen understanding of international economic and financial issues.

with a simple system of VaR limits. Starting in 1990, VaR numbers were combined with P&L's in a report for each day's 4:15 PM Treasury meeting in New York. Those reports, with comments from the Treasury group, were forwarded to chairman Weatherstone. One of the architects of the new VaR measure was Till Guldimann. His career with JP Morgan had positioned him to help develop and then promote the VaR measure within the firm. Guldimann formed a small team to develop the service that is now known as RiskMetrics. It comprised a detailed technical document as well as a covariance matrix for several hundred key factors, which was updated daily. Both were distributed without charge over the Internet (Holton, 2002, p. 20). The service was rolled out with considerable fanfare in October 1994. Launched at a time of global concerns about derivatives and leverage, the timing for RiskMetrics was perfect. RiskMetrics was not a technical breakthrough. While the RiskMetrics Technical Document contained original ideas, for the most part, it described practices that were already widely used. Its linear VaR measure was arguably less sophisticated than Wilson's (1993). The important contribution of RiskMetrics was that it publicized VaR to a wide audience.

3.3 Preconditions for successful implementation of Value-at-Risk methodology

Although advanced methods and systems for measuring and managing risks are a necessary condition for having a business impact, they are not by themselves a sufficient condition. Experience has shown that at least two other preconditions, in addition to having the proper VaR methods and systems, need to be met in practice before VaR will have a significant business impact: the risk management organization must be capable of using VaR information to its advantage and, secondly, it must have the incentives to do so (Alexander, 2000, p. 65). For many institutions the main challenges to getting business impact is not necessarily developing VaR and risk adjusted performance measures (RAPM) systems, but rather ensuring that the risk management organization, processes and culture are in place to utilize, and take advantage of, the information (Alexander, 2000, p. 65).

The first precondition that must be met in order for an institution to leverage VaR and, by extension, RAPM into a true business impact is that the institution be organizationally capable of using the information to support its decision-making process (Alexander, 2000, p. 66). Risk comparability and the fungibility of risk capital imply that risk capital limits can, and should, be dynamically allocated across diverse business activities, allowing it to flow to wherever attractive business opportunities emerge. Many organizations find that market or credit risk lines are "sticky" and that, as a consequence, opportunities are being lost; those institutions that have managed to gain the most impact from VaR behave as if it is fungible, with senior management working together as a team, ensuring that while the overall risk capital limits are respected across the trading businesses, risk capital nonetheless flows to where it is needed within the trading organization

(Alexander, 2000, p. 67). This implies a fundamental redesign of the capital management processes and limit structures in addition to a robust and technically correct VaR methodology.

The lack of close cooperation between people responsible for managing the returns and those responsible for managing the risks leads to a stalemate and an inability to actually use VaR information to support proactive portfolio management. While each of the two possible organizational realignment options (e.g. putting both return and risk management responsibilities with the front or within portfolio management) can be optimal in practice, depending upon the type of business being considered, and therefore may coexist within the same organization, it is clear that one must be chosen before active portfolio management based on VaR methodology can proceed (Alexander, 2000, p. 67-68).

The second precondition that must be met in order for an institution for a VaR system to have a business impact is that the institution has the incentive and opportunities to use the information. Managing capital and using VaR and RAPM measures bottom-up at the transaction level typically do not succeed until senior management recognizes top-down that capital is not a free good. This typically does not occur until management recognises that the 8-12 per cent Return on Equity (ROE) is simply not adequate (Alexander, 2000, p. 68). Until then, there is often very little incentive for the organization to use VaR and RAPM information, even if it were available and the management organization were in place. In general, experience has shown that the incentive to use VaR information is driven by two important considerations: first, the organization must view capital as a scarce resource that needs to be adequately compensated and, secondly, the organization must face non-trivial choices in terms of the types of businesses that could be undertaken given that scarce capital base. Broadly speaking, if management recognizes that capital is scarce and must be allocated between real business alternatives, then VaR and RAPM measures will begin to have real business impact.

It is often thought that the third and final precondition for achieving business impact from VaR numbers is that they be technically correct. A more accurate (and more controversial) statement would be that they be directionally correct, adequate for the business and, most importantly, are actually used to support risk management decisions. In summary, VaR measures and systems are not by themselves sufficient to guarantee business impact: they must also be complemented by changes in the risk management organization and incentives. In point of fact, many institutions have obtained far more impact out of far less in terms of technical sophistication simply because they have put equal focus on these other two dimensions (Alexander, 2000, p. 68).

3.4   Opportunities for using Value-at-Risk forecasts

There are many areas where VaR can potentially have a significant business impact. VaR can be applied consistently across a wide variety of diverse risky positions and portfolios, allowing the relative importance of each to be directly compared and aggregated. While there is a wide variety of standard risk measures available for characterizing the individual risks in a trading or derivatives portfolio (e.g. delta, gamma, vega, shifts, rotations) or credit portfolio (e.g. ratings, exposure numbers, watch lists), they provide little guidance when trying to interpret the relative importance of each individual risk factor to the portfolio's bottom line or for aggregating the different risk categories to a business unit or institution level. The ability to do so correctly allows an institution to gain a deeper understanding of the relative importance of its different risk positions and to gauge better its aggregate risk exposure relative to its aggregate risk appetite. VaR accomplishes these objectives by defining a common metric that can be applied universally across all risk positions or portfolios: the maximum possible loss within a known confidence interval over a given holding period. Besides being able to be applied universally across all risk categories, including market, credit, operational and insurance risks, this metric can be expressed either as returns or monetary units, and this makes it meaningful for all levels of management. It therefore serves as a relevant focal point for discussing risks at all levels within the institution, creating a risk dialogue and culture that is otherwise difficult to achieve given the otherwise technical nature of the issues.

The comparability of VaR across different asset classes leads to the second important reason for calculating VaR. Because VaR can be calculated in monetary units and is designed to cover most, but not all, of the losses that might face a risk business, it also has the intuitive interpretation as the amount of economic or equity capital that must be held to support that particular level of risky business activity. In fact, the definition of VaR is completely compatible with the role of equity as perceived by many financial institutions: while reserves or provisions are held to cover expected losses incurred in the normal course of business, equity capital is held to provide a capital cushion against any potential unexpected losses. Since an institution cannot be expected to hold capital to cover all unexpected losses with 100 per cent certainty, the level of this capital cushion must be determined within prudent solvency guidelines over a reasonable time horizon needed to identify and resolve problem situations. The philosophy that economically-determined VaR is the relevant measure for determining capital requirements for risk businesses is also being increasingly adopted by regulators and supervisors. Unfortunately, while there is a convergence in terms of the acceptance of VaR as the relevant determinant of capital adequacy for most risk businesses in concept and even a few of the relevant parameters (e.g. a 99 per cent confidence interval/10-day holding period horizon), the actual calculation rules are left up to the individual institution. This is unfortunate because there exists a wide variety of different methods, each presenting the institution with non-trivial trade-offs.

Another important characteristic of VaR is that it takes account of the correlations between different risk factors. If two risks offset each other, the VaR allows for this offset and reports a low overall risk. If the same two risks don't offset each other, the VaR takes this into account as well and gives a higher risk estimate. Clearly, a risk measure that accounts for correlations is essential in order to handle portfolio risks in a statistically meaningful way. Finally, VaR information can also be used in several other ways (Dowd, 2002, p.10-11):

- Senior management can use it to set their overall risk target, and determine risk targets and position limits down the line. If the firm wants to increase its risks, it would increase the overall VaR target, and vice versa.

- Since VaR provides information about the maximum amount a firm is likely to lose with a certain confidence level, it can be used to determine capital allocation. It can be used to determine capital requirements at the level of the firm, but also down to the level of the individual investment decision: the riskier the activity, the higher the VaR and greater the capital requirement.

- VaR can be very useful for reporting and disclosing purposes, and firms increasingly make a point of reporting VaR information in their annual reports[17]

- VaR information can be used to assess the risks of different investment opportunities before decisions are made. VaR-based decision rules can guide investment, hedging and trading decisions, and do so taking account of the implications of alternative choices for the portfolio risk as a whole[18].

- VaR information can be used to implement portfolio-wide hedging strategies that are otherwise rarely possible (Dowd, 1999).

- VaR information can be used to provide new remuneration rules for traders, managers and other employees that take account of the risks they take, and so discourage the excessive risk-taking that occurs when employees are rewarded on the basis of profits alone, without any reference to the risks they took to get those profits. VaR can help provide for a more consistent and integrated approach to the management of different risks, leading also to greater risk transparency and disclosure, and better strategic management.

3.5   Criticism and limitations of Value-at-Risk methodology

Probably the most obvious criticism of VaR as a risk measure is that it is completely backwards looking, oriented towards past events and historical data. This means that VaR takes no account of the future events and developments that can have significant influence on the riskiness of a particular position, that might be predictable by other means. Unfortunately this is a just and undeniable critique that also applies to majority of other risk measures, with the exception of stress testing and scenario analysis, which on the other hand have their own shortcoming, as

---

[17] For more on the use of VaR for reporting and disclosure purposes see Dowd, 2000 or Jorion, 2001.
[18] For further information on VaR-based decision rules see Dowd, 1999.

described earlier. The second, related problem of VaR is more practical. Even in a stationary environment it is difficult to estimate the loss distribution accurately, particularly for large portfolios, and many seemingly sophisticated risk management systems are based on relatively crude statistical models for the loss distribution. However, this is not an argument against using VaR. Rather, it calls for improvements in the way loss distributions are estimated and for prudence in the practical implementation of risk management models based on estimated loss distributions. In particular, risk measures based on the loss distribution, such as VaR, should be complemented by information from hypothetical scenarios. Moreover, forward-looking information reflecting the expectations of market participants, such as implied volatilities, should be used in conjunction with statistical estimates in calibrating models of the loss distribution. Unfortunately, this approach is also inherently faulty since it is necessarily based on past information (McNeil, Frey, Embrechts, 2005, p.36). These serious constraints of VaR as a risk measure are exactly the reason why the regulators require regular stress testing and encourage scenario analysis. Only by combining the advantages and strong points of backwards looking risk measure such as VaR and forward looking risk measures such as stress testing and scenario analysis can an institution hope to construct a sound and robust risk measurement system.

Following the release of JP Morgan's RiskMetrics and the widespread adoption of VaR measures, there was somewhat of a backlash against VaR. Criticisms followed three themes:
   1. different VaR implementations produced inconsistent results;
   2. VaR is conceptually flawed as a measure of risk;
   3. widespread use of VaR entails systemic risks.

Critics of the first issue include Beder (1995) and Marshall and Seigel (1997). Beder (1995) performed an analysis using Monte Carlo and historical VaR measures to calculate sixteen different VaR measurements for three portfolios. The tested VaR measurements for each portfolio tended to be inconsistent, leading Beder (1995) to describe VaR as "*seductive but dangerous*". In retrospect, this indictment seems harsh. Beder's (1995) analysis employed different VaR metrics, different covariance matrices and historical VaR measures with very low sample sizes. It came as no surprise that Beder obtained disparate VaR measurements. Despite its shortcomings, Beder's (1995) paper is historically important as an early critique of VaR. It was cited frequently in the ensuing VaR debate. To make matters worse, work by Marshall and Siegel (1997) showed that VaR models were exposed to considerable implementation risk as well, so even theoretically similar models could give quite different VaR estimates because of the differences in the ways in which the models are implemented. It is therefore difficult for VaR advocates to deny that VaR estimates can be very imprecise. The danger here is obvious: if VaR estimates are too inaccurate and users take them seriously, they could take on much bigger risks and lose much more than they had bargained for. As Hoppe (1998) put it: "*believing a spuriously precise estimate of risk is worse than admitting the irreducible unreliability of one's estimate. False certainty is more dangerous than acknowledged ignorance*" (Hoppe, 1998, p. 50). Nassim Taleb, a famous derivatives trader put the same point in a different way: "*You are worse off relying on misleading information than on not having any information at all. If you give a pilot an altimeter that is sometimes defective he will crash the plane. Give him nothing and he will look out the window*" (Taleb, 1997a, p. 37).

Of more concern were criticisms suggesting that VaR measures were conceptually flawed. A key issue was the validity of the statistical and other assumptions underlying VaR, and both Nassim Taleb (1997a,b) and Richard Hoppe (1998,1999) were very critical of the naive transfer of mathematical and statistical models from the physical sciences where they were well suited to social systems where they were often invalid. Such applications often ignore important features of social systems - the ways in which intelligent agents learn and react to their environment, the non-stationarity and dynamic interdependence of many market processes, and so forth - features that undermine the plausibility of many models and leave VaR estimates wide open to major errors (Taleb, 1997a, p. 445). A good example of this problem is suggested by Hoppe (1999, p. 1): Long Term Capital Management (LTCM) had a risk model that suggested that the loss it suffered in the summer and autumn of 1998 was 14 times the standard deviation of its returns, and a 14-sigma event shouldn't occur once in the entire history of the universe. So LTCM was either incredibly unlucky or it had a very poor risk measurement model (Dowd, 2002, p.12). Taleb (1997a,b) was also critical of the tendency of some VaR proponents to overstate the usefulness of VaR. He was particularly dismissive of Philippe Jorion's (1997) claim that VaR might have prevented disasters such as Orange County. Taleb's response was that these disasters had other causes - especially, excessive leverage. As he put it, a Wall Street clerk would have picked up these excesses with an abacus, and VaR defenders overlook the point that there are simpler and more reliable risk measures than VaR (Taleb, 1997b). Taleb is clearly right because any simple duration analysis should have revealed the rough magnitude of Orange County's interest-rate exposure. So in the case of Orange County the problem was not the absence of VaR, as such, but the absence of any basic risk measurement at all. Similar criticisms of VaR were also made by Culp, Miller, Neves (1997): they point out that the key issue is not how VaR is measured, but how it is used; they also point out that VaR measures would have been of limited use in averting these disasters, and might actually have been misleading in some cases.

The third line of criticism suggests that, if many market participants use VaR to allocate capital or maintain market risk limits, they will have a tendency to simultaneously liquidate positions during periods of market turmoil. This risk is similar to that of portfolio insurance, which contributed to the stock market crash of 1987, but there are differences. Stock positions tend mostly to be long because short selling comprises only a small fraction of equity transactions. Portfolio insurance programs in 1987 were designed to protect against a falling market, so they responded to the crash in lockstep. In other markets, positions may be long or short. In fixed income markets, there are lenders and borrowers. In commodities markets, there are buyers and sellers. In foreign exchange markets, every forward position is long one currency but short another. If VaR measures compel speculators in these markets to reduce positions, this will affect both long and short positions, so liquidations will tend to offset. Taleb (1997a) pointed out that VaR players are dynamic hedgers, and need to revise their positions in the face of changes in market prices. If everyone uses VaR, there is then a danger that this hedging behaviour will make uncorrelated risks become very correlated - and firms will bear much greater risk than their VaR models might suggest. Taleb's argument is all the more convincing because he wrote this before the summer 1998 financial crisis, where this sort of problem was widely observed. Similarly, Danielsson (2001) and Basak, Shapiro (2001) suggested good reasons to believe that poorly thought through regulatory VaR constraints could destabilise the financial system by inducing banks to increase their risk-taking: for example, a VaR cap can give risk managers an incentive to protect themselves against mild losses, but not against larger ones.

The above stated problems are common to all risk measurement systems, and are not unique to VaR. Unfortunately VaR has its own distinctive flaws and limitations.

The first problem connected directly to parametric VaR is the idea of forecasting a correlation matrix. Forecast of the correlation matrix gives a point estimate in the future. The errors that result from correlation effects, dominate the errors in market movements at the time. So the correlation methodology for VaR is inherently flawed (Holton, 2002, p. 24). Such concerns have a practical tone, but underlying them are philosophical issues first identified by Markowitz (1952). If probabilities are subjective, it makes no sense to speak of the accuracy of a VaR measure or of a forecast of a correlation matrix. From a subjective perspective, a VaR measurement or a correlation matrix is merely an objective representation of a user's subjective perceptions.

A serious limitation of VaR as a risk measure is that it forecasts the most a firm can lose p percent of time (e.g. 99%), but tells nothing about what the loss can be on the remaining $1-p$ (e.g. 1%) percent of occasions. If a tail event (a loss in excess of VaR) does occur, it is natural to expect to lose more than the forecasted VaR, but the VaR figure itself gives no indication of how much that might be. This is a serious problem that can lead to some awkward consequences. A trader or asset manager might enter into deals that produce small gains under most circumstances and the occasional very large loss. If the probability of loss is low enough, then this position would have a low VaR and so appear to have little risk, and yet the firm would now be exposed to the danger of a very large loss. A single VaR figure can also give a misleading impression of relative risk of a particular position. For example, two positions with equal VaR at some given confidence level and holding period, but one position might involve much heavier tail losses than the other. The VaR measure taken on its own would incorrectly suggest that both positions were equally risky (Dowd, 2002, p. 28). Another problem with VaR was pointed out by Ju and Pearson (1999). If VaR measures are used to control or remunerate risk-taking, traders will have an incentive to seek out positions where risk is over- or underestimated and trade them. They will therefore take on more risk than suggested by VaR estimates, so VaR estimates will be biased downwards. Ju and Pearson (1999) suggest that the magnitude of these underestimates can be very substantial. Another drawback is that VaR can discourage diversification. A good example of this effect is provided by Dowd (2002). For example, if there are 100 possible future states of the world, each with the same probability. There are 100 different assets, each earning reasonable money in 99 states, but suffering a big loss in one state. Each of these assets loses in a different state, so this means that one of them will certainly suffer a large loss. If a investor invest in one of these assets only, then the VaR will be negative at the 95% confidence level, because the probability of incurring a loss is 1%. However, diversifying the investments and investing in all assets, means that the investor is certain to incur a big loss. The VaR of the diversified portfolio is therefore much larger than the VaR of the undiversified one. This simple example shows that VaR measure can discourage diversification of risks because it fails to take into account the magnitude of losses in excess of VaR (Dowd, 2002, p. 29).

VaR risk measures are also open to criticism from a very different direction. Artzner, Delbaen, Eber, Heath (1997,1999) have used an axiomatic approach to the problem of defining a satisfactory risk measure. They set out certain attributes that a good risk measure should satisfy, and call risk measures that satisfy these axioms "coherent". A coherent risk measure ρ assigns to each loss X a risk measure $\rho(X)$ such that the following conditions hold (Artzner, Delbaen, Eber, Heath, 1999):

$\rho(tX) = t\rho(X)$	(homogeneity)	(3.9)
$\rho(X) \geq \rho(Y)$, if $X \leq Y$	(monotonicity)	(3.10)
$\rho(X + n) = \rho(X) - n$	(risk-free condition)	(3.11)
$\rho(X) + \rho(Y) \leq \rho(X + Y)$	(sub-additivity)	(3.12)

for any number n and positive number t. These conditions guarantee that the risk function is convex, which in turn corresponds to risk aversion. That is:

$$\rho(tX + (1 - t)Y) \leq t\rho(X) + (1 - t)\rho(Y) \qquad (3.13)$$

The first and second conditions are reasonable conditions to impose a priori, and together imply that the function $\rho(\cdot)$ is convex. The risk-free condition means that the addition of a riskless asset to a portfolio will decrease its risk because it will increase the value of end-of-period portfolio. According to the last condition a risk measure is sub-additive if the measured risk of the sum of positions X and Y is less than or equal to the sum of the measured risks of the individual positions considered on their own. VaR is not a coherent risk measure because it does not necessarily satisfy the sub-additivity condition. VaR can only be made to be sub-additive if a usually implausible assumption is imposed of returns being normally (or slightly more generally, elliptically) distributed (Artzner, Delbaen, Eber, Heath, 1999, p. 217). Sub-additivity matters for a number of reasons (Dowd, 2002, p. 30):

- If risks are sub-additive, then adding risks together would give an overestimate of combined risk, and this means that a sum of risks can be used as a conservative estimate of combined risk. This facilitates decentralised decision-making within a firm, because a supervisor can always use the sum of the risks of the units reporting to him as a conservative risk measure. But if risks are not sub-additive, adding them together gives an underestimate of combined risks, and this makes the sum of risks effectively useless as a risk measure. In risk management, it is desirable for risk estimates to be unbiased or biased conservatively.
- If regulators use non-sub-additive risk measures to set capital requirements, a financial firm might be tempted to break itself up to reduce its regulatory capital requirements, because the sum of the capital requirements of the smaller units would be less than the capital requirement of the firm as a whole.
- Non-sub-additive risk measures can also tempt agents trading on an organised exchange to break up their accounts, with separate accounts for separate risks, in order to reduce their margin requirements. This could be a matter of serious concern for the exchange because the margin requirements on the separate accounts would no longer cover the combined risks.

A very serious shortcoming of VaR is that it provides no handle on the extent of the losses that might be suffered beyond the threshold amount indicated by this measure. VaR is incapable of distinguishing between situations where losses in the tail are only a bit worse, and those where they are overwhelming. Indeed, VaR merely provides a lowest bound for losses in the tail of the loss distribution and has a bias toward optimism instead of the conservatism that ought to prevail in risk management.

An alternative measure that does quantify the losses that might be encountered in the tail is conditional value-at-risk, or CVaR. Both VaR and CVaR require the user to a priori specify confidence level and holding period. While VaR represents a maximum loss one expects at a determined confidence level for a given holding period, CVaR is the loss one expects to suffer, provided that the loss is equal to or greater than VaR. Formally, CVaR at the 100cl% confidence level is (adapted from McNeil, Frey, Embrechts, 2005, p. 45):

$$CVaR[cl,r] \equiv -E\{r \mid r \leq -VaR[cl,r]\} \qquad (3.14)$$

Graphical representation of CVaR and its connection to VaR is presented in figure 12.

Figure 12 - CVaR and VaR

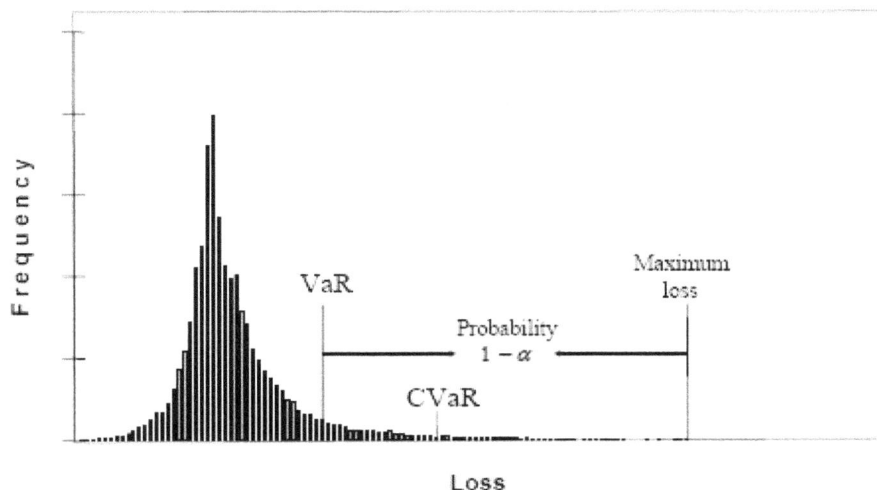

As a tool in optimisation modelling, CVaR has superior properties to VaR in many respects. It maintains consistency with VaR by yielding the same results in the limited settings where VaR computations are tractable, i.e., for normal distributions (or a more general class of "elliptical" distributions (Rockafellar, Uryasev, 2001, p. 2)); for portfolios with such simple distributions, working with CVaR, VaR, or minimum variance (Markowitz, 1952) is equivalent (Rockafellar, Uryasev, 2001). Most importantly for applications, however, CVaR can be expressed by a remarkable minimization formula. This formula can readily be incorporated into problems of optimisation with respect to $x \in X$ that are designed to minimize risk or shape it within bounds. Significant shortcuts are thereby achieved while preserving crucial problem features like convexity. CVaR and its minimization formula were first developed in the paper by Rockafellar and Uryasev (1999).

For continuous loss distributions, the CVaR at a given confidence level is the expected loss given that the loss is greater than the VaR at that level, or for that matter, the expected loss given that the loss is greater than or equal to the VaR. For distributions with possible discontinuities, however, it has a more subtle definition and can differ from either of those quantities, which for convenience in comparison can be designated by $CVaR^+$ and $CVaR^-$, respectively. $CVaR^+$ is also known as "mean shortfall" (Mausser, Rosen, 1999), although the seemingly identical term "expected shortfall" has been interpreted in other ways in Acerbi, Nordio (2001); Acerbi, Tasche (2001), with the latter paper taking it as a synonym for CVaR itself), while "tail VaR" is a term that has been suggested for $CVaR^-$ (Artzner, Delbaen, Eber, Heath, 1999). Unlike $CVaR^+$ and $CVaR^-$, CVaR is seen to be a coherent measure of risk in the sense of Artzner, Delbaen, Eber, Heath (1999). Although recently being proclaimed as a "superior" risk measure CVaR also has its shortcomings. Alexander, Baptista (2003) find that under certain conditions, the presence of CVaR constraint will cause a risk-averse agent to select a portfolio that has a smaller standard deviation than the one that would have been selected in the absence of CVaR constraints. In other conditions CVaR constraints cause a highly risk-averse agent to select a portfolio that has larger standard deviation. Since a CVaR constraint is tighter than the VaR constraint when the CVaR and VaR bounds coincide, these implications are also true but to a lesser extent if a VaR constraint is imposed. Consequently, a CVaR constraint is more effective than a VaR constraint as a tool to control slightly risk-averse agents but has a more perverse effect on highly risk-averse agents, such as pension funds (Alexander, Baptista, 2003, p.2). These findings significantly undermine the status of a "superior" risk measure and weaken the main argument put forward against VaR by the advocates of CVaR.

CVaR is still not widely used in financial industry, but it plays an important role in insurance industry due to its focus on extreme events. CVaR has some advantages over VaR when used in portfolio optimisation but its use in measuring market risk and forming of capital requirements is still questionable since it, under certain conditions, suffers from similar problems that are put forward as main critiques of VaR. Furthermore, CVaR as a measure of risk is not recognised by the Basel Committee, meaning that the banks will continue to research and develop VaR models to make them more appropriate for forming of capital requirements. All things considering, recognising all its imperfections and flaws, at present, VaR is the most popular and widespread modern risk measure in existence.

4   CALCULATING VALUE-AT-RISK FOR MARKET RISK EXPOSURE

Slightly confusing for the organizations considering implementing VaR measure is the fact that, although all institutions begin with the same generic definition, the actual calculation methods used can markedly differ. In fact, it seems that just as each institution has a unique name for its VaR, each also has a unique technical implementation, and while there is some convergence in terms of high-level approaches for measuring market risk, convergence in technical approaches is much farther off when discussing the measurement of credit, insurance and operational risks. In all fairness, the different technical implementations are based in part on theoretical grounds, in part on systems considerations, and in part on the institutional and strategic context in which the calculations are employed to measure and control risks. But the myriad of different context-specific methods only serves to highlight the need to evaluate carefully the trade-offs between the different methods when deciding which method is best suited to a particular business. The purpose of this chapter is to give a concise technical overview of some of the most prevalent techniques used for calculating VaR, clearly stating their (implicit) assumptions and their relative strengths and weaknesses from a theoretical as well as a practical perspective. Although VaR measurement techniques are becoming more prevalent for a wide variety of different risk classes (e.g. market, credit, insurance, operational, business volume and behavioural risks), in order to frame the issues in manageable terms the focus here is primarily on market or price risks.

4.1   Time series modelling

Financial asset prices are observed in the present, and will have been observed in the past, but it is not possible to determine exactly what they will be in the future. Financial asset prices are random variables, not deterministic variables. A random variable, also called a stochastic variable or variate, is a real-valued function that is defined over a sample space with probability measure. A value x of a random variable X may be thought of as a number that is associated with a chance outcome (Brockwell, Davis, 1991, p. 8). Each outcome is determined by a chance event, and so has a probability measure. This probability measure is represented by the probability density function of the random variable. For any probability density function $g(x)$, the corresponding distribution function is defined as $G(x)=Prob(X<x) = \int_{-\infty}^{x} g(x)dx$. It is not necessary to specify both density and distribution. Given the density it is possible to calculate the distribution, and conversely since $g(x) = G'(x)$ (Alexander, 2001, p. 4).

As is the common practice in risk literature, the time series will be analysed through logarithmic returns of held assets. In general, when dealing with time series analysis, it is far easier to work with financial returns, instead of prices of assets. In financial markets the modelling procedures for return data and for price data are different and thus the statistical concepts and methods that apply to return data do not apply to price data. For example, volatility and correlation are concepts that only apply to stationary processes. It makes no sense to try to estimate volatility or correlation based on price data. Campbell, Lo and MacKinlay (1997) give the main reasons for using logarithmic returns in analysis of financial time series. First, for average investor, return of an asset is easy to understand and it represents a scale-free presentation of the investment opportunity. Second, compared to prices of assets, returns have some attractive statistical properties, such as stationarity.

A random variable is lognormally distributed when its logarithms are normally distributed. A lognormal density function is not symmetrical; it is bounded by zero on the low side but can, in theory, reach infinitely high values. This ensures that the asset price (or portfolio value) is never negative even if the returns themselves are unbounded. The logarithmic returns make more sense over long horizon periods because it allows for interim income to earn returns. For this reason it is commonly assumed that financial assets (bonds and shares) and possibly commodity prices are better represented by lognormal than by normal variates. If the return process of an asset:

$$r_t = (P_t - P_{t-1})/P_{t-1} \qquad (4.1)$$

is normally distributed then (Tsay, 2002, p. 4):

$$P_t/P_{t-1} = 1 + r_t \qquad \text{and}$$
$$ln(P_t/P_{t-1}) \approx r \text{ (when } r \text{ is small, } ln(1 + r) \approx r) \qquad (4.2)$$

Therefore $ln(P_t/P_0)$ is normally distributed and P_t/P_0 is lognormally distributed. This argument is based on investment assets and would not apply to interest rates (Alexander, 2001, p. 4). The argument also shows that the return over small time intervals is approximated by the first difference in the log prices. The general model for the log returns $\{r_{it}; i = 1,..., N; t = 1,..., T\}$ is its joint distribution function (Tsay, 2002, p. 9):

$$F_r(r_{11},...,r_{N1}; r_{12},...,r_{N2};...; r_{1T},...,r_{NT}; Y; \theta) \qquad (4.3)$$

Y – state vector consisting of variables that summarize the environment in which asset returns are determined,
θ – vector of parameters that determine the distribution function $F_r(.)$

The probability distribution $F_r(.)$ governs the stochastic behaviour of the returns r_{it} and Y. In majority of financial studies, the state vector Y is considered as a priori given and the main point of interest is the conditional distribution of returns. The goal of time series analysis is to estimate the unknown parameter vector θ and to draw statistical inference about behaviour of returns given the information on historical returns. It is hard to predict price variations of financial assets so it is usual to assume that successive returns are relatively independent of each other. This means that uncertainty will increase as the holding period increases, the distribution will become more dispersed and its variance will increase. Put another way, the variance of n-day returns will increase with n. Therefore it is not possible to compare n-day variance with m-day variance on the same scale. It is standard to assume statistically independent returns and to express a standard deviation in annual terms.

Two random variables X and Y are independent if and only if their joint density function $h(x, y)$ is simply the product of two marginal densities. That is, if X has density $f(x)$ and Y has density $g(y)$ then X and Y are independent if and only if $h(x, y)$ $=f(x)g(y)$ (Hamilton, 1994, p. 742). Thus in financial markets the annual volatility is defined as (Alexander, 2001, p. 5):

$$\text{Annual volatility} = (100\sigma\sqrt{A})\% \qquad\qquad (4.4)$$

where A is an annualising factor, the number of returns per year. The annualising factor is a normalizing constant: the variance increases with the holding period but the annualising factor decreases. The number of trading days (or risk days) per year is usually taken for the conversion of a daily standard deviation into an annualised percentage; that is, often $A = 250$ or 252 days. In this way volatilities of returns of different frequencies may be compared on the same scale in a volatility term structure.

4.1.1 Linear stochastic processes

When analysing a financial time series using formal statistical methods, it is useful to regard the observed return series, $(r_1, r_2,..., r_T)$, as a particular realisation of a stochastic process (Enders, 2004, p. 49). This realisation is often denoted $\{r_t\}$, while, in general, the stochastic process itself will be the family of random variables $\{R_t\}_{-\infty}^{+\infty}$ defined on an appropriate probability space (Mills, 2004, p. 8). The stochastic process can be described by a T-dimensional probability distribution, so that the relationship between a realisation and a stochastic process is analogous to that between the sample and the population in classical statistics. A fundamental theorem in time series analysis, known as Wold's decomposition (Hamilton, 1994, chapter 3.8), states that every weakly stationary[19], purely non-deterministic,

---

[19] A time series is considered strictly stationary if the joint distribution of $(r_{t1},...,r_{tk})$ is the same as $(r_{t1+t},...,r_{tk+t})$ for all t, where k is a positive integer and $(t_1,...,t_k)$ is a series of k positive integers. This means that for a time series to be strictly stationary, the joint distribution of the observed variable needs to be time invariant. This condition is very restrictive and cannot be defended in the empirical studies of financial series. A time series is said to be weakly stationary if both the mean of r_t and the covariance between r_t and r_{t-l} are time invariant, where l is an arbitrary positive integer. This means that a time series is

stochastic process $(r_t - \mu)$ can be written as a linear combination (or linear filter) of a sequence of uncorrelated random variables[20]. The basic building block in time series modelling is a sequence $\{\varepsilon_t\}_{t=-\infty}^{\infty}$ whose elements have mean zero and variance σ^2:

$$E(\mu) = 0 \qquad\qquad (4.5)$$
$$E(\varepsilon^2) = \sigma^2 \qquad\qquad (4.6)$$

for which the ε's are uncorrelated across time[21]:

$$E(\varepsilon_t \varepsilon_\tau) = 0 \quad for\ t \neq \tau \qquad\qquad (4.7)$$

A process satisfying Equations 4.5 to 4.7 is described as a white noise process. A stronger condition requiring the ε's to be independent across time as well as satisfying Equations 4.5 and 4.6 is called independent white noise process:

$$\varepsilon_t,\ \varepsilon_\tau\ independent\ for\ t \neq \tau \qquad\qquad (4.8)$$

---

weakly stationary if the expected value of the series equals its mean which is a constant, $E(r_t) = \mu$ and covariance between r_t and some prior observation r_{t-l} is constant and changes only with l, $Cov(r_t,\ r_{t-l}) = \gamma_l$. Necessary conditions for both the strictly and weakly stationary time series is that the first two moments of r_t are finite. If the time series r_t is normally distributed, the weak stationarity is equivalent to strict stationarity. In the finance literature it is common to assume that an asset return series is weakly stationary (Tsay, 2002, p. 23).

[20] Purely non-deterministic process means that any linearly deterministic components have been subtracted from $(r_t - \mu)$. Such a component is one that can be perfectly predicted from past values of itself and examples commonly found are a (constant) mean, as is implied by writing the process as $(r_t - \mu)$, periodic sequences, and polynomial or exponential sequences in t. A formal discussion of this theorem can be found in Brockwell and Davis (1991, chapter 5.7).

[21] When the linear dependence between r_t and its past values r_{t-l} is of interest, the concept of correlation is generalized to autocorrelation. The correlation coefficient between r_t and r_{t-l} is called the lag-l autocorrelation of r_t and is denoted by ρ_l, which under the weak stationarity assumption is a function of only l. Specifically:

$$\hat{\rho}_l = \frac{\sum_{t=l+1}^{T}(r_t - \bar{r})(r_{t-l} - \bar{r})}{\sum_{t=1}^{T}(r_t - \bar{r})^2},\quad 0 \leq l < T-1$$

where $\bar{r}$ is the sample mean $\bar{r} = \sum_{t=1}^{T} r_t / T$ for a given sample of returns $\{r_t\}_{t=1}^{T}$. From the equation, $\rho_0 = 1$, $\rho_l = \rho_{-l}$, and $-1 \leq \rho_l \leq 1$. In addition, a weakly stationary series r_t is not serially correlated if and only if $\rho_l = 0$ for all $l > 0$. If $\{r_t\}$ is an identically and independently distributed (IID) sequence satisfying $E(r_t^2) < \infty$ then $\hat{\rho}_l$ is asymptotically normal with mean zero and variance $1/T$ for any fixed positive integer l. The test statistic is the usual t ratio, which is $\sqrt{T}\hat{\rho}_l$ and follows asymptotically the standard normal distribution (Box, Jenkins, and Reinsel 1994, p. 26).

If all the conditions 4.5 to 4.8 are satisfied and $\varepsilon_t \sim N(0, \sigma^2)$ the process is called a Gaussian white noise process (Hamilton, 1994, p. 48).

A financial time series r_t is linear if it can be written as (Tsay, 2002, p. 27):

$$r_t = \mu + \sum_{i=0}^{\infty} \alpha_i \varepsilon_{t-i} \tag{4.9}$$

where μ is the mean of r_t, $\alpha_0 = 1$ and $\{\varepsilon_t\}$ is a white noise series. For a linear time series in Equation 4.9, the dynamic structure of r_t is governed by the coefficients α_i, which are called the α-weights of r_t in the time series literature (Tsay, 2002, p. 28).

If r_t is weakly stationary, by using the independence of $\{\varepsilon_t\}$ its mean and variance are obtained as:

$$E(r_t) = \mu, \qquad V(r_t) = \sigma_{\varepsilon}^2 \sum_{i=0}^{\infty} \alpha_i^2 \tag{4.10}$$

where σ_{ε}^2 is the variance of ε_t. The lag-l autocovariance of r_t is (Tsay, 2002, p. 28):

$$\gamma_l = Cov(r_t, r_{t-l}) = E\left[\left(\sum_{i=0}^{\infty} \alpha_i \varepsilon_{t-i} \right) \left(\sum_{j=0}^{\infty} \alpha_j \varepsilon_{t-l-j} \right) \right] = E\left(\sum_{i,j=0}^{\infty} \alpha_i \alpha_j \varepsilon_{t-i} \varepsilon_{t-l-j} \right)$$

$$= \sum_{j=0}^{\infty} \alpha_{j+l} \alpha_j E(\varepsilon_{t-l-j}^2) = \sigma_{\varepsilon}^2 \sum_{j=0}^{\infty} \alpha_j \alpha_{j+l} \tag{4.11}$$

Consequently, the α-weights are related to the autocorrelations of r_t as follows:

$$\rho_l = \frac{\gamma_l}{\gamma_0} = \frac{\sum_{i=0}^{\infty} \alpha_i \alpha_{i+l}}{1 + \sum_{i=1}^{\infty} \alpha_i^2}, \quad l \geq 0 \tag{4.12}$$

where $\alpha_0 = 1$.

The white noise process is transformed into a process r_t by what is called a linear filter (Box, Jenkins, Reinsel, 1994, p. 9):

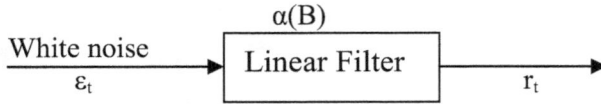

$$
\begin{array}{c}
\alpha(B) \\
\text{White noise} \xrightarrow{} \boxed{\text{Linear Filter}} \xrightarrow{} \\
\varepsilon_t \qquad\qquad\qquad\qquad\qquad r_t
\end{array}
$$

where B is a backward shift operator, defined by $Br_t = r_{t-1}$; hence $B^m r_t = r_{t-m}$.

The linear filtering operation simply takes a weighted sum of previous random shocks ε_t:

$$
\begin{aligned}
r_t &= \mu + \varepsilon_t + \alpha_{1}\varepsilon_{t-1} + \alpha_2\varepsilon_{t-2} + \dots \\
&= \mu + \alpha(B)\varepsilon_t
\end{aligned}
\qquad (4.13)
$$

In general, μ is a parameter that determines the level of the process, and

$$
\alpha(B) = 1 + \alpha_1 B + \alpha_2 B^2 + \dots
\qquad (4.14)
$$

is a linear operator that transforms ε_t into r_t, and is called the transfer of the filter.

The sequence $\alpha_1, \alpha_2, \dots$ formed by the weights may be infinite. If the sequence is finite, or infinite but absolutely summable meaning that $\sum_{j=0}^{\infty} |\alpha_j| < \infty$, the filter is considered stable and process r_t is stationary. In that case, parameter μ represents the mean about which the process varies. If the process is infinite and not absolutely summable, process r_t is nonstationary and μ has no specific meaning except as a reference point for the level of the process.

It is possible however, for a linear filter of a white noise process to result in a non-linear stationary process r_t, the variance, $V(r_t)$ is a constant for all t but the conditional variance $V(r_t | r_{t-1}, \dots, r_{t-n})$ depends on the observed prior value and thus can change from period to period.

4.1.1.1   Autoregressive (AR) process

Autoregressive models are the simplest and the most well known linear time series models, representing the time series as a function of its own lagged values. For example, the autoregressive model of order 1, the AR(1) model, is represented by (Hamilton, 1994, p. 53):

$$
r_t = \alpha_0 + \alpha_1 r_{t-1} + \varepsilon_t
\qquad (4.15)
$$

where $\varepsilon_t \sim IID(0, \sigma)$. The constant term α_0 models a trend in the series either upwards ($\alpha_0 > 0$) or downwards ($\alpha_0 < 0$). The lag coefficient α determines the stability of the process. If $|\alpha| > 1$ the time series will explode, that is $r_t \to \pm\infty$ as $t \to \infty$. The special case $|\alpha| = 1$ gives the random walk model[22], and it is only when $|\alpha| < 1$ that the process defined by (4.15) will be stationary.

Conditional on the past return r_{t-1}, AR(1) model implies that:

$$E(r_t \mid r_{t-1}) = \alpha_0 + \alpha_1 r_{t-1}, \quad V(r_t \mid r_{t-1}) = V(\varepsilon_t) = \sigma_\varepsilon^2 \qquad (4.16)$$

Given the past return (r_{t-1}) the current return (r_t) is centred around $\alpha_0 + \alpha_1 r_{t-1}$ with variability σ_ε^2. This is a Markov property such that conditional on r_{t-1} the return r_t is not correlated with r_{t-i} for $i > 1$ (Tsay, 2002, p. 30). A generalization of the AR(1) model is the AR(p) model:

$$r_t = \alpha_0 + \alpha_1 r_{t-1} + \ldots + \alpha_p r_{t-p} + \varepsilon_t \qquad (4.17)$$

where p is a non-negative integer.

This model says that the past p values r_{t-i} $(i=1,\ldots, p)$ jointly determine the conditional expectation of r_t given the past data.

Assuming that the time series is weakly stationary, the $E(r_t) = \mu$, $V(r_t) = \gamma_0$, and $Cov(r_t, r_{t-j}) = \gamma_j$, where μ and γ_0 are constant and γ_j is a function of j not t. The mean, variance and autocorrelations of the series is obtained as follows (Tsay, 2002, p. 29). Taking the expectation of Equation 4.15:

$$E(r_t) = \alpha_0 + \alpha_1 E(r_{t-1}) \qquad (4.18)$$

Under the stationarity condition $E(r_t) = E(r_{t-1}) = \mu$ and hence:

---

[22] Random walk model is related to geometric Brownian motion, a process that underlies the efficient market hypothesis related to basic option pricing models. Fundamental assumption of the efficient market hypothesis is that asset prices follow a process:

$$dP/P = r\,dt + \sigma\,dZ$$

where P is the price of an asset, r and σ are constants representing the drift in asset prices and the volatility of returns respectively, and Z is a Wiener process. That is, increments dZ are independent and normally distributed with mean zero and variance dt. Random walk model is obtained by applying Ito's lemma to the geometric Brownian motion. The random walk process that will be followed by log prices is:

$$\ln P_t = c + \ln P_{t-1} + \varepsilon_t$$

where $c = r - \sigma^2/2$ and the error term $\varepsilon_t \sim NID(0, \sigma^2)$, is the returns process. The random walk model is commonly applied to model log prices in efficient financial markets. The random walk model allows for trends in asset prices through constant term c that corresponds to the expected return (Alexander, 2001, p. 320).

$$\mu = \alpha_0 + \alpha_1 \mu \quad \text{or} \quad E(r_t) = \mu = \frac{\alpha_0}{1-\alpha_1} \tag{4.19}$$

The obtained equation has two important implications for r_t. The mean of r_t exists only if $\alpha_1 \neq 1$, and the mean of r_t is zero if and only if $\alpha_0 = 0$. Thus, for a stationary AR(1) process, the constant term α_0 is related to the mean of r_t and $\alpha_0 = 0$ implies that $E(r_t) = 0$.

Using $\alpha_0 = (1 - \alpha_1)\mu$, the AR(1) model can be written as:

$$r_t - \mu = \alpha_1(r_{t-1} - \mu) + \varepsilon_t \tag{4.20}$$

which gives:

$$r_t - \mu = \varepsilon_t + \alpha_1 \varepsilon_{t-1} + \ldots + \alpha_1^i \varepsilon_{t-i} = \sum_{i=0}^{\infty} \alpha_1^i \varepsilon_{t-i} \tag{4.21}$$

Meaning that $(r_t - \mu)$ is a linear function of ε_{t-i} for $i \geq 0$. Using this and the independence of the series $\{\varepsilon_t\}$, it is obvious that $E[(r_t - \mu)\varepsilon_{t+1}] = 0$. Under the assumption of stationarity, the $Cov(r_{t-1}, \varepsilon_t) = E[(r_{t-1} - \mu)\varepsilon_t] = 0$. This means that r_{t-1} occurred before time t and ε_t does not depend on past information. The variance of the expected return in Equation 4.20 is:

$$V(r_t) = \alpha_1^2 V(r_{t-1}) + \sigma_\varepsilon^2 \tag{4.22}$$

Under the stationarity assumption, $V(r_t) = V(r_{t-1})$, so that (Hamilton, 1994, p. 53):

$$V(r_t) = \frac{\sigma_\varepsilon^2}{1-\alpha_1^2} \tag{4.23}$$

given that $\alpha_1^2 < 1$. The requirement of $\alpha_1^2 < 1$ results from the fact that the variance of a random variable is bounded and non-negative. The weak stationarity of AR(1) model implies that $-1 < \alpha_1 < 1$. Given that $-1 < \alpha_1 < 1$, the independence of $\{\varepsilon_t\}$ series and by Equation 4.21 it can be easily shown that the mean and the variance of r_t are finite. In addition, by the Cauchy-Schwartz inequality, all the autocovariances of r_t are finite (Tsay, 2002, p. 30). Therefore, the AR(1) model is weakly stationary. The necessary and sufficient condition for the AR(1) model in Equation 4.15 to be weakly stationary is $|\alpha_1| < 1$.

Multiplying Equation 4.21 by ε_t, using the independence between ε_t and r_{t-1}, and taking the expectation, yields the result:

$$E[\varepsilon_t(r_t - \mu)] = E[\varepsilon_t(r_{t-1} - \mu)] + E(\varepsilon_t^2) = E(\varepsilon_t^2) = \sigma_\varepsilon^2 \tag{4.24}$$

Multiplying Equation 4.20 by $(r_{t-l} - \mu)$, taking expectation, and using the previously obtained result from Equation 4.24 gives (Tsay, 2002, p. 31):

$$\gamma_l = \begin{cases} \alpha_1 \gamma_1 + \sigma_\varepsilon^2 & if \quad l = 0 \\ \alpha_1 \gamma_{l-1} & if \quad l > 0 \end{cases} \qquad (4.25)$$

Consequently, for a weakly stationary AR(1) model $V(r_t) = \gamma_0$ and $\gamma_l = \alpha_1 \gamma_{l-1}$, for $l > 0$. Furthermore, the autocorrelation function (ACF) of r_t satisfies $\rho_l = \alpha_1 \rho_{l-1}$, for $l \geq 0$. Because $\rho_0 = 1$, $\rho_l = \alpha_1^l$. This result says that the ACF of a weakly stationary AR(1) series decays exponentially with rate α_1 and starting value $\rho_0 = 1$. For a positive α_1, the plot of ACF of an AR(1) model shows an exponential decay. For a negative α_l, the plot consists of two alternating exponential decays with rate α_1^2.

It is easy to generalize the calculation of mean and variance of a stationary AR(p) model. For an AR(p) model the mean is equal to, $E(r_t) = \alpha_0 / (1 - \alpha_1 - \ldots - \alpha_p)$ and $V(r_t) = \gamma_0 = \alpha_1 \gamma_1 + \ldots + \alpha_p \gamma_p + \sigma^2$. The ACF of a stationary AR(p) series satisfies the difference equation (Tsay, 2002, p. 35):

$$(1 - \alpha_1 B - \ldots - \alpha_p B^p)\rho_l = 0, \quad for \; l > 0 \qquad (4.26)$$

The plot of ACF of a stationary AR(p) model shows a mixture of damping sine and cosine patterns and exponential decays depending on the nature of its characteristic roots.

4.1.1.2   Moving average (MA) process

After the autoregressive process the moving average is the second building block for models of stationary time series, but its use is in the modelling of a white noise process. Moving average can be treated as an infinite order AR model with parameter constraints. A infinite order AR model can be made practical by forcing the coefficients α_i to satisfy some constraints so that they are determined by a finite number of parameters. A simple representation of this approach is (Hamilton, 1994, p. 50):

$$r_t = \alpha_0 + \theta_1 \varepsilon_{t-1} + \theta_1^2 \varepsilon_{t-2} + \ldots + \theta_1^i \varepsilon_{t-i} + \varepsilon_t \qquad (4.27)$$

where all the coefficients depend on a single parameter θ_1 that is derived from $\alpha_i = -\theta_1^i$ for $i \geq 1$. For the model to be stationary the absolute value of θ_1 must be less than 1, otherwise the series and θ_1^i would explode. If $|\theta_1| < 1$, then $\theta_1^i \to 0$ as $i \to \infty$, which results in a situation where the contribution of r_{t-i} to r_t decays exponentially as i increases. More distant observations have less effect on the current observed value of the variable than recent ones.

The above equation can be rewritten as (Tsay, 2002, p. 43):

$$r_t = \alpha_0(1 - \theta_1) + \varepsilon_t - \theta_1\varepsilon_{t-1} \tag{4.28}$$

from which it is clearly visible that r_t is composed of two parts: a constant term (α_0) and a weighted average of shocks ε_t and ε_{t-1}, which are white noise.

MA(q) model is of the form (Hamilton, 1994, p. 51):

$$r_t = \alpha_0 + \varepsilon_t + \theta_1\varepsilon_{t-1} + \dots + \theta_q\varepsilon_{t-q} \quad \text{where} \quad q > 0 \tag{4.29}$$

MA model is weakly stationary resulting from its characteristic that it is a finite linear combination of white noise sequences which first two moments are time invariant. For example, taking the expectation of MA(1) model results in (Tsay, 2002, p. 44):

$$E(r_t) = \alpha_0 \tag{4.30}$$

which is time invariant. Taking the variance of MA(1) gives:

$$V(r_t) = \sigma_\varepsilon^2 + \theta_1^2\sigma_\varepsilon^2 = (1 + \theta_1^2)\sigma_\varepsilon^2 \tag{4.31}$$

and again, $V(r_t)$ is time invariant. This also applies to general MA(q) models. The constant term of an MA model is the mean of the series and the variance of an MA(q) model is (Mills, 2004, p. 15):

$$V(r_t) = (1 + \theta_1^2 + \dots + \theta_q^2)\sigma_\varepsilon^2 \tag{4.32}$$

Setting the constant α_0 in an MA(1) model equal to 0, multiplying it by r_{t-l}, and taking the expectation yields:

$$\gamma_1 = -\theta_1\sigma_\varepsilon^2 \quad \text{and} \quad \gamma_l = 0, \text{ for } l > 1 \tag{4.33}$$

Using the fact that $V(r_t) = (1 + \theta_1^2)\sigma_\varepsilon^2$ gives (Mills, 2004, p. 14):

$$\rho_0 = 1, \quad \rho_1 = \frac{-\theta_1}{1 + \theta_1^2}, \quad \rho_l = 0 \quad for \quad l > 1 \tag{4.34}$$

Thus, for an MA(1) model, the lag-1 ACF is not zero, but all higher order ACFs are zero. In other words, the ACF of an MA(1) model cuts off at lag 1. For an MA(q) model, the lag-q ACF is not zero, but $\rho_l = 0$ for $l > q$ (Mills, 2004, p. 24). Consequently, a MA(q) series is only linearly related to its first q lagged values and hence is a "finite-memory" model. Order of MA model can be identified with the use of its ACF. For a time series with ACF ρ_l, if $\rho_q \neq 0$, but $\rho_l = 0$, the time series follows an MA(q) model. Because an MA model has finite memory its point forecasts converge to the mean of the series quickly. In general, for a MA(q) model, multi step ahead forecasts go to the mean after the q-th step (Tsay, 2002).

4.1.1.3 Mixed Autoregressive Moving average (ARMA) process

Simple autoregressive (AR) and moving average (MA) models can easily become troublesome and computationally intensive because of the need for high order model that results in an overwhelming number of parameters to describe the dynamic structure of the data. To overcome this difficulty an autoregressive moving average (ARMA) model can be implemented. ARMA model is a combination of AR and MA models in a compact form that keeps the number of parameters relatively small.

Time series r_t follows an ARMA(1,1) model if it satisfies (Brockwell, Davis, 2002, p. 55):

$$r_t - \alpha_1 r_{t-1} = \alpha_0 + \varepsilon_t + \theta_1 \varepsilon_{t-1} \qquad\qquad (4.35)$$

The left-hand side of the equation is the AR component of the ARMA model and the right-hand side is the MA component. For an ARMA model to function it is required that $\alpha_1 + \theta_1 \neq 0$, because if this inequality is not satisfied, there is a cancellation in the left-hand and the right-hand side of the equation and the ARMA process is reduced to a white noise series.

Properties of the ARMA(1,1) models are generalizations of those of AR(1) models with some minor modifications to handle the impact of the MA(1) component. Taking the expectation of Equation 4.35 yields (Tsay, 2002, p. 49):

$$E(r_t) - \alpha_1 E(r_{t-1}) = \alpha_0 + E(\varepsilon_t) + \theta_1 E(\varepsilon_{t-1}) \qquad\qquad (4.36)$$

Because $E(\varepsilon_i) = 0$ for all i, the mean of r_t is

$$E(r_t) = \mu = \alpha_0 / (1 - \alpha_1) \qquad\qquad (4.37)$$

provided that the series is weakly stationary. This result is exactly the same as that of the AR(1) model in Equation 4.15. If the series r_t is weakly stationary, then $V(r_t) = V(r_{t-1})$ and variance under an ARMA(1,1) process is (Tsay, 2002, p. 49):

$$V(r_t) = \frac{(1 - 2\alpha_1 \theta_1 + \theta_1^2)\sigma_\varepsilon^2}{1 - \alpha_1^2} \qquad\qquad (4.38)$$

Because the variance is positive it is necessary that $\alpha_1^2 < 1$ (i.e., $|\alpha_1| < 1$). Again, this is precisely the same stationarity condition as that of the AR(1) model. The autocovariance function of r_t for $l = 1$ is:

$$\gamma_1 - \alpha_1 \gamma_0 = -\theta_1 \sigma_\varepsilon^2 \tag{4.39}$$

where $\gamma_l = Cov(r_t, r_{t-l})$. This result is different from that of the AR(1) case for which $\gamma_l - \alpha_1 \gamma_0 = 0$. However, for autocovariance at $l = 2$:

$$\gamma_2 - \alpha_1 \gamma_1 = 0 \quad for \quad l > 1 \tag{4.40}$$

and is identical to that of the AR(1) case. In fact, the same technique yields

$$\gamma_l - \varphi_1 \gamma_{l-1} = 0, \text{ for } l > 1 \tag{4.41}$$

In terms of ACF, the previous results show that for a stationary ARMA(1,1) model (Box, Jenkins, Reinsel, 1994, p. 81):

$$\rho_1 = \alpha_1 - \frac{\theta_1 \sigma_\varepsilon^2}{\gamma_0}, \quad \rho_l = \alpha_1 \rho_{l-1} \quad for \quad l > 1 \tag{4.42}$$

Thus, the ACF of an ARMA(1,1) model behaves very much like that of an AR(1) model except that the exponential decay starts with lag 2. Consequently, the ACF of an ARMA(1,1) model does not cut off at any finite lag. The PACF of an ARMA(1, 1) model does not cut off at any finite lag either. It behaves very much like that of an MA(1) model except that the exponential decay starts with lag 2 instead of lag 1. The stationarity condition of an ARMA(1,1) model is the same as that of an AR(1) model, and the ACF of an ARMA(1,1) exhibits a similar pattern like that of an AR(1) model except that the pattern starts at lag 2.

A general ARMA(p, q) model with p autoregressive terms and q moving average terms is in the form (Tsay, 2002, p. 50):

$$r_t = \alpha_0 + \sum_{i=1}^{p} \alpha_i r_{t-i} + \varepsilon_t + \sum_{i=1}^{q} \theta_i \varepsilon_{t-i} \tag{4.43}$$

The AR and MA models are special cases of the ARMA(p, q) model. Using the back-shift operator, the model can be written as (Hamilton, 1994, p. 59):

$$(1 - \alpha_1 B - ... -\alpha_p B^p) r_t = \alpha_0 + (1 - \theta_1 B - ... -\theta_q B^q) \varepsilon_t \tag{4.44}$$

The polynomial $1 - \alpha_1 B - ... -\alpha_p B^p$ is the AR polynomial of the model. Similarly, $1 - \theta_1 B - ... - \theta_q B^q$ is the MA polynomial. It is important that there are no common factors between the AR and MA polynomials; otherwise the order *(p, q)* of the model can be reduced. Like a pure AR model, the AR polynomial introduces the characteristic equation of an ARMA model. If all of the solutions of the characteristic equation are less than 1 in absolute value, then the ARMA model is weakly stationary. In this case, the unconditional mean of the model is $E(r_t) = \alpha_0/(1 - \alpha_1 - ... -\alpha_p)$.

In practice, the theoretical mean, variance and autocorrelations are unknown to the researcher. Given that the time series is stationary the sample mean, variance and autocorrelations can be used to estimate the parameters of the actual data generating process. In the identification of the ARMA model sample autocorrelation function (ACF) and sample partial autocorrelation function (PACF) can be compared to the various theoretical functions to help identify the true nature of the underlying process. A simple visual inspection of the correlogram may help to reach a conclusion that the series exhibits autocorrelation patterns that can be modelled by a certain AR or MA model. A more robust method of identification is to use some statistical test of autocorrelation.

There are a number of tests for significance of autocorrelation and one of the most common is the Box-Pierce Q test. The Q-statistic is used to test whether a group of autocorrelations is significantly different from zero. A problem with Box-Pierce Q statistic is that it works poorly even in moderately large samples (Enders, 2004, p. 68). Ljung and Box developed a superior small sample measure. Ljung-Box Q-statistic is the lth autocorrelation of the *T*-squared returns, and calculates whether the size of the movement at time *t* has any useful information to predict the size of the movement at time *t+l*. Ljung-Box Q-statistic is (Engle, Mezrich, 1995, p. 112):

$$Q(p) = T(T+2)\sum_{l=1}^{p} \frac{\hat{\rho}_l^2}{T-l} \qquad (4.45)$$

where *T* is the sample size, *l* number of autocorrelation lags included in the statistic, and $\hat{\rho}_l^2$ is the squared sample autocorrelation at lag *l*. Ljung-Box Q-statistic is used as a lack-of-fit test for a departure from randomness. Under the null hypothesis that the model fit is adequate, the test statistic is asymptotically chi-square distributed with *m* degrees of freedom. The Ljung-Box Q-statistic can also serve to check if the residuals from an estimated ARMA (p, q) model behave as a white noise process.

The chance of using an ARMA process to model a financial return series is quite low, especially in the developed markets. Returns on financial assets themselves are usually not dependent (correlated), otherwise traders could forecast daily returns. This claim is often challenged in less developed markets where autocorrelation in returns is not an unusual thing to find. Returns squared are usually dependent; meaning that volatility can be forecasted, but not the direction of the change of a variable. Because of this characteristic of financial markets the concept of ARMA models is highly relevant in volatility modelling. As a matter of fact, the generalized autoregressive conditional heteroskedastic (GARCH) model can be regarded as an ARMA model, albeit nonstandard, for the ε_t^2 series (Tsay, 2002, p. 48).

4.1.2 Generalized Autoregressive Conditional Heteroskedasticity (GARCH) process

Volatility is a fundamental characteristic of financial markets whose measuring and forecasting is always important. Volatility is a measure of the intensity of random or unpredictable changes in asset returns. Constant volatility models such as ARMA only refer to the unconditional volatility of a returns process. Processes that model unconditional volatility presume a constant variance of the time series throughout the whole data generation process. Such volatility can be defined in terms of the variance parameter of the unconditional distribution of a stationary returns process. In fact, unconditional volatility is only defined if it is assumed that a stationary stochastic process generates the asset return series, but this assumption seems far more reasonable than many other assumptions that are commonly made in financial models.

Time-varying volatility models describe a process for the conditional volatility. A conditional distribution, in this context, is a distribution that governs a return at a particular instant in time. In more general terms, a conditional distribution is any distribution that is conditioned on a set of known values for some of the variables, that is, on information set (Alexander, 2001, p. 12). In time series models the information set at time t, I_t is often taken as all the past values that were realized in the process. Conditional volatility at time t is the square root of the variance of the conditional distribution at time t. The conditional mean at time t is denoted $E_t(r_t|r_{t-i})$ or μ_t and the conditional variance at time t is denoted $V_t(r_t|r_{t-i})$ or σ_t^2 (Engle, 1982, p. 988).

An estimation procedure for the time-varying parameters of the conditional distributions is based on a model where anything that has happened in the past is not considered to be an observation on the current random variable. Its value is known, and so past observations become part of the information set. That is, the actual rather than the expected values of anything that happened in the past will be used to estimate the current value of a time-varying volatility parameter. Put another way, the current (and future) conditional distributions of the random variable will be "conditioned" on the current information set.

The difference between constant and time-varying volatility models is illustrated in figure 13.

Figure 13 - The a) constant and b) time varying volatility

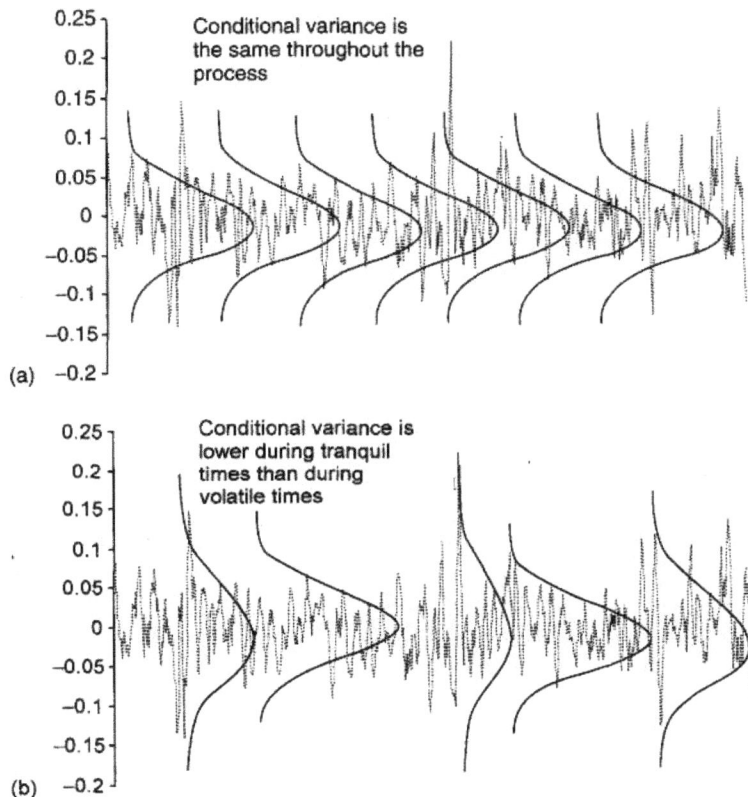

(a)

(b)

Source: Alexander C.: Market Models. Chichester: John Wiley & Sons, 2001. p. 13.

The majority of time varying volatility models assume that returns are normally distributed, in which case each conditional distribution is completely determined by its conditional mean and its conditional variance. Both the conditional mean and the conditional variance could change at every time period throughout the process, but for the purposes of estimating and forecasting conditional volatility it is often assumed that the conditional mean is a constant. The conditional volatility has no place in the standard framework for linear regression, because standard linear regression assumes that returns are homoskedastic - that is, their conditional variance is the same throughout the process (Kennedy, 2003, p. 48) (this assumption is depicted in Figure 13a). The term conditional heteroskedasticity means that the conditional variance changes over time (depicted in Figure 13b). The episodes of high and low volatility are often called volatility clusters. This phenomenon shows the possibility of forecasting volatility. High volatility periods tend to persist before falling to lower levels. Financial returns also tend to be leptokurtic[23], which makes them even harder to model since they are not even asymptotically normal. These characteristics of financial time series were noted in the early works of Mandelbrot (1963), Fama (1965), Clark (1973) and Blattberg and Gonedes (1974). This early research led to modelling financial returns as IID draws from thick tailed distributions such as Student's t and a family of distributions known as Stable Paretian distributions.

Until a decade ago the focus of most financial econometrics and financial time series modelling was centred on the conditional first moments of a presumed theoretical distribution, and any temporal dependence in the higher order moments was treated as random noise. The increased interest in risk management in financial theory has necessitated the development of new econometric time series models that take into account time variation of variances and covariances. The goal of every volatility model is to describe the historical pattern of volatility and use this to forecast the future. Volatility can be thought of as a random variable that follows a stochastic process. Discovering the underlying stochastic process is the task of every volatility model. Financial data shows that volatility clusters vary significantly in their persistence i.e. life span. Volatility clusters can be very short-lived, lasting only hours, or they may last for decades. These long-term volatilities are usually driven by certain economic processes or/and institutional changes. The primary source of changes in market prices is the arrival of news about the asset's fundamental value. If the news arrives in rapid succession, the returns exhibit a volatility cluster (Engle, Mezrich, 1995, p. 112). At the highest frequencies, the most likely sources of volatility are the turbulences included through trading. The frequency of the data dictates which types of volatility can be observed. Low frequency data (monthly, weekly) allows only low frequency or macroeconomic volatility to be observed. High frequency data is more revealing about the true nature of the volatility and its' properties (Wright, Bollerslev, 1999).

Unfortunately, use of data at frequencies higher than once a day introduces more complex features, such as a typical shape of volatility over a trading day, the bounce caused by bid and ask prices and the autocorrelation due to stale prices and irregular trading rates (Engle, Mezrich, 1995, p. 112). Following the same logic, if the frequency of the data is too high the low frequency volatility clustering cannot be observed.

Given the apparent lack of any structural dynamic economic theory which could explain the variation in the higher order moments, particularly instrumental in the development of this area has been the autoregressive conditional heteroskedastic (ARCH) class of models first introduced by Robert Engle in his paper "Autoregressive Conditional Heteroscedasticity with Estimates of Variance of

---

[23] Leptokurtosis = fat tails, expresion used to describe the forth moment of the probability distribution that differs from the normal distribution by being slimmer in the middle and having longer, fatter tails (Gujarati, 2003, p. 886).

United Kingdom Inflation" from 1982. The key insight of Engle's ARCH model is in the distinction between the conditional and unconditional second order moments. While the unconditional covariance matrix may be time invariant, the conditional variances and covariances of particular variables can often depend significantly on their previous states. For many issues in finance, such as option pricing, term structure of interest rates, general dynamic asset pricing relationships and especially risk management, understanding the true nature of temporal dependence is of utmost importance. From the perspective of econometric inference, the loss in asymptotic efficiency from neglected heteroskedasticity can be large. When evaluating economic forecasts, a much more accurate estimate of the forecast error uncertainty is available by conditioning the available information set. While the first empirical applications of the ARCH model was concerned with modelling inflationary uncertainty, the methodology has subsequently proven very useful in capturing temporal dependency in financial returns. For financial data it is more appropriate to use a generalization of this model, the symmetric Generalized Autoregressive Conditional Heteroskedasticity (GARCH) model introduced by Tim Bollerslev (1986) in his paper "Generalized Autoregressive Conditional Heteroskedasticity". Based on this pioneering work, many different GARCH models have been developed, notably the exponential GARCH model of Daniel Nelson (1991) - one of the first asymmetric GARCH models to be introduced. For excellent reviews of literature on GARCH models in finance, see Bollerslev, Chou, Kroner (1992), Bera, Higgins (1993) and Palm (1996).

The moving average model of volatility that was described in chapter 4.1.1.2 assumes that asset returns are independent and identically distributed (IID). There is no time-varying volatility assumption in any of the weighted moving average methods, be it a simple moving average or an exponential moving average. Moving average models only provide an estimate of the unconditional volatility, assumed to be a constant, and the current estimate is taken as the forecast. The volatility estimates do change over time, but this can only be attributed to noise or sampling errors in a moving average model (Alexander, 2000, p. 129).

In a GARCH model, returns are assumed to be generated by a stochastic process with time-varying volatility. Instead of modelling the data after they have been collapsed into a single unconditional distribution, a GARCH model introduces more detailed assumptions about the conditional distributions of returns. These conditional distributions change over time in an autocorrelated way, in fact the conditional variance, is in it self an autoregressive process. Volatility clustering implies a strong autocorrelation in squared returns, so a simple method for detecting volatility clustering is to calculate the first-order autocorrelation coefficient in squared returns. A wide established approach to detecting volatility clusters is the Ljung-Box Q-statistic calculated on the squared returns. Another powerful test for detecting autoregressive conditional heteroskedasticity in the data is Engle's ARCH test. Engle's hypothesis test for the presence of autoregressive conditional heteroskedasticity (ARCH) effects tests the null hypothesis that a time series of sample residuals consists of independently and identically distributed (IID) Gaussian disturbances, i.e., that no ARCH effects exist. Given sample residuals obtained from a curve fit (e.g., a regression model), Engle's ARCH test tests for the presence of pth order ARCH effects by regressing the squared residuals on a constant and the lagged values of the previous p squared residuals. Under the null hypothesis, the asymptotic test statistic, $T(R^2)$, where T is the number of squared residuals included in the regression and R^2 is the sample multiple correlation coefficient, is asymptotically chi-square distributed with p degrees of freedom (Hamilton, 1994, p. 665)[24].

GARCH volatility forecasts are very flexible and can be adapted to any time period. The forward volatilities that are generated by GARCH models can have many applications. Valuing path-dependent options or volatility options, measuring risk capital requirements, calibration of binomial trees - all of these require forecasts of forward volatilities that have a mean-reverting property. Perhaps the most important of all the advantages of GARCH models is that they are based on a statistical theory that is justified by empirical evidence. Unlike constant volatility models, there is no need to impose unrealistic assumptions to force it into a framework that is inconsistent with its basic assumptions. This coherency has led to many applications of GARCH models to measuring financial risks and pricing and hedging of options.

4.1.2.1   Properties of GARCH process

A simple linear regression can provide a model for the conditional mean of a return process. In a factor model regression the expected value of a stock return will change over time, as specified by its relationship with the market return and any other explanatory variables. This expectation is the conditional mean. The classical linear regression model assumes that the unexpected return ε_t, that is, the error process in the model, is homoskedastic. In other words, the error process has a constant variance $V(\varepsilon_t) = \sigma^2$ whatever the value of the dependent variable. Unlike the classical econometric models that presume constant variance of a variable, GARCH model allows the conditional variance to change over time as a function of past errors, leaving the unconditional variance constant (Alexander, 2001, p. 69). The fundamental idea in GARCH is to add a second equation to the standard regression model: the conditional variance equation (Enders, 2004, p.112). This equation describes the evolution of the conditional variance of the unexpected return process, $V_t(\varepsilon_t) = \sigma_t^2$. The dependent variable, the input to the GARCH volatility model, is always a return series, and accordingly a GARCH model consists of two equations. The first equation is the conditional mean equation. This can be anything, but since the focus of GARCH is on the conditional variance equation it is usual to have a very simple conditional mean equation. Many of the GARCH models used in practice take the simplest possible conditional mean equation $r_t = c + \varepsilon_t$, where c is a constant. In this case the unexpected return ε_t, is just the mean deviation return, because the constant will be the average of returns over the data period. In some

---

[24] Other tests for ARCH effects can be found in Bollerslev, Chou, Kroner (1992, p. 8) and Bollerslev, Engle, Nelson (1994, p. 2974).

circumstances it is better to use a time-varying conditional mean, but on the other hand, using to many parameters in the conditional mean equation might lead to convergence problems. If there is significant autocorrelation in returns, autoregressive moving average conditional mean should be used to model the returns.

The second equation in a GARCH model is the conditional variance equation. Different GARCH models arise because the conditional variance equations are specified in different forms. There is a fundamental distinction between the symmetric GARCH models that are used to model ordinary volatility clustering and the asymmetric GARCH models that are designed to capture leverage effects. In symmetric GARCH the conditional mean and conditional variance equations can be estimated separately. This kind of estimation is not possible for asymmetric GARCH models making their estimation more complex (Alexander, 2001, p. 70). Underlying every GARCH model there is also an unconditional returns distribution. The unconditional distribution of a GARCH process will be stationary under certain conditions imposed on the GARCH parameters and if necessary these conditions can be imposed on the estimation.

4.1.2.2   Symmetric GARCH Models

Symmetric GARCH models are the most widely used GARCH models. They are based on the idea of equally weighting the positive and negative returns to produce conditional volatility forecasts. If the time series can be represented by a stationary ARMA model $r_t = \alpha_0 + \alpha_1 r_{t-1} + \varepsilon_t$ the conditional mean of r_{t+1} is:

$$E_t r_{t+1} = \alpha_0 + \alpha_1 r_t \qquad (4.46)$$

With the conditional mean forecast of r_{t+1} the forecast error variance is $E_t[(r_{t+1} - \alpha_0 - \alpha_1 r_t)^2] = E_t \varepsilon_{t+1}^2 = \sigma^2$. On the other hand, if the unconditional forecast is used, the forecast will always be the long-run mean of $\{r_t\}$ sequence that is equal to $\alpha_0/(1-\alpha_1)$. The unconditional forecast error variance is (Enders, 2004, p. 113):

$$E\{[r_{t+1} - \alpha_0/(1-\alpha_1)]^2\} \quad = E[(\varepsilon_{t+1} + \alpha_1 \varepsilon_t + \alpha_1^2 \varepsilon_{t-1} + \alpha_1^3 \varepsilon_{t-2} + ...)^2]$$
$$= \sigma^2/(1-\alpha_1^2) \qquad (4.47)$$

Since $1/(1-\alpha_1^2) > 1$, the unconditional forecast has a greater variance than the conditional forecast. Conditional forecasts are preferred to unconditional ones because they take into account the current and past realizations of a series.

In case that the variance of $\{\varepsilon_t\}$ is not constant, any tendency for a sustained movements in the variance can be estimated using an ARMA model. One way of forecasting conditional variance in this case is by using AR(q) process using squares of estimated residuals (Enders, 2004, p. 114):

$$\hat{\varepsilon}_t^2 = \alpha_0 + \alpha_1\hat{\varepsilon}_{t-1}^2 + \alpha_2\hat{\varepsilon}_{t-2}^2 + ... + \alpha_q\hat{\varepsilon}_{t-q}^2 + v_t \qquad (4.48)$$

where v_t is a white-noise process.

If the values of α_1, α_2, ... , α_n all equal zero, the estimated variance is simply a constant α_0. Otherwise, the conditional variance of r_t evolves according to the autoregressive process given in Equation 4.48. Conditional variance at $t+1$ can be forecasted using Equation 4.48:

$$E_t\hat{\varepsilon}_{t+1}^2 = \alpha_0 + \alpha_1\hat{\varepsilon}_t^2 + \alpha_2\hat{\varepsilon}_{t-1}^2 + ... + \alpha_q\hat{\varepsilon}_{t+1-q}^2 \qquad (4.49)$$

A process that models the conditional variance in this fashion is called autoregressive conditional heteroskedastic (ARCH) model. The model for $\{r_t\}$ and the conditional variance are best estimated simultaneously using maximum likelihood techniques, so the linear specification of Equation 4.48 is not the most convenient. It is simpler to specify v_t as a multiplicative disturbance as proposed by Engle (1982, p. 999):

$$\varepsilon_t = v_t\sqrt{\alpha_0 + \alpha_1\varepsilon_{t-1}^2} \qquad (4.50)$$

where v_t is a white-noise process such that $\sigma_v^2 = 1$, v_t and ε_{t-1} are independent, and α_0 and α_1 are constants such that $\alpha_0 > 0$ and $0 < \alpha_1 < 1$. Since v_t is a white noise and independent of ε_{t-1} it is obvious that the elements of $\{\varepsilon_t\}$ have a mean zero and are uncorrelated (Hamilton, 1994, p. 48).

Since $Ev_t = 0$,
$$E\varepsilon_t = E[v_t(\alpha_0 + \alpha_1\varepsilon_{t-1}^2)^{1/2}]$$
$$= Ev_tE(\alpha_0 + \alpha_1\varepsilon_{t-1}^2)^{1/2} = 0$$

Since $Ev_tEv_{t-i} = 0$, it also follows that

$$E\varepsilon_t\varepsilon_{t-i} = 0, \quad i \neq 0$$

In ARCH model the error structure $\{\varepsilon_t\}$ is serially uncorrelated, meaning that there is no linear dependence between them, but the errors are not independent since they are related through their second moment (variance). The conditional variance itself is an autoregressive process resulting in conditionally heteroskedastic errors. Since v_t and ε_{t-1} are independent and $Ev_t = 0$, the conditional mean of ε_t is (Enders, 2004, p. 115):

$$E(\varepsilon_t^2 \mid \varepsilon_{t-1}, \varepsilon_{t-2}, ...) = E_{t-1}v_tE_{t-1}(\alpha_0 + \alpha_1\varepsilon_{t-1}^2)^{1/2} = 0 \qquad (4.51)$$

The influence of sequence $\{\varepsilon_t\}$, given by Equation 4.50, influences profoundly the conditional variance. Because $Ev_t^2 = 1$, the variance of ε_t conditioned on the past history of ε_{t-1}, ε_{t-2}, ... is (Enders, 2004, p. 115):

$$E[\varepsilon_t^2 \mid \varepsilon_{t-1}, \varepsilon_{t-2}, ...] = \alpha_0 + \alpha_1 \varepsilon_{t-1}^2 \qquad (4.52)$$

As can be seen from Equation 4.52 the conditional variance of ε_t is dependent on the realized value of ε_{t-1}^2. If the realized value of ε_{t-1}^2 is large, the conditional variance at moment t will also be large. As opposed to usual regression, the coefficients α_0 and α_1 have to be restricted. In order to ensure that the conditional variance can never be negative it is necessary to assume that both α_0 and α_1 positive. To ensure the stability of the process it is necessary to restrict α_1 that $0 < \alpha_1 < 1$ (Nelson, Cao 1992, p. 229). It makes no difference whether the market movement is positive or negative, since all unexpected returns are squared. Due to the influence of ε_t on r_t, the conditional heteroskedasticity in $\{\varepsilon_t\}$ will result in $\{r_t\}$ being heteroskedastic also. Thus, the ARCH model is able to capture periods of tranquillity and pronounced volatility in the $\{r_t\}$ series. The conditional mean and variance of $\{r_t\}$ series are given by (Enders, 2004, p. 117):

$$E_{t-1} r_t = \alpha_0 + \alpha_1 r_{t-1}$$
$$V(r_t | r_{t-1}, r_{t-2}, ...) = E_{t-1}(r_t - \alpha_0 - \alpha_1 r_{t-1})^2$$
$$= E_{t-1}(\varepsilon_t)^2 = \alpha_0 + \alpha_1(\varepsilon_{t-1})^2 \qquad (4.53)$$

Since α_1 and ε_{t-1}^2 cannot be negative, the minimum value for the conditional variance is α_0. For any nonzero realization of ε_{t-1} the conditional variance of r_t is positively related to α_1. The unconditional mean and variance of r_t are obtained by solving the difference equation for r_t and taking expectation. For a sufficiently long series, the solution is given by (Enders, 2004, p. 117):

$$r_t = \frac{\alpha_0}{1-\alpha_1} + \sum_{i=0}^{\infty} \alpha_1^i \varepsilon_{t-i} \qquad (4.54)$$

The unconditional expectation of Equation 4.54 is $Er_t = \alpha_0/(1-\alpha_1)$. The unconditional variance of r_t follows directly from Equation 4.54:

$$V(r_t) = \sum_{i=0}^{\infty} \alpha_1^{2i} V(\varepsilon_{t-i}) \qquad (4.55)$$

Knowing that the unconditional variance of ε_t is constant and equal to $\alpha_0/(1-\alpha_1)$, it follows that

$$V(r_t) = \left(\frac{\alpha_0}{1-\alpha_1}\right)\left(\frac{1}{1-\alpha_1^2}\right) \qquad (4.56)$$

Higher order ARCH (q) process developed by Engle (1982) are given by:

$$\varepsilon_t = v_t \sqrt{\alpha_0 + \sum_{i=1}^{q} \alpha_i \varepsilon_{t-i}^2} \qquad\qquad (4.57)$$

In ARCH(q) process all shocks from ε_{t-1} to ε_{t-q} have a direct effect on ε_t, so that the conditional variance acts like an autoregressive process of order q.

In empirical applications of the ARCH model a relatively long lag in conditional variance equation is often necessary, and to avoid violating the non-negativity constraint on variance parameters, a fixed lag structure has to be imposed. ARCH models are not often used in financial markets because the simple GARCH models perform much better. ARCH model with exponentially declining lag coefficients is equivalent to a GARCH(1,1) model so the GARCH process actually models an infinite ARCH process, with sensible constraints on coefficients and using only very few parameters (Bollerslev, 1986, p. 308). Since ARCH model needs very many lags to get close to a standard symmetrical GARCH(1,1) model, which has only three parameters, the use of standard ARCH models for financial volatility estimation is not recommended.

ARCH model exhibits several other weaknesses (Tsay, 2002, p. 86):
1. The model assumes that positive and negative shocks have the same effects on volatility because it depends on the square of the previous shocks. In practice, it is well documented that price of a financial asset responds differently to positive and negative shocks (see e.g. Black, 1976, Christie, 1982, and Schwert, 1989b).
2. The ARCH model is rather restrictive. For instance, α_1^2 of an ARCH(1) model must be in the interval [0, 1/3] if the series is to have a finite fourth moment. The constraints become more complicated for a higher order ARCH models.
3. The ARCH model does not provide any new insight for understanding the source of variations of a financial time series. It only provides a mechanical way to describe the behaviour of the conditional variance. It gives no indication about what causes such behaviour to occur.
4. ARCH models are likely to over predict the volatility because they respond slowly to large isolated shocks to the return series.

GARCH model extends the ARCH model by allowing for both the longer memory and a more flexible lag structure. In a GARCH model ε_t denotes a real-valued discrete-time stochastic process whose conditional distribution is assumed to be normal (other probability distributions could also be applied such as Student's t) and ψ_t the information set (σ-field) of all information up till time t. Next period's variance is forecasted by the GARCH (p, q) process in the following way (Bollerslev, 1986, p. 309):

$$\varepsilon_t | \psi_{t-1} \sim N(0, \sigma_t^2) \qquad\qquad (4.58)$$

$$\sigma_t^2 = \alpha_0 + \sum_{i=1}^{q} \alpha_i \varepsilon_{t-i}^2 + \sum_{i=1}^{p} \beta_i \sigma_{t-i}^2 \qquad (4.59)$$

$$\sigma_t^2 = \alpha_0 + A(L)\varepsilon_t^2 + B(L)\sigma_t^2 \qquad (4.60)$$

$p \geq 0, \quad q > 0$
$\alpha_0 > 0, \quad \alpha_i \geq 0, \quad i = 1,...,q$
$\beta_i \geq 0, \qquad\qquad i = 1,...,p$

α, β – GARCH parameters
σ_t^2 – variance at time (t)
ε_t – residual at time (t)

when $p = 0$ the process is reduced to the ARCH(q) process, and when $p=q=0$, the process becomes a white noise series (ε). In the ARCH(q) process the conditional variance is specified as a linear function of past sample variances, whereas the GARCH(p, q) process uses also lagged conditional variances.

Putting it into another perspective, the full GARCH(p, q) model adds q autoregressive terms to the ARCH(p) specification, and in the recursive form the conditional variance equation can be written as (Lamoureux, Lastrapes, 1990, p. 226):

$$\sigma_t^2 = \alpha_0 + \alpha_1 \varepsilon_{t-1}^2 + ... + \alpha_p \varepsilon_{t-p}^2 + \beta_1 \sigma_{t-1}^2 + ... + \beta_q \sigma_{t-q}^2 \qquad (4.61)$$

$\alpha_0 > 0, \alpha_1, ..., \alpha_p, \beta_1, ..., \beta_q \geq 0 \quad \varepsilon_t | I_t \sim N(0, \sigma_t^2)$

However, it is rarely necessary to use more than a GARCH(1,1) model, which has just one lagged error square and one autoregressive term. Using the standard notation for the GARCH constant ω, the GARCH error coefficient α and the GARCH lag coefficient β, the symmetric GARCH(1,1) model is (Duan, 1997, p. 98):

$$\sigma_t^2 = \omega + \alpha \varepsilon_{t-1}^2 + \beta \sigma_{t-1}^2 \qquad (4.62)$$

$\omega > 0, \quad \alpha, \beta \geq 0$

This "vanilla" GARCH model may also be written as (Alexander, 2000, p. 136):

$$\begin{aligned}
\sigma_t^2 &= \omega + \alpha \varepsilon_{t-1}^2 + \beta \sigma_{t-1}^2 \\
&= \omega + \alpha \varepsilon_{t-1}^2 + \beta(\omega + \alpha \varepsilon_{t-2}^2 + \beta(\omega + \alpha \varepsilon_{t-3}^2 + \beta(...))) \\
&= \omega/(1-\beta) + \alpha(\varepsilon_{t-1}^2 + \beta \varepsilon_{t-2}^2 + \beta^2 \varepsilon_{t-3}^2 + ...) \qquad (4.63)
\end{aligned}$$

In this form the GARCH(1,1) model is equivalent to an infinite ARCH model with exponentially declining weights.

The size of the parameters α and β determines the short-run dynamics of the resulting volatility time series. Large GARCH lag coefficients β indicate that shocks to conditional variance take a long time to die out, so volatility is persistent. Large GARCH error coefficients α mean that volatility reacts intensely to market movements, and so if alpha is relatively high and beta is relatively low, volatilities tend to be spikier. In financial markets it is common to estimate lag coefficients based on daily observations in excess of 0.8 and error coefficients of no more than 0.2 (Alexander, 2001, p. 73).

Putting $\sigma_t^2 = \sigma^2$ for all t in (4.62) gives an expression for the long-term steady-state variance in a GARCH(1,1) model (Chou, 1988, p. 282):

$$\sigma^2 = \omega/(1 - \alpha - \beta) \tag{4.64}$$

The sum $\alpha + \beta$ must be less than 1 if the returns process is to be stationary. Only in this case will the GARCH volatility term structure converge to a long-term average level of volatility that is determined by Equation 4.64.

An explicit generating equation for ARCH and GARCH processes is given by (Li, Ling, McAleer, 2001, p. 2):

$$\varepsilon_t = \eta_t \sqrt{\sigma_t^2} \tag{4.65}$$

where $\eta_t \sim IID\ N(0,1)$ and σ_t^2 is given by Equation 4.59. Since σ_t^2 is a function of elements of the information set (ψ_{t-1}) and therefore is fixed when conditioning on ψ_{t-1}, ε_t as given in Equation 4.65 will be conditionally normal with

$$E(\varepsilon_t \mid \psi_{t-1}) = \sqrt{\sigma_t^2} E(\eta_t \mid \psi_{t-1}) = 0$$

and variance $V(\varepsilon_t \mid \psi_{t-1}) = \sigma_t^2 V(\eta_t \mid \psi_{t-1}) = \sigma_t^2$. This means that the process described in Equation 4.65 is the same as the GARCH process in Equation 4.58. This generating equation reveals that GARCH process actually rescales the underlying Gaussian innovation process (η_t) by multiplying it with the conditional standard deviation (σ_t^2), which is a function of the information set (ψ_{t-1}).

The GARCH(p, q) process is wide-sense stationary with $E(\varepsilon_t)=0$, $V(\varepsilon_t)=\alpha_0(1-A(1)-B(1))^{-1}$ and $cov(\varepsilon_t, \varepsilon_s) = 0$ for $t \neq s$ if and only if $A(1)+B(1)<1$. The GARCH(p, q) process can be interpreted as an autoregressive moving average process in ε_t^2 of orders $m=max\{p,q\}$ and p, respectively (Bollerslev, 1986, p. 310).

Presuming that the process starts indefinitely far in the past with $2m$ finite initial moments and structure of the GARCH process, $\alpha_1 + \beta_1 < 1$ suffices for wide-sense stationarity. A necessary and sufficient condition for existence of the $2m^{th}$ moment in a GARCH(1,1) process is (Bollerslev, 1986, p. 311):

$$\mu(\alpha_1, \beta_1, m) = \sum_{j=0}^{m} \binom{m}{j} a_j \alpha_1^j \beta_1^{m-j} < 1 \qquad (4.66)$$

where

$$a_0 = 1, \ a_j = \prod_{i=1}^{j}(2j-1), \ j=1,... \qquad (4.67)$$

The $2m^{th}$ moment can be expressed by the recursive equation:

$$E(\varepsilon_t^{2m}) = a_m \left[\sum_{n=0}^{m-1} a_n^{-1} E(\varepsilon_t^{2n}) \alpha_0^{m-n} \binom{m}{m-n} \mu(\alpha_1, \beta_1, n) \right] \times [1 - \mu(\alpha_1, \beta_1, m)]^{-1} \ (4.68)$$

As ε_t is conditionally normal, by symmetry it follows that if the first $2m^{th}$ moments exist, $E(\varepsilon_t^{2m-1}) = 0$. This directly relates to the fact that skewness coefficient (third moment) must be equal to zero. For $\beta_1 = 0$, Equation 4.66 reduces to the well-known condition for the ARCH(1) process, $a_m \alpha_1^m < 1$ (Engle, 1982, p. 992). If $\alpha_1 > (a_m)^{-1/m}$ in the ARCH(1) process, the $2m^{th}$ moment does not exist, whereas in the GARCH(1,1) process, even if $\sum_{i=1}^{\infty} \delta_i = \alpha_1(1-\beta_1)^{-1} > (a_m)^{-1/m}$, the $2m^{th}$ moment might exist because of the longer memory in GARCH process (Bollerslev, 1986, p. 311).

Higher moments indicate further interesting information about the nature of the GARCH process. If $3\alpha_1^2 + 2\alpha_1\beta_1 + \beta_1^2 < 1$, the fourth-order moment (kurtosis) exists and since (Drost, Nijman, 1993, p. 916):

$$E(\varepsilon_t^2) = \alpha_0(1-\alpha_1-\beta_1)^{-1} \qquad (4.69)$$

and

$$E(\varepsilon_t^4) = 3\alpha_0^2(1+\alpha_1+\beta_1)\left[(1-\alpha_1-\beta_1)(1-\beta_1^2-2\alpha_1\beta_1-3\alpha_1^2)\right]^{-1} (4.70)$$

The coefficient of kurtosis is therefore (Bollerslev, 1986, p. 312):

$$\kappa = (E(\varepsilon_t^4) - 3E(\varepsilon_t^2)^2)E(\varepsilon_t^2)^{-2}$$
$$= 6\alpha_1^2(1-\beta_1^2-2\alpha_1\beta_1-3\alpha_1^2)^{-1} \qquad (4.71)$$

which is greater than zero by assumption, and hence greater than assumed under normal distribution. This means that a GARCH(1,1) process is leptokurtic, meaning that it has heavier tails than assumed under normal distribution, a property that the process shares with the ARCH(q) process.

The property of being leptokurtic, although the probability distribution of stochastic variable (ε) is normal, makes the ARCH and GARCH processes very convenient for modelling fat tailed observations, a characteristic that is usually displayed by asset returns. The lack of this property would mean that the modelling of heavy tailed behaviour of asset returns would require other, more computationally demanding distributions such as Student's t, GED or a mixture of normal distributions. In fact Nelson (1990) demonstrated that under suitable conditions, as time interval goes to zero, a GARCH(1,1) process approaches a continuous time process whose stationary unconditional distribution is Student's t.

The GARCH(1,1) process is the most common specification for GARCH volatility models, being relatively easy to estimate and generally having robust coefficients that are interpreted naturally in terms of long-term volatilities and short-run dynamics. However, it should be stressed that all three parameter estimates, and particularly that of ω, will be sensitive to the data period used in the estimation of GARCH parameters. Thus the choice of historic data will affect the current volatility forecasts. In particular, long-term volatility forecasts will be influenced by the inclusion of stress events in the historic data (Alexander, 2001, p. 75).

In finance, the return of a security may depend on its volatility. To model such a phenomenon, Engle, Lilien and Robins (1987) introduced the ARCH in the mean (ARCH-M) model in which the conditional mean is a function of conditional variance of the process (Engle, Lilien, Robins, 1987, p. 395):

$$r_t = g(z_{t-1}, \sigma_t^2) + \sigma_t \varepsilon_t \qquad (4.72)$$

where z_{t-1} is a vector of predetermined variables, g is some function of z_{t-1} and σ_t^2 is generated by an ARCH(q) process. The most simple ARCH-M model has $g(z_{t-1}, \sigma_t^2) = \delta\sigma_t^2$. When σ_t^2 follows a GARCH process, Equation 4.72 will become a GARCH in the mean (GARCH-M) equation. A simple GARCH(1, 1)-M model can be written as (Lucchetti, Rossi, 2005, p. 310):

$$r_t = \mu + c\sigma_t^2 + a_t , \; a_t = \sigma_t \varepsilon_t$$
$$\sigma_t^2 = \omega + \alpha a_{t-1}^2 + \beta\sigma_{t-1}^2 \qquad (4.73)$$

where μ and c are constant. The parameter c is called the risk premium parameter. A positive c indicates that the return is positively related to its past volatility. The formulation of the GARCH-M model in Equation 4.73 implies that there are serial correlations in the return series r_t. These serial correlations are introduced by correlations in the volatility process $\{\sigma_t^2\}$. The existence of risk premium is, therefore, another reason that some historical stock returns have serial correlations.

Most financial markets have GARCH volatility forecasts that mean-revert. That is, there is a convergence in term structure forecasts to the long-term average volatility level, and by the same token the time series of any GARCH volatility forecast will be stationary. However, currencies and commodities tend to have volatilities that are not as mean reverting as the volatility of other types of financial assets. In fact, they may not mean-revert at all (Hsieh, 1989, Kroner, Kneafsey, Claessens, 1993, Diebold, Hahn, Tay, 1999, Giot, Laurent, 2002). In some currency markets not only are exchange rates themselves a random walk, but the volatilities of exchange rates may also be random walks. In this case the usual stationary GARCH models will not apply.

When $\alpha + \beta = 1$ the recursion equation can be simplified by letting $\beta = \lambda$ and rewriting the GARCH (1,1) model as (Yu, So, 2002, p. 3):

$$\sigma_t^2 = \omega + (1-\lambda)\varepsilon_{t-1}^2 + \lambda\sigma_{t-1}^2 \qquad (0 \leq \lambda \leq 1) \qquad\qquad (4.74)$$

In this form the unconditional variance is no longer defined and term structure forecasts do not converge. Since in this case the variance process is non-stationary, Equation 4.74 is called the integrated GARCH (I-GARCH) model. When $\omega = 0$ the I-GARCH model becomes an EWMA model, hence EWMA may be viewed as simple GARCH models without ω and with constant term structures (Giot, Laurent, 2003, p. 645).

I-GARCH is often encountered in foreign exchange markets but it is not unusual to find it in some stock indexes (Alexander, 2001, p.76-77). It is interesting that very often currency and the equity index I-GARCH models have persistence parameters that are near 0.94, the same as the RiskMetrics daily data persistence parameter (RiskMetrics, 1996, p. 97).

Another symmetric variation of the general form of GARCH model is the components GARCH model. When a GARCH model is estimated over a rolling data window, different long-term volatility levels will be estimated, corresponding to different estimates of the GARCH parameters. The components GARCH model extends this idea to allow variation of long-term volatility within the estimation period (Engle, Lee, 1993a, 1993b, Engle, Mezrich, 1995). It is most useful in currency and commodity markets, where GARCH models are often close to being integrated and so convergent term structures that fit the market implied volatility term structure cannot be generated. The components model is an attempt to regain the convergence in GARCH term structures in currency markets, by allowing for a time-varying long-term volatility.

The GARCH(1,1) conditional variance may be written in the form (Alexander, 2001, p. 78):

$$\sigma_t^2 = (1 - \alpha - \beta)\sigma^2 + \alpha\varepsilon_{t-1}^2 + \beta\sigma_{t-1}^2$$
$$= \sigma^2 + \alpha(\varepsilon_{t-1}^2 - \sigma^2) + \beta(\sigma_{t-1}^2 - \sigma^2) \qquad (4.75)$$

Where σ^2 is defined by Equation 4.64. In components GARCH σ^2 is replaced by a time-varying permanent component given by (Connor, 2001, p. 3):

$$q_t = \omega + \rho(q_{t-1} - \omega) + \zeta(\varepsilon_{t-1}^2 - \sigma_{t-1}^2) \qquad (4.76)$$

Therefore the conditional variance equation in the components GARCH model is:

$$\sigma_t^2 = q_t + \alpha(\varepsilon_{t-1}^2 - q_{t-1}) + \beta(\sigma_{t-1}^2 - q_{t-1}) \qquad (4.77)$$

Equations 4.76 and 4.77 together define the components GARCH model. If $\rho = 1$, the permanent component to which long-term volatility forecasts mean-revert is just a random walk. While the components model has an attractive specification for currency markets, parameter estimation is, unfortunately not straightforward. Estimates may lack robustness and it seems difficult to recommend the use of the components model - except in the event that its specification has passed rigorous diagnostic tests.

4.1.2.3 Asymmetric GARCH Models

An important feature of financial returns known as "leverage effect", that was first documented by Black (1976) describes the tendency for changes in the financial returns, especially in the stock market, to be negatively correlated with changes in stock volatility. A part of this phenomenon can be explained by the fixed costs that companies incur, such as financial and operational leverage. Lowering of stock price reduces the value of company's equity relative to its debt, thus raising its debt to equity ratio, which raises the volatility of a stock making them riskier to hold. Black (1976) argues that the response of stock volatility to the direction of returns is too large to be explained by leverage alone. This conclusion is also supported by the work of Christie (1982) and Schwert (1989b). Simply stated, if volatility is higher following a negative return than it is following a positive return, then the autocorrelation between yesterday's return and today's squared return will be large and negative.

A very simple test of this effect is to compute the first-order autocorrelation coefficient between lagged returns and current squared returns (Alexander, 2001, p. 68):

$$\frac{\sum_{t=2}^{T} r_t^2 r_{t-1}}{\sqrt{\sum_{t=2}^{T} r_t^4 \sum_{t=2}^{T} r_{t-1}^2}} \qquad (4.78)$$

If the first-order autocorrelation coefficient is negative and the corresponding Ljung-Box Q-test is significantly different from zero, then there is asymmetry in volatility clustering which a symmetric GARCH model will not adequately capture. In such a case one of the asymmetric GARCH models should be employed.

It is interesting that empirical research using robust test statistics that are much more sophisticated than the simple Ljung-Box Q-test procedure, (see Hagerud, 1997a) has found that relatively few stocks show signs of asymmetric volatility clustering. Hagerud (1997a) finds that only 12 out of his sample of 45 Nordic stocks exhibited a noticeable leverage effect. The volatility skew may still be very pronounced in these stocks, so where implied volatility smiles have noticeable skew effects, these may or may not be indicative of a leverage effect.

Literally dozens of different variants of asymmetric GARCH models have been proposed and tested in a vast research literature. However, asymmetric GARCH models have a fairly limited practical use. It is a good thing to be able to include the possibility of asymmetry in the GARCH model so that any leverage effect will be captured, but one should do so with caution because the estimation of asymmetric GARCH models can be much more difficult than the estimation of symmetric GARCH models.

To overcome some weaknesses of the GARCH model in handling financial time series, Nelson (1991) proposed the exponential GARCH (EGARCH) model. The conditional variance equation in the E-GARCH model is defined in terms of a standard normal variate z_t. In particular, to allow for asymmetric effects between positive and negative asset returns, he considers the weighted innovation (Nelson, 1991, p. 351):

$$g(z_t) = \lambda z_t + \varphi(|z_t| - E(|z_t|)) \qquad (4.79)$$

where λ and φ are real constants. The parameter φ allows for the asymmetry in the model. If $\varphi = 0$ then a positive surprise ($\varepsilon_{t-j} > 0$) has the same effect on volatility as a negative surprise of the same magnitude. If $-1 < \varphi < 0$, a positive surprise increases volatility less than a negative surprise. If $\varphi < -1$, a positive surprise actually reduces volatility while a negative surprise increases volatility. A number of researchers have found evidence of asymmetry in stock price behaviour – negative surprises seem to increase volatility more than positive surprises of the same magnitude (Black, 1976, Pagan, Schwert, 1990, Engle, Ng, 1991).

Both z_t and $|z_t| - E(|z_t|)$ are zero-mean IID sequences with continuous distributions. Therefore, $E[g(z_t)] = 0$. The asymmetry of $g(z_t)$ can be seen by rewriting Equation 4.79 as (Tsay, 2002, p. 102):

$$g(z_t) = \begin{cases} (\lambda + \varphi)z_t - \varphi E(|z_t|) & if \quad z_t \geq 0 \\ (\lambda - \varphi)z_t - \varphi E(|z_t|) & if \quad z_t < 0 \end{cases}$$

(4.80)

For the standard Gaussian random variable ε_t, $E(|z_t|) = \sqrt{2/\pi}$. For the standardized Student's t distribution $E(|z_t|)$ equals (McDonald, 1996, p. 430):

$$E(|z_t|) = \cfrac{1}{\sqrt{\sigma}B\left(\cfrac{1}{2},\cfrac{v}{2}\right)\left(1+\cfrac{2z^2}{v\sigma^2}\right)^{\frac{v+1}{2}}}$$

(4.81)

where B is a beta function[25], and v is degrees of freedom.

An EGARCH(p, q) model can be written as (Nelson, 1991, p. 354):

$$\ln \sigma_t^2 = \omega + \frac{1 + \beta_1 B + ... + \beta_p B^p}{1 - \alpha_1 B - ... - \alpha_q B^q} g(z_{t-1})$$

(4.82)

where ω, α and β are not restricted to be nonnegative, B is the back-shift (lag) operator such that $Bg(z_t) = g(z_{t-1})$, and $1 + \beta_1 B + ... + \beta_p B^p$ and $1 - \alpha_1 B - ... - \alpha_q B^q$ are polynomials with absolute values of their zeros greater than one. Based on this representation, some properties of the EGARCH model can be obtained in a similar manner as those of the GARCH model. For instance, the unconditional mean of $ln(\sigma_t^2)$ is ω. However, the model differs from the GARCH model in several ways. First, it uses logged conditional variance to relax the positiveness constraint of model coefficients. Second, the use of $g(z_t)$ enables the model to respond asymmetrically to positive and negative lagged values of ε_t. Several studies have found that the exponential GARCH model fits financial data very well, often better

---

[25] Beta function, B(p,q), is defined by (McDonald, 1996, p. 455):

$$B(p,q) = \int_0^\infty t^{p-1}(1-t)^{q-1}\, dt = \int_0^\infty \frac{t^{p-1}}{(1+t)^{p+q}}\, dt$$

for positive p and q. B(p,q) can also be expressed in terms of a gamma function:

$$B(p,q) = \frac{\Gamma(p)\Gamma(q)}{\Gamma(p+q)}$$

than other GARCH models. Even without significant leverage effects, the logarithmic specification appears to have considerable advantages (Taylor, 1994, Heynen, Kemna, Vorst, 1994). Unfortunately, exponential GARCH is difficult to use for volatility forecasting because there is no analytic form for the volatility term structure. Some additional properties of the EGARCH model can be found in Nelson (1991) and Karanasos, Kim (2003).

The asymmetric GARCH or A-GARCH model of Engle and Ng (1993) is easier to estimate than E-GARCH and its volatility term structure forecasts may be generated in a simple analytic way. The conditional variance equation for A-GARCH model is (Engle, Ng, 1993, p. 1755):

$$\sigma_t^2 = \omega + \alpha(\varepsilon_{t-1} - \lambda)^2 + \beta\sigma_{t-1}^2 \qquad (4.83)$$

with constraints $\omega > 0$, α, β, $\lambda \geq 0$

For the purpose of option pricing and hedging Duan (1997) advocates the non-linear asymmetric GARCH or N-GARCH model (Alexander, 2001, p. 81):

$$r_t = r - 0.5\sigma_t^2 + \sigma_t\xi_t$$
$$\sigma_t^2 = \omega + \alpha\sigma_{t-1}^2(\xi_{t-1} - \theta - \lambda)^2 + \beta\sigma_{t-1}^2$$
$$\xi_t = \varepsilon_t + \lambda \qquad (4.84)$$

When volatility is stochastic the perfect markets assumption that is necessary for a risk-neutral probability measure no longer holds, but Duan (1997) shows that a form of local risk neutrality does hold if prices follow this model. Thus option prices can be calculated as discounted expected values under a unique risk neutral probability measure, in the usual way.

The QGARCH model developed by Sentana (1991) is:

$$\sigma_t^2 = \sigma^2 + \psi'x_{t-q} + x_{t-q}'Ax_{t-q} + \sum_{i=1}^{p}\beta_i\sigma_{t-i}^2 \qquad (4.85)$$

where $x_{t-q} = (r_{t-1}, ..., r_{t-q})'$. The linear term in the model allows for asymmetry. The off-diagonal elements of A matrix account for interaction effect of lagged values of x_t on the conditional variance. The various quadratic variance functions proposed in the literature are nested in Equation 4.85 (Palm, 1996, p. 212). The augmented GARCH (GAARCH) model of Bera and Lee (1990) assumes $\psi = 0$. Engle's ARCH model restricts $\psi = 0$, $\beta_i = 0$ and A matrix to be diagonal. The asymmetric GARCH model of Engle (1990) and Engle and Ng (1993) assumes A to be diagonal. The linear standard deviation model by Robinson (1991) restricts $\beta_i = 0$, $\sigma^2 = \rho^2$, $\psi = 2\rho\varphi$ and $A = \varphi\varphi'$, a matrix of rank 1. The conditional variance then becomes $\sigma_t^2 = (\rho + \varphi'x_{t-q})^2$.

TGARCH and GJR-GARCH models are similar to the EGARCH model in spirit but have better forecasting properties (Engle, Mezrich, 1995, p. 114). Zakoian (1994) and Glosten, Jagannathan and Runkle (1993) introduced the models independently of each other and it was examined and compared with other asymmetric models in Engle and Ng (1993). The model gives a bigger coefficient to squared returns when they are negative than when they are positive. The TGARCH model and the GJR-GARCH model do the same thing in a slightly different manner. The TGARCH model accounts for the asymmetry by allowing two different coefficients into the conditional volatility equation, and the GJR-GARCH model, in case of a negative surprise adds to volatility forecast via an indicator function.

The Threshold GARCH (TGARCH) put forward by Zakoian is given by (Palm, 1996, p. 212):

$$\sigma_t^2 = \omega + \sum_{i=1}^{q}(\alpha_i^+ \varepsilon_{t-i}^{2+} + \alpha_i^- \varepsilon_{t-i}^{2-}) + \sum_{j=1}^{p}\beta_j \sigma_{t-j}^2 \tag{4.86}$$

where $\varepsilon_t^{2+} = \max\{\varepsilon_t^2, 0\}$ and $\varepsilon_t^{2-} = \min\{\varepsilon_t^2, 0\}$. TGARCH account for asymmetry by allowing coefficients ε_t^{2+} and ε_t^{2-} to differ.

The GJR-GARCH put forward by Glosten, Jagannathan and Runkle is given by (Hagerud, 1997b, p. 3):

$$\sigma_t^2 = \omega + \sum_{i=1}^{q}[\alpha_1 + \gamma_i I_t]\varepsilon_{t-i}^2 + \sum_{j=1}^{p}\beta_j \sigma_{t-j}^2 \tag{4.87}$$

$I_t = 1 \ if \ \varepsilon_{t-i} < 0$
$I_t = 0 \ if \ \varepsilon_{t-i} \geq 0$

Positive surprises have an impact of α while negative surprises have an impact of α + γ.

As shown in Hentschel (1995) many members of the GARCH family of models (taking p = q = 1) can be embedded in a Box-Cox transformation of the absolute GARCH model:

$$(\sigma_t^\lambda - 1)/\lambda = \omega + \alpha \sigma_{t-1}^\lambda f^v(\varepsilon_{t-1}) + \beta(\sigma_{t-1}^\lambda - 1)/\lambda \tag{4.88}$$

where $f(\varepsilon_t) = |\varepsilon_t - b| - c(\varepsilon_t - b)$ is the news impact curve introduced by Pagan and Schwert (1990). For $\lambda > 1$, Box-Cox transformation is convex, for $\lambda < 1$, it is concave. For $\lambda = v = 1$ and $|c| \leq 1$ expression (4.88) specializes to become the AGARCH model. The model for the conditional standard deviation suggested by Schwert (1989a) arises when $\lambda = v = 1$ and $b = c = 0$. The EGARCH model for $p = q = 1$ arises from Equation 4.88 when $\lambda = 0$, $v = 1$ and $b = 0$. The TGARCH model is obtained when $\lambda = v = 1$, $b = 0$ and $|c| \leq 1$. The GARCH model arises if $\lambda = v = 2$

and $c = 0$ whereas the GJR-GARCH is obtained when $\lambda = v = 2$ and $b = 0$. The non-linear ARCH model of Higgins and Bera (1992) leaves λ free and v equal to λ with $b = c = 0$. The asymmetric power ARCH (APARCH) of Ding, Granger and Engle (1993) leaves λ free and equal to v, $b = 0$ and $|c| \leq 1$. Sentana's (1991) QGARCH is not nested in the specification (4.88). Nesting existing GARCH models in a general specification like the one given in Equation 4.88 highlights the relationships between these models and offers opportunities for testing sequences of nested hypotheses regarding the functional form for conditional second order moments.

4.1.2.4 Specification and estimation of GARCH models

The choice of data window for GARCH model parameter estimation is crucial for successful inference of VaR estimates. When choosing the length of the observation period there is a trade-off between the amount of data needed for parameter estimates to be stable as the data window is rolled, and the need for the model to reflect current market conditions. Daily or intra-day returns are usually used for GARCH estimation, because GARCH effects at lower frequencies are not so apparent. In choosing the time span of historical data used for estimating a GARCH model, the first consideration is whether major market events from several years ago should be influencing present forecasts. For example, including a national stock crash or some other special events in GARCH models will have the effect of raising current long-term volatility forecasts by several per cent. Several years of daily data should be used, enough to ensure that parameter estimates are relatively stable as the data window is rolled, but not so much that these estimates do not reflect changes in current market conditions. When there are outliers in the data, however far in the past, they can upset convergence of the GARCH model and result in misleading parameter estimates. A very long data period with several outliers is unlikely to be suitable because extreme moves from very long ago can have a great influence on the long-term volatility forecasts made today. The long-term level of volatility to which a current volatility term structure will converge depends on the estimates of the GARCH parameters. For example, in the GARCH(1,1) model the long-term volatility is related to the GARCH constant ω (Alexander, 2001, p. 85). All parameter estimates, and in particular the estimate of the GARCH constant, are sensitive to the historic data used for the model. Thus even if the market has been stable for some time, the estimate of long-term volatility can be high if the data period covers several years with many extreme market movements. It is for this reason that in choosing how far to go back with the data, one has to take a view of whether or not current forecasts should be influenced by events that occurred many years ago.

If the GARCH parameter estimates vary considerably when the model is rolled over time it may be that the model is not well specified. Hamilton and Susmel (1994) give evidence to suggest that specification of the GARCH model will depend on the current market regime.

Following Bollerslev's original paper from 1986, GARCH model parameters can be efficiently estimated by maximum likelihood. Maximum likelihood is a standard method for fitting the parameters of a density function. Under the classical assumptions of linear regression ordinary least squares estimation and maximum likelihood estimation are equal, so there is no explicit need for likelihood methods when estimating linear models or testing linear restrictions on their parameters (Gujarati, 2003, p. 112). However, non-linear statistical models are usually estimated by maximum likelihood because maximum likelihood estimators (MLEs) are almost always consistent (Johnston, DiNardo, 1997, p. 63).

The likelihood of observation x on a random variable is the value of its density function at x, written $f(x, \theta)$, where $\theta = (\theta_1, ..., \theta_q)$ are the parameters of the density function. The likelihood function of an independent set of observations $(x_1, ..., x_n)$ on the same random variable with density function $f(\theta)$ is the product of the likelihoods of each point, that is (Davidson, MacKinnon, 2004, p. 400):

$$L(\theta \mid x_1, ..., x_n) = \prod f(x_i, \theta) \qquad (4.89)$$

For given random sample data $(x_1, ..., x_n)$ the value of the likelihood will depend on θ.

As θ ranges over all possible values for all parameters the likelihood function describes a $(q + 1)$ dimensional surface. The greater the value of the likelihood, the more probable are the parameter values, based on the given sample data. Different sample data will give different values of the likelihood, so the values of the parameters that generate the highest likelihood will depend on the choice of the sample data.

The maximum likelihood estimator of θ is the value of θ that maximizes the likelihood function, given the sample data:

$$MLE\ \theta = arg\ max\ L(\theta \mid x_1, ..., x_n) \qquad (4.90)$$

The MLE of a parameter θ solves

$$\partial L(\theta \mid x_1, ..., x_n) / \partial \theta_i = 0 \qquad (i = 1, ..., q) \qquad (4.91)$$

provided the matrix of second derivatives is negative definite. Being a product of density functions which are typically fairly complex, it is not straightforward to calculate the derivatives of $L(\theta \mid x_1, ..., x_n)$. It is much easier to differentiate the log-likelihood function $ln\ L(\theta \mid x_1, ..., x_n)$, that is, the sum of the log densities (Engle, 1984, p. 780):

$$\ln L(\theta \mid x_1, ..., x_n) = \sum \ln f(x_i, \theta) \qquad (4.92)$$

Since the optima of L are the same as those of $\ln L$, it is standard to find the MLE as the value of θ that maximizes the log-likelihood (Alexander, 2001. p. 449). MLEs do not necessarily have good small-sample properties, but under standard data regularity conditions, MLEs are consistent, asymptotically normally distributed and asymptotically efficient. That is, they have the lowest variance of all consistent asymptotically normal estimators. In fact the asymptotic covariance matrix of MLEs achieves the Cramer-Rao lower bound for the variance of unbiased estimators (Kennedy, 2003, p. 33). This bound is the inverse of the information matrix $I(\theta)$, where

$$I(\theta) = -E(\partial^2 \ln L(\theta) / \partial\theta\partial\theta') \qquad (4.93)$$

Information matrix equals minus the expected values of the second derivatives of the log-likelihood function. In large samples MLEs have the minimum variance property, with covariance matrix $I(\theta)^{-1}$. Statistical inference on MLEs follows from the convergence of their distribution to the multivariate normal $N(\theta, I(\theta)^{-1})$ (Alexander, 2001, p. 449).

Another feature that makes MLEs among the best of the classical estimators is that the MLE of any continuous function $g(\theta)$ of a parameter θ is $g(\hat{\theta})$, where $\hat{\theta}$ is the MLE of θ. Thus it is a simple matter to find MLEs of standard transformations or products of parameters if the individual parameter MLEs are known.

Most algorithms are iterative, that is, the parameter estimates are updated using a scheme (Alexander, 2001, p. 94):

$$\theta_{i+1} = \theta_i + \lambda_i \delta_i$$

where λ_i is a step length and δ_i is a direction vector chosen so that the likelihood of the data under θ_{i+1} is greater than the likelihood under θ_i. The gradient descent methods that are used for GARCH model estimation in most software packages define the direction vector in terms of the gradient of the likelihood function and the Hessian matrix of second derivatives of the likelihood function, both evaluated at θ_i.

The point to emphasize is that the first-order conditions are easily solved since they are all linear. Calculating the appropriate sums may be tedious, but the methodology is straightforward. Unfortunately, this is not the case in estimating an ARCH or GARCH model since the first-order equations are non-linear. Instead, the solution requires some sort of search algorithm. The simplest way to illustrate the issue is to introduce an ARCH(1) error process into the simple regression model where the residuals(errors) are generated by:

$$\varepsilon_t = y_t - \beta x_t$$

In a classical regression framework where the values of $\{\varepsilon_t\}$ are drawn from a normal distribution having a mean of zero and a constant variance σ^2 the likelihood of any realization of ε_t is given by (Vose, 2000, p. 237):

$$L_t = \left(\frac{1}{\sqrt{2\pi\sigma^2}}\right)\exp\left(\frac{-\varepsilon_t^2}{2\sigma^2}\right) \tag{4.94}$$

where L_t is the likelihood of ε_t.

Since the realizations of $\{\varepsilon_t\}$ are independent, the likelihood of the joint realizations of ε_1, ε_2,..., ε_T is the product in the individual likelihoods. Hence, if all have the same variance, the likelihood of the joint realizations is (Enders, 2004. p. 138):

$$L = \prod_{t=1}^{T}\left(\frac{1}{\sqrt{2\pi\sigma^2}}\right)\exp\left(\frac{-\varepsilon_t^2}{2\sigma^2}\right) \tag{4.95}$$

Written in more convenient logarithmic form the likelihood is (Enders, 2004. p. 138):

$$\ln L = -\frac{T}{2}\ln(2\pi) - \frac{T}{2}\ln\sigma^2 - \frac{1}{2\sigma^2}\sum_{t=1}^{T}(\varepsilon_t)^2 \tag{4.96}$$

Under the presumption of ARCH(1) process ε_t is given by:

$$\varepsilon_t = v_t\sqrt{\sigma_t^2} \tag{4.97}$$

Although the conditional variance of ε_t is not constant, it is clear that Equation (4.96) that is valid for linear regression, needs a modification to be applied to ARCH process. Since each realization of ε_t has the conditional variance σ_t^2, the joint likelihood of realization ε_1 through ε_T is (Enders, 2004, p. 139):

$$L = \prod_{t=1}^{T}\left(\frac{1}{\sqrt{2\pi\sigma_t^2}}\right)\exp\left(\frac{-\varepsilon_t^2}{2\sigma_t^2}\right) \tag{4.98}$$

This gives the log likelihood function (Enders, 2004, p. 140):

$$\ln L = -\frac{T}{2}\ln(2\pi) - 0.5\sum_{t=1}^{T}\ln\sigma_t^2 - 0.5\sum_{t=1}^{T}(\varepsilon_t^2/\sigma_t^2) \tag{4.99}$$

If $\varepsilon_t = y_t - \beta x_t$ and the conditional variance is a ARCH(1) process $\sigma_t^2 = \alpha_0 + \alpha_1\varepsilon_{t-1}^2$ substituting for σ_t^2 and y_t yields (Enders, 2004, p. 140):

$$\ln L = -\frac{T-1}{2}\ln(2\pi) - 0.5\sum_{t=2}^{T}\ln(\alpha_0 + \alpha_1\varepsilon_{t-1}^2) - 0.5\sum_{t=2}^{T}\left[\frac{(y_t - \beta x_t)^2}{\alpha_0 + \alpha_1\varepsilon_{t-1}^2}\right] \quad (4.100)$$

Once the $(y_{t-1} - \beta_{t-1})^2$ is substituted for ε_{t-1}^2 it is possible to maximize *ln L* with respect to α_0, α_1 and β.

Ignoring the term in *ln(2π)* because it does not affect the estimates, the log-likelihood of a single observation r_t for a normal symmetric GARCH model is (Bollerslev, 1987, p. 501):

$$L_t = -\frac{1}{2}\left[\ln\sigma_t^2 + (\varepsilon_t^2/\sigma_t^2)\right] \quad (4.101)$$

and ΣL_t, should be maximized with respect to the variance parameters θ. In the case of GARCH(1,1) the variance parameters are $\theta = (\omega, \alpha, \beta)'$. The first derivatives may be written as (Alexander, 2001, p. 95):

$$\partial L_t/\partial\theta = (1/(2\sigma_t^2))\left[(\varepsilon_t^2/\sigma_t^2) - 1\right]g_t \quad (4.102)$$

where the gradient vector g_t is:

$$g_t = \partial\sigma_t^2/\partial\theta \quad (4.103)$$

These derivatives may be calculated recursively, taking the ordinary least squares estimate of unconditional variance as pre-sample estimates of ε_t^2 and σ_t^2 and calculating the gradient vectors by the recursion:

$$g_t = z_t + \beta g_{t-1} \quad (4.104)$$

where $z_t = (1, \varepsilon_{t-1}^2, \sigma_{t-1}^2)$. The algorithm may take a long time unless analytic derivatives are used to calculate the gradient[26]. This problem has limited the usefulness of GARCH models with Student's t distribution, for very leptokurtic data, since they require numerical derivatives to be calculated at each iteration. Solving the first-order conditions $\partial_t/\partial\theta = 0$ yields a set of non-linear equations in the parameters that may be solved using some quasi-Newton variable metric algorithm (McNeil, Frey, Embrecht, 2005, p.152), such as the Davidon-Fletcher-Powell (DFP) or the Berndt-Hall-Hall-Hausmann (BHHH) algorithm recommended by Bollerslev (1986). The BHHH iteration is:

---

[26] For further discussion see Davidson, MacKinnon, 2004, Chapter 10.

$$\theta_{i+1} = \theta_i + \lambda_i H_t^{-1} g_i \qquad\qquad (4.105)$$

where λ_t is a variable step length chosen to maximize the likelihood in the appropriate direction, H_i is the Hessian matrix $\Sigma(g_i g_t')$ and $g_i = \Sigma g_t$, both evaluated at θ_i. The iteration is deemed to have converged when the gradient vector g equals zero (McCullough, Renfo, 1998, p. 6).

Sometimes convergence problems arise because the more parameters in the GARCH model the flatter the likelihood function becomes, therefore the more difficult it is to maximize. The likelihood function becomes like the surface of the moon (in many dimensions) so it may be that only a local optimum is achieved. In that case a different set of estimates may be obtained when the starting values for the iteration are changed. In order to ensure that the estimates correspond to a global optimum of the likelihood function it is necessary to run the model with many starting values and each time record the likelihood of the optima. If this type of convergence problem is encountered a more parsimonious parameterisation of the GARCH model should be used. Convergence problems with GARCH models can also arise because the gradient algorithm used to maximize the likelihood function has hit a boundary. If there are obvious outliers in the data then it is very likely that the iteration will return the value 0 or 1 for either the alpha or the beta parameter (or both). It may be safe to remove a single outlier if the circumstances that produced the outlier are thought to be unlikely to happen in future. Alternatively, changing the starting values of the parameters, or changing the data set so that the likelihood function has a different gradient at the beginning of the search might mitigate the boundary problem. Otherwise the GARCH model specification will have to be changed. A sure sign of using the wrong GARCH model is when the iteration refuses to converge at all, even after the data outliers have been removed, starting values changed and different data period chosen. Most univariate GARCH models should encounter few convergence problems if the model is well specified and the data are well behaved. This applies especially to the most simple, but often the most robust of the GARCH models, the normally distributed GARCH(1,1) model. Changes in the data will induce some changes in the coefficient estimates, but if the appropriate model is chosen, parameter estimates should not change greatly as the new data arrives, except when there are structural breaks in the data generation process.

If a GARCH model is capturing volatility clustering adequately, the returns should have no significant autoregressive conditional heteroskedasticity once they have been standardized by their conditional volatility (Andersen, Bollerslev, Diebold, Labys, 1999a and Andersen, Bollerslev, Diebold, Ebens, 2000). An indication of the success of GARCH models to really capture the volatility clustering is that, even in very high-frequency exchange rate data where GARCH effects are strong and complex, returns are nearly normally distributed when divided by their conditional volatility (Zangari, 1996b, p. 7). Standard tests for autoregressive conditional heteroskedasticity are based on autocorrelation in squared returns. Returns themselves may not be autocorrelated, but if volatility clustering is present in the data they will not be independent because squared returns will be autocorrelated. Therefore a simple test for a GARCH model is that the standardized returns squared, $r_t'^2 = r_t^2 / \hat{\sigma}_t^2$ where $\hat{\sigma}_t^2$ is the estimate of the GARCH conditional variance, should have no autocorrelation. Such tests may be based on an autocorrelation test statistic such as the Ljung-Box Q test statistic or the Engle's ARCH test. If there is no autocorrelation in the squared standardized returns the GARCH model is well specified. If several GARCH models account equally well for GARCH effects the GARCH model which gives the highest likelihood in post-sample predictive tests should be chosen, while taking into account the parsimony of the model.

4.1.2.5   GARCH Volatility Term Structure

Term structure volatility forecasts are forecasts of the volatility of *h*-day returns for every maturity *h*. Return r_{th} over the next *h* days at time *t*, is approximately given by:

$$r_{th} = ln\ P_{t+h} - ln\ P_t \qquad\qquad (4.106)$$

where P_t denotes the price at time *t*. Converting the forecasted variance $V(r_{th})$ for every *h* to a volatility gives the volatility term structure. The underlying model for both equally weighted moving averages and EWMA is a constant volatility model, so term structure volatility forecasts that are consistent with moving average models will be constant. If the return process is independent and identically distributed (IID) with constant variance σ^2, taking variances of the r_{th} gives $V(r_{th}) = h\sigma^2$ (Diebold, Hickman, Inoue, Schuermann, 1997, p. 2). If there are *A* returns a year, then the number of *h*-day returns per year is *A/h*, and annualising $V(r_{th})$ into a volatility gives:

h-day volatility = $100\sqrt{(A/h)}\sqrt{(h\sigma^2)} = 100\sqrt{(A\sigma^2)}$ = 1-day volatility

In general, the square root of time rule states that if 1-period returns are IID then *h*-period standard deviations are just $\sqrt{h}$ times the 1-period standard deviation. Although very simple and useful the square root of time rule it is not supported by empirical observations (Bollerslev, Chou, Kroner, 1992) and (Diebold, Hickman, Inoue, Schuermann, 1997, p. 3).

The failure of square root of time scaling in a non IID environment and the nature of the associated erroneous long-horizon volatility estimates can be easily shown by a simple GARCH(1,1) process. The GARCH (1,1) process for 1-day returns is:

$$y_t = \sigma_t \varepsilon_t \qquad \sigma_t^2 = \omega + \alpha\, y_t^2 + \beta\sigma_{t-1}^2 \qquad \varepsilon_t \sim NID(0,1) \quad t = 1, ..., T \quad (4.107)$$

Drost and Nijman (1993) in their study of temporal aggregation of GARCH processes show that, under regularity conditions, a sample path of a h-day return series follows a GARCH (1,1) process with (Drost, Nijman, 1993, p. 913):

$$\sigma_{(h)t}^2 = \omega_{(h)} + \beta_{(h)}\sigma_{(h)t-1}^2 + \alpha_{(h)}y_{(h)t-1}^2 \tag{4.108}$$

where

$$\omega_{(h)} = h\omega\frac{1-(\beta+\alpha)^h}{1-(\beta+\alpha)}$$

$$\alpha_{(h)} = (\beta+\alpha)^h - \beta_{(h)}$$

and $|\beta_{(h)}|<1$ is the solution of the quadratic equation (Drost, Nijman, 1993, p. 916),

$$\frac{\beta_{(h)}}{1+\beta_{(h)}^2} = \frac{a(\beta+\alpha)^h - b}{a(1+(\beta+\alpha)^{2h})-2b} \tag{4.109}$$

where

$$a = h(1-\beta)^2 + 2h(h-1)\frac{(1-\beta-\alpha)^2(1-\beta^2-2\beta\alpha)}{(\kappa-1)(1-(\beta+\alpha)^2)}$$

$$+4\frac{(h-1-h(\beta+\alpha)+(\beta+\alpha)^h)(\alpha-\beta\alpha(\beta+\alpha))}{1-(\beta+\alpha)^2}$$

$$b = (\alpha - \beta\alpha(\beta+\alpha))\frac{1-(\beta+\alpha)^{2h}}{1-(\beta+\alpha)^2}$$

and κ is the kurtosis of y_t.[27] The Drost-Nijman formula is the key to correct conversion of 1-day volatility to h-day volatility. It is obvious that the square root of time scaling formula does not look like the Drost-Nijman formula. If, however, the scaling formula were an accurate approximation to the Drost-Nijman formula, it would still be very useful because of its simplicity and intuitive appeal. Unfortunately, that is not the case. As h → ∞, analysis of the Drost-Nijman formula reveals that α → 0 and β → 0, which means that temporal aggregation produces gradual disappearance of volatility fluctuations. Scaling by a square root of time, in contrast, magnifies volatility fluctuations, which is completely opposite. Term structure forecasts that are constructed from GARCH models mean-revert to the long-term level of volatility at a speed that is determined by the estimated GARCH parameters[28]. This is the great advantage of GARCH over moving average methods,

---

[27] Bollerslev (1986, p. 312) shows that a necessary and sufficient condition for the existence of a finite fourth moment is $3\alpha^2 + 2\alpha\beta + \beta^2 < 1$.

[28] For detailed discussion on temporal aggregation of GARCH processes see Drost, Nijman (1993).

which are based on the assumption of constant volatility term structures. In the GARCH(1,1) model the 1-day forward variance forecast is (Alexander, 2001, p. 100):

$$\hat{\sigma}_{t+1}^2 = \hat{\omega} + \hat{\alpha}\varepsilon_t^2 + \hat{\beta}\hat{\sigma}_t^2 \tag{4.110}$$

Although the unexpected return at time $t + j$ is unknown for $j > 0$, $E(\varepsilon_{t+j}^2) = \sigma_{t+j}^2$, so the j-step ahead forecasts are computed iteratively as:

$$\hat{\sigma}_{t+j}^2 = \hat{\omega} + (\hat{\alpha} + \hat{\beta})\hat{\sigma}_{t+j-1}^2 \tag{4.111}$$

Putting $\hat{\sigma}_{i+j}^2 = \hat{\sigma}^2$ for all j gives the steady-state variance estimate

$$\hat{\sigma}^2 = \hat{\omega}/(1 - \hat{\alpha} - \hat{\beta}) \tag{4.112}$$

that determines the long-term volatility level to which GARCH(1,1) term structure forecasts converge if $\hat{\alpha} + \hat{\beta} < 1$.

The forecasts from an asymmetric A-GARCH model (4.83) also have a simple analytic form. The one-step-ahead forecast is (Engle, Ng, 1993, p. 1754-1755):

$$\hat{\sigma}_{t+1}^2 = \hat{\omega} + \hat{\alpha}(\varepsilon_t - \hat{\lambda})^2 + \hat{\beta}\hat{\sigma}_t^2 \tag{4.113}$$

and the steady-state variance estimate is

$$\hat{\sigma}^2 = (\hat{\omega} + \hat{\alpha}\hat{\lambda}^2)/(1 - \hat{\alpha} - \hat{\beta}) \tag{4.114}$$

Comparison of (4.112) and (4.114) shows that the leverage coefficient λ from A-GARCH model has the effect of increasing long-term volatility forecasts, all other things held constant. That is, if the ω, α and β estimates were not changed very much by moving from a symmetric GARCH(1,1) to an A-GARCH(1,1) model, the long-term volatility forecasts from the A-GARCH model would be higher than those from a symmetric GARCH model. However, there will be a change in the ω, α and β estimates and the steady-state variance estimate in (4.114) should not differ from the GARCH(1,1) steady state given by (4.112). The most noticeable differences between the forecasts made by symmetric and asymmetric GARCH models are in the short-term volatility forecasts following a large fall in market price. Comparison of (4.111) with (4.113) shows that the difference between one-step ahead variance forecasts will be dominated by the term $\hat{\alpha}\hat{\lambda}(\hat{\lambda} - 2\varepsilon_t)$. Differences in volatility forecasts may be considerable if a very large unexpected negative return is experienced at time *t*, as shown in table 5.

Table 5 - The approximate influence of size of λ on increase in 1-day volatility forecast

Lambda		0.15	0.125	Alpha 0.1	0.075	0.05
	0.0001	0.868	0.793	0.709	0.614	0.501
$\varepsilon_t = -0.01$	0.0005	1.961	1.790	1.601	1.386	1.132
	0.001	2.806	2.562	2.291	1.984	1.620
	0.0001	1.937	1.769	1.582	1.370	1.119
$\varepsilon_t = -0.05$	0.0005	4.341	3.963	3.544	3.070	2.506
	0.001	6.154	5.618	5.025	4.352	3.553
	0.0001	2.739	2.501	2.237	1.937	1.582
$\varepsilon_t = -0.1$	0.0005	6.131	5.597	5.006	4.336	3.540
	0.001	8.682	7.925	7.089	6.139	5.012

Source: Alexander, 2001. p. 100.

As it can be seen from table 5, in case of a major shock in the market (e.g. $\varepsilon_t = -0.1$), the one day forecast volatility can differ by more than three times, depending on the size of lambda (λ). GARCH forecast of *h*-period variance is the sum of the instantaneous GARCH forecast variances, plus the double sum of the forecast autocovariances between returns (Alexander, 2001. p. 100):

$$r_{t,h} = \sum_{j=1}^{h} r_{t+j} \qquad V_t(r_{t,h}) = \sum_{i=1}^{h} V_t(r_{t+i}) + \sum_i \sum_j \mathrm{cov}_t(r_{t+i}, r_{i+j}) \quad (4.115)$$

The double sum is very small compared to the first sum on the right-hand side of the variance equation and in the majority of cases the conditional mean equation in a GARCH model is simply a constant, so the double sum is zero. Hence it is usual to ignore the second term and construct *h*-day forecasts simply by adding the *j*-step-ahead GARCH variance forecasts. Since all 1-day forward variance forecasts are computed it is also a simple matter to generate *h*-day forward volatility forecasts at any future date. The speed of convergence of the GARCH(1,1) volatility term structure depends on the estimate of $\alpha + \beta$. The smaller the sum, more rapid is the convergence to the long-term volatility estimate that is determined by Equation 4.110. The half-life of the return to the long-term average is determined by $1/(1 - \alpha - \beta)$. For example, if $\alpha + \beta$ is estimated as 0.95 it is 20 days, and if $\alpha + \beta$ is estimated as 0.99 it is 100 days.

4.2 Parametric approaches to calculating Value-at-Risk

The main difference among numerous VaR methods is related to the estimation of distribution that adequately describes the returns of the undertaken position in financial markets. The most commonly used VaR models in the world are parametric, and assume in advance a particular theoretical shape of the cumulative distribution of a variable (commodity price, stock price, interest rate, etc.). The distinguishing feature of estimating VaR using parametric approaches is that it requires an explicit specification of the statistical distribution from which the data is drawn. A parametric approach can be thought of as fitting curves through the data and then reading the VaR from the fitted curve. In making use of a parametric approach, it is necessary to take account of both the statistical distribution and the type of data to which it is applied. Parametric VaR can be calculated under the assumption that the arithmetic returns are normally distributed with mean μ_r and standard deviation σ_r. To derive the VaR, it is necessary to obtain the critical value of r_t, r^*, such that the probability that r_t, exceeds r^* is equal to the chosen confidence level (Dowd, 2002, p. 42):

$$r^* = \mu_r + \alpha_{cl}\sigma_r \qquad (4.116)$$

where α_{cl} is the standard normal variate corresponding to the chosen confidence level. Thus, for a chosen confidence level cl, α_{cl} is the value of the standard normal variate such that $1 - cl$ of the probability density lies to the left, and cl of the probability density lies to the right. For example, under the normal distribution if the confidence level is 99%, the value of α_{cl} is 2.33 (Kohler, 1994, p. 912). The return r_t is related to the negative of the loss/profit divided by the earlier asset value, P_{t-1} (Dowd, 2002, p. 42):

$$r_t = (P_t - P_{t-1})/P_{t-1} = - Loss_t/P_{t-1} \qquad (4.117)$$

This gives the relationship between r^*, the critical value of P_t, P^* value corresponding to a loss equal to VaR, and the VaR itself:

$$r_t^* = (P^* - P_{t-1})/P_{t-1} = - VaR/P_{t-1} \qquad (4.118)$$

Substituting Equation 4.116 into Equation 4.118 and rearranging them gives the VaR equation (Dowd, 2002, p. 42):

$$VaR = -(\mu_r + \alpha_{cl}\sigma_r)P_{t-1} \qquad (4.119)$$

Unfortunately, this approach assigns a positive probability of the asset value, P_t, becoming negative. This drawback can be avoided by working with geometric (logarithmic) returns rather than arithmetic returns. For logarithmic returns the critical value of R, R^*, that is the direct analogue of r^* is:

$$R^* = \mu_R + \alpha_{cl}\sigma_R \qquad (4.120)$$

The critical value P^* (i.e., the value of P_t corresponding to a loss equal to VaR), is obtained as (Dowd, 2002, p. 43):

$$R^* = \ln P^* - \ln P_{t-1} => \ln P^* = R^* + \ln P_{t-1}$$
$$=> P^* = \exp [R^* + \ln P_{t-1}] = \exp [\mu_R + \alpha_{cl}\sigma_R + \ln P_{t-1}]$$
$$=> VaR = P_{t-1} - P^* = P_{t-1} - \exp [\mu_R + \alpha_{cl}\sigma_R + \ln P_{t-1}] \qquad (4.121)$$

This formula gives the lognormal VaR, which is consistent with normally distributed geometric returns. The lognormal VaR has the attraction of ruling out the possibility of negative asset (or portfolio) values. The lognormal VaR can never exceed P_{t-1} because the loss/profit data is bounded above by P_{t-1} and this is a generally desirable property because it ensures that an investor cannot lose more than the invested amount.

4.2.1 Normally distributed VaR

The most frequently used distribution in finance is the normal (Gaussian) distribution primarily because of the central limit theorem[29]. Consequently, the normal distribution is often used when the distribution of sample means is of interest, more generally, when dealing with quantiles and probabilities near the centre of the distribution. A random variable (X) is normally distributed with mean μ and variance σ^2 if the probability that the value x, which is a function of $f(x)$, obeys the following probability density function (Holton, 2003, p. 133):

$$f(x) = \frac{1}{\sigma\sqrt{2\pi}} \exp\left(-\frac{1}{2}\frac{(x-\mu)^2}{\sigma^2} \right) \qquad (4.122)$$

where X is defined over $-\infty < x < \infty$

Every random variable X that is normally distributed can be transformed into a standardised normal random variable (Z) if variable X is linearly transformed into $X = \mu + z\sigma$ (Šošić, Serdar, 1997, p. 248):

$$Z = \frac{x-\mu}{\sigma} \qquad X \sim N(\mu,\sigma^2) \qquad Z \sim N(0,1) \qquad (4.123)$$

The mean of a standardized distribution is 0, and standard deviation is equal to 1. With the help of standardized variable Z, the standardized normal distribution can be written as (Šošić, Serdar, 1997, p. 248):

---

[29] Central limit theorem says that the means of samples of a random variable drawn from an unknown but well-behaved distribution are asymptotically (i.e., in the limit) normally distributed (Johnston, DiNardo, 1997, p. 55).

$$f(Z) = \frac{1}{\sqrt{2\pi}} \exp\left(-\frac{1}{2}Z^2\right) \tag{4.124}$$

which does not depend on the unknown parameters μ and σ. The implication is that it is very simple to calculate the probabilities of any state of the variable X by using the linear transformation to Z. The probability that the value of variable Z is in interval $[z_x;z_y]$ is:

$$P(z_x < Z \leq z_y) = \int_{z_x}^{z_y} f(z)dz = F(z_y) - F(z_x) \tag{4.125}$$

Because of the fact that normal distribution uses only the mean and standard deviation of the variable to describe its' distribution it is very simple to work with (Gujarati, 2003, p. 888). The third moment of the normal distribution, the skewness, is zero (i.e., so the normal distribution is symmetric) and the fourth moment, the kurtosis (which measures tail fatness), equals three[30]. The normality assumption has the additional attraction of making it easy to get good estimators of the parameters. Under normality, the least squares regression will give the best linear unbiased estimators of parameters, the same as those obtained by maximum likelihood approach (Davidson, MacKinnon, 2004, p. 399). In order to calculate VaR with the desired confidence level, and using the assumption of normal distribution, it is only necessary to estimate the μ and σ (Dowd, 2002, p. 78):

$$VaR = \alpha_{cl}\sigma_r - \mu_r \tag{4.126}$$

One of the appealing features of parametric approaches is that the formulas they provide for VaR estimation also allow for estimation of risk measures at any confidence level or holding period. If μ_r and σ_r are the mean and standard deviation of the observed returns over a given period (e.g., a day), then the mean and standard deviation of the data set over hp such periods are (Dowd, 2002, p. 79):

$$\mu_r(hp) = hp\,\mu_r \quad \sigma_r^2(hp) = hp\,\sigma_r^2 \rightarrow \sigma_r(hp) = \sqrt{hp}\,\sigma_r \tag{4.127}$$

Substituting Equation 4.127 into Equation 4.126 gives the formula for VaR over an arbitrary holding period hp and confidence level cl:

$$VaR(hp, cl) = \alpha_{cl}\sqrt{hp}\,\sigma_r - hp\,\mu_r \tag{4.128}$$

This makes it very easy to measure VaR once the values of σ_r and μ_r are known. These equations show that VaR will rise with the confidence level. However, the effects of a rising holding period are ambiguous, as the first terms in the formula

---

[30] In most statistical and econometric software packages the equation for calculating kurtosis is modified to equal zero (κ - 3), for easier interpretation.

rises with *hp*, but the second terms fall as *hp* rises. Since the first term relates to σ_r and the second to μ_r the effects of a rising *hp* on VaR depends on the relative sizes of μ_r and σ_r. Furthermore, since the first term rises with the square root of *hp*, whilst the second terms rise proportionately with *hp*, the second terms will become more prominent as *hp* gets larger. It is very informative to look at the entire VaR surface, as it conveys much more information than single point estimates. The usual (i.e. $\mu > 0$, $\sigma = 1$) normal VaR surface is shown in figure 14. The magnitudes of VaR will vary with the parameters, but the basic shape will always be the same: the VaR rises with the confidence level, and initially rises with the holding period, but as the holding period continues to rise, the VaR eventually peaks, turns down and becomes negative. The VaR is therefore highest when the confidence level is highest and holding period is high but not too high. Away from its peak, the VaR surface has nicely curved convex isoquants: these are shown in the figure 14 by the different shades on the VaR surface.

Figure 14 - Normal VaR surface against confidence level and holding period ($\mu = 0.1$, $\sigma = 1$)

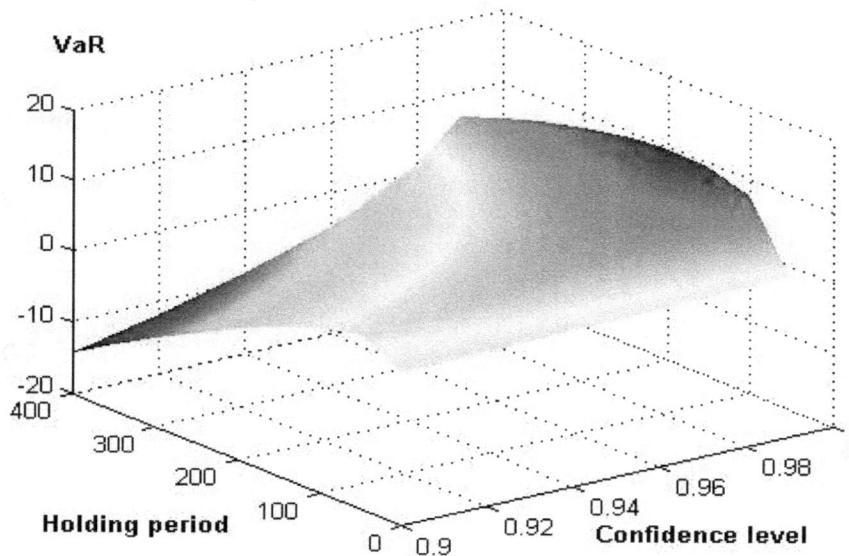

Figure 14 showing the VaR-holding period chart is very different from the VaR figure obtained by applying the square root of time rule, which is recommended under the Basle regulations on bank capital adequacy (Basel Committee on Banking Supervision, 1996a, p. 44). According to this rule, VaRs over longer holding periods can be approximated by taking a VaR measured over a short holding period and scaling it up by the square root of the desired holding period. If VaR over a 1-day holding period is *VaR(1,cl)*, then the VaR over a holding period of *hp* days, *VaR(hp,cl)*, is given by:

$$VaR(hp, cl) = \sqrt{hp}\; VaR(1, cl) \qquad\qquad\qquad (4.129)$$

This formula produces a VaR that always rises as the holding period increases, although at a decreasing rate, as illustrated in figure 15.

Figure 15 - Normal VaR surface against confidence level and holding period ($\mu = 0$, $\sigma = 1$)

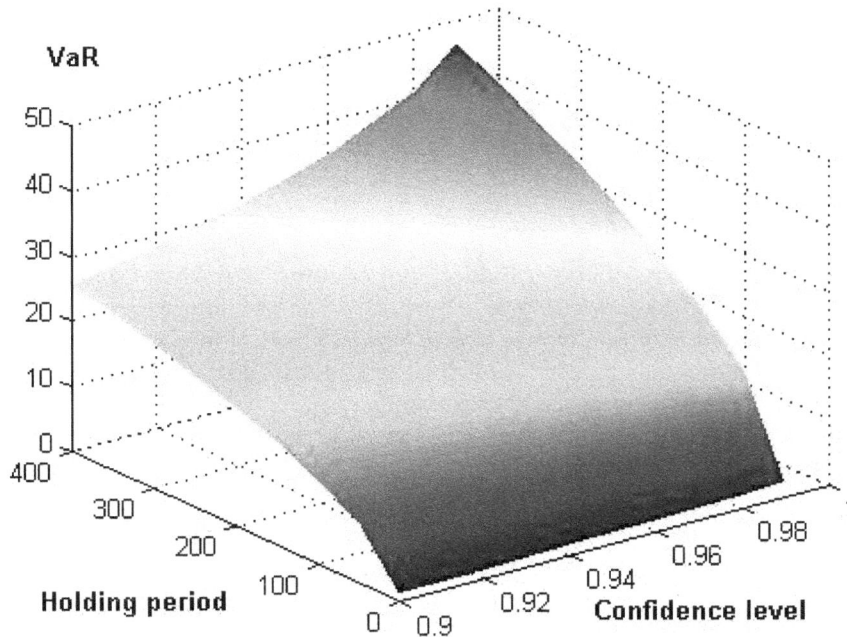

It is very useful to compare the surfaces in figures 14 and 15. In figure 14 the VaR becomes increasingly strongly negative, whilst the square root of time VaR in figure 15 becomes increasingly strongly positive as holding period gets larger. In figure 15, VaR rises with both confidence level and holding period. It never turns down, and the VaR surface spikes upward as the confidence level and holding period approach their maximum values. It is important to emphasise that the difference between the surfaces in figures 14 and 15 is due entirely to the fact that μ is positive in the first case and zero in the second. This simple example shows the importance of the mean that characterises a particular time series.

The normality assumption, whether applied to profit and loss data or returns, also has a number of potential disadvantages. One of the greatest advantages of normal distribution is at the same time its main weakness; the fact that it uses only the first two moments to describe the entire distribution (Guermat, Harris, 2002, p. 410). Furthermore, under the normal distribution returns are not limited, and this means that VaR might produce forecasts of losses larger than the initial investment. However, it is usually the case (e.g., due to limited liability and similar constraints)[31] that the losses are bounded, and the failure of the normality assumption to respect constraints on the maximum loss can lead to gross overestimates of risk.

A second potential problem is one of statistical plausibility. As mentioned already, the normality assumption is often justified by reference to the central limit theorem, but the central limit theorem applies only to the central mass of the density function, and not to its extremes. It follows that normality can be justified by reference to the central limit theorem only when dealing with more central quantiles and probabilities. When dealing with extremes - that is, when the confidence level is either very low or very high, the use of extreme value theorem is recommended (see Hongwei, Wei, 1999, McNeil, 1999, Embrechts, 2000). The extreme value theorem clearly shows that normal distribution should not be used to model the tails of the distribution[32].

The third problem of using normal distribution in modelling of financial data is that most financial returns have excess kurtosis (fat tails). Disregarding excess kurtosis can lead to major problems in risk management. Excess kurtosis implies that tails of a distribution are heavier than normal, and this means that VaR (at the relatively high confidence levels) will be greater. For example, VaR at the 95% confidence level, under the standard normality assumption is 1.645σ, but the Student's t VaR is 2.015σ, which is 22% greater (Kohler, 1994, p. 912-915). Furthermore, the proportional difference between the two VaRs gets bigger with the confidence level (e.g., at the 99% confidence level, the normal VaR is 2.326σ, but the Student's t VaR is 3.365σ, which is almost 44% higher) (Kohler, 1994, p. 912-915). This means that if the returns are assumed to be normal when they are actually fat-tailed, VaR will be underestimated and these underestimates are likely to be particularly large when dealing with VaR at high confidence levels.

The use of normal distribution is especially questionable in developing and shallow markets such as those of transition countries (see e.g. Žiković, 2006a, Žiković, Bezić, 2006). As stated earlier, the normally distributed mean-variance VaR takes into account only the first two moments of the distributions, and completely neglects the third and fourth moment around the mean (skewness and kurtosis). It is a well-documented fact that distribution of stock returns in the developed markets is asymmetric (negatively skewed) and leptokurtotic (has fatter tails than described by the normal distribution) (Mandelbrot, 1963, Fama, 1965, Bollerslev, 1986, Schwert 1990, Schwert, Seguin 1990). Because of these drawbacks, VaR calculation based on assumption of normality of distribution, including the Normal Monte Carlo

---

[31] Losses greater than the initial investment are only possible in portfolios containing financial derivatives, such as futures, swaps and short positions in options (Kolb, 2003, p. 201).

[32] For detailed discussion of Extreme Value Theory and its applications see Embrechts, Resnick, Samorodnitsky, 1997, Bensalah, 2002, Gilli, Kellezi, 2003.

simulation, when faced with empirical distribution that clearly is not normal, perform poorly.

4.2.2   VaR with Student's t distribution

One way of accommodating excess kurtosis is to use a Student's t distribution instead of normal distribution. The Student's t distribution is usually defined as a one-parameter distribution. If $t(v)$ is distributed as a Student's t with v degrees of freedom, where v is a positive integer, then $t(v)$ is distributed as the ratio of a standard normal distribution and the square root of a chi-squared distribution that is divided by v, where the chi-squared itself has v degrees of freedom (Gujarati, 2003, p. 890-892). Student's t distribution has: a mean of zero, provided $v > 1$, which is necessary for the mean to be finite; a variance of $v/(v - 2)$, provided $v > 2$, which is necessary for the variance to be finite; a zero skewness, provided $v > 3$, which is necessary for the skewness to be finite, although the distribution is always symmetric, and a kurtosis of $3(v - 2)/(v - 4)$, provided $v > 4$, which is necessary for the kurtosis to be finite (Evans, Hastings, Peacock, 2000, p. 179-180). In the case where $v = 1$, Student's t distribution becomes a Lorentzian (Cauchy) distribution, which is a member of the stable Lévy family of distributions (Blattberg, Gonedes, 1974, p. 245).

Student's t probability density function is given by (Shaw, 2006, p. 44):

$$y = f(x \mid v) = \frac{\Gamma\left(\dfrac{v+1}{2}\right)}{\Gamma\left(\dfrac{v}{2}\right)} \frac{1}{\sqrt{v\pi}} \frac{1}{\left(1 + \dfrac{x^2}{v}\right)^{\frac{v+1}{2}}} \qquad (4.130)$$

where $\Gamma(\,\cdot\,)$ is the Gamma function.

In risk measurement it is preferable to deal with a generalised Student's t distribution that allows the values of the mean and standard deviation to be set by the user. If a and b are defined as location and scale parameters, the generalised Student's t variate, $t(a,b,v)$, is related to the original Student's t by the equation $t(a,b,v) = a + bt(v)$. Assuming that the moments are finite, this generalised t distribution has mean μ, variance $b^2 v/(v - 2)$, skewness 0 and kurtosis $3(v - 2)/(v - 4)$. If $\alpha_{cl,v}$ is the inverse function (i.e., VaR, if the data is in loss/profit form) of the original Student's t for confidence level cl and v degrees of freedom, then the inverse function or VaR of the generalised Student's t is $a + b\alpha_{cl,v}$. If parameter b is substituted for the standard deviation σ, VaR becomes $a + \sigma\sqrt{(v-2)/v}\,\alpha_{cl,v}$. This gives the solution for VaR which is distributed as Student's t with mean a, standard deviation σ, and kurtosis *3(v - 2)/(v - 4)* (Dowd, 2002, p. 84-85). To make use of it in practice, *a* and σ are chosen to match the observed mean and standard deviation, and v is chosen to approximate the observed kurtosis in the data set. An alternative to calculating VaR with Student's t distribution is suggested by Huisman, Koedjik and Pownall (1998). They suggest that instead of fitting the Student's t distribution by matching the number of degrees of freedom to the empirical kurtosis, it is possible to set the degrees of freedom equal to the inverse of a Hill estimator of the tail index, modified to correct for small-sample bias. The problem with this approach is that it produces an implied kurtosis equal to *3(v - 2)/(v - 4)* that may not equal the empirical kurtosis. The parameters of the Student's t VaR equation can also be estimated using least squares (LS) or maximum likelihood (ML) methods. However, these two approaches are in the case of Student's t distribution distinctly different. In choosing between them, the ML method is theoretically superior only if the correct Student's t distribution is applied. Results reported by Lucas (2000) suggest that the LS estimators are better in the face of possible misspecification, meaning that for risk management purposes, the LS approach to estimating Student's t parameters is superior.

When modelling a relatively high excess kurtosis, Student's t distribution will have a relatively low value for v, and for relatively low excess kurtosis a relatively high value for v. Using the same notation as before, VaR is equal to (Dowd, 2002, p. 83):

$$VaR(hp, cl) = \alpha_{cl,v} \sqrt{hp} \sqrt{(v-2)/v} \sigma_r - hp\mu_r \qquad (4.131)$$

This Student's t VaR formula differs from the earlier normal VaR formula, Equation 4.128, in that the confidence level term, $\alpha_{cl,v}$ refers to a Student's t distribution instead of a normal one, and so depends on the value of v as well as *cl*. The Student's t VaR formula also includes the additional multiplier term $\sqrt{(v-2)/v}$, which moderates the effect of the standard deviation on the VaR. Since the Student's t distribution converges to the normal distribution as v gets larger, Student's t distribution can be regarded as a generalisation of the normal distribution that produces higher than normal kurtosis when v is finite. However, as v gets large, $\alpha_{cl,v}$ approaches its normal equivalent α_{cl}, $\sqrt{(v-2)/v}$ approaches 1, and Student's t VaR, given in Equation 4.131, approaches the normal VaR - Equation 4.128.

The Student's t VaR surface with positive mean is shown in figure 16. Similar to the normal VaR surface the Student's t VaR initially rises with the confidence level and holding period until it reaches its maximum. As holding period continues to rise, the surface eventually turns down again, enters negative territory, and then becomes ever more strongly negative as the holding period gets longer. The VaR surface falls off at lower confidence levels first, and it takes a very long time for it to fall off at higher confidence levels, especially in the cases of low number of degrees of freedom – high kurtosis value. The surface is similar to the normal VaR surface but the VaR values are significantly higher due to the effect of higher kurtosis.

Figure 16 - Student's t VaR surface against confidence level and holding period ($\mu =$ 0.1, $\sigma = 1$, $\upsilon = 4$)

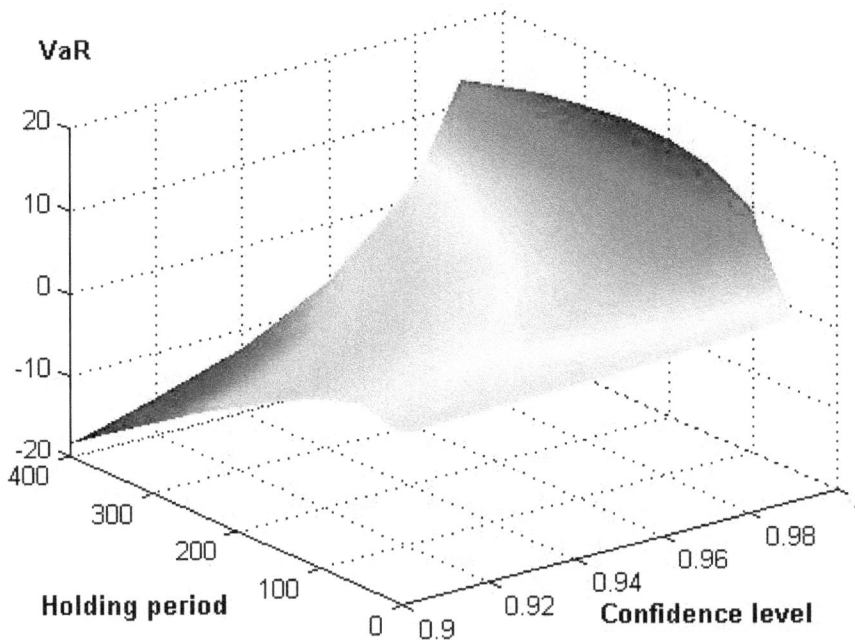

Again, as with the normal VaR surface, the mean term can make a big difference in estimating risk, particularly over longer holding periods. In figure 17 Student's t VaR has a $\mu = 0$, which means that it rises with both confidence level and holding period. It never turns down, and the VaR surface spikes upward as the confidence level and holding period approach their maximum values.

Figure 17 - Student's t VaR surface against confidence level and holding period ($\mu = 0$, $\sigma = 1$, $\upsilon = 4$)

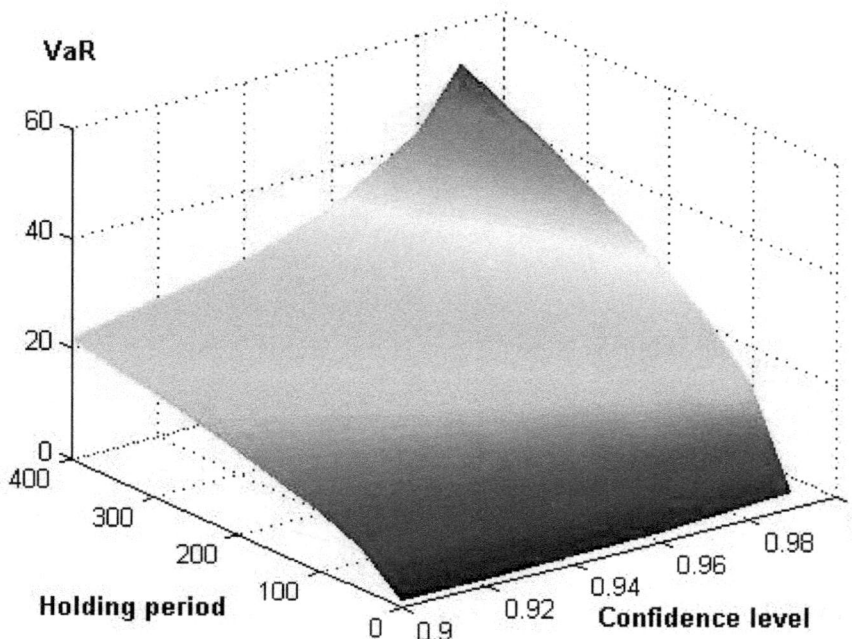

The Student's t VaR is very closely related to the normal VaR, and has many of the same properties. In particular, it behaves in much the same way as normal VaR in the face of changes in *cl* and *hp*. It rises with *cl*; for $\mu_r > 0$, it tends to rise initially with *hp*, and then peak and fall, the same as in the case of normal distribution.

The great advantage of the Student's t distribution over the normal distribution is its ability to handle excess kurtosis. Unfortunately the Student's t distribution also has its problems. Same as the normal distribution, it fails to respect constraints on maximum possible losses, and can produce misleadingly high risk estimates as a result. When used at very high or very low confidence levels, it has the drawback of not being consistent with extreme value theory. This means that from a theoretical point of view a Student's t distribution should not be used for measuring VaR at extreme confidence levels. The Student's t distribution suffers from an additional problem that does not affect the normal distribution. The Student's t distribution is not stable except for two special cases - when υ is 1 (Cauchy distribution), and when υ is infinite (normal distribution) (Davidson, MacKinnon, 2004, p. 136). Student's t distribution is not stable in the more general case when υ is greater than 1 but finite. As a consequence this means that the Student's t VaR formula cannot be relied on when forecasting VaR over long holding periods (Dowd, 2002, p. 84).

4.2.3 Lognormally distributed VaR

A popular alternative to modelling financial returns by normal or Student's t distribution is to assume that geometric returns are normally distributed, which is equal to assuming that the value of a portfolio at the end of a holding period is lognormally distributed. VaR model based on this preposition is usually referred to as lognormal VaR. The lognormal cumulative distribution function is defined as (McDonald, 1996, p. 430):

$$LN(y; \mu, \sigma) = \frac{1}{2} + \frac{(\ln(y) - \mu)}{\sqrt{2\pi}\sigma} {}_1F_1\left[\frac{1}{2}; \frac{3}{2}; -\frac{(\ln(y) - \mu)^2}{2\sigma^3}\right] \qquad (4.132)$$

where ${}_1F_1[]$ denotes the confluent hypergeometric series[33].

Lognormal VaR is characterized by a probability density function that it asymmetric and has a distinctive long tail on its right-hand side and at the left-hand side cuts-off at zero. This means that the value of a portfolio is bounded to be always positive.

The lognormal VaR is given by the following formula (Dowd, 2002, p. 85):

$$VaR(hp, cl) = P_{t-1} - \exp\left[-hp\,\mu_R + \alpha_{cl}\sqrt{hp}\,\sigma_R + \ln P_{t-1}\right] \qquad (4.133)$$

Equation 4.133 generalises the earlier lognormal VaR equation - Equation 4.121 by allowing for an arbitrary holding period. While Student's t distribution can account for excess kurtosis, it does not allow for skewness in the data. Skewness of a lognormal distribution is positive and increases with the variance, $\mu_3 = (e^{\sigma^2} - 1)\sqrt{(e^{\sigma^2} - 1)}$. The lognormal assumption has the attraction of ruling out the possibility of a positive-value portfolio becoming a negative-value one: in this case, the VaR can never exceed the value of a portfolio. The lognormal VaR surface with positive mean is illustrated in figure 18. Similar to the normal and Student's t VaR the lognormal VaR initially rises with the confidence level and holding period until it reaches an upper bound. This bound is given by the initial

---

[33] Generalized hypergeometric series is defined by (McDonald, 1996, p. 455-456):

$$ {}_pF_q\left[a_1, a_2, ..., a_p; b_1, b_2, ..., b_q; x\right] = \sum_{i=0}^{\infty} \frac{(a_1)_i (a_2)_i ... (a_p)_i x^i}{(b_1)_i (b_2)_i ... (b_q)_i\, i!} $$

where $(a)_n = (a)(a+1)(a+2)...(a+n-1) = \dfrac{\Gamma(a+n)}{\Gamma(a)}$ for $1 \leq n$,

Confluent hypergeometric series is a special case of the generalized hypergeometric series with (p = q = 1):

$$ {}_1F_1\left[a_1; b_1; x\right] = \sum_{i=0}^{\infty} \frac{(a_1)_i x^i}{(b_1)_i\, i!} $$

value of a portfolio. The VaR surface then flattens out along this ceiling for a period of time. As holding period continues to rise, the surface eventually turns down again and becomes smaller as the holding period gets longer. Same as in the case of Student's t VaR surface, the lognormal VaR surface falls off much faster at lower confidence levels first, but takes a long time to decrease at higher confidence levels. The VaR surface always turns down eventually, regardless of the confidence level, as long as the mean return is positive. The reason for this is the same as for normal and Student's t VaR. The mean term becomes more important than the standard deviation term as the holding period rises, since it grows at a faster rate.

Figure 18 - Lognormal VaR surface against confidence level and holding period (μ = 0.1, σ = 1, I = 1€)

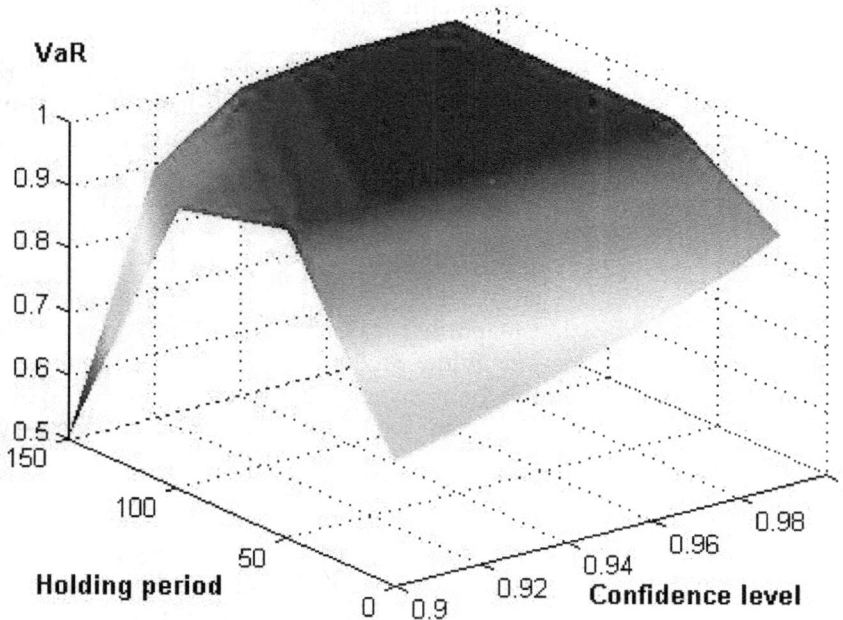

A lognormal VaR surface with a zero mean term shown in figure 19 acts analogous to normal and Student's t VaR surface. VaR quickly hit its ceiling, set by the size of the initial investment, and stays at its maximum forever.

Figure 19 - Lognormal VaR surface against confidence level and holding period (μ = 0, σ = 1, I = 1€)

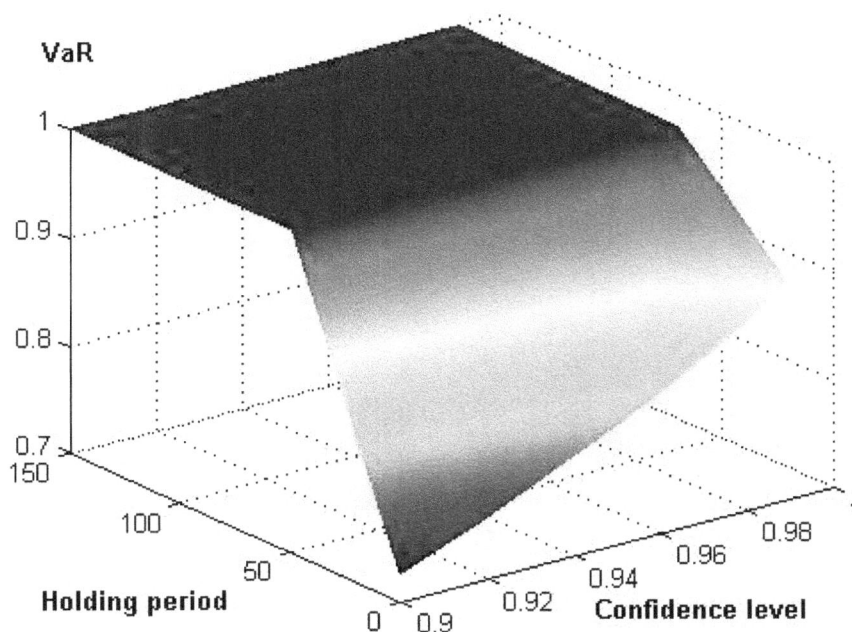

An important implication of any asymmetric distribution is that long and short positions have asymmetric risk exposures. A long position loses if the market goes down, and a short position loses if the market goes up, but with any symmetric distribution the VaR on a long position and the VaR on a short position are mirror images of each other, reflecting the symmetry of the lower and upper tails of the distribution. With the asymmetric distribution, such as lognormal, the most a long position can lose is the value of its investment, but a short position can make much larger losses than the initial investment.

Since the lognormal approach is consistent with a geometric Brownian motion process for the underlying asset price, which is one of its main advantages, it also suffers from the same drawbacks, meaning that it also cannot accommodate fat tails in geometric returns. A simple solution to this problem is to replace the assumption that the geometric returns are normally distributed with the assumption that they are distributed as Student's t. Log - Student's t VaR can be written as:

$$VaR(hp,cl) = P_{t-1} - \exp\left[- hp\mu_R + \alpha_{cl,\upsilon}\sqrt{hp}\sqrt{(\upsilon-2)/\upsilon}\sigma_R + \ln P_{t-1}\right] \quad (4.134)$$

Log - Student's t VaR approach should combine the benefits of the geometric returns with the fatter tails of Student's t distribution. For the same reason as the normal and Student's t distribution, lognormal distribution is also not suitable for measuring VaR at extreme confidence levels.

4.2.4   Miscellaneous parametric approaches to calculating VaR

Besides using Student's t and lognormal distribution, other approaches can be used to handle excess kurtosis and asymmetry in the financial data. Some of the most widely accepted approaches are: Stable Lévy processes, elliptical distribution, hyperbolic distribution and mixture of normal distributions. A short overview of theses approaches is presented in this chapter of the book.

4.2.4.1   Stable Lévy processes

Non-normal stable Lévy processes, also known as α-stable or stable Paretian processes were first suggested as plausible representations of financial return processes by Mandelbrot and Fama in the 1960s (Mandelbrot, 1963, Fama, 1965) as a means of accommodating fat tails of financial return data. At the same time, stable Lévy processes also have a certain theoretical plausibility because they arise from a generalised version of the central limit theorem. Stable Lévy processes generally lack conventional closed-form solutions for their density or distribution functions, but can instead be represented by their characteristic function (Mantegna, Stanley, 2000, p. 25):

$$\ln \phi(x) = \begin{cases} i\mu x - \gamma \mid x \mid^{\alpha} [1 - i\beta(x/\mid x \mid)\tan(\pi\alpha/2)] \\ i\mu x - \gamma \mid x \mid [1 + i\beta(x/\mid x \mid)(2/\pi)\ln \mid x \mid] \end{cases} \quad if \quad \begin{matrix} \alpha \neq 1 \\ \alpha = 1 \end{matrix} \quad (4.135)$$

This function has four parameters: a stability index, α, lying in the range $0 < \alpha \leq 2$; a skewness parameter, β, lying in the range $-1 \leq \beta \leq 1$ and taking the value 0 if the distribution is symmetric; a location parameter, μ, that is a real number; and a positive scale parameter, γ. The Lévy process has some interesting special cases (adapted from Dowd, 2002, p. 395):

$$Stability \quad index(\alpha) \begin{cases} = 2 \quad Levy\,process \; = Normal \;\; distribution \\ < 2 \quad Levy \quad process \quad has \qquad \sigma^2 \to \infty \\ = 1, \beta = 0 \quad Levy\,process \; = Cauchy \;\; distribution \end{cases} \quad (4.136)$$

Except for the normal special case (i.e., provided α < 2), all stable Lévy processes have probability density functions that converge to power-law tails with exponent 1 + α (Dowd, 2002, p. 265):

$$p(x) \sim 1/x^{1+\alpha} \qquad\qquad\qquad (4.137)$$

meaning that stable Lévy processes have infinite variance and heavy tails. Non-normal Lévy processes are suitable for modelling heavy tails but have a serious disadvantage of having infinite variance. Besides the ability to capture fat tails Lévy processes have other properties that make them potentially very attractive for modelling financial data. Stable Lévy processes have domains of attraction, which means that any distribution close to a stable Lévy distribution will have similar properties to this distribution. This is important because it indicates that small departures from a stable Lévy process (e.g., because of errors in the data) should not produce serious errors in any inferences made using stable Lévy processes. Second attractive property of stable Lévy processes is stability, which means that the sum of two independent Lévy processes with the same index α is itself a Lévy process with index α. This property means that the distribution retains its shape when summed. The third attractive property is scale-invariance or self-similarity, which means that stable Lévy process can be rescaled over one time period so that it has the same distribution over another. This property leads to the stable Lévy scaling law (Mantegna, Stanley, 2000, p. 71):

$$Z(t) = Z(\Delta t)^{1/\alpha} \tag{4.138}$$

where Z is a stable Lévy process defined over a given period, and $Z(t)$ is the equivalent stable Lévy process defined over period t. Stable Lévy processes scale at a rate $1/\alpha$. This means that the square root of time rule (i.e., where $Z(t)$ grows with the square root of t) only applies in a special case, when $\alpha = 2$ and $Z(t)$ is a geometric Brownian motion, which is the same as saying that Z is normally distributed. Mittnik, Paolella and Rachev have provided considerable evidence to support the applicability of stable Lévy processes to financial returns data (Mittnik, Paolella, Rachev, 2000). Their work also suggests that stable Lévy processes can be regarded as (partial) alternatives to GARCH processes for modelling financial returns, because GARCH models also lead to fat-tailed return distributions (Mittnik, Paolella, Rachev, 2000, p. 389-390). Stable Lévy processes also have their drawbacks. Perhaps the most obvious is that the applicability of non-normal stable Lévy processes is undermined by widespread evidence that the variances of financial returns are finite (although this evidence has been challenged (e.g. Mittnik, Paolella, Rachev, 2000, p. 391)). There is also some evidence that financial return processes are not always scale-invariant (Cont, Potters, Bouchaud, 1997, p. 5). Another problem with these kinds of distributions are the power law tails, which decay too slowly from the point of view of financial modelling. Furthermore, in practice the distribution of price changes for larger time intervals converge to a normal distribution, the fact that is not consistent with the stable Lévy processes (Lehnert, Wolff, 2001, p. 2).

The stated problems can be overcome by taking the Lévy distribution in the central part and introducing a cut-off in the far tails that is faster than the Lévy power law tails. The Lévy distribution with a cut-off and exponentially declining tails was introduced in the field of physics by Mantegna and Stanley and is known as a truncated Lévy flight (TLF). This cut-off ensures that the variance will be finite and the distribution will asymptotically converge to a normal distribution. To model financial prices over time the truncated Lévy flight can be constructed by the sum of independent and identically distributed random variables described by a truncated Lévy distribution. Lévy flights have been observed experimentally in physical systems and have been used very successfully to describe for instance the spectral random walk of a single molecule embedded in a solid. In all these cases an unavoidable cut-off in the tails of the distribution is always present, which ensures the finiteness of the second moment of the process (Lehnert, Wolff, 2001, p. 4). One possible cut-off is the exponential function, for which the characteristic function has been developed (Koponen, 1995). Lehnert and Wolff (2001) corrected the mistake in characteristic function of Koponen (1995), and give the correct version (Lehnert, Wolff, 2001, p. 4):

$$\Psi_{TL}(k,\mu,C,\alpha,\lambda,\beta) = i\mu k - C^{\alpha}\left\{\frac{\lambda^{\alpha}-(k^2+\lambda^2)^{\alpha/2}}{\cos(\pi\alpha/2)}\cos(\varepsilon)[1+i\,\mathrm{sgn}(k)\beta\tan(\varepsilon)]\right\}$$

$$\varepsilon = \alpha \quad \arctan\left(\frac{|k|}{\lambda}\right) \qquad\qquad\qquad (4.139)$$

where μ is a location parameter, $C > 0$ is a scale parameter, α is the characteristic exponent determining the shape of the distribution and especially the fatness of the tails ($0 < \alpha \leq 2$, but $\alpha \neq 1$) and λ is the so-called cut-off parameter, which determines the speed of the decay and as a result the cut-off region. The parameter β ($\beta \in [-1,1]$) determines the skewness when $\beta \neq 0$, the distribution is skewed to the right when $-1 < \beta < 0$ and skewed to the left when $0 < \beta < 1$. For $\lambda \to +0$ the truncated Lévy distribution reduces to the Lévy distribution. In contrast to the stable Lévy distribution the exponential cut-off ensures that all moments exist. The density function is only known analytically when $\lambda \to \infty$, $\beta = 0$, $\alpha = 1$, (Cauchy distribution) and $\lambda \to \infty$, $\beta = 0$, $\alpha = 2$ (Gaussian distribution). However, for the symmetric case the value of the density of the Lévy distribution is known at the origin and in the far tails. In all other situations the density must be generated numerically. Accurate numerical values for the density ψL can be calculated by Fourier-transforming the characteristic function and evaluating the integral numerically (Lehnert, Wolff, 2001, p. 4). Because the variance of TLF is finite, it will eventually converge to a normal distribution. Hence, a TLF is a stochastic process that behaves like a stable Lévy process for relatively short periods, but eventually converges to a normal distribution in the long run.

4.2.4.2 Elliptical and Hyperbolic Distributions

A simple approach to modelling fat tails is to use elliptical distributions, as suggested in recent research papers (Eberlein, Keller, Prause, 1998, Bauer, 2000). The name elliptical distribution comes from the fact that their log-density is an ellipse; by comparison, the log-density of a normal distribution is a parabola. These distributions are symmetric distributions with a less constrained kurtosis, and include the normal as a special case when the kurtosis is equal to three. They also have the attraction of having a straightforward VaR formula. If the returns distribution is elliptical with location and scale parameters equal to μ and δ, VaR is given by (Bauer, 2000, p. 456-457):

$$VaR = - \alpha_{cl}\delta - \mu \tag{4.140}$$

where α_{cl} is the percentile of the standard form elliptical distribution. In the special case of the normal distribution, α_{cl} will be the percentile of the standard normal distribution. Elliptical distributions are easy to work with at the individual-position level, as well as at the aggregate portfolio level. To estimate the elliptical VaR, all that is needed is an estimate of the two parameters μ and δ. Location parameter (μ) can be estimated as a mean of a sample by conventional methods, and the scale parameter (δ) can be estimated by using a maximum likelihood procedure. A further generalisation of elliptical distributions is the family of generalised hyperbolic distributions. These distributions include the hyperbolic and normal inverse Gaussian distributions as special cases, as well as the elliptical and normal distributions. They can also accommodate excess kurtosis, but have forbidding density functions and, special cases aside, do not yield closed-form solutions for VaR. Elliptical and hyperbolic distributions are theoretically attractive, because they can be regarded as generalisations of the normal distribution, that can be applied at both the position and portfolio level (Eberlein, Keller, Prause, 1998).

4.2.4.3   Normal Mixture Approach

Another attractive alternative, suggested by Zangari (1996b) and Venkataraman (1997), is to model returns using a mixture-of-normals approach. This process assumes that most of the time the returns are drawn from one normal process, but occasionally returns are drawn from another normal process with a higher variance. If p_x is the probability that a standardized return was generated from the normal distribution N_x, where N_x is defined by its mean μ_x and variance σ_x^2. A typical two variable normal mixture process is (Zangari, 1996b, p. 10):

$$Normal\ mixture\ process = p_1N_1(\mu_1,\ \sigma_1^2) + p_2N_2(\mu_2,\ \sigma_2^2) \tag{4.141}$$

Since the normal mixture model can assign large probabilities to more extreme returns the standardized returns are modelled as the sum of a normal return (n_t), with mean zero and variance σ_n^2, and another normal return β_t, with mean and variance that occurs each period with probability p. Standardized return $R(t)$ is generated from a following model (Zangari, 1996b, p. 11):

$$R_t = n_t + \delta_t\beta_t \tag{4.142}$$

where $\delta_t = 1$ with probability p, or $\delta_t = 0$ with probability $1 - p$. When $\delta_t = 1$, the standardized return is normally distributed with $\mu_{\beta(t)}$ and variance $\sigma_\beta^2 + \sigma_n^2$. Otherwise it is distributed normally with mean zero and variance σ_n^2. Modelling the returns in this way results in very large or very low values that occur more frequently than under an unadjusted normal distribution. For a mixture of two random variables the kurtosis of the mixture is $3[p\sigma_1^4 + (1-p)\sigma_2^4] / [p\sigma_1^2 + (1-p)\sigma_2^2]^2$, which is greater than 3 provided $\sigma_1^2 \neq \sigma_2^2$ and $0 < p < 1$ (Lagnado, Delianedis, Tikhonov, 2000, p. 4).

Normal mixture approaches have a number of merits: they are conceptually simple, they can accommodate any reasonable degree of kurtosis, they make use of the standard linear normal estimates of variances and correlations, and so retain much of the tractability of normal approaches and (at least for portfolios with a small number of different assets) they require relatively few additional parameters (Dowd, 2002, p. 93). However, implementing the normal mixtures approach requires the estimation of the parameters involved, which is a very demanding task. The most obvious approach to parameter estimation is maximum likelihood, but unfortunately, the normal mixture likelihood function does not have a global maximum, and this makes a standard ML approach unusable (Dowd, 2002, p. 94). Zangari and Venkataraman suggest alternative solutions to this problem, Zangari (1996b) suggests involving a Gibbs sampling tool, and Venkataraman (1997) suggests involving quasi-Bayesian maximum likelihood[34]. Implementing a normal mixtures approach also raises a problem of modelling the correlation between the individual risk factors, including the δ_t binary terms. The normal mixtures approach can also be generalised to allow the unobserved selection variable δ_t, to depend on an unobserved state, and this state can be modelled as a Markov chain. The Markov chain approach is suggested by Billio and Pelizzon (1997), and has the advantage of allowing for volatility clustering, which the normal mixtures approach does not. However, it also requires more parameters than the mixtures approach, and is far harder to implement.

4.2.5   RiskMetrics methodology

RiskMetrics describes a methodology based on J.P. Morgan's approach to quantifying market risk in portfolios of fixed-income instruments, equities, foreign exchange, commodities, and their derivatives in the financial markets. The data consists of spot prices or rates, volatilities and correlation matrices for more than 30 countries (RiskMetrics, 1996, p. 17). It is an outgrowth of recent trends in financial markets, the growth of trading, securitization, derivatives, focus on performance evaluation, indexing and the risk-return trade of in investing and the product of many years of developing a common framework for measuring market risk that is rooted historically in the pioneering work of Markowitz toward the modern portfolio theory (Phelan, 1995, p. 6). The practice of quantifying risk on the basis of value-at-risk developed along side of management practices over trading functions, where there is a need to mark-to-market trading positions frequently at prevailing prices and rates in order to project income over short horizons.

---

[34] Details of these solutions can be found in their respective articles. See also Hamilton (1994) chapter 22.

The RiskMetrics VaR measures are based on a forecast variance-covariance matrix. RiskMetrics simply consists of three large variance-covariance matrices of the returns including major FX rates, money market rates, equity indices, bonds and some key commodities. The first is a one-day matrix (i.e. a variance-covariance matrix relevant for VaR measures corresponding to one-day returns) the second is a one-month (25-day) matrix and the third is a "regulatory" matrix for compliance with the Basle Committee proposals (Alexander, 2000, p. 278). RiskMetrics data is based on moving average methods, which are standard statistical estimation techniques where it is usual to take the current moving average estimate of variance (or covariance) to be the one-step-ahead forecast. J.P. Morgan has applied the exponentially weighted moving average (EWMA) methodology to produce 1-day and 1-month matrices. To provide VaR measures of holding periods other than one day or one month it is possible to follow the Basle Committee recommendations and use the square root of time rule. This unrealistic assumption of constant volatility which underlies this rule generally means that such VaR measures can substantially over estimate the risk in tranquil times, and underestimate it in periods of high volatility. Those who are unwilling to accept VaR measures based on the assumption that current levels of volatility will remain the same forever are therefore limited by RiskMetrics. There is no other possibility to produce VaR measures for 1-week holding periods or indeed any holding period other than 1-day or 1-month. However a good VaR model will produce VaR numbers for every holding period from 1-day (or less than a day), 2-days, 3-days up to 1-year or even more.

The RiskMetrics "regulatory" matrix is constructed exactly according to the Basle Committee proposals, and is based on equally weighted moving averages over the past year of data. Equally weighted averages is a standard statistical method for estimating unconditional variances and covariances, but when it is applied to financial markets the "ghost effects" which result from this type of conditionally heteroskedastic data can pose substantial problems (Alexander, 2000, p. 280). When there is a large movement in the underlying time series such as a jump in market price, an equally weighted average of squared returns will jump up the very next day. This is as an accurate reflection of the clustering behaviour of volatility in financial markets. However, there are serious problems with this approach: Firstly, a large, squared return will continue to keep volatility estimates high for exactly one year (or however long the moving average is) whereas the underlying volatility will have long ago returned to normal levels. Secondly, exactly after the passage of the time length of the moving average from a major market event that caused the spike, the equally weighted volatility estimate will jump down again as abruptly as it jumped up. But there is nothing special about that day - what is seen is just a ghost of what happened one year ago, a correction in the estimate which is by then long over due. If the average is taken over fewer observations, this correction will be much bigger in short-term volatility estimates. Because of this "ghost effect", any extreme event, which has occurred during the last year, could have a big effect on VaR measures based on the RiskMetrics regulatory matrix. Whether the VaR measures are increased or decreased by the "ghost effect" depends on the portfolio construction (Alexander, 2000, p. 281).

Being aware of the problems induced by the "ghost effect" produced in equally weighted averages, J.P. Morgan decided to construct the daily and monthly matrices that use exponentially weighted moving averages (EWMA). Because past observations are weighted by applying EWMA, they are actually weighted by the smoothing constant (decay factor) λ which is between 0 and 1. The weighting is done by multiplying an observation that occurred n days ago by λ^n, which is very small for large n. Thus extreme events have less of an impact on variances and covariances as they move further into the past, and the "ghost effects" should no longer appear. This is indeed the case in the RiskMetrics one-day matrix, where EWMA is applied to squared daily returns. The RiskMetrics model assumes that returns are generated according to the following model (RiskMetrics, 1996, p. 73):

$$r_{i,t} = \sigma_{i,t}\varepsilon_{i,t} \quad \varepsilon_{i,t} \sim N(0, 1)$$

$$\varepsilon_t \sim MVN(0, R_t) \quad \varepsilon_t = [\varepsilon_{1t}, \varepsilon_{2t}, ..., \varepsilon_{Nt}] \tag{4.143}$$

where R_t is an $N \times N$ time dependent correlation matrix. The variance of each return, $\sigma_{i,t}^2$ and the correlation between returns, $\rho_{ij,t}$, are functions of time. The property that the distribution of returns is normal given a time dependent mean and correlation matrix assumes that returns follow a conditional normal distribution - conditional on time. The term μ_i is excluded from the Equation 4.143 because the RiskMetrics presumes that the daily mean return is equal to zero. For a given set of T returns, the equally and exponentially weighted standard deviation is calculated as (RiskMetrics, 1996, p. 78):

Equally weighted standard deviation:

$$\sigma = \sqrt{\frac{1}{T}\sum_{t=1}^{T}(r_t - \bar{r})^2} \tag{4.144}$$

Exponentially weighted standard deviation (EWMA):

$$\sigma = \sqrt{(1-\lambda)\sum_{t=1}^{T}\lambda^{t-1}(r_t - \bar{r})^2} \tag{4.145}$$

The exponentially weighted moving average model depends on the parameter λ ($0 < \lambda < 1$) that is often referred to as the decay factor or smoothing constant. This parameter determines the relative weights that are applied to the observations and the effective amount of data used in estimating volatility.

The EWMA estimator in Equation 4.145 is constructed by using an approximation (RiskMetrics, 1996, p. 79):

$$\sum_{j=1}^{T}\lambda^{j-1} \cong \frac{1}{(1-\lambda)} \tag{4.146}$$

These two expressions are equivalent in the limit, i.e., as $T \to \infty$. For purpose of comparison to the equally weighted factor *1/T*, the more appropriate version of the EWMA is:

$$\lambda^{t-1} / \sum_{j=1}^{T} \lambda^{j-1} \tag{4.147}$$

rather than *$(1-\lambda)\lambda^{t-1}$*. When $\lambda = 1$, the above Equation 4.147 collapses to *1/T*.

An attractive feature of the exponentially weighted estimator is that it can be written in recursive form, which is used as a basis for making volatility forecasts. In order to derive the recursive form, it is assumed that an infinite amount of data is available. Assuming that the sample mean is zero, period *t+1* variance forecast, given the data available at time *t* (one day earlier) is derived as (RiskMetrics, 1996, p. 81):

$$\begin{aligned}
\sigma_{1,t+1|t}^2 &= (1-\lambda) \sum_{i=0}^{\infty} \lambda^i r_{1,t-i}^2 \\
&= (1-\lambda)\left(r_{1,t}^2 + \lambda r_{1,t-1}^2 + \lambda^2 r_{1,t-2}^2 + \ldots\right) \\
&= (1-\lambda)r_{1,t}^2 + \lambda(1-\lambda)\left(r_{1,t-1}^2 + \lambda r_{1,t-2}^2 + r_{1,t-3}^2\right) \\
&= \lambda \sigma_{1,t|t-1}^2 + (1-\lambda)r_{1,t}^2
\end{aligned} \tag{4.148}$$

The 1-day RiskMetrics volatility forecast is given by the expression:

$$\sigma_{1,t+1|t} = \sqrt{\lambda \sigma_{1,t|t-1}^2 + (1-\lambda)r_{1,t}^2} \tag{4.149}$$

The subscript "*t+1|t*" is read as the time *t+1* forecast given information up to and including time *t*. The subscript "*t|t-1*" is read in a similar fashion. This notation underscores the fact that the variance is treated as time-dependent. The fact that this period's variance forecast depends on last period's variance is consistent with the observed autocorrelation in squared returns observed in the empirical studies (see e.g. Engle, 1982, Engle, Takatoshi, Lin, 1990, Day, Lewis, 1992).

RiskMetrics produces volatility and correlation forecasts for almost 100.000 time series (Allen, Boudoukh, Saunders, 2004, p. 236). Since these parameters comprise a covariance matrix, the optimal decay factors for each variance and covariance forecast are not independent of one another. RiskMetrics applies one optimal decay factor to the entire covariance matrix. That is, RiskMetrics uses one decay factor for the daily volatility and correlation matrix and one for the monthly volatility and correlation matrix. This decay factor is determined from individual variance forecasts across all time series.

The definition of the time *t+1* forecast of the variance of the return r_{t+1} made one period earlier is simply $E_t\left[r_{t+1}^2\right] = \sigma_{t+1|t}^2$, the expected value of the squared return one-period earlier. The variance forecast error is $\varepsilon_{t+1|t} = r_{t+1}^2 - \sigma_{t+1|t}^2$. It follows that the expected value of the forecast error is zero, i.e., $E_t(\varepsilon_{t+1|t}) = E_t(r_{t+1}^2) - \sigma_{t+1|t}^2 = 0$. Based on this relation a natural requirement for choosing λ is to minimize average squared errors. When applied to daily forecasts of variance, this leads to the (daily) root mean squared prediction error (RMSE), which is given by (RiskMetrics, 1996, p. 244):

$$RMSE = \sqrt{\frac{1}{T}\sum_{t=1}^{T}\left(r_{t+1}^2 - \hat{\sigma}_{t+1|t}^2(\lambda)\right)^2} \qquad (4.150)$$

In practice, the optimal decay factor λ^* is found by searching for the smallest RMSE over different values of λ. The goal is to find the decay factor that produces the best forecasts (i.e., minimizes the forecast measures). With each time series it processes, RiskMetrics associates an optimal decay factor that minimizes the root mean squared error of the variance forecast. For the daily and monthly data sets only one optimal decay factor from 100.000 time series is calculated. RiskMetrics calculates the one optimal decay factor in the following steps (RiskMetrics, 1996, p. 99):

$\hat{\lambda}_i$ = *i*th optimal decay factor

$N (i = 1, 2,\ldots, N)$ = number of time series in the RiskMetrics database

τ_i = *i*th RMSE associated with $\hat{\lambda}_i$ (τ_i is the minimum RMSE for the *i*th time series)

1. Finding Π, the sum of all N minimal RMSE's, τ_i's:

$$\Pi = \sum_{i=1}^{N}\tau_i \qquad (4.151)$$

2. Relative error measure is given by:

$$\theta_i = \tau_i / \left(\sum_{i=1}^{N}\tau_i\right) \qquad (4.152)$$

3. The weight ϕ_i is defined as:

$$\phi_i = \theta_i^{-1} / \sum_{i=1}^{N}\theta_i^{-1} \qquad (4.153)$$

where

$$\sum_{i=1}^{N} \phi_i = 1 \qquad\qquad (4.154)$$

4. The optimal decay factor is defined as:

$$\tilde{\lambda} = \sum_{i=1}^{N} \phi_i \hat{\lambda}_i \qquad\qquad (4.155)$$

As can be seen, the optimal decay factor applied by RiskMetrics is a weighted average of individual optimal decay factors where the weights are a measure of individual forecast accuracy. By applying this methodology to both daily and monthly returns RiskMetrics found that the optimal decay factor for the daily data set is 0.94, and the optimal decay factor for the monthly data set is 0.97 (RiskMetrics, 1996, p. 100).

The elements of the one-day matrix appear very similar to GARCH one-day forecasts. However, there are substantial difficulties to producing EWMA estimates relevant for the RiskMetrics one-month forecasts. Since the EWMA methodology is only really applicable to one-step-ahead forecasting, the correct approach would be to smooth 25-day returns, but there is not enough data. Instead, J.P. Morgan have applied exponential smoothing to the 25-day equally weighted variance, which will be full of 25-day "ghost effects". But this has the effect of augmenting the very "ghost features" which they seek to diminish: After a major market movement the equally weighted 25-day series jumps up immediately - as does the GARCH 25-day series. But the RiskMetrics monthly data hardly reacts at all, at first, and then it gradually increases over the next 25 days to reach a maximum exactly 25 days after the event. The proof of this is simple (Alexander, 2000, p. 282):

Setting the s_t^2 to be a 25-day historic variance series, the monthly variance forecast is equal to $\hat{\sigma}_t^2 = \lambda \hat{\sigma}_{t-1}^2 + (1-\lambda)s_{t-1}^2$. Clearly $\hat{\sigma}_t^2 > \hat{\sigma}_{t-1}^2 \iff s_{t-1}^2 > \hat{\sigma}_{t-1}^2$. At the occurrence of "ghost effect", s_t^2 drops dramatically, and so the maximum value of $\hat{\sigma}_t^2$ will occur at that point.

Although backtests performed first by J. P. Morgan and later by other market participants lent support to the RiskMetrics model, its basic assumptions were shown to be questionable from several points of view (Alexander, 2000, Pafka, Kondor, 2001). Moreover, the existence of fat tails in real market data is in a clear conflict with RiskMetrics' assumption of normally distributed returns, which can lead to a gross underestimation of risk. Even the makers of RiskMetrics system acknowledge that there are serious limitations to using the restrictive assumptions of the system (Zangari, 1996b, p. 7-8), (Zangari, 1996c, p. 26). Furthermore, serious doubt has recently been raised as to the stability and information content of the empirical covariance matrices used by the model for calculating the risk of portfolios (Galluccio, Bouchaud, Potters, 1998, Laloux, Cizeau, Bouchaud, Potters, 1999, Plerou, Gopikrishnan, Rosenow, Amaral, Stanley, 1999).

The key to understanding the reasonably successful performance of RiskMetrics, can be found in the paper by Nelson (1992) who showed that even misspecified models can estimate volatility rather accurately. More explicitly, Nelson (1992) shows that if the return generating process is well approximated by diffusion, a broad class of even misspecified ARCH models can provide consistent estimates of the conditional volatility. Since RiskMetrics can be considered as an IGARCH(1,1) model the results of Nelson (1992) offer a natural explanation for the success of RiskMetrics in estimating volatility. Actually, in the RiskMetrics framework, this estimate is used as a one-day ahead volatility forecast, nevertheless it seems that this does not significantly worsen its accuracy. However, if one uses this estimate to calculate (as often required by regulators) a multiperiod forecast using the simple square root of time rule, the quality of the forecast is bound to decline with the number of periods.

It is very often found that despite the presence of fat tails in the data, for many distributions the 5% quantile is roughly -1.65 times the standard deviation (Pafka, Kondor, 2001, p. 4). For example, the 5% quantile of the Student's t distribution with 7 degrees of freedom (which is leptokurtic and has a kurtosis of 5 similar to the typical kurtosis of returns in financial markets) is -1.60, very close to -1.65, or, conversely, the -1.65 percentile is 4.6%. For higher significance levels (e.g. 99%) the effect of fat tails becomes much stronger, and therefore the VaR is seriously underestimated if one assumes normality. For example, the 1% quantile of the Student's t distribution considered above is -2.54, which is significantly larger than under the normality assumption (-2.33), while the percentile corresponding to -2.33 is 1.43%. Therefore, it can be concluded that the satisfactory performance of RiskMetrics in estimating VaR is mainly the artefact of the choice of the significance level of 95%. However, existing capital adequacy regulations require 99% confidence, and at this level RiskMetrics systematically underestimates risk (Pafka, Kondor, 2001, p. 5).

4.2.6   Simulation approach to calculating VaR - Monte Carlo simulation

Monte Carlo methods are a widely used class of computational algorithms for simulating the behaviour of various physical and mathematical systems. They are distinguished from other simulation methods by being stochastic, that is nondeterministic in some manner - usually by using random numbers (or more often pseudo-random numbers) - as opposed to deterministic algorithms. In general, Monte Carlo methods are used in mathematics to solve various problems by generating suitable random numbers and observing that fraction of the numbers obeying some property or properties. The method is useful for obtaining numerical solutions to problems that are too complicated to solve analytically. The most common application of the Monte Carlo method is Monte Carlo integration.

Deterministic methods of numerical integration operate by taking a number of evenly spaced samples from a function. In general, this works very well for functions of one variable. However, for functions of vectors, deterministic quadrature methods can be very inefficient. To numerically integrate a function of a two-dimensional vector, equally spaced grid points over a two-dimensional surface are required. For instance a 10x10 grid requires 100 points. If the vector has 100 dimensions, the same spacing on the grid would require 10^{100} points – that's far too many to be computed. 100 dimensions is by no means unreasonable, since in finance, a "dimension" is usually equivalent to a degree of freedom. Monte Carlo methods provide a way out of this exponential time-increase. As long as the function in question is reasonably well-behaved, it can be estimated by randomly selecting points in 100-dimensional space, and taking some kind of average of the function values at these points. By the law of large numbers, this method will display convergence – i.e. quadrupling the number of sampled points will halve the error, regardless of the number of dimensions (Campbell, Lo, MacKinlay, 1997, p. 386).

A refinement of this method is to somehow make the points random, but more likely to come from regions of high contribution to the integral than from regions of low contribution, such as Latin Hypercube sampling (Vose, 2000, p. 59). In other words, the points should be drawn from a distribution similar in form to the integrand. Understandably, doing this precisely is just as difficult as solving the integral in the first place, but there are approximate methods available: from simply making up an integrable function thought to be similar, to one of the adaptive routines. A similar approach involves using low-discrepancy sequences instead - the quasi-Monte Carlo method. Quasi-Monte Carlo methods can often be more efficient at numerical integration because the sequence "fills" the area better and samples more of the most important points that can make the simulation converge to the desired solution more quickly (Papageorgiou, Traub, 1996, p. 63-64).

Monte Carlo method does not require truly random numbers to be useful. Much of the most useful techniques use deterministic, pseudo-random sequences, making it easy to test and re-run simulations. The only quality usually necessary to make good simulations is for the pseudo-random sequence to appear "random enough" in a certain sense. What this means depends on the application, but typically quasi random numbers should pass a series of statistical tests (Holton, 2003, 207-209). Testing that the numbers are uniformly distributed or follow another desired distribution when a large enough number of elements of the sequence is considered one of the simplest.

In many applications of Monte Carlo, the underlying process is simulated directly, and there is no need to even write down the differential equations that describe the behaviour of the system. The only requirement is that the mathematical system be described by probability density functions (pdf's). Once the pdf's are known, the Monte Carlo simulation can proceed by random sampling from the pdf's. Many simulations are then performed and the desired result is taken as an average over the number of observations (which may be a single observation or perhaps millions of observations). In many practical applications, the statistical error (variance) for this average result can be predicted, and hence an estimate can be obtained of the number of Monte Carlo trials that are needed to achieve a given error (Holton, 1998, p. 61). Assuming that the evolution of the particular system can be described by probability density functions (pdf's), then the Monte Carlo simulation can proceed by sampling from these pdf's, which necessitates a fast and effective way to generate random numbers uniformly distributed on the interval [0,1]. The outcomes of these random samplings, or trials, must be accumulated or tallied in an appropriate manner to produce the desired result, but the essential characteristic of Monte Carlo is the use of random sampling techniques (and perhaps other algebra to manipulate the outcomes) to arrive at a solution of the problem at hand. In contrast, a conventional numerical solution approach would start with the mathematical model of the system, discrediting the differential equations and then solving a set of algebraic equations for the unknown state of the system. It is natural to think that Monte Carlo methods are used to simulate random, or stochastic, processes, since these can be described by pdf's. However, this coupling is actually too restrictive because many Monte Carlo applications have no apparent stochastic content, such as the evaluation of a definite integral or the inversion of a system of linear equations. However, in these cases and others, the desired solution can be posed in terms of pdf's, and while this transformation may seem artificial, this step allows the system to be treated as a stochastic process for the purpose of simulation and hence Monte Carlo methods can be applied to simulate the system.

The primary components of a Monte Carlo simulation method include the following:
- Probability distribution functions (pdf's) - the mathematical system must be described by a set of pdf's.
- Random number generator - a source of random numbers uniformly distributed on the unit interval must be available.
- Sampling rule - a prescription for sampling from the specified pdf's, assuming the availability of random numbers on the unit interval, must be given.
- Scoring (or tallying) - the outcomes must be accumulated into overall tallies or scores for the quantities of interest.
- Error estimation - an estimate of the statistical error as a function of the number of trials and other quantities must be determined.
- Variance reduction techniques - methods for reducing the variance in the estimated solution to reduce the computational time for Monte Carlo simulation
- Parallelization and vectorization - algorithms to allow Monte Carlo methods to be implemented efficiently on advanced computer architectures.

In the world of risk management Monte Carlo method is a name for any approach to risk measurement that involves the simulation of a parametric model for risk-factor changes. As such, the method can be either conditional or unconditional, depending on whether the model adopted is a dynamic time series model or a static distributional model. The first step of the method is the choice of the model and the calibration of this model to historical data $X_{t-n+1},\ldots, X_t$. This should be a model from which the simulations can be readily performed, since in the second stage, m independent realizations of risk-factor changes are generated for the next period. Similarly to the historical simulation method the simulated realizations from the loss distribution are obtained. The simulated loss data are used to estimate risk measures, often this is done by simple order statistic, but it would also be possible to base the inference on fitted univariate distributions, or to use an extreme value model to model the tails of the simulated realizations (McNeil, Frey, Embrechts, 2005, p. 52). Illustration of the process for Monte Carlo VaR calculation is given in Figure 20.

Figure 20 – Illustration of the Monte Carlo VaR calculation

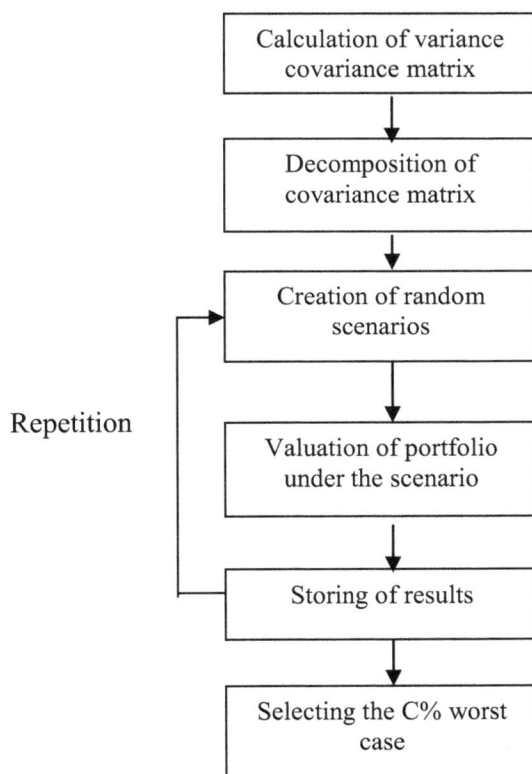

Source: Marrison Chris: The Fundamentals of Risk measurement. New York: McGraw Hill, 2002. p.119

The use of the Monte Carlo means that the researcher is free to choose the number of simulations m, with the only constraint being the computational time. Generally m is chosen to be much larger than n so that more accurate estimation of empirical VaR are obtained than in the case of historical simulation VaR (McNeil, Frey, Embrechts, 2005, p. 52).

The underlying stochastic process that governs the dynamics of asset prices may be calibrated for the asset's future values. A popular, simple stochastic process is the geometric Brownian motion given by (Jorion, 2001, p. 292):

$$dS_t/S_t = \mu_t dt + \sigma_t dW_t \tag{4.156}$$

where S_t is the asset price at time t, W_t is a standard Wiener process, and μ_t and σ_t are the drift and the volatility parameters, respectively. The solution to this stochastic differential equation is (Bao, Lee, Saltoglu, 2004, p. 5):

$$S_t = S_0 \exp\left(\left[\mu_t - \frac{1}{2}\sigma_t^2\right]t + \sigma_t W_t\right) \tag{4.157}$$

Simulating S_t amounts to simulating W_t. Since the goal is to predict one-step-ahead VaR, it can be written as (Bao, Lee, Saltoglu, 2004, p. 5):

$$S_t = S_{t-1} \exp\left(\left[\mu_t - \frac{1}{2}\sigma_t^2\right] + \sigma_t z_t\right) \tag{4.158}$$

where z_t is simulated from a standard normal distribution. The calculation is performed N times, from which the empirical α-th quantile of $r_t \equiv ln\ (St/St - 1)$ is estimated. When σ_t^2 is estimated from the unconditional variance $\frac{1}{t-2}\sum_{j=1}^{t-1}\left(r_j - \hat{\mu}_j\right)^2$ with $\mu_t = \frac{1}{t-1}\sum_{j=1}^{t-1}r_j$ the VaR model is known as Normal Monte Carlo (MC). When σ_t^2 is estimated by the EWMA conditional variance model $\sigma_t^2 = \omega + (1-\lambda)\varepsilon_{t-1}^2 + \lambda\sigma_{t-1}^2$, it is known as EWMA Monte Carlo (EWMA MC). The Monte Carlo method does not solve the problem of finding a distributional function for a random variable and any results that are obtained will only be as good as the model that is used (Jorion, 2001, p. 226). In a market risk context a dynamic model seems desirable and a GARCH structure with a heavy tailed conditional distribution might be considered. For large portfolios the computational cost of the Monte Carlo approach can be considerable, as every simulation requires the revaluation of the portfolio. This is particularly problematic if the portfolio contains many derivatives that cannot be priced in closed, analytical form. However, to create experiments using a Monte Carlo method is fraught with dangers. Each market variable has to be modelled according to an estimated distribution as well as the relationships between distributions (such as correlation or less obvious non-linear relationships, for which copulas are becoming prominent). Using the Monte Carlo approach means one is committed to the use of such distributional assumptions and the estimations one makes (Jorion, 2001, p. 226). These distributions can become inappropriate, and if unconditional variances and covariances are used as inputs into Monte Carlo simulation it reacts slowly to changing market conditions. To build and keep current a Monte Carlo risk management system requires continual re-estimation, a good reserve of analytic and statistical skills, and non-automated decision-making.

4.3 Non-parametric and semi-parametric approaches to calculating Value-at-Risk

The non-parametric approaches seek to estimate VaR without making strong assumptions about the distribution of profits and losses or returns. The essence of these approaches is to let the data speak for itself as much as possible, and use the empirical distribution of returns and not some assumed theoretical distribution to estimate the VaR. All non-parametric approaches are based on the underlying assumption that the near future will be sufficiently like the recent past (Pritsker, 2001, p. 3). This means that the data from the recent past can be efficiently used to forecast risks in the near future, an assumption that may or may not be valid in any given context.

The first and the most popular non-parametric approach is historical simulation (HS). Historical simulation is, loosely speaking, a histogram-based approach, and it is conceptually simple, easy to implement, very widely used, and has a fairly good historical track record. Non-parametric estimation can also be performed by using more complex methods such as; bootstrap methods and non-parametric density estimation methods.

4.3.1 Historical simulation

Historical simulation is the most well known member of nonparametric family of VaR models. The main characteristic of nonparametric approach is the calculation of VaR without making apriori assumptions about the shape of the distribution of realized returns. Nonparametric approach, unlike the parametric approach that a priori assigns a theoretical distribution to a random variable, empirically determines the distribution of the observed variable, and the VaR figure is easily computed via order statistics from the desired quantile of the cumulative distribution function. Historical simulation is based on two elementary assumptions (Manganelli, Engle, 2001, p. 10):
  1) future will be similar to the past, from the data obtained from the recent past, the risk in the near future can be calculated,
  2) realized returns are independently and identically distributed (IID) through time.

Unfortunately, these assumptions do not hold in practice, as it will be tested and proven in remainder of the book. When comparing only classical historical simulation and normally distributed mean-variance VaR, it is the authors' opinion that historical simulation approach to calculating VaR would be better suited for calculating market risk in capital market of transition countries for several reasons (Žiković, 2005b, p. 74):

1) volatilities of stocks are time varying (heteroskedastic),
2) coefficients of correlation between stocks are not stationary, they often change very dramatically and suddenly in very short time intervals,
3) distribution of returns of stocks is asymmetric and has fat tails,
4) existence of sufficient number of extreme events.

In his study Žiković (2006a) finds that simple historical simulation with longer observation windows gives satisfactory unconditional coverage when applied to illiquid markets of EU member candidate states.

The main advantages of historical simulation compared to the other methods of estimating VaR are (Dowd, 2002, p. 72):

- the method is theoretically simple,
- it is easy to implement in practice,
- data used can be easily obtained from stock exchanges or from specialized companies, such as Bloomberg, Reuters and DataStream,
- obtained VaR figures are simple to present to the top management,
- since it is not parametric in its' nature, asymmetry and kurtosis can be easily included in the calculation of VaR,
- there is no need for the calculation of the variance-covariance matrices, which greatly lowers the computational and time burden.

Besides all the stated advantages, historical simulation also exhibits some serious problems when compared to other methods of calculating VaR. The principle disadvantage of historical simulation method is that it computes the empirical cumulative distribution function of the portfolio returns by assigning an equal probability weight of $1/N$ to each day's return. This is equivalent to assuming that the risk factors, and hence the historically simulated returns are independently and identically distributed (IID) through time. This assumption is unrealistic because it is known that the volatility of asset returns tends to change through time, and that periods of high and low volatility tend to cluster together (e.g. Bollerslev, 1986, Schwert, 1989b). One of the most serious critiques on account of historical simulation is the fact that it completely depends on the past events and data that is used as a basis for the calculation of VaR. Another serious problem of historical simulation that is not noticeable in the developed markets but is clearly present in the transition countries is the lack of a larger number of observations that is required for the historical simulation. Other potential drawbacks of historical simulation are (Dowd, 2002, p. 72-73):

- if the time period used for the calculation of VaR is characterized by low volatility and includes no extreme events, historical simulation can underestimate the true level of risk,
- if the time period used for the calculation of VaR is characterized by high volatility and includes numerous extreme events, historical simulation can overestimate the true level of risk,

- historical simulation is known to react poorly to one-time changes that happen in the observation period, such as currency devaluation,
- the method can react very slowly to sudden changes in the market, especially if the observation period used for the calculation of VaR is long,
- the method is known to suffer from "ghost effect", meaning that high losses that occurred in relatively distant past continue to effect the level of VaR until they disappear from the observation period (Allen, Boudoukh, Saunders, 2004, p. 49),
- VaR is limited to the highest losses that happened in the observation period disregarding the current market volatility.

Banks often rely on VaR's from historical simulations (HS VaR). The value of VaR is calculated as the *100cl* percentile or the *(T+1)cl* order statistic of the set of pseudo portfolio returns. In principle it is easy to construct a time series of historical portfolio returns using current portfolio holdings and historical asset returns. In practice, however, historical asset prices for the assets held today may not be available. Examples where difficulties arise include derivatives, individual bonds with various maturities, private equity, new public companies, merged companies and so on. For these cases "pseudo" historical prices must be constructed using either pricing models, factor models or some ad hoc considerations (Pallotta, Zenti, 2000, p. 5). The current assets without historical prices can for example be matched to "similar" assets by capitalization, industry, leverage, and duration. Historical pseudo asset prices and returns can then be constructed using the historical prices on these substitute assets (Jorion, 2001, p. 221):

$$r_{w,t} = \sum_{i=1}^{N} w_{i,T} r_{i,t} \equiv W'_T R_t, \qquad t = 1, 2, ..., T \qquad (4.159)$$

Historical simulation VaR can be expressed as:

$$HS - VaR^p_{T+1|T} \equiv r_w\big((T+1)p\big) \qquad (4.160)$$

where $r_w\big((T+1)p\big)$ is taken from the set of ordered pseudo returns $\{r_w(1), r_w(2), ..., r_w(T)\}$. If *(T+1)p* is not an integer value then the two adjacent observations can be interpolated to calculate the VaR. Historical simulation has some serious problems, which have been well-documented (Hendricks, 1996, Pritsker, 2001). Perhaps most importantly, historical simulation does not properly incorporate conditionality into the VaR forecast. The only source of dynamics in the HS VaR is the fact that the sample window is updated with the passing of time. However, this source of conditionality is minor in practice.

Historical simulation is based on the concept of rolling windows. The process of calculating VaR by historical simulation begins by choosing a length (*n*) of the window of observations, which usually ranges from two months to two years.

Calculated portfolio returns within the observation window are sorted and the desired quantile is given by the return x_i that satisfies the condition that j out of n observations do not exceed it. The probability that j out of n observations do not exceed some fixed value of observed variable x follows a binomial distribution (Kendall, Stuart, 1973, p. 348):

$$P\{j.observations \leq x\} = \binom{n}{j}\{F(x)\}^j \{1 - F(x)\}^{n-j} \qquad (4.161)$$

It follows that the probability of at least i observations in the selected sample not exceeding x also follows a binomial distribution (Kendall, Stuart, 1973, p. 348):

$$G_i(x) = \sum_{j=i}^{n} \binom{n}{j}\{F(x)\}^j \{1 - F(x)\}^{n-j} \qquad (4.162)$$

$G_i(x)$ is the distribution function of the order statistic and thus also of the VaR.

To compute the VaR the following day, the whole window is moved forward by one observation and the entire procedure is repeated. Historical simulation method assigns equal probability weight of 1/N to each observation. This means that the historical simulation estimate of VaR at the cl confidence level corresponds to the N(1-cl) lowest return in the N period rolling sample. Because a crash is the lowest return in the N period sample, the N(1-cl) lowest return after the crash, turns out to be the (N(1-cl)-1) lowest return before the crash. If the N(1-cl) and (N(1-cl)-1) lowest returns happen to be very close in magnitude, the crash actually has almost no impact on the historical simulation estimate of VaR for the long positions in a portfolio of securities.

Although historical simulation makes no explicit assumptions about the distribution of portfolio returns, an implicit assumption is hidden behind the procedure: the distribution of portfolio returns doesn't change within the window. From this implicit assumption several problems may arise in using this method in practice. From the assumption that all the returns within the observation window used in historical simulation have the same distribution, it follows that all the returns of the time series also have the same distribution: if $y_{t\text{-window}},...,y_t$ and $y_{t+1\text{-window}},...,y_{t+1}$ are independently and identically distributed (IID), then also y_{t+1} and $y_{t\text{-window}}$ have to be IID, by the transitive property. Another serious problem of the historical simulation is the fact that for the empirical quantile estimator to be consistent, the size of observation window must go to infinity (Manganelli, Engle, 2001, p. 10). The length of the observation window hides another serious problem. Forecasts of VaR under historical simulation are meaningful only if the historical data used in the calculations have the same distribution. The length of the window must satisfy two contradictory properties: it must be large enough, in order to make statistical inference significant, and it must not be too large, to avoid the risk of taking observations outside of the current volatility cluster. Clearly, there is no easy solution to this problem. If the market is moving from a period of low volatility to a period of high volatility, VaR forecasts based on the historical simulation will underestimate the true risk of a position since it will take some time before the observations from the low volatility period leave the observation window.

From the Equation 4.160 it can be seen that HS VaR changes significantly only if the observations around the order statistic $r_w((T+1)cl)$ change significantly. For instance, when using a 250-day moving window for a 1% HS VaR, only the second and third smallest returns will matter for the calculation. Including a crash in the sample, which now becomes the smallest return, may therefore not change the HS VaR very much if the new second smallest return is similar to the previous one. Moreover, the lack of a properly-defined conditional model in the historical simulation methodology implies that it does not allow for the construction of a term structure of VaR. Calculating a 1% 1-day HS-VaR may be possible on a window of 250 observations, but calculating a 10-day 1% VaR on 250 daily returns is not. Often the 1-day VaR is simply scaled by the square root of time, but this extrapolation is only valid under the assumption of IID daily returns, which is not valid, as proven in the chapter 4.1.2.5.

Finally, VaR forecasts based on historical simulation may present predictable jumps, due to the discreteness of extreme returns. If VaR of a portfolio is computed using a rolling window of N days and today's return is a large negative number, it is easy to predict that the VaR estimate will jump upward, because of today's observation. The same effect (reversed) will reappear exactly after N days, when the large observation drops out of the observation window (Manganelli, Engle, 2001, p. 10).

4.3.2 Historical simulation using non-parametric density estimation

Evaluating the trade-off between long and short sample observation windows is complicated by the fact that the historical simulation approach does not produce a statistical measure of precision. In fact, as Kupiec (1995) notes, typical VaR models of all types lack the ability to measure this precision or goodness-of-fit property ex ante. Kupiec (1995) shows how an approximation to the variance of estimated VaR can provide additional useful information about the VaR estimate. Jorion (1996) suggests that VaR always be reported with confidence intervals and shows that it is possible to improve the efficiency of VaR estimates using their standard errors. Quantifying the uncertainty in the estimated VaR for an unknown return distribution would address the issues raised by Kupiec (1995). Pritsker (1996) notes that it is possible to compute a standard error in a Monte Carlo VaR analysis. Pritsker suggests that a Monte Carlo estimate and standard error can be used to construct a confidence interval around the estimate from any VaR model. This approach, while feasible, may not be desirable for several reasons, but the most obvious is the fact that parametric representation introduces unwanted assumptions about the portfolio return distribution. A nonparametric representation requires bootstrapping from the set of sample observations to obtain a standard error. Unfortunately, bootstrapping approach cannot generate any information about the tail of the return distribution beyond the smallest sample observation. The usefulness of a precision measure goes beyond the point made by Kupiec (1995). With information about the precision of the estimate, it would be easier to evaluate whether large deviations of returns from the predicted VaR are evidence of model problems. This potentially has an impact on regulatory capital. Under the Basle market risk rules a bank is required to maintain additional capital if the daily return losses were greater than daily VaR more than four times in a year (Basle Committee on Banking Supervision, 1996b, p. 7). The relation between the number of "exceptions" and the severity of the penalty is based on the assumption that the VaR is estimated without error. However, supervisors of banks may discount exceptions if they can be explained as not arising from model error. To the extent that the bank and its supervisor can use precision information to explain such exceptions as being unrelated to the quality of the VaR model, the supervisor may elect not to require the greater capital requirements.

Density estimation deals with the construction of an estimated density function from observed data (Silverman, 1986, p. 1). It also deals with associated issues such as how to present a data set, how to investigate its properties (e.g., such as possible bimodality, skewness, etc.), and how to use density estimates as inputs in other tasks. Density estimation comes in two basic forms: parametric density estimation, which imposes the distribution on the data, and non-parametric density estimation, which tries to use the empirical data and let it shape the distribution.

The most common way of representing data is the histogram. Given an origin x_0 and a binwidth (or bandwidth) h, the bins of the histogram can be defined as the intervals (Dowd, 2002, p. 251):

$$[x_0 + mh, x_0 + (m + 1)h] \qquad (4.163)$$

which have been arbitrarily chosen to be closed on the left (i.e., so data on the left boundary are included in the interval) and open on the right (i.e., so data on the right boundary are excluded from the interval). The histogram itself is then defined as (Dowd, 2002, p. 251):

$$f(x) = (1/nh)\#X_i \qquad (4.164)$$

where $\# X_i$, is the number of observations in the same bin as x. The choice of both origin X_0, and binwidth h, can make a big difference to the final results, particularly the binwidth. There is a trade-off in choosing binwidth: a wider binwidth smoothes out irrelevant noise in the data, but a binwidth that is too wide smoothes out valuable information as well. Histograms predominantly depend on arbitrary judgements, and can be misleading. Histograms can also be inefficient, and the discontinuities of histograms can sometimes cause problems when they are used as surrogate density functions in other routines.

Fortunately, there are many alternatives to histograms, and one of these is the so-called naive estimator. The naive estimator replaces Equation 4.164 with:

$$f(x) = (1/2nh)[No. \ of \ X_1, ..., X_n \ in \ range \ (x-h, \ x+h)]$$ (4.165)

Although similar to Equation 4.164, the naïve estimator does not depend on a choice of origin x_0. The naive estimator constructs a histogram by treating each observation as falling at the centre of a sampling interval, and that is way there is no need to specify the origin x_0. However, the choice of binwidth remains making the estimates discontinuous. It is helpful to express the naive estimator in terms of weighting functions. If the weight function is defined by (Silverman, 1986, p. 12):

$$w(x) = \begin{cases} 1/2 & if \ |x| < 1 \\ 0 & if \ |x| \geq 1 \end{cases}$$ (4.166)

the naive estimator can be written as:

$$\hat{f}(x) = (1/n)\sum_{i=1}^{n}(1/h)w((x - X_i)/h)$$ (4.167)

It is clear that the naive estimator is determined by a rather naive, choice of weight function. A superior alternative to both the histogram and naive estimators is the kernel estimator. The kernel is a generalisation of the naive estimator, and replaces the naive weight function given in Equation 4.166 with a kernel function $K(x)$ that satisfies the condition (Dowd, 2002, p. 253):

$$\int_{-\infty}^{\infty}K(x)dx = 1$$ (4.168)

$K(x)$ is the probability density function, but it can also be a discrete or piecewise function. Given the kernel function, the kernel estimator can be defined as:

$$\hat{f}(x) = (1/nh)\sum_{i=1}^{n}K((x - X_i)/h)$$ (4.169)

Provided that $K(x)$ is non-negative everywhere, the kernel estimator will be well behaved with smooth derivatives, and this means that the kernel estimator given in Equation 4.169 can be treated as a probability density function.

Kernel places mini-density functions around each data point, and the kernel itself is the sum of these "mini-densities" and has a total area underneath it of 1. The kernel estimator can be pictured as placing "bumps" around each of the recorded observations. The shape of these bumps is determined by the kernel function $K(x)$ and the bandwidth h determines their width. As the sample size grows, the net sum of all the smoothed points approaches the true probability density function, whatever that may be, irrespective of the method of smoothing the data. This is because the influence of each point becomes arbitrarily small as the sample size grows, so the choice of kernel imposes no restrictions on the results asymptotically. In a small sample there may be differences, which can be examined by using different kernels. The smoothing is accomplished by spreading each data point with a kernel, usually a probability density function centred on the data point, and the bandwidth. To use kernels, a kernel function $K(x)$ and a bandwidth h have to be chosen. In making the decisions about choice of a kernel function $K(x)$ and a bandwidth h, one should remember that the objective is to find an estimator $\hat{f}$ that is close to the true but unknown density function f, and a natural measure of the closeness of fit at a point x is the mean square error (MSE) (Dowd, 2002, p. 254):

$$MSE_x(\hat{f}(x)) = E[\hat{f}(x) - f(x)]^2 = [E\hat{f}(x) - f(x)]^2 + \operatorname{var}(\hat{f}(x))$$
$$= [bias(\hat{f}(x))]^2 + \operatorname{var}(\hat{f}(x)) \qquad (4.170)$$

where $\operatorname{var}(\hat{f}(x))$ is the variance of $\hat{f}(x)$. The MSE is thus the bias squared plus the variance, which indicates that there is a trade-off between the bias and variance of $\hat{f}(x)$. The global measure (mean integrated square error - MISE) of the closeness of fit of $\hat{f}(x)$ to $f(x)$ can be found by integrating the MSE over x.

$$MISE(\hat{f}) = E \int [\hat{f}(x) - f(x)]^2 dx$$
$$= \int [E\hat{f}(x) - f(x)]^2 dx + \int \operatorname{var}(\hat{f}(x)) dx \qquad (4.171)$$

The kernel function that minimises the MISE is the following, known as the Epanechnikov kernel (Silverman, 1986, p. 39-40):

$$K_e(x) = \begin{cases} [3/(4\sqrt{5})](1-0.2x^2) & -\sqrt{5} \le x \le \sqrt{5} \\ & if \\ 0 & otherwise \end{cases} \qquad (4.172)$$

However, there are also many other useful kernels that are nearly as efficient as the Epanechnikov kernel (Silverman, 1986, p. 43). These include the biweight, triangular, rectangular and Gaussian kernels, which are respectively:

Biweight kernel:
$$\begin{cases} (15/16)(1-x^2)^2 & |x| < 1 \\ 0 & otherwise \end{cases} \qquad (4.173)$$

Triangular kernel:

$$\begin{cases} 1 - |x| & |x| < 1 \\ 0 & otherwise \end{cases}$$ (4.174)

Rectangular kernel:

$$\begin{cases} 1/2 & |x| < 1 \\ 0 & otherwise \end{cases}$$ (4.175)

Gaussian kernel:

$$\left(1/\sqrt{2\pi}\right)e^{-0.5x^2}$$ (4.176)

After having chosen a kernel function, there still remains the issue of optimal bandwidth (h). One obvious solution is to choose h subjectively, by plotting out kernel estimates for different bandwidths, and choosing the one that seems right for the data at hand. However, there are also certain automatic rules, which include least squares and likelihood cross-validation, for choosing h if the suitable kernel function is determined. For example, when using Gaussian kernel the optimal bandwidth is (Silverman, 1986, p. 45):

$$H_{opt} = 1.06\sigma n^{-1/5}$$ (4.177)

which enables the estimate of the optimal bandwidth directly from the data, using a sample estimate of σ. It is important to stress that using of a Gaussian kernel density estimator does not assume that the data follow a normal or any other distribution nor make the ultimate estimation of the VaR normal or even parametric. To compensate for potential oversmoothing of the data, Silverman suggests the modified optimal bandwidth:

$$h_{opt} = 1.06An^{-1/5}$$ (4.178)

$$A = min[\sigma, interquartile\ range/1.34]$$

Silverman's findings suggest that this bandwidth should provide a close fit for a wide range of distributions.

The kernel approach is intuitive and straightforward to apply, and its properties are fairly well understood. However, it does have one practical problem. Since the bandwidth is fixed across the whole sample, a kernel that provides a good degree of smoothing over the central part of the distribution will often leave spurious noise in the tail. But if this noise is smoothed, there is a danger that the central part of the distribution will oversmooth and useful information will be lost: it is difficult to deal with the tail properly without oversmoothing the main part of the distribution.

A solution to this problem is to use adaptive methods in which the bandwidth is allowed to depend on how the observations are distributed. One such method is based on the variable kernel estimator (Dowd, 2002, p. 256):

$$\hat{f}(x) = (1/n)\sum_{j=1}^{n}\left(1/(hd_{j,k})\right)K\left((x - X_j)/(hd_{j,k})\right) \qquad (4.179)$$

where $d_{j,k}$ is the distance between X_j and the kth nearest of the other data points. The bandwidth of the kernel placed on the observation X_j is proportional to $d_{j,k}$. In this way sparser data will have flatter kernels placed on them.

Other solutions to the problem of oversmoothing the central or tail part of the distribution include: nearest neighbour method, in which the bandwidth applied to an observation depends on the distance between that observation and its near neighbours; maximum penalised likelihood methods, which are maximum likelihood methods adjusted for the roughness of the empirical density function; and orthogonal series estimators, which are Fourier transform methods[35].

Naïve estimator and especially kernel functions methods are tailor-made for VaR estimation, and density estimation theory suggests that they should produce better non-parametric estimates of VaR than those expected under historical simulation. The historical simulation approach is essentially density estimation with a histogram and a histogram is rarely the best way to handle a data set. This reasoning suggests that some of the more advanced density estimation approaches — particularly kernel methods — should produce superior VaR estimates. This is the logic behind the historical kernel approach to VaR proposed by Butler and Schachter (1998). This type of approach suggests the VaR can be estimated by first estimating the density of a given set of return observations, using some preferred density estimation approach. Having estimated the density function, it can then be inverted to infer the percentile or quantile that corresponds to the VaR. The confidence internals for VaR estimates can then be obtained by using some appropriate method (e.g., using order statistics, bootstrap or Monte Carlo approaches to confidence-interval estimation). Butler and Schachter (1998) applied a historical kernel approach to real trading portfolios, and found that the adaptive kernel approaches generally led to higher VaR estimates, but the choice of kernel otherwise made relatively little difference to VaR estimates (Butler, Schachter, 1998, p. 380-381). To the extent that the choice of kernel did make a difference, they concluded that the best ones were the adaptive Epanechnikov and adaptive Gaussian kernels.

---

[35] For more on these methods, see Silverman (1986, ch. 2 and 5).

4.3.3 Bootstrapping

A broad interpretation of bootstrap methods argues that they are defined by replacing an unknown distribution function F, by its empirical estimator, $\hat{F}$, in a functional form for an unknown quantity of interest (Hall, 1994, p. 2342). The name bootstrap was introduced by Efron (1979), who pointed out that bootstrap methods (in the sense of replacing F with $\hat{F}$) had been in use long before his paper. But he was the first to perceive the breadth of this class of methods. The vast range of applications of bootstrap methods would not be possible without a facility for extremely rapid simulation. The elementary question that arises when using bootstrap methods is how does one decide which functionals of F should be estimated. Given the functional f_t it is necessary to determine the value t_0 of t that solves the equation (Hall, 1994, p. 2345):

$$E\{f_t(F_0, F_1)|F_0\} = 0 \tag{4.180}$$

where $F = F_0$ denotes the population distribution function and $\hat{F} = F_1$ is the distribution function of the sample. Conditioning on F_0 serves to stress that the expectation is taken with respect to the distribution F_0. Equation 4.180 is called the population equation because the properties of the population are required if the equation is to be solved exactly. For example, if $\theta_0 = \theta(F_0)$ denotes a true parameter value, such as the rth power of a mean (Hall, 1994, p. 2345):

$$\theta_0 = \left\{\int x dF_0(x)\right\}^r \tag{4.181}$$

Let $\hat{\theta} = \theta(F_1)$ be the bootstrap estimator of θ_0 such as the rth power of the sample mean:

$$\hat{\theta} = \left\{\int x dF_1(x)\right\}^r = \overline{X}^r \tag{4.182}$$

Where $\hat{F} = F_1$ is the empirical distribution function of the sample from which $\overline{X}$ is computed. To obtain an approximate solution of the population Equation 4.180 the following assumptions are made. Let F_2 denote the distribution function of a sample drawn from F_1 (conditional on F_1). Replacing the pair (F_0, F_1) in Equation 4.180 by (F_1, F_2) transforms the population equation into (Hall, 1994, p. 2346):

$$E\{f_t(F_1, F_2)|F_1\} = 0 \tag{4.183}$$

Equation 4.183 is called the sample equation since everything is known about it, once the sample distribution function F_1 is known, and its solution $\hat{t}_0$ is a function of the sample values. The $\hat{t}_0$ and $E\{f_t(F_1, F_2)|F_1\}$ are called the bootstrap estimators of t_0 and $E\{f_t(F_0, F_1)|F_0\}$ respectively. They are obtained by replacing F_0 by F_1 in the formulae for t_0 and $E\{f_t(F_0, F_1)|F_0\}$. There are two approaches of treating F_1 and F_2, suitable for nonparametric and parametric problems respectively. In both approaches, inference is based on a sample H of n random (independent and identically distributed) observations of the population. In the nonparametric case, F_1 is simply the empirical distribution function of H.; that is, the distribution function of the distribution that assigns mass n^{-1} to each point in H. The associated empirical probability measure assigns to a region R a value equal to the proportion of the sample that lies within R. Similarly, F_2 is the empirical distribution function of a sample drawn at random from the population with distribution function F_1; that is, the empirical distribution of a sample H^* drawn randomly, with replacement, from H. If the population is denoted by H_0 a nest of sampling operations is formed: H is drawn at random from H_0 and H^* is drawn at random from H (Hall, 1994, p. 2346).

In the parametric case, F_0 is assumed completely known up to a finite vector λ_0 of unknown parameters. To indicate this dependence, it can be written, $F_0 = F_{(\lambda_0)}$, an element of a class $\{F_{(\lambda)}, \lambda \in \Lambda\}$ of possible distributions. Let $\hat{\lambda}$ be an estimator of λ_0 computed from H, often (but not necessary) the maximum likelihood estimator. Since $\hat{\lambda}$ is a function of sample values, it can be also written as $\lambda(H)$. In this case $F_1 = F_{(\hat{\lambda})}$, the distribution function obtained by replacing "true" parameter values by their sample estimates. Let H^* denote the sample drawn at random from the distribution with distribution function $F_{(\hat{\lambda})}$ (not simply drawn from H with replacement), and let $\hat{\lambda}^* = \lambda(H)^*$ denote the version of $\hat{\lambda}$ computed from H^* instead of H. Then it can be written, $F_2 = F_{(\hat{\lambda}^*)}$. Unfortunately with time series data the standard bootstrap method relevant for IID observations is not valid. If returns are not IID, bootstrapping and can lead to biased results, because the presence of autocorrelation and heteroskedasticity in the data is ignored. Some of the suggested alternatives are: recursive bootstrap, moving block bootstrap and the stationary bootstrap (Maddala, Li, 1996, p. 464).

4.3.3.1   The recursive bootstrap

To deal with the lagged dependent variables and serially correlated errors with a well specified structure (for example ARMA(p,q) model) a recursive bootstrap method introduced by Freedman and Peters (1984) can be used. In the recursive bootstrap method the model is estimated by OLS, or some other consistent method. From this fitted model the residuals are obtained and resampled. With the resampled residuals, the bootstrap samples are generated recursively. For example, in case of a regression model with AR(1) errors:

$$y_t = \beta x_t + u_t$$
$$u_t = \rho u_{t-1} + e_t$$

where $e_t \sim IID(0, \sigma^2)$, the first equation is estimated by OLS, and then using the estimated residuals $\hat{u}_t$, the $\hat{\rho}_t$ is estimated using Cochrane-Orcutt or Prais-Winstein procedures and the is $\hat{e}_t$ obtained. The $\hat{e}_t$ are resampled and using a recursive procedure the $\hat{u}_t$ are generated, as well as the bootstrap sample on y_t.

4.3.3.2   Moving block bootstrap

Application of the recursive bootstrap methods is straightforward if the error distribution is specified to be a stationary ARMA(p,q) process with known p and q. However, if the structure of serial correlation is not tractable or is misspecified, the residual based methods will give inconsistent estimates (if lagged dependent variables are present in the system). Other approaches that do not require fitting the data into parametric form have been developed to deal with general dependent time series data. Carlstein (1986) first introduced the idea of bootstrapping non-overlapping blocks of observations rather than the individual observations. A more general bootstrap procedure applicable to stationary time series data, in which the blocks of observations are overlapping was introduced later by Künsch (1989). The methods of Carlstein (non-overlapping blocks) and Künsch (overlapping blocks) both divide the data of n observations into blocks of length l and select b of these blocks (with repeats allowed) by resampling with replacement all the possible blocks. Since there are only b blocks in the Carlstein procedure and $n - l + 1$ blocks in Künsch procedure, the probability of missing entire blocks in the Carlstein scheme is far greater and for this reason it is not popular in practice.

4.3.3.3   The stationary bootstrap

The pseudo time series generated by the moving block method is not stationary, even if the original series $\{x_t\}$ is stationary. To correct this, Politis and Romano (1994) suggested the stationary bootstrap method. The basic steps for the stationary bootstrap are the same as those of the moving block bootstrap. However, there is a major difference between the sampling schemes of the moving block bootstrap and the stationary bootstrap. The stationary bootstrap resamples the data blocks of random length, where the length of each block has a geometric distribution with parameter p, while the moving block bootstrap resamples blocks of data of the same length. Presently there does not exist a way to optimally choose the parameters k and p, and their choice is left to individual judgement.

4.3.4   Age-weighted Historical simulation

When relaxing the assumption that returns are IID, it might be reasonable to assume that simulated returns from the recent past better represent today portfolio's risk than returns from the distant past. Boudoukh, Richardson, and Whitelaw, BRW hereafter, used this idea to introduce a generalization of the historical simulation and assign a relatively higher amount of probability weight to returns from the more recent past (Boudoukh, Richardson, Whitelaw, 1998).

The BRW approach combines RiskMetrics and historical simulation methodologies, by applying exponentially declining weights to past returns of the portfolio (Boudoukh, Richardson, Whitelaw, 1998, p. 64). Each of the most recent N returns of the portfolio, y_t, y_{t-1}, ..., y_{t-N+1}, is associated a weight, $\frac{1-\lambda}{1-\lambda^N}, \left(\frac{1-\lambda}{1-\lambda^N}\right)\lambda, ..., \left(\frac{1-\lambda}{1-\lambda^N}\right)\lambda^{N-1}$ respectively[36]. After the probability weights are assigned, VaR is calculated based on the empirical cumulative distribution function of returns with the modified probability weights. The basic historical simulation method can be considered as a special case of the more general BRW method in which the decay factor λ is set equal to 1.

The BRW method involves a simple modification of the historical simulation. However, the modification makes a large difference (see e.g. Boudoukh, Richardson, Whitelaw, 1998, Pallotta, Zenti, 2000, Pritsker, 2001). In a recent study Žiković (2006b) finds that the BRW approach is superior to historical simulation for a range of confidence levels even in small and illiquid markets of EU member candidate states. Under the BRW approach, the most recent return receives probability weight of just over 1% for $\lambda = 0.99$ and a weight of over 3% for $\lambda = 0.97$. In both cases, this means that if the most recent observation is the worst loss of the N days, it automatically becomes the VaR estimate at 1% confidence level.

The BRW method appears to remedy one of the main problems of historical simulation since very large losses are immediately reflected in VaR forecasts. The simplest way to implement BRW approach is to construct a history of N hypothetical returns that the portfolio would have earned if held for each of the previous N days, $r_{t-1}, ..., r_{t-N}$ and then assign exponentially declining probability weights $w_{t-1}, ..., w_{t-N}$ to the return series[37]. Given the probability weights, VaR at the cl percent confidence level can be approximated from $G(.; t;N)$, the empirical cumulative distribution function of r based on return observations $r_{t-1}, ..., r_{t-N}$ (Pritsker, 2001, p. 6).

$$G(x;t,N) = \sum_{i=1}^{N} 1_{\{r_{t-i} \le x\}} w_{t-i} \qquad (4.184)$$

---

[36] The role of the term $\frac{1-\lambda}{1-\lambda^N}$ is to ensure that the weights sum to 1.

[37] The weights sum to 1 and are exponentially declining at rate λ ($0 < \lambda \le 1$)

$$\sum_{i=1}^{N} w_{t-i} = 1$$

$$w_{t-i-1} = \lambda w_{t-i}$$

Because the empirical cumulative distribution function, unless smoothed, for example via kernel smoothing as suggested by Butler and Schachter (1998), is discrete, the solution for VaR at the *cl* confidence level will typically not correspond to a particular return from the return history. Instead, the BRW solution for VaR at the *cl* percent confidence level can be between a return that has a cumulative distribution that is less than *cl*, and one that has a cumulative distribution that is higher than *cl*. These returns can be used as estimates of the BRW VaR model at confidence level *cl*. The estimate that understates VaR at the *cl* percent confidence level (upper limit) is given by (Pritsker, 2001, p. 7):

$$BRW^u(t \mid \lambda, N, cl) = \inf(r \in \{r_{t-1}, \dots r_{t-1-N}\} \mid G(r; t, N) \geq cl) \qquad (4.185)$$

and the estimator of lower limit is given by:

$$BRW^o(t \mid \lambda, N, cl) = \sup(r \in \{r_{t-1}, \dots r_{t-1-N}\} \mid G(r; t, N) \leq cl) \qquad (4.186)$$

where λ is the exponential weight factor, N is the length of the history of returns used to compute VaR, and *cl* is the VaR confidence level.

$BRW^u(t \mid \lambda, N, cl)$ is the lowest return of the N observations whose empirical cumulative probability is greater than *cl*, and $BRW^o(t \mid \lambda, N, cl)$ is the highest return whose empirical cumulative probability is less than *cl*.

The main issue in evaluation of BRW based VaR, as a risk measure, is the extent to which VaR forecasts based on the BRW method respond to changes in the underlying risk factors. It is important to know under what circumstances risk estimates increase when using the $BRW^u(t \mid \lambda, N, cl)$ estimator. The result is provided in the following proposition (Pritsker, 2001, p. 25):

If $r_t > BRW^u(t, \lambda, N)$ then $BRW^u(t+1, \lambda, N) \geq BRW^u(t, \lambda, N)$.

When BRW VaR is estimated for returns during time period *t+1*, the return at time *t−N* is dropped from the sample, the return at time *t* receives weight $\frac{1-\lambda}{1-\lambda^N}$ and the weight on all other returns is λ times their earlier values. Consequently, *r(cl)* is defined as:

$$r(cl) = \{r_{t-1}, i = 1, \dots N \mid G(r_{t-1}; t, N) \leq cl\}$$

To verify this proposition, it suffices to examine how much probability weight the VaR estimate at time *t+1* places below $BRW^u(t, \lambda, N)$. In the paper by Pritsker

(2001) there is an error in the proposition and the correct proposition is (Žiković, 2006b, p. 7):

Case 1: $r_{t-N} \notin r(cl)$ - in this case, since by assumption, $r_t \notin r(cl)$ then:

$$G(BRW^u(t, \lambda, N); t+1, \lambda, N) < \lambda G(BRW^u(t, \lambda, N)). \text{ Therefore,}$$

$$BRW^u(t+1, \lambda, N) = \inf(r \in \{r_t, ... r_{t-1-N}\} \mid G(r; t+1, \lambda, N) \geq cl) \geq BRW^u(t, \lambda, N)$$

Case 2: $r_{t-N} \in r(cl)$ - in this case, since $r_t \in r(cl)$ by assumption, then:

$$G(BRW^o(t, \lambda, N); t+1, \lambda, N) < \lambda G(BRW^o(t, \lambda, N)). \text{ Therefore,}$$

$$BRW^o(t+1, \lambda, N) = \sup(r \in \{r_t, ... r_{t-1-N}\} \mid G(r; t+1, \lambda, N) \leq cl) \leq BRW^o(t, \lambda, N)$$

The proposition shows that when losses at time t are bounded below the BRW VaR estimate at time t, the BRW VaR estimate for time $t+1$ will indicate that risk at time $t+1$ is no greater than it was at time t. To understand the importance of this proposition, it suffices to examine the case when today's BRW VaR estimate for tomorrow's return is conditionally correct, but since risk changes with returns, tomorrow's return will influence risk for the day after tomorrow. Under these circumstances, an important question is what is the probability that a VaR estimate that is correct today will increase tomorrow. The answer provided by the proposition is that tomorrow's VaR estimate will not increase with probability $1-cl$. So, for example, if cl is equal to 1%, then a VaR estimate that is correct today will not increase tomorrow with probability 99%.

Although the BRW approach suffers from the explained logical inconsistency, this approach still represents a significant improvement over the historical simulation, since it drastically simplifies the assumptions needed in the parametric models and it incorporates a more flexible specification than the historical simulation approach. To better understand the connection to historical simulation and the assumptions behind the BRW approach, BRW quantile estimator can be expressed as (Manganelli, Engle, 2001, p. 11):

$$\hat{q}_{t+1, cl} = \sum_{j=t-N+1}^{t} y_j I\left(\sum_{i=1}^{N} f_i(\lambda; N) I(y_{t+1-i} \leq y_j) = cl\right) \qquad (4.187)$$

where $f_i(\lambda; N)$ are the weights associated with return y_i and $I(\cdot)$ is the indicator function. If $f_i(\lambda; N) = 1/N$, BRW quantile estimator equals the historical simulation estimator. The main difference between BRW approach and historical simulation is in the specification of the quantile process. With historical simulation each return is given the same weight, while with the BRW approach returns have different weights, depending on how old the observations are. Strictly speaking, none of these models is completely nonparametric, since a parametric specification is proposed for the quantile. Boudoukh, Richardson, Whitelaw in their original paper set λ equal to 0.97 and 0.99, as in their framework no statistical method is available to estimate this unknown parameter (Boudoukh, Richardson, Whitelaw, 1998, p. 66).

4.3.5   Hull-White model of Historical simulation

One common approach to calculating VaR involves assuming that daily percentage changes in the underlying market variables are conditionally multivariate normal with the mean percentage change in each market variable being zero. This is often referred to as the "model building" approach. If the daily change in the portfolio value is linearly dependent on daily changes in market variables that are normally distributed, its probability distribution is also normal. The variance of the probability distribution, and hence the percentile of the distribution corresponding to VaR, can be calculated in a straightforward way from the variance-covariance matrix for the market variables. In circumstances where the linear assumption is inappropriate, the change in the portfolio value is often approximated as a quadratic function of percentage changes in the market variables. This allows the first few moments of the probability distribution of the change in the portfolio value to be calculated analytically so that the required percentile of the distribution can be estimated. An alternative approach to handling non-linearity is to use Monte Carlo simulation. On each simulation trial daily changes in the market variables are sampled from their multivariate distribution and the portfolio is revalued. This enables a complete probability distribution for the daily change in the portfolio value to be determined. The advantage of the model building approach is that the underlying variance-covariance matrix can be updated using an exponentially weighted moving average (EWMA) model. The disadvantage is that the market variables are assumed to be conditionally multivariate normal. The model building approach takes no account of skewness or kurtosis in the distributions of market variables and no account of non-linear correlations between market variables. Historical simulation, by contrast, has the advantage that it accurately reflects the historical multivariate probability distribution of market variables. Its main disadvantage is that it incorporates no volatility updating.

Hull and White (1998a) approach provides one way of bridging the gap between the model building and historical simulation approaches. It shows how the model building approach can be modified to incorporate some of the attractive features of the historical simulation approach. The probability distribution of a market variable, when scaled by an estimate of its volatility, is often found to be approximately stationary. This suggests that historical simulation can be improved by taking account of the volatility changes experienced during the period covered by the historical data. For example, if the current volatility of a market variable is 1.5% per day and two months ago the volatility was only 1% per day, the data observed two months ago understates the changes that can be expected at present. On the other hand, if the volatility was 2% per day two months ago the reverse is true (Hull, White, 1998a, p. 284).

Hull, White (1998a) premise is that the relevant regime change is encapsulated in the volatility measure, thus all that is needed for a historical data to reflect current market conditions is to update the sample using today's volatility. This ensures that the historical sample is a more appropriate reflection of current market conditions. The intuitive reason for this updating system is that it provides an inclusion of today's volatility in VaR forecasts. This is an attempt to refute the argument that is often posed for the irrelevance of past data, and the fact that market conditions change dynamically and can therefore not be reflected in a historical risk estimate. The Hull, White (1998a) procedure for forecasting VaR for day T is the following. Let $r_{t,i}$ be the historical return on asset i on day t in a historical sample, $\sigma_{t,i}$ is the historical EWMA forecast of the volatility of the return on asset i for day t, made at the end of day $t - 1$, and $\sigma_{T,i}$ is the most recent forecast of the volatility of asset i. The historical returns in the data set, $r_{t,i}$, are replaced with volatility-adjusted returns, $z_{t,i}$, given by (Hull, White, 1998a, p. 284):

$$z_{t,i} = \frac{\sigma_{T,i} r_{t,i}}{\sigma_{t,i}} \tag{4.188}$$

Actual returns in any period t are therefore increased (or decreased), depending on whether the current forecast of volatility is greater (or less than) the EWMA forecast of volatility for period t. The set of returns needed for historical simulation are calculated by using Equation 4.159 instead of the original data set $r_{t,i}$, and the HS VaR is estimated in the traditional way, by assigning equal weights to the $\{z_{i,t}\}$ set.

The Hull-White approach has a number of advantages relative to the traditional equally weighted and the BRW age-weighted approaches (Hull, White, 1998a):

- It takes account of volatility changes in a natural and direct way, whereas equally weighted historical simulation ignores volatility changes and the BRW approach treats volatility changes in a restrictive manner.
- It produces risk estimates that are appropriately sensitive to current volatility estimates, and so enables the incorporation of information from EWMA forecasts into HS VaR estimation.
- It obtains VaR forecasts that can exceed the maximum loss in the historical data set; in periods of high volatility, historical returns are scaled upwards, and the return series used in the Hull-White procedure will have values that exceed actual historical losses. This is a major advantage over traditional historical simulation, which prevents the VaR forecasts from being any bigger than the losses in historical data set.
- Empirical evidence presented by Hull and White indicates that their approach produces superior VaR estimates to the BRW approach (Hull, White, 1998a, p. 19).

4.3.6   Hybrid Historical simulation (HHS)

A new hybrid (semi-parametric) VaR model proposed in this book, which will hereafter be called "Hybrid historical simulation" (HHS), is based on the combination of nonparametric bootstrapping of standardized residuals and parametric GARCH volatility forecasting. The HHS model is designed to combine the best features of nonparametric and parametric VaR approaches, but it is designed to do so in a simple and straightforward way. The HHS model is designed to successfully capture the two most conspicuous characteristics of financial asset returns, namely strong time varying volatility and excess kurtosis relative to the normal distribution. In the HHS model leptokurtosis and asymmetry are accounted for by the nonparametric part of the model, while the parametric – ARMA GARCH part of the model is suggested for removing autocorrelation and heteroskedasticity from the data. ARMA GARCH volatility modelling is introduced to create IID observations, suitable for bootstrapping. While successfully dealing with leptokurtosis, asymmetry, autocorrelation and heteroskedasticity in the data, the HHS model developed in this book is not as computationally intensive as some other approaches that are based on extreme value theory, mixtures of distributions or stable Paretian distributions. Furthermore, HHS model is far easier to understand and implement in practice. The number of parameters that have to be estimated in HHS model is small, and its' number is determined by the GARCH specification structure. My suggestion is to use the simplest GARCH specification possible to keep the model as robust as possible to misspecification and model risk.

While greatly differing in approaches, some of the models discussed so far are able to account for strong time varying volatility and excess kurtosis relative to the normal distribution. Simplistic methods, such as historical simulation and parametric variance-covariance approaches, cannot adequately account for the volatility clustering and usually perform poorly in practice (Manganelli, Engle, 2001, Balaban, Bayar, Faff, 2004). The least sophisticated parametric method, which can still capture the volatility clustering and leptokurtosis in the data, is the basic GARCH model. In academic community the inadequacy of the normal AR(1) GARCH(1,1) model for in and out of sample forecasting became obvious not long after its inception, and was superseded by replacing the normality assumption by the Student's t distribution, whereby the degrees of freedom parameter is interpreted as an additional distributional shape parameter and is estimated jointly with the location and scale model parameters. While better than a normal GARCH model, particularly for more extreme (1% or less) VaR thresholds, the Student's t GARCH can also be improved by generalizing both the parametric form of the time varying volatility and the distributional assumption (Mittnik, Paolella, 2000, Giot, Laurent, 2004).

There now exist a wide variety of generalizations of the functional form of volatility, and a large number of candidate distributions for the innovation sequence. Several combinations of distributions have proven to be capable of capturing most of the various empirical features of returns and delivering reasonably accurate out of the sample predictions of the entire distribution of a future returns or just particular quantiles, as is needed for VaR forecasting[38]. Unfortunately, these approaches have the drawbacks of requiring a relatively large number of parameters that cannot be solved in a closed, analytical form, and can result in negative scale parameters, both of which exacerbate the numeric computation of the maximum likelihood estimate, and bars use of less sophisticated software. Furthermore, the more volatility models get complex, estimated parameters become unstable making such models vulnerable to parameter misspecification and model risk. Similarly, the EGARCH model introduced by Nelson (1991), which possesses some theoretical advantages over the GARCH model, is known to be very problematic in practice, with the choice of starting values being extremely critical for successful likelihood maximization (Frachot, 1995, Franses, van Dijk, 1996).

A similar critique that applies to more complex volatility models also applies to the distributional assumption of the VaR model, in that the density (required for the likelihood function) and distribution function (for computing the VaR) may not be expressible in closed analytical form. Examples include the hyperbolic distribution and Gauss-Laplace mixtures (Haas, Mittnik, Paolella, 2005), non-central Student's t (Campbell, Siddique, 1999, Broda, Paolella, 2006), geometric stable and stable Paretian distributions. These distributions require complex numeric procedures such as numeric integration, special function libraries, fast Fourier transform methods, multivariate root finding, etc., which cannot be found in most of the software packages and require considerable intellectual effort. Needles to say that the increase in number of parameters inevitably leads to parameter instability and estimation problems.

Nonparametric approaches require less effort and can easily account for leptokurtosis, asymmetry and to some extent even volatility clustering in the financial data. On the negative side, nonparametric approaches depend too much on the historical data set, react slowly to changes in the market and are subject to predictable jumps in their forecasts of volatility. The simplest nonparametric approach, historical simulation, provides a flexible and intuitive framework for risk analysis, but its basic version uses only the realized path of returns and therefore produces risk indicators with high variance. When the goal is to model returns for a horizon longer than data frequency, simulation approaches, such as, Monte Carlo simulation or bootstrapping techniques can be seen as sensible choices. Usually, the approach based on Monte Carlo simulation uses a set of stochastic differential equations for generating returns over the time horizon. Monte Carlo simulation uses arbitrary distributional assumptions, imposing the structure of risk that it is supposed to investigate. Unlike Monte Carlo simulation, the bootstrapping approach can be seen as a variation of the historical simulation approach, where it resamples from the empirical distribution of portfolio returns. Bootstrapping can be viewed as mixing Monte Carlo and historical simulation. This method guarantees that the multivariate properties of original data are preserved and is flexible enough to incorporate an

---

[38] see Alexander, 2001, Ch. 9 and 10; Bao, Lee, Saltoglu, 2004.

update of both mean and volatility. Unfortunately, bootstrapping is based on a rather strict assumption that excess returns are identically and independently distributed. If returns are not IID, they are unsuitable for bootstrapping and can lead to biased results, because, for example, the eventual presence of autocorrelation and volatility clusters is ignored. To avoid this problem, it is possible to modify the basic bootstrapping scheme by weighting the realized observations.

As was discussed previously in chapter 4.3.4, Boudoukh, Richardson, Whitelaw (1998) showed how weighting of historical observations can be performed by exponentially decreasing the impact of past observations. The second, more appealing way is by incorporating volatility updating in future scenarios, and here there are several options. Hull and White (1998) show how to take into account volatility clusters into the basic historical simulation method (without bootstrapping), by scaling observations by the ratio of current over past conditional EWMA volatility forecasts. McNeil and Frey (2000) propose a bootstrapping approach, where the residuals of the ARMA-GARCH model follow an Extreme value (EV) distribution. Of course, instead of using an ARMA model, mean updating can be incorporated in future scenarios using different models, ranging from simple EWMA techniques to structural models.

The new HHS approach developed in this book is based on the modification of recursive bootstrap procedure developed by Freedman and Peters (1984). This means that the proposed HHS model does not impose any theoretical distribution on the data since it uses empirical (historical) distribution of the return series. Two main problems with empirical data are the heteroskedasticity and presence of autocorrelation. In order to successfully implement bootstrapping the returns should not have any of these characteristics, meaning that they should be identically and independently distributed (IID). In the HHS model autocorrelations can be removed by modelling the conditional mean as an ARMA process. Heteroskedasticity can be removed by modelling returns as a second moment by using GARCH process. In modeling of residuals the proposed HHS approach uses the general specification of the form:

$$r_t = \varphi(x) + \varepsilon_t, \quad \varepsilon_t \sim (0, \sigma_t)$$

$$\sigma_t^2 = \alpha_0 + \sum_{i=1}^{q} \alpha_i \varepsilon_{t-i}^2 + \sum_{i=1}^{p} \beta_i \sigma_{t-i}^2 \qquad (4.189)$$

$$z_t = \varepsilon_t / \sigma_t$$

where φ is some functional form, x is a vector of explanatory variables (observed at time t or lagged), ε_t is the disturbance term with zero mean and standard deviation σ_t, which follows a GARCH(p, q) process. Because of its simplicity and a good track record, HHS model uses the ARMA process as the functional form of φ.

The HHS model can be implemented in practice by applying the following steps:

1) Any autocorrelation in the returns is removed by fitting an ARMA(p,q) model to the historical observations, making the residuals identically and independently distributed:

$$r_t = \alpha_0 + \sum_{i=1}^{p} \alpha_i r_{t-i} + \sum_{i=1}^{q} \theta_i \varepsilon_{t-i} + \varepsilon_t$$

$$\varepsilon_t = \eta_t \sqrt{\sigma_t^2} \qquad\qquad \eta_t \sim IID\ N(0,1) \qquad\qquad (4.190)$$

2) GARCH(p,q) model is fitted to the obtained residuals:

$$\sigma_t^2 = \omega + \sum_{i=1}^{q} \alpha_i \varepsilon_{t-i}^2 + \sum_{i=1}^{p} \beta_i \sigma_{t-i}^2 \qquad\qquad (4.191)$$

3) To obtain standardized residuals $\{z_t\}$, residuals obtained from ARMA(p,q) fitting $\{\varepsilon_t\}$ are divided by conditional GARCH(p,q) volatility forecasts that where calculated for the same point in time:

$$z_t = \frac{\varepsilon_t}{\sigma_t} \qquad\qquad (4.192)$$

Under the GARCH hypothesis the set of standardized residuals are independently and identically distributed and therefore suitable for bootstrapping. To ensure that the standardized residuals are truly IID, diagnostic tests, specifically Ljung-Box Q test for standardized residuals and squared standardized residuals, and Engle's ARCH test are applied. The p-statistics of model parameters indicate whether the GARCH model is well specified. If the obtained standardized residuals are not IID, some other autoregressive conditional heteroskedasticity model should be applied (i.e. IGARCH, GJR-GARCH, EGARCH, APARCH or higher order GARCH model).

4) Identically and independently distributed standardized residual returns $\{z_t\}$ are bootstrapped for a large number of times, e.g. 30,000 times, to obtain a standardized historical time series Θ. Because bootstrapping is applied to IID residuals the results are unbiased:

$$z = \{z_1, z_2, ..., z_t\}\ z_i \in \Theta \qquad\qquad (4.193)$$

5) After obtaining the bootstrapped standardized residuals the calculation of VaR is straightforward. The HHS model uses the Hull-White idea of volatility updating the standardized residuals $\{z_t\}$ and scales them by the latest GARCH volatility forecast ($\hat{\sigma}_{t+1}$) to obtained a series of historical residuals that have been updated by forecasted volatility to reflect the current market conditions $\{\hat{z}_{t+1}\}$.

$$\hat{z}_{t+1} = z_t \times \hat{\sigma}_{t+1}^2 \tag{4.194}$$

6) The simulated returns $\hat{r}_{t+1}$ are obtained by using updated historical residuals $\{\hat{z}_{t+1}\}$, in the Equation (4.190):

$$\hat{r}_{t+1} = \alpha_0 + \sum_{i=1}^{p} \alpha_i r_{t-i+1} + \sum_{i=1}^{q} \theta_i \hat{z}_{t-i+1} + \hat{z}_{t+1} \tag{4.195}$$

HHS model allows for the VaR at the arbitrary confidence levels *cl* to be obtained in several ways. HHS VaR can be approximated from $G(.; t;N)$, the empirical cumulative distribution function of $\{\hat{r}_t\}$ based on return observations $\hat{r}_{t-1}, ..., \hat{r}_{t-N}$, and the procedure is the same as the one used for obtaining BRW VaR forecasts described in chapter 4.3.4. HHS VaR can also be calculated by applying a smooth density estimator such as kernel. Following the results obtained by Silverman (1986) and Butler and Schachter (1998) the best choice would be the adaptive Gaussian or adaptive Epanechnikov kernel.

HHS model has another attractive characteristic; the observation period from which the standardized residuals are obtained can be modeled in two ways. The first option is to let observation period freely grow with the passing of time, resulting in slightly more conservative VaR estimates, but which are extremely resilient to extreme events. The second option is to arbitrary set the length of the observation period, allowing the VaR estimates to be less conservative but also less appropriate for capturing extreme events. The choice of length of the observation period is purely arbitrary but in author's opinion should in no case be shorter than one year of daily data. Testing of the HHS model, its backtesting performance, and characteristics are presented in chapter 6 of the book.

Hybrid historical simulation (HHS) has a number of attractions:
- It combines the non-parametric attractions of nonparametric approaches with a sophisticated, parametric GARCH treatment of volatility.
- It successfully captures autocorrelation and heteroskedasticity in the data.
- It is far easier to implement than other approaches such as extreme value theory, mixtures of distributions or stable Paretian distributions that are successful at capturing asymmetry and kurtosis.
- Number of parameters that have to be estimated is small compared to other approaches, and depend on the choice of volatility forecasting model.
- It is computationally fast.
- It minimizes the "ghost effect" since the extreme events in the data set are minimized via volatility updating. For example, an extreme event in the data set that happened during a period of increased volatility will have much less influence on the VaR forecasts during the tranquil times because the current

GARCH driven volatility forecasts actually decrease the value of such extreme events.

- Residuals do not follow any predefined distribution making the model more robust to model risk.
- Bootstrapping is applied to IID residuals, making the results unbiased.
- Unlike most of the nonparametric approaches, HHS model uses all available information about the dynamics of the asset price assigning equal weight to positive and negative returns (response to the positive and negative shocks can be made asymmetric by using an Asymmetric instead of Symmetric GARCH model).
- Unlike most of the nonparametric approaches, HHS model allows the VaR forecasts that can exceed the maximum historical loss in the data set. HHS VaR forecasts are not limited by the maximum loses that occurred in the historical data set.
- It instantaneously reacts to changes in the market volatility regime unlike most of the nonparametric models that, depending on the length of the observation window react rather slowly.
- It maintains the correlation structure in the return data without modelling the variance covariance matrix or assuming the conditional distribution of asset returns as is the case with parametric approaches.

5   BACKTESTING MARKET RISK MODELS

One of the most important tasks in risk management is backtesting. Backtesting is the process of quantitative VaR model evaluation. It uses a formal statistical framework to determine whether VaR model's risk estimates are consistent with the assumptions on which the model is based. This consists of verifying whether actual loses are in line with projected losses (Jorion, 2001, p. 129). It involves systematically comparing the history of VaR forecasts with associated portfolio returns. Backtesting is essential for risk managers who need to check if the VaR models are well calibrated. If the VaR model is not well calibrated, it should be re-examined for faulty assumptions, wrong parameters or inaccurate modelling. Backtesting is also paramount to central banks due to the Basle Committee's allowance of VaR models in the internal rating approach used for calculating capital requirements.

5.1   Backtesting preconditions

The first requirement in backtesting is to obtain a suitable data set. This is not as easy as it sounds, since return data is typically calculated according to standard principles of accounting prudence, and this often means that assets are understated in value and fluctuations of their values are smoothed over. However, for risk measurement purposes it is more important that the return data reflect underlying volatility rather than accounting prudence.

The return data also need cleaning to get rid of components that are not directly related to current or recent market risk-taking. Such components include fee income, hidden profits/losses from trades carried out at prices different from the mid bid-ask spread, return earned from other forms of risk-taking (e.g., high yields on bonds with high credit risks), and unrealised returns and provisions against future losses. It is also necessary to take account of the impact of the internal funding regime that underlies the institution's trading activity, and the impact of intra-day trading on both returns and risk measures[39]. In order to compare returns against market risk the return data should either be cleaned so that it reflects the return at the end of the day market risk positions, or hypothetical return data obtained by revaluing trading positions from one day to the next should be used.

Having obtained the clean data, it can be very useful to draw up a chart showing the time series of both daily returns and risk measures. Such a chart shows how these series have behaved over time, and gives a good visual indication of the behaviour of the outliers or exceptions. It also shows how many exceptions there were, how big they were, and whether they show any pattern. Such a chart gives a good indication of possible underlying causes (Dowd, 2002, p. 180):

---

[39] For more on these issues see Deans, 2000, p. 265-269.

- A relatively large number of extreme observations indicate that the risk measures are probably too low.
- A relatively small number of tail observations, or none at all, indicates that the risk measures are probably too high.
- If there are major differences between high and low exceptions, then the return measures might be biased.
- If the risk lines show flatness, or excessive smoothness, then risk measures are not being updated sufficiently quickly.
- If returns are close to zero much of the time, then there is relatively little trading taking place and this suggests that positions are illiquid.
- Abrupt changes in risk lines suggest changes in volatility or changes in the way risks are estimated.

The errors in VaR estimation depend on the reasonabless of assumptions made when calculating VaR.

Possibly the most important assumption to be made is the choice of the theoretical distribution that describes the distribution of empirical data. The assumptions about the theoretical distribution of returns, as well as other assumptions made when calculating VaR, can be judged by whether the VaR measure provides the correct conditional and unconditional risk coverage. A VaR measure achieves the correct unconditional coverage if the portfolio losses exceed the *cl* percent VaR *1-cl* percent of the time. Because the losses are expected to exceed *cl* percent VaR *1-cl* percent of the time, a VaR measure that satisfies the unconditional coverage is correct on average.

Correct conditional coverage means that as the risk of a portfolio changes daily, so should the VaR estimate change, and provide the correct VaR figure daily, and not on average. Although it is probably unrealistic for VaR to provide the exact coverage for every time period, a good VaR measure should at least go so far as to increase, when the risk of a portfolio appears to be increasing.

5.2   Statistical backtests based on the frequency of tail losses

All statistical tests are based on the principle of first selecting a significance level, and then estimating the probability associated with the null hypothesis being true[40]. Typically, the null hypothesis is accepted if the estimated value of this probability, the estimated p-value, exceeds the chosen significance level, and rejected otherwise. The higher the significance level, the more likely it is to accept the null hypothesis, and the less likely is to incorrectly reject a true model (i.e., to make a Type I error). However, it also means that it is more likely to incorrectly accept a false model (i.e., to make a Type II error). Any statistical test therefore involves a trade-off between these two types of possible errors.

In principle, a significance level should be selected to take account of the likelihoods of these errors (and, in theory, their costs as well) and strike an appropriate balance between them. However, it is very common to select some arbitrary significance level such as 5% or 10% and apply that level in all the tests. A significance level of this magnitude gives the model a certain benefit of the doubt, and implies that the model will be rejected only if the evidence against it is reasonably strong: for example, if the selected significance level is 10%, the model is adequate if the obtained p-value estimate is greater than 10%. A test can be said to be reliable if it is likely to avoid both types of error when used with an appropriate significance level.

---

[40] The problem of hypothesis testing can be stated as follows. Assuming a random variable X with a known probability density function $f(x;\theta)$, where θ is the parameter of the distribution. Having obtained a random sample of size n, the point estimator $\hat{\theta}$ is obtained. Since the true θ is not known, a question arises whether the estimator $\hat{\theta}$ is the true representation of θ, for instance $\theta = \theta^*$, where θ^* is a specific numerical value of θ. The task is to test whether the the random sample comes from probability density function $f(x;\theta) = \theta^*$. In statistics, $\theta = \theta^*$ is called the null (maintained) hypothesis and is generally denoted by H_0. The null hypothesis is tested against an alternative hypothesis denoted by H_1, which can simply be $\theta \neq \theta^*$. To test the validity of null hypothesis the sample information is used to obtain the test statistic. Very often the test statistic is the point estimator of the unknown parameter. The next step is to find the probability distribution of the test statistic and use the confidence interval or test of significance approach to test the null hypothesis (Gujarati, 2003, p. 905). In the language of hypothesis testing the established confidence interval is called the acceptance region and the area outside the acceptance region is called critical region, or region of rejection of the null hypothesis. The lower and upper limits of the acceptance region (which demarcate it from rejection regions) are called the critical values. When deciding to reject or not to reject the null hypothesis any researcher is likely to commit two types of errors (Gujarati, 2003, p. 907-908):
1) rejecting the null hypothesis when it is in fact correct – type I error, or
2) accepting the null hypothesis when it is in fact false – type II error.

5.2.1 Frequency of tail losses test – Kupiec test

Perhaps the most widely used test is the basic frequency of tail losses test (Kupiec, 1995). Kupiec proposed a test based on the proportion of failures. The setup for this test is the classic framework for a sequence of successes and failures, also known as Bernoulli trials. The number of exceptions (x) follows a binomial probability distribution (Jorion, 2001, p. 133):

$$f(x) = \binom{T}{x}(1 - cl)^x \, cl^{T-x} \qquad (5.1)$$

T - sample size
cl - confidence level

The expected value of x is $E(x) = (1-cl)T$ and variance $V(x) = cl(1-cl)T$. For large values of T, by the central limit theorem, binominal distribution can be approximated by the normal distribution (Jorion, 2001, p. 133):

$$z = \frac{x - (1 - cl)T}{\sqrt{cl(1 - cl)T}} \approx N(0,1) \qquad (5.2)$$

Kupiec (1995) developed approximate 95% confidence regions for binominal test. These regions are defined by the tail points of the log-likelihood ratio (Crouhy, Galai, Mark, 2001, p. 248):

$$LR = -2\ln[cl^{T-N}(1 - cl)^N] + 2\ln\left[\left(1 - \frac{N}{T}\right)^{T-N}\left(\frac{N}{T}\right)^N\right] \qquad (5.3)$$

The LR test is uniformly most powerful for a given sample size and is asymptotically distributed as chi-square with one degree of freedom under the null hypothesis that ($1-cl$) is the true probability. Kupiec (1995) also proposes a second test that is based on the time that elapses before the first return greater than forecasted VaR is observed. Let $\widetilde{X}$ be a random variable that denotes the number of days until the first excess return is observed. The probability of observing the first excess return at time X is given by:

$$P(\widetilde{X} = X) = (1 - cl)cl^{X-1} \qquad (5.4)$$

Given a realization X of $\widetilde{X}$, the LR test for the null hypothesis that ($1-cl$) percent is (Crouhy, Galai, Mark, 2001, p. 248):

$$LR(X, 1-cl) = -2\ln[(1-cl)cl^{X-1}] + 2\ln\left[\left(1-\frac{1}{X}\right)^{X-1}\left(\frac{1}{X}\right)\right] \quad (5.5)$$

Under the null hypothesis, *LR(X, 1-cl)* is distributed as chi-square with one degree of freedom. This test is inferior to basic Kupiec test because it uses less information. The test only uses the information about the occurence of the previous excess return, and disregards everything else. It is best regarded as a diagnostic that can be used alongside more powerful tests.

The Kupiec test has a simple intuition, is very easy to apply and does not require a great deal of information. However, it also has some drawbacks (Dowd, 2002, p. 182):

- The Kupiec test is not reliable except with very large sample sizes. Frequency-of-tail-loss tests have even more difficulty as the holding period rises. For a longer holding period than a day, the test can be applied in one of two ways: by straightforward temporal aggregation (working with returns and VaR over a period of *h* days), and by using rolling h-day windows with 1-day steps (Tilman, Brusilovskiy, 2001, p. 85-86). Unfortunately, the first approach cuts down the sample size by a factor of *h,* and the second is difficult to implement. When backtesting, it is probably best to work with data of daily frequency, or more than daily frequency, if that is feasible.
- Since it focuses exclusively on the frequency of tail losses, the Kupiec test throws away potentially valuable information about the sizes of tail losses. The Kupiec test also throws away useful information about the pattern of tail losses over time. If the model is correct, then not only should the observed frequency of tail losses be close to the frequency predicted by the model, but the sequence of observed indicator values that take the value 1 if the loss exceeds VaR and 0 otherwise should be independently and identically distributed. One way to test this prediction is suggested by Manganelli and Engle (2001, p. 9-12): if *hit$_t$* is the value of the indicator in period *t* minus the VaR tail probability, 1 - *cl,* then *hit$_t$* should be uncorrelated with any other variables in the current information set. This prediction can be tested by specifying a set of variables in the current information set and regressing *hit$_t$* against them: if the prediction is satisfied, these variables should have jointly insignificant regression coefficients.

5.2.2 Conditional backtesting test – Christoffersen test

A useful adaptation to the Kupiec approach is the conditional backtesting approach suggested by Christoffersen (1998). Christoffersen developed a backtesting model that separates the particular hypotheses being tested, and then tests each hypothesis separately. For example, the full null hypothesis in a standard frequency of tail losses test is that the model generates a correct frequency of exceptions and, in addition, that exceptions are independent of each other. The second assumption is usually subsidiary and made only to simplify the test. However, it raises the possibility that the model could fail the test, not because it generates the wrong frequency of failures, as such, but because failures are not independent of each other. The Christoffersen approach is designed to avoid this problem. To use it, the joint null hypothesis is divided into its constituent parts, thus giving two distinct sub-hypotheses: the sub-hypothesis that the model generates the correct frequency of tail losses, and the sub-hypothesis that tail losses are independent. If the appropriate assumptions for the alternative hypotheses are made, then each of these hypotheses has a likelihood ratio test. The sub-hypotheses can be tested separately, as well as the original joint hypothesis that the model has the correct frequency of independently distributed tail losses. For $h = 1$ step-ahead VaR predictions, $\hat{\kappa}_\lambda(1,t)$, and observed actual returns r_{t+1}, the Boolean sequence indicating the presence or absence of VaR violations is defined as (Hartz, Mittnik, Paolella, 2006, p. 10):

$$I_{t+1} = I_{(-\infty,\hat{\kappa}_\lambda(1,t))}(r_{t+1}) \tag{5.6}$$

With $T_1 = \sum_{t=1}^{T} I_{t+1}$ the number of violations and $T_0 = T - T_1$ the number of non-violations, the empirical downfall probability is given by $\hat{\lambda} = T^{-1}\sum_{t=1}^{T} I_{t+1} = T_1/T$. For a correct VaR prediction model, the violation sequence I_{t+1} is expected to be (Christoffersen, 1998, p. 5):

H_0: $I_{t+1} \sim IID(Bernoulli(\lambda)$ \hfill (5.7)

Testing this null hypothesis is twofold. One part is testing the unconditional coverage, or that the observed downfall probability is equal to the specified downfall probability (unconditional coverage). The second part tests whether the violations are IID. For the first part, the likelihood value under hypothesis that $\hat{\lambda} = \lambda$ is (Hartz, Mittnik, Paolella, 2006, p. 11):

$$L(\lambda) = \prod_{t=1}^{T}(1-\lambda)^{1-I_{t+1}}\lambda^{I_{t+1}} = (1-\lambda)^{T_0}\lambda^{T_1} \tag{5.8}$$

while the observed likelihood is given by $L(\hat{\lambda}) = (1-\hat{\lambda})^{T_0}\hat{\lambda}^{T_1}$. Using the likelihood ratio test statistic and the corresponding, asymptotically valid p-value tests the unconditional coverage (Christoffersen, 1998, p. 6):

$$LR_{uc} = -2\ln\left[L(\lambda)/L(\hat{\lambda})\right] \sim \chi_1^2 \qquad P_{uc} = 1 - F_{\chi_1^2}(LR_{uc}) \tag{5.9}$$

P_{uc} is the probability of getting a sample that conforms even less to the null hypothesis than the sample. For P_{uc} below the set significance level the null hypothesis is rejected. The *LRuc* test is an unconditional test since it simply counts exceptions over the entire period. However, in the presence of time dependent heteroskedasticity, the conditional accuracy of interval forecasts is an important issue. Interval forecasts that ignore such variance dynamics may have correct unconditional coverage but, at any given time, will have incorrect conditional coverage. In such cases, the *LRuc* test is of limited use since it will classify inaccurate VaR estimates as acceptably accurate. For testing the independence of I_{t+1} as in Christoffersen (1998), let Λ be the transition probability matrix for a first order Markov sequence (Hartz, Mittnik, Paolella, 2006, p. 11):

$$\Lambda = \begin{bmatrix} \lambda_{00} & \lambda_{01} \\ \lambda_{10} & \lambda_{11} \end{bmatrix} \tag{5.10}$$

where λ_{ij} are the proportions given by $\lambda_{ij} = prop(I_t = i$ and $I_{t+1} = j)$, $i,j = 0,1$. With T_{ij}, $i,j = 0,1$ the number of observations with a j following an i, the observed probabilities are given by (Christoffersen, 1998, p. 6):

$$\lambda_{01} = \frac{T_{01}}{T_{00} + T_{01}} \qquad\qquad \lambda_{11} = \frac{T_{11}}{T_{10} + T_{11}} \tag{5.11}$$

and $\lambda_{00} = 1 - \lambda_{01}$, $\lambda_{10} = 1 - \lambda_{11}$. The likelihood value under the null ($\lambda_{01} = \lambda_{11} = \lambda$) is $L(\hat{\lambda}) = (1 - \hat{\lambda})^{T_0}\,\hat{\lambda}^{T_1}$ and the observed likelihood is given by (Hartz, Mittnik, Paolella, 2006, p. 11):

$$L(\hat{\Lambda}) = (1 - \hat{\lambda}_{01})^{T_{00}}\,\hat{\lambda}_{01}^{T_{01}}\,(1 - \hat{\lambda}_{11})^{T_{10}}\,\hat{\lambda}_{11}^{T_{11}} \tag{5.12}$$

Likelihood ratio test statistic and corresponding p-value are (Hartz, Mittnik, Paolella, 2006, p. 11):

$$LR_{ind} = -2\ln\left[L(\hat{\lambda})/L(\hat{\Lambda})\right] \sim \chi_1^2 \qquad P_{ind} = 1 - F_{\chi_1^2}(LR_{ind}) \tag{5.13}$$

The *LRind* statistic is the likelihood ratio statistic for the null hypothesis of serial independence against the alternative of first-order Markov dependence.

The *LRcc* test, adapted from the more general test proposed by Christoffersen (1998) is a test of correct conditional coverage. The test involves two hypotheses $\hat{\lambda} = \lambda$ and $I_{t+1} \sim IID$. The likelihood ratio test statistic with corresponding p-value is given by (Christoffersen, 1998 p. 9):

$$LR_{cc} = -2\ln\left[L(\lambda)/L(\hat{\Lambda})\right] = LR_{uc} + LR_{ind} \sim \chi_2^2$$
$$P_{cc} = 1 - F_{\chi_2^2}(LR_{cc}) \tag{5.14}$$

The finite sample critical values for the regulatory parameter values of $(k,\alpha) = (1,1)$ are shown in table 6.

Table 6 - Critical values for LRuc and LRcc statistics

	Significance level		
	1%	5%	10%
	LRuc Statistic		
Asymptotic χ2(1)	6,635	3,842	2,706
Finite-sample	5,497 (0,5%)	5,025 (9,5%)	3,555 (12,2%)
	LRcc Statistic		
Asymptotic χ2(2)	9,210	5,992	4,605
Finite-sample	6,007 (0,2%)	5,015 (1,1%)	5,005 (11,8%)

Note: The finite-sample critical values for the *LRuc* and *LRcc* test statistics for the lower 1 percent quantile ($\alpha = 1$) are based on 10,000 simulations of sample size $T = 250$. The percentages in parentheses are the quantiles that correspond to the asymptotic critical values under the finite-sample distribution.

The finite-sample critical values from table 6 are obtained by simulation and shows significant differences between the two distributions that must be accounted for when drawing statistical inference.

As can be concluded from above discussion, Christoffersen approach helps to separate testable hypotheses about the dynamic structure of excess losses from testable hypotheses about the frequency of excess losses. This is potentially useful because it indicates not only whether models fail backtesting, but also helps to identify the reason why.

5.3   Statistical backtests based on the size of tail losses

Statistical backtests based on the frequency of tail losses focus exclusively on the frequency of tail losses, and effectively throw away information about the size of these losses. Size of tail losses is potentially very useful for assessing model adequacy, and tests using such information could be considered more reliable than tests that use only the information about the frequency of tail losses and in case of Christoffersen (1998) test the information about the independence of losses. Statistical backtests based on the size of tail losses seek to test if the values of tail losses are consistent with those forecasted by the tested VaR model.

A simple test of size of tail loss can be conducted by taking a sample of return observations and estimating VaR for a chosen confidence level. After that the sign of the returns is reversed to make loss observations positive the sample is truncated to eliminate all observations except those involving losses higher than calculated VaR (Dowd, 2002, p. 185). In this way the empirical distribution of tail-loss observations is obtained. The distributional assumptions on which the risk model is based is used to predict the distribution of tail loss observations, and test whether the two distributions are the same. The significance of the difference between these two distributions can be tested by using a standard distribution-difference test (e.g., the Kolmogorov-Smirnov or Kuiper test). The main difference between the backtests based on the frequency of tail losses and backtests based on the size of tail losses is that the sizes of tail losses test take account of the size of losses exceeding VaR and the frequency of tail losses tests do not. The Kupiec (1995) test or Christoffersen (1998) test will not be able to tell the difference between a VaR model that generates tail losses compatible with the model, and a VaR model that generates tail losses incompatible with the model, provided that they have the right tail-loss frequencies. By contrast, size of tail losses tests do take account of the difference between the two models, and should be able to distinguish between them. The most well known backtest from this group of tests are the Crnkovic-Drachman backtest and a backtest based on Berkowitz transformations.

5.3.1   Crnkovic-Drachman Backtest Procedure

Crnkovic and Drachman (Crnkovic, Drachman, 1996) developed an approach that evaluates VaR models by testing the difference between the empirical return distribution and the predicted return distribution, across whole range of values. Their argument is that each return observation can be classified into a percentile of the forecast return distribution, and if the model is good, the return observations classified in this way should be uniformly distributed and independent of each other. This line of reasoning suggests two distinct tests (Dowd, 2002, p. 188). The first test is designed to test whether the classified observations are distributed as uniform $U(0,1)$. This can be performed by testing whether the empirical distribution of classified observations matches the predicted distribution of classified observations. The second test in the Crnkovic-Drachman backtest procedure is a test of the independence of classified return observations. Crnkovic and Drachman suggest testing for independence with the BDS test suggested by Brock, Dechert and Scheinkman. The BDS test is powerful but quite involved and data-intensive, and perhaps a simpler test of independence like likelihood ratio test (Christoffersen, 1998) could be used.

The first Crnkovic-Drachman test is a test of whether the predicted and realized return distributions are the same, and practically equal to the simple sizes of tail losses test applied to all observations rather than just tail losses. The main difference between the size of tail losses test and the first Crnkovic-Drachman test is the location of the threshold that separates return observations into tail observations and non-tail ones. Another difference lies in the choice of the distance test between the predicted and empirical distributions. Kolmogorov-Smirnov statistic used in the size of tail losses test tends to be more sensitive around the median value of the distribution and less sensitive around the extremes. This means that the Kolmogorov-Smirnov statistic is less likely to detect differences between the tails of the distributions than differences between their central masses, and this can be a problem for VaR estimation, where the tails of the distribution are of interest. An alternative that avoids this latter problem is Kuiper's statistic, and it is for this reason that Crnkovic and Drachman prefer the Kuiper statistic to Kolmogorov-Smirnov. The Kuiper statistic is the sum of the maximum amount by which each distribution exceeds the other, and its critical values can be determined in same manner as with Kolmogorov-Smirnov statistic. However, Crnkovic and Drachman (1996, p. 140) report that the Kuiper's test statistic is very data-intensive: results begin to deteriorate with less than 1,000 observations, and are of little validity for less than 500. Both these statistics assume that the parameters of the distributions are known, and if estimates are used instead of known true parameters, these test procedures cannot be relied upon and alternative tests should be used, such as Lillifors test[41], or Monte Carlo methods. Both these tests are therefore open to objections, and how useful they might be in practice remains controversial. Crnkovic-Drachman test can be regarded as a special case of the sizes of tail losses test, and this special case occurs when the sizes of tail losses test is used with a very low threshold. Making the tail larger (by using the Crnkovic-Drachman test) gives more observations and hence greater precision (lower variance). On the other hand if the extreme observations are particularly distinctive for any reason, then including the central observations by using the Crnkovic-Drachman test can bias the results. This means that Crnkovic-Drachman test should only be used when the whole empirical distribution of returns is relevant to tail losses. In terms of variance-bias trade-off, this would be the case only if concerns about variance dominated concerns about bias. If the goal is to minimize variance and bias, the basic sizes of tail losses test is the preferred test (Dowd, 2002, p. 189).

5.3.2 Test based on Berkowitz transformations

There is also another, more useful, size-based approach to backtesting. Crnkovic, Drachman (1996) approach transforms the distribution of classified returns to IID $U(0, 1)$ distributed. Instead of testing these predictions directly, Berkowitz (2001) suggests transforming classified observations to make them normal under the null

---

[41] The Lilliefors test for goodness of fit to a normal distribution evaluates the hypothesis that variable X has a normal distribution with unspecified mean and variance, against the alternative that variable X does not have a normal distribution. This test compares the empirical distribution of X with a normal distribution having the same mean and variance as X. If the result of hypothesis test is H = 1 it means that the hypothesis that X has a normal distribution should be rejected, if H = 0 the hypothesis of normality should not be rejected at the p% significance level. Lilliefors test is similar to the Kolmogorov-Smirnov test, but is better suited for evaluating empirical data because it adjusts for the fact that the parameters of the normal distribution are estimated from variable X rather than specified in advance.

hypothesis. This is done by applying an inverse normal transformation to the uniform series[42]. When the data is transformed to follow normal distribution, a wider array of powerful statistical tools can be applied, than under uniform distribution. One possible use of such a procedure is to test the null hypothesis that z_t is IID N(0,1) against a fairly general first-order autoregressive process with a possibly different mean and variance. Alternative process can be written as (Dowd, 2002, p. 190):

$$z_t - \mu = \rho(z_{t-1} - \mu_i) + \varepsilon_t \tag{5.15}$$

The null hypothesis states that $\mu = 0$, $\rho = 0$ and σ^2, the variance of ε_t is equal to 1. The log-likelihood function associated with Equation 5.15 is (Berkowitz, 2001, p. 468):

$$L = -\frac{1}{2}\ln(2\pi) - \frac{1}{2}\ln\left[\sigma^2/(1-\rho)^2\right] - \frac{[z_1 - \mu/(1-\rho)]^2}{2\sigma^2/(1-\rho)^2} - \frac{(T-1)}{2}\ln(2\pi)$$
$$-\frac{(T-1)}{2}\ln(\sigma^2) - \left[z_{t-1} - \sum_{t=2}^{T}\frac{(z_t - \mu - \rho z_{t-1})^2}{2\sigma^2}\right] \tag{5.16}$$

The likelihood ratio test statistic for the null hypothesis is:

$$LR = -2\left[L(0,1,0) - L(\hat{\mu}, \hat{\sigma}^2, \hat{\rho})\right] \tag{5.17}$$

where $\hat{\mu}, \hat{\sigma}^2$ and $\hat{\rho}$ are maximum likelihood estimates of the parameters. Likelihood ratio is distributed as χ_3^2, chi-squared with three degrees of freedom. The null hypothesis can be tested against this alternative hypothesis by obtaining maximum likelihood estimates of the parameters, deriving the value of the LR statistic, and comparing that value against the critical value for a χ_3^2. This is a powerful test because the alternative hypothesis is quite general and because, unlike the Crnkovic-Drachman test or sizes of tail losses test, this approach captures both aspects of the null hypothesis - uniformity/normality and independence, within a single test (Dowd, 2002, p. 191). Berkowitz approach can also be adapted to test whether the sizes of tail losses are consistent with expectations under the null hypothesis. The point here is that if the underlying data has fatter tails than the VaR model presumes, the transformed z_t will also be leptokurtic. This prediction can be tested by transforming tail loss data and noting that their likelihood function is a truncated normal log-likelihood function. The LR test is constructed in the same way as before. Estimated parameters are used as inputs into truncated log-likelihood function, whose values are than used in Equation 5.17, and compared to the resulting test value against the critical value that is distributed as χ_3^2 under the null hypothesis.

---

[42] If x_t is IID U(0,1), then $z_t = \Phi^{-1}(x_t)$ is IID N(0,1).

5.4 Forecast evaluation approaches to backtesting

The forecast evaluation approach was suggested by Lopez (1998, 1999) and is motivated by the evaluation methods often used to rank the forecasts of macroeconomic models. This approach allows for ranking of different competing models, but does not give any formal statistical indication of model adequacy. In ranking them, it also allows to take account of any particular concerns one might have. For example, higher losses can be given greater weight because of greater concern about higher losses. Furthermore, because they are not statistical tests, forecast evaluation approaches do not suffer from the low power of standard tests such as the Kupiec (1995) test. This makes forecast evaluation approach very attractive for backtesting with the small data sets typically available in practice. A forecast evaluation process has four key inputs, and a single output, a final score for each model. The first input is a set of paired observations of returns for each period and their associated VaR forecasts. The second input is a loss function that gives each observation a score depending on how the observed return compares to the VaR forecast for that period. Thus, if L_t is the loss made over period t, and VaR_t is the forecast VaR for that period, the loss function L_t assigns the following value to the period t observation (Blanco, Ihle, 1998, p. 1):

$$C_t = \begin{cases} f(L_t, VaR_t) \, if & L_t > VaR_t \\ g(L_t, VaR_t) \, if & L_t \leq VaR_t \end{cases} \tag{5.18}$$

where $f(L_t, VaR_t) \geq g(L_t, VaR_t)$ to ensure that tail losses do not receive a lower value than other return observations. The third input is a benchmark that serves to distinguish between good and bad VaR models. The fourth input is a score function, which takes as its inputs the loss function and benchmark values. If the benchmark equals the expected value of C_t, under the null hypothesis that the VaR model is good, a quadratic probability score (QPS) function can be used, suggested by Lopez (1999, p. 47):

$$QPS = (2/n) \sum_{t=1}^{n} (C_t - p)^2 \tag{5.19}$$

The QPS function can take values in the range [0, 2], and the closer the QPS value is to zero, the better the model. QPS function can be used to rank VaR models, with the better models having lower scores. The QPS criterion also has the attractive property that it encourages honest reporting by the banks. If a bank wishes to minimise its QPS score, it will report its VaR figures sincerely (Lopez, 1999, p. 47-48). This is a useful property in situations where a supervisor and the VaR modeller are different, and where the supervisor might be concerned about the VaR modeller reporting false VaR forecasts to alter the results of the backtest. Lopez also reports that the forecast evaluation approach distinguishes better between good and bad VaR models than the Kupiec test (Lopez, 1999, p. 51-60).

5.4.1   Size adjusted frequency of tail losses approach – Lopez test

To implement forecast evaluation, it is necessary to specify the loss function, and a number of different loss functions have been proposed in the literature. The simplest loss function is the binomial loss function proposed by Lopez (1998), which gives an observation a value of 1 if it involves a tail loss, and a value of 0 otherwise. Equation 5.18 therefore takes the form (Lopez, 1998, p. 7):

$$C_t = \begin{cases} 1 & if \quad L_t > VaR_t \\ 0 & if \quad L_t \leq VaR_t \end{cases} \qquad\qquad (5.20)$$

This Lopez binomial loss function is intended for the users that are concerned only with the frequency of tail losses. The benchmark for this loss function is p, the expected value of $E(C_t)$. This loss function actually only shows what can be seen from the Kupiec test. Ranking the VaR models by the Lopez binomial function and (preferring the models with the minimal score) is in all aspects completely the same as ranking the competing VaR models by the highest p value of the Kupiec test. In the same way, as all frequency of tail losses tests, it also ignores the magnitude of tail losses. In an attempt to remedy this defect Lopez (1998) himself suggests a second, size-adjusted, loss function (Lopez, 1998, p. 8):

$$C_t = \begin{cases} 1 + (L_t - VaR_t)^2 & if \quad L_t > VaR_t \\ 0 & if \quad L_t \leq VaR_t \end{cases} \qquad\qquad (5.21)$$

This loss function allows for the sizes of tail losses to influence the final rating of VaR model. VaR model that generates higher tail losses would generate higher values under this size adjusted loss function than a VaR model that generates lower tail losses, ceteris paribus. However, with this loss function, there is no longer a straightforward condition for the benchmark, and the benchmark has to be estimated by some other means. One way to do so is suggested by Lopez (1998, p. 13). He suggests that under assumption that the observed returns are independent and identically distributed an empirical loss function and a value of the final score can be derived by repeating the operation a large number of times, and using the average final score as the estimate of the benchmark. However, if the VaR model is parametric, simpler and more direct approaches can be used to estimate the benchmark. For example, return data can be simulated under the null hypothesis using Monte Carlo methods, and the average of final scores can be taken as the benchmark.

5.4.2   Blanco-Ihle test

The Lopez size adjusted loss function loses some of its intuition, because squared monetary returns have no practical real life interpretation. Accordingly, Blanco and Ihle (1998) suggest a different size-loss function (Blanco, Ihle, 1998, p. 1):

$$C_t = \begin{cases} \dfrac{L_t - VaR_t}{VaR_t} & \text{if} \quad L_t > VaR_t \\ 0 & \text{if} \quad L_t \le VaR_t \end{cases} \qquad (5.22)$$

Blanco-Ihle loss function gives each tail-loss observation a weight equal to the tail loss divided by VaR. The loss function ensures that higher tail losses get awarded higher values without the impaired intuition introduced by squaring the tail loss. The benchmark for this forecast evaluation procedure is also easy to derive: the benchmark is the expected value of the difference between the tail loss and the VaR, divided by the VaR itself, and this is equal to the difference between the expected tail loss and the VaR, divided by the VaR. Blanco and Ihle (1998) also suggest a second approach that incorporates concerns about both the frequency and the size of tail losses. If $C_t^{frequency}$ is the Lopez (1998) frequency loss function, given by Equation 5.20, and C_t^{size} is the Blanco-Ihle size (1998) loss function, given by Equation 5.22, they suggest an alternative loss function that is a weighted average of both, with the weighing factor reflecting relative concern about the two sources of loss. Blanco-Ihle (1998) is an excellent test for comparing competing VaR models that report the same frequency of tail losses, and whose tail losses are IID. Ranking VaR models by Blanco-Ihle approach is one of the best approaches to distinguish between such VaR models.

5.5   Comparison of backtesting models

Comparison of competing VaR models can also be done by using standard statistical measures. VaR models' risk measures can be compared either to the average results of all competing VaR models, or to those predicted by each individual model. VaR models can also be ranked based on more formal tests, and this can be done in two ways. The first and the easiest way is to take a statistical backtest procedure and rank VaR models by means of their resulting p-values: the better the model, the higher the p-value. As already noted this is the same as ranking VaR models by the binomial Lopez test. This approach is easy to carry out, but it is also statistically not too reliable.

A more sophisticated approach is suggested by Christoffersen, Hahn, Inoue (2001). Their approach not only allows for testing of the VaR models, but also allows pair wise comparisons of models in a rigorous fashion using an appropriate statistical framework. Comparing risk measures to the model-average measures, can give some feel for which models produce higher or more volatile risk estimates. By comparing the risk estimates of VaR models to predicted measures, the VaR models can be ranked by the closeness of their forecasts to predicted values. Some of the procedures are discussed in Hendricks (1996)[43].

For the purpose of comparing alternative VaR models Mean Absolute Percentage Error (MAPE) and Root Mean Squared Error (RMSE) measures are used. MAPE is a combined measure of both bias and bunching. The impact of bias in the measurement of tail events is clear. If the procedure for measuring tail events is biased so that in every 100-day period there are two observations of 1%-tail events MAPE equals 1. MAPE measure is similar to a standard deviation measure. If it were based on the difference between the observed number of tail events and the sample mean number of tail events it would be even closer to the standard deviation measure. Since the windows are overlapping, standard tests of statistical significance cannot be used. MAPE is calculated as follows. For each period of 100 consecutive days for which estimates are made, the absolute difference between the actual number of tail events and the expected number of tail events is calculated. If the indicator variable is both unbiased and independent, the number of tail events is supposed to equal VaR confidence level. The measure is set equal to the mean of these absolute differences. Denoting r^{tail} as the number of extreme events observed in the time window h, which is as suggested by Boudoukh, Richardson and Whitelaw (1998) set at 100 days, *(1-cl)h* is the number of expected extreme events in the period h.

The Mean Absolute Percentage Error (MAPE) constructed according to instructions given in Boudoukh, Richardson, Whitelaw (1998, p. 66) is:

$$MAPE = \frac{1}{h}\sum_{t=S}^{S+h}\left|r^{tail} - (1-cl)h\right| \qquad\qquad (5.23)$$

Smaller deviations from the expected value indicate better VaR measure.

Root Mean Squared Error (RMSE) measure examines the degree to which the VaR forecasts tend to vary around the realized returns for a given date. The root mean squared error (RMSE) for each VaR approach can be calculated by taking the square root of the mean (over all sample dates) of the squares of the daily biases (Balaban, Bayar, Faff, 2004, p. 11):

---

[43] Hendricks (1996) uses nine alternative measures: mean relative bias, root mean-squared relative bias, percentage volatility of risk measures, fraction of outcomes covered, multiple needed to attain desired coverage, average tail loss to VaR, maximum tail loss to VaR, correlations between risk measure and returns and mean relative bias for scaled risk measures.

$$RMSE = \sqrt{\frac{\sum_{i=1}^{T} |r_i^2 - VaR_i^2|}{T}} \qquad\qquad (5.24)$$

Each of these measures looks at a different aspect of model performance, and very often, different measures do not produce the same rankings of alternative VaR models. However, different measures can give a feel for the relative strengths and weaknesses of different VaR models, and in this way they allow for a more informed view of VaR model adequacy.

6   MEASURING MARKET RISK IN TRANSITION COUNTRIES

Majority of the transition markets are all exposed to very similar processes of strong inflow of foreign direct and portfolio investments, and offer possibilities of huge profits for investors. These countries represent a very interesting opportunity for foreign and domestic banks, investment funds, insurance companies and other investors. Banks and investment funds when investing in these financial markets employ the same risk measurement models for measuring market risk and forming of provision as they do in the developed markets. This means that risk managers in banks operating in transition countries de facto presume similar or even equal characteristics and behaviour in these markets, as they would expect in developed markets. This is a dangerous assumption, which is not founded on empirical research.

Using VaR models, which are created and suited for developed and liquid markets in developing markets, raises important questions: Do the VaR models developed and tested in developed and liquid financial markets apply to the volatile and shallow financial markets of transition countries? Do the commonly used VaR models adequately capture market risk of these markets or are they only giving a false sense of security?

The errors in VaR estimation depend on how reasonable are the assumptions made when calculating VaR. Probably the most important assumption to be made in a VaR model is the choice of the theoretical distribution that describes the distribution of empirical data. The assumption about the theoretical distribution of returns, as well as other assumptions made when calculating VaR, can be judged by whether a VaR model provides the correct conditional and unconditional risk coverage. A VaR model achieves the correct unconditional coverage if the portfolio losses exceed the *cl* percent VaR, *1-cl* percent of the time. Because the losses are expected to exceed *cl* percent VaR *1-cl* percent of the time, a VaR model that satisfies the unconditional coverage is correct on average. Correct conditional coverage means that as the risk of a portfolio changes daily, so should the VaR estimate change, and provide the correct VaR figure daily, and not on average. Although it is probably unrealistic for a VaR model to provide the exact coverage for every time period, a good VaR model should at least go so far as to increase, when the risk of a portfolio appears to be increasing and vice versa.

Employing VaR models in forming of bank's provisions that are not suited to financial markets they are used on, can have serious consequences for any investor. This can result in significant losses in trading portfolio that could pass undetected by the employed risk measurement models, leaving the investors unprepared for such events. Banks could also be penalized by the regulators, via higher scaling factor when forming their market risk provisions, due to the use of a faulty risk measurement model (Hendricks, Hirtle, 1997, p. 4).

6.1 A summary of empirical research on VaR estimation and model comparison

According to published research, VaR models based on moving average volatility models seem to perform the worst. Otherwise, there is no straightforward result, and it is impossible to establish a ranking among the models. The results are very sensitive to the type of loss functions used, the chosen probability level of VaR, the period being turbulent or normal etc. Some researchers also find a trade-off between model sophistication and uncertainty.

Hendricks (1996) in his famous study tested twelve VaR models (variance-covariance VaR based on equally weighted moving average approach with 50, 125, 250, 500, and 1,250 days observation periods, variance-covariance VaR with varying exponentially weighted moving averages and historical simulation VaR with 125, 250, 500, and 1,250 days observation periods). Hendricks (1996) finds that in almost all cases the approaches cover the risk that they are intended to cover. In addition, the twelve approaches tend to produce risk estimates that do not differ greatly in average size, although historical simulation approaches yield somewhat larger 99th percentile risk measures than the variance-covariance approaches. Despite the similarity in the average size of the risk estimates, his investigation reveals differences, some times substantial, among the various VaR approaches. In terms of variability over time, the VaR approaches using longer observation periods tend to produce less variable results than those using short observation periods or those using weighting schemes. Jackson, Maude, Perraudin (1998) conclude that simulation-based VaR models yield more accurate measures of tail probabilities than parametric VaR models. They find that parametric VaR analysis tracks the time-series behaviour of volatility better and yield slightly superior volatility forecasts compared to non-parametric, simulation-based techniques (though the differences are generally not statistically significant). In their study the parametric VaR models that yield the best forecasts have relatively short window lengths and large weighting factors. But such models are very poor at fitting the tails of return distributions and capital requirements based on them tend to be too low. De Raaji, Raunig (1998) analyse six different VaR approaches. They test two methods based on the variance-covariance approach with equally and exponentially weighted moving averages, two methods based on historical simulation with different historical period lengths and two VaR model based on mixtures of normal distributions with equally and exponentially weighted moving averages. De Raaji and Raunig (1998) comparison of the various VaR models revealed that the resulting VaR forecasts differ extremely for identical portfolios. With linear portfolios, differences sometimes exceeded 200% when the methods are compared with the EWMA-based variance-covariance approach as the benchmark. Even average differences fell into the 25 to 59% range. The results are consistent with the conjecture that methods that do not incorporate excess kurtosis tend to underestimate VaR at the 99% confidence interval. On the other hand, the same methods tend to overestimate VaR at the 95% confidence interval.

Lehar, Scheicher, Schittenkopf (2002) find that more complex volatility models (GARCH and Stochastic volatility) are unable to improve on constant volatility models for VaR forecast, although they do for option pricing. Wong, Cheng, Wong (2002) conclude that GARCH models, often found superior in forecasting volatility, consistently fail the Basel backtest. Several papers investigate the issue of trade-off in model choice; for example Caporin (2003c) finds that the EWMA compared to GARCH-based VaR forecast provides the best efficiency at a lower level of complexity. Bams, Wielhouwer (2000) draw similar conclusions, although sophisticated tail modelling results in better VaR estimates but with more uncertainty. Supposing that data generating process is close to be integrated, the use of the more general GARCH model introduces estimation error, which might result in the superiority of EWMA. Guermat, Harris (2002) show that EWMA-based VaR forecasts are excessively volatile and unnecessarily high, when returns do not have conditionally normal distribution but fat tails. This is because EWMA puts too much weight on extremes. According to Brooks, Persand (2003), the relative performance of different models depends on the loss function used. However, GARCH models provide reasonably accurate VaR. Christoffersen, Hahn, Inoue (2001) show that different models (EWMA, GARCH, Implied Volatility) might be optimal for different probability levels.

A study by Berkowitz, O'Brien (2002) examines the VaR models used by six leading US financial institutions. Their results indicate that these models are in some cases highly inaccurate: banks sometimes experienced high losses much larger than their models predicted, which suggests that these models are poor at dealing with fat tails and extreme events. Their results also indicate that banks' models have difficulty dealing with changes in volatility. In addition, a comparison of banks' models with a simple univariate parametric GARCH model indicates that the latter gives roughly comparable coverage of high losses, but also tends to produce lower VaR figures and is much better at dealing with volatility changes. These results suggest that the banks' structural models embody so many approximations and other implementation compromises that they lose any edge over much simpler models such as GARCH. Their findings could also be interpreted as a suggestion that banks would be better off ditching their structural risk models in favour of much simpler GARCH models. Similar findings are also reported by Lucas (2000) who finds that sophisticated risk models based on estimates of complete variance-covariance matrices fail to perform much better than simpler univariate VaR models that require only volatility estimates.

Although there is an abundance of research papers dealing with VaR and market risk measurement and management all of the existing VaR models are developed and tested in mature, developed and liquid markets (e.g.: Harvey, Whaley, 1992, Boudoukh, Richardson, Whitelaw, 1998, Hull, White, 1998a,b, Brook, Clare,

Persand, 2000, Manganelli, Engle, 2001, Alexander, 2001 etc). Quantitative testing of VaR models in other, less developed or developing financial market is scarce (e.g. Parrondo, 1997, Hagerud, 1997, Santoso, 2000, Sinha, Chamu, 2000, Magnusson, Andonov, 2002, Fallon, Sabogal, 2004, Valentinyi-Endrész, 2004, Žiković, 2005b, 2006a, 2006b, Žiković, Bezić, 2006).

Parrondo (1997) analysed the performance of VaR measures in emerging markets. He concludes that emerging markets are characterised by high instability, which considerably decreases the efficiency of the usual statistical methods. In this type of markets, jumps or discontinuities characterize the temporal behaviour of macroeconomic factors, such as FX or interest rates, and these discontinuities are usually followed by periods of large volatilities which slowly relax back to normal levels. The presence of such discontinuities indicates that the rate of change of a factor of interest can be no longer modelled by normal random variables. Additionally, the existence of well differentiable periods of large volatility which slowly relax to low volatility shows that the rate of change cannot be considered as uncorrelated over time. Parrondo (1997) shows that ARCH type processes can play an important role in calculating VaR in emerging markets.

VaR estimation and volatility forecasting in Nordic countries was analysed by Hagerud (1997b) and Magnusson, Andonov (2002). Hagerud (1997b) investigated 45 equity return series from Nordic stock exchanges in Helsinki, Stockholm, Oslo and Copenhagen. The study investigated whether asymmetric GARCH models might have been the data generating process of those series. Hagerud found that relatively few Nordic stocks show signs of asymmetric volatility clustering. Only 12 out of 45 stocks exhibited a noticeable leverage effect. Magnusson and Andonov (2002) study some aspects of the influence of capital adequacy requirements (CAR) on financial stability in Iceland. They conclude that Icelandic market is characterised by relatively high volatility and relatively small diversification of the economy, suggesting that Icelandic banking sector should increase its capital coverage above the mandatory minimum during the upswing of the economy. They also find that tested approaches fail to provide universal methodology or hardly any guidance about the optimal size of the CAR.

Santoso (2000) tries to identify the best approach to calculating market risk for Indonesian banks and to provide guidelines for banks' management in the choice of the most appropriate internal model. He compares the results of the BIS standardised and internal model based on variance-covariance VaR model using the data obtained from Indonesian banks. Santoso (2000) finds that by using the normality assumption, VaR does not satisfy the backtesting requirement. Furthermore, his results vary depending on the probability level, used with the employed model.

Sinha, Chamu (2000) compare the performance of three different methods of calculating VaR in the context of Mexican and Latin American securities. They examine weaknesses of these methods by using five different tests: test based on the time until first failure, test based on failure rate, test based on expected value, test based on autocorrelation, and test based on (rolling) mean absolute percentage error. In their study BRW historical simulation performs better than the historical simulation method and they conclude that BRW VaR gives estimates as precise as the stochastic simulation method, but with lower analytical and computational resources. Furthermore, they find that historical simulation and RiskMetrics methodology can lead to serious errors in estimating VaR in the world of volatile markets.

Soczo (2001) published an interesting paper in which he did not analyse the statistical validity of VaR models in transition economies but investigated the difference between Basel standardised approach and VaR model based approach in forming capital requirements for market risk. The average difference between the capital charges based on Internal and Standardised Method for the portfolio of Hungarian securities was 21.2%, which is nearly three times larger than the average standard capital requirement. It is clear that financial institutions will not use the Internal Method to calculate the capital charge because of its large extra charges and costs compared to the Standardised Method. Soczo (2001) concluded that the large difference between capital charges determined by the Internal and Standardised Model are derived from the fact that the young Hungarian market, is more volatile than developed markets. According to Jorion (2001) volatility of shares and bonds is significantly lower in the US market. In the Hungarian market the typical volatility of shares forming the test portfolios was between 2% and 5%, which is much larger than volatility in the US market. Soczo (2001) points out that these conditions should be considered by the Hungarian regulatory agencies so that Internal Models would become attractive for financial institutions.

Fallon, Sabogal (2004) by using coefficient of variation as a relative risk measure failed to provide conclusive evidence that the historical simulation VaR is a reliable for measuring risk at high confidence level in the Colombian stock market. Although, they could not reject the null hypothesis in all the cases, their finding can be explained by the fact that they did not use enough historical monthly observations to make it statistically significant, which can distort the results obtained at certain confidence levels.

Valentinyi-Endrész (2004) performed the analysis on daily log-returns of the Hungarian stock index (BUX) for the period 1995-2002. She compares VaR forecast of different unconditional and conditional models (MA, EWMA, AR-GARCH, AR-GARCH with structural break dummies). The obtained results are very sensitive to the type of loss functions used, the chosen probability level of VaR, the period being turbulent or normal etc. When testing VaR forecasts in-sample Valentinyi-Endrész (2004) finds that the performance of various models depends on choice of confidence level. At 5% confidence level majority of the models provide adequate coverage. However, for 1% and 0.5% confidence level none of the tested models ensured VaR forecasts high enough to cover losses at those probabilities. When testing out-of-the-sample almost all the models fail according to the Christoffersen test, but at 5% none is rejected by the Kupiec test. At 99% confidence level only two

VaR models based on GARCH volatilities with structural breaks and the EWMA models are not rejected. Across various evaluation criterions simple moving average model with 500-day observation window seems to be the worst. VaR models with structural breaks and EWMA outperformed others in the sense that the number of hits stayed in a narrow band around the theoretical values.

Žiković (2005b) developed a semiparametric VaR model that uses EWMA volatility forecasting and tested it on Croatian VIN and CROBEX index and Slovenian SBI 20 index. All the tested stock indexes showed significant departure from normality, significant autocorrelation and presence of heteroskedasticity. The model performed far superiorly to historical simulation and BRW historical simulation but also failed to properly capture the dynamics of SBI 20 index at extreme confidence levels. Based on the performed tests on CROBEX and VIN index Žiković (2006b) concluded that historical simulation VaR models should not be used for high confidence level estimates (above 95%), especially VaR models based on shorter rolling windows. The obtained results show that although BRW VaR approach also has its flaws, especially when testing for temporal dependence in the tail events, it brings significant improvement to historical simulation with minimal additional computational effort.

Žiković, Bezić (2006) investigate the stock indexes of the EU member candidate states. CROBEX (Croatia), SOFIX (Bulgaria), BBETINRM (Romania) and XU100 (Turkey) index all show clear positive trend in a longer time period. With the exception of XU100 index all other analysed indexes exhibit asymmetry, leptokurtosis and based on performed tests of normality, it can be said with great certainty that these returns are not normally distributed. Employed tests show significant autocorrelation and ARCH effects in the squared returns of all the analysed indexes. These phenomena violate normality assumption, as well as the IID assumption that is a necessary requirement for the proper implementation of historical simulation. Results point to the conclusion that even though historical simulation provided correct unconditional coverage for tested indexes at most of the confidence levels, use of historical simulation (especially based on shorter observation periods) is not recommendable in these markets.

Besides the study of Hungarian stock index (BUX) by Valentinyi-Endrész (2004) in the VaR literature there are no quantitative research papers dealing with empirical VaR model comparison or volatility forecasting in the financial markets of transition countries besides my own.

6.2   Data and methodology

Data used in the analyses of performance of VaR models are the daily log returns from analysed indexes of transition countries. The returns are collected from Bloomberg web site for the period 01.01.2000 - 31.12.2005. Because of different working days in analysed countries the data set ranges from minimum of 1414 observations for Slovakian SKSM index to maximum of 1554 observations for Latvian RIGSE index. To secure the same out-of-the-sample VaR backtesting period for all of the tested indexes, the out-of-the-sample data sets are formed by taking out 500 of the latest observations from each index. The rest of the observations (ranging from 914 observations for SKSM index to 1054 observations for RIGSE index) are used as presample observations needed for VaR starting values and volatility model calibration.

Regarding the volatility modelling, the data shows that GARCH representation will be necessary to adequately capture the dynamics of data generating processes of analysed stock indexes. The dynamics of the data generating processes are complex because changes in the efficiency[44] of the market alter the long-run level and persistence of volatility. Furthermore, there is ample of empirical evidence on a positive relationship between trading volume and volatility. Thus, the rapid expansion of stock markets in transition countries might have contradictory impacts on volatility: supposing that some predictability (significant AR term) is present in the series, increasing efficiency tends to lower the level and persistence of volatility, but larger volume might push its level up. Volatility can be raised due to other reasons too, for example when news in the return series arrives more often and are of larger magnitude than usual (shift in the volatility of error term). The increasing integration of the local stock markets into international capital markets may only further amplify this effect.

The appropriate log-likelihood objective function needed for estimation of GARCH model parameters is obtained via maximum likelihood estimation. The log-likelihood objective is calculated in three steps:

1) Given the vector of current parameter values and the observed series, the log-likelihood function infers the process innovations (residuals) by inverse filtering. This inference operation solves for the current innovation:

$$\varepsilon_t = -\alpha_0 + r_t - \sum_{i=1}^{R}\alpha_i r_{t-i} - \sum_{j=1}^{M}\theta_j \varepsilon_{t-j}$$

This rearranged Equation 4.44 serves as a whitening filter, transforming a correlated process into uncorrelated white noise process.

2) The log-likelihood function then uses the inferred innovations to infer the corresponding conditional variances via recursive substitution into the model-dependent conditional variance equation.

3) Finally, the function uses the inferred innovations and conditional variances to evaluate the appropriate log-likelihood objective function.

---

[44] Efficiency is used in terms of speed of prices adjusting to new information ariving to the market.

Since conditional mean equation and conditional variance equation are recursive it is necessary to secure an adequate presample data set to initiate the inverse filtering.

To determine the basic statistical characteristics of daily returns of tested stock indexes summary statistics are calculated and a series of normality test is performed. All of the tests are performed over the entire observation period for every analysed index. The simplest test of normality is to analyse the third and fourth moment around the mean of the empirical distribution. Third moment around the mean, asymmetry, in the case of normal distribution should be zero (Šošić, Serdar, 1997, p. 71). Negative asymmetry means that the distribution is skewed to the left, which implies that there is a greater chance of experiencing negative returns, and vice versa. Fourth moment around the mean, kurtosis, in the case of normal distribution should be three (Šošić, Serdar, 1997, p. 76). Most of the statistical software packages modify the equation for kurtosis to equal zero for normal distribution, to ease the interpretation. Excess kurtosis higher than zero means that the distribution has fatter tails than normal distribution, meaning that more extreme events occur more frequently than it would be expected under normal distribution. More sophisticated tests for normality of distribution are Lilliefors test and Jarque-Bera test.

The Lilliefors test for goodness of fit to a normal distribution evaluates the hypothesis that variable X has a normal distribution with unspecified mean and variance, against alternative that variable X does not have a normal distribution. This test compares the empirical distribution of X with a normal distribution having the same mean and variance as X. If the result of hypothesis test is H = 1 it means that the hypothesis that X has a normal distribution should be rejected, if H = 0 the hypothesis should not be rejected at the 5% significance level. Lilliefors test is similar to the Kolmogorov-Smirnov test, but is better suited for evaluating empirical data because it adjusts for the fact that the parameters of the normal distribution are estimated from variable X rather than specified in advance.

The Jarque-Bera test for goodness-of-fit to a normal distribution evaluates the hypothesis that variable X has a normal distribution with unspecified mean and variance, against the alternative that variable X does not have a normal distribution. The test is based on the sample skewness and kurtosis of variable X. If the result of hypothesis test is H = 1 it means that the hypothesis that variable X has a normal distribution should be rejected, if H = 0 the hypothesis should not be rejected at the 5% significance level. The Jarque-Bera test determines whether the sample skewness and kurtosis are unusually different than their expected values, as measured by a chi-square statistic (Gujarati, 2003, p.148).

Jarque-Bera test of normality is calculated as (Gujarati, 2003, p.148):

$$JB = n\left[\frac{S^2}{6} + \frac{(K-3)^2}{24}\right]$$
(6.1)

n – number of observations in the sample
S – skewness of the sample
K – kurtosis of the sample

Under the null hypothesis of normality, Jarque-Bera statistic is distributed as a chi-square statistic with two degrees of freedom.

Returns on financial assets themselves are usually not dependent (correlated), otherwise traders could forecast daily returns. Returns squared are usually dependent, this meaning that volatility can be forecasted, but not the direction of the change of a variable. Calculating sample autocorrelation (ACF) and sample partial correlation function (PACF) at 5% significance level tests the independence of the data. Wide established approaches to detecting volatility clustering, which is autoregression in the squared returns, are the Ljung-Box Q-statistic and Engle's ARCH test. Ljung-Box Q-statistic is the lth autocorrelation of the *T*-squared returns, and calculates whether the size of the movement at time *t* has any useful information to predict the size of the movement at time *t+l*. Engle's hypothesis test for the presence of autoregressive conditional heteroskedasticity (ARCH) effects tests the null hypothesis that a time series of sample residuals consists of independently and identically distributed (IID) Gaussian disturbances, i.e., that no ARCH effects exist. Given sample residuals obtained from a curve fit (e.g., a regression model), Engle's ARCH test tests for the presence of Mth order ARCH effects by regressing the squared residuals on a constant and the lagged values of the previous *M* squared residuals. Under the null hypothesis, the asymptotic test statistic, $T(R^2)$, where *T* is the number of squared residuals included in the regression and R^2 is the sample multiple correlation coefficient, which is asymptotically chi-square distributed with *M* degrees of freedom.

The return data is tested for autocorrelation both in log returns as well as squared log returns. Autocorrelation in log returns is tested by ACF, PACF and mean adjusted Ljung-Box Q-statistic. Autocorrelation in squared log returns is tested by ACF, PACF, Ljung-Box Q-statistic and ARCH test. When autocorrelation is detected in the log returns the most parsimonious ARMA(p, q) model adequate to remove autocorrelation is fitted to the data. When autocorrelation is detected in the squared log returns the most parsimonious GARCH model is fitted to the ARMA filtered (if necessary) data to remove heteroskedasticity from the time series.

The log return series $r_t=100*ln(P_t/P_{t-1})$ is specified as an ARMA-GARCH process and is estimated by maximum likelihood estimation (MLE):

$$r_t = \alpha_0 + \sum_{i=1}^{p}\alpha_i r_{t-i} + \varepsilon_t + \sum_{i=1}^{q}\theta_i \varepsilon_{t-i}$$

$$\varepsilon_t = \eta_t \sqrt{\sigma_t^2}$$

$$\sigma_t^2 = \alpha_0 + \sum_{i=1}^{q} \alpha_i \varepsilon_{t-i}^2 + \sum_{i=1}^{p} \beta_i \sigma_{t-i}^2$$

where $\eta_t \sim IID\ N(0,1)$

After ARMA-GARCH filtering the obtained innovation series is scaled by GARCH conditional variance to obtain standardized innovations. If the employed ARMA-GARCH model successfully captures the dynamics of the data generating process, standardised innovations should be independently and identically distributed. Presumption of IID in standardised innovations is tested by ACF, PACF and Ljung-Box Q-statistic. If the tests do not discover autocorrelation in the standardized innovations employed ARMA can be considered adequate. Squared standardised innovations are tested for autocorrelation and ARCH effects through ACF, PACF, Ljung-Box Q-statistic and ARCH test. The most parsimonious GARCH model that passes the tests of autocorrelation and ARCH effects in the squared standardized innovations is chosen to describe the volatility dynamics of the return series.

In the following analysis VaR models based on historical simulation are calculated as quantiles of empirical distribution with an equally weighted moving observations window. Normal variance-covariance VaR is calculated as equally weighted moving average with observation window length of 250 returns (approximately 1 year). RiskMetrics model is calculated as described in the RiskMetrics Technical document (1996), with lambda set at 0.94. Similarly, EWMA Monte Carlo Model uses the same lambda value of 0.94 to calculate the variance estimation. Normal Monte Carlo uses 250-day equally weighted moving observations window. Both Monte Carlo models are calculated based on 5.000 simulations. BRW VaR is calculated as described by Boudoukh, Richardson, Whitelaw (1998), with the same suggested decay factors of 0.97 and 0.99. GARCH-RiskMetrics is a parametric approach to VaR similar to RiskMetrics model but uses GARCH volatility forecasting instead of EWMA volatility forecasting. HHS model developed earlier by the author is calculated as described in chapter 4.3.6, uses the same GARCH volatility forecasting as GARCH-RiskMetrics model, with unbounded observation window length and its quantiles are calculated via order statistics.

6.3   Characteristics of stock market indexes in transition countries

In the following section, statistical characteristics of the stock indexes from transition countries are analysed. The return series are tested for normality and presence of autocorrelation and heteroskedasticity. The most parsimonious ARMA-GARCH model is fitted to the return series to obtain independently and identically distributed standardised innovations. For transition economies such as those of European transition countries, a short history of market economy and active trading in the financial markets presents a significant problem in a serious and statistically significant analysis. Because of the short time series of returns of individual stocks as well as their highly variable liquidity it is practical to analyse the stock indexes of these countries.

6.3.1 Slovenia – SBI20 index

Trading on the Ljubljana Stock Exchange (LSE) started in 1989. The SBI20 index was launched in 1989 with the initial value of 1000 points.

The analysis of the SBI20 stock index is performed for the period 03.01.2000. – 31.12.2005. In this observation period the obtained sample from SBI20 index consists of 1462 daily index value observations. The evolution of index values and its returns is displayed in Figures 21, 22 and 23.

Figure 21 - Daily values of SBI20 index, period 03.01.2000 - 31.12.2005 (1462 observations)

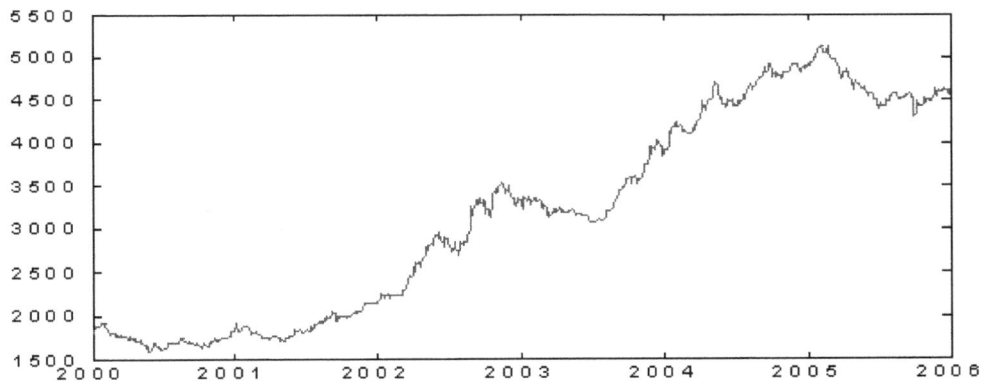

Figure 22 - Daily log returns of SBI20 index, period 03.01.2000 - 31.12.2005 (1461 observations)

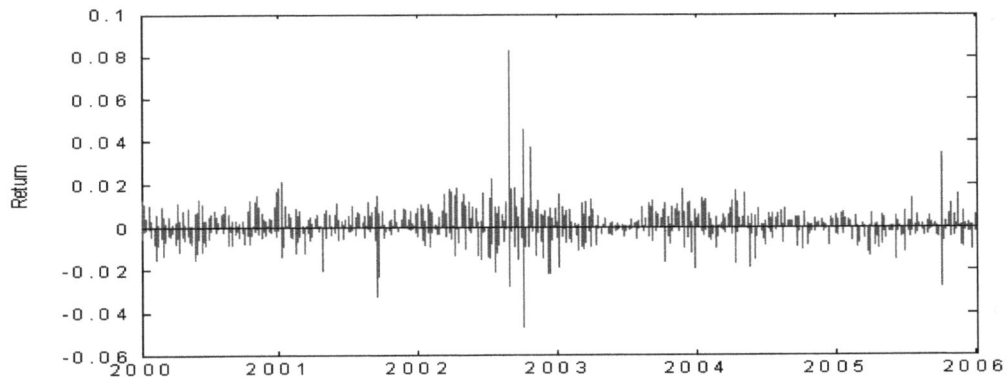

Figure 23 - Histogram of daily log returns of SBI20 index, period 03.01.2000 - 31.12.2005 (1461 observations)

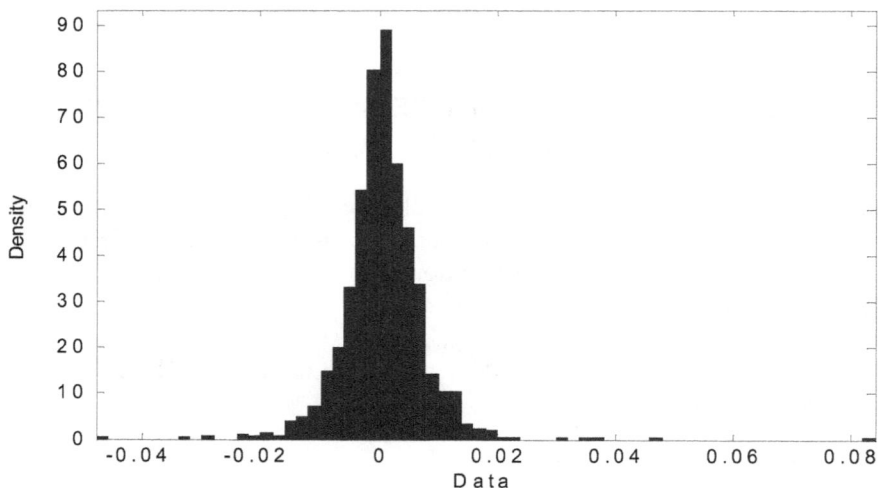

From figures 21, 22 and 23 it is visible that there is significant volatility clustering and presence of extreme positive and negative returns, which motivates a conditional volatility model that accounts for time varying volatility.

Basic descriptive statistics for SBI20 index in the period 03.1.2000 - 31.12.2005 are presented in table 7.

Table 7 - Basic statistics for SBI20 index daily log returns, period 03.01.2000 - 31.12.2005 (1461 observations)

Mean	0.000644
Median	0.0005
Minimum	-0.04767
Maximum	0.083109
Standard deviation	0.006888
Skewness	1.1188
Kurtosis	21.647

Mean and median of daily returns significantly differ, which is in breach of normality assumption. Both mean and median differ from zero and show a significant positive trend. Skewness and excess kurtosis of the index are also significantly different from zero assumed under normality. In the observed period SBI20 index experienced extreme daily returns. The highest daily gain in the analysed period was 8,31%, while the highest daily loss amounted to − 4,77%. Asymmetry is significantly positive (1,1188) meaning that the distribution slopes to the right and positive returns are expected to occur more frequently than negative ones. Excess kurtosis of 21,647 indicates that the empirical probability distribution of SBI20 index has significantly fatter tails than assumed under normal distribution. The high value of kurtosis for this index indicates to the investors investing on Slovenian stock exchange that they can expect high, both positive and negative returns on their investments. Combining the third and fourth moment of the SBI20 index with the mean and standard deviation, it can be concluded that in the observed period, positive returns were more frequent than negative returns, and the magnitude of the positive returns was significantly higher than the magnitude of loses. These characteristics of SBI20 index resulted in a strong positive trend and continually increasing index values. To determine if the daily returns of SBI20 index are normally distributed, normality of empirical distribution is tested by Jarque-Bera test and Lilliefors test. Normality tests for the SBI20 index are presented in table 8.

Table 8 - Normality tests for SBI20 index daily log returns, period 03.01.2000 - 31.12.2005 (1461 observations)

Jarque-Bera test	21,404
(p value)	0
Lilliefors test	0.077501
(p value)	0

Both normality tests show that the hypothesis of normality of returns for SBI20 index, for the entire analysed period, should be rejected at 5% significance level. Probability values of distribution of returns being normal, according to both normality tests are zero, strongly indicating that there is no possibility that the returns on this index are normally distributed. The distribution of SBI20 index returns is leptokurtotic and not symmetrical i.e. it skews to the right, as can be seen from figures 23 and 24, as well as from table 9.

Figure 24 - Probability plot for SBI20 index daily log returns, period 03.01.2000 - 31.12.2005 (1461 observations)

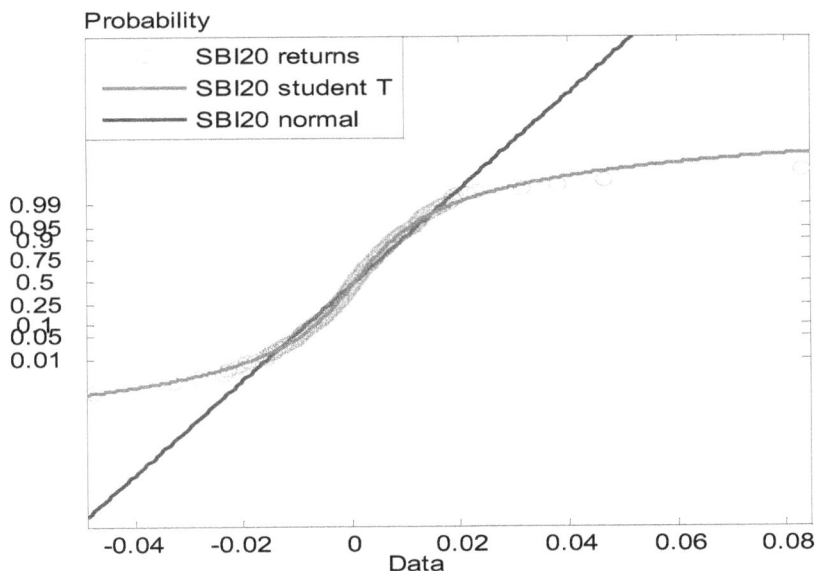

Table 9 - Parameters of fitted Normal and Students' T distribution to SBI20 index daily log returns, period 03.01.2000 - 31.12.2005 (1461 observations)

Distribution: Normal			Distribution: t location-scale			
Log likelihood: 4780.57			Log likelihood: 4942.64			
Mean: 0.00066644			Mean: 0.000637			
Variance: 4.82E-05			Variance: 4.70E-05			
Parameter	Estimate	Std. Err.	Parameter	Estimate	Std. Err.	
mu	0.00066644	0.0001892	mu	0.000637	0.00015	
sigma	0.0069414	0.00013386	sigma	0.004607	0.000165	
			df	3.64915	0.400123	
Estimated covariance of parameter estimates:			Estimated covariance of parameter estimates:			
	mu	sigma		mu	sigma	df
mu	3.58E-08	1.05E-24	mu	2.25E-08	3.68E-10	9.67E-07
sigma	1.05E-24	1.79E-08	sigma	3.68E-10	2.71E-08	4.49E-05
			df	9.67E-07	4.49E-05	0.160099

Figure 24 and table 9 show that the true empirical distribution of SBI20 index daily returns is far better approximated by a Student's t distribution with 3,65 degrees of freedom, than it is by normal distribution.

Since the assumption of IID returns underlies the logic behind most of the VaR models it is necessary to test whether returns of the analysed time series are indeed IID. First, the presence of autocorrelation in SBI20 daily log returns is tested by examining its sample autocorrelation and sample partial correlation function (Figure 25), and calculating Ljung-Box Q-statistic for mean adjusted SBI20 returns (Table 10).

Figure 25 - Sample autocorrelation and sample partial correlation function of SBI20 index daily log returns, period 03.01.2000 - 02.12.2003 (961 observations)

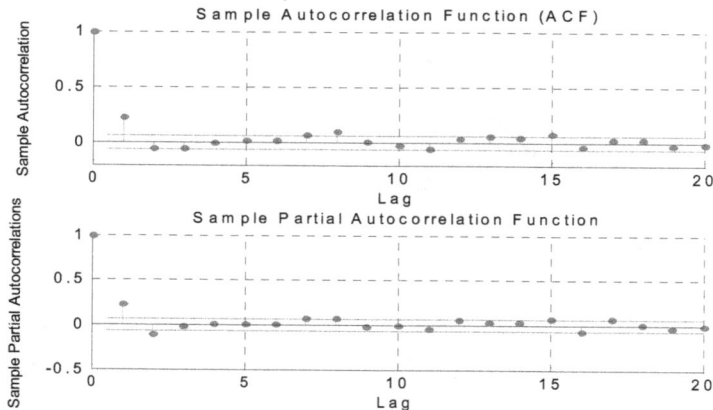

Table 10 - Ljung-Box-Pierce Q-test for mean adjusted SBI20 index daily log returns, period 03.01.2000 - 02.12.2003 (961 observations)

Period (days)	H	p-value	Statistic	Critical value
5	1	0	102.7	11.07
10	1	0	124.94	18.307
15	1	0	145.81	24.996
20	1	0	150.62	31.41

Sample autocorrelation, sample partial correlation function and Ljung-Box Q-statistic found the presence of autocorrelation in the SBI20 daily log returns meaning that the Slovenian stock market is not very efficient since the direction of the market can be predicted. To extract the autocorrelation from the data it will be necessary to use an ARMA (p, q) model. After the presence of autocorrelation in the daily log returns has been investigated it is necessary to test the squared log returns for presence of autocorrelation i.e. heteroskedasticity. Presence of heteroskedasticity in SBI20 returns is tested by examining its sample autocorrelation and sample partial correlation function of squared returns (Figure 26), calculating Ljung-Box Q-statistic for mean adjusted squared SBI20 returns (Table 11) and ARCH test for mean adjusted SBI20 returns (Table 12).

Figure 26 - Sample autocorrelation and sample partial correlation function of squared SBI20 index daily log returns, period 03.01.2000 - 02.12.2003 (961 observations)

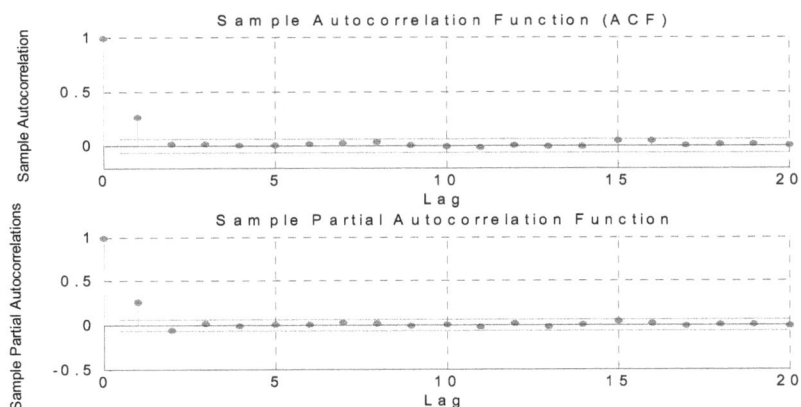

Table 11 - Ljung-Box-Pierce Q-test for mean adjusted squared SBI20 index daily log returns, period 03.01.2000 - 02.12.2003 (961 observations)

Period (days)	H	p-value	Statistic	Critical value
5	1	0	114.24	11.07
10	1	0	119.16	18.307
15	1	0	123.3	24.996
20	1	0	129.19	31.41

Table 12 - ARCH test for mean adjusted SBI20 index daily log returns, period 03.01.2000 - 02.12.2003 (961 observations)

Period (days)	H	p-value	Statistic	Critical value
5	1	0	115.37	11.07
10	1	0	117	18.307
15	1	0	120.19	24.996
20	1	0	121.36	31.41

Sample autocorrelation and sample partial correlation function of squared returns, as well as the Ljung-Box Q-statistic and Engle's ARCH test confirm that there is significant autocorrelation and ARCH effects present in SBI20 daily log returns i.e. volatility tends to cluster together (periods of low volatility are followed by further periods of low volatility and vice versa), meaning that the returns on SBI20 index are not IID. The results are that much more indicative when considering that the hypothesis of IID was rejected for all the tested time lags (5, 10, 15 and 20 days). Since the employed tests discovered significant autocorrelation and heteroskedasticity in the SBI20 daily returns it is necessary to model the data in order to obtain independently and identically distributed returns. Because autocorrelation has been detected in both returns and squared returns, SBI20 index returns will be modelled as an ARMA-GARCH process, in order to deal with both types of dependence. Estimated ARMA-GARCH parameters for SBI20 index are given in table 13.

Table 13 - Estimated ARMA-GARCH parameters for SBI20 index daily log returns, period 03.01.2000 - 02.12.2003 (961 observations)

Mean: ARMA(2,0)
Variance: GARCH(1,1)

Conditional Probability Distribution: Gaussian

Parameter	Value	Standard error	T statistic
C	5.14E-04	0.000171	3.0146
AR(1)	4.26E-01	0.034087	12.4995
AR(2)	-1.41E-01	0.0302	-4.6581
K	6.69E-06	1.25E-06	5.3528
GARCH(1)	0.50069	0.049385	10.1385
ARCH(1)	0.39003	0.037382	10.4337

All of the estimated parameters are statistically significant according to their t statistics. The obtained model is a normally distributed AR(2)-GARCH(1,1) model:

$$r_t = 0.000514 + 0.426r_{t-1} - 0.141r_{t-2} + \varepsilon_t$$

$$\sigma_t^2 = 6.69E - 06 + 0.39003\varepsilon_{t-1}^2 + 0.50069\sigma_{t-1}^2$$

The conditional volatility model for SBI20 index is far from being integrated and places unusually little importance on past conditional volatility, but places a lot of weight on previous period's residual. The plot of fitted AR-GARCH model innovations, conditional standard deviations and observed SBI20 index daily log returns are given in figure 27.

Figure 27 - Plot of fitted AR-GARCH model innovations, conditional standard deviations and observed SBI20 index daily log returns, period 03.01.2000 - 02.12.2003

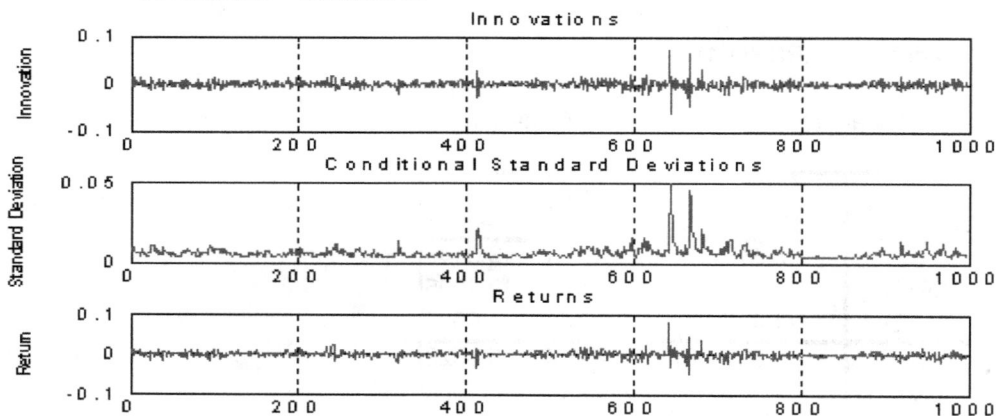

If the fitted AR-GARCH model is appropriate for describing the dynamics of underlying data generating process the standardised innovation from such AR-GARCH model should be independently and identically distributed (Figure 28). The adequacy of fitted AR-GARCH model can be statistically tested in the same manner as returns and squared returns.

Figure 28 - Standardised innovations from fitted AR-GARCH model for SBI20 index daily log returns, period 03.01.2000 - 02.12.2003

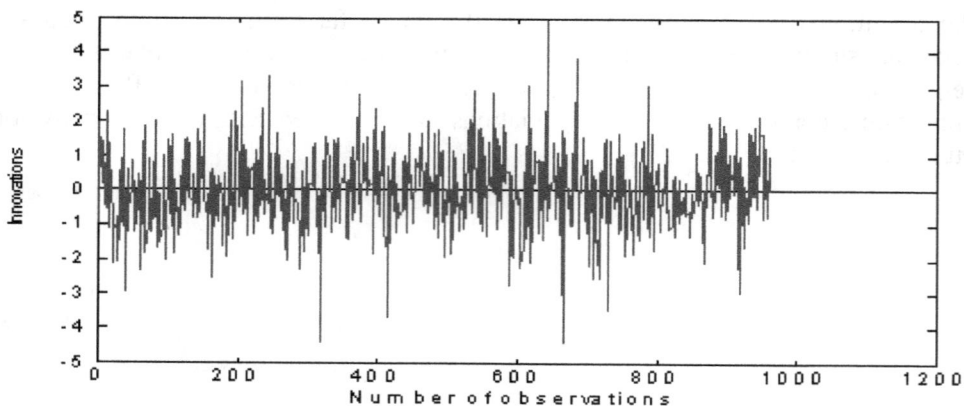

Sample autocorrelation, sample partial correlation function and Ljung-Box Q-statistic of standardised innovation detect no presence of autocorrelation in the standardised innovations from fitted AR-GARCH model, meaning that the conditional mean model (AR(2)) successfully captured the autocorrelation present in SBI20 returns (Figure 29, Table 14).

Figure 29 - Sample autocorrelation and sample partial correlation function of standardized innovations from SBI20 index daily log returns, period 03.01.2000 - 02.12.2003

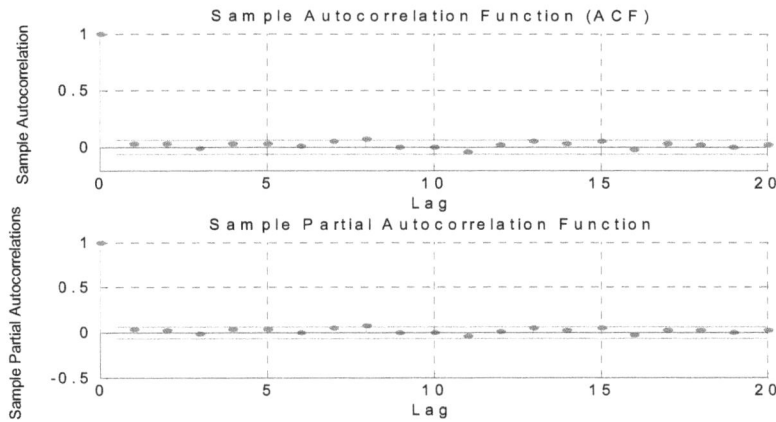

Table 14 - Ljung-Box-Pierce Q-test for standardised innovations from SBI20 index daily log returns, period 03.01.2000 - 02.12.2003

Period (days)	H	p-value	Statistic	Critical value
5	0	0.524	4.1783	11.07
10	0	0.2764	12.1305	18.307
15	0	0.1084	21.9763	24.996
20	0	0.2309	24.2667	31.41

Sample autocorrelation and sample partial correlation function, Ljung-Box Q-statistic of squared standardised innovation and ARCH test of standardised innovations detect no presence of autocorrelation in the squared standardised innovations from fitted AR-GARCH model. This indicates that the conditional variance model (GARCH(1,1)) successfully captured the heteroskedasticity present in SBI20 returns (Figure 30, Tables 15, 16).

Figure 30 - Sample autocorrelation and sample partial correlation function of squared standardized innovations from SBI20 index daily log returns, period 03.01.2000 - 02.12.2003

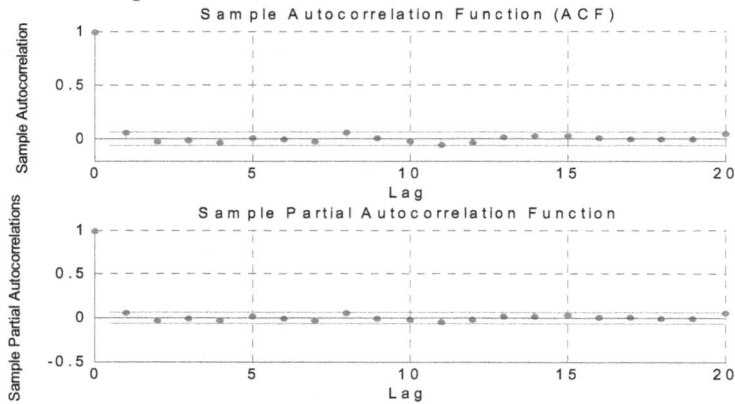

Table 15 - Ljung-Box-Pierce Q-test for squared standardised innovations from SBI20 index daily log returns, period 03.01.2000 - 02.12.2003

Period (days)	H	p-value	Statistic	Critical value
5	0	0.3754	5.3434	11.07
10	0	0.439	10.0165	18.307
15	0	0.4149	15.5158	24.996
20	0	0.5279	18.9068	31.41

Table 16 - ARCH test for standardised innovations from SBI20 index daily log returns, period 03.01.2000 - 02.12.2003

Period (days)	H	p-value	Statistic	Critical value
5	0	0.3354	5.7108	11.07
10	0	0.406	10.4012	18.307
15	0	0.4614	14.8614	24.996
20	0	0.5486	18.5899	31.41

Findings of the performed tests imply that the fitted AR(2)-GARCH(1,1) model adequately describes the dynamics of SBI20 index daily returns.

6.3.2 Hungary – BUX index

Trading on the Budapest Stock Exchange (BSE) started in 1990. The BUX index was launched in 1991 with the initial value of 1000 points.

The analysis of the BUX stock index is performed for the period 04.01.2000. – 31.12.2005. In this observation period the obtained sample from BUX index consists of 1502 daily index value observations. The evolution of index values and returns is displayed in Figures 31, 32 and 33.

Figure 231 - Daily values of BUX index, period 04.01.2000 - 31.12.2005 (1502 observations)

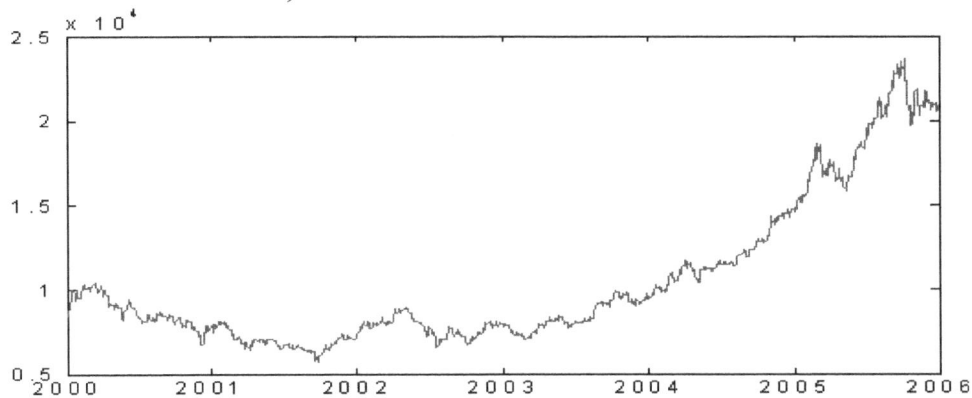

Figure 32 - Daily log returns of BUX index, period 04.01.2000 - 31.12.2005 (1501 observations)

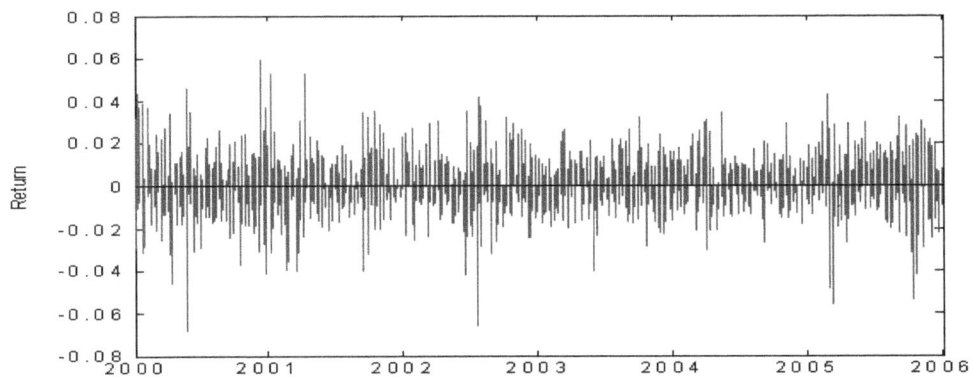

Figure 33 - Histogram of daily log returns of BUX index, period 04.01.2000 - 31.12.2005 (1501 observations)

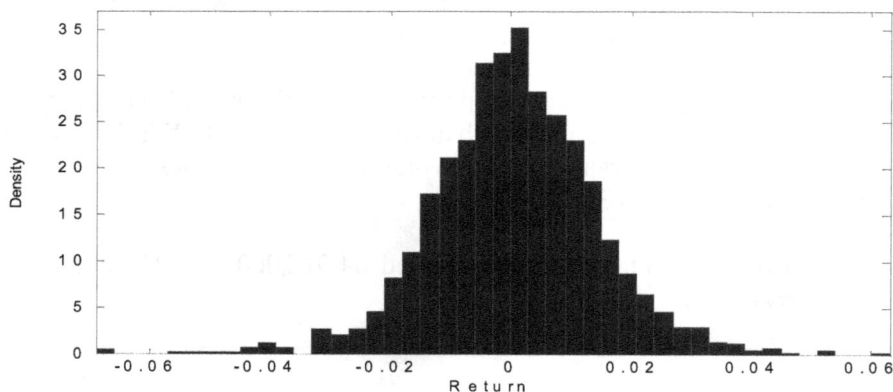

From figures 31, 32 and 33 it is visible that there is significant volatility clustering and presence of extreme positive and negative returns, which motivates a conditional volatility model that accounts for time varying volatility. Basic descriptive statistics for BUX index in the period 04.01.2000 - 31.12.2005 are presented in table 17.

Table 17 - Basic statistics for BUX index daily log returns, period 04.01.2000 - 31.12.2005 (1501 observations)

Mean	0.000579
Median	0.00051
Minimum	-0.06874
Maximum	0.060043
Standard deviation	0.013921
Skewness	-0.11694
Kurtosis	4.6873

Mean and median of daily returns are very similar and show a significant positive trend. Skewness and excess kurtosis are different from zero. In the observed period BUX index experienced extreme daily returns. The highest daily gain in the analysed period was 6%, while the highest daily loss amounted to – 6,87%. Asymmetry is slightly negative (-0,1169) meaning that the distribution slopes slightly to the left and negative returns are expected to occur slightly more frequently than positive. Excess kurtosis of 4,687 indicates that the empirical probability distribution of BUX index has fatter tails than assumed under normal distribution. Combining the third and fourth moment of the BUX index with the mean and standard deviation, it can be concluded that although in the entire observation period, negative returns were more frequent than positive returns, the magnitude of the positive returns was significantly higher than the magnitude of loses, resulting in a strong positive trend for BUX index. These characteristics of

BUX index resulted in a strong positive trend and continually increasing index values. To determine if the daily returns of BUX index are normally distributed, normality of empirical distribution is tested by Jarque-Bera test and Lilliefors test. Normality tests for the BUX index are presented in table 18.

Table 18 - Normality tests for BUX index daily log returns, period 04.01.2000 - 31.12.2005 (1501 observations)

Jarque-Bera test	180.16
(p value)	0
Lilliefors test	0.031092
(p value)	0

Both normality tests show that the hypothesis of normality of returns for BUX index, for the entire analysed period, should be rejected at 5% significance level. Probability values of distribution of returns being normal, according to both normality tests are zero, strongly indicating that there is no possibility that the returns on this index are normally distributed. The distribution of BUX index returns is leptokurtotic and not symmetrical i.e. it skews to the left, as can be seen from figures 33 and 34, and from table 19.

Figure 34 - Probability plot for BUX index daily log returns, period 04.01.2000 - 31.12.2005. (1501 observations)

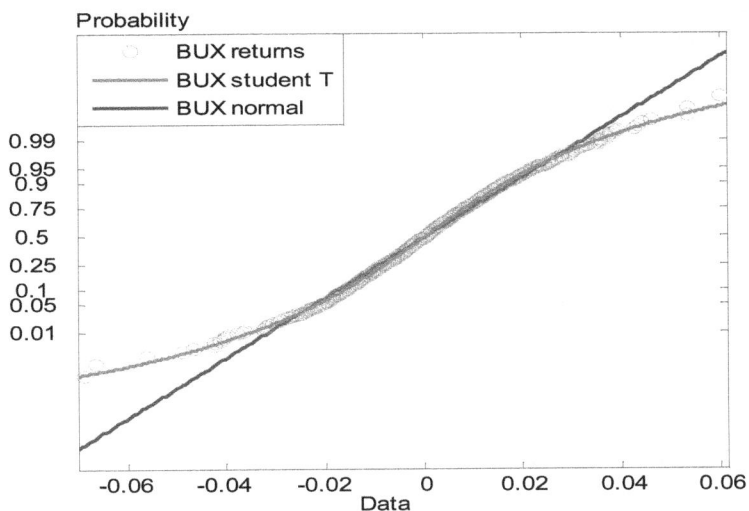

Table 19 - Parameters of fitted Normal and Students' T distribution to BUX index daily log returns, period 04.01.2000 - 31.12.2005. (1501 observations)

Distribution:	Normal		Distribution:	t location-scale	
Log likelihood:	3968.66		Log likelihood:	4004.15	
Mean:	0.000598		Mean:	0.000553	
Variance:	0.000189		Variance:	0.000191	

Parameter	Estimate	Std. Err.	Parameter	Estimate	Std. Err.
mu	0.000598	0.00037	mu	0.000553	0.000344
sigma	0.013758	0.000262	sigma	0.011299	0.000364
			df	6.06188	0.95123

Estimated covariance of parameter estimates:

	mu	sigma			mu	sigma	df
mu	1.37E-07	-1.14E-23		mu	1.18E-07	3.32E-09	1.01E-05
sigma	-1.14E-23	6.85E-08		sigma	3.32E-09	1.32E-07	0.000239
				df	1.01E-05	0.000239	0.904839

Figure 34 and table 19 show that the true empirical distribution of BUX index daily returns is somewhat better approximated by a Student's t distribution with 6,06 degrees of freedom, than it is by normal distribution, although the difference in log-likelihoods of two distributions is not large.

Presence of autocorrelation in BUX daily log returns is tested by examining its sample autocorrelation and sample partial correlation function (Figure 35), and calculating Ljung-Box Q-statistic for mean adjusted BUX returns (Table 20).

Figure 35 - Sample autocorrelation and sample partial correlation function of BUX index daily log returns, period 04.01.2000 - 12.01.2004 (1001 observations)

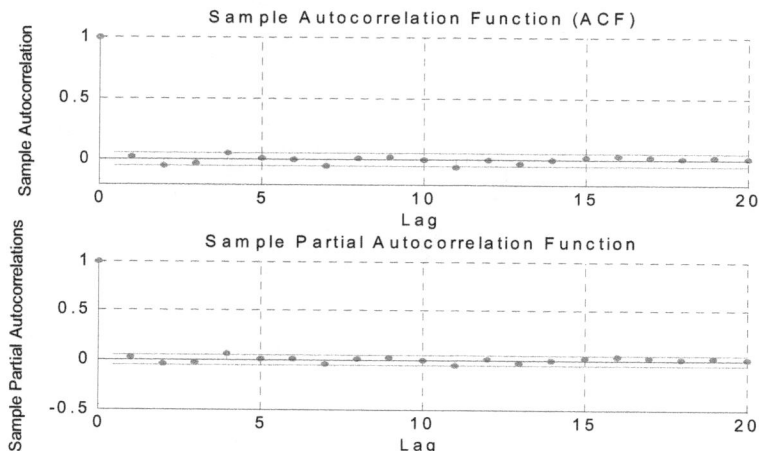

Table 20 - Ljung-Box-Pierce Q-test for mean adjusted BUX index daily log returns, period 04.01.2000 - 12.01.2004 (1001 observations)

Period (days)	H	p-value	Statistic	Critical value
5	0	0.05606	10.774	11.07
10	0	0.095619	16.143	18.307
15	0	0.068003	23.832	24.996
20	0	0.11443	27.792	31.41

As expected, sample autocorrelation, sample partial correlation function and Ljung-Box Q-statistic found no evidence of autocorrelation in the BUX daily log returns. Since there is no autocorrelation in the BUX index returns there is no need to fit a conditional mean model to the data.

Presence of heteroskedasticity in BUX returns is tested by examining its sample autocorrelation and sample partial correlation function of squared returns (Figure 36), calculating Ljung-Box Q-statistic for mean adjusted squared BUX returns (Table 21) and ARCH test for mean adjusted BUX returns (Table 22).

Figure 36 - Sample autocorrelation and sample partial correlation function of squared BUX index daily log returns, period 04.01.2000 - 12.01.2004 (1001 observations)

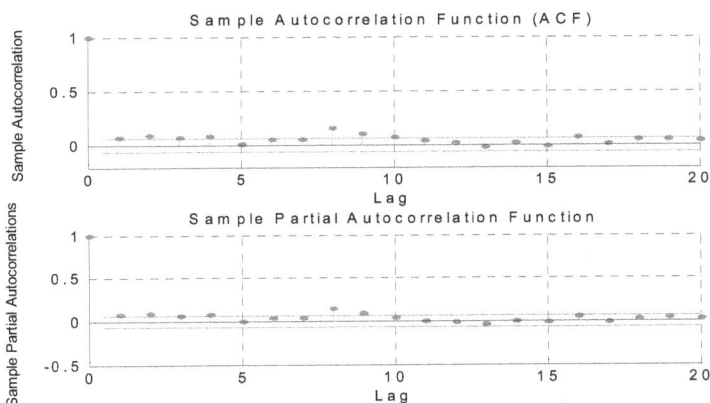

Table 21 - Ljung-Box-Pierce Q-test for mean adjusted squared BUX index daily log returns, period 04.01.2000 - 12.01.2004 (1001 observations)

Period (days)	H	p-value	Statistic	Critical value
5	1	1.31E-10	54.997	11.07
10	1	0	131.75	18.307
15	1	0	142.91	24.996
20	1	0	165.01	31.41

Table 22 - ARCH test for mean adjusted BUX index daily log returns, period
04.01.2000 - 12.01.2004 (1001 observations)

Period (days)	H	p-value	Statistic	Critical value
5	1	6.91E-08	41.659	11.07
10	1	3.23E-13	80.979	18.307
15	1	4.67E-12	86.383	24.996
20	1	1.94E-10	87.599	31.41

Sample autocorrelation and sample partial correlation function of squared returns, as well as the Ljung-Box Q-statistic and Engle's ARCH test confirm that there is significant autocorrelation and ARCH effects present in BUX daily log returns, meaning that the returns on BUX index are not IID. The results are that much more indicative when considering that the hypothesis of IID was rejected for all the tested time lags (5, 10, 15 and 20 days).

Since the employed tests discovered significant heteroskedasticity in the BUX daily returns it is necessary to model the data in order to obtain independently and identically distributed returns. Because autocorrelation has been detected only in squared returns, BUX index returns will be modelled as a simple GARCH process, without having to model the conditional mean. Estimated GARCH parameters for BUX index are given in table 23.

Table 23 - Estimated GARCH parameters for BUX index daily log returns, period
04.01.2000 - 12.01.2004 (1001 observations)

Mean: ARMA(0,0)
Variance: GARCH(1,1)

Conditional Probability Distribution: Gaussian

Parameter	Value	Standard error	T statistic
C	9.89E-05	0.000438	0.2259
K	8.59E-06	2.86E-06	3.0081
GARCH(1)	0.89067	0.022978	38.7618
ARCH(1)	0.066215	0.014394	4.6001

According to their t statistics all of the estimated parameters are statistically significant, except the mean drift that is statistically insignificant and will be assumed to equal zero. The obtained model is a normally distributed GARCH(1,1) model:

$$\sigma_t^2 = 8.59E - 06 + 0.0662153\varepsilon_{t-1}^2 + 0.890679\sigma_{t-1}^2$$

The plot of fitted GARCH model innovations, conditional standard deviations and observed BUX index daily log returns are given in figure 37.

Figure 37 - Plot of fitted ARMA-GARCH model innovations, conditional standard deviations and observed BUX index daily log returns, period 04.01.2000 - 12.01.2004

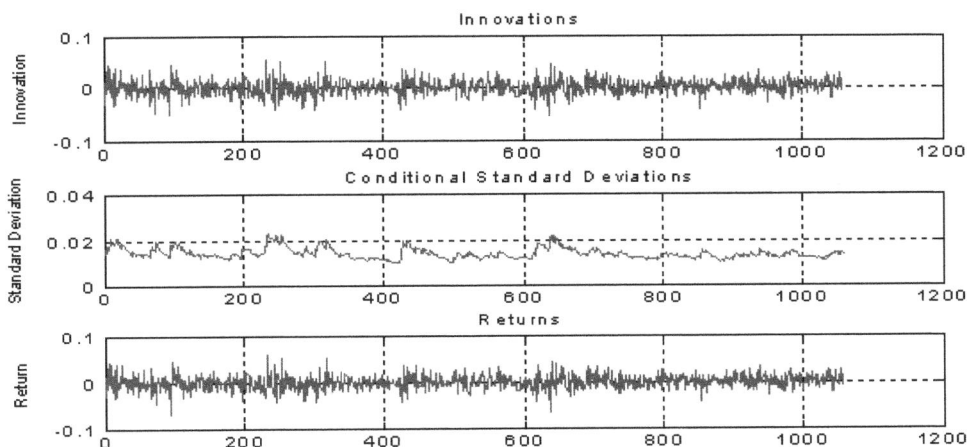

If the fitted GARCH model is appropriate for describing the dynamics of underlying data generating process the standardised innovation from such GARCH model should be independently and identically distributed (Figure 38). The adequacy of fitted GARCH model is tested in the same manner as returns and squared returns.

Figure 38 - Standardised innovations from fitted ARMA-GARCH model for BUX index daily log returns, period 04.01.2000 - 12.01.2004

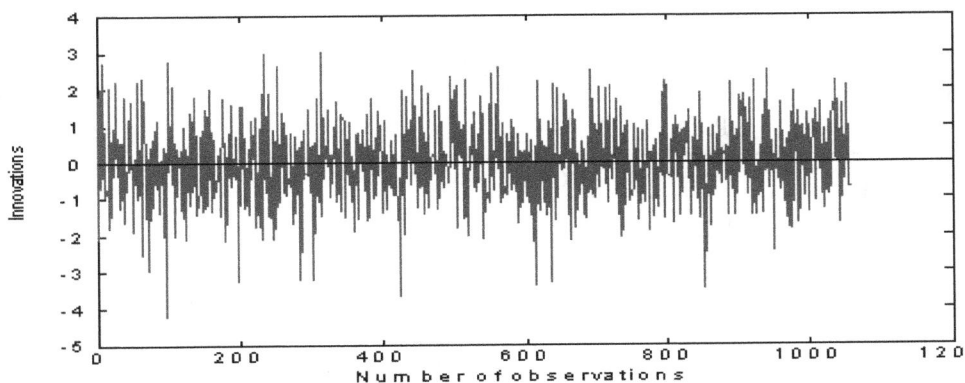

Sample autocorrelation, sample partial correlation function, Ljung-Box Q-statistic of squared standardised innovation and ARCH test of standardised innovations detect no presence of autocorrelation in the squared standardised innovations from fitted

GARCH model. This indicates that the conditional variance model (GARCH(1,1)) successfully captured the heteroskedasticity present in BUX returns (Figure 39, Tables 24, 25).

Figure 39 - Sample autocorrelation and sample partial correlation function of squared standardized innovations from BUX index daily log returns, period 04.01.2000 - 12.01.2004

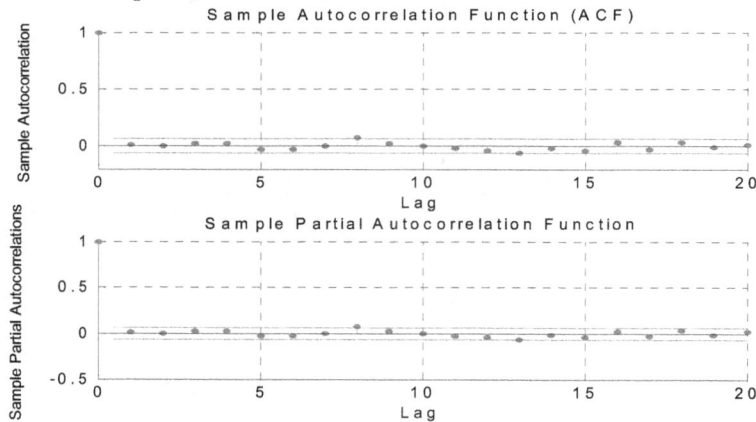

Table 24 - Ljung-Box-Pierce Q-test for squared standardised innovations from BUX index daily log returns, period 04.01.2000 - 12.01.2004

Period (days)	H	p-value	Statistic	Critical value
5	0	0.83429	2.106	11.07
10	0	0.42206	10.212	18.307
15	0	0.22556	18.744	24.996
20	0	0.32226	22.342	31.41

Table 25 - ARCH test for standardised innovations from BUX index daily log returns, period 04.01.2000 - 12.01.2004

Period (days)	H	p-value	Statistic	Critical value
5	0	0.84798	2.0084	11.07
10	0	0.43952	10.011	18.307
15	0	0.22147	18.832	24.996
20	0	0.37595	21.365	31.41

Findings of the performed tests imply that the fitted GARCH(1,1) model adequately describes the dynamics of BUX index daily returns.

6.3.3 Poland – WIG20 index

Trading on the Warsaw Stock Exchange (WSE) started in 1991. The WIG20 index was launched in 1991 with the initial value of 1000 points.

The analysis of the WIG20 stock index is performed for the period 03.01.2000 – 31.12.2005. In this observation period the obtained sample from WIG20 index consists of 1506 daily index value observations. The evolution of index values and returns is displayed in Figures 40, 41 and 42.

Figure 40 - Daily values of WIG20 index, period 03.01.2000 - 31.12.2005 (1506 observations)

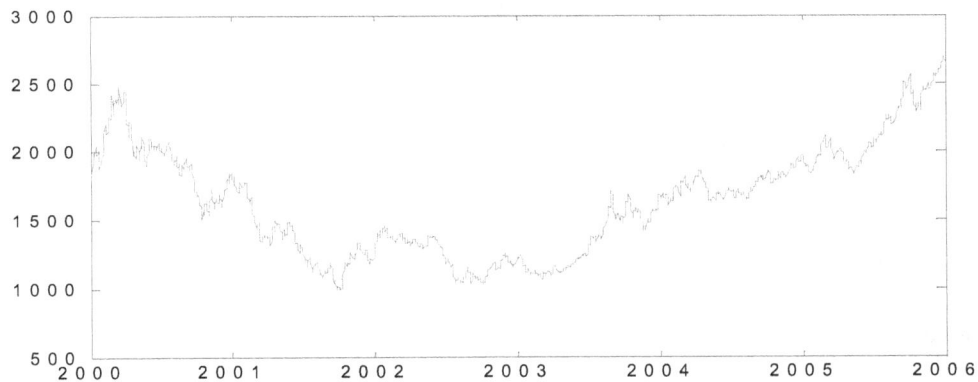

Figure 41 - Daily log returns of WIG20 index, period 03.01.2000 - 31.12.2005 (1505 observations)

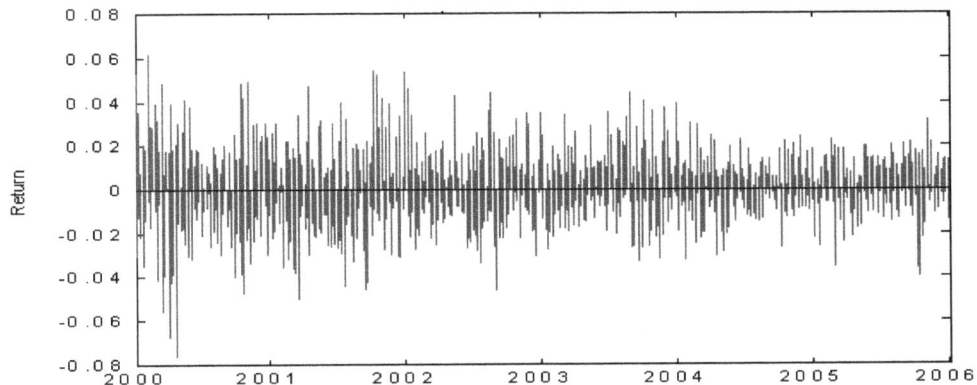

Figure 42 - Histogram of daily log returns of WIG20 index, period 03.01.2000 -
31.12.2005 (1505 observations)

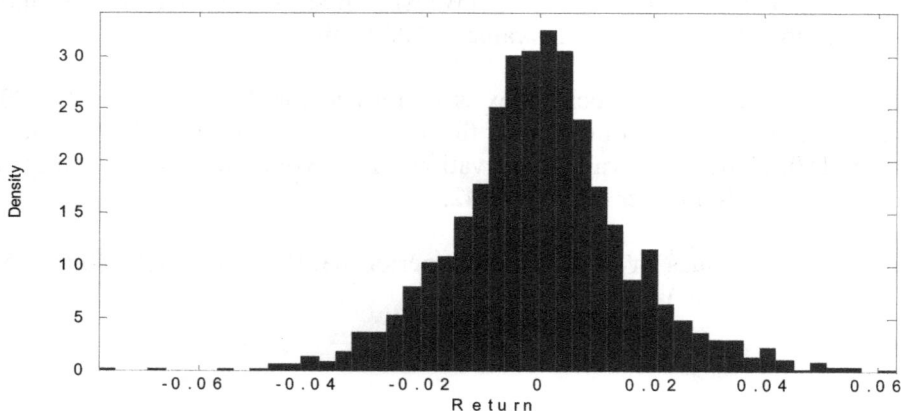

From figures 40, 41 and 42 it is visible that there is significant volatility clustering
and presence of extreme positive and negative returns, which motivates a
conditional volatility model that accounts for time varying volatility. Basic
descriptive statistics for WIG20 index in the period 03.01.2000 - 31.12.2005 are
presented in table 26.

Table 26 - Basic statistics for WIG20 index daily log returns, period 03.01.2000 -
31.12.2005 (1505 observations)

Mean	0.000239
Median	0.00019
Minimum	-0.07706
Maximum	0.062461
Standard deviation	0.01561
Skewness	0.069375
Kurtosis	4.4498

Mean and median of daily returns are similar and close to zero, which is the usual
simplifying assumption in risk management. Excess kurtosis of WIG20 index is
significantly different from zero, but skewness is very close to being zero, meaning
that the empirical distribution of WIG20 index is almost perfectly symmetrical.
These values are very similar to the values obtained for Hungarian BUX index. In
the observed period WIG20 index experienced extreme daily returns, which are
again very similar to the ones from BUX index. The highest daily gain in the
analysed period was 6,25%, while the highest daily loss amounted to – 7,7%.
Asymmetry is very close to zero so it can be assumed that expectance of occurrence
of positive and negative returns is equal. Excess kurtosis of 4,45, which is almost
equal to BUX index indicates that the empirical probability distribution of WIG20
index has fatter tails than assumed under normal distribution.

By observing the graphical representation of evolution of WIG20 index daily values (Figure 40) and knowing the first four moments of WIG20 index, it can be concluded that in the long run WIG20 index did not experience a strong trend of any direction but after a drift that occurred during the observation period, returned to its starting values. The fact that the frequency of occurrence of positive and negative returns was the same, mean and median are close to zero and kurtosis of the index being higher than normal can explain the particular shape of WIG20 index values.

To determine if the daily returns of WIG20 index are normally distributed, normality of empirical distribution is tested by Jarque-Bera test and Lilliefors test. Normality tests for the WIG20 index are presented in table 27.

Table 27 - Normality tests for WIG20 index daily log returns, period 03.01.2000 - 31.12.2005 (1505 observations)

Jarque-Bera test	131.94
(p value)	0
Lilliefors test	0.053572
(p value)	0

Both normality tests show that the hypothesis of normality of returns for WIG20 index, for the entire analysed period, should be rejected at 5% significance level. Probability values of distribution of returns being normal, according to both normality tests are zero, strongly indicating that there is no possibility that the returns on this index are normally distributed. The distribution of WIG20 index returns is leptokurtotic but symmetrical, as can be seen from figures 42 and 43, and from table 28.

Figure 43 - Probability plot for WIG20 index daily log returns, period 03.01.2000 - 31.12.2005 (1505 observations)

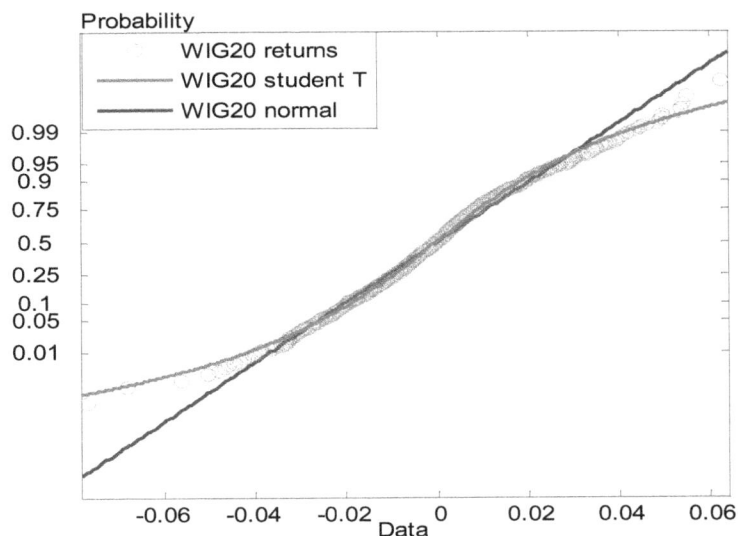

Table 28 - Parameters of fitted Normal and Students' T distribution to WIG20 index daily log returns, period 03.01.2000 - 31.12.2005 (1505 observations)

Distribution: Normal			Distribution: t location-scale			
Log likelihood: 3780.36			Log likelihood: 3812.35			
Mean: 0.000101			Mean: -0.00015			
Variance: 2.53E-04			Variance: 2.62E-04			
Parameter	Estimate	Std. Err.	Parameter	Estimate	Std. Err.	
mu	0.000101	0.000427	mu	-0.00015	0.000393	
sigma	0.015919	0.000302	sigma	0.012781	0.000459	
			df	5.30544	0.842059	
Estimated covariance of parameter estimates:			Estimated covariance of parameter estimates:			
	mu	sigma		mu	sigma	df
mu	1.82E-07	-1.36E-24	mu	1.55E-07	8.30E-09	1.70E-05
sigma	-1.36E-24	9.13E-08	sigma	8.30E-09	2.11E-07	2.88E-04
			df	1.70E-05	2.88E-04	0.709064

Figure 43 and table 28 show that the true empirical distribution of WIG20 index daily returnsis somewhat better approximated by a Student's t distribution with 5,31 degrees of freedom, than it is by normal distribution, although the difference in log-likelihoods of two distributions is not large.

Presence of autocorrelation in WIG20 daily log returns is tested by examining its sample autocorrelation, sample partial correlation function (Figure 44) and calculating Ljung-Box Q-statistic for mean adjusted WIG20 returns (Table 29).

Figure 44 - Sample autocorrelation and sample partial correlation function of WIG20 index daily log returns, period 03.01.2000 - 08.01.2004 (1005 observations)

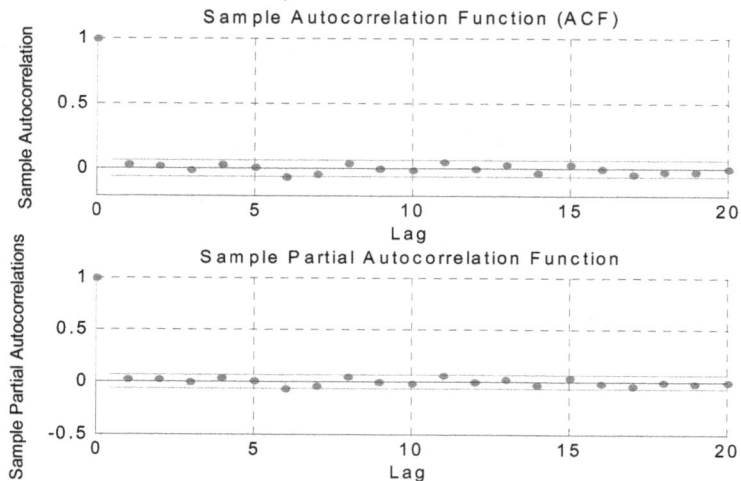

Table 29 - Ljung-Box-Pierce Q-test for mean adjusted WIG20 index daily log returns, period 03.01.2000 - 08.01.2004 (1005 observations)

Period (days)	H	p-value	Statistic	Critical value
5	0	0.45948	4.6545	11.07
10	0	0.29123	11.908	18.307
15	0	0.17114	20.021	24.996
20	0	0.26554	23.486	31.41

As expected, sample autocorrelation, sample partial correlation function and Ljung-Box Q-statistic found no evidence of autocorrelation in the WIG20 daily log returns. Since there is no autocorrelation in the WIG20 index returns there is no need to fit a conditional mean model to the data.

Presence of heteroskedasticity in WIG20 returns is tested by examining its sample autocorrelation, sample partial correlation function of squared returns (Figure 45), calculating Ljung-Box Q-statistic for mean adjusted squared WIG20 returns (Table 30) and ARCH test for mean adjusted WIG20 returns (Table 31).

Figure 45 - Sample autocorrelation and sample partial correlation function of squared WIG20 index daily log returns, period 03.01.2000 - 08.01.2004 (1005 observations)

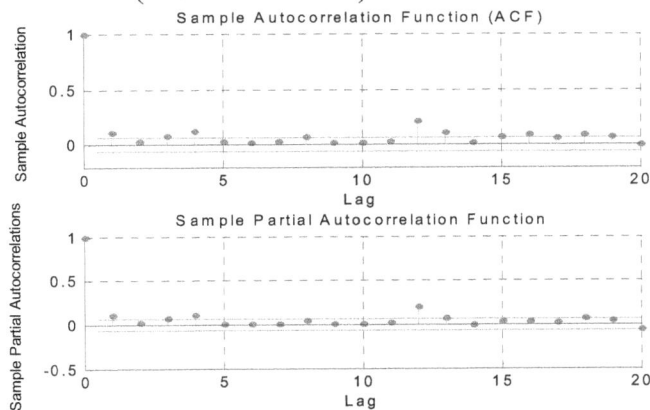

Table 30 - Ljung-Box-Pierce Q-test for mean adjusted squared WIG20 index daily log returns, period 03.01.2000 - 08.01.2004 (1005 observations)

Period (days)	H	p-value	Statistic	Critical value
5	1	0	108.31	11.07
10	1	0	151.55	18.307
15	1	0	308.37	24.996
20	1	0	395.1	31.41

Table 31 - ARCH test for mean adjusted WIG20 index daily log returns, period 03.01.2000 - 08.01.2004 (1005 observations)

Period (days)	H	p-value	Statistic	Critical value
5	1	1.52E-14	73.982	11.07
10	1	6.68E-14	84.455	18.307
15	1	0	161.64	24.996
20	1	0	177.78	31.41

Sample autocorrelation and sample partial correlation function of squared returns, as well as the Ljung-Box Q-statistic and Engle's ARCH test confirm that there is significant autocorrelation and ARCH effects present in WIG20 daily log returns, meaning that the returns on WIG20 index are not IID. The results are that much more indicative when considering that the hypothesis of IID was rejected for all the tested time lags (5, 10, 15 and 20 days).

Since the employed tests discovered significant heteroskedasticity in the WIG20 daily returns it is necessary to model the data in order to obtain independently and identically distributed returns. Because autocorrelation has been detected only in squared returns, WIG20 index returns will be modelled as a simple GARCH process, without having to model the conditional mean. Estimated GARCH parameters for WIG20 index are given in table 32.

Table 32 - Estimated GARCH parameters for WIG20 index daily log returns, period 03.01.2000 - 08.01.2004 (1005 observations)

Mean: ARMA(0,0)
Variance: GARCH(1,1)

Conditional Probability Distribution: Gaussian

Parameter	Value	Standard error	T statistic
C	0.0001624	0.000532	0.305
K	5.60E-06	2.72E-06	2.0611
GARCH(1)	0.93292	0.018124	51.4755
ARCH(1)	0.047987	0.011846	4.0511

According to their t statistics all of the estimated parameters are statistically significant, except the mean drift that is statistically insignificant and will be assumed to equal zero. The obtained model is a normally distributed GARCH(1,1) model:

$$\sigma_t^2 = 5.6E - 06 + 0.047987\varepsilon_{t-1}^2 + 0.93292\sigma_{t-1}^2$$

The plot of fitted GARCH model innovations, conditional standard deviations and observed WIG20 index daily log returns are given in figure 46.

Figure 46 - Plot of fitted ARMA- GARCH model innovations, conditional standard deviations and observed WIG20 index daily log returns, period 03.01.2000 - 08.01.2004

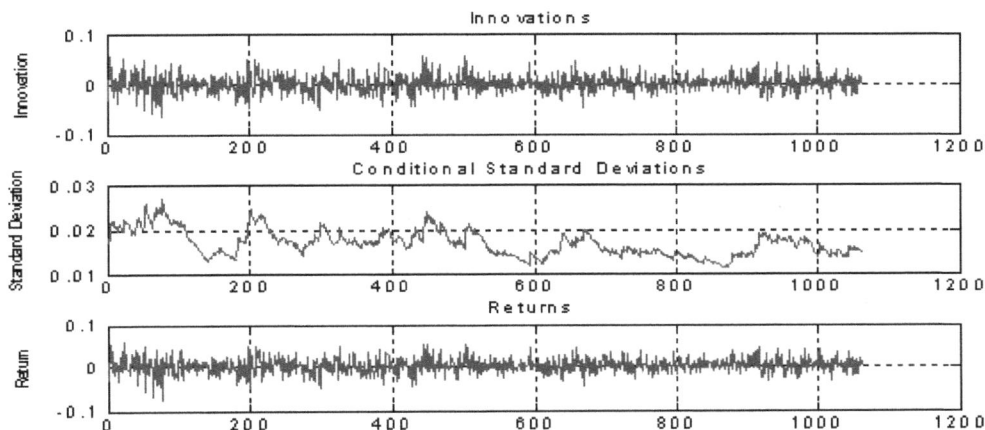

If the fitted GARCH model is appropriate for describing the dynamics of underlying data generating process the standardised innovation from such GARCH model should be independently and identically distributed (Figure 47). The adequacy of fitted GARCH model is tested in the same manner as returns and squared returns.

Figure 47 - Standardised innovations from fitted ARMA- GARCH model for WIG20 index daily log returns, period 03.01.2000 - 08.01.2004

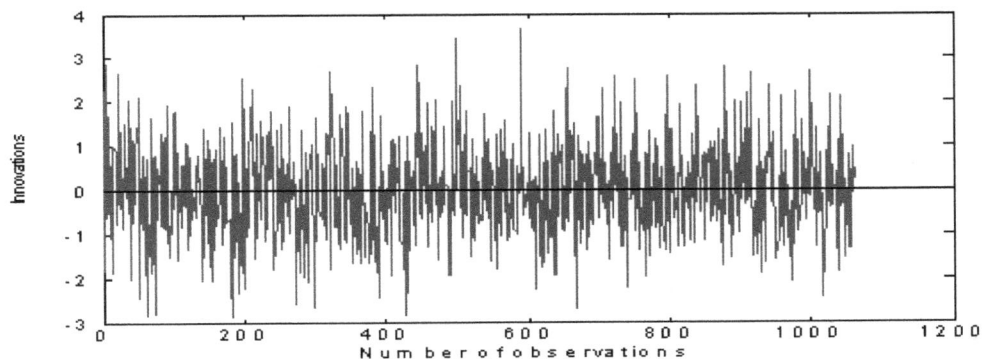

Sample autocorrelation, sample partial correlation function, Ljung-Box Q-statistic of squared standardised innovation and ARCH test of standardised innovations detect no presence of autocorrelation in the squared standardised innovations from fitted GARCH model. This indicates that the conditional variance model (GARCH(1,1))

successfully captured the heteroskedasticity present in WIG20 returns (Figure 48, Tables 33, 34).

Figure 48 - Sample autocorrelation and sample partial correlation function of squared standardized innovations from WIG20 index daily log returns, period 03.01.2000 - 08.01.2004

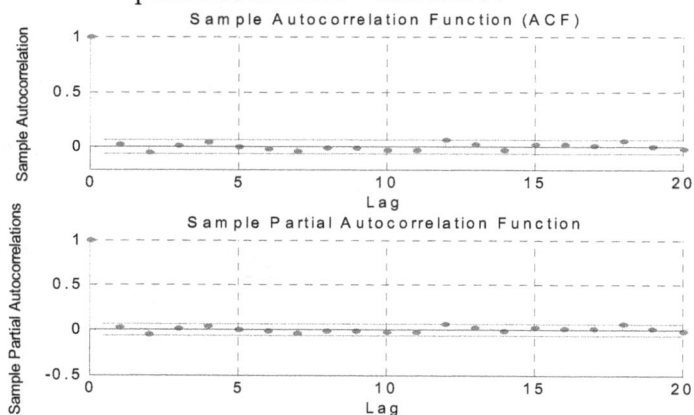

Table 33 - Ljung-Box-Pierce Q-test for squared standardised innovations from WIG20 index daily log returns, period 03.01.2000 - 08.01.2004

Period (days)	H	p-value	Statistic	Critical value
5	0	0.37118	5.3809	11.07
10	0	0.49832	9.3599	18.307
15	0	0.37816	16.059	24.996
20	0	0.417	20.666	31.41

Table 34 - ARCH test for standardised innovations from WIG20 index daily log returns, period 03.01.2000 - 08.01.2004

Period (days)	H	p-value	Statistic	Critical value
5	0	0.44246	4.7868	11.07
10	0	0.62775	8.0112	18.307
15	0	0.49155	14.452	24.996
20	0	0.54474	18.649	31.41

Findings of the performed tests imply that the fitted GARCH(1,1) model adequately describes the dynamics of WIG20 index daily returns.

6.3.4   Czech Republic – PX50 index

Trading on the Prague Stock Exchange (PSE) started in 1993. The PX50 index was launched in 1994 with the initial value of 100 points.

The analysis of the PX50 stock index is performed for the period 05.01.2000 – 31.12.2005. In this observation period the obtained sample from PX50 index consists of 1503 daily index value observations. The evolution of index values and returns is displayed in Figures 49, 50 and 51.

Figure 49 - Daily values of PX50 index, period 05.01.2000 - 31.12.2005 (1503 observations)

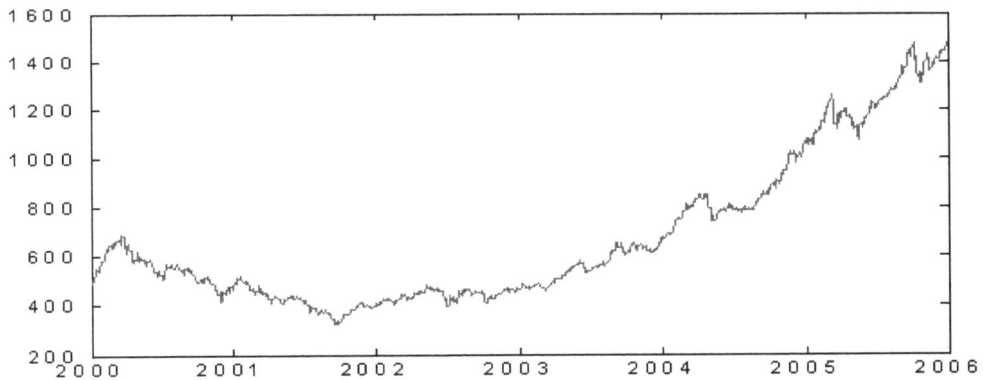

Figure 50 - Daily log returns of PX50 index, period 05.01.2000 - 31.12.2005 (1502 observations)

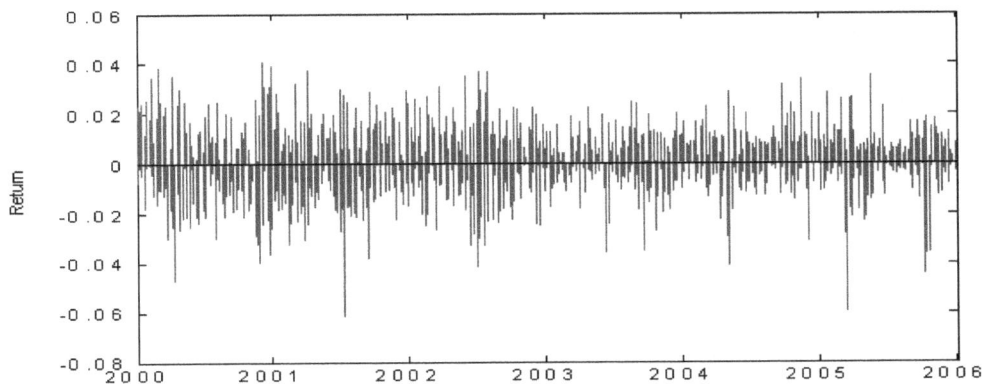

Figure 51 - Histogram of daily log returns of PX50 index, period 05.01.2000 - 31.12.2005 (1502 observations)

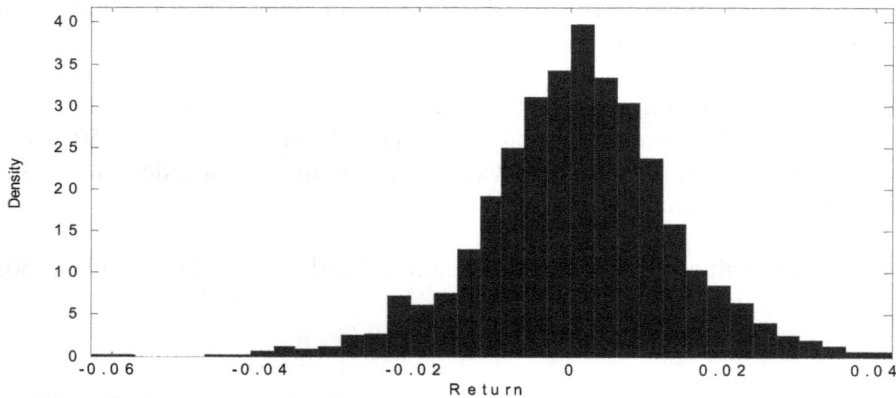

From figures 49, 50 and 51 it is visible that there is significant volatility clustering and presence of extreme positive and negative returns, which motivates a conditional volatility model that accounts for time varying volatility. Basic descriptive statistics for PX50 index in the period 05.01.2000 - 31.12.2005 are presented in table 35.

Table 35 - Basic statistics for PX50 index daily log returns, period 05.01.2000 - 31.12.2005 (1502 observations)

Mean	0.00074
Median	0.000961
Minimum	-0.06205
Maximum	0.041785
Standard deviation	0.012581
Skewness	-0.26716
Kurtosis	4.3604

Mean and median of daily returns differ significantly, which is in breach of normality assumption. Both mean and median differ significantly from zero and show a significant positive trend that is even stronger than detected in SBI20 and BUX index. Skewness and excess kurtosis are different from zero. In the observed period PX50 index experienced extreme daily returns. The highest daily gain in the analysed period was 4,18%, while the highest daily loss amounted to – 6,21%, which is again very similar to situation already encountered in BUX and WIG20 index. Asymmetry is slightly negative (-0,267) meaning that the distribution slopes slightly to the left and negative returns are expected to occur more frequently than positive, similarly to BUX index, only more pronounced. Excess kurtosis of 4,36 indicates that the empirical probability distribution of PX50 index has slightly fatter tails than assumed under normal distribution, a characteristic that is shared with BUX and WIG20 index.

Combining the third and fourth moment of the PX50 index with the mean and standard deviation, it can be concluded that although in the entire observation period, negative returns were more frequent than positive returns, the magnitude of the positive returns was significantly higher than the magnitude of loses, resulting in a strong positive trend for PX50 index. These characteristics of PX50 index, similar to BUX index, resulted in a strong positive trend and continually increasing index values. To determine if the daily returns of PX50 index are normally distributed, normality of empirical distribution is tested by Jarque-Bera test and Lilliefors test. Normality tests for the PX50 index are presented in table 36.

Table 36 - Normality tests for PX50 index daily log returns, period 05.01.2000 - 31.12.2005 (1502 observations)

Jarque-Bera test	132.67
(p value)	0
Lilliefors test	0.040504
(p value)	0

Both normality tests show that the hypothesis of normality for PX50 index, for the entire analysed period, should be rejected at 5% significance level. Probability values of distribution of returns being normal, according to both normality tests are zero, strongly indicating that there is no possibility that the returns on this index are normally distributed. The distribution of PX50 index returns is leptokurtotic and not symmetrical i.e. it skews to the left, as can be seen from figures 51 and 52, and from table 37. Figure 52 and table 37 show that the true empirical distribution of PX50 index daily returns is somewhat better approximated by a Student's t distribution with 7,18 degrees of freedom, than it is by normal distribution, although the difference in log-likelihoods of two distributions is minimal.

Figure 52 - Probability plot for PX50 index daily log returns, period 05.01.2000 - 31.12.2005 (1502 observations)

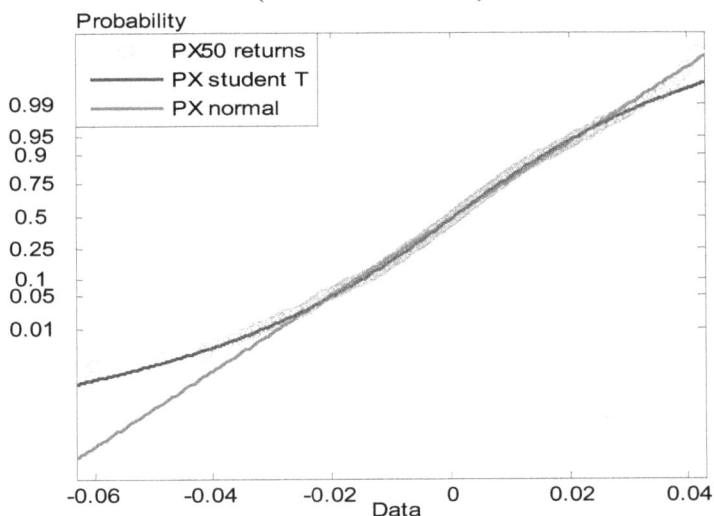

Table 37 - Parameters of fitted Normal and Students' T distribution to PX50 index daily log returns, period 05.01.2000 - 31.12.2005 (1502 observations)

Distribution: Normal			Distribution: t location-scale			
Log likelihood: 4077.72			Log likelihood: 4098.36			
Mean: 0.000679			Mean: 0.000797			
Variance: 1.63E-04			Variance: 1.64E-04			
Parameter	Estimate	Std. Err.	Parameter	Estimate	Std. Err.	
mu	0.000679	0.000343	mu	0.000797	0.000326	
sigma	0.01277	0.000243	sigma	0.010894	0.000364	
			df	7.18162	1.39813	
Estimated covariance of parameter estimates:			Estimated covariance of parameter estimates:			
	mu	sigma		mu	sigma	df
mu	1.18E-07	1.58E-24	mu	1.07E-07	-2.85E-09	-1.27E-05
sigma	1.58E-24	5.89E-08	sigma	-2.85E-09	1.32E-07	3.73E-04
			df	-1.27E-05	3.73E-04	1.95477

Presence of autocorrelation in PX50 daily log returns is tested by examining its sample autocorrelation and sample partial correlation function (Figure 53), and calculating Ljung-Box Q-statistic for mean adjusted PX50 returns (Table 38).

Figure 53 - Sample autocorrelation and sample partial correlation function of PX50 index daily log returns, period 05.01.2000 - 08.01.2004 (1002 observations)

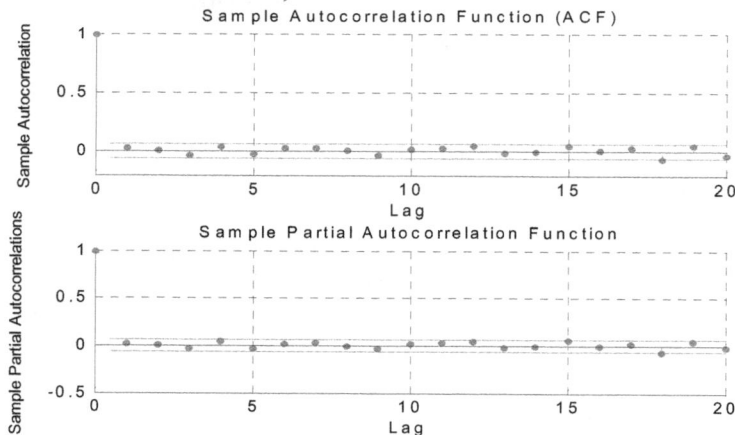

Table 38 - Ljung-Box-Pierce Q-test for mean adjusted PX50 index daily log returns, period 05.01.2000 - 08.01.2004 (1002 observations)

Period (days)	H	p-value	Statistic	Critical value
5	0	0.21194	7.119	11.07
10	0	0.45371	9.8504	18.307
15	0	0.34321	16.602	24.996
20	0	0.3119	22.541	31.41

As expected, sample autocorrelation, sample partial correlation function and Ljung-Box Q-statistic found no evidence of autocorrelation in the PX50 daily log returns. Since there is no autocorrelation in the PX50 index returns there is no need to fit a conditional mean model to the data. Presence of heteroskedasticity in PX50 returns is tested by examining its sample autocorrelation and sample partial correlation function of squared returns (Figure 54), calculating Ljung-Box Q-statistic for mean adjusted squared PX50 returns (Table 39) and ARCH test for mean adjusted PX50 returns (Table 40).

Figure 54 - Sample autocorrelation and sample partial correlation function of squared PX50 index daily log returns, period 05.01.2000 - 08.01.2004 (1002 observations)

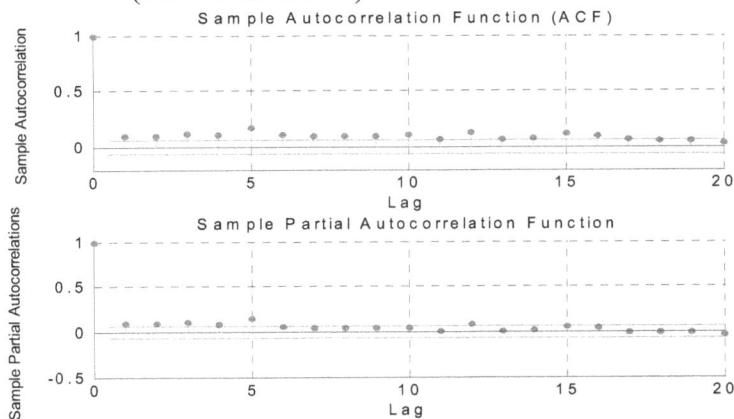

Table 39 - Ljung-Box-Pierce Q-test for mean adjusted squared PX50 index daily log returns, period 05.01.2000 - 08.01.2004 (1002 observations)

Period (days)	H	p-value	Statistic	Critical value
5	1	0	128.49	11.07
10	1	0	224.87	18.307
15	1	0	286.84	24.996
20	1	0	316.2	31.41

Table 40 - ARCH test for mean adjusted PX50 index daily log returns, period 05.01.2000 - 08.01.2004 (1002 observations)

Period (days)	H	p-value	Statistic	Critical value
5	1	0	89.424	11.07
10	1	0	110.38	18.307
15	1	0	117.94	24.996
20	1	3.33E-16	120.03	31.41

Sample autocorrelation and sample partial correlation function of squared returns, as well as the Ljung-Box Q-statistic and Engle's ARCH test confirm that there is significant autocorrelation and ARCH effects present in PX50 daily log returns, meaning that the returns on PX50 index are not IID. The results are that much more indicative when considering that the hypothesis of IID was rejected for all the tested time lags (5, 10, 15 and 20 days).

Since the employed tests discovered significant heteroskedasticity in the PX50 daily returns it is necessary to model the data in order to obtain independently and identically distributed returns. Because autocorrelation has been detected only in squared returns, PX50 index returns will be modelled as a simple GARCH process, without having to model the conditional mean. Estimated GARCH parameters for PX50 index are given in table 41.

Table 41 - Estimated GARCH parameters for PX50 index daily log returns, period 05.01.2000 - 08.01.2004 (1002 observations)

Mean: ARMA(0,0)
Variance: GARCH(1,1)

Conditional Probability Distribution: Gaussian

Parameter	Value	Standard error	T statistic
C	0.000755	0.000396	1.9084
K	4.69E-06	2.18E-06	2.1481
GARCH(1)	0.90381	0.026029	34.7227
ARCH(1)	0.069603	0.018137	3.8376

According to their t statistics all of the estimated parameters are statistically significant. The obtained model is a normally distributed GARCH(1,1) model:

$$r_t = 0.000755 + \varepsilon_t$$

$$\sigma_t^2 = 4.69E - 06 + 0.069603\varepsilon_{t-1}^2 + 0.90381\sigma_{t-1}^2$$

The plot of fitted GARCH model innovations, conditional standard deviations and observed PX50 index daily log returns are given in figure 54.

Figure 54 - Plot of fitted ARMA-GARCH model innovations, conditional standard deviations and observed PX50 index daily log returns, period 05.01.2000 - 08.01.2004

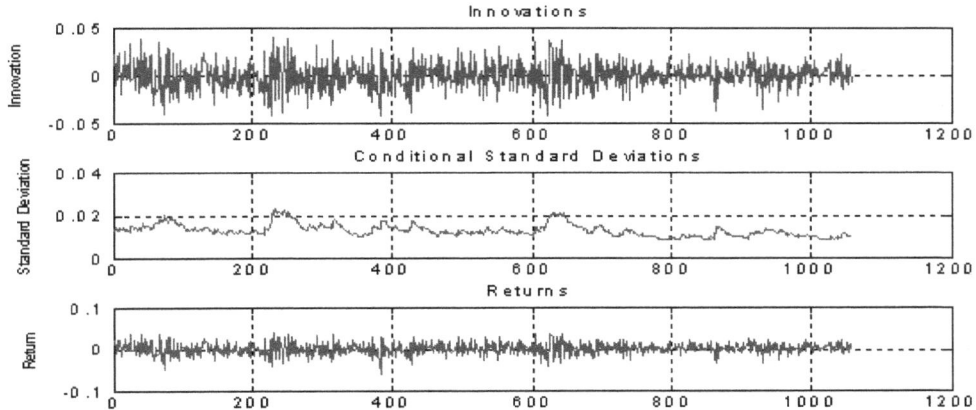

If the fitted GARCH model is appropriate for describing the dynamics of underlying data generating process the standardised innovation from such GARCH model should be independently and identically distributed (Figure 55). The adequacy of fitted GARCH model is tested in the same manner as returns and squared returns.

Figure 55 - Standardised innovations from fitted ARMA-GARCH model for PX50 index daily log returns, period 05.01.2000 - 08.01.2004

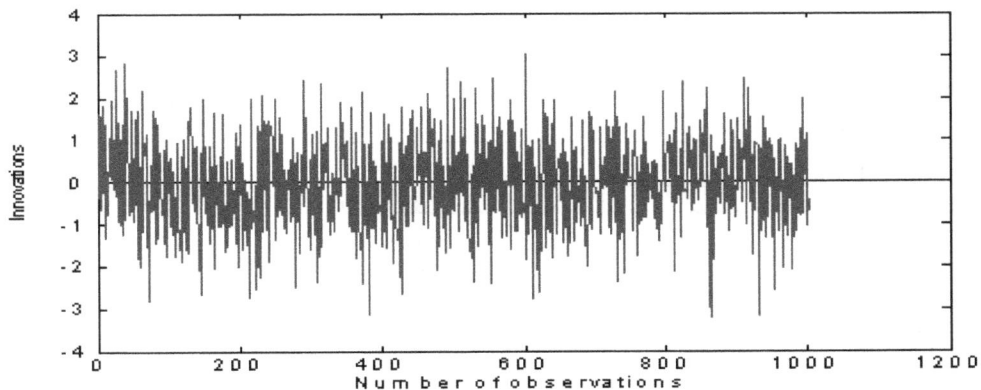

Sample autocorrelation, sample partial correlation function, Ljung-Box Q-statistic of squared standardised innovation and ARCH test of standardised innovations detect no presence of autocorrelation in the squared standardised innovations from fitted GARCH model. This indicates that the conditional variance model (GARCH(1,1))

successfully captured the heteroskedasticity present in PX50 returns (Figure 56, Tables 42, 43).

Figure 56 - Sample autocorrelation and sample partial correlation function of squared standardized innovations from PX50 index daily log returns, period 05.01.2000 - 08.01.2004

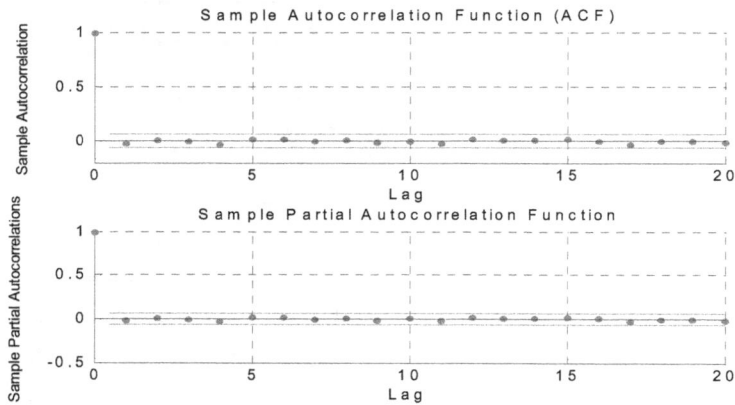

Table 42 - Ljung-Box-Pierce Q-test for squared standardised innovations from PX50 index daily log returns, period 05.01.2000 - 08.01.2004

Period (days)	H	p-value	Statistic	Critical value
5	0	0.88062	1.765	11.07
10	0	0.98444	2.8643	18.307
15	0	0.99272	4.9282	24.996
20	0	0.9991	5.8371	31.41

Table 43 - ARCH test for standardised innovations from PX50 index daily log returns, period 05.01.2000 - 08.01.2004

Period (days)	H	p-value	Statistic	Critical value
5	0	0.88664	1.7179	11.07
10	0	0.97824	3.1282	18.307
15	0	0.99045	5.1839	24.996
20	0	0.99843	6.2966	31.41

Findings of the performed tests imply that the fitted GARCH(1,1) model adequately describes the dynamics of PX50 index daily returns.

6.3.5   Slovakia – SKSM index

Trading on the Bratislava Stock Exchange (BSSE) started in 1993. The SKSM index was launched in 1994 with the initial value of 100 points.

The analysis of the SKSM stock index is performed for the period 07.01.2000 – 31.12.2005. In this observation period the obtained sample from SKSM index consists of 1415 daily index value observations. The evolution of index values and returns is displayed in Figures 57, 58 and 59.

Figure 57 - Daily values of SKSM index, period 07.01.2000 - 31.12.2005 (1415 observations)

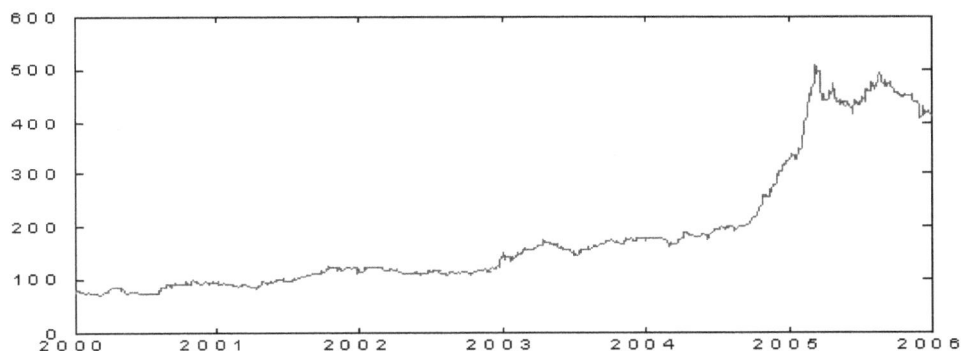

Figure 58 - Daily log returns of SKSM index, period 07.01.2000 - 31.12.2005 (1414 observations)

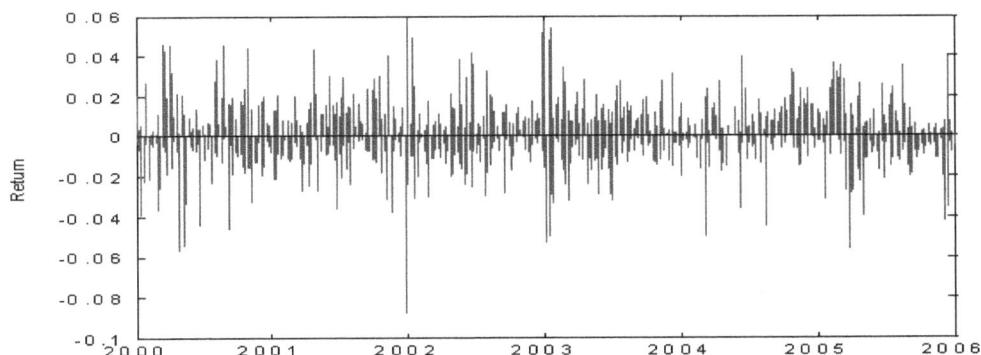

Figure 59 - Histogram of daily log returns of SKSM index, period 07.01.2000 - 31.12.2005 (1414 observations)

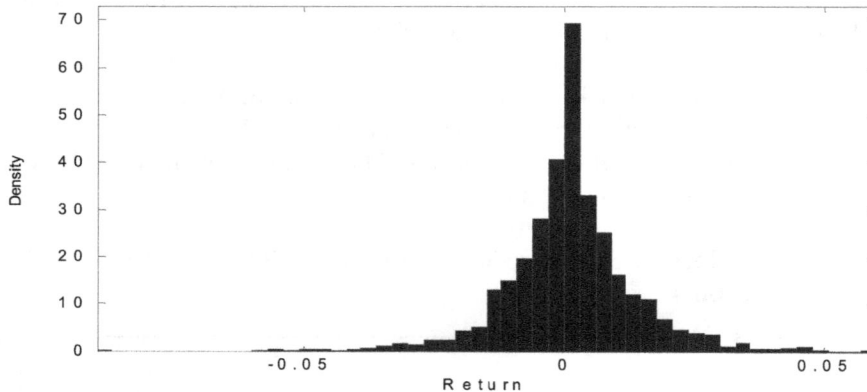

From figures 57, 58 and 59 it is visible that there is significant volatility clustering and presence of extreme positive and negative returns, which motivates a conditional volatility model that accounts for time varying volatility.

Basic descriptive statistics for SKSM index in the period 07.01.2000 - 31.12.2005 are presented in table 44.

Table 44 - Basic statistics for SKSM index daily log returns, period 07.01.2000 - 31.12.2005 (1414 observations)

Mean	0.001184
Median	0.0003
Minimum	-0.08817
Maximum	0.059591
Standard deviation	0.013255
Skewness	-0.11384
Kurtosis	7.4742

Mean and median of daily returns differ significantly, which is in breach of normality assumption. Both mean and median differ significantly from zero. Mean shows a very positive trend that is much more pronounced than in SBI20, BUX and PX50 index. Skewness and excess kurtosis are different from zero. In the observed period SKSM index experienced extreme daily returns. The highest daily gain in the analysed period was 5,96%, while the highest daily loss amounted to − 8,82%, which is again very similar to situation already encountered in BUX, WIG20 and PX50 index. Asymmetry is slightly negative (-0,1138) and almost identical to BUX index, meaning that the distribution slopes slightly to the left and negative returns are expected to occur more frequently than positive. Excess kurtosis of 7,47 indicates that the empirical probability distribution of SKSM index has significantly fatter tails than assumed under normal distribution. Excess kurtosis is much higher than detected in BUX, WIG20 and PX50 but still significantly lower than recorded in SBI20 index.

Combining the third and fourth moment of the SKSM index with its mean and standard deviation, it can be concluded that although in the entire observation period, negative returns were more frequent than positive returns, the magnitude of the positive returns was significantly higher than the magnitude of loses, resulting in a strong positive trend for SKSM index. These characteristics of SKSM index, similar to BUX and PX50 index, resulted in a strong positive trend and continually increasing index values. To determine if the daily returns of SKSM index are normally distributed, normality of empirical distribution is tested by Jarque-Bera test and Lilliefors test. Normality tests for the SKSM index are presented in table 45.

Table 45 - Normality tests for SKSM index daily log returns, period 07.01.2000 - 31.12.2005 (1414 observations)

Jarque-Bera test	1,176.9
(p value)	0
Lilliefors test	0.094636
(p value)	0

Both normality tests show that the hypothesis of normality of returns for SKSM index, for the entire analysed period, should be rejected at 5% significance level. Probability values of distribution of returns being normal, according to both normality tests are zero, strongly indicating that there is no possibility that the returns on this index are normally distributed. The distribution of SKSM index returns is leptokurtotic and almost symmetrical i.e. it skews slightly to the left, as can be seen from figures 59 and 60, as well as from table 46. Figure 60 and table 46 show that the true empirical distribution of SKSM index daily returns is far better approximated by a Student's t distribution with 2,33 degrees of freedom, than it is by normal distribution.

Figure 60 - Probability plot for SKSM index daily log returns, period 07.01.2000 - 31.12.2005 (1414 observations)

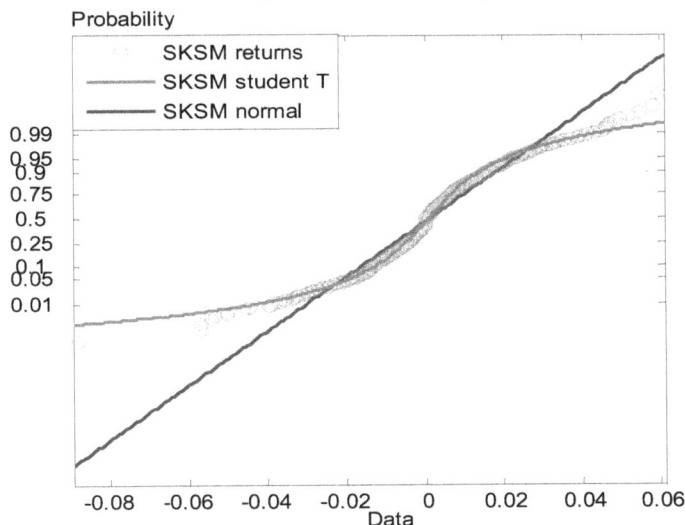

Table 46 - Parameters of fitted Normal and Students' T distribution to SKSM index daily log returns, period 07.01.2000 - 31.12.2005 (1414 observations)

Distribution:	Normal		Distribution:	t location-scale	
Log likelihood:	3764.92		Log likelihood:	3913.97	
Mean:	0.001344		Mean:	0.000974	
Variance:	1.81E-04		Variance:	4.03E-04	

Parameter	Estimate	Std. Err.	Parameter	Estimate	Std. Err.
mu	0.001344	0.000373	mu	0.000974	0.000262
sigma	0.013461	0.000264	sigma	0.007566	0.000334
			df	2.33126	0.212427

Estimated covariance of parameter estimates:

	mu	sigma			mu	sigma	df
mu	1.39E-07	1.10E-23		mu	6.87E-08	8.19E-09	5.24E-06
sigma	1.10E-23	6.96E-08		sigma	8.19E-09	1.11E-07	5.12E-05
				df	5.24E-06	5.12E-05	0.045125

Presence of autocorrelation in SKSM daily log returns is tested by examining its sample autocorrelation, sample partial correlation function (Figure 61) and calculating Ljung-Box Q-statistic for mean adjusted SKSM returns (Table 47).

Figure 61 - Sample autocorrelation and sample partial correlation function of SKSM index daily log returns, period 07.01.2000 - 09.10.2003 (914 observations)

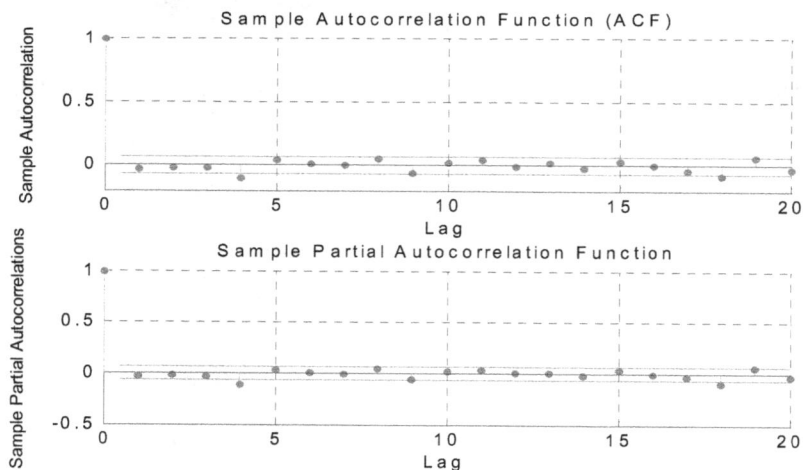

Table 47 - Ljung-Box-Pierce Q-test for mean adjusted SKSM index daily log returns, period 07.01.2000 - 09.10.2003 (914 observations)

Period (days)	H	p-value	Statistic	Critical value
5	0	0.07474	10.018	11.07
10	1	0.007697	23.964	18.307
15	1	0.023616	27.686	24.996
20	1	0.012973	36.625	31.41

Sample autocorrelation, sample partial correlation function and Ljung-Box Q-statistic found the presence of autocorrelation in the SKSM daily log returns meaning that the Slovakian stock market is not very efficient since the direction of the market can be predicted. To extract the autocorrelation from the data it will be necessary to use an ARMA (p, q) model.

After the presence of autocorrelation in the daily log returns has been investigated it is necessary to test the squared log returns for presence of autocorrelation i.e. heteroskedasticity. Presence of heteroskedasticity in SKSM returns is tested by examining its sample autocorrelation and sample partial correlation function of squared returns (Figure 62), calculating Ljung-Box Q-statistic for mean adjusted squared SKSM returns (Table 48) and ARCH test for mean adjusted SKSM returns (Table 49).

Figure 62 - Sample autocorrelation and sample partial correlation function of squared SKSM index daily log returns, 07.01.2000 - 09.10.2003 (914 observations)

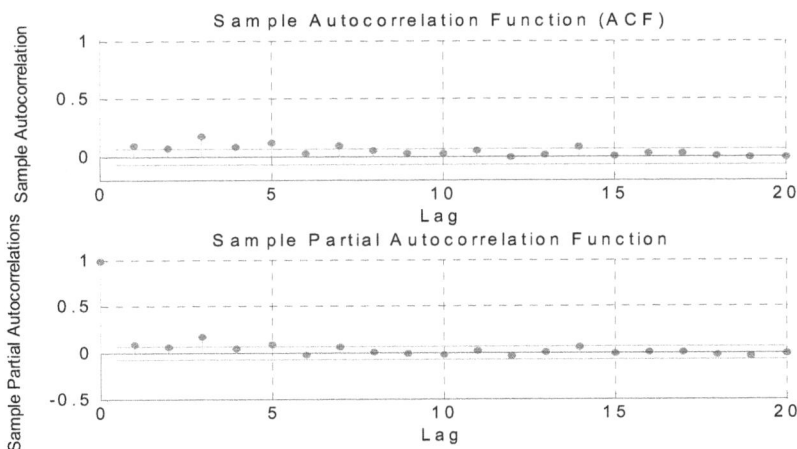

Table 48 - Ljung-Box-Pierce Q-test for mean adjusted squared SKSM index daily log returns, period 07.01.2000 - 09.10.2003 (914 observations)

Period (days)	H	p-value	Statistic	Critical value
5	1	0	99.655	11.07
10	1	0	116.37	18.307
15	1	0	128.62	24.996
20	1	0	131.99	31.41

Table 49 - ARCH test for mean adjusted SKSM index daily log returns, period 07.01.2000 - 09.10.2003 (914 observations)

Period (days)	H	p-value	Statistic	Critical value
5	1	3.66E-15	76.922	11.07
10	1	6.95E-13	79.28	18.307
15	1	3.19E-12	87.276	24.996
20	1	9.36E-11	89.419	31.41

Sample autocorrelation and sample partial correlation function of squared returns, as well as the Ljung-Box Q-statistic and Engle's ARCH test confirm that there is significant autocorrelation and ARCH effects present in SKSM daily log returns, meaning that the returns on SKSM index are not IID.

Since the employed tests discovered significant autocorrelation and heteroskedasticity in the SKSM daily returns it is necessary to model the data in order to obtain independently and identically distributed returns. Because autocorrelation has been detected in both returns and squared returns, SKSM index returns will be modelled as an ARMA-GARCH process in order to deal with both types of dependence. Estimated ARMA-GARCH parameters for SKSM index are given in table 50.

Table 50 - Estimated ARMA-GARCH parameters for SKSM index daily log returns, period 07.01.2000 - 09.10.2003 (914 observations)

Mean: ARMA(0,1)
Variance: GARCH(1,1)

Conditional Probability Distribution: Gaussian

Parameter	Value	Standard error	T statistic
C	6.89E-04	0.000413	1.6675
MA(1)	-5.75E-02	0.030394	-1.8232
K	1.27E-05	2.85E-06	4.4377
GARCH(1)	0.85016	0.025413	33.4541
ARCH(1)	0.07733	0.013561	5.7025

All of the estimated parameters are statistically significant according to their t statistics. The obtained model is a normally distributed MA(1)-GARCH(1,1) model:

$$r_t = 0.000689 - 0.0575\varepsilon_{t-1} + \varepsilon_t$$

$$\sigma_t^2 = 1.27E - 05 + 0.07733\varepsilon_{t-1}^2 + 0.85016\sigma_{t-1}^2$$

Similarly to SBI20 index the conditional volatility model for SKSM index is also far from being integrated. The plot of fitted MA-GARCH model innovations, conditional standard deviations and observed SKSM index daily log returns are given in figure 63.

Figure 63 - Plot of fitted MA-GARCH model innovations, conditional standard deviations and observed SKSM index daily log returns, period 07.01.2000 - 09.10.2003

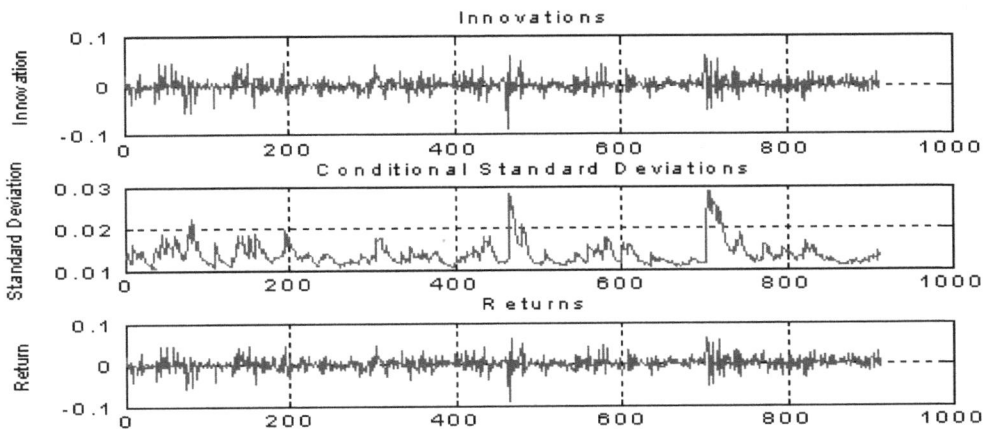

If the fitted MA-GARCH model is appropriate for describing the dynamics of underlying data generating process the standardised innovation from such MA-GARCH model should be independently and identically distributed (Figure 64). The adequacy of fitted MA-GARCH model can be statistically tested in the same manner as returns and squared returns.

Figure 64 - Standardised innovations from fitted MA-GARCH model for SKSM index daily log returns, period 07.01.2000 - 09.10.2003

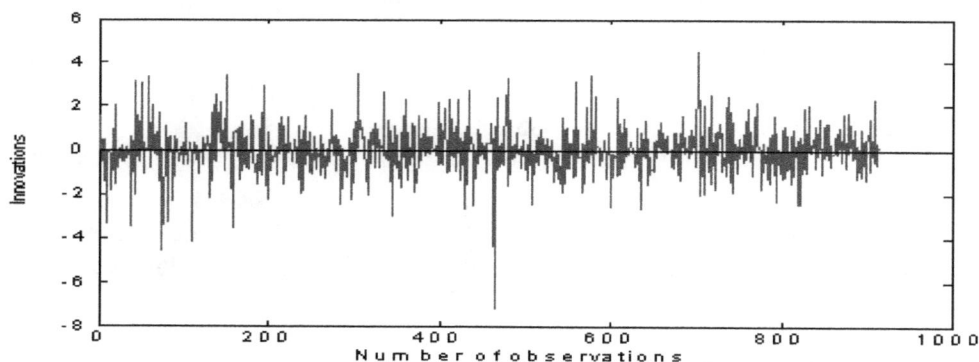

Sample autocorrelation, sample partial correlation function and Ljung-Box Q-statistic of standardised innovation detect no presence of autocorrelation in the standardised innovations from fitted MA-GARCH model, meaning that the conditional mean model (MA(1)) successfully captured the autocorrelation present in SKSM returns (Figure 65, Table 51).

Figure 65 - Sample autocorrelation and sample partial correlation function of standardized innovations from SKSM index daily log returns, period 07.01.2000 - 09.10.2003

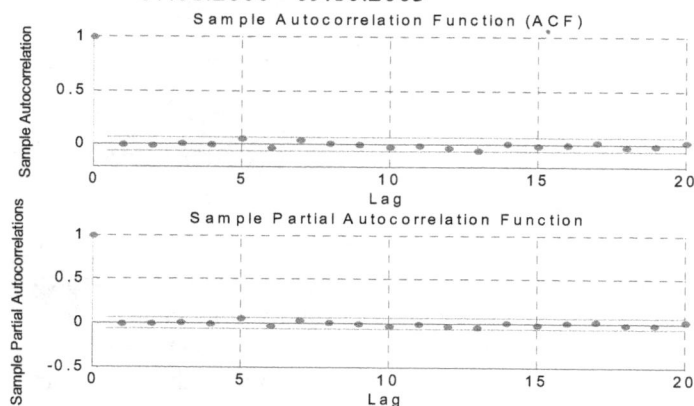

Table 51 - Ljung-Box-Pierce Q-test for standardised innovations from SKSM index daily log returns, period 07.01.2000 - 09.10.2003

Period (days)	H	p-value	Statistic	Critical value
5	0	0.3267	5.795	11.07
10	0	0.2251	12.9738	18.307
15	0	0.3267	16.8706	24.996
20	0	0.1401	26.8302	31.41

Sample autocorrelation and sample partial correlation function, Ljung-Box Q-statistic of squared standardised innovation and ARCH test of standardised innovations detect no presence of autocorrelation in the squared standardised innovations from fitted MA-GARCH model. This indicates that the conditional variance model (GARCH(1,1)) successfully captured the heteroskedasticity present in SKSM returns (Figure 66, Tables 52, 53).

Figure 66 - Sample autocorrelation and sample partial correlation function of squared standardized innovations from SKSM index daily log returns, period 07.01.2000 - 09.10.2003

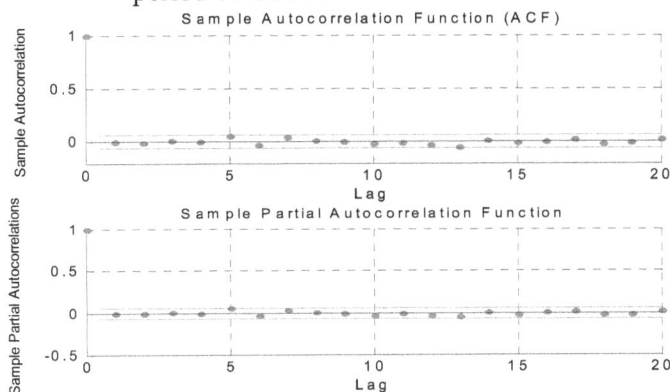

Table 52 - Ljung-Box-Pierce Q-test for squared standardised innovations from SKSM index daily log returns, period 07.01.2000 - 09.10.2003

Period (days)	H	p-value	Statistic	Critical value
5	0	0.64116	3.383	11.07
10	0	0.77893	6.4188	18.307
15	0	0.83564	9.7422	24.996
20	0	0.94041	11.217	31.41

Table 53 - ARCH test for standardised innovations from SKSM index daily log returns, period 07.01.2000 - 09.10.2003

Period (days)	H	p-value	Statistic	Critical value
5	0	0.64372	3.3662	11.07
10	0	0.76362	6.5887	18.307
15	0	0.81669	10.048	24.996
20	0	0.93267	11.485	31.41

Findings of the performed tests imply that the fitted MA(1)-GARCH(1,1) model adequately describes the dynamics of SKSM index daily returns.

6.3.6 Croatia – CROBEX index

Although a small country, up until 2007 Croatia had two stock exchanges, Zagreb Stock Exchange (ZSE) and Varaždin Stock Exchange (VSE). Although the Varaždin stock exchange does not exist anymore and all of the securities are now trading only on ZSE, VIN index is included in this analysis since it existed during the studied period. Trading on the Zagreb Stock Exchange (ZSE) started in 1991. The CROBEX index was launched on 1 September 1997 with the initial value of 1000 points.

The analysis of the CROBEX stock index is performed for the period 04.01.2000 – 31.12.2005. In this observation period the obtained sample from CROBEX index consists of 1435 daily index value observations. The evolution of index values and returns is displayed in Figures 67, 68 and 69.

Figure 67 - Daily values of CROBEX index, period 04.01.2000 - 31.12.2005 (1435 observations)

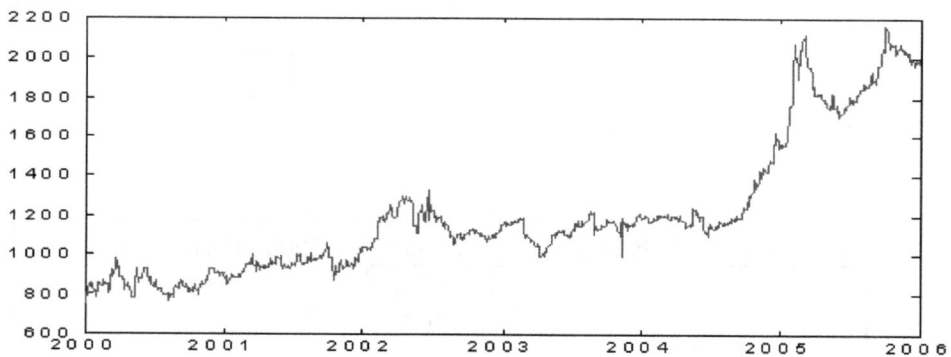

Figure 68 - Daily log returns of CROBEX index, period 04.01.2000 - 31.12.2005 (1434 observations)

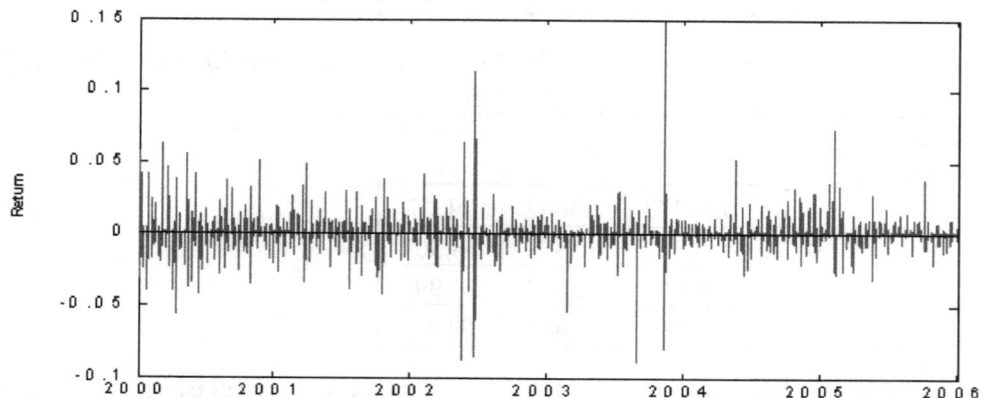

Figure 69 - Histogram of daily log returns of CROBEX index, period 04.01.2000 - 31.12.2005 (1434 observations)

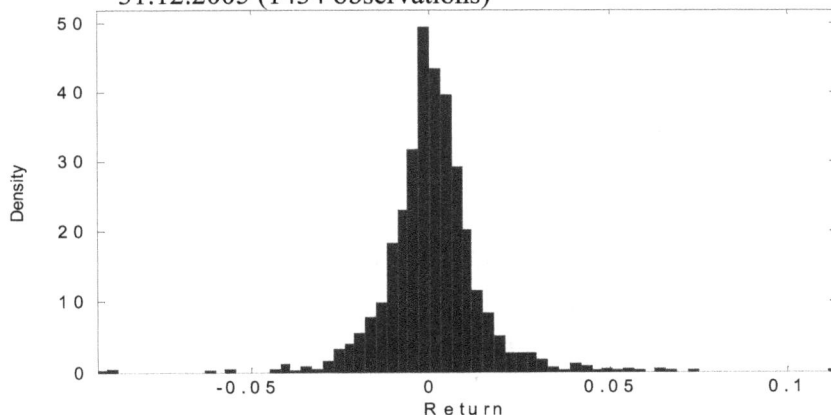

From figures 67, 68 and 69 it is visible that there is significant volatility clustering and presence of extreme positive and negative returns, which motivates a conditional volatility model that accounts for time varying volatility.

Basic descriptive statistics for CROBEX index in the period 04.01.2000 - 31.12.2005 are presented in table 54.

Table 54 - Basic statistics for CROBEX index daily log returns, period 04.01.2000 - 31.12.2005 (1434 observations)

Mean	0.000683
Median	0.000164
Minimum	-0.09032
Maximum	0.14979
Standard deviation	0.014751
Skewness	0.75377
Kurtosis	18.369

Mean and median of daily returns differ significantly, which is in breach of normality assumption. Both mean and median differ significantly from zero. Mean shows a very positive trend similar to SBI20, BUX and PX50 index. Skewness and excess kurtosis of the index are also significantly different from zero assumed under normality. In the observed period CROBEX index experienced extreme daily returns. The highest daily gain in the analysed period was a huge 14,98%, while the highest daily loss amounted to – 9,03%. Asymmetry is significantly positive (0,754), similar to SBI20 index, meaning that the distribution slopes to the right and positive returns are expected to occur more frequently than negative ones. Excess kurtosis of 18,369 indicates that the empirical probability distribution of CROBEX index has significantly fatter tails than assumed under normal distribution. The value of excess kurtosis is close to the value found for SBI20 index, and much higher than the values for BUX, WIG20, PX50 and SKSM index. The high value of excess kurtosis for this index indicates to the investors investing on ZSE that they can expect high, both positive and negative returns on their investments. Combining the third and fourth moment of the CROBEX index with the mean and standard deviation, it can be concluded that in the observed period, positive returns were more frequent than negative returns, and the magnitude of the positive returns was significantly higher than the magnitude of loses. These characteristics of CROBEX index, very similar to SBI20 index, resulted in a strong positive trend and continually increasing index values.   To determine if the daily returns of CROBEX index are normally distributed, normality of empirical distribution is tested by Jarque-Bera test and Lilliefors test. Normality tests for the CROBEX index are presented in table 55.

Table 55 - Normality tests for CROBEX index daily log returns, period 04.01.2000 - 31.12.2005 (1434 observations)

Jarque-Bera test	14,202
(p value)	0
Lilliefors test	0.10855
(p value)	0

Both normality tests show that the hypothesis of normality of returns for CROBEX index, for the entire analysed period, should be rejected at 5% significance level. Probability values of distribution of returns being normal, according to both normality tests are zero, strongly indicating that there is no possibility that the returns on this index are normally distributed. The distribution of CROBEX index returns is leptokurtotic and not symmetrical i.e. it skews to the right, as can be seen from figures 69 and 70, and from table 56. Figure 70 and table 56 show that the true empirical distribution of CROBEX index daily returns is much better approximated by a Student's t distribution with 2,75 degrees of freedom, than it is by a normal.

Figure 70 - Probability plot for CROBEX index daily log returns, period 04.01.2000 - 31.12.2005. (1434 observations)

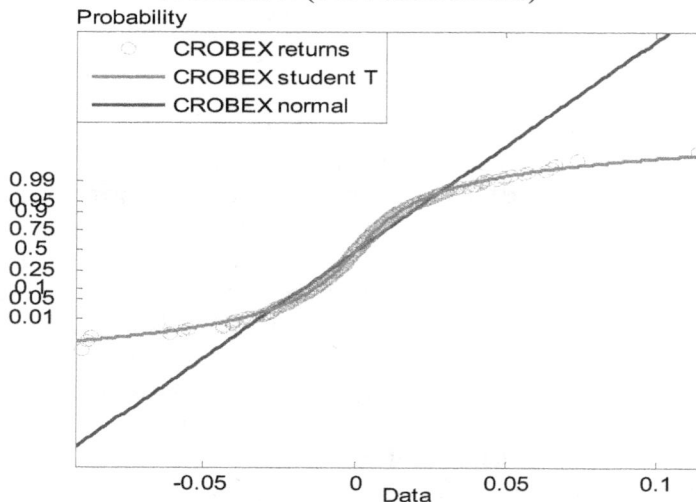

Table 56 - Parameters of fitted Normal and Students' T distribution to CROBEX index daily log returns, period 04.01.2000 - 31.12.2005. (1434 observations)

Distribution: Normal			Distribution: t location-scale			
Log likelihood: 3850.32			Log likelihood: 4049.3			
Mean: 0.000637			Mean: 0.000466			
Variance: 0.000195			Variance: 0.000245			
Parameter	Estimate	Std. Err.	Parameter	Estimate	Std. Err.	
mu	0.000637	0.00038	mu	0.000466	0.000275	
sigma	0.013973	0.000269	sigma	0.008173	0.000302	
			df	2.7481	0.241739	
Estimated covariance of parameter estimates:			Estimated covariance of parameter estimates:			
	mu	sigma		mu	sigma	df
mu	1.45E-07	2.13E-24	mu	7.55E-08	-2.11E-10	-1.75E-07
sigma	2.13E-24	7.24E-08	sigma	-2.11E-10	9.13E-08	4.78E-05
			df	-1.75E-07	4.78E-05	0.058438

Presence of autocorrelation in CROBEX daily log returns is tested by examining its sample autocorrelation and sample partial correlation function (Figure 71) and calculating Ljung-Box Q-statistic for mean adjusted CROBEX returns (Table 57).

Figure 71 - Sample autocorrelation and sample partial correlation function of CROBEX index daily log returns, period 04.01.2000 - 21.10.2003 (934 observations)

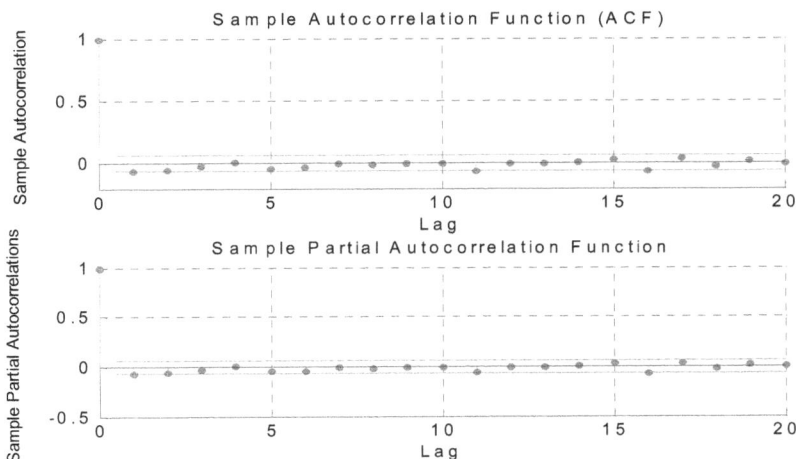

Table 57 - Ljung-Box-Pierce Q-test for mean adjusted CROBEX index daily log returns, period 04.01.2000 - 21.10.2003 (934 observations)

Period (days)	H	p-value	Statistic	Critical value
5	0	0.38439	5.2651	11.07
10	0	0.758	6.6503	18.307
15	0	0.70777	11.617	24.996
20	0	0.69091	16.41	31.41

As expected, sample autocorrelation and sample partial correlation function and Ljung-Box Q-statistic found no evidence of autocorrelation in the CROBEX daily log returns. Since there is no autocorrelation in the CROBEX index returns there is no need to fit a conditional mean model to the data. Presence of heteroskedasticity in CROBEX returns is tested by examining its sample autocorrelation, sample partial correlation function of squared returns (Figure 72), calculating Ljung-Box Q-statistic for mean adjusted squared CROBEX returns (Table 58) and ARCH test for mean adjusted CROBEX returns (Table 59).

Figure 72 - Sample autocorrelation and sample partial correlation function of squared CROBEX index daily log returns, period 04.01.2000 - 21.10.2003 (934 observations)

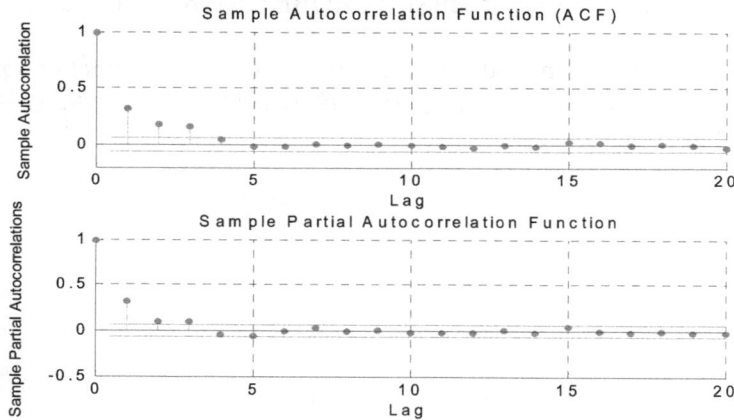

Table 58 - Ljung-Box-Pierce Q-test for mean adjusted squared CROBEX index daily log returns, period 04.01.2000 - 21.10.2003 (934 observations)

Period (days)	H	p-value	Statistic	Critical value
5	1	0	239.83	11.07
10	1	0	241.44	18.307
15	1	0	243.25	24.996
20	1	0	245.21	31.41

Table 59 - ARCH test for mean adjusted CROBEX index daily log returns, period 04.01.2000 - 21.10.2003 (934 observations)

Period (days)	H	p-value	Statistic	Critical value
5	1	0	168.9	11.07
10	1	0	171.58	18.307
15	1	0	173.86	24.996
20	1	0	174.16	31.41

Sample autocorrelation, sample partial correlation function of squared returns, as well as the Ljung-Box Q-statistic and Engle's ARCH test confirm that there is significant autocorrelation and ARCH effects present in CROBEX daily log returns, meaning that the returns on CROBEX index are not IID. The results are that much more indicative when considering that the hypothesis of IID was rejected for all the tested time lags (5, 10, 15 and 20 days).

Since the employed tests discovered significant heteroskedasticity in the CROBEX daily returns it is necessary to model the data in order to obtain independently and identically distributed returns. Because autocorrelation has been detected only in squared returns, CROBEX index returns will be modelled as a simple GARCH process, without having to model the conditional mean. Estimated GARCH parameters for CROBEX index are given in table 60.

Table 60 - Estimated GARCH parameters for CROBEX index daily log returns, period 04.01.2000 - 21.10.2003 (934 observations)

Mean: ARMA(0,0)
Variance: GARCH(1,1)

Conditional Probability Distribution: Gaussian

Parameter	Value	Standard error	T statistic
C	4.25E-04	0.000389	1.0917
K	1.06E-05	3.96E-06	2.664
GARCH(1)	0.8323	0.033011	25.2126
ARCH(1)	0.11082	0.024	4.6175

According to their t statistics all of the estimated parameters are statistically significant, except the mean drift that is statistically insignificant and will be assumed to equal zero. The obtained model is a normally distributed GARCH(1,1) model:

$$r_t = \varepsilon_t$$

$$\sigma_t^2 = 1.06E - 05 + 0.11082\varepsilon_{t-1}^2 + 0.8323\sigma_{t-1}^2$$

The plot of fitted GARCH model innovations, conditional standard deviations and observed CROBEX index daily log returns are given in figure 73.

Figure 73 - Plot of fitted GARCH model innovations, conditional standard deviations and observed CROBEX index daily log returns, period 04.01.2000 - 21.10.2003

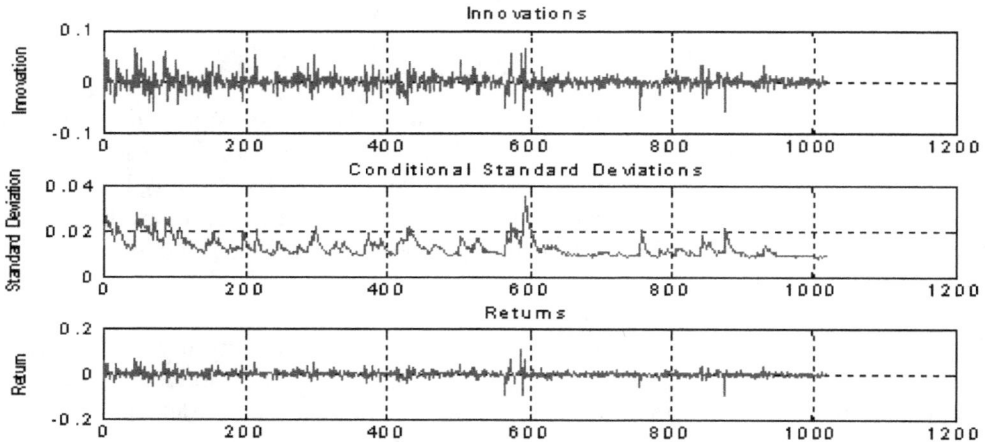

If the fitted GARCH model is appropriate for describing the dynamics of underlying data generating process the standardised innovation from such GARCH model should be independently and identically distributed (Figure 74). The adequacy of fitted GARCH model is tested in the same manner as returns and squared returns.

Figure 74 - Standardised innovations from fitted GARCH model for CROBEX index daily log returns, period 04.01.2000 - 21.10.2003

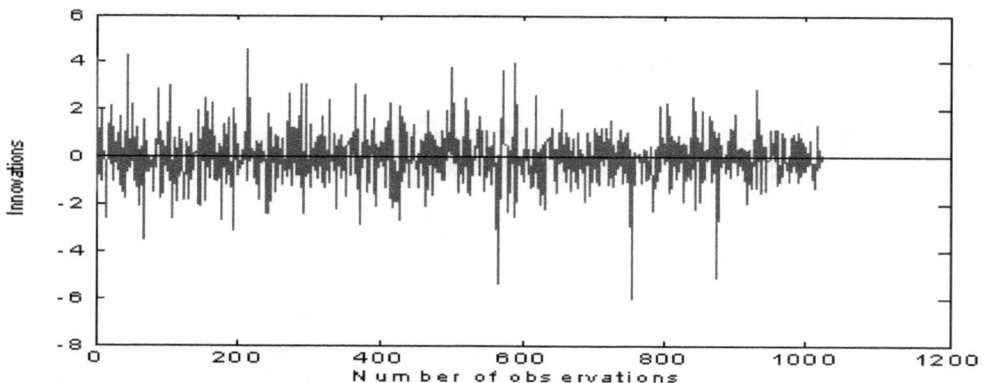

Sample autocorrelation, sample partial correlation function, Ljung-Box Q-statistic of squared standardised innovation and ARCH test of standardised innovations detect no presence of autocorrelation in the squared standardised innovations from fitted GARCH model. This indicates that the conditional variance model (GARCH(1,1))

successfully captured the heteroskedasticity present in CROBEX returns (Figure 75, Tables 61, 62).

Figure 75 - Sample autocorrelation and sample partial correlation function of squared standardized innovations from CROBEX index daily log returns, period 04.01.2000 - 21.10.2003

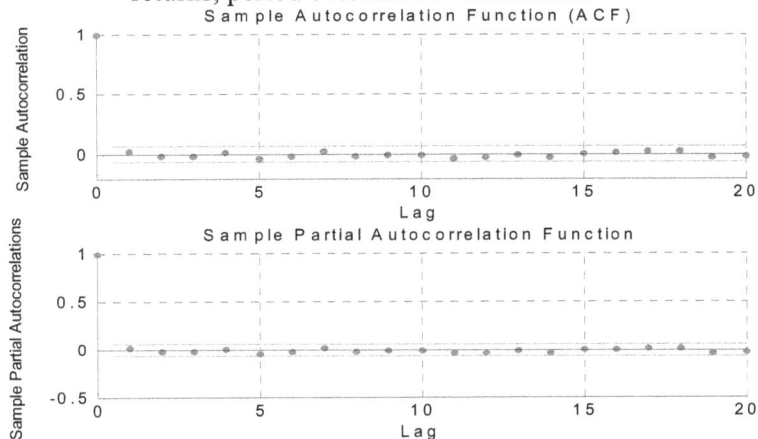

Table 61 - Ljung-Box-Pierce Q-test for squared standardised innovations from CROBEX index daily log returns, period 04.01.2000 - 21.10.2003

Period (days)	H	p-value	Statistic	Critical value
5	0	0.98968	0.56199	11.07
10	0	0.9911	2.4841	18.307
15	0	0.99916	3.3801	24.996
20	0	0.99996	3.8649	31.41

Table 62 - ARCH test for standardised innovations from CROBEX index daily log returns, period 04.01.2000 - 21.10.2003

Period (days)	H	p-value	Statistic	Critical value
5	0	0.99116	0.52561	11.07
10	0	0.9914	2.463	18.307
15	0	0.99918	3.3709	24.996
20	0	0.99997	3.7849	31.41

Findings of the performed tests imply that the fitted GARCH(1,1) model adequately describes the dynamics of CROBEX index daily returns.

6.3.7   Croatia – VIN index

Trading on the Varaždin Stock Exchange (VSE) started in 1993. The VIN index was launched on 1 January 1997 with the initial value of 1000 points. From 2007 Varaždin stock exchange does not exist anymore and all of the securities are now trading only on ZSE. VIN index is included in our analysis since it existed during the studied period.

The analysis of the VIN stock index is performed for the period 04.01.2000 – 31.12.2005. In this observation period the obtained sample from VIN index consists of 1481 daily index value observations. The evolution of index values and returns is displayed in Figures 76, 77 and 78.

Figure 76 - Daily values of VIN index, period 04.01.2000 - 31.12.2005 (1481 observations)

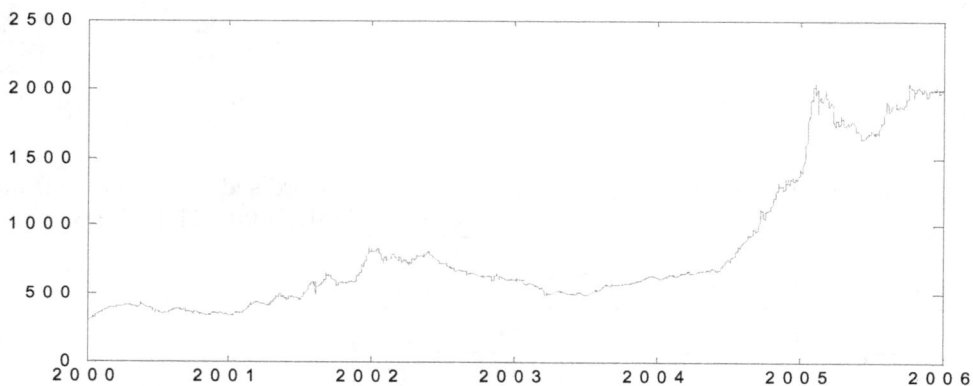

Figure 77 - Daily log returns of VIN index, period 04.01.2000 - 31.12.2005 (1480 observations)

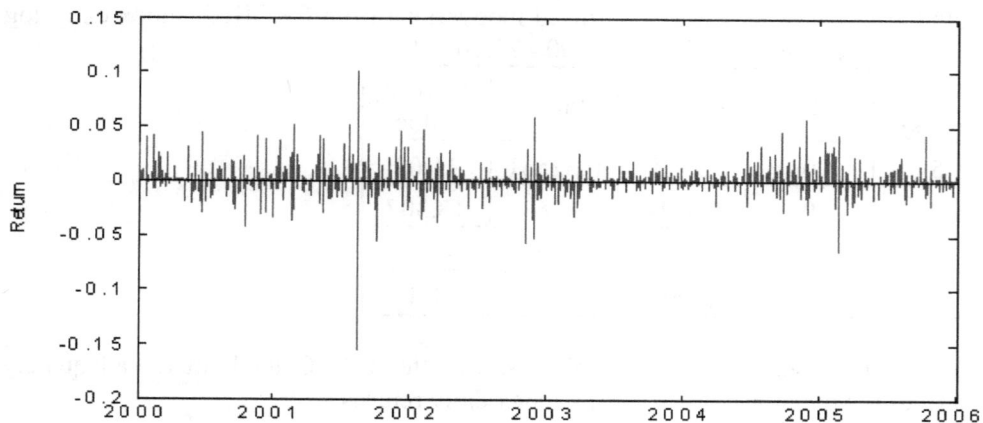

Figure 78 - Histogram of daily log returns of VIN index, period 04.01.2000 - 31.12.2005 (1480 observations)

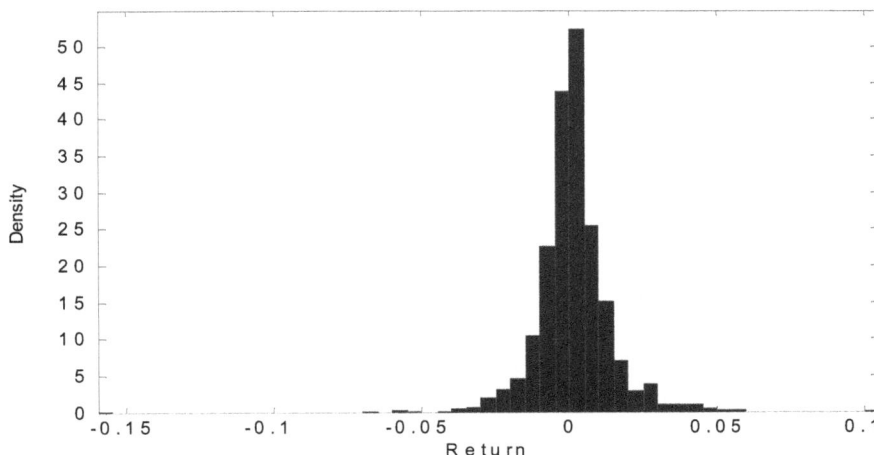

From figures 76, 77 and 78 it is visible that there is significant volatility clustering and presence of extreme positive and negative returns, which motivates a conditional volatility model that accounts for time varying volatility.

Basic descriptive statistics for VIN index in the period 04.01.2000 - 31.12.2005 are presented in table 63.

Table 63 - Basic statistics for VIN index daily log returns, period 04.01.2000 - 31.12.2005 (1480 observations)

Mean	0.001286
Median	0.000534
Minimum	-0.1567
Maximum	0.10186
Standard deviation	0.012806
Skewness	-0.6828
Kurtosis	23.689

Mean and median of daily returns differ significantly, which is in breach of normality assumption. Both mean and median differ significantly from zero. Mean shows a very strong positive trend similar to SKSM index. Skewness and excess kurtosis are different from zero. In the observed period VIN index experienced extreme daily returns. The highest daily gain in the analysed period was 10,19%, while the highest daily loss amounted to huge – 15,67%. Asymmetry is negative (-0,6828) and very close to value of PX50 index, meaning that the distribution slopes to the left and negative returns are expected to occur more frequently than positive. Excess kurtosis of 23,69 indicates that the empirical probability distribution of VIN index has significantly fatter tails than assumed under normal distribution. Excess kurtosis is much higher than detected in other indexes with SBI20 and CROBEX index having the most similar values.

Although significant linear dependence could be expected between CROBEX and VIN index, since they both represent the same market their descriptive statistics, in particular higher moments around the mean, tell a different story. Both CROBEX and VIN index have significant positive means and medians in the entire analysed period. This clearly points to the conclusion that securities composing these two indexes had a steady positive mean, resulting in considerable capital gains for the investors. In the analysed period VIN index was less volatile and more profitable than CROBEX. For the entire analysed period VIN index had negative skewness of −0,6828, while CROBEX index had positive skewness of 0,754. This fact is very important for the investors meaning that the probability of positive returns occurring is far greater when investing in CROBEX index than in VIN index although they represent the same market. Pronounced kurtosis shows that investors investing on Varaždin stock exchange can expect to experience even higher profits/losses than when investing on Zagreb stock exchange. Combining the third and fourth moment of the VIN index with its mean and standard deviation, it can be concluded that although in the entire observation period, negative returns were more frequent than positive returns, the magnitude of the positive returns was significantly higher than the magnitude of loses, resulting in a strong positive trend for VIN index. These characteristics of VIN index, similar to BUX, PX50, CROBEX and SKSM index, resulted in a strong positive trend and continually increasing index values.

To determine if the daily returns of VIN index are normally distributed, normality of empirical distribution is tested by Jarque-Bera test and Lilliefors test. Normality tests for the VIN index are presented in table 64.

Table 64 - Normality tests for VIN index daily log returns, period 04.01.2000 - 31.12.2005 (1480 observations)

Jarque-Bera test	26,430
(p value)	0
Lilliefors test	0.10509
(p value)	0

Both normality tests show that the hypothesis of normality of returns for VIN index, for the entire analysed period, should be rejected at 5% significance level. Probability values of distribution of returns being normal, according to both normality tests are zero, strongly indicating that there is no possibility that the returns on this index are normally distributed. The distribution of VIN index returns is leptokurtotic and not symmetrical i.e. it skews to the left, as can be seen from figures 78 and 79, as well as from table 65. Figure 79 and table 65 show that the true empirical distribution of VIN index daily returns is far better approximated by a Student's t distribution with 2,33 degrees of freedom, than it is by normal distribution.

Figure 79 - Probability plot for VIN index daily log returns, period 04.01.2000 - 31.12.2005 (1480 observations)

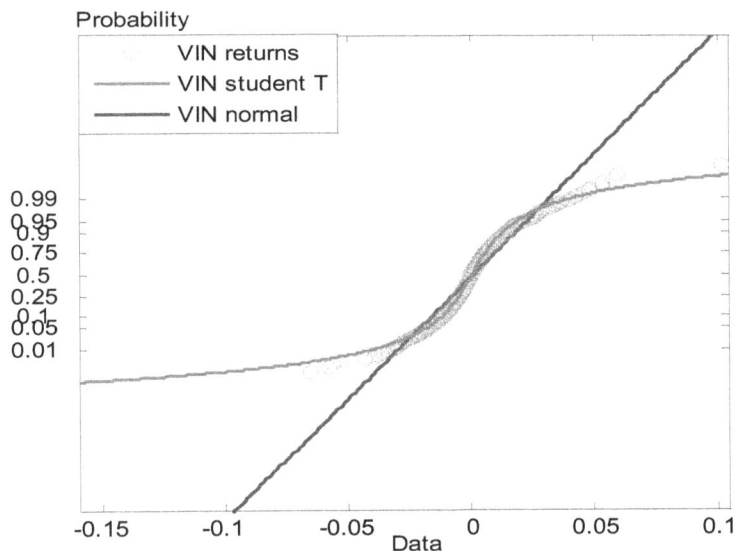

Table 65 - Parameters of fitted Normal and Students' T distribution to VIN index daily log returns, period 04.01.2000 - 31.12.2005 (1480 observations)

Distribution: Normal			Distribution: t location-scale		
Log likelihood: 3989.65			Log likelihood: 4243.54		
Mean: 0.001267			Mean: 0.000639		
Variance: 0.000172			Variance: 0.000335		
Parameter	Estimate	Std. Err.	Parameter	Estimate	Std. Err.
mu	0.001267	0.000354	mu	0.000639	0.000233
sigma	0.013102	0.000251	sigma	0.006851	0.000274
			df	2.32543	0.191813

Estimated covariance of parameter estimates:			Estimated covariance of parameter estimates:			
	mu	sigma		mu	sigma	df
mu	1.25E-07	-5.26E-24	mu	5.45E-08	6.01E-09	4.23E-06
sigma	-5.26E-24	6.28E-08	sigma	6.01E-09	7.53E-08	3.57E-05
			df	4.23E-06	3.57E-05	0.036792

Presence of autocorrelation in VIN daily log returns is tested by examining its sample autocorrelation and sample partial correlation function (Figure 80), and calculating Ljung-Box Q-statistic for mean adjusted VIN returns (Table 66).

Figure 80 - Sample autocorrelation and sample partial correlation function of VIN index daily log returns, period 04.01.2000 - 04.12.2003 (980 observations)

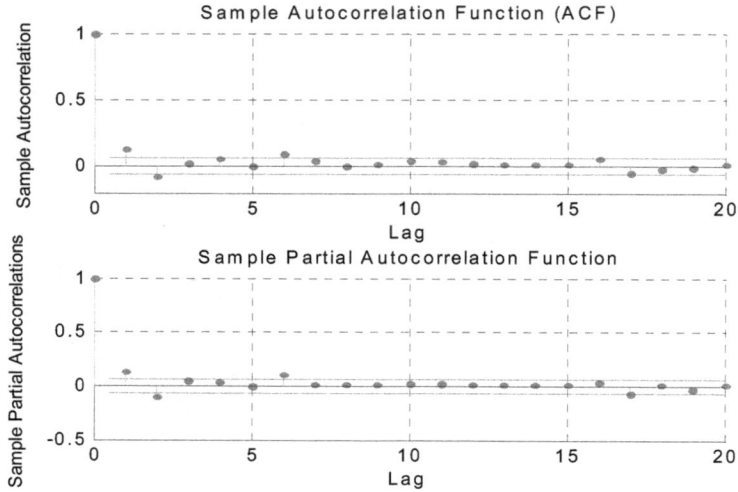

Table 66 - Ljung-Box-Pierce Q-test for mean adjusted VIN index daily log returns, period 04.01.2000 - 04.12.2003 (980 observations)

Period (days)	H	p-value	Statistic	Critical value
5	1	2.03E-09	49.194	11.07
10	1	1.38E-11	72.617	18.307
15	1	1.89E-10	77.632	24.996
20	1	2.47E-09	81.185	31.41

Sample autocorrelation, sample partial correlation function and Ljung-Box Q-statistic found the presence of autocorrelation in the VIN daily log returns meaning that the Varaždin stock market is not very efficient since the direction of the market can be predicted. To extract the autocorrelation from the data it will be necessary to use an ARMA (p, q) model.

After the presence of autocorrelation in the daily log returns has been investigated it is necessary to test the squared log returns for presence of autocorrelation i.e. heteroskedasticity. Presence of heteroskedasticity in VIN returns is tested by examining its sample autocorrelation and sample partial correlation function of squared returns (Figure 81), calculating Ljung-Box Q-statistic for mean adjusted squared VIN returns (Table 67) and ARCH test for mean adjusted VIN returns (Table 68).

Figure 81 - Sample autocorrelation and sample partial correlation function of squared VIN index daily log returns, period 04.01.2000 - 04.12.2003 (980 observations)

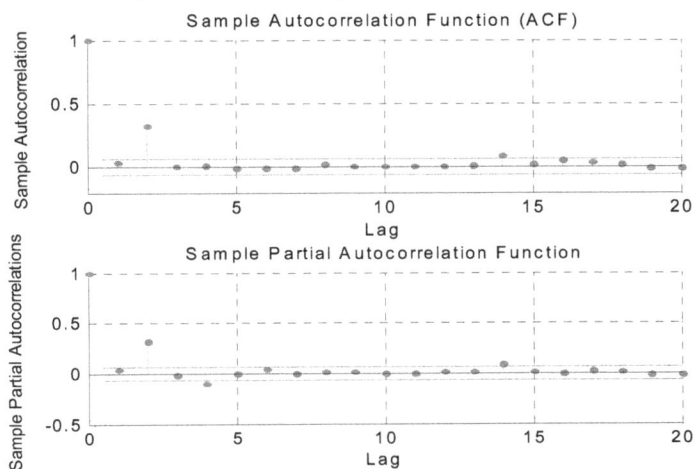

Table 67 - Ljung-Box-Pierce Q-test for mean adjusted squared VIN index daily log returns, period 04.01.2000 - 04.12.2003 (980 observations)

Period (days)	H	p-value	Statistic	Critical value
5	1	0	139.94	11.07
10	1	0	140.6	18.307
15	1	0	150.57	24.996
20	1	0	156.2	31.41

Table 68 - ARCH test for mean adjusted VIN index daily log returns, period 04.01.2000 - 04.12.2003 (980 observations)

Period (days)	H	p-value	Statistic	Critical value
5	1	0	147.3	11.07
10	1	0	148.29	18.307
15	1	0	157.28	24.996
20	1	0	158.84	31.41

Sample autocorrelation and sample partial correlation function of squared returns, as well as the Ljung-Box Q-statistic and Engle's ARCH test confirm that there is significant autocorrelation and ARCH effects present in VIN daily log returns, meaning that the returns on VIN index are not IID.

Since the employed tests discovered significant autocorrelation and heteroskedasticity in the VIN daily returns it is necessary to model the data in order to obtain independently and identically distributed returns. Because autocorrelation has been detected in both returns and squared returns, VIN index returns will be modelled as an ARMA-GARCH process in order to deal with both types of dependence. Estimated ARMA-GARCH parameters for VIN index are given in table 69.

Table 69 - Estimated ARMA-GARCH parameters for VIN index daily log returns, period 04.01.2000 - 04.12.2003 (980 observations)

Mean: ARMA(1,0)
Variance: GARCH(1,1)

Conditional Probability Distribution: Gaussian

Parameter	Value	Standard error	T statistic
C	-7.23E-05	0.000367	-0.1968
AR(1)	1.45E-01	0.034035	4.2476
K	1.25E-05	1.51E-06	8.2774
GARCH(1)	0.78932	0.022073	35.7604
ARCH(1)	0.1405	0.020087	6.9949

According to their t statistics all of the estimated parameters are statistically significant, except the mean drift that is statistically insignificant and will be assumed to equal zero. The obtained model is a normally distributed AR(1)-GARCH(1,1) model:

$$r_t = -0.0000723 + 0.145r_{t-1} + \varepsilon_t$$

$$\sigma_t^2 = 1.25E - 05 + 0.1405\varepsilon_{t-1}^2 + 0.78932\sigma_{t-1}^2$$

Similarly to SBI20 and SKSM index the conditional volatility model for VIN index is also far from being integrated. The plot of fitted AR-GARCH model innovations, conditional standard deviations and observed VIN index daily log returns are given in figure 82.

Figure 82 - Plot of fitted AR-GARCH model innovations, conditional standard
deviations and observed VIN index daily log returns, period 04.01.2000
- 04.12.2003

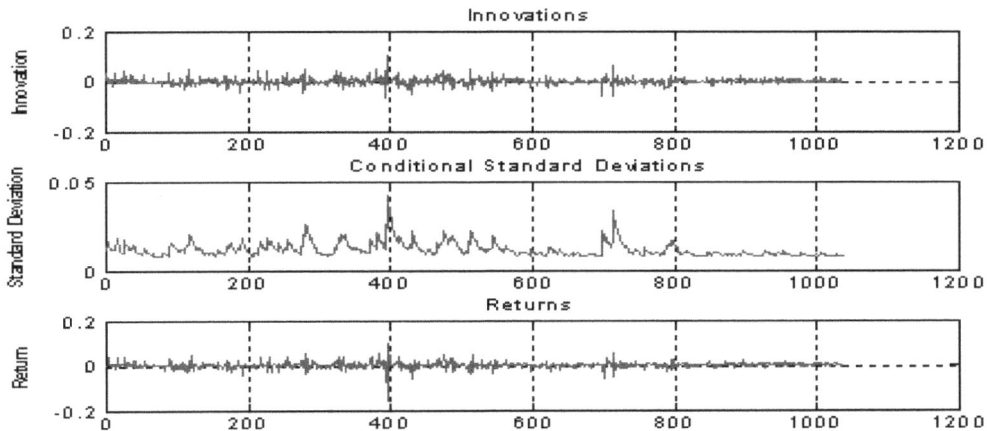

If the fitted AR-GARCH model is appropriate for describing the dynamics of
underlying data generating process the standardised innovation from such AR-
GARCH model should be independently and identically distributed (Figure 83). The
adequacy of fitted AR-GARCH model can be statistically tested in the same manner
as returns and squared returns.

Figure 83 - Standardised innovations from fitted AR-GARCH model for VIN index
daily log returns, period 04.01.2000 - 04.12.2003

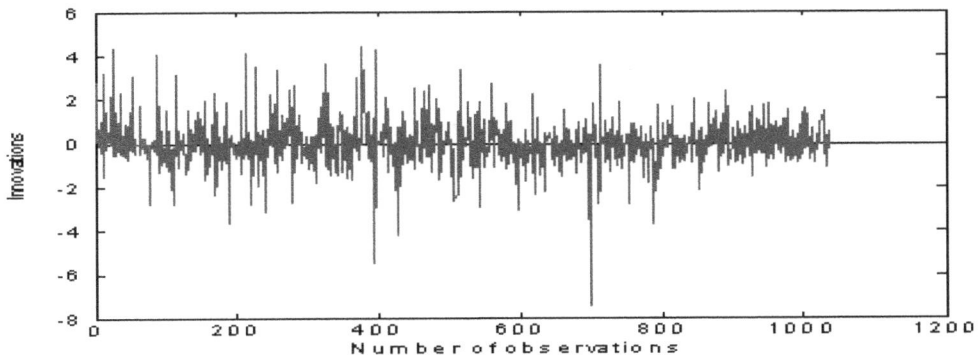

Sample autocorrelation, sample partial correlation function and Ljung-Box Q-
statistic of standardised innovation detect no presence of autocorrelation in the
standardised innovations from fitted AR-GARCH model, meaning that the
conditional mean model (AR(1)) successfully captured the autocorrelation present in
VIN returns (Figure 84, Table 70).

Figure 84 - Sample autocorrelation and sample partial correlation function of standardized innovations from VIN index daily log returns, period 04.01.2000 - 04.12.2003

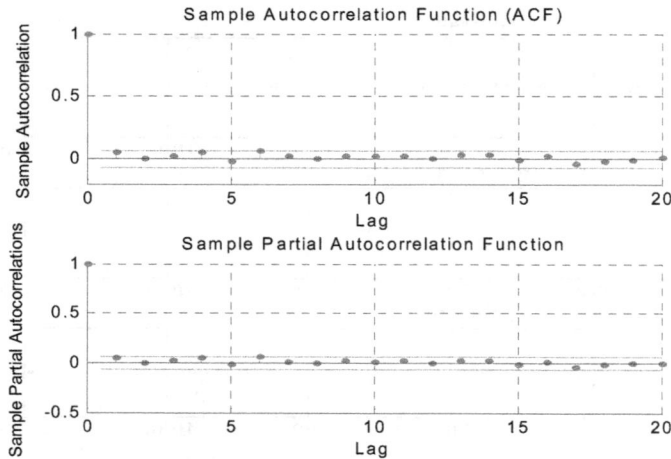

Table 70 - Ljung-Box-Pierce Q-test for standardised innovations from VIN index daily log returns, period 04.01.2000 - 04.12.2003

Period (days)	H	p-value	Statistic	Critical value
5	0	0.3503	5.5707	11.07
10	0	0.3744	10.7862	18.307
15	0	0.5987	13.0465	24.996
20	0	0.7874	14.8054	31.41

Sample autocorrelation and sample partial correlation function, Ljung-Box Q-statistic of squared standardised innovation and ARCH test of standardised innovations detect no presence of autocorrelation in the squared standardised innovations from fitted AR-GARCH model. This indicates that the conditional variance model (GARCH(1,1)) successfully captured the heteroskedasticity present in VIN returns (Figure 85, Tables 71, 72).

Figure 85 - Sample autocorrelation and sample partial correlation function of squared standardized innovations from VIN index daily log returns, period 04.01.2000 - 04.12.2003

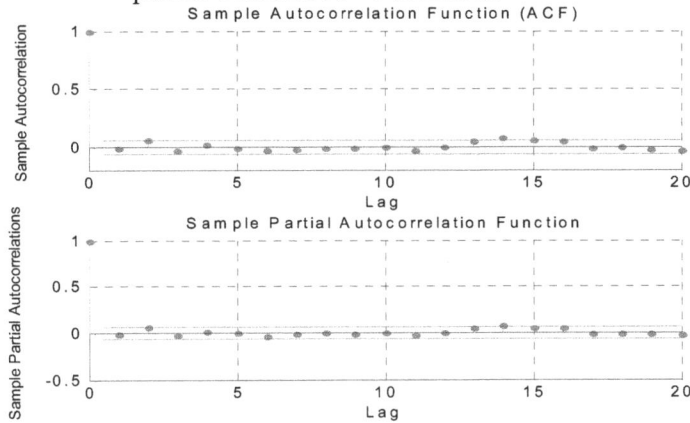

Sample Autocorrelation Function (ACF)

Sample Partial Autocorrelation Function

Table 71 - Ljung-Box-Pierce Q-test for squared standardised innovations from VIN index daily log returns, period 04.01.2000 - 04.12.2003

Period (days)	H	p-value	Statistic	Critical value
5	0	0.3896	5.2203	11.07
10	0	0.73875	6.8583	18.307
15	0	0.19945	19.324	24.996
20	0	0.26924	23.407	31.41

Table 72 - ARCH test for standardised innovations from VIN index daily log returns, period 04.01.2000 - 04.12.2003

Period (days)	H	p-value	Statistic	Critical value
5	0	0.42952	4.8894	11.07
10	0	0.76363	6.5886	18.307
15	0	0.2003	19.304	24.996
20	0	0.30075	22.76	31.41

Findings of the performed tests imply that the fitted AR(1)-GARCH(1,1) model adequately describes the dynamics of VIN index daily returns.

6.3.8   Estonia – TALSE index

Trading on the Tallin Stock Exchange (TSE-OMX) started in 1995. The TALSE (later changed its name into OMX Tallin Index) index was launched in 1996 with the initial value of 100 points.

The analysis of the TALSE stock index is performed for the period 03.01.2000 – 31.12.2005. In this observation period the obtained sample from TALSE index consists of 1522 daily index value observations. The evolution of index values and returns is displayed in Figures 86, 87 and 88.

Figure 86 - Daily values of TALSE index, period 03.01.2000 - 31.12.2005 (1522 observations)

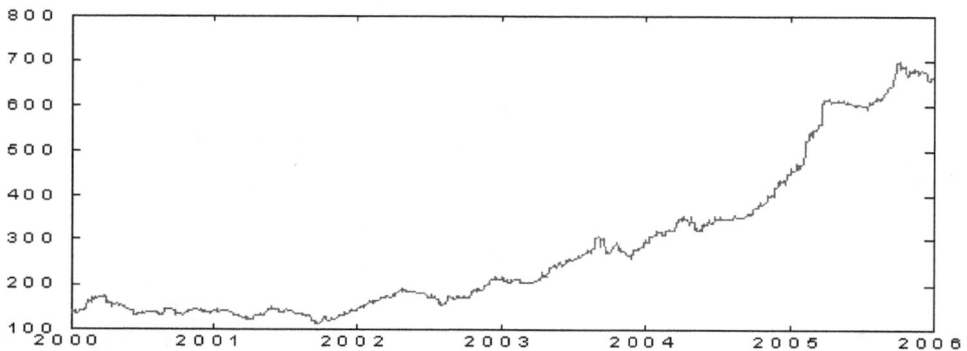

Figure 87 - Daily log returns of TALSE index, period 03.01.2000 - 31.12.2005 (1521 observations)

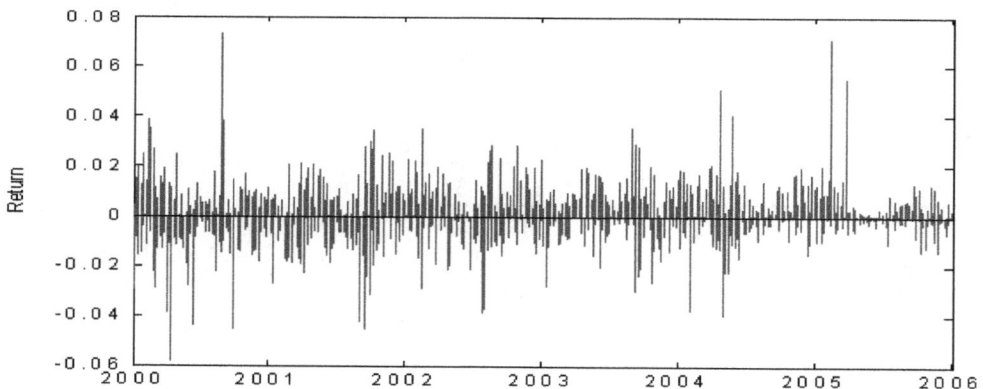

Figure 88 - Histogram of daily log returns of TALSE index, period 03.01.2000 - 31.12.2005 (1521 observations)

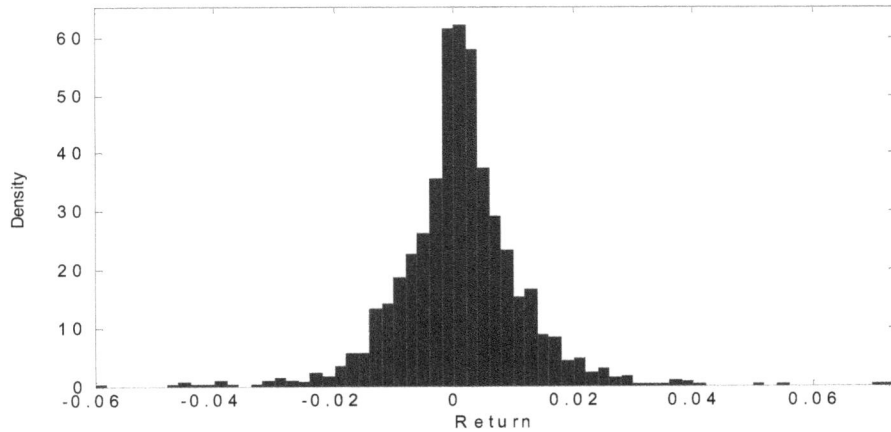

From figures 86, 87 and 88 it is visible that there is significant volatility clustering and presence of extreme positive and negative returns, which motivates a conditional volatility model that accounts for time varying volatility.

Basic descriptive statistics for TALSE index in the period 03.01.2000 - 31.12.2005 are presented in table 73.

Table 73 - Basic statistics for TALSE index daily log returns, period 03.01.2000 - 31.12.2005 (1521 observations)

Mean	0.001016
Median	0.000965
Minimum	-0.05874
Maximum	0.073425
Standard deviation	0.010472
Skewness	0.22481
Kurtosis	9.0341

Mean and median of daily returns are very similar and show a significant positive trend that is similar to SBI20 and VIN index. Excess kurtosis and skewness of TALSE index are different from zero. In the observed period TALSE index experienced extreme daily returns. The highest daily gain in the analysed period was 7,34%, while the highest daily loss amounted to − 5,87%. Asymmetry is slightly positive (0,2248), meaning that the distribution slopes slightly to the right and positive returns are expected to occur more frequently than negative. Excess kurtosis of 9,03 indicates that the empirical probability distribution of TALSE index has significantly fatter tails than assumed under normal distribution. Excess kurtosis is similar to excess kurtosis detected in CEE countries.

Combining the third and fourth moment of the TALSE index with the mean and standard deviation, it can be concluded that in the observed period, frequency of positive and negative returns was very similar but the magnitude of the positive returns was significantly higher than the magnitude of loses. These characteristics of TALSE index, very similar to CEE countries, resulted in a strong positive trend. To determine if the daily returns of TALSE index are normally distributed, normality of empirical distribution is tested by Jarque-Bera test and Lilliefors test. Normality tests for the TALSE index are presented in table 74.

Table 74 - Normality tests for TALSE index daily log returns, period 03.01.2000 - 31.12.2005 (1521 observations)

Jarque-Bera test	2,311.2
(p value)	0
Lilliefors test	0.079737
(p value)	0

Both normality tests show that the hypothesis of normality of returns for TALSE index, for the entire analysed period, should be rejected at 5% significance level. Probability values of distribution of returns being normal, according to both normality tests are zero, strongly indicating that there is no possibility that the returns on this index are normally distributed. The distribution of TALSE index returns is leptokurtotic and slightly asymmetrical i.e. it skews slightly to the right, as can be seen from figures 88 and 89, as well as from table 75. Figure 89 and table 75 show that the true empirical distribution of TALSE index daily returns is far better approximated by a Student's t distribution with 3,02 degrees of freedom, than it is by normal distribution.

Figure 89 - Probability plot for TALSE index daily log returns, period 03.01.2000 - 31.12.2005 (1521 observations)

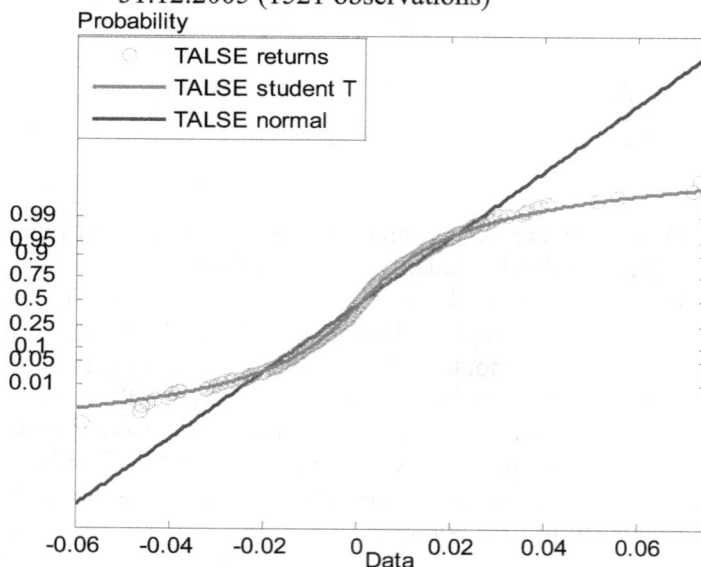

Table 75 - Parameters of fitted Normal and Students' T distribution to TALSE index daily log returns, period 03.01.2000 - 31.12.2005 (1521 observations)

Distribution: Normal			Distribution: t location-scale			
Log likelihood: 4359.9			Log likelihood: 4498.75			
Mean: 0.00103			Mean: 0.000981			
Variance: 1.17E-04			Variance: 1.40E-04			
Parameter	Estimate	Std. Err.	Parameter	Estimate	Std. Err.	
mu	0.00103	0.000288	mu	0.000981	0.000223	
sigma	0.010798	0.000204	sigma	0.006871	0.000262	
			df	3.0153	0.298383	
Estimated covariance of parameter estimates:			Estimated covariance of parameter estimates:			
	mu	sigma		mu	sigma	df
mu	8.32E-08	-3.25E-24	mu	4.98E-08	1.56E-10	1.86E-07
sigma	-3.25E-24	4.16E-08	sigma	1.56E-10	6.84E-08	5.49E-05
			df	1.86E-07	5.49E-05	0.089033

Presence of autocorrelation in TALSE daily log returns is tested by examining its sample autocorrelation and sample partial correlation function (Figure 90), and calculating Ljung-Box Q-statistic for mean adjusted TALSE returns (Table 76).

Figure 90 - Sample autocorrelation and sample partial correlation function of TALSE index daily log returns, period 03.01.2000 - 15.01.2004 (1021 observations)

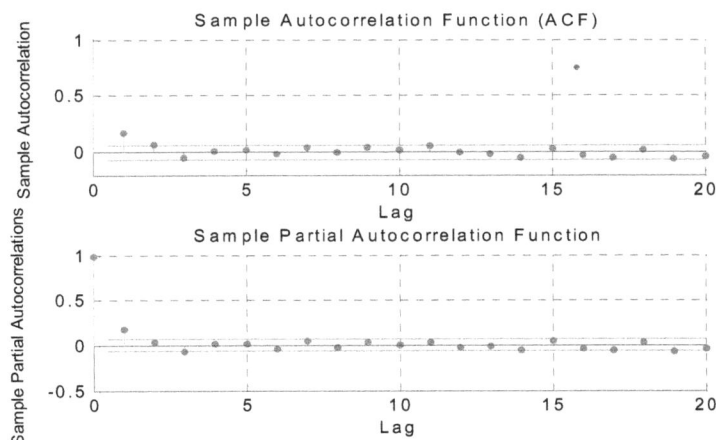

Table 76 - Ljung-Box-Pierce Q-test for mean adjusted TALSE index daily log returns, period 03.01.2000 - 15.01.2004 (1021 observations)

Period (days)	H	p-value	Statistic	Critical value
5	1	2.23E-07	39.136	11.07
10	1	2.66E-07	50.009	18.307
15	1	8.12E-07	57.027	24.996
20	1	1.69E-06	63.989	31.41

Sample autocorrelation, sample partial correlation function and Ljung-Box Q-statistic found the presence of autocorrelation in the TALSE daily log returns meaning that the Estonian stock market is not very efficient since the direction of the market can be predicted. To extract the autocorrelation from the data it will be necessary to use an ARMA (p, q) model.

After the presence of autocorrelation in the daily log returns has been investigated it is necessary to test the squared log returns for presence of autocorrelation i.e. heteroskedasticity. Presence of heteroskedasticity in TALSE returns is tested by examining its sample autocorrelation and sample partial correlation function of squared returns (Figure 91), calculating Ljung-Box Q-statistic for mean adjusted squared TALSE returns (Table 77) and ARCH test for mean adjusted TALSE returns (Table 78).

Figure 91 - Sample autocorrelation and sample partial correlation function of squared TALSE index daily log returns, period 03.01.2000 - 15.01.2004 (1021 observations)

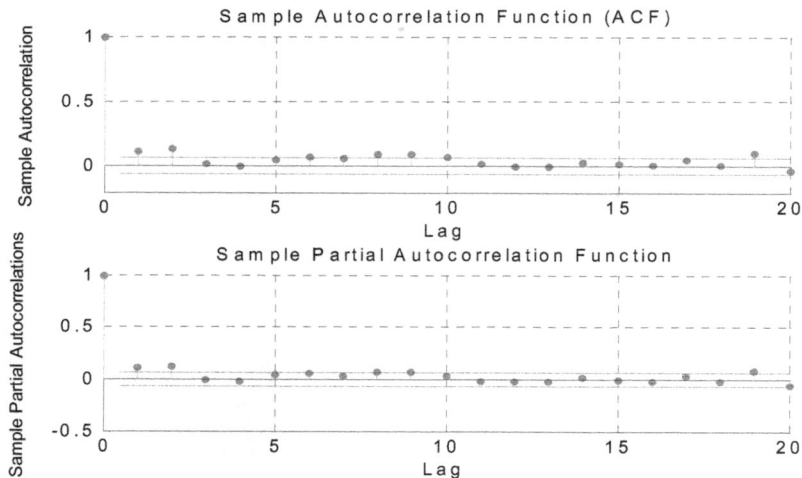

Table 77 - Ljung-Box-Pierce Q-test for mean adjusted squared TALSE index daily log returns, period 03.01.2000 - 15.01.2004 (1021 observations)

Period (days)	H	p-value	Statistic	Critical value
5	1	3.66E-07	38.067	11.07
10	1	1.10E-10	67.961	18.307
15	1	1.48E-09	72.691	24.996
20	1	3.08E-12	97.829	31.41

Table 78 - ARCH test for mean adjusted TALSE index daily log returns, period 03.01.2000 - 15.01.2004 (1021 observations)

Period (days)	H	p-value	Statistic	Critical value
5	1	4.25E-06	32.735	11.07
10	1	8.83E-07	47.16	18.307
15	1	2.86E-05	47.688	24.996
20	1	1.52E-06	64.279	31.41

Sample autocorrelation and sample partial correlation function of squared returns, as well as the Ljung-Box Q-statistic and Engle's ARCH test confirm that there is significant autocorrelation and ARCH effects present in TALSE daily log returns, meaning that the returns on TALSE index are not IID. Since the employed tests discovered significant autocorrelation and heteroskedasticity in the TALSE daily returns it is necessary to model the data in order to obtain independently and identically distributed returns. Because autocorrelation has been detected in both returns and squared returns, TALSE index returns will be modelled as an ARMA-GARCH process in order to deal with both types of dependence. Estimated ARMA-GARCH parameters for TALSE index are given in table 79.

Table 79 - Estimated ARMA-GARCH parameters for TALSE index daily log returns, period 03.01.2000 - 15.01.2004 (1021 observations)

Mean: ARMA(0,2)
Variance: GARCH(1,1)

Conditional Probability Distribution: Gaussian

Parameter	Value	Standard error	T statistic
C	9.60E-04	0.000425	2.2614
MA(1)	2.16E-01	0.035403	6.0955
MA(2)	9.23E-02	0.033881	2.7252
K	6.76E-06	1.84E-06	3.673
GARCH(1)	0.84035	0.026909	31.2295
ARCH(1)	0.10469	0.018945	5.5263

All of the estimated parameters are statistically significant according to their t statistics. The obtained model is a normally distributed MA(2)-GARCH(1,1) model:

$$r_t = 0.00096 + 0.216\varepsilon_{t-1} + 0.0923\varepsilon_{t-2} + \varepsilon_t$$

$$\sigma_t^2 = 6.76E - 06 + 0.10469\varepsilon_{t-1}^2 + 0.84035\sigma_{t-1}^2$$

The plot of fitted MA-GARCH model innovations, conditional standard deviations and observed TALSE index daily log returns are given in figure 92.

Figure 92 - Plot of fitted MA-GARCH model innovations, conditional standard deviations and observed TALSE index daily log returns, period 03.01.2000 - 15.01.2004

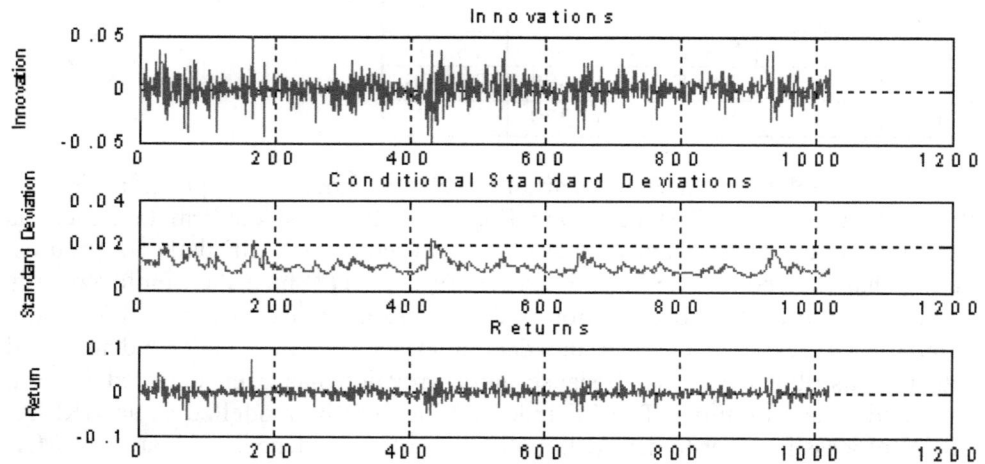

If the fitted MA-GARCH model is appropriate for describing the dynamics of underlying data generating process the standardised innovation from such MA-GARCH model should be independently and identically distributed (Figure 93). The adequacy of fitted MA-GARCH model can be statistically tested in the same manner as returns and squared returns.

Figure 93 - Standardised innovations from fitted MA-GARCH model for TALSE index daily log returns, period 03.01.2000 - 15.01.2004

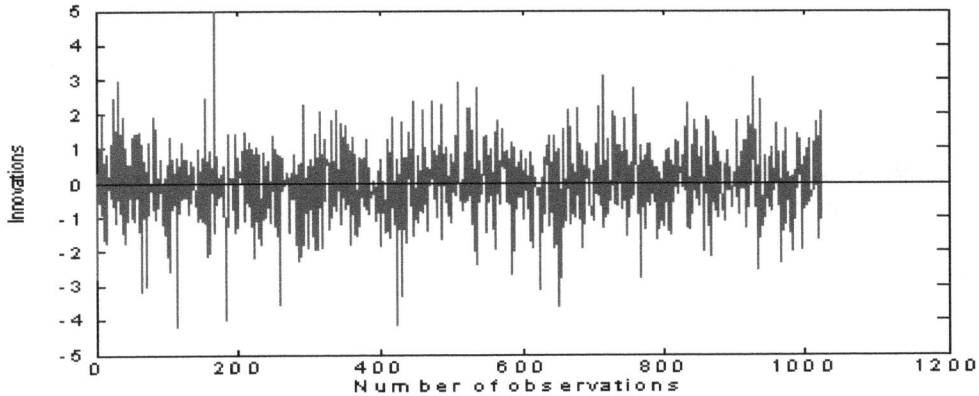

Sample autocorrelation, sample partial correlation function and Ljung-Box Q-statistic of standardised innovation detect no presence of autocorrelation in the standardised innovations from fitted MA-GARCH model, meaning that the conditional mean model (MA(2)) successfully captured the autocorrelation present in TALSE returns (Figure 94, Table 80).

Figure 94 - Sample autocorrelation and sample partial correlation function of standardized innovations from TALSE index daily log returns, period 03.01.2000 - 15.01.2004

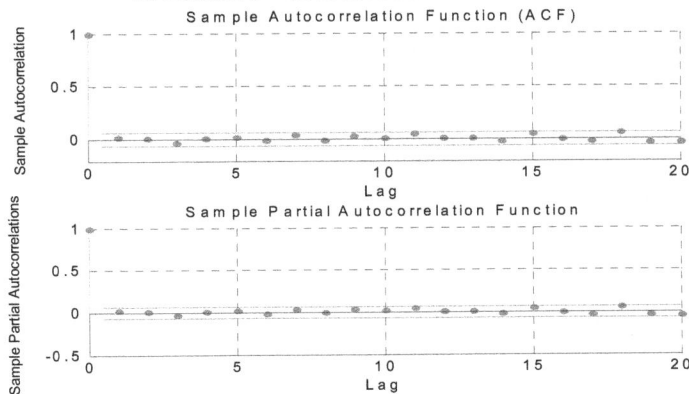

Table 80 - Ljung-Box-Pierce Q-test for standardised innovations from TALSE index daily log returns, period 03.01.2000 - 15.01.2004

Period (days)	H	p-value	Statistic	Critical value
5	0	0.84405	2.0367	11.07
10	0	0.83724	5.7322	18.307
15	0	0.69937	11.73	24.996
20	0	0.56092	18.402	31.41

Sample autocorrelation and sample partial correlation function, Ljung-Box Q-statistic of squared standardised innovation and ARCH test of standardised innovations detect no presence of autocorrelation in the squared standardised innovations from fitted MA-GARCH model. This indicates that the conditional variance model (GARCH(1,1)) successfully captured the heteroskedasticity present in TALSE returns (Figure 95, Tables 81, 82).

Figure 95 - Sample autocorrelation and sample partial correlation function of squared standardized innovations from TALSE index daily log returns, period 03.01.2000 - 15.01.2004

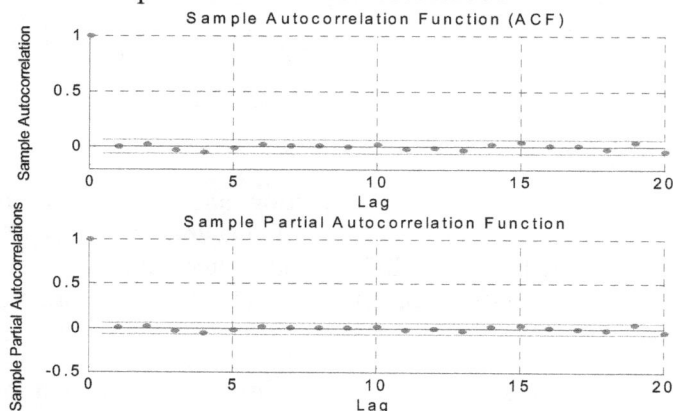

Table 81 - Ljung-Box-Pierce Q-test for squared standardised innovations from TALSE index daily log returns, period 03.01.2000 - 15.01.2004

Period (days)	H	p-value	Statistic	Critical value
5	0	0.47174	4.5612	11.07
10	0	0.83132	5.8057	18.307
15	0	0.85566	9.4005	24.996
20	0	0.82156	14.174	31.41

Table 82 - ARCH test for standardised innovations from TALSE index daily log returns, period 03.01.2000 - 15.01.2004

Period (days)	H	p-value	Statistic	Critical value
5	0	0.45389	4.6976	11.07
10	0	0.82656	5.8639	18.307
15	0	0.87868	8.9777	24.996
20	0	0.83088	13.992	31.41

Findings of the performed tests imply that the fitted MA(2)-GARCH(1,1) model adequately describes the dynamics of TALSE index daily returns.

6.3.9   Latvia – RIGSE index

Trading on the Riga Stock Exchange (RSE-OMX) started in 1993. The RIGSE (later changed its name into OMX Riga Index) index was launched in 2000 with the initial value of 100 points.

The analysis of the RIGSE stock index is performed for the period 03.01.2000 – 31.12.2005. In this observation period the obtained sample from RIGSE index consists of 1555 daily index value observations. The evolution of index values and returns is displayed in Figures 96, 97 and 98.

Figure 96 - Daily values of RIGSE index, period 03.01.2000 - 31.12.2005 (1555 observations)

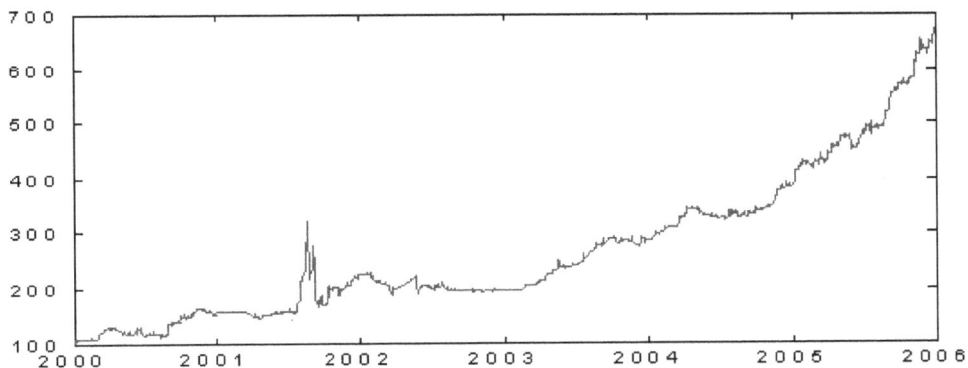

Figure 97 - Daily log returns of RIGSE index, period 03.01.2000 - 31.12.2005 (1554 observations)

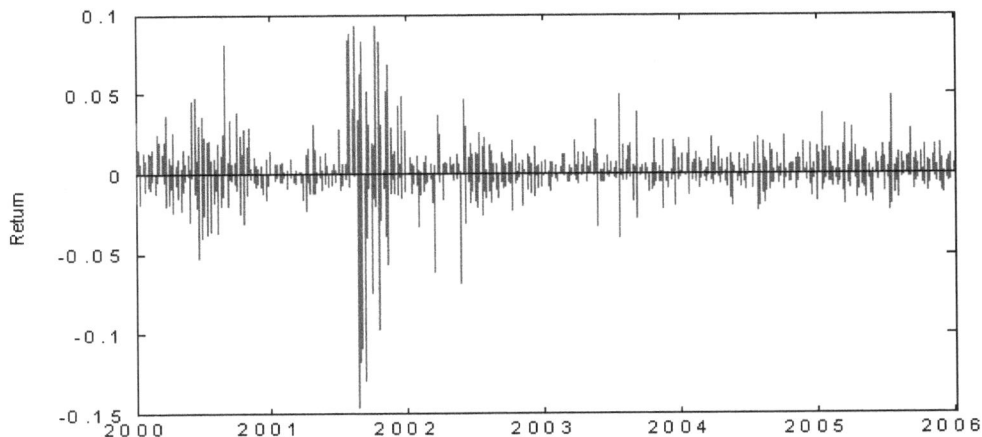

Figure 98 - Histogram of daily log returns of RIGSE index, period 03.01.2000 - 31.12.2005 (1554 observations)

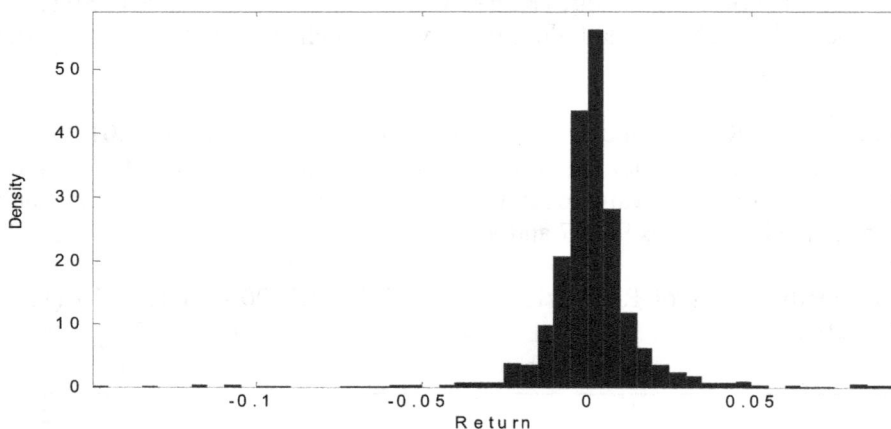

From figures 96, 97 and 98 it is visible that there is significant volatility clustering and presence of extreme positive and negative returns, which motivates a conditional volatility model that accounts for time varying volatility. Basic descriptive statistics for RIGSE index in the period 03.01.2000 - 31.12.2005 are presented in table 83.

Table 83 - Basic statistics for RIGSE index daily log returns, period 03.01.2000 - 31.12.2005 (1554 observations)

Mean	0.001202
Median	0.000608
Minimum	-0.14705
Maximum	0.094609
Standard deviation	0.016286
Skewness	-1.2783
Kurtosis	23.563

Mean and median of daily returns are significantly different and show a significant positive trend that is similar to TALSE index. Skewness and excess kurtosis are different from zero. In the observed period RIGSE index experienced extreme daily returns. The highest daily gain in the analysed period was 9,46%, while the highest daily loss amounted to – 14,71%, maximum values very similar to VIN index. Asymmetry is negative (-1,278), meaning that the distribution slopes to the left and negative returns are expected to occur more frequently than positive. Excess kurtosis of 23,563 indicates that the empirical probability distribution of RIGSE index has significantly fatter tails than assumed under normal distribution. Excess kurtosis is much higher than detected in TALSE index and majority of CEE countries but very similar to Croatian indexes.

Combining the third and fourth moment of the RIGSE index with its mean and standard deviation, it can be concluded that although in the entire observation period, negative returns were more frequent than positive returns, the magnitude of the positive returns was significantly higher than the magnitude of loses, resulting in a strong positive trend for RIGSE index. These characteristics of RIGSE index, very similar to CEEC indexes, resulted in a strong positive trend for the index. To determine if the daily returns of RIGSE index are normally distributed, normality of empirical distribution is tested by Jarque-Bera test and Lilliefors test. Normality tests for the RIGSE index are presented in table 84.

Table 84 - Normality tests for RIGSE index daily log returns, period 03.01.2000 - 31.12.2005 (1554 observations)

Jarque-Bera test	27,721
(p value)	0
Lilliefors test	0.15709
(p value)	0

Both normality tests show that the hypothesis of normality of returns for RIGSE, for the entire analysed period, should be rejected at 5% significance level. Probability values of distribution of returns being normal, according to both normality tests are zero, strongly indicating that there is no possibility that the returns on this index are normally distributed. The distribution of RIGSE index returns is leptokurtotic and asymmetrical i.e. it skews strongly to the left, as can be seen from figures 98 and 99, as well as from table 85. Figure 99 and table 85 show that the true empirical distribution of RIGSE index daily returns is far better approximated by a Student's t distribution with 1,61 degrees of freedom, than it is by normal distribution. Student's t distribution with 1,61 degrees of freedom has a finite mean because $df > 1$, but infinite variance since $df < 2$, meaning that the empirical distribution of RIGSE index could be treated as being nearly a Lorentzian distribution.

Figure 99 - Probability plot for RIGSE index daily log returns, period 03.01.2000 - 31.12.2005 (1554 observations)

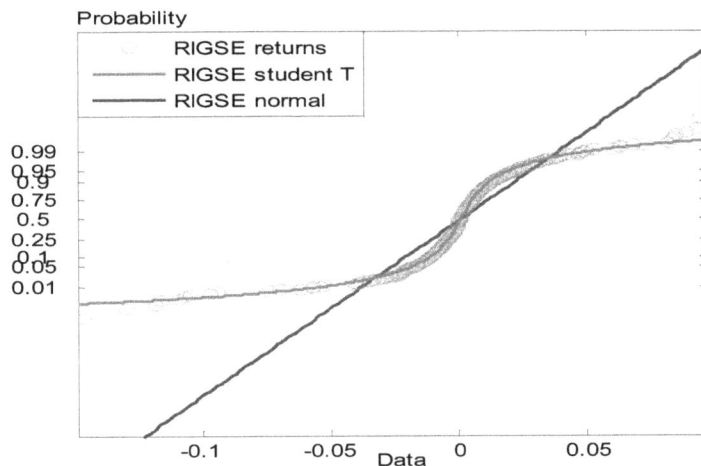

Table 85 - Parameters of fitted Normal and Students' T distribution to RIGSE index
daily log returns, period 03.01.2000 - 31.12.2005 (1554 observations)

Distribution: Normal			Distribution: t location-scale			
Log likelihood: 3836.88			Log likelihood: 4442.56			
Mean: 0.001056			Mean: 0.00076			
Variance: 2.80E-04			Variance: Inf			
Parameter	Estimate	Std. Err.	Parameter	Estimate	Std. Err.	
mu	0.001056	0.000442	mu	0.00076	0.000193	
sigma	0.016731	0.000312	sigma	0.005559	0.00023	
			df	1.60802	0.100002	
Estimated covariance of parameter estimates:			Estimated covariance of parameter estimates:			
	mu	sigma		mu	sigma	df
mu	1.95E-07	6.34E-25	mu	3.71E-08	2.02E-09	8.26E-07
sigma	6.34E-25	9.76E-08	sigma	8.26E-07	1.44E-05	1.00E-02
			df	8.26E-07	1.44E-05	0.01

Presence of autocorrelation in RIGSE daily log returns is tested by examining its
sample autocorrelation, sample partial correlation function (Figure 100) and
calculating Ljung-Box Q-statistic for mean adjusted RIGSE returns (Table 86).

Figure 100 - Sample autocorrelation and sample partial correlation function of
RIGSE index daily log returns, period 03.01.2000 - 15.01.2004 (1054
observations)

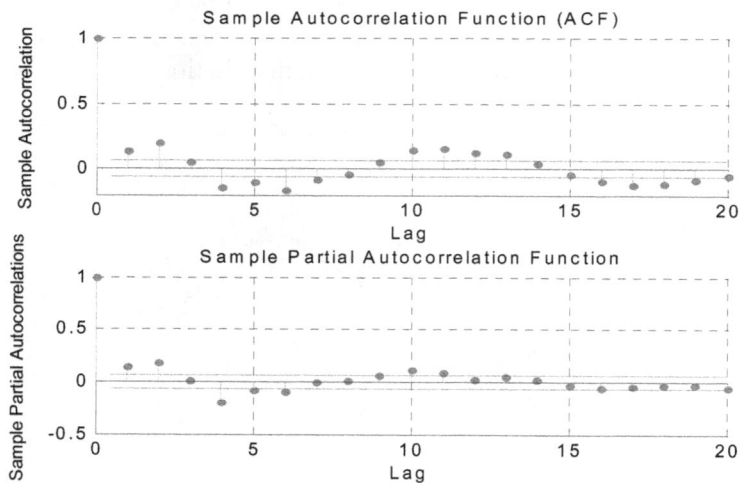

Table 86 - Ljung-Box-Pierce Q-test for mean adjusted RIGSE index daily log
returns, period 03.01.2000 - 15.01.2004 (1054 observations)

Period (days)	H	p-value	Statistic	Critical value
5	1	0	116.27	11.07
10	1	0	193.79	18.307
15	1	0	268.27	24.996
20	1	0	326.72	31.41

Sample autocorrelation, sample partial correlation function and Ljung-Box Q-statistic found the presence of autocorrelation in the RIGSE daily log returns meaning that the Latvian stock market is not very efficient since the direction of the market can be predicted. To extract the autocorrelation from the data it will be necessary to use an ARMA (p, q) model.

After the presence of autocorrelation in the daily log returns has been investigated it is necessary to test the squared log return for presence of autocorrelation i.e. heteroskedasticity. Presence of heteroskedasticity in RIGSE returns is tested by examining its sample autocorrelation and sample partial correlation function of squared returns (Figure 101), calculating Ljung-Box Q-statistic for mean adjusted squared RIGSE returns (Table 87) and ARCH test for mean adjusted RIGSE returns (Table 88).

Figure 101 - Sample autocorrelation and sample partial correlation function of squared RIGSE index daily log returns, period 03.01.2000 - 15.01.2004 (1054 observations)

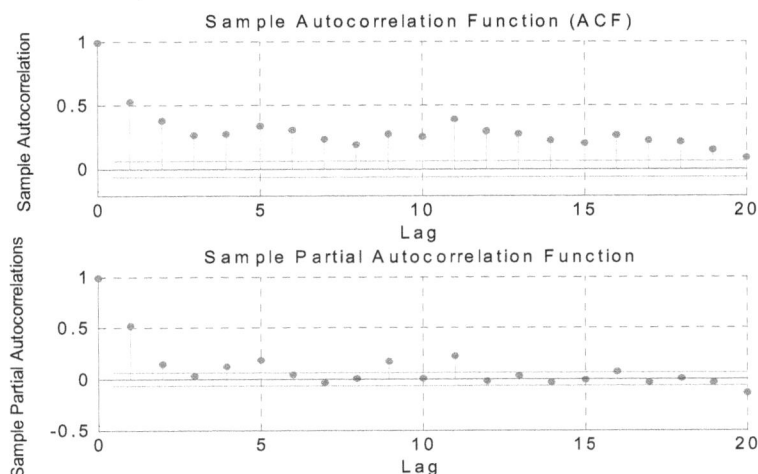

Table 87 - Ljung-Box-Pierce Q-test for mean adjusted squared RIGSE index daily log returns, period 03.01.2000 - 15.01.2004 (1054 observations)

Period (days)	H	p-value	Statistic	Critical value
5	1	0	1089.1	11.07
10	1	0	1631	18.307
15	1	0	2320.2	24.996
20	1	0	2650.4	31.41

Table 88 - ARCH test for mean adjusted RIGSE index daily log returns, period 03.01.2000 - 15.01.2004 (1054 observations)

Period (days)	H	p-value	Statistic	Critical value
5	1	0	514.28	11.07
10	1	0	548.49	18.307
15	1	0	601.38	24.996
20	1	0	623.8	31.41

Sample autocorrelation and sample partial correlation function of squared returns, as well as the Ljung-Box Q-statistic and Engle's ARCH test confirm that there is significant autocorrelation and ARCH effects present in RIGSE daily log returns, meaning that the returns on RIGSE index are not IID. The results are that much more indicative when considering that the hypothesis of IID was rejected for all the tested time lags (5, 10, 15 and 20 days). Since the employed tests discovered significant autocorrelation and heteroskedasticity in the RIGSE daily returns it is necessary to model the data in order to obtain independently and identically distributed returns. Because autocorrelation has been detected in both returns and squared returns, RIGSE index returns will be modelled as an ARMA-GARCH process in order to deal with both types of dependence. Estimated ARMA-GARCH parameters for RIGSE index are given in table 89.

Table 89 - Estimated ARMA-GJR GARCH parameters for RIGSE index daily log returns, period 03.01.2000 - 15.01.2004 (1054 observations)

Mean: ARMA(0,1)
Variance: GJR GARCH(1,1)

Conditional Probability Distribution: Gaussian

Parameter	Value	Standard error	T statistic
C	0.000755	0.000396	1.9084
MA(1)	-0.13221	0.059682	-2.2152
K	4.69E-06	2.18E-06	2.1481
GARCH(1)	0.90381	0.026029	34.7227
ARCH(1)	0.069603	0.018137	3.8376
Leverage(1)	-0.39327	0.098331	-3.9994

Significant leverage effect was discovered in the RIGSE daily log returns. To incorporate this characteristic of RIGSE index, the conditional volatility model had to be specified as a GJR-GARCH model. All of the estimated parameters are statistically significant according to their t statistics. The obtained model is a normally distributed MA(1)-GJR GARCH(1,1) model:

$$r_t = 0.000755 - 0.13221\varepsilon_{t-1} + \varepsilon_t$$

$$\sigma_t^2 = 64.69E - 06 + [0.069603 - 0.39327I_t]\varepsilon_{t-1}^2 + 0.90381\sigma_{t-1}^2$$

The plot of fitted MA-GJR GARCH model innovations, conditional standard deviations and observed RIGSE index daily log returns is given in figure 102.

Figure 102 - Plot of fitted MA-GJR GARCH model innovations, conditional standard deviations and observed RIGSE index daily log returns, period 03.01.2000 - 15.01.2004

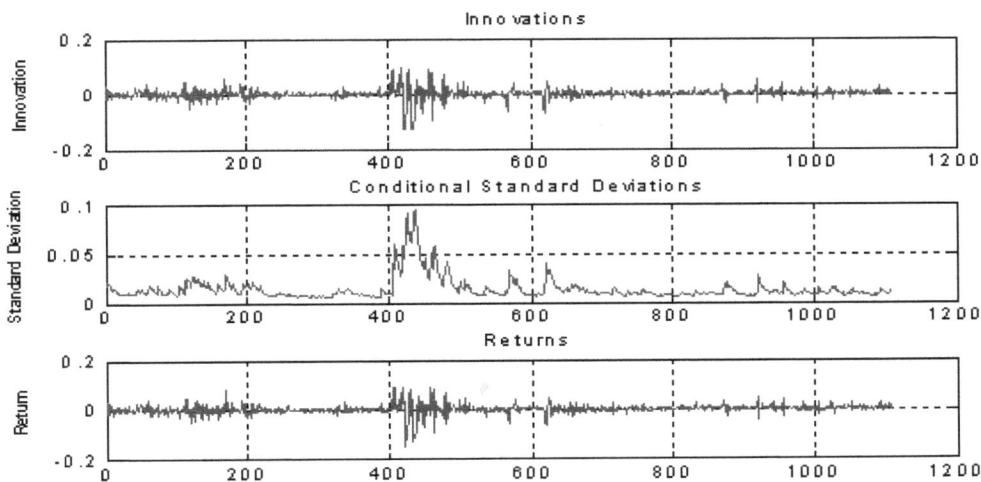

If the fitted MA-GJR GARCH model is appropriate for describing the dynamics of underlying data generating process the standardised innovation from such MA-GJR GARCH model should be independently and identically distributed (Figure 103). The adequacy of fitted MA-GJR GARCH model can be statistically tested in the same manner as returns and squared returns.

Figure 103 - Standardised innovations from fitted MA-GJR GARCH model for RIGSE index daily log returns, period 03.01.2000 - 15.01.2004

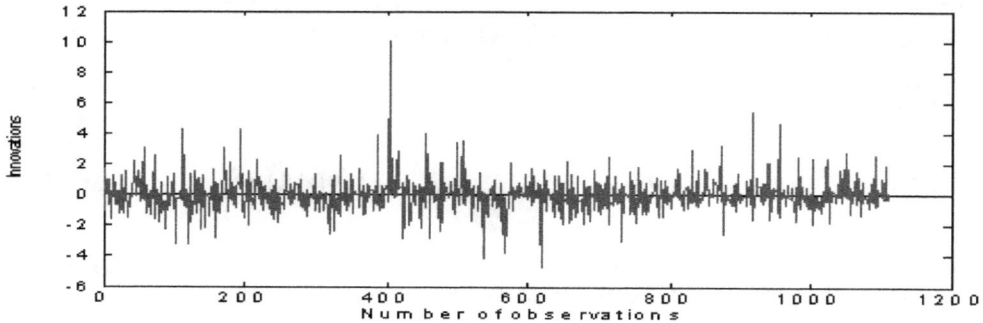

Sample autocorrelation, sample partial correlation function and Ljung-Box Q-statistic of standardised innovation detect no presence of autocorrelation in the standardised innovations from fitted MA-GJR GARCH model, meaning that the conditional mean model (MA(1)) successfully captured the autocorrelation present in RIGSE returns (Figure 104, Table 90).

Figure 104 - Sample autocorrelation and sample partial correlation function of standardized innovations from RIGSE index daily log returns, period 03.01.2000 - 15.01.2004

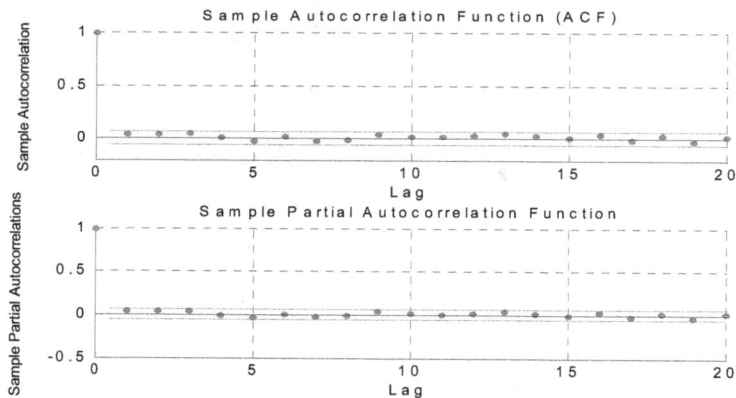

Table 90 - Ljung-Box-Pierce Q-test for standardised innovations from RIGSE index daily log returns, period 03.01.2000 - 15.01.2004

Period (days)	H	p-value	Statistic	Critical value
5	0	0.15415	8.0381	11.07
10	0	0.27108	12.213	18.307
15	0	0.23456	18.556	24.996
20	0	0.32222	22.342	31.41

Sample autocorrelation, sample partial correlation function, Ljung-Box Q-statistic of squared standardised innovation and ARCH test of standardised innovations detect no presence of autocorrelation in the squared standardised innovations from fitted MA-GJR GARCH model. This indicates that the conditional variance model (GJR GARCH(1,1)) successfully captured the heteroskedasticity present in RIGSE returns (Figure 105, Tables 91, 92).

Figure 105 - Sample autocorrelation and sample partial correlation function of squared standardized innovations from RIGSE index daily log returns, period 03.01.2000 - 15.01.2004

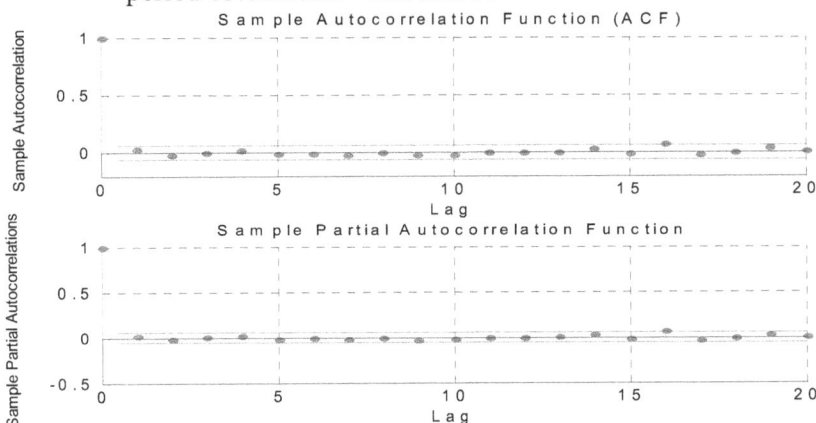

Table 91 - Ljung-Box-Pierce Q-test for squared standardised innovations from RIGSE index daily log returns, period 03.01.2000 - 15.01.2004

Period (days)	H	p-value	Statistic	Critical value
5	0	0.86265	1.9012	11.07
10	0	0.97805	3.1356	18.307
15	0	0.99369	4.8001	24.996
20	0	0.83904	13.829	31.41

Table 92 - ARCH test for standardised innovations from RIGSE index daily log returns, period 03.01.2000 - 15.01.2004

Period (days)	H	p-value	Statistic	Critical value
5	0	0.85756	1.9387	11.07
10	0	0.97914	3.0935	18.307
15	0	0.99401	4.7546	24.996
20	0	0.84601	13.687	31.41

Findings of the performed tests imply that the fitted MA(1)-GJR GARCH(1,1) model adequately describes the dynamics of RIGSE index daily returns.

6.3.10 Lithuania – VILSE index

Trading on the Vilnius Stock Exchange (VSE-OMX) started in 1993. The VILSE (later changed its name into OMX Vilnius Index) index was launched in 2000 with the initial value of 100 points.

The analysis of the VILSE stock index is performed for the period 03.01.2000 – 31.12.2005. In this observation period the obtained sample from VILSE index consists of 1504 daily index value observations. The evolution of index values and returns is displayed in Figures 106, 107 and 108.

Figure 106 - Daily values of VILSE index, period 04.01.2000 - 31.12.2005 (1504 observations)

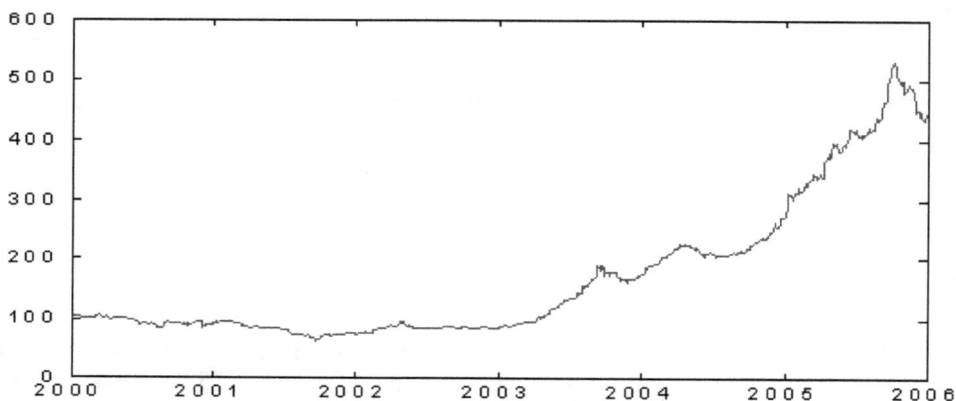

Figure 107 - Daily log returns of VILSE index, period 04.01.2000 - 31.12.2005 (1503 observations)

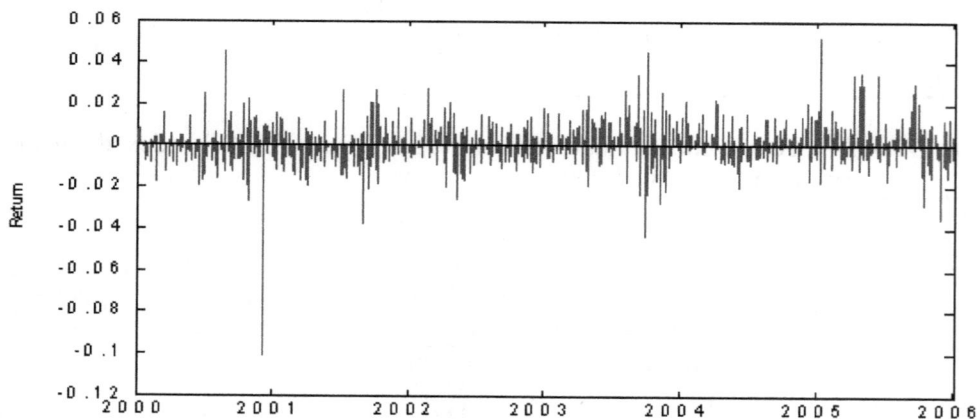

Figure 108 - Histogram of daily log returns of VILSE index, period 04.01.2000 - 31.12.2005 (1503 observations)

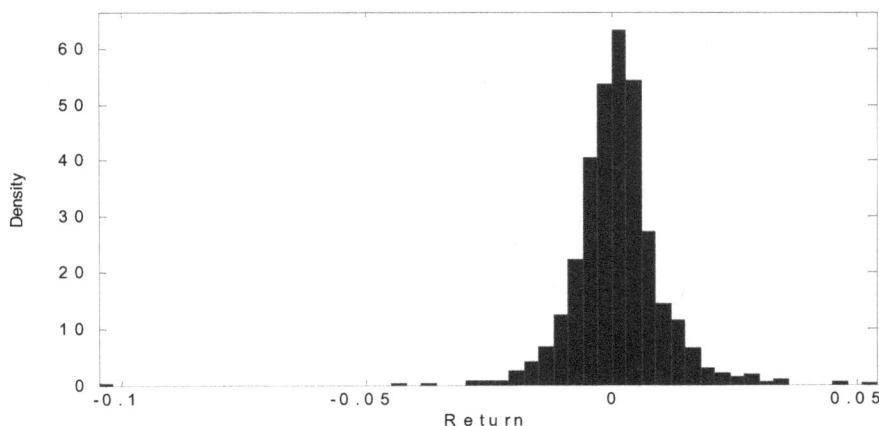

From figures 106, 107 and 108 it is visible that there is significant volatility clustering and presence of extreme positive and negative returns, which motivates a conditional volatility model that accounts for time varying volatility.

Basic descriptive statistics for VILSE index in the period 04.01.2000 - 31.12.2005 are presented in table 93.

Table 93 - Basic statistics for VILSE index daily log returns, period 04.01.2000 - 31.12.2005 (1503 observations)

Mean	0.000993
Median	0.000814
Minimum	-0.10216
Maximum	0.053092
Standard deviation	0.008965
Skewness	-0.64913
Kurtosis	17.469

Mean and median of daily returns are very similar and show a strong positive trend that is similar to TALSE and RIGSE index. Skewness and excess kurtosis are different from zero. In the observed period VILSE index experienced extreme daily returns. The highest daily gain in the analysed period was 5,31%, while the highest daily loss amounted to – 10,22%, similar values to RIGSE index. Asymmetry is negative (-0.649), a characteristic shared with RIGSE index, meaning that the distribution slopes to the left and negative returns are expected to occur more frequently than positive. Excess kurtosis of 17.469 indicates that the empirical probability distribution of VILSE index has significantly fatter tails than assumed under normal distribution. Excess kurtosis is similar to the value detected for RIGSE index, and greater than detected in TALSE index and majority of CEE countries.

Combining the third and fourth moment of the VILSE index with its mean and standard deviation, it can be concluded that although in the entire observation period, negative returns were more frequent than positive returns, the magnitude of the positive returns was significantly higher than the magnitude of loses, resulting in a strong positive trend for VILSE index. These characteristics of VILSE index, very similar to RIGSE index and CEEC indexes, resulted in a strong positive trend for the index. To determine if the daily returns of VILSE index are normally distributed, normality of empirical distribution is tested by Jarque-Bera test and Lilliefors test. Normality tests for the VILSE index are presented in table 94.

Table 94 - Normality tests for VILSE index daily log returns, period 04.01.2000 - 31.12.2005 (1503 observations)

Jarque-Bera test	13,174
(p value)	0
Lilliefors test	0.083442
(p value)	0

Both normality tests show that the hypothesis of normality of returns for VILSE index, for the entire analysed period, should be rejected at 5% significance level. Probability values of distribution of returns being normal, according to both normality tests are zero, strongly indicating that there is no possibility that the returns on this index are normally distributed. The distribution of VILSE index returns is leptokurtotic and asymmetrical i.e. it skews slightly to the left, as can be seen from figures 108 and 109, as well as from table 95. Figure 109 and table 95 show that the true empirical distribution of VILSE index daily returns is far better approximated by a Student's t distribution with 3,3 degrees of freedom, than it is by normal distribution.

Figure 109 - Probability plot for VILSE index daily log returns, period 04.01.2000 - 31.12.2005 (1503 observations)

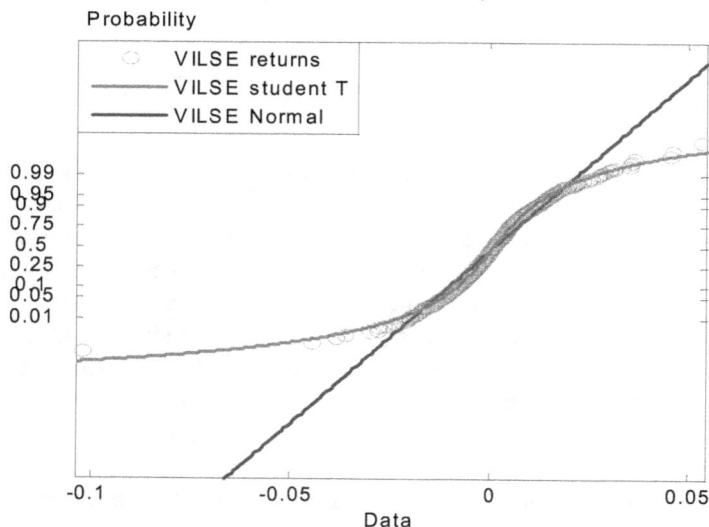

Table 95 - Parameters of fitted Normal and Students' T distribution to VILSE index daily log returns, period 04.01.2000 - 31.12.2005 (1503 observations)

Distribution:	Normal			Distribution:	t location-scale		
Log likelihood:	4953.66			Log likelihood:	5125.24		
Mean:	0.000993			Mean:	0.000822		
Variance:	8.04E-05			Variance:	8.55E-05		
Parameter	Estimate	Std. Err.		Parameter	Estimate	Std. Err.	
mu	0.000993	0.000231		mu	0.000822	0.000181	
sigma	0.008965	0.000164		sigma	0.005797	0.000199	
				df	3.29562	0.316159	
Estimated covariance of parameter estimates:				Estimated covariance of parameter estimates:			
	mu	sigma			mu	sigma	df
mu	5.35E-08	1.13E-24		mu	3.26E-08	7.86E-10	1.33E-06
sigma	1.13E-24	2.68E-08		sigma	7.86E-10	3.95E-08	4.23E-05
				df	1.33E-06	4.23E-05	0.099957

Presence of autocorrelation in VILSE daily log returns is tested by examining its sample autocorrelation, sample partial correlation function (Figure 110) and calculating Ljung-Box Q-statistic for mean adjusted VILSE returns (Table 96).

Figure 110 - Sample autocorrelation and sample partial correlation function of VILSE index daily log returns, period 04.01.2000 - 29.12.2003 (1003 observations)

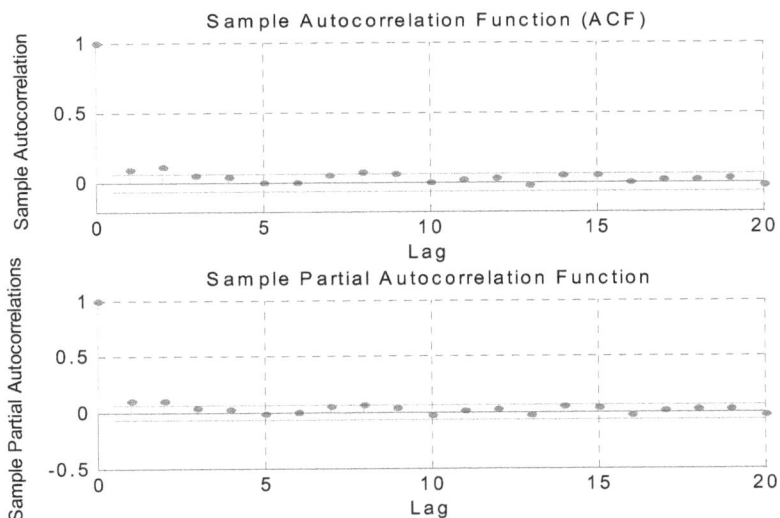

Table 96 - Ljung-Box-Pierce Q-test for mean adjusted VILSE index daily log returns, period 04.01.2000 - 29.12.2003 (1003 observations)

Period (days)	H	p-value	Statistic	Critical value
5	1	4.25E-11	57.368	11.07
10	1	2.38E-12	76.543	18.307
15	1	6.69E-14	96.242	24.996
20	1	8.18E-13	101.05	31.41

Sample autocorrelation, sample partial correlation function and Ljung-Box Q-statistic found a highly structured mean in the VILSE daily log returns, meaning that the Lithuanian stock market is not very efficient since the direction of the market can be predicted. To extract this structure from the data it will be necessary to use a more elaborate ARMA (p, q) model.

After the presence of autocorrelation in the daily log returns has been investigated it is necessary to test the squared log returns for presence of autocorrelation i.e. heteroskedasticity. Presence of heteroskedasticity in VILSE returns is tested by examining its sample autocorrelation and sample partial correlation function of squared returns (Figure 111), calculating Ljung-Box Q-statistic for mean adjusted squared VILSE returns (Table 97) and ARCH test for mean adjusted VILSE returns (Table 98).

Figure 111 - Sample autocorrelation and sample partial correlation function of squared VILSE index daily log returns, period 04.01.2000 - 29.12.2003 (1003 observations)

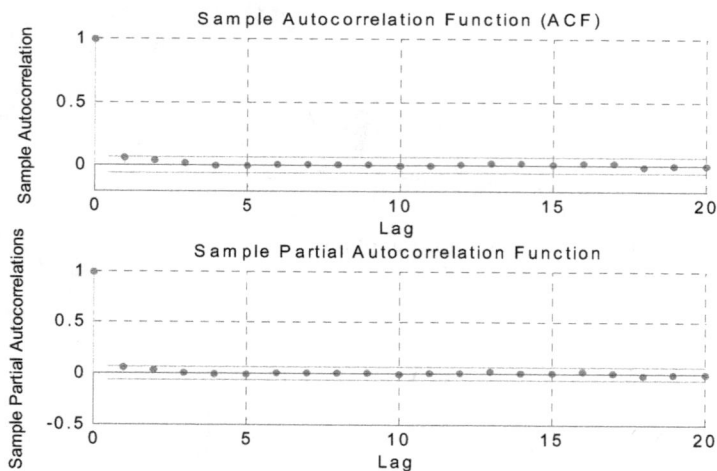

Table 97 - Ljung-Box-Pierce Q-test for mean adjusted squared VILSE index daily log returns, period 04.01.2000 - 29.12.2003 (1003 observations)

Period (days)	H	p-value	Statistic	Critical value
5	1	0.028743	12.482	11.07
10	0	0.19802	13.481	18.307
15	0	0.45209	14.991	24.996
20	0	0.66683	16.786	31.41

Table 98 - ARCH test for mean adjusted VILSE index daily log returns, period 04.01.2000 - 29.12.2003 (1003 observations)

Period (days)	H	p-value	Statistic	Critical value
5	1	0.044145	11.392	11.07
10	0	0.28124	12.057	18.307
15	0	0.59921	13.04	24.996
20	0	0.81555	14.289	31.41

Sample autocorrelation and sample partial correlation function of squared returns, as well as the Ljung-Box Q-statistic and Engle's ARCH test confirm that there is some autocorrelation and ARCH effects present in VILSE daily log returns, meaning that the returns on VILSE index are not IID.

Since the employed tests discovered significant autocorrelation and heteroskedasticity in the VILSE daily returns it is necessary to model the data in order to obtain independently and identically distributed returns. Because autocorrelation has been detected in both returns and squared returns, VILSE index returns will be modelled as an ARMA-GARCH process in order to deal with both types of dependence. Estimated ARMA-GARCH parameters for VILSE index are given in table 99.

Table 99 - Estimated ARMA-GARCH parameters for VILSE index daily log
returns, period 04.01.2000 - 29.12.2003 (1003 observations)

Mean: ARMA(2,1)
Variance: GARCH(1,1)

Conditional Probability Distribution: Gaussian

Parameter	Value	Standard error	T statistic
C	1.19E-06	6.87E-06	0.1725
AR(1)	1.08050	0.039787	27.1573
AR(2)	-0.08366	0.037544	-2.2284
MA(1)	-0.96844	0.011306	-85.6547
K	1.31E-05	2.10E-06	6.2469
GARCH(1)	0.55848	0.054464	10.254
ARCH(1)	0.25825	0.037792	6.8336

According to their t statistics all of the estimated parameters are statistically significant, except the mean drift that is statistically insignificant and will be assumed to equal zero. The obtained model is a normally distributed ARMA(2,1)-GARCH(1,1) model:

$$r_t = 1.0805 r_{t-1} - 0.08366 r_{t-2} - 0.96844 \varepsilon_{t-1} + \varepsilon_t$$

$$\sigma_t^2 = 1.31E - 05 + 0.25825 \varepsilon_{t-1}^2 + 0.55848 \sigma_{t-1}^2$$

Similarly to SBI20 and SKSM index, although more pronounced, the conditional volatility model for VILSE index is far from being integrated and places unusually little importance on past conditional volatility, but places a lot of weight on previous period residual. The plot of fitted ARMA-GARCH model innovations, conditional standard deviations and observed VILSE index daily log returns are given in figure 112.

Figure 112 - Plot of fitted ARMA-GARCH model innovations, conditional standard
deviations and observed VILSE index daily log returns, period
04.01.2000 - 29.12.2003

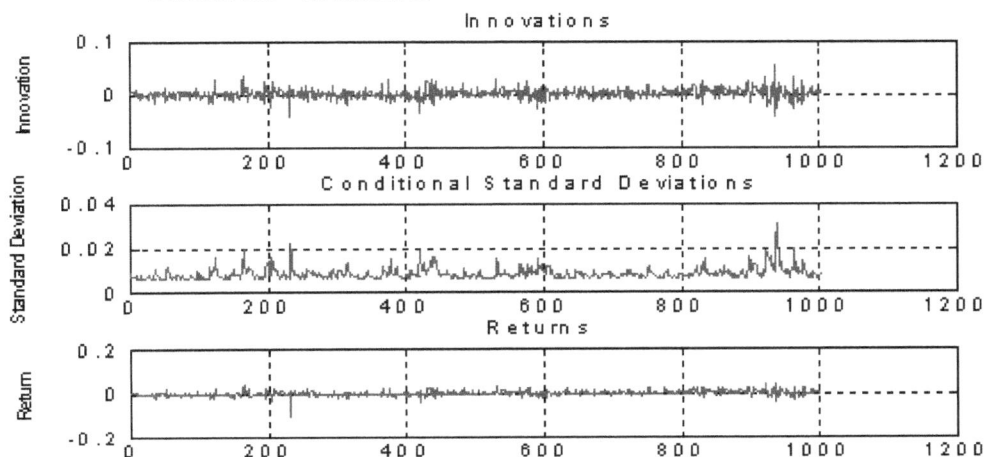

If the fitted ARMA-GARCH model is appropriate for describing the dynamics of
underlying data generating process the standardised innovation from such ARMA-
GARCH model should be independently and identically distributed (Figure 113).
The adequacy of fitted ARMA-GARCH model can be statistically tested in the same
manner as returns and squared returns.

Figure 113 - Standardised innovations from fitted ARMA- GARCH model for
VILSE index daily log returns, period 04.01.2000 - 29.12.2003

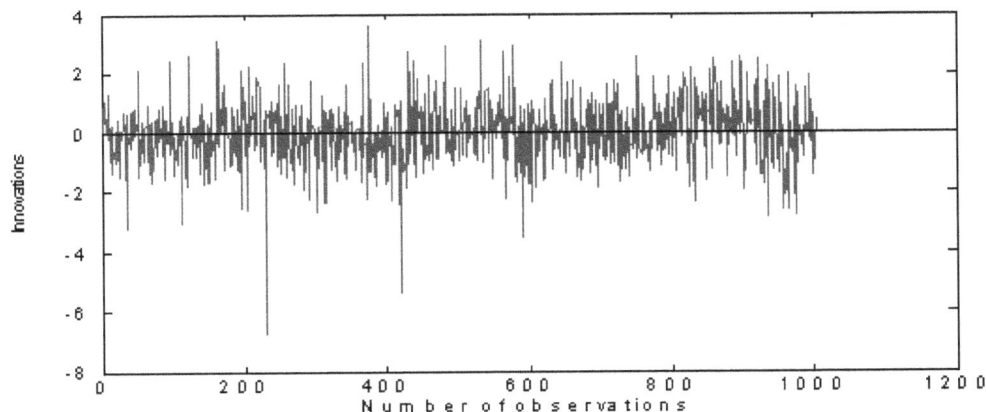

Sample autocorrelation, sample partial correlation function and Ljung-Box Q-
statistic of standardised innovation detect no presence of autocorrelation in the
standardised innovations from fitted ARMA-GARCH model, meaning that the
conditional mean model (ARMA(2,1)) successfully captured the structure present in
VILSE returns (Figure 114, Table 100).

Figure 114 - Sample autocorrelation and sample partial correlation function of standardized innovations from VILSE index daily log returns, period 04.01.2000 - 29.12.2003

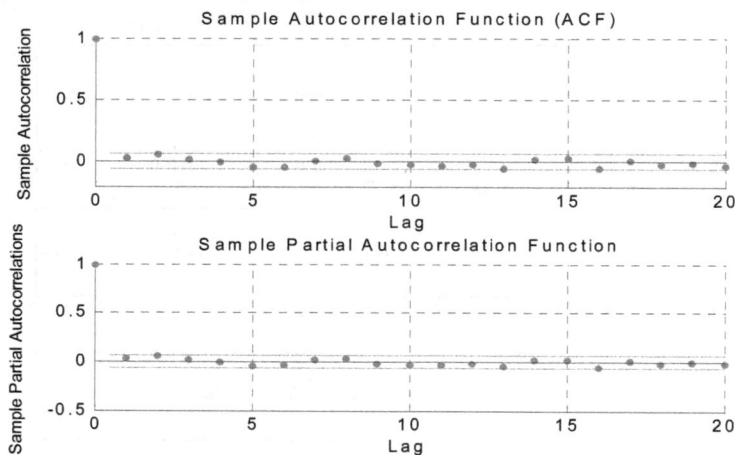

Table 100 - Ljung-Box-Pierce Q-test for standardised innovations from VILSE index daily log returns, period 04.01.2000 - 29.12.2003

Period (days)	H	p-value	Statistic	Critical value
5	0	0.18318	7.5447	11.07
10	0	0.38686	10.632	18.307
15	0	0.40118	15.716	24.996
20	0	0.45764	20.005	31.41

Sample autocorrelation and sample partial correlation function, Ljung-Box Q-statistic of squared standardised innovation and ARCH test of standardised innovations detect no presence of autocorrelation in the squared standardised innovations from fitted ARMA-GARCH model. This indicates that the conditional variance model (GARCH(1,1)) successfully captured the heteroskedasticity present in VILSE returns (Figure 115, Tables 101, 102).

Figure 115 - Sample autocorrelation and sample partial correlation function of squared standardized innovations from VILSE index daily log returns, period 04.01.2000 - 29.12.2003

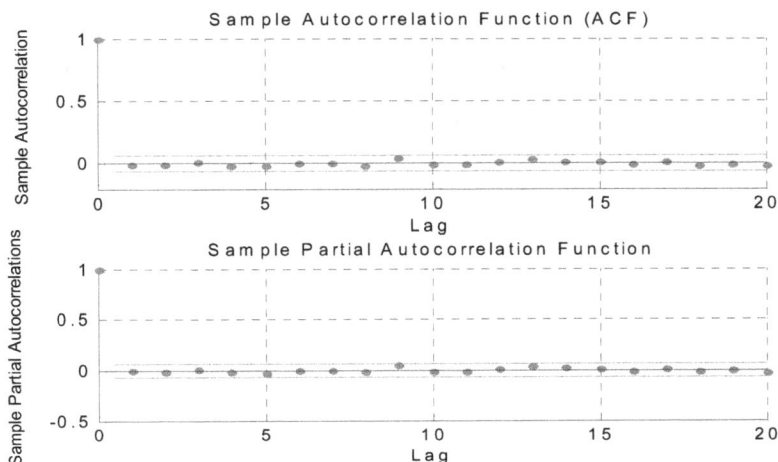

Sample Autocorrelation Function (ACF)

Sample Partial Autocorrelation Function

Table 101 - Ljung-Box-Pierce Q-test for squared standardised innovations from VILSE index daily log returns, period 04.01.2000 - 29.12.2003

Period (days)	H	p-value	Statistic	Critical value
5	0	0.93683	1.2814	11.07
10	0	0.95183	3.8981	18.307
15	0	0.97934	6.0242	24.996
20	0	0.99561	7.2933	31.41

Table 102 - ARCH test for standardised innovations from VILSE index daily log returns, period 04.01.2000 - 29.12.2003

Period (days)	H	p-value	Statistic	Critical value
5	0	0.93793	1.2706	11.07
10	0	0.95734	3.7647	18.307
15	0	0.98051	5.954	24.996
20	0	0.99592	7.2139	31.41

Findings of the performed tests imply that the fitted ARMA(2,1)-GARCH(1,1) model adequately describes the dynamics of VILSE index daily returns.

6.3.11 Cyprus – CYSMGENL index

Trading on the Cyprus Stock Exchange (CSE) started in 1996. The CYSMGENL index was launched in 1997 with the initial value of 1000 points.

The analysis of the CYSMGENL stock index is performed for the period 04.01.2000 – 31.12.2005. In this observation period the obtained sample from CYSMGENL index consists of 1510 daily index value observations. The evolution of index values and returns is displayed in Figures 116, 117 and 118.

Figure 116 - Daily values of CYSMGENL index, period 04.01.2000 - 31.12.2005 (1510 observations)

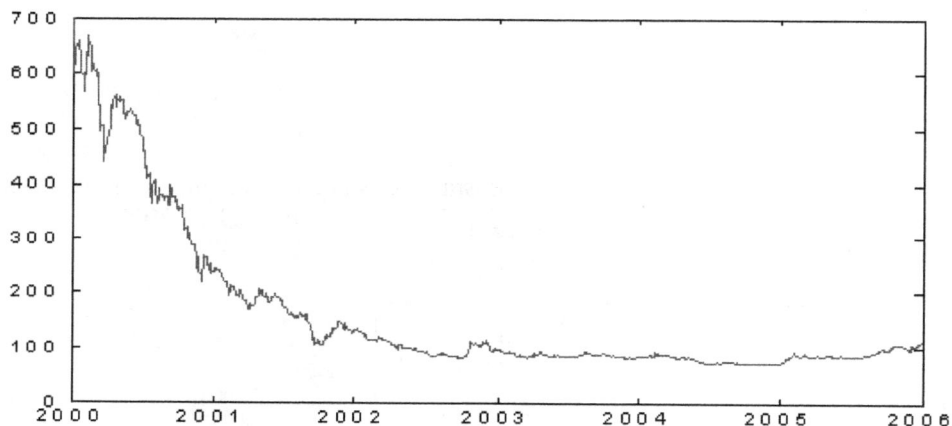

Figure 117 - Daily log returns of CYSMGENL index, period 04.01.2000 - 31.12.2005 (1509 observations)

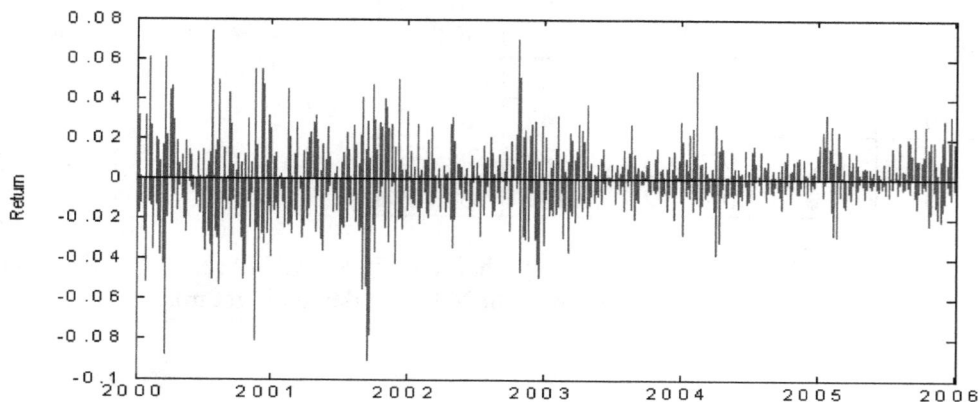

Figure 118 - Histogram of daily log returns of CYSMGENL index, period 04.01.2000 - 31.12.2005 (1509 observations)

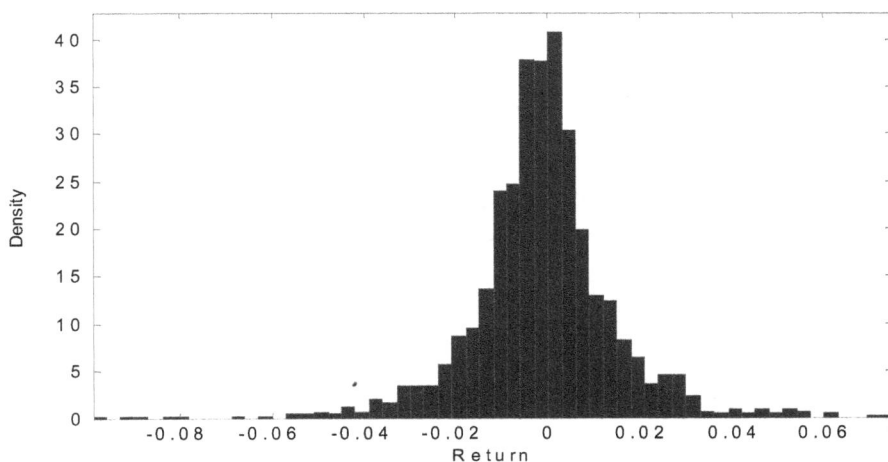

From figures 116, 117 and 118 it is visible that there is significant volatility clustering and presence of extreme positive and negative returns, which motivates a conditional volatility model that accounts for time varying volatility.

Basic descriptive statistics for CYSMGENL index in the period 04.01.2000 - 31.12.2005 are presented in table 103.

Table 103 - Basic statistics for CYSMGENL index daily log returns, period 04.01.2000 - 31.12.2005 (1509 observations)

Mean	-0.00123
Median	-0.00108
Minimum	-0.09877
Maximum	0.074742
Standard deviation	0.015849
Skewness	-0.28268
Kurtosis	7.8347

Mean and median of daily returns are similar and differ significantly from zero. Mean and median show a very strong negative trend as opposed to CEEC, Baltic and Croatian indexes. Skewness and excess kurtosis are different from zero. In the observed period CYSMGENL index experienced extreme daily returns. The highest daily gain in the analysed period was 7,47%, while the highest daily loss amounted to − 9,88%. Asymmetry is slightly negative (-0,2827), meaning that the distribution slopes slightly to the left and negative returns are expected to occur more frequently than positive. Excess kurtosis of 7,83 indicates that the empirical probability distribution of CYSMGENL index has fatter tails than assumed under normal distribution. Excess kurtosis is similar to excess kurtosis of TALSE and SKSM index.

By observing the graphical representation of evolution of CYSMGENL index daily values (Figure 115) and knowing the first four moments of CYSMGENL index, it can be concluded that CYSMGENL index has almost noting in common with other analysed indexes (CEEC, Baltic countries and Croatia).

During the entire observation period the value of index declined sharply as opposed to other indexes. The fact that the skewness of returns is negative, mean and median are significantly negative and kurtosis of the index being higher than normal can help explain the declining trend of CYSMGENL index values. To determine if the daily returns of CYSMGENL index are normally distributed, normality of empirical distribution is tested by Jarque-Bera test and Lilliefors test. Normality tests for the CYSMGENL index are presented in table 104.

Table 104 - Normality tests for CYSMGENL index daily log returns, period 04.01.2000 - 31.12.2005 (1509 observations)

Jarque-Bera test	1,483.4
(p value)	0
Lilliefors test	0.084385
(p value)	0

Both normality tests show that the hypothesis of normality of returns for CYSMGENL index, for the entire analysed period, should be rejected at 5% significance level. Probability values of distribution of returns being normal, according to both normality tests are zero, strongly indicating that there is no possibility that the returns on this index are normally distributed. The distribution of CYSMGENL index returns is leptokurtotic and slightly asymmetrical i.e. it skews slightly to the left, as can be seen from figures 118 and 119, as well as from table 105.

Figure 119 and table 105 show that the true empirical distribution of CYSMGENL index daily returns is far better approximated by a Student's t distribution with 2,75 degrees of freedom, than it is by normal distribution.

Figure 119 - Probability plot for CYSMGENL index daily log returns, period 04.01.2000 - 31.12.2005. (1509 observations)

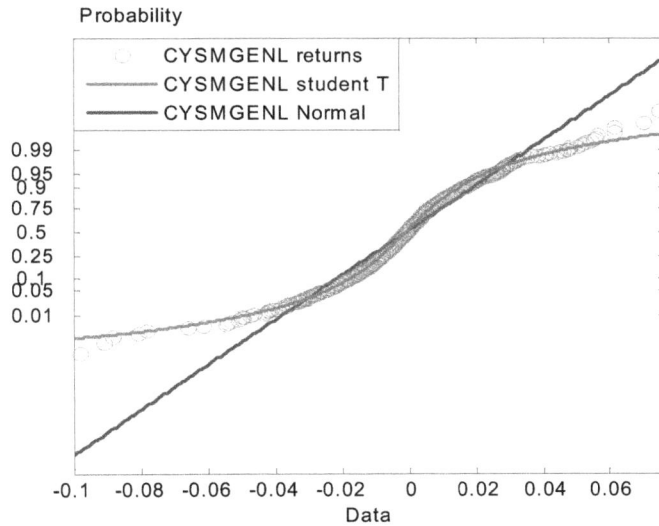

Table 105 - Parameters of fitted Normal and Students' T distribution to CYSMGENL index daily log returns, period 04.01.2000 - 31.12.2005. (1509 observations)

Distribution: Normal			Distribution: t location-scale			
Log likelihood: 4113.59			Log likelihood: 4270.95			
Mean: -0.00123			Mean: -0.00127			
Variance: 2.51E-04			Variance: 3.44E-04			
Parameter	Estimate	Std. Err.	Parameter	Estimate	Std. Err.	
mu	-0.00123	0.000408	mu	-0.00127	0.000306	
sigma	0.015849	0.000289	sigma	0.009679	0.000359	
			df	2.74813	0.243471	
Estimated covariance of parameter estimates:			Estimated covariance of parameter estimates:			
	mu	sigma		mu	sigma	df
mu	1.66E-07	-1.84E-23	mu	9.38E-08	2.40E-09	1.68E-06
sigma	-1.84E-23	8.33E-08	sigma	2.40E-09	1.29E-07	6.06E-05
			df	1.68E-06	6.06E-05	0.059278

Presence of autocorrelation in CYSMGENL daily log returns is tested by examining its sample autocorrelation, sample partial correlation function (Figure 120) and calculating Ljung-Box Q-statistic for mean adjusted CYSMGENL returns (Table 106).

Figure 120 - Sample autocorrelation and sample partial correlation function of CYSMGENL index daily log returns, period 04.01.2000 - 12.01.2004 (1009 observations)

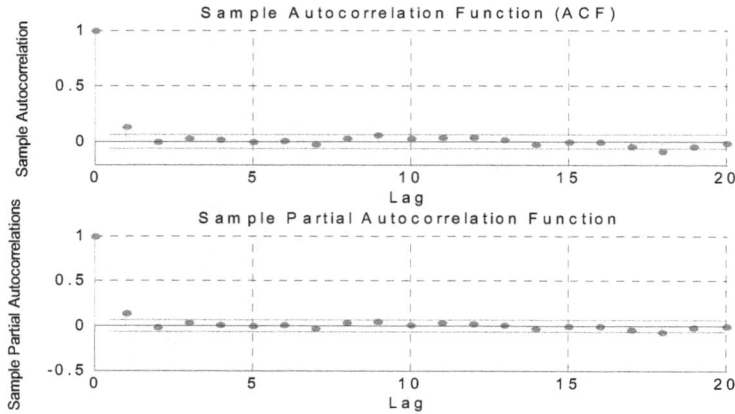

Table 106 - Ljung-Box-Pierce Q-test for mean adjusted CYSMGENL index daily log returns, period 04.01.2000 - 12.01.2004 (1009 observations)

Period (days)	H	p-value	Statistic	Critical value
5	1	6.17E-06	31.916	11.07
10	1	2.64E-06	44.535	18.307
15	1	5.00E-06	52.318	24.996
20	1	1.67E-05	57.582	31.41

Sample autocorrelation, sample partial correlation function and Ljung-Box Q-statistic found the presence of autocorrelation in the CYSMGENL daily log returns meaning that the Cyprus stock market is not very efficient since the direction of the market can be predicted. To extract the autocorrelation from the data it will be necessary to use an ARMA (p, q) model.

After the presence of autocorrelation in the daily log returns has been investigated it is necessary to test the squared log returns for presence of autocorrelation i.e. heteroskedasticity. Presence of heteroskedasticity in CYSMGENL returns is tested by examining its sample autocorrelation and sample partial correlation function of squared returns (Figure 121), calculating Ljung-Box Q-statistic for mean adjusted squared CYSMGENL returns (Table 107) and ARCH test for mean adjusted CYSMGENL returns (Table 108).

Figure 121 - Sample autocorrelation and sample partial correlation function of squared CYSMGENL index daily log returns, period 04.01.2000 - 12.01.2004 (1009 observations)

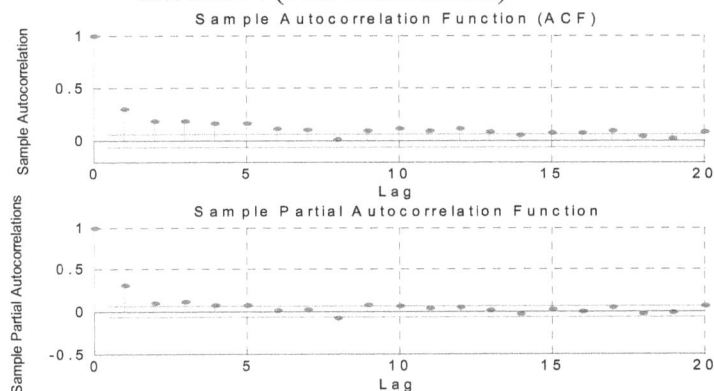

Table 107 - Ljung-Box-Pierce Q-test for mean adjusted squared CYSMGENL index daily log returns, period 04.01.2000 - 12.01.2004 (1009 observations)

Period (days)	H	p-value	Statistic	Critical value
5	1	0	387.42	11.07
10	1	0	488.33	18.307
15	1	0	581.85	24.996
20	1	0	646.6	31.41

Table 108 - ARCH test for mean adjusted CYSMGENL index daily log returns, period 04.01.2000 - 12.01.2004 (1009 observations)

Period (days)	H	p-value	Statistic	Critical value
5	1	0	233.48	11.07
10	1	0	260.67	18.307
15	1	0	272.86	24.996
20	1	0	285.34	31.41

Sample autocorrelation and sample partial correlation function of squared returns, as well as the Ljung-Box Q-statistic and Engle's ARCH test confirm that there is significant autocorrelation and ARCH effects present in CYSMGENL daily log returns, meaning that the returns on CYSMGENL index are not IID.

Since the employed tests discovered significant autocorrelation and heteroskedasticity in the CYSMGENL daily returns it is necessary to model the data in order to obtain independently and identically distributed returns. Because autocorrelation has been detected in both returns and squared returns, CYSMGENL index returns will be modelled as an ARMA-GARCH process in order to deal with both types of dependence. Estimated ARMA-GARCH parameters for CYSMGENL index are given in table 109.

Table 109 - Estimated ARMA-GARCH parameters for CYSMGENL index daily log returns, period 04.01.2000 - 12.01.2004 (1009 observations)

Mean: ARMA(1,0)
Variance: GARCH(1,1)

Conditional Probability Distribution: Gaussian

Parameter	Value	Standard error	T statistic
C	-1.35E-03	0.000384	-3.518
AR(1)	1.30E-01	0.032421	4.0209
K	6.04E-06	1.80E-06	3.3528
GARCH(1)	0.79835	0.018353	43.4985
ARCH(1)	0.19802	0.024501	8.0821

According to their t statistics all of the estimated parameters are statistically significant. The obtained model is a normally distributed AR(1)-GARCH(1,1) model:

$$r_t = -0.00135 + 0.13r_{t-1} + \varepsilon_t$$

$$\sigma_t^2 = 6.04E - 06 + 0.19802\varepsilon_{t-1}^2 + 0.79835\sigma_{t-1}^2$$

Conditional volatility model for CYSMGENL index is very close to being integrated. The plot of fitted AR-GARCH model innovations, conditional standard deviations and observed CYSMGENL index daily log returns are given in figure 122.

Figure 122 - Plot of fitted AR-GARCH model innovations, conditional standard deviations and observed CYSMGENL index daily log returns, period 04.01.2000 - 12.01.2004

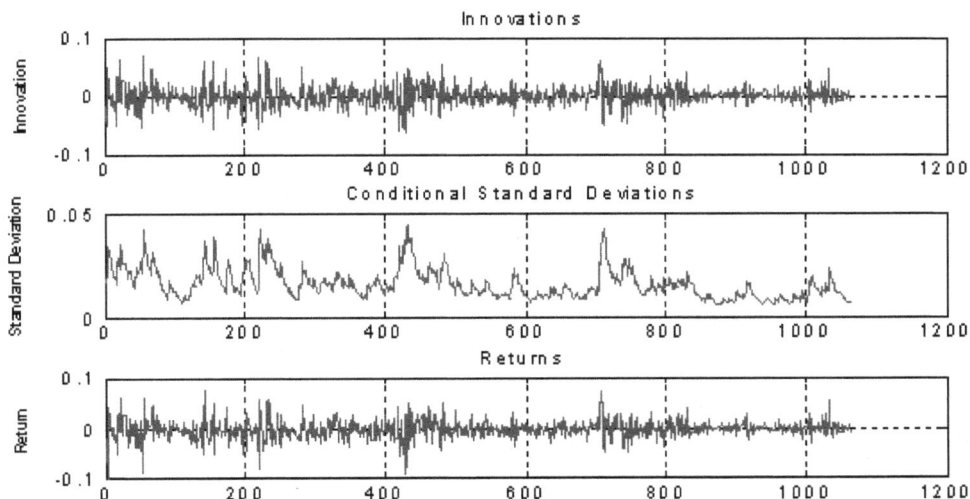

If the fitted AR-GARCH model is appropriate for describing the dynamics of underlying data generating process the standardised innovation from such AR-GARCH model should be independently and identically distributed (Figure 123). The adequacy of fitted AR-GARCH model can be statistically tested in the same manner as returns and squared returns.

Figure 123 - Standardised innovations from fitted AR-GARCH model for CYSMGENL index daily log returns, period 04.01.2000 - 12.01.2004

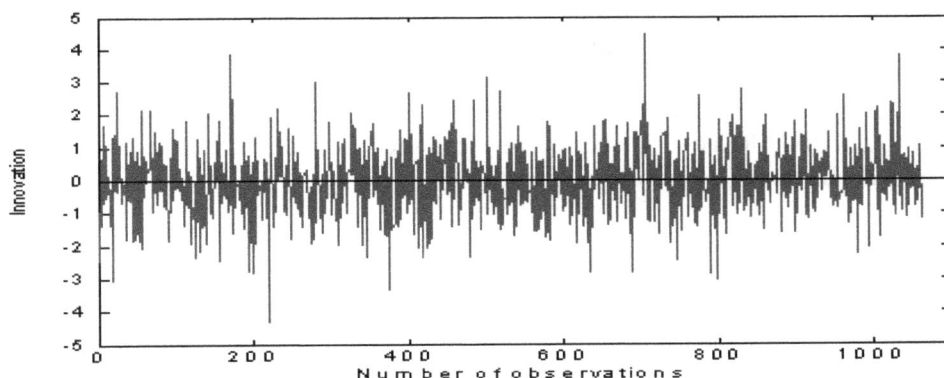

Sample autocorrelation, sample partial correlation function and Ljung-Box Q-statistic of standardised innovation detect no presence of autocorrelation in the standardised innovations from fitted AR-GARCH model, meaning that the conditional mean model (AR(1)) successfully captured the autocorrelation present in CYSMGENL returns (Figure 124, Table 110).

Figure 124 - Sample autocorrelation and sample partial correlation function of standardized innovations from CYSMGENL index daily log returns, period 04.01.2000 - 12.01.2004

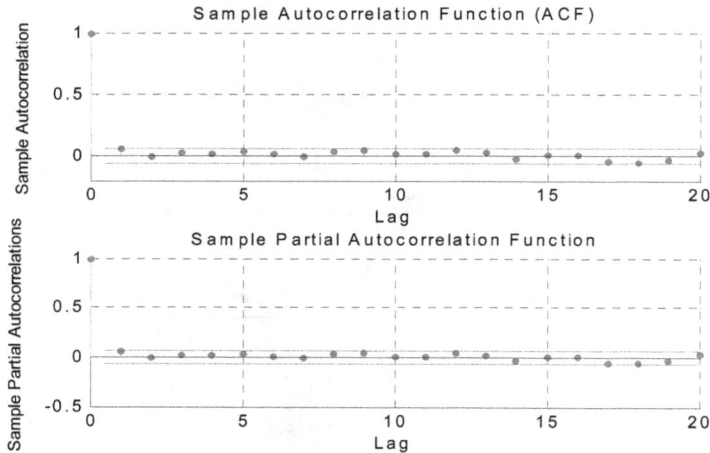

Table 110 - Ljung-Box-Pierce Q-test for standardised innovations from CYSMGENL index daily log returns, period 04.01.2000 - 12.01.2004

Period (days)	H	p-value	Statistic	Critical value
5	0	0.12773	8.5649	11.07
10	0	0.1564	14.379	18.307
15	0	0.16928	20.07	24.996
20	0	0.13642	26.959	31.41

Sample autocorrelation and sample partial correlation function, Ljung-Box Q-statistic of squared standardised innovation and ARCH test of standardised innovations detect no presence of autocorrelation in the squared standardised innovations from fitted AR-GARCH model. This indicates that the conditional variance model (GARCH(1,1)) successfully captured the heteroskedasticity present in CYSMGENL returns (Figure 125, Tables 111, 112).

Figure 125 - Sample autocorrelation and sample partial correlation function of squared standardized innovations from CYSMGENL index daily log returns, period 04.01.2000 - 12.01.2004

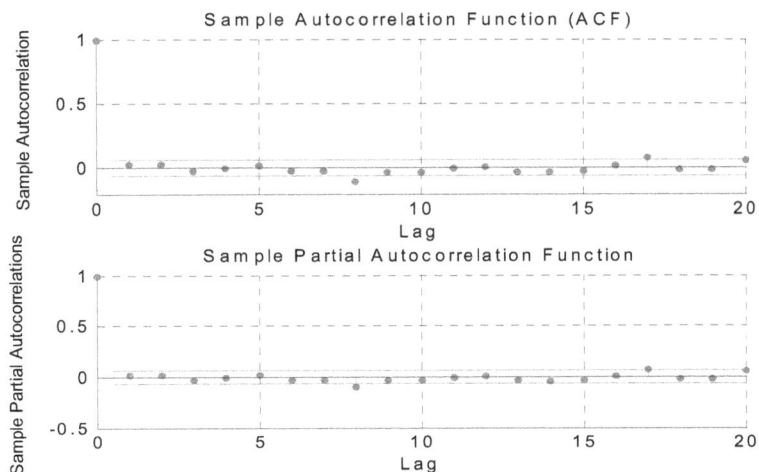

Table 111 - Ljung-Box-Pierce Q-test for squared standardised innovations from CYSMGENL index daily log returns, period 04.01.2000 - 12.01.2004

Period (days)	H	p-value	Statistic	Critical value
5	0	0.70052	2.9965	11.07
10	0	0.092424	16.26	18.307
15	0	0.2025	19.253	24.996
20	0	0.055892	30.947	31.41

Table 112 - ARCH test for standardised innovations from CYSMGENL index daily log returns, period 04.01.2000 - 12.01.2004

Period (days)	H	p-value	Statistic	Critical value
5	0	0.73516	2.7715	11.07
10	0	0.15003	14.533	18.307
15	0	0.31102	17.132	24.996
20	0	0.088025	28.987	31.41

Findings of the performed tests imply that the fitted AR(1)-GARCH(1,1) model adequately describes the dynamics of CYSMGENL index daily returns.

6.3.12 Malta – MALTEX index

Trading on the Malta Stock Exchange (MSE) started in 1991. The MALTEX index was launched in 1995 with the value of 1000 points.

The analysis of the MALTEX stock index is performed for period 03.01.2000 – 31.12.2005. In this observation period the obtained sample from MALTEX index consists of 1480 daily index value observations. The evolution of index values and returns is displayed in Figures 126, 127 and 128.

Figure 126 - Daily values of MALTEX index, period 03.01.2000 - 31.12.2005 (1480 observations)

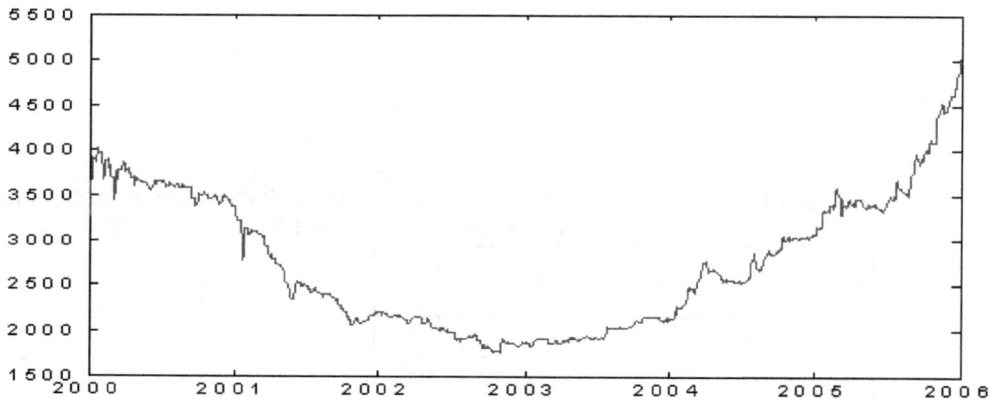

Figure 127 - Daily log returns of MALTEX index, period 03.01.2000 - 31.12.2005 (1479 observations)

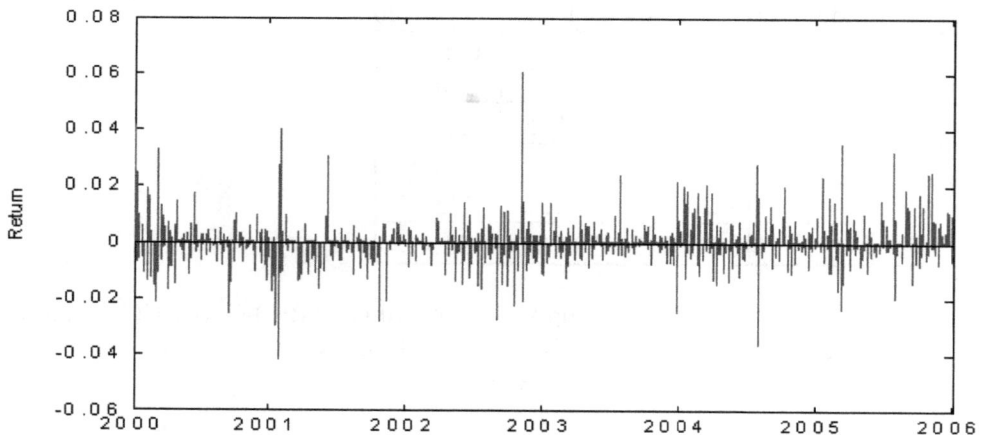

Figure 128 - Histogram of daily log returns of MALTEX index, period 03.01.2000 -
      31.12.2005 (1479 observations)

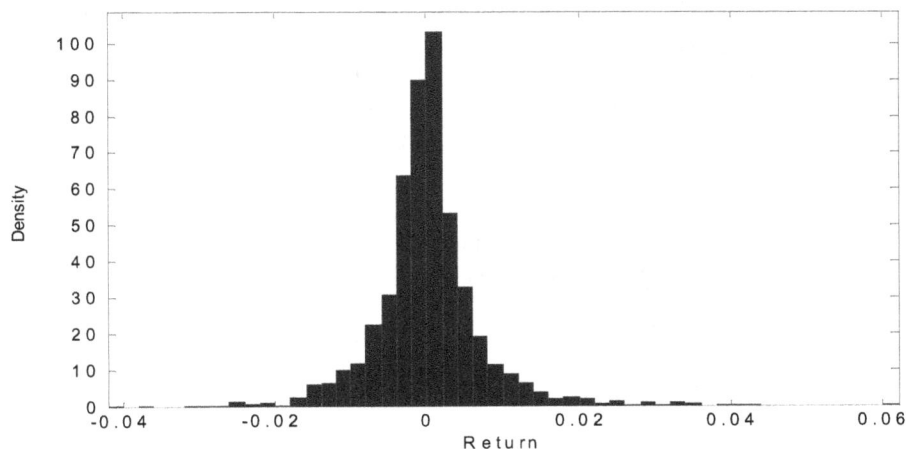

From figures 126, 127 and 128 it is visible that there is significant volatility
clustering and presence of extreme positive and negative returns, which motivates a
conditional volatility model that accounts for time varying volatility.

Basic descriptive statistics for MALTEX index in the period 03.01.2000 -
31.12.2005 are presented in table 113.

Table 113 - Basic statistics for MALTEX index daily log returns, period 03.01.2000
      - 31.12.2005 (1479 observations)

Mean	0.000285
Median	0
Minimum	-0.04189
Maximum	0.060972
Standard deviation	0.007483
Skewness	0.90336
Kurtosis	11.149

Mean and median of daily returns are similar and close to zero. Skewness and excess
kurtosis of the index are significantly different from zero assumed under normality.
In the observed period MALTEX index experienced extreme daily returns. The
highest daily gain in the analysed period was 6,1%, while the highest daily loss
amounted to − 4,2%. Asymmetry is significantly positive (0,90336), as opposed to
CYSMGENL index, meaning that the distribution slopes to the right and positive
returns are expected to occur more frequently than negative ones. Excess kurtosis of
11,149 indicates that the empirical probability distribution of MALTEX index has
significantly fatter tails than assumed under normal distribution. The value of excess
kurtosis is close to the value found for CYSMGENL index.

From graphical representation of evolution of MALTEX index daily values (Figure 126) and knowing the first four moments of MALTEX index, it can be concluded that in the long run MALTEX index did not experience a strong trend of any direction but after a drift that occurred during the observation period, slightly surpassed its starting values. To determine if the daily returns of MALTEX index are normally distributed, normality of empirical distribution is tested by Jarque-Bera test and Lilliefors test. Normality tests for the MALTEX index are presented in table 114.

Table 114 - Normality tests for MALTEX index daily log returns, period 03.01.2000 - 31.12.2005 (1479 observations)

Jarque-Bera test	4,278.2
(p value)	0
Lilliefors test	0.11459
(p value)	0

Both normality tests show that the hypothesis of normality of returns for MALTEX index, for the entire analysed period, should be rejected at 5% significance level. Probability values of distribution of returns being normal, according to both normality tests are zero, strongly indicating that there is no possibility that the returns on this index are normally distributed. The distribution of MALTEX index returns is leptokurtotic and asymmetrical i.e. it skews to the right, as can be seen from figures 128 and 129, as well as from table 115. Figure 129 and table 115 show that the true empirical distribution of MALTEX index daily returns is far better approximated by a Student's t distribution with 2,04 degrees of freedom, than it is by normal distribution.

Figure 129 - Probability plot for MALTEX index daily log returns, period 03.01.2000 - 31.12.2005 (1479 observations)

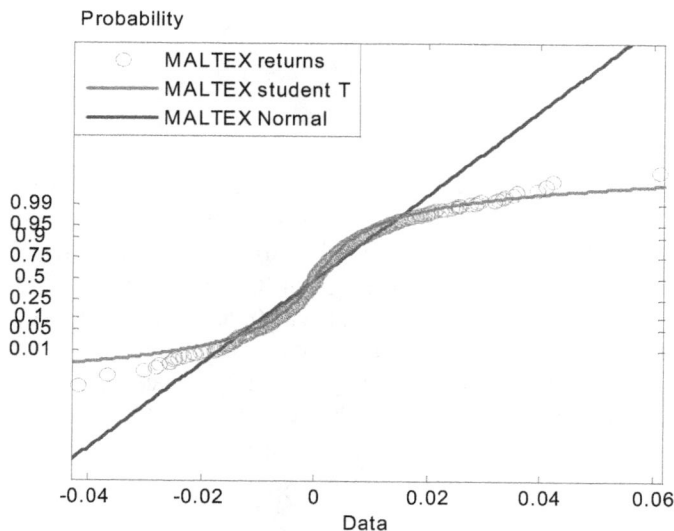

Table 115 - Parameters of fitted Normal and Students' T distribution to MALTEX index daily log returns, period 03.01.2000 - 31.12.2005 (1479 observations)

Distribution: Normal			Distribution: t location-scale			
Log likelihood: 5141.71			Log likelihood: 5411.64			
Mean: 0.000285			Mean: -7.01E-05			
Variance: 5.60E-05			Variance: 7.38E-04			
Parameter	Estimate	Std. Err.	Parameter	Estimate	Std. Err.	
mu	0.000285	0.000195	mu	-7.01E-05	0.000121	
sigma	0.007483	0.000138	sigma	0.003665	0.000149	
			df	2.03706	0.151887	
Estimated covariance of parameter estimates:			Estimated covariance of parameter estimates:			
	mu	sigma		mu	sigma	df
mu	3.79E-08	-3.80E-24	mu	1.46E-08	6.53E-10	6.55E-07
sigma	-3.80E-24	1.90E-08	sigma	6.53E-10	2.22E-08	1.55E-05
			df	6.55E-07	1.55E-05	0.02307

Presence of autocorrelation in MALTEX daily log returns is tested by examining its sample autocorrelation, sample partial correlation function (Figure 130) and calculating Ljung-Box Q-statistic for mean adjusted MALTEX returns (Table 116).

Figure 130 - Sample autocorrelation and sample partial correlation function of MALTEX index daily log returns, period 03.01.2000 - 18.12.2003 (979 observations)

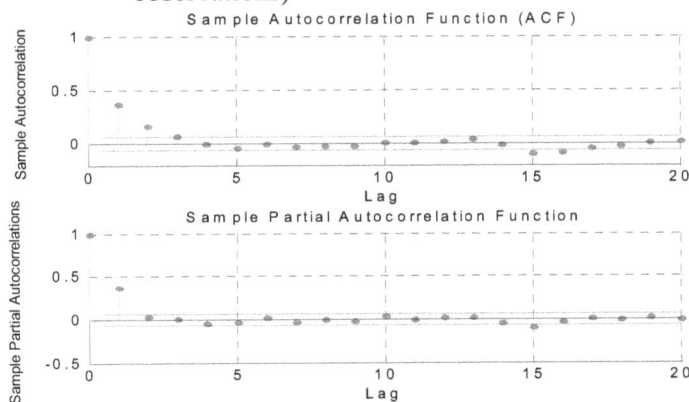

Table 116 - Ljung-Box-Pierce Q-test for mean adjusted MALTEX index daily log returns, period 03.01.2000 - 18.12.2003 (979 observations)

Period (days)	H	p-value	Statistic	Critical value
5	1	0	257.38	11.07
10	1	0	258.61	18.307
15	1	0	264.35	24.996
20	1	0	277.57	31.41

Sample autocorrelation, sample partial correlation function and Ljung-Box Q-statistic found the presence of autocorrelation in the MALTEX daily log returns meaning that the stock market in Malta is not very efficient since the direction of the market can be predicted. To extract the autocorrelation from the data it will be necessary to use an ARMA (p, q) model.

After the presence of autocorrelation in the daily log returns has been investigated it is necessary to test the squared log returns for presence of autocorrelation i.e. heteroskedasticity. Presence of heteroskedasticity in MALTEX returns is tested by examining its sample autocorrelation and sample partial correlation function of squared returns (Figure 131), calculating Ljung-Box Q-statistic for mean adjusted squared MALTEX returns (Table 117) and ARCH test for mean adjusted MALTEX returns (Table 118).

Figure 131 - Sample autocorrelation and sample partial correlation function of squared MALTEX index daily log returns, period 03.01.2000 - 18.12.2003 (979 observations)

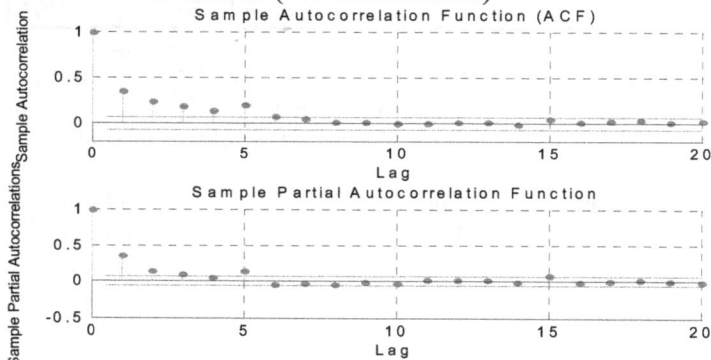

Table 117 - Ljung-Box-Pierce Q-test for mean adjusted squared MALTEX index daily log returns, period 03.01.2000 - 18.12.2003 (979 observations)

Period (days)	H	p-value	Statistic	Critical value
5	1	0	348.59	11.07
10	1	0	359.69	18.307
15	1	0	362.68	24.996
20	1	0	367.72	31.41

Table 118 - ARCH test for mean adjusted MALTEX index daily log returns, period 03.01.2000 - 18.12.2003 (979 observations)

Period (days)	H	p-value	Statistic	Critical value
5	1	0	158.43	11.07
10	1	0	168.72	18.307
15	1	0	174.29	24.996
20	1	0	175.17	31.41

Sample autocorrelation and sample partial correlation function of squared returns, as well as the Ljung-Box Q-statistic and Engle's ARCH test confirm that there is significant autocorrelation and ARCH effects present in MALTEX daily log returns, meaning that the returns on MALTEX index are not IID.

Since the employed tests discovered significant autocorrelation and heteroskedasticity in the MALTEX daily returns it is necessary to model the data in order to obtain independently and identically distributed returns. Because autocorrelation has been detected in both returns and squared returns, MALTEX index returns will be modelled as an ARMA-GARCH process in order to deal with both types of dependence. Estimated ARMA-GARCH parameters for MALTEX index are given in table 119.

Table 119 - Estimated ARMA-GARCH parameters for MALTEX index daily log returns, period 03.01.2000 - 18.12.2003 (979 observations)

Mean: ARMA(1,0)
Variance: GARCH(1,1)

Conditional Probability Distribution: Gaussian

Parameter	Value	Standard error	T statistic
C	-5.36E-04	0.0002	-2.676
AR(1)	2.75E-01	0.029654	9.2824
K	6.71E-06	1.04E-06	6.434
GARCH(1)	0.64587	0.045722	14.1259
ARCH(1)	0.18561	0.027638	6.7156

According to their t statistics all of the estimated parameters are statistically significant. The obtained model is a normally distributed AR(1)-GARCH(1,1) model:

$$r_t = -0.000536 + 0.275 r_{t-1} + \varepsilon_t$$

$$\sigma_t^2 = 6.71E - 06 + 0.18561 \varepsilon_{t-1}^2 + 0.64587 \sigma_{t-1}^2$$

When modelling the mean process as an AR(1) process the constant term is significant and negative. The value of the constant drift from AR(1) model can explain some similarities between MALTEX and CYSMGENL index. Unlike CYSMGENL index, conditional volatility model for MALTEX index is far from being integrated and similar to SBI20 and SKSM index. It places unusually little importance on past conditional volatility, but places a lot of weight on previous period's residual. The plot of fitted AR-GARCH model innovations, conditional standard deviations and observed MALTEX index daily log returns are given in figure 132.

Figure 132 - Plot of fitted AR-GARCH model innovations, conditional standard deviations and observed MALTEX index daily log returns, period 03.01.2000 - 18.12.2003

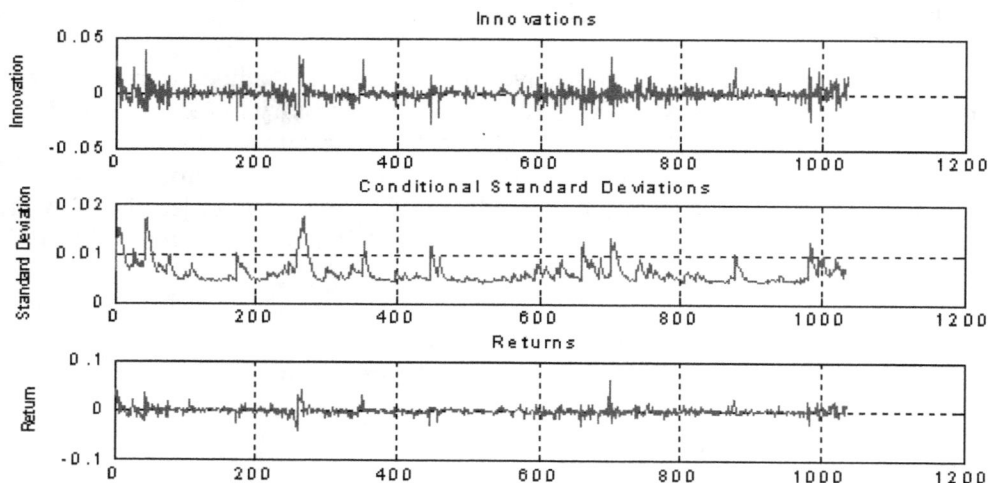

If the fitted AR-GARCH model is appropriate for describing the dynamics of underlying data generating process the standardised innovation from such AR-GARCH model should be independently and identically distributed (Figure 133). The adequacy of fitted AR-GARCH model can be statistically tested in the same manner as returns and squared returns.

Figure 133 - Standardised innovations from fitted AR-GARCH model for MALTEX index daily log returns, period 03.01.2000 - 18.12.2003

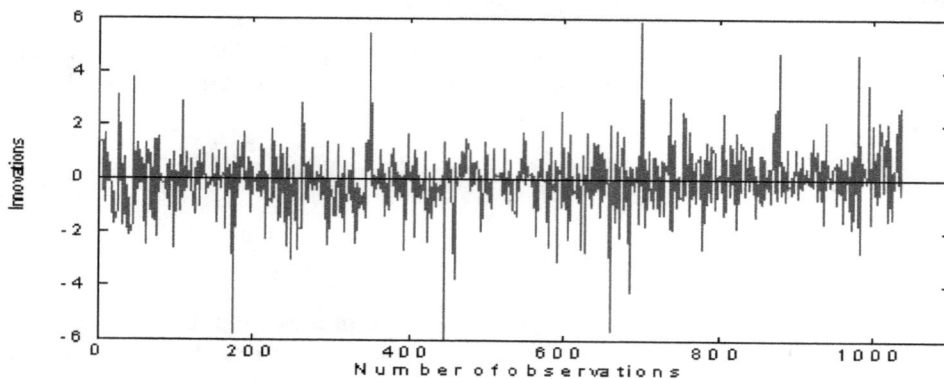

Sample autocorrelation, sample partial correlation function and Ljung-Box Q-statistic of standardised innovation detect no presence of autocorrelation in the standardised innovations from fitted AR-GARCH model meaning that the conditional mean model (AR(1)) successfully captured the autocorrelation present in MALTEX returns (Figure 134, Table 120).

Figure 134 - Sample autocorrelation and sample partial correlation function of standardized innovations from MALTEX index daily log returns, period 03.01.2000 - 18.12.2003

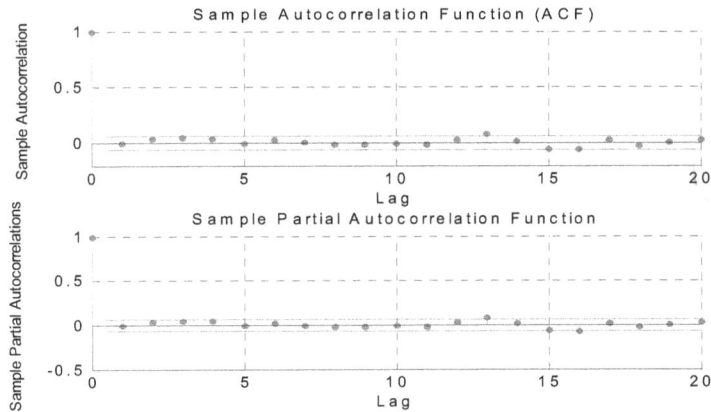

Table 120 - Ljung-Box-Pierce Q-test for standardised innovations from MALTEX index daily log returns, period 03.01.2000 - 18.12.2003

Period (days)	H	p-value	Statistic	Critical value
5	0	0.24563	6.679	11.07
10	0	0.63465	7.9405	18.307
15	0	0.20429	19.212	24.996
20	0	0.22266	24.465	31.41

Sample autocorrelation and sample partial correlation function, Ljung-Box Q-statistic of squared standardised innovation and ARCH test of standardised innovations detect no presence of autocorrelation in the squared standardised innovations from fitted AR-GARCH model. This indicates that the conditional variance model (GARCH(1,1)) successfully captured the heteroskedasticity present in MALTEX returns (Figure 135, Tables 121, 122).

314

Figure 135 - Sample autocorrelation and sample partial correlation function of squared standardized innovations from MALTEX index daily log returns, period 03.01.2000 - 18.12.2003

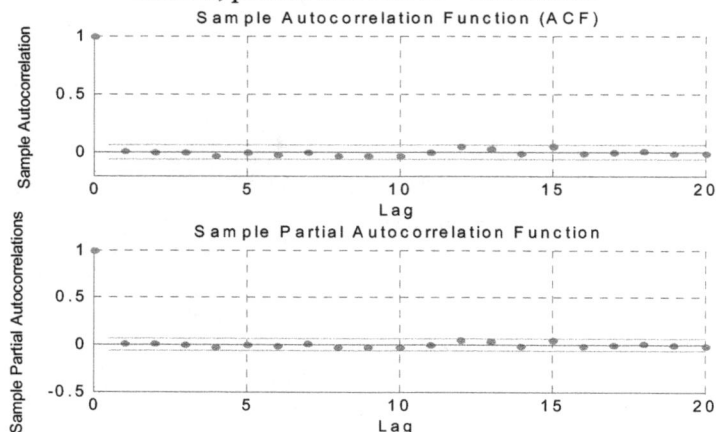

Table 121 - Ljung-Box-Pierce Q-test for squared standardised innovations from MALTEX index daily log returns, period 03.01.2000 - 18.12.2003

Period (days)	H	p-value	Statistic	Critical value
5	0	0.97042	0.89729	11.07
10	0	0.94952	3.9512	18.307
15	0	0.73767	11.209	24.996
20	0	0.93016	11.567	31.41

Table 122 - ARCH test for standardised innovations from MALTEX index daily log returns, period 03.01.2000 - 18.12.2003

Period (days)	H	p-value	Statistic	Critical value
5	0	0.97694	0.80138	11.07
10	0	0.94551	4.0404	18.307
15	0	0.71799	11.479	24.996
20	0	0.91821	11.937	31.41

Findings of the performed tests imply that the fitted AR(1)-GARCH(1,1) model adequately describes the dynamics of MALTEX index daily returns.

6.3.13 Summary of findings

From graphical representation of the realized returns of stock indexes from transition countries it can be concluded that volatility clustering and occurrence of extreme positive and negative returns is a common characteristic shared by all of the tested indexes.

Overall basic statistics and normality test for daily log returns of all the tested indexes, in period 01.1.2000 - 31.12.2005. are presented in table 123.

Table 123 - Basic statistics and normality tests for daily log returns of stock indexes from EU new member states and Croatia, period 01.1.2000 - 31.12.2005.

	SBI20	BUX	WIG20	PX50	SKSM	CROBEX	VIN	TALSE	RIGSE	VILSE	CYSMGENL	MALTEX
Sample size	1461	1501	1505	1502	1414	1434	1480	1521	1554	1503	1509	1479
Mean	0.000644	0.000579	0.000239	0.00074	0.001184	0.000683	0.001286	0.001016	0.001202	0.000993	-0.0012254	0.000285
Median	0.0005	0.00051	0.00019	0.000961	0.0003	0.000164	0.000534	0.000965	0.000608	0.000814	-0.0010817	0
Minimum	-0.047674	-0.068735	-0.077057	-0.062054	-0.088167	-0.090324	-0.1567	-0.058741	-0.14705	-0.10216	-0.098768	-0.041892
Maximum	0.083109	0.060043	0.062461	0.041785	0.059591	0.14979	0.10186	0.073425	0.094609	0.053092	0.074742	0.060972
Standard deviation	0.006888	0.013921	0.01561	0.012581	0.013255	0.014751	0.012806	0.010472	0.016286	0.008965	0.015849	0.007483
Skewness	1.1188	-0.11694	0.069375	-0.26716	-0.11384	0.75377	-0.6828	0.22481	-1.2783	-0.64913	-0.28268	0.90336
Kurtosis	21.647	4.6873	4.4498	4.3604	7.4742	18.369	23.689	9.0341	23.563	17.469	7.8347	11.149
Jarque-Bera test	21,404	180.16	131.94	132.67	1,176.90	14,202	26,430	2,311.20	27,721	13,174	1,483.40	4,278.20
(p value)	0	0	0	0	0	0	0	0	0	0	0	0
Lilliefors test	0.077501	0.031092	0.053572	0.040504	0.094636	0.10855	0.10509	0.079737	0.15709	0.083442	0.084385	0.11459
(p value)	0	0	0	0	0	0	0	0	0	0	0	0

From table 123 and individual statistical analyses of stock indexes from transition countries, performed in the previous chapters, it can be determined all of the indexes are characterised by having fatter tails than presumed under normal distribution. In the observed period, all of the tested indexes exhibit varying degrees of asymmetry, with seven indexes having negative skewness and five indexes having positive skewness. Due to pronounced leptokurtosis and asymmetry of empirical return distributions of stock indexes from transition countries it comes as no surprise that according to both Lilliefors and Jarque-Bera test of normality none of the tested indexes is normally distributed. The results from normality tests are also confirmed by the histograms and probability plots of tested indexes.

By examining the sample autocorrelation functions, sample partial autocorrelation functions of mean adjusted returns and by calculating the Ljung-Box Q-statistics for mean adjusted returns it can be concluded that in eight out of twelve tested stock indexes autocorrelation in the returns of stock indexes was detected. Sample autocorrelation functions, sample partial autocorrelation functions of squared mean adjusted returns, Ljung-Box Q-statistics for squared mean adjusted returns and Engle's ARCH tests all detected significant heteroskedasticity in all of the tested stock indexes.

Since autocorrelation in returns was detected for most of the stock indexes from transition countries, and presence of heteroskedasticity was discovered in all of the stock indexes, the return and volatility processes of tested indexes are modelled as ARMA-GARCH processes. After estimating the parameters of ARMA-GARCH processes and fitting the models, the innovations (residuals) from the process are obtained. Through analysis of sample autocorrelation functions and sample partial autocorrelation functions of standardised innovations as well as calculating the Ljung-Box Q-statistics for standardised innovations it can be concluded that the ARMA process used to model the conditional mean captured the autocorrelation present in the mean adjusted returns of the analysed stock indexes. Likewise, sample autocorrelation functions, sample partial autocorrelation functions of squared standardised innovations as well as Ljung-Box Q-statistics and ARCH tests confirm that GARCH conditional volatility process captured the heteroskedasticity present in the mean adjusted squared returns of the analysed stock indexes. This means that after fitting ARMA-GARCH models to stock indexes from transition countries, which are not identically and independently distributed, obtained standardised innovations are identically and independently distributed. The importance and implications of these findings are explained and discussed in Chapter 6.5.

6.4   Backtesting results

In this chapter the backtesting results for twelve analysed VaR are presented and their performance according to different criteria is analysed. The calculated VaR figures are for a one-day ahead horizon and 95 and 99 percent confidence level, i.e. the five and one percent lower tail of the return distribution. The performance of twelve VaR models is tested on 500 out-of-the-sample daily return observations. The reported VaR figures from each VaR model are compared with the realized changes in index values. Twelve VaR models are analysed across twelve indexes from transition countries. Performance of each VaR model will be evaluated based on seven criterions – tests.

First test is the Kupiec test, a simple expansion of the failure rate, which is prescribed by the Basel Committee on Banking Supervision. The set-up for this test is the classic framework for a sequence of successes and failures, also known as Bernoulli trials. Since a good risk measurement should secure that VaR exceedences are independent through time, since any clustering of VaR failures could easily force a bank into bankruptcy the Christoffersen independence test is calculated. It tests whether VaR exceedences are IID. Results of Christoffersen unconditional test (UC) are also reported but in the author's opinion they provide a somewhat distorted image of the relative performance of VaR models. Since Christoffersen unconditional test is distributed as chi-square with one degree of freedom, deviations from the expected value of the test that occur on the conservative side (i.e. number of exceedences is lower than the excepted value) are treated more severely, a characteristic that is not compatible with regulators desire to increase the safety of the banking sector. From the regulatory standpoint Kupiec binomial test is preferred to Christoffersen unconditional test because it is more desirable to have positive than negative deviations. The same logic extends to the Christoffersen conditional coverage (CC) test, which also should be considered with a serious reserve since it automatically puts in a disadvantage VaR models that report a lower number of VaR exceedences per confidence level than expected.

Furthermore, two forecast evaluation approaches are used to evaluate the relative performance of tested VaR models. This approach allows for ranking of different competing models, but does not give any formal statistical indication of model adequacy. In ranking them, it takes account of any particular concerns one might have. For example, higher losses can be given greater weight because of concern about higher losses. Furthermore, because they are not statistical tests, forecast evaluation approaches do not suffer from the low power of standard tests such as the Kupiec test. This makes forecast evaluation approach very attractive for backtesting with the small data sets typically available in practice. The first forecast evaluation approach is the Lopez size-adjusted loss function (1998). Second is the Blanco-Ihle (1998) loss function that gives each tail-loss observation a weight equal to the tail loss divided by the VaR. The loss function ensures that higher tail losses get awarded higher values without the impaired intuition introduced by squaring the tail loss. Blanco-Ihle is an excellent test for comparing competing VaR models that report the same frequency of tail losses, and whose tail losses are IID. Ranking VaR models by Blanco-Ihle approach is one of the best approaches to distinguish between such VaR tests.

Forecasting performance of VaR models is also evaluated by two statistical loss functions. First measure of forecasting performance of the tested VaR models is the root mean squared error (RMSE) measure, which examines the degree to which the VaR forecasts tend to vary around the realized returns for a given date. Smaller deviations from the expected value indicate better VaR measure. Second measure of forecasting performance of the tested VaR models is the mean absolute percentage error measure (MAPE) for measuring bunching proposed by Boudoukh, Richardson, and Whitelaw (1998). MAPE is a combined measure of both bias and bunching. Smaller deviations from the expected value indicate better VaR measure. Size of tail loss test is not calculated directly but it is used indirectly through Lopez size adjusted test and Blanco-Ihle test. Crnkovic-Drachman test is not used in the evaluation of VaR models because Kuiper's test statistic that it uses is very data-intensive - results begin to deteriorate with less than 1,000 observations. Furthermore, the statistic assumes that the parameters of the distributions are known, which is a very unrealistic assumption. Performance of each VaR model is evaluated for each individual index, based on every performance test. The summary of VaR models performance is presented in backtesting tables in tables 124-147. Significance level for VaR model acceptance is set at 10% to secure a more rigorous backtesting criterion.

The first row of backtesting tables reports the actual rates at which violations occurred for the twelve stock indexes. Second row reports the p value for Kupiec test of a particular VaR model. Third row reports the p value for Christoffersen unconditional coverage test. Fourth row reports the p value for Christoffersen independence test. Fifth row reports the p value for Christoffersen conditional coverage test. Sixth row reports the score of the Lopez size-adjusted loss function. Seventh row reports the score of the Blanco-Ihle loss function. Eighth and ninth row report the RMSE and MAPE values. Tenth row shows the value of average VaR according to each VaR model for the duration of the testing period.

SBI20 index

Performance of tested VaR models for Slovenian SBI20 index at 95 and 99% confidence level is given in tables 124 and 125. According to Kupiec test at 95% confidence level most of the tested VaR models did not pass the test. Historical simulation models with 50 and 100 day rolling window failed the test and reported the observed frequency of failures of 7% and 6,6% respectively. Historical simulation based on 250 and 500 day rolling window passed the Kupiec test, as well as both BRW models. Normal variance covariance and RiskMetrics VaR models both failed the Kupiec test with observed frequencies of failures of 6,2% and 6,6%. Similarly, both Normal Monte Carlo and EWMA Monte Carlo models also failed the test with frequencies of failures of 6,2% and 6,8%. GARCH-RiskMetrics model and HHS model both passed the Kupiec test at 95% confidence level. With frequency of failure of 7% (40% more than expected) HS 50 is the model with highest reported frequency of failures. At 99% confidence level situation is similar, with historical simulation models with 50 and 100 day rolling window again failing the test with frequencies of failures of 3% and 1,8%. Historical simulation based on 250 and 500 day rolling window and BRW model with $\lambda = 0.99$ passed the Kupiec test. BRW model with $\lambda = 0.97$, Normal variance covariance, RiskMetrics, Normal Monte Carlo and EWMA Monte Carlo VaR models as well as the GARCH-RiskMetrics model all failed the Kupiec test at 99% confidence level, with RiskMetrics model having the highest frequency of failures of 3,6% - more than three times of expected frequency. HHS model successfully passed the Kupiec test at 99% confidence level. According to Christoffersen independence test at 95% confidence level all of the tested VaR models failed at 10% significance level except GARCH-RiskMetrics and HHS model. At 99% confidence level HS 50, HS 250, HS 500, RiskMetrics and EWMA Monte Carlo VaR models failed the Christoffersen independence test. Based on Lopez test at 95% confidence level VaR model with the worst ranking based on underestimation of risk is the HS 50 model, and the worst ranking model based on overestimation of risk is the HS 500 model. The best ranked VaR model is the GARCH-RiskMetrics model. At 99% confidence level VaR model with the worst ranking based on underestimation of risk is the RiskMetrics model. None of the VaR models overestimated the risk at 99% confidence level. The best ranked VaR model is the HS 500 model. Based on Blanco-Ihle test at 95% confidence level the best ranking VaR model is the HS 500 model and the worst is the RiskMetrics model, meaning that it experienced the highest losses in excess of forecasted VaR. At 99% confidence level the best ranking VaR model is again the HS 500 model and the worst is again the RiskMetrics model. According to RMSE measure, at 95% confidence level, the best performing VaR model is Normal Monte Carlo and the worst ranked model is GARCH-RiskMetrics model. At 99% confidence level the best ranking VaR model is again the Normal Monte Carlo and the worst ranked model is the HS 500 model. According to MAPE measure, at 95% confidence level, the best performing VaR model is the HS 500 and the worst ranked model is the EWMA Monte Carlo model. At 99% confidence level the best ranking VaR model is the HS 500 model and the worst ranked model is the RiskMetrics model. In the analysed period, at 95% confidence level, VaR model with the lowest average VaR was the HS 50 model (0,763%), HS 500 model reported the highest average VaR of 0,95%. The difference between the lowest and the highest average VaR at 95% confidence level is 24,51%. At 99% confidence level, VaR model with the lowest average VaR was the RiskMetrics model (1,129%), HS 500 model again reported the highest average VaR of 1,716%. The difference between the lowest and the highest average VaR at 99% confidence level is 51,99%.

Table 124 - Backtesting results and diagnostics of 500 VaR forecasts for SBI20 index daily log returns, 95% confidence level, period 03.12.2003 -31.12.2005

	HS 50	HS 100	HS 250	HS 500	BRW λ=0,97	BRW λ=0,99	Normal VCV	Risk Metrics	Normal MC	EWMA MC	GARCH RM	HHS
Number of failures	35	33	29	21	29	26	31	33	31	34	25	28
Frequency of failures	0.07	0.066	0.058	0.042	0.058	0.052	0.062	0.066	0.062	0.068	0.05	0.056
Kupiec test (p value)	0.019643	0.045412	0.17647	0.75905	0.17647	0.36861	0.09445	0.045412	0.09445	0.03026	0.44706	0.23168
Christoffersen UC test (p value)	0.052333	0.11684	0.42294	0.3992	0.42294	0.83842	0.23456	0.11684	0.23456	0.079233	1	0.54553
Christoffersen IND test (p value)	0.001662	0.003907	0.004448	0.058758	0.004448	0.046153	0.001687	0.000668	0.001687	0.001066	0.51405	0.7268
Christoffersen CC test (p value)	0.001084	0.004549	0.012694	0.11749	0.012694	0.13415	0.003562	0.000896	0.003562	0.001013	0.80823	0.7837
Lopez test	10.165	8.1521	4.1267	-3.9049	4.1364	1.1193	6.1315	8.1599	6.1342	9.1591	0.087587	3.1102
Blanco-Ihle test	28.035	23.843	15.928	10.322	20.364	15.269	17.138	30.033	17.351	27.907	10.905	14.873
RMSE	0.007954	0.007795	0.008109	0.009046	0.008717	0.00844	0.00776	0.007906	0.007748	0.008147	0.009329	0.008447
MAPE	2.2718	1.8404	1.389	1.3042	1.3741	1.3242	1.6434	2.2219	1.8728	2.7681	1.8304	2.0673
Average VaR	-0.007631	-0.007843	-0.00835	-0.009502	-0.008609	-0.00875	-0.008025	-0.007725	-0.007996	-0.007902	-0.009209	-0.008285
Acceptance (Kupiec test)	NO	NO	YES	YES	YES	YES	NO	NO	NO	NO	YES	YES
Christoffersen IND test	NO	NO	NO	NO	NO	NO	NO	NO	NO	NO	YES	YES

Table 125 - Backtesting results and diagnostics of 500 VaR forecasts for SBI20 index daily log returns, 99% confidence level, period 03.12.2003 -31.12.2005

	HS 50	HS 100	HS 250	HS 500	BRW λ=0,97	BRW λ=0,99	Normal VCV	Risk Metrics	Normal MC	EWMA MC	GARCH RM	HHS
Number of failures	15	9	7	5	10	7	10	18	11	16	8	7
Frequency of failures	0.03	0.018	0.014	0.01	0.02	0.014	0.02	0.036	0.022	0.032	0.016	0.014
Kupiec test (p value)	6.15E-05	0.031102	0.13232	0.38404	0.013244	0.13232	0.013244	1.16E-06	0.005208	1.73E-05	0.06711	0.13232
Christoffersen UC test (p value)	0.000286	0.10602	0.39657	1	0.047896	0.39657	0.047896	6.10E-06	0.019918	8.40E-05	0.21487	0.39657
Christoffersen IND test (p value)	0.007142	0.14477	0.078954	0.034295	0.52246	0.65537	0.18573	0.023097	0.23191	0.010905	0.60964	0.65537
Christoffersen CC test (p value)	3.72E-05	0.093525	0.1492	0.10646	0.11517	0.63195	0.058871	2.73E-06	0.032579	1.71E-05	0.40678	0.63195
Lopez test	10.067	4.045	2.0447	0.01972	5.0421	2.0273	5.0646	13.085	6.0652	11.078	3.0313	2.0276
Blanco-Ihle test	9.0629	3.6694	3.5894	1.2881	3.816	2.0738	6.0303	12.174	6.2616	9.972	3.0783	2.5829
RMSE	0.013481	0.014417	0.014085	0.016685	0.015729	0.016029	0.011075	0.011344	0.010972	0.011485	0.01329	0.013854
MAPE	1.9576	1.0474	1.0449	0.85037	0.88279	0.88529	1.5137	2.7955	1.7631	2.5262	0.8803	0.90274
Average VaR	-0.013248	-0.014728	-0.014543	-0.017157	-0.015591	-0.016409	-0.011633	-0.011289	-0.011501	-0.011398	-0.013024	-0.013495
Acceptance (Kupiec test)	NO	NO	YES	YES	NO	YES	NO	NO	NO	NO	NO	YES
Christoffersen IND test	NO	YES	NO	NO	YES	YES	YES	NO	YES	NO	YES	YES

BUX index

Performance of tested VaR models for Hungarian BUX index at 95 and 99% confidence level is given in tables 126 and 127. According to Kupiec test at 95% confidence level most of the tested VaR models passed the test. The only two VaR models that did not pass the test were the historical simulation models with 100 and 250 day rolling window. Observed frequency of failures for the HS 100 model is 7% and 6,4% for HS 250 model. With frequency of failure of 7% (40% more than expected) HS 50 is the model with highest reported frequency of failures. At 99% confidence level situation is different with all of the historical simulation models (HS 50, 100, 250 and 500) failing the test with frequencies of failures ranging from 3% for HS 50 to 2% for HS 500 model. BRW model with $\lambda = 0.97$ failed the Kupiec test at 99% confidence level with reported frequency of failures of 2,4%. Normal variance covariance and Normal Monte Carlo model also failed the test with frequency of failures of 2% and 1,8% respectively. BRW model with $\lambda = 0.99$, RiskMetrics, EWMA Monte Carlo, GARCH-RiskMetrics and HHS model all passed the test. With frequency of failure of 3% (three times more than expected) HS 50 is the model with highest reported frequency of failures. According to Christoffersen independence test both at 95% and 99% confidence level all of the tested VaR models passed the test at 10% significance level. Based on Lopez test at 95% confidence level VaR model with the worst ranking based on underestimation of risk is the HS 100 model, and the worst ranking model based on overestimation of risk is the GARCH-RiskMetrics model. The best ranked VaR model is the Normal variance-covariance model. At 99% confidence level VaR model with the worst ranking based on underestimation of risk is the HS 50 model, and the worst ranking model based on overestimation of risk is the HHS model. The best ranked VaR model is the RiskMetrics model. Based on Blanco-Ihle test at 95% confidence level the best ranking VaR model is the GARCH-RiskMetrics model and the worst is the HS 50 model, meaning that it experienced the highest losses in excess of forecasted VaR. At 99% confidence level the best ranking VaR model is the HHS model and the worst is again the HS 50 model. According to RMSE measure, at 95% confidence level, the best performing VaR model is HS 250 model and the worst ranked model is GARCH-RiskMetrics model. At 99% confidence level the best ranking VaR model is Normal Monte Carlo and the worst ranked model is the HHS model. According to MAPE measure, at 95% confidence level, the best performing VaR model is the BRW model with $\lambda = 0.97$ and the worst ranked model is the HS 250 model. At 99% confidence level the best ranking VaR model is the RiskMetrics model and the worst ranked model is the HS 50 model. In the analysed period, at 95% confidence level, VaR model with the lowest average VaR was the HS 250 model (1,67%), HS 500 model reported the highest average VaR of 2,179%. The difference between the lowest and the highest average VaR at 95% confidence level is 30,48%. At 99% confidence level, VaR model with the lowest average VaR was the Normal Monte Carlo model (2,59%), HHS model reported the highest average VaR of 3,229%. The difference between the lowest and the highest average VaR at 99% confidence level is 24,67%.

Table 126 - Backtesting results and diagnostics of 500 VaR forecasts for BUX index daily log returns, 95% confidence level, period 13.01.2004 -31.12.2005

	HS 50	HS 100	HS 250	HS 500	BRW λ=0.97	BRW λ=0.99	Normal VCV	Risk Metrics	Normal MC	EWMA MC	GARCH RM	HHS
Number of failures	30	35	32	29	24	28	25	24	23	26	13	20
Frequency of failures	0.06	0.07	0.064	0.058	0.048	0.056	0.05	0.048	0.046	0.052	0.026	0.04
Kupiec test (p value)	0.13085	0.019643	0.066371	0.17647	0.52865	0.23168	0.44706	0.52865	0.61007	0.36861	0.99449	0.82115
Christoffersen UC test (p value)	0.31923	0.052333	0.16777	0.42294	0.83639	0.54553	1	0.83639	0.67759	0.83842	0.006901	0.28848
Christoffersen IND test (p value)	0.38133	0.74804	0.50453	0.80199	0.11931	0.7268	0.51405	0.44939	0.95076	0.58221	0.40428	0.8236
Christoffersen CC test (p value)	0.41509	0.14455	0.30911	0.70292	0.29099	0.7837	0.80823	0.73535	0.91545	0.84187	0.01837	0.55533
Lopez test	5.2759	10.275	7.2889	4.2652	-0.78307	3.2533	0.23754	-0.82547	-1.7616	1.1879	-11.878	-4.8435
Blanco-Ihle test	19.888	17.421	17.581	15.349	13.365	15.136	13.125	8.6934	13.133	9.7005	4.8039	6.8498
RMSE	0.017181	0.016047	0.015485	0.016156	0.017665	0.016195	0.016353	0.018	0.016255	0.017585	0.019635	0.017916
MAPE	1.7132	2.4489	3.3566	2.7132	1.2244	2.0948	2.399	1.8279	2.5312	1.8828	2.788	2.7207
Average VaR	-0.017613	-0.017203	-0.016699	-0.017617	-0.018508	-0.017606	-0.018009	-0.019939	-0.017907	-0.01888	-0.021785	-0.019935
Acceptance (Kupiec test)	YES	NO	NO	YES	YES	YES	YES	YES	YES	YES	YES	YES
Christoffersen IND test	YES	YES	YES	YES	YES	YES	YES	YES	YES	YES	YES	YES

Table 127 - Backtesting results and diagnostics of 500 VaR forecasts for BUX index daily log returns, 99% confidence level, period 13.01.2004 -31.12.2005

	HS 50	HS 100	HS 250	HS 500	BRW λ=0.97	BRW λ=0.99	Normal VCV	Risk Metrics	Normal MC	EWMA MC	GARCH RM	HHS
Number of failures	15	12	9	10	12	6	10	5	9	7	3	3
Frequency of failures	0.03	0.024	0.018	0.02	0.024	0.012	0.02	0.01	0.018	0.014	0.006	0.006
Kupiec test (p value)	6.15E-05	0.001901	0.031102	0.013244	0.001901	0.23708	0.013244	0.38404	0.031102	0.13232	0.73638	0.73638
Christoffersen UC test (p value)	0.000286	0.007663	0.10602	0.047896	0.007663	0.66302	0.047896	1	0.10602	0.39657	0.33148	0.33148
Christoffersen IND test (p value)	0.33489	0.44186	0.56529	0.18573	0.44186	0.70234	0.18573	0.75037	0.14477	0.65537	0.84892	0.84892
Christoffersen CC test (p value)	0.000871	0.021257	0.22956	0.058871	0.021257	0.84538	0.058871	0.95065	0.093525	0.63195	0.61281	0.61281
Lopez test	10.14	7.1458	4.1033	5.1092	7.116	1.0945	5.1087	0.062911	4.1078	2.0782	-1.9531	-1.9587
Blanco-Ihle test	7.1688	7.0205	4.1127	4.2704	5.5231	3.6922	4.1703	2.0634	4.1898	2.7537	1.2737	1.0693
RMSE	0.026958	0.028692	0.025458	0.025101	0.027397	0.029133	0.023905	0.026593	0.023793	0.02602	0.028905	0.030469
MAPE	2.0249	1.4963	1.0524	1.1845	1.596	0.53865	1.1845	0.41646	0.93516	0.76309	0.82544	0.82544
Average VaR	-0.025895	-0.027832	-0.026848	-0.027295	-0.027718	-0.029934	-0.026144	-0.027923	-0.025963	-0.027256	-0.030811	-0.03229
Acceptance (Kupiec test)	NO	NO	NO	NO	NO	YES	NO	YES	NO	YES	YES	YES
Christoffersen IND test	YES	YES	YES	YES	YES	YES	YES	YES	YES	YES	YES	YES

WIG20 index

Performance of tested VaR models for Polish WIG20 index at 95 and 99% confidence level is given in tables 128 and 129. According to Kupiec test at 95% confidence level all of the tested VaR models passed the test. At 99% confidence level historical simulation models with 50 and 100 day rolling window failed the test and reported the observed frequency of failures of 2,8% and 2% respectively. BRW model with $\lambda = 0.97$ failed the Kupiec test at 99% confidence level with reported frequency of failures of 2,4%. RiskMetrics, Normal Monte Carlo and EWMA Monte Carlo model also failed the test all with frequency of failures of 2%. HS 250, HS 500, BRW model with $\lambda = 0.99$, Normal variance-covariance, GARCH-RiskMetrics and HHS model all passed the test. With frequency of failure of 2,8% (almost three times more than expected) HS 50 is the model with highest reported frequency of failures. According to Christoffersen independence test both at 95% and 99% confidence level all of the tested VaR models passed the test at 10% significance level. Based on Lopez test at 95% confidence level VaR model with the worst ranking based on underestimation of risk is the HS 50 model, and the worst ranking model based on overestimation of risk is the GARCH-RiskMetrics model. The best ranked VaR model is the HS 100 model. At 99% confidence level VaR model with the worst ranking based on underestimation of risk is the HS 50 model, and the worst ranked models based on overestimation of risk are the HS 500 and BRW model with $\lambda = 0.99$. The best ranked VaR model is the HS 250 model. Based on Blanco-Ihle test at 95% confidence level the best ranking VaR model is the GARCH-RiskMetrics model and the worst is the HS 50 model, meaning that it experienced the highest losses in excess of forecasted VaR. At 99% confidence level the best ranking VaR model is again the GARCH-RiskMetrics model and the worst is again the HS 50 model. According to RMSE measure, at 95% confidence level, the best performing VaR model is HS 50 model and the worst ranked model is GARCH-RiskMetrics model. At 99% confidence level the best ranking VaR model is EWMA Monte Carlo and the worst ranked model is the BRW model with $\lambda = 0.99$. According to MAPE measure, at 95% confidence level, the best performing VaR model is the RiskMetrics model and the worst ranked models are GARCH-RiskMetrics and HHS model. At 99% confidence level the best ranking VaR model is the HHS model and the worst ranked model is the HS 50 model. In the analysed period, at 95% confidence level, VaR model with the lowest average VaR was the HS 50 model (1,596%), GARCH-RiskMetrics model reported the highest average VaR of 2,124%. The difference between the lowest and the highest average VaR at 95% confidence level is 33,08%. At 99% confidence level, VaR model with the lowest average VaR was the EWMA Monte Carlo model (2,386%), HS 500 model reported the highest average VaR of 3,032%. The difference between the lowest and the highest average VaR at 99% confidence level is 27,07%.

Table 128 – Backtesting results and diagnostics of 500 VaR forecasts for WIG20 index daily log returns, 95% confidence level, period 09.01.2004 -31.12.2005

	HS 50	HS 100	HS 250	HS 500	BRW λ=0,97	BRW λ=0,99	Normal VCV	Risk Metrics	Normal MC	EWMA MC	GARCH RM	HHS
Number of failures	27	25	20	14	24	16	19	24	19	24	12	12
Frequency of failures	0.054	0.05	0.04	0.028	0.048	0.032	0.038	0.048	0.038	0.048	0.024	0.024
Kupiec test (p value)	0.29612	0.44706	0.82115	0.98919	0.52865	0.96571	0.87277	0.52865	0.87277	0.52865	0.99739	0.99739
Christoffersen UC test (p value)	0.6852	1	0.28848	0.014162	0.83639	0.048624	0.19939	0.83639	0.19939	0.83639	0.003118	0.003118
Christoffersen IND test (p value)	0.70388	0.48092	0.8236	0.36861	0.4182	0.53106	0.74834	0.91433	0.74834	0.91433	0.44186	0.44186
Christoffersen CC test (p value)	0.85693	0.78005	0.55533	0.032938	0.70539	0.11762	0.4169	0.97325	0.4169	0.97325	0.009425	0.009425
Lopez test	2.2228	0.19328	-4.8406	-10.891	-0.81766	-8.8517	-5.8471	-0.83096	-5.8488	-0.82832	-12.903	-12.887
Blanco-Ihle test	17	14	10	5	13	9	9	10.586	9	11	4.5414	5.6689
RMSE	0.015101	0.016021	0.017438	0.018652	0.016576	0.01722	0.016947	0.015295	0.016859	0.015272	0.019303	0.017948
MAPE	1.005	1.803	2.0449	2.4938	1.7307	2.0998	1.9551	0.73815	1.9551	0.99252	2.7232	2.7232
Average VaR	-0.015961	-0.017153	-0.018792	-0.020642	-0.017523	-0.018759	-0.018536	-0.016665	-0.01847	-0.016634	-0.021238	-0.019842
Acceptance (Kupiec test)	YES	YES	YES	YES	YES	YES	YES	YES	YES	YES	YES	YES
Christoffersen IND test	YES	YES	YES	YES	YES	YES	YES	YES	YES	YES	YES	YES

Table 129 – Backtesting results and diagnostics of 500 VaR forecasts for WIG20 index daily log returns, 99% confidence level, period 09.01.2004 -31.12.2005

	HS 50	HS 100	HS 250	HS 500	BRW λ=0,97	BRW λ=0,99	Normal VCV	Risk Metrics	Normal MC	EWMA MC	GARCH RM	HHS
Number of failures	14	10	5	4	9	4	6	10	10	10	5	6
Frequency of failures	0.028	0.02	0.01	0.008	0.018	0.008	0.012	0.02	0.02	0.02	0.01	0.012
Kupiec test (p value)	0.000206	0.013244	0.38404	0.56039	0.031102	0.56039	0.23708	0.013244	0.013244	0.013244	0.38404	0.23708
Christoffersen UC test (p value)	0.000914	0.047896	1	0.64143	0.10602	0.64143	0.66302	0.047896	0.047896	0.047896	1	0.66302
Christoffersen IND test (p value)	0.39933	0.18573	0.75037	0.7993	0.14477	0.7993	0.70234	0.52246	0.52246	0.52246	0.75037	0.70234
Christoffersen CC test (p value)	0.002874	0.058871	0.95065	0.8687	0.093525	0.8687	0.84538	0.11517	0.11517	0.11517	0.95065	0.84538
Lopez test	9.0919	5.0863	0.038835	-0.97314	4.0622	-0.97341	1.0504	5.0646	5.0597	5.0717	0.020414	1.022
Blanco-Ihle test	5.0301	4.9045	1.4832	0.91814	3.1877	1.0352	2.201	2.8371	2.633	3.1793	0.65868	0.71743
RMSE	0.023573	0.025369	0.027317	0.028519	0.026224	0.028731	0.025029	0.02245	0.024785	0.022384	0.028329	0.027947
MAPE	1.8703	1.2294	0.59102	0.70574	0.99002	0.70574	1	1.2369	1.4339	1.2369	0.46135	0.34663
Average VaR	-0.024292	-0.026287	-0.029079	-0.03032	-0.027273	-0.030297	-0.026618	-0.023982	-0.026314	-0.023861	-0.030037	-0.029671
Acceptance (Kupiec test)	NO	NO	YES	YES	NO	YES	YES	NO	NO	NO	YES	YES
Christoffersen IND test	YES	YES	YES	YES	YES	YES	YES	YES	YES	YES	YES	YES

PX50 index

Performance of tested VaR models for Czech PX50 index at 95 and 99% confidence level is given in tables 130 and 131. According to Kupiec test at 95% confidence level all of the tested VaR models passed the test except HS 50 model with frequency of failures of 6,4%, which is 28% more than expected. At 99% confidence level historical simulation models HS 50, HS 100 and HS 250 failed the test with frequencies of failures ranging from 2,8% for HS 50 to 1,6% for HS 250 model. BRW model with $\lambda = 0.97$ failed the Kupiec test at 99% confidence level with reported frequency of failures of 1,8%. Normal variance covariance and RiskMetrics failed the test with reported frequency of failures of 2% and 1,6% respectively. Both Normal Monte Carlo and EWMA Monte Carlo failed the test with reported frequency of failures of 2% and 1,8% respectively. GARCH-RiskMetrics model also failed the test with frequency of failures of 1,6%. HS 500, BRW model with $\lambda = 0.99$ and HHS are the only models that successfully passed the Kupiec test at 99% confidence level. With frequency of failure of 2,8% (almost three times more than expected) HS 50 is the model with highest reported frequency of failures. According to Christoffersen independence test at 95% confidence level HS 50, HS 250 and HS 500 models failed the test at 10% significance level. At 99% confidence level all of the tested VaR models passed the Christoffersen independence test. Based on Lopez test at 95% confidence level VaR model with the worst ranking based on underestimation of risk is the HS 50 model, and the worst ranking model based on overestimation of risk is the GARCH-RiskMetrics model. The best ranked VaR model is the HS 100 model. At 99% confidence level VaR model with the worst ranking based on underestimation of risk is the HS 50 model. None of the VaR models overestimated the risk at 99% confidence level. The best ranked VaR model is the BRW model with $\lambda = 0.99$. Based on Blanco-Ihle test at 95% confidence level the best ranking VaR model is the GARCH-RiskMetrics model and the worst is the HS 50 model, meaning that it experienced the highest losses in excess of forecasted VaR. At 99% confidence level the best ranking VaR model is the HHS model and the worst is again the HS 50 model. According to RMSE measure, at 95% confidence level, the best performing VaR model is HS 250 model and the worst ranked model is GARCH-RiskMetrics model. At 99% confidence level the best ranking VaR model is Normal Monte Carlo and the worst ranked model is the BRW model with $\lambda = 0.99$. According to MAPE measure, at 95% confidence level, the best performing VaR models are HS 100 and BRW model with $\lambda = 0.97$, and the worst ranked model is the HS 250 model. At 99% confidence level the best ranking VaR model is the BRW model with $\lambda = 0.99$ and the worst ranked model is the HS 50 model. In the analysed period, at 95% confidence level, VaR model with the lowest average VaR was the HS 250 model (1,366%), GARCH-RiskMetrics model reported the highest average VaR of 1,823%. The difference between the lowest and the highest average VaR at 95% confidence level is 33,46%. At 99% confidence level, VaR model with the lowest average VaR was the EWMA Monte Carlo model (2,198%), BRW model with $\lambda = 0.99$ reported the highest average VaR of 3,036%. The difference between the lowest and the highest average VaR at 99% confidence level is 38,13%.

Table 130 - Backtesting results and diagnostics of 500 VaR forecasts for PX50 index daily log returns, 95% confidence level, period 09.01.2004 -31.12.2005

	HS 50	HS 100	HS 250	HS 500	BRW λ=0,97	BRW λ=0,99	Normal VCV	Risk Metrics	Normal MC	EWMA MC	GARCH RM	HHS
Number of failures	32	25	26	21	22	21	20	20	21	22	13	13
Frequency of failures	0.064	0.05	0.052	0.042	0.044	0.042	0.04	0.04	0.042	0.044	0.026	0.026
Kupiec test (p value)	0.066371	0.44706	0.36861	0.75905	0.6879	0.75905	0.82115	0.82115	0.75905	0.6879	0.99449	0.99449
Christoffersen UC test (p value)	0.16777	1	0.83842	0.3992	0.53008	0.3992	0.28848	0.28848	0.3992	0.53008	0.006901	0.006901
Christoffersen IND test (p value)	0.056742	0.51405	0.046153	0.058758	0.33241	0.28078	0.23401	0.23401	0.28078	0.33241	0.33905	0.33905
Christoffersen CC test (p value)	0.062886	0.80823	0.13415	0.11749	0.51332	0.39179	0.28041	0.28041	0.39179	0.51332	0.016469	0.016469
Lopez test	7.3137	0.32282	1.2847	-3.7566	-2.7728	-3.7368	-4.7609	-4.7898	-3.7574	-2.7822	-11.838	-11.823
Blanco-Ihle test	33.235	30.34	21.409	17.267	20.267	19.712	15.661	13.426	16.176	14.329	8.4172	9.8957
RMSE	0.015802	0.014549	0.013307	0.015149	0.015772	0.014311	0.014661	0.01515	0.014677	0.014947	0.017261	0.016152
MAPE	1.9751	1.995	2.6509	1.9352	1.1995	2.0524	2.182	1.5885	2.4239	1.7456	2.3591	2.3591
Average VaR	-0.014415	-0.014413	-0.013662	-0.015611	-0.015256	-0.014706	-0.0154	-0.015471	-0.01536	-0.015153	-0.018231	-0.017064
Acceptance (Kupiec test)	NO	YES	YES	YES	YES	YES	YES	YES	YES	YES	YES	YES
Christoffersen IND test	NO	YES	NO	NO	YES	YES	YES	YES	YES	YES	YES	YES

Table 131 - Backtesting results and diagnostics of 500 VaR forecasts for PX50 index daily log returns, 99% confidence level, period 09.01.2004 -31.12.2005

	HS 50	HS 100	HS 250	HS 500	BRW λ=0,97	BRW λ=0,99	Normal VCV	Risk Metrics	Normal MC	EWMA MC	GARCH RM	HHS
Number of failures	14	9	8	7	9	6	10	8	10	9	8	7
Frequency of failures	0.028	0.018	0.016	0.014	0.018	0.012	0.02	0.016	0.02	0.018	0.016	0.014
Kupiec test (p value)	0.000206	0.031102	0.06711	0.13232	0.031102	0.23708	0.013244	0.06711	0.013244	0.031102	0.06711	0.13232
Christoffersen UC test (p value)	0.000914	0.10602	0.21487	0.39657	0.10602	0.66302	0.047896	0.21487	0.047896	0.10602	0.21487	0.39657
Christoffersen IND test (p value)	0.39933	0.56529	0.60964	0.65537	0.56529	0.70234	0.18573	0.60964	0.18573	0.56529	0.60964	0.65537
Christoffersen CC test (p value)	0.002874	0.22956	0.40678	0.63195	0.22956	0.84538	0.058871	0.40678	0.058871	0.22956	0.40678	0.63195
Lopez test	9.1682	4.1618	3.0849	2.0791	4.1205	1.0862	5.134	3.1149	5.1349	4.1204	3.0823	2.0611
Blanco-Ihle test	11.536	9.9184	3.1027	2.7535	7.0154	3.3922	6.0369	5.1612	6.1094	5.4901	3.0785	2.0755
RMSE	0.025003	0.024644	0.02696	0.027823	0.026294	0.029557	0.021107	0.021945	0.020894	0.021593	0.024848	0.027341
MAPE	1.7905	1.1596	1.0125	0.81546	1.1521	0.75312	1.3117	1.0549	1.3117	1.1796	1.0549	0.88778
Average VaR	-0.023011	-0.024503	-0.028144	-0.029201	-0.025858	-0.030363	-0.022449	-0.02243	-0.022193	-0.021981	-0.025785	-0.028168
Acceptance (Kupiec test)	NO	NO	NO	YES	NO	YES	NO	NO	NO	NO	NO	YES
Christoffersen IND test	YES	YES	YES	YES	YES	YES	YES	YES	YES	YES	YES	YES

SKSM index

Performance of tested VaR models for Slovakian SKSM index at 95 and 99% confidence level is given in tables 132 and 133. According to Kupiec test at 95% confidence level all of the tested VaR models passed the test except HS 50 model with frequency of failures of 7,4%, which is 48% more than expected. At 99% confidence level historical simulation models with 50 and 100 day rolling window failed the test and reported the observed frequency of failures of 3,2% and 2,6% respectively. BRW model with $\lambda = 0.97$ failed the Kupiec test at 99% confidence level with reported frequency of failures of 1,8%. Normal variance covariance and RiskMetrics failed the test with reported frequency of failures of 2,4% and 3% respectively. Both Normal Monte Carlo and EWMA Monte Carlo failed the test with reported frequency of failures of 2,4% and 3,2% respectively. GARCH-RiskMetrics model also failed the test with frequency of failures of 1,6%. HS 250, HS 500, BRW model with $\lambda = 0.99$ and HHS model successfully passed the Kupiec test at 99% confidence level. With frequency of failure of 3,2% (more than three times more than expected) HS 50 and EWMA Monte Carlo are models with the highest reported frequency of failures. According to Christoffersen independence test at 95% confidence level BRW model with $\lambda = 0.97$ failed the test at 10% significance level. At 99% confidence level all of the tested VaR models passed the Christoffersen independence test. Based on Lopez test at 95% confidence level VaR model with the worst ranking based on underestimation of risk is the HS 50 model, and the worst ranking model based on overestimation of risk is the GARCH-RiskMetrics model. The best ranked VaR model is the HS 500 model. At 99% confidence level VaR model with the worst ranking based on underestimation of risk is the HS 50 model. None of the VaR models overestimated the risk at 99% confidence level. The best ranked VaR model is the BRW model with $\lambda = 0.99$. Based on Blanco-Ihle test at 95% confidence level the best ranking VaR model is the GARCH-RiskMetrics model and the worst is the HS 50 model, meaning that it experienced the highest losses in excess of forecasted VaR. At 99% confidence level the best ranking VaR model is the HHS model and the worst is the EWMA Monte Carlo model. According to RMSE measure, at 95% confidence level, the best performing VaR model is HS 250 model and the worst ranked model is GARCH-RiskMetrics model. At 99% confidence level the best ranking VaR model is EWMA Monte Carlo and the worst ranked model is the BRW model with $\lambda = 0.99$. According to MAPE measure, at 95% confidence level, the best performing VaR model is the BRW model with $\lambda = 0.97$, and the worst ranked model is the EWMA Monte Carlo model. At 99% confidence level the best ranking VaR model is the BRW model with $\lambda = 0.99$ and the worst ranked model is the HS 50 model. In the analysed period, at 95% confidence level, VaR model with the lowest average VaR was the HS 50 model (1,43%), GARCH-RiskMetrics model reported the highest average VaR of 2,088%. The difference between the lowest and the highest average VaR at 95% confidence level is 46,01%. At 99% confidence level, VaR model with the lowest average VaR was the EWMA Monte Carlo model (2,432%), BRW model with $\lambda = 0.99$ reported the highest average VaR of 3,875%. The difference between the lowest and the highest average VaR at 99% confidence level is 59,33%.

Table 132 - Backtesting results and diagnostics of 500 VaR forecasts for SKSM index daily log returns, 95% confidence level, period 10.10.2003 -31.12.2005

	HS 50	HS 100	HS 250	HS 500	BRW λ=0,97	BRW λ=0,99	Normal VCV	Risk Metrics	Normal MC	EWMA MC	GARCH RM	HHS
Number of failures	37	29	29	25	28	24	21	24	21	30	16	22
Frequency of failures	0.074	0.058	0.058	0.05	0.056	0.048	0.042	0.048	0.042	0.06	0.032	0.044
Kupiec test (p value)	0.007661	0.17647	0.17647	0.44706	0.23168	0.52865	0.75905	0.52865	0.75905	0.13085	0.96571	0.6879
Christoffersen UC test (p value)	0.02112	0.42294	0.42294	1	0.54553	0.83639	0.3992	0.83639	0.3992	0.31923	0.048624	0.53008
Christoffersen IND test (p value)	0.43839	0.80199	0.54743	0.80616	0.067983	0.87753	0.89924	0.44939	0.89924	0.87822	0.30316	0.15421
Christoffersen CC test (p value)	0.051887	0.70292	0.60529	0.97034	0.15752	0.96735	0.69532	0.73535	0.69532	0.60182	0.084226	0.29756
Lopez test	12.362	4.3648	4.3368	3.32085	3.3136	-0.69014	-3.7182	-0.70877	-3.715	5.3094	-8.8052	-2.7396
Blanco-Ihle test	32.462	30.93	22.868	20.569	25.843	21.288	16.828	24.047	17.048	26.185	9.7456	15.288
RMSE	0.0162	0.016772	0.015581	0.01598	0.017609	0.016813	0.017435	0.01737	0.017438	0.016809	0.019772	0.016895
MAPE	2.4988	2.5062	1.9352	2.5436	1.0075	1.5511	2.3591	1.813	2.3591	2.6883	2.02	1.9177
Average VaR	-0.014295	-0.015258	-0.015254	-0.015886	-0.016192	-0.016445	-0.017629	-0.017316	-0.017573	-0.016632	-0.020881	-0.017428
Acceptance (Kupiec test)	NO	YES	YES	YES	YES	YES	YES	YES	YES	YES	YES	YES
Christoffersen IND test	YES	YES	YES	YES	NO	YES	YES	YES	YES	YES	YES	YES

Table 133 - Backtesting results and diagnostics of 500 VaR forecasts for SKSM index daily log returns, 99% confidence level, period 10.10.2003 -31.12.2005

	HS 50	HS 100	HS 250	HS 500	BRW λ=0,97	BRW λ=0,99	Normal VCV	Risk Metrics	Normal MC	EWMA MC	GARCH RM	HHS
Number of failures	16	13	7	7	9	5	12	15	12	16	8	6
Frequency of failures	0.032	0.026	0.014	0.014	0.018	0.01	0.024	0.03	0.024	0.032	0.016	0.012
Kupiec test (p value)	1.73E-05	0.000646	0.13232	0.13232	0.031102	0.38404	0.001901	6.15E-05	0.001901	1.73E-05	0.06711	0.23708
Christoffersen UC test (p value)	8.40E-05	0.00274	0.39657	0.39657	0.10602	1	0.007663	0.000286	0.007663	8.40E-05	0.21487	0.66302
Christoffersen IND test (p value)	0.30316	0.40428	0.65537	0.65537	0.56529	0.75037	0.44186	0.33489	0.44186	0.53106	0.60964	0.70234
Christoffersen CC test (p value)	0.000258	0.007951	0.63195	0.63195	0.22956	0.95065	0.021257	0.000871	0.021257	0.00036	0.40678	0.84538
Lopez test	11.183	8.191	2.0911	2.0785	4.1269	0.07547	7.1608	10.173	7.1703	11.182	3.1078	1.0709
Blanco-Ihle test	10.404	9.9805	2.9491	2.4079	5.9708	2.5385	6.5735	10.357	7.2017	11.23	3.9468	2.2656
RMSE	0.028019	0.029633	0.032989	0.032981	0.034227	0.03787	0.024553	0.024769	0.024294	0.023984	0.028172	0.033007
MAPE	1.7731	1.182	0.798	0.798	0.67581	0.32918	1.6185	1.4738	1.6185	1.5187	0.83791	0.53865
Average VaR	-0.026811	-0.028625	-0.034518	-0.034636	-0.033225	-0.038751	-0.025799	-0.025112	-0.025505	-0.024323	-0.029532	-0.034199
Acceptance (Kupiec test)	NO	NO	YES	YES	NO	YES	NO	NO	NO	NO	NO	YES
Christoffersen IND test	YES	YES	YES	YES	YES	YES	YES	YES	YES	YES	YES	YES

CROBEX index

Performance of tested VaR models for Croatian CROBEX index at 95 and 99% confidence level is given in tables 134 and 135. According to Kupiec test at 95% confidence level all of the tested VaR models passed the test except HS 50 model with frequency of failures of 6,2%, which is 24% more than expected. At 99% confidence level historical simulation models with 50 and 100 day rolling window failed the test and reported the observed frequency of failures of 3% and 2% respectively. BRW model with $\lambda = 0.97$ failed the Kupiec test at 99% confidence level with reported frequency of failures of 1,6%. All other tested VaR model successfully passed the Kupiec test at 99% confidence level. With frequency of failure of 3% (three times more than expected) HS 50 is the model with highest reported frequency of failures. According to Christoffersen independence test at 95% confidence level HS 250, Normal variance-covariance and Normal Monte Carlo all failed the test at 10% significance level. At 99% confidence level HS 250, Normal variance-covariance and Normal Monte Carlo again failed the test. Based on Lopez test at 95% confidence level VaR model with the worst ranking based on underestimation of risk is the HS 50 model, and the worst ranking model based on overestimation of risk is the GARCH-RiskMetrics model. The best ranked VaR model is the BRW model with $\lambda = 0.97$. At 99% confidence level VaR model with the worst ranking based on underestimation of risk is the HS 50 model, and the worst ranking models based on overestimation of risk are the HS 500 and HHS model. The best ranked VaR model is the Normal Monte Carlo model. Based on Blanco-Ihle test at 95% confidence level the best ranking VaR model is the GARCH-RiskMetrics model and the worst is the HS 50 model, meaning that it experienced the highest losses in excess of forecasted VaR. At 99% confidence level the best ranking VaR model is the HHS model and the worst is the HS 50 model. According to RMSE measure, at 95% confidence level, the best performing VaR model is HS 250 model and the worst ranked model is Normal variance-covariance model. At 99% confidence level the best ranking VaR model is GARCH-RiskMetrics and the worst ranked model is the BRW model with $\lambda = 0.99$. According to MAPE measure, at 95% confidence level, the best performing VaR model is the EWMA Monte Carlo model, and the worst ranked models are Normal variance-covariance and Normal Monte Carlo model. At 99% confidence level the best ranking VaR model is the GARCH-RiskMetrics and the worst ranked model is the HS 50 model. In the analysed period, at 95% confidence level, VaR model with the lowest average VaR was the HS 50 model (1,478%), Normal variance-covariance model reported the highest average VaR of 2,225%. The difference between the lowest and the highest average VaR at 95% confidence level is 50,54%. At 99% confidence level, VaR model with the lowest average VaR was the HS 50 model (2,446%), BRW model with $\lambda = 0.99$ reported the highest average VaR of 3,924%. The difference between the lowest and the highest average VaR at 99% confidence level is 60,43%.

Table 134 - Backtesting results and diagnostics of 500 VaR forecasts for CROBEX index daily log returns, 95% confidence level, period 22.10.2003 -31.12.2005

	HS 50	HS 100	HS 250	HS 500	BRW λ=0,97	BRW λ=0,99	Normal VCV	Risk Metrics	Normal MC	EWMA MC	GARCH RM	HHS
Number of failures	31	29	19	19	25	24	12	14	12	18	10	15
Frequency of failures	0.062	0.058	0.038	0.038	0.05	0.048	0.024	0.028	0.024	0.036	0.02	0.03
Kupiec test (p value)	0.09445	0.17647	0.87277	0.87277	0.44706	0.52865	0.99739	0.98919	0.99739	0.91354	0.99954	0.98014
Christoffersen UC test (p value)	0.23456	0.42294	0.19939	0.19939	1	0.83639	0.003118	0.014162	0.003118	0.13135	0.000493	0.027102
Christoffersen IND test (p value)	0.15605	0.10028	0.032264	0.19222	0.51405	0.12501	0.027589	0.36861	0.027589	0.67408	0.18573	0.4635
Christoffersen CC test (p value)	0.1804	0.18794	0.04435	0.18755	0.80823	0.30179	0.001119	0.032938	0.001119	0.29326	0.000961	0.066479
Lopez test	6.1687	4.169	-5.8536	-5.863	0.12804	-0.86802	-12.921	-10.933	-12.922	-6.9207	-14.956	-9.9313
Blanco-Ihle test	13.818	13.061	9.6827	8.8005	9.577	8.4617	4.4041	4.7839	4.4015	6.3368	2.2733	3.9777
RMSE	0.015429	0.015861	0.015219	0.015399	0.016196	0.015591	0.021814	0.019276	0.021747	0.018715	0.018409	0.016545
MAPE	2.0798	3.0998	2.2469	2.4464	1.9476	2.5835	3.5262	2.1172	3.5262	1.2444	2.6958	1.6384
Average VaR	-0.014779	-0.015614	-0.015582	-0.015833	-0.015967	-0.015902	-0.022251	-0.01845	-0.022171	-0.017691	-0.019059	-0.017096
Acceptance (Kupiec test)	NO	YES	YES	YES	YES	YES	YES	YES	YES	YES	YES	YES
Christoffersen IND test	YES	YES	NO	YES	YES	YES	NO	YES	NO	YES	YES	YES

Table 135 - Backtesting results and diagnostics of 500 VaR forecasts for CROBEX index daily log returns, 99% confidence level, period 22.10.2003 -31.12.2005

	HS 50	HS 100	HS 250	HS 500	BRW λ=0,97	BRW λ=0,99	Normal VCV	Risk Metrics	Normal MC	EWMA MC	GARCH RM	HHS
Number of failures	15	10	4	2	8	4	4	5	5	6	3	2
Frequency of failures	0.03	0.02	0.008	0.004	0.016	0.008	0.008	0.01	0.01	0.012	0.006	0.004
Kupiec test (p value)	6.15E-05	0.013244	0.56039	0.87661	0.06711	0.56039	0.56039	0.38404	0.38404	0.23708	0.73638	0.87661
Christoffersen UC test (p value)	0.0002857	0.047896	0.64143	0.12504	0.21487	0.64143	0.64143	1	1	0.66302	0.33148	0.12504
Christoffersen IND test (p value)	0.4635	0.18573	0.019432	0.89904	0.60964	0.7993	0.019432	0.75037	0.034295	0.70234	0.84892	0.89904
Christoffersen CC test (p value)	0.0010599	0.058871	0.058453	0.30589	0.40678	0.8687	0.058453	0.95065	0.10646	0.84538	0.61281	0.30589
Lopez test	10.069	5.0609	-0.97907	-2.9957	3.044	-0.98632	-0.98636	0.017483	0.015329	1.0214	-1.9958	-2.9974
Blanco-Ihle test	4.3127	3.5935	0.87702	0.14551	2.4558	0.52729	0.51622	0.88054	0.58828	1.1896	0.14931	0.083191
RMSE	0.029054	0.038777	0.041378	0.040298	0.036371	0.043355	0.031372	0.027644	0.031219	0.026686	0.026499	0.027443
MAPE	2.4464	1.4988	1.1646	0.6808	0.8803	0.66584	1.1646	0.67581	1.414	0.89776	0.39401	0.64339
Average VaR	-0.024464	-0.032315	-0.038967	-0.038865	-0.031749	-0.039239	-0.031893	-0.026243	-0.031698	-0.025224	-0.026955	-0.027827
Acceptance (Kupiec test)	NO	NO	YES	YES	NO	YES	YES	YES	YES	YES	YES	YES
Christoffersen IND test	YES	YES	NO	YES	YES	YES	NO	YES	NO	YES	YES	YES

VIN index

Performance of tested VaR models for Croatian VIN index at 95 and 99% confidence level is given in tables 136 and 137. According to Kupiec test at 95% confidence level all of the tested VaR models passed the test except HS 250 model with frequency of failures of 6,2%, which is 24% more than expected. At 99% confidence level historical simulation models HS 50, HS 100 and HS 250 failed the test with frequencies of failures ranging from 2,8% for HS 50 to 1,8% for HS 100 and HS 250 models. BRW model with $\lambda = 0.97$ failed the Kupiec test at 99% confidence level with reported frequency of failures of 2,2%. Normal variance covariance failed the test with reported frequency of failures of 1,8%. Both Normal Monte Carlo and EWMA Monte Carlo failed the test with reported frequency of failures of 2% and 1,6% respectively. HS 500, BRW model with $\lambda = 0.99$, RiskMetrics, GARCH-RiskMetrics and HHS model successfully passed the Kupiec test at 99% confidence level. With frequency of failure of 2,8% (almost three times more than expected) HS 50 is the model with highest reported frequency of failures. According to Christoffersen independence test at 95% confidence level HS 50, HS 250, HS 500, BRW model with $\lambda = 0.99$, Normal variance-covariance and Normal Monte Carlo all failed the test at 10% significance level. At 99% confidence level all of the tested VaR models passed the Christoffersen independence test. Based on Lopez test at 95% confidence level VaR model with the worst ranking based on underestimation of risk is the HS 250 model, and the worst ranking model based on overestimation of risk is the GARCH-RiskMetrics model. The best ranked VaR model is the Normal variance-covariance model. At 99% confidence level VaR model with the worst ranking based on underestimation of risk is the HS 50 model, and the worst ranking model based on overestimation of risk is the HHS model. The best ranked VaR model is the RiskMetrics model. Based on Blanco-Ihle test at 95% confidence level the best ranking VaR model is the GARCH-RiskMetrics model and the worst is the HS 250 model, meaning that it experienced the highest losses in excess of forecasted VaR. At 99% confidence level the best ranking VaR model is the HHS model and the worst is the HS 50 model. According to RMSE measure, at 95% confidence level, the best performing VaR model is HS 50 model and the worst ranked model is GARCH-RiskMetrics model. At 99% confidence level the best ranking VaR model is HS 100 and the worst ranked model is the HHS. According to MAPE measure, at 95% confidence level, the best performing VaR model is the HS 50 model, and the worst ranked model is the HS 250 model. At 99% confidence level the best ranking VaR model is the RiskMetrics and the worst ranked model is the HS 50 model. In the analysed period, at 95% confidence level, VaR model with the lowest average VaR was the HS 50 model (1,231%), GARCH-RiskMetrics model reported the highest average VaR of 1,87%. The difference between the lowest and the highest average VaR at 95% confidence level is 51,91%. At 99% confidence level, VaR model with the lowest average VaR was the HS 100 model (2,057%), HHS model reported the highest average VaR of 3,032%. The difference between the lowest and the highest average VaR at 99% confidence level is 47,4%.

Table 136 - Backtesting results and diagnostics of 500 VaR forecasts for VIN index daily log returns, 95% confidence level, period 05.12.2003 -31.12.2005

	HS 50	HS 100	HS 250	HS 500	BRW λ=0,97	BRW λ=0,99	Normal VCV	Risk Metrics	Normal MC	EWMA MC	GARCH RM	HHS
Number of failures	28	29	31	30	26	26	24	15	23	21	9	21
Frequency of failures	0.056	0.058	0.062	0.06	0.052	0.052	0.048	0.03	0.046	0.042	0.018	0.042
Kupiec test (p value)	0.23168	0.17647	0.09445	0.13085	0.36861	0.36861	0.52865	0.98014	0.61007	0.75905	0.99983	0.75905
Christoffersen UC test (p value)	0.54553	0.42294	0.23456	0.31923	0.83842	0.83842	0.83639	0.027102	0.67759	0.3992	0.000169	0.3992
Christoffersen IND test (p value)	0.078667	0.10028	0.043184	0.000142	0.19094	0.046153	0.025213	0.33489	0.018082	0.89924	0.56529	0.17427
Christoffersen CC test (p value)	0.17749	0.18794	0.06389	0.000438	0.41646	0.13415	0.079985	0.054634	0.056106	0.69532	0.00072	0.27852
Lopez test	3.2346	4.2086	6.2531	5.2377	1.1927	1.2065	-0.81034	-9.893	-1.81	-3.8652	-15.924	-3.8647
Blanco-Ihle test	23.664	17.943	24.71	19.313	16.345	17.277	15.182	7.236	15.2	11.884	3.6972	8.5437
RMSE	0.013741	0.013956	0.014151	0.013964	0.014482	0.014224	0.015436	0.016753	0.015388	0.015465	0.018077	0.0147
MAPE	1.8454	2.4589	3.9277	3.5611	1.9127	2.8329	2.9227	1.985	3.1546	2.0773	2.9825	2.3117
Average VaR	-0.01231	-0.012789	-0.012429	-0.013203	-0.01335	-0.013187	-0.014571	-0.0164	-0.014478	-0.014788	-0.018701	-0.014858
Acceptance (Kupiec test)	YES	YES	NO	YES	YES	YES	YES	YES	YES	YES	YES	YES
Christoffersen IND test	NO	YES	NO	NO	YES	YES	NO	YES	NO	YES	YES	YES

Table 137 - Backtesting results and diagnostics of 500 VaR forecasts for VIN index daily log returns, 99% confidence level, period 05.12.2003 -31.12.2005

	HS 50	HS 100	HS 250	HS 500	BRW λ=0,97	BRW λ=0,99	Normal VCV	Risk Metrics	Normal MC	EWMA MC	GARCH RM	HHS
Number of failures	14	9	9	5	11	5	9	5	10	8	4	2
Frequency of failures	0.028	0.018	0.018	0.01	0.022	0.01	0.018	0.01	0.02	0.016	0.008	0.004
Kupiec test (p value)	0.000206	0.031102	0.031102	0.38404	0.005208	0.38404	0.031102	0.38404	0.013244	0.06711	0.56039	0.87661
Christoffersen UC test (p value)	0.000914	0.10602	0.10602	1	0.019918	1	0.10602	1	0.047896	0.21487	0.64143	0.12504
Christoffersen IND test (p value)	0.39933	0.56529	0.56529	0.75037	0.23191	0.75037	0.56529	0.75037	0.52246	0.60964	0.7993	0.89904
Christoffersen CC test (p value)	0.002874	0.22956	0.22956	0.95065	0.032579	0.95065	0.22956	0.95065	0.11517	0.40678	0.8687	0.30589
Lopez test	9.1213	4.0988	4.0944	0.057024	6.0978	0.070308	4.0924	0.04708	5.0936	3.0585	-0.96664	-2.9805
Blanco-Ihle test	8.4332	6.3572	5.2555	2.3557	6.1694	3.2121	4.9405	2.1155	5.0865	3.0538	0.98664	0.42578
RMSE	0.022011	0.020693	0.022049	0.024453	0.025203	0.024054	0.021564	0.02406	0.021397	0.022153	0.026078	0.030105
MAPE	2.0848	1.0125	1.6409	1.1746	1.5112	0.73317	1.6409	0.51372	1.8903	0.90274	0.72818	0.58853
Average VaR	-0.020682	-0.020573	-0.022192	-0.025586	-0.024036	-0.024941	-0.021603	-0.023525	-0.02141	-0.021669	-0.026449	-0.030316
Acceptance (Kupiec test)	NO	NO	NO	YES	NO	YES	NO	YES	NO	NO	YES	YES
Christoffersen IND test	YES	YES	YES	YES	YES	YES	YES	YES	YES	YES	YES	YES

TALSE index

Performance of tested VaR models for Estonian TALSE index at 95 and 99% confidence level is given in tables 138 and 139. According to Kupiec test at 95% confidence level all of the tested VaR models passed the test except HS 50 model with frequency of failures of 6,8%, which is 36% more than expected. At 99% confidence level historical simulation models with 50 and 100 day rolling window failed the test and reported the observed frequency of failures of 2,2% and 1,8% respectively. EWMA Monte Carlo model failed the Kupiec test at 99% confidence level with reported frequency of failures of 1,8%. Other models successfully passed the Kupiec test at 99% confidence level. With frequency of failure of 2,2% (more than two times more than expected) HS 50 is the model with highest reported frequency of failures. According to Christoffersen independence test at 95% confidence level HS 50, HS 100, HS 250, both BRW models with $\lambda = 0.97$ and 0.99, RiskMetrics and EWMA Monte Carlo all failed the test at 10% significance level. At 99% confidence level all of the tested VaR models passed the Christoffersen independence test. Based on Lopez test at 95% confidence level VaR model with the worst ranking based on underestimation of risk is the HS 50 model, and the worst ranking model based on overestimation of risk is the GARCH-RiskMetrics model. The best ranked VaR model is the BRW model with $\lambda = 0.97$. At 99% confidence level VaR model with the worst ranking based on underestimation of risk is the HS 50 model, and the worst ranking model based on overestimation of risk is the HHS model. The best ranked VaR model is the BRW model with $\lambda = 0.99$. Based on Blanco-Ihle test at 95% confidence level the best ranking VaR model is the GARCH-RiskMetrics model and the worst is the HS 50 model, meaning that it experienced the highest losses in excess of forecasted VaR. At 99% confidence level the best ranking VaR model is the HHS model and the worst is the HS 50 model. According to RMSE measure, at 95% confidence level, the best performing VaR model is HS 50 model and the worst ranked model is GARCH-RiskMetrics model. At 99% confidence level the best ranking VaR model is HS 50 and the worst ranked model is the HHS. According to MAPE measure, at 95% confidence level, the best performing VaR model is the BRW model with $\lambda = 0.97$, and the worst ranked model is the GARCH-RiskMetrics model. At 99% confidence level the best ranking VaR model is the BRW model with $\lambda = 0.97$ and the worst ranked model is the HS 50 model. In the analysed period, at 95% confidence level, VaR model with the lowest average VaR was the HS 50 model (0,843%), GARCH-RiskMetrics model reported the highest average VaR of 1,5%. The difference between the lowest and the highest average VaR at 95% confidence level is 77,94%. At 99% confidence level, VaR model with the lowest average VaR was the HS 50 model (1,411%), HHS model reported the highest average VaR of 2,51%. The difference between the lowest and the highest average VaR at 99% confidence level is 77,89%.

Table 138 - Backtesting results and diagnostics of 500 VaR forecasts for TALSE index daily log returns, 95% confidence level, period 16.01.2004 -31.12.2005

	HS 50	HS 100	HS 250	HS 500	BRW λ=0,97	BRW λ=0,99	Normal VCV	Risk Metrics	Normal MC	EWMA MC	GARCH RM	HHS
Number of failures	34	28	16	12	25	19	10	21	11	22	7	9
Frequency of failures	0.068	0.056	0.032	0.024	0.05	0.038	0.02	0.042	0.022	0.044	0.014	0.018
Kupiec test (p value)	0.03026	0.23168	0.96571	0.99739	0.44706	0.87277	0.99954	0.75905	0.99886	0.6879	0.99998	0.99983
Christoffersen UC test (p value)	0.079233	0.54553	0.048624	0.003118	1	0.19939	0.000493	0.3992	0.001297	0.53008	1.41E-05	0.000169
Christoffersen IND test (p value)	0.005762	0.017199	0.010905	0.28312	0.03444	0.032264	0.52246	0.058758	0.48129	0.076916	0.65537	0.56529
Christoffersen CC test (p value)	0.004739	0.048769	0.005603	0.007121	0.10685	0.04435	0.001881	0.11749	0.004421	0.17178	7.30E-05	0.00072
Lopez test	9.1711	3.1586	-8.8873	-12.909	0.12809	-5.887	-14.924	-3.9028	-13.921	-2.8942	-17.962	-15.948
Blanco-Ihle test	26.382	21.514	11.746	7.053	16.11	11.148	5.3851	13.346	5.8481	17.91	2.2999	3.5721
RMSE	0.010627	0.010744	0.01182	0.012556	0.011145	0.011463	0.013587	0.01302	0.013546	0.013012	0.015362	0.013803
MAPE	2.1895	2.5212	3.2643	3.4638	1.9027	2.4788	3.2793	2.7531	3.1995	3.3317	3.9327	3.4763
Average VaR	-0.008432	-0.009014	-0.011033	-0.012488	-0.009476	-0.010634	-0.013561	-0.011337	-0.01349	-0.011208	-0.014998	-0.0133
Acceptance (Kupiec test)	NO	YES	YES	YES	YES	YES	YES	YES	YES	YES	YES	YES
Christoffersen IND test	NO	NO	NO	YES	NO	NO	YES	NO	YES	NO	YES	YES

Table 139 - Backtesting results and diagnostics of 500 VaR forecasts for TALSE index daily log returns, 99% confidence level, period 16.01.2004 -31.12.2005

	HS 50	HS 100	HS 250	HS 500	BRW λ=0,97	BRW λ=0,99	Normal VCV	Risk Metrics	Normal MC	EWMA MC	GARCH RM	HHS
Number of failures	11	9	6	2	6	5	2	6	3	9	1	1
Frequency of failures	0.022	0.018	0.012	0.004	0.012	0.01	0.004	0.012	0.006	0.018	0.002	0.002
Kupiec test (p value)	0.005208	0.031102	0.23708	0.87661	0.23708	0.38404	0.87661	0.23708	0.73638	0.031102	0.96025	0.96025
Christoffersen UC test (p value)	0.019918	0.10602	0.66302	0.12504	0.66302	1	0.12504	0.66302	0.33148	0.10602	0.02824	0.02824
Christoffersen IND test (p value)	0.23191	0.56529	0.70234	0.89904	0.70234	0.75037	0.89904	0.70234	0.84892	0.56529	0.94947	0.94947
Christoffersen CC test (p value)	0.032579	0.22956	0.84538	0.30589	0.84538	0.95065	0.30589	0.84538	0.61281	0.22956	0.089933	0.089933
Lopez test	6.0801	4.064	1.0349	-2.9751	1.063	0.028851	-2.9646	1.0492	-1.9633	4.0552	-3.9826	-3.988
Blanco-Ihle test	8.1953	5.48	1.7801	0.93433	5.2915	1.2642	1.6517	4.1732	1.7272	5.4396	0.84619	0.45831
RMSE	0.016023	0.018176	0.020874	0.024226	0.017741	0.021049	0.019621	0.018381	0.019459	0.018047	0.021677	0.025894
MAPE	1.2768	1.0025	0.86035	0.85287	0.58105	0.73067	0.85287	0.90274	1.02	1.0075	0.96509	0.96509
Average VaR	-0.014105	-0.016086	-0.02031	-0.024507	-0.016394	-0.020452	-0.01991	-0.016709	-0.019732	-0.016341	-0.021213	-0.025102
Acceptance (Kupiec test)	NO	NO	YES	YES	YES	YES	YES	YES	YES	NO	YES	YES
Christoffersen IND test	YES	YES	YES	YES	YES	YES	YES	YES	YES	YES	YES	YES

RIGSE index

Performance of tested VaR models for Latvian RIGSE index at 95 and 99% confidence level is given in tables 140 and 141. According to Kupiec test at 95% confidence level all of the tested VaR models passed the test, except the historical simulation models with 50 and 500 day rolling window, which reported the observed frequency of failures of 6,8% and 6,2% respectively. With frequency of failure of 6,8% (36% more than expected) HS 50 is the model with highest reported frequency of failures. At 99% confidence level historical simulation models with 50 and 100 day rolling window failed the test and reported the observed frequency of failures of 3,4% and 2,2% respectively. BRW model with $\lambda = 0.97$ failed the Kupiec test at 99% confidence level with reported frequency of failures of 2,2%. Normal variance-covariance model also failed the test with frequency of failures of 1,6%. All other VaR models passed the test. With frequency of failure of 3,4% (more than three times more than expected) HS 50 is the model with highest reported frequency of failures. According to Christoffersen independence test at 95% confidence level HS 500 model failed the test at 10% significance level. At 99% confidence level all of the tested VaR models passed the Christoffersen independence test. Based on Lopez test at 95% confidence level VaR model with the worst ranking based on underestimation of risk is the HS 50 model, and the worst ranking model based on overestimation of risk is the GARCH-RiskMetrics model. The best ranked VaR model is the BRW model with $\lambda = 0.99$. At 99% confidence level VaR model with the worst ranking based on underestimation of risk is again the HS 50 model, and the worst ranking model based on overestimation of risk is again the GARCH-RiskMetrics model. The best ranked VaR model is the EWMA Monte Carlo model. Based on Blanco-Ihle test at 95% confidence level the best ranking VaR model is the GARCH-RiskMetrics model and the worst is the HS 50 model, meaning that it experienced the highest losses in excess of forecasted VaR. At 99% confidence level the best ranking VaR model is again the GARCH-RiskMetrics model and the worst is again the HS 50 model. According to RMSE measure, at 95% confidence level, the best performing VaR model is HS 250 model and the worst ranked model is GARCH-RiskMetrics model. At 99% confidence level the best ranking VaR model is HS 50 and the worst ranked model is again the GARCH-RiskMetrics model. According to MAPE measure, at 95% confidence level, the best performing VaR model is the RiskMetrics model and the worst ranked model is the GARCH-RiskMetrics model. At 99% confidence level the best ranking VaR model is the BRW model with $\lambda = 0.99$ and the worst ranked model is the HS 50 model. In the analysed period, at 95% confidence level, VaR model with the lowest average VaR was the HS 50 model (1,093%), GARCH-RiskMetrics model reported the highest average VaR of 1,651%. The difference between the lowest and the highest average VaR at 95% confidence level is 51,05%. At 99% confidence level, VaR model with the lowest average VaR was the HS 50 model (1,602%), GARCH-RiskMetrics model reported the highest average VaR of 2,335%. The difference between the lowest and the highest average VaR at 99% confidence level is 45,76%.

Table 140 - Backtesting results and diagnostics of 500 VaR forecasts for RIGSE index daily log returns, 95% confidence level, period 16.01.2004 -31.12.2005

	HS 50	HS 100	HS 250	HS 500	BRW λ=0,97	BRW λ=0,99	Normal VCV	Risk Metrics	Normal MC	EWMA MC	GARCH RM	HHS
Number of failures	34	28	29	31	29	25	18	20	19	23	8	20
Frequency of failures	0.068	0.056	0.058	0.062	0.058	0.05	0.036	0.04	0.038	0.046	0.016	0.04
Kupiec test (p value)	0.03026	0.23168	0.17647	0.09445	0.17647	0.44706	0.91354	0.82115	0.87277	0.61007	0.99994	0.82115
Christoffersen UC test (p value)	0.079233	0.54553	0.42294	0.23456	0.42294	1	0.13135	0.28848	0.19939	0.67759	5.21E-05	0.28848
Christoffersen IND test (p value)	0.81973	0.60744	0.54743	0.042634	0.54743	0.80616	0.24571	0.8236	0.21997	0.95076	0.60964	0.19617
Christoffersen CC test (p value)	0.20883	0.73004	0.60529	0.063201	0.60529	0.97034	0.16333	0.55533	0.20686	0.91545	0.000245	0.24693
Lopez test	9.1564	3.1278	4.1272	6.1376	4.1184	0.11691	-6.912	-4.9139	-5.9116	-1.9125	-16.976	-4.9344
Blanco-Ihle test	17.852	12.865	12.027	13.151	11.767	10.833	7.046	7.5287	7.0526	7.6632	1.4951	5.0509
RMSE	0.011239	0.011055	0.010752	0.01104	0.012071	0.011201	0.012159	0.012568	0.012132	0.012384	0.015685	0.012558
MAPE	1.9401	2.3067	2.1845	2.9102	1.6958	1.8329	1.5387	1.3965	1.5436	1.6658	3.0599	1.5985
Average VaR	-0.010932	-0.011253	-0.011	-0.011242	-0.012175	-0.011563	-0.012877	-0.012913	-0.01285	-0.012682	-0.016513	-0.013069
Acceptance (Kupiec test)	NO	YES	YES	NO	YES	YES	YES	YES	YES	YES	YES	YES
Christoffersen IND test	YES	YES	YES	NO	YES	YES	YES	YES	YES	YES	YES	YES

Table 141 - Backtesting results and diagnostics of 500 VaR forecasts for RIGSE index daily log returns, 99% confidence level, period 16.01.2004 -31.12.2005

	HS 50	HS 100	HS 250	HS 500	BRW λ=0,97	BRW λ=0,99	Normal VCV	Risk Metrics	Normal MC	EWMA MC	GARCH RM	HHS
Number of failures	17	11	4	2	11	4	8	6	7	5	1	1
Frequency of failures	0.034	0.022	0.008	0.004	0.022	0.008	0.016	0.012	0.014	0.01	0.002	0.002
Kupiec test (p value)	4.60E-06	0.005208	0.56039	0.87661	0.005208	0.56039	0.06711	0.23708	0.13232	0.38404	0.96025	0.96025
Christoffersen UC test (p value)	2.33E-05	0.019918	0.64143	0.12504	0.019918	0.64143	0.21487	0.66302	0.39657	1	0.02824	0.02824
Christoffersen IND test (p value)	0.60145	0.48129	0.7993	0.89904	0.23191	0.7993	0.60964	0.70234	0.65537	0.75037	0.94947	0.94947
Christoffersen CC test (p value)	0.000113	0.051948	0.8687	0.30589	0.032579	0.8687	0.40678	0.84538	0.63195	0.95065	0.089933	0.089933
Lopez test	12.061	6.0342	-0.9927	-2.9961	6.035	-0.99064	3.0194	1.0201	2.0188	0.021055	-3.9983	-3.998
Blanco-Ihle test	4.8962	2.3797	0.38057	0.18473	2.4853	0.50577	1.0754	1.2635	1.0365	1.3705	0.080799	0.09282
RMSE	0.015468	0.017143	0.019708	0.021219	0.017556	0.01954	0.017499	0.018083	0.017347	0.017725	0.022678	0.022633
MAPE	2.2768	1.4439	0.56608	0.50125	1.3865	0.39152	1.0349	0.59601	0.80549	0.84539	0.75062	0.75062
Average VaR	-0.016021	-0.018241	-0.020951	-0.022318	-0.018448	-0.020865	-0.01878	-0.018776	-0.018601	-0.018419	-0.023354	-0.023326
Acceptance (Kupiec test)	NO	NO	YES	YES	NO	YES	NO	YES	YES	YES	YES	YES
Christoffersen IND test	YES	YES	YES	YES	YES	YES	YES	YES	YES	YES	YES	YES

VILSE index

Performance of tested VaR models of Lithuanian VILSE index at 95 and 99% confidence level is given in tables 142 and 143. According to Kupiec test at 95% confidence level all of the tested VaR models passed the test, except the historical simulation models with 50 and 100 day rolling window, which reported the observed frequency of failures of 8,6% and 7,8% respectively. With frequency of failure of 8,6% (72% more than expected) HS 50 is the model with highest reported frequency of failures. At 99% confidence level historical simulation models with 50 and 100 day rolling window failed the test and reported the observed frequency of failures of 3,6% and 2,8% respectively. BRW model with $\lambda = 0.97$ also failed the Kupiec test at 99% confidence level with reported frequency of failures of 2,8%. All other VaR models passed the test. With frequency of failure of 3,6% (more than three times more than expected) HS 50 is the model with highest reported frequency of failures. According to Christoffersen independence test at 95% confidence level all tested VaR model failed the test at 10% significance level, except BRW model with $\lambda = 0.97$. At 99% confidence level HS 100, HS 250, both BRW models with $\lambda = 0.97$ and 0.99, RiskMetrics and EWMA Monte Carlo model all failed the Christoffersen independence test. Based on Lopez test at 95% confidence level VaR model with the worst ranking based on underestimation of risk is the HS 50 model, and the worst ranking model based on overestimation of risk is the GARCH-RiskMetrics model. The best ranked VaR model is the BRW model with $\lambda = 0.99$. At 99% confidence level VaR model with the worst ranking based on underestimation of risk is again the HS 50 model, and the worst ranking model based on overestimation of risk is the HHS model. The best ranked VaR model is the Normal variance-covariance model. Based on Blanco-Ihle test at 95% confidence level the best ranking VaR model is the GARCH-RiskMetrics model and the worst is the HS 50 model, meaning that it experienced the highest losses in excess of forecasted VaR. At 99% confidence level the best ranking VaR model is the HHS model and the worst is again the HS 50 model. According to RMSE measure, at 95% confidence level, the best performing VaR model is HS 50 model and the worst ranked model is GARCH-RiskMetrics model. At 99% confidence level the best ranking VaR model is HS 50 and the worst ranked model is the HS 500 model. According to MAPE measure, at 95% confidence level, the best performing VaR model is the BRW model with $\lambda = 0.99$ and the worst ranked model is the HS 50 model. At 99% confidence level the best ranking VaR model is the RiskMetrics model and the worst ranked model is the HS 50 model. In the analysed period, at 95% confidence level, VaR model with the lowest average VaR was the HS 50 model (0,845%), GARCH-RiskMetrics model reported the highest average VaR of 1,336%. The difference between the lowest and the highest average VaR at 95% confidence level is 58,11%. At 99% confidence level, VaR model with the lowest average VaR was the HS 50 model (1,363%), HS 500 model reported the highest average VaR of 2,197%. The difference between the lowest and the highest average VaR at 99% confidence level is 61,19%.

Table 142 - Backtesting results and diagnostics of 500 VaR forecasts for VILSE index daily log returns, 95% confidence level, period 30.12.2003 -31.12.2005

	HS 50	HS 100	HS 250	HS 500	BRW λ=0,97	BRW λ=0,99	Normal VCV	Risk Metrics	Normal MC	EWMA MC	GARCH RM	HHS
Number of failures	43	39	25	23	29	25	18	17	16	16	13	14
Frequency of failures	0.086	0.078	0.05	0.046	0.058	0.05	0.036	0.034	0.032	0.032	0.026	0.028
Kupiec test (p value)	0.000251	0.002701	0.44706	0.61007	0.17647	0.44706	0.91354	0.94408	0.96571	0.96571	0.99449	0.98919
Christoffersen UC test (p value)	0.000762	0.007699	1	0.67759	0.42294	1	0.13135	0.082169	0.048624	0.048624	0.006901	0.014162
Christoffersen IND test (p value)	0.029397	0.008042	0.000737	0.002456	0.32643	0.005742	0.023097	0.016105	0.096153	0.000825	0.039413	0.054505
Christoffersen CC test (p value)	0.000323	0.000856	0.003357	0.009344	0.44817	0.022044	0.024262	0.012199	0.035856	0.000533	0.003117	0.00777
Lopez test	18.184	14.175	0.14534	-1.8595	4.1354	0.14027	-6.9078	-7.9126	-8.9062	-8.9044	-11.934	-10.914
Blanco-Ihle test	30.204	22.116	16.314	15.316	16.824	15.491	7.8505	8.1307	8.0754	9.3643	5.1213	7.5836
RMSE	0.010079	0.010956	0.011019	0.010712	0.010556	0.010842	0.012348	0.012115	0.012296	0.0119	0.013243	0.011956
MAPE	4.0274	3.6608	2.6683	2.5162	1.6683	1.6035	2.4589	2.2095	2.5935	2.4713	3.0374	2.788
Average VaR	-0.00845	-0.009783	-0.010386	-0.010461	-0.00955	-0.010216	-0.012466	-0.0116	-0.012396	-0.011314	-0.013361	-0.011931
Acceptance (Kupiec test)	NO	NO	YES	YES	YES	YES	YES	YES	YES	YES	YES	YES
Christoffersen IND test	NO	NO	NO	NO	YES	NO	NO	NO	NO	NO	NO	NO

Table 143 - Backtesting results and diagnostics of 500 VaR forecasts for VILSE index daily log returns, 99% confidence level, period 30.12.2003 -31.12.2005

	HS 50	HS 100	HS 250	HS 500	BRW λ=0,97	BRW λ=0,99	Normal VCV	Risk Metrics	Normal MC	EWMA MC	GARCH RM	HHS
Number of failures	18	14	6	2	14	6	5	7	5	6	3	2
Frequency of failures	0.036	0.028	0.012	0.004	0.028	0.012	0.01	0.014	0.01	0.012	0.006	0.004
Kupiec test (p value)	1.16E-06	0.000206	0.23708	0.87661	0.000206	0.23708	0.38404	0.13232	0.38404	0.23708	0.73638	0.87661
Christoffersen UC test (p value)	6.10E-06	0.000914	0.66302	0.12504	0.000914	0.66302	1	0.39657	1	0.66302	0.33148	0.12504
Christoffersen IND test (p value)	0.15539	0.054505	0.05405	0.89904	0.054505	0.05405	0.75037	0.002146	0.75037	0.000984	0.84892	0.89904
Christoffersen CC test (p value)	1.32E-05	0.000645	0.1422	0.30589	0.000645	0.1422	0.95065	0.006287	0.95065	0.003989	0.61281	0.30589
Lopez test	13.089	9.0837	1.051	-2.9686	9.0538	1.0378	0.036003	2.0388	0.040021	1.0466	-1.9749	-2.9748
Blanco-Ihle test	8.9673	7.4494	3.5403	1.8309	4.2634	2.2339	2.0295	2.3925	2.4341	3.244	1.4887	1.4817
RMSE	0.014861	0.016259	0.018865	0.021069	0.017528	0.020536	0.017912	0.01732	0.017768	0.017044	0.018655	0.019146
MAPE	2.7955	1.9676	0.83541	0.92519	2.0349	0.83541	0.70075	0.61596	0.70075	0.86534	0.94763	0.92519
Average VaR	-0.013633	-0.015692	-0.018899	-0.021971	-0.017056	-0.020839	-0.018564	-0.017246	-0.018362	-0.016854	-0.018897	-0.019396
Acceptance (Kupiec test)	NO	NO	YES	YES	NO	YES	YES	YES	YES	YES	YES	YES
Christoffersen IND test	YES	NO	NO	YES	NO	NO	YES	NO	YES	NO	YES	YES

CYSMGEN index

Performance of tested VaR models for Cyprus CYSMGEN index at 95 and 99% confidence level is given in tables 144 and 145. According to Kupiec test at 95% confidence level all of the tested VaR models passed the test except HS 50 model with frequency of failures of 6,4%, which is 28% more than expected. At 99% confidence level historical simulation models with 50 and 100 day rolling window failed the test and reported the observed frequency of failures of 2,8% and 2,6% respectively. BRW model with $\lambda = 0.97$ failed the Kupiec test at 99% confidence level with reported frequency of failures of 1,8%. Normal variance-covariance and Normal Monte Carlo model also failed the Kupiec test at 99% confidence level with reported frequency of failures of 1,6%. Other models successfully passed the Kupiec test at 99% confidence level. With frequency of failure of 2,8% (almost three times more than expected) HS 50 is the model with highest reported frequency of failures. According to Christoffersen independence test at 95% confidence level HS 50, HS 100, both BRW models with $\lambda = 0.97$ and 0.99 and Normal variance-covariance model all failed the test at 10% significance level. At 99% confidence level HS 50, HS 100 and both BRW models with $\lambda = 0.97$ and 0.99 failed the Christoffersen independence test. Based on Lopez test at 95% confidence level VaR model with the worst ranking based on underestimation of risk is the HS 50 model, and the worst ranking model based on overestimation of risk is the HHS model. The best ranked VaR model is the HS 250 model. At 99% confidence level VaR model with the worst ranking based on underestimation of risk is again the HS 50 model, and the worst ranking model based on overestimation of risk is again the HHS model. The best ranked VaR model is the EWMA Monte Carlo model. Based on Blanco-Ihle test at 95% confidence level the best ranking VaR model is the HHS model and the worst is the HS 100 model, meaning that it experienced the highest losses in excess of forecasted VaR. At 99% confidence level the best ranking VaR model is again the HHS model and the worst is the HS 50 model. According to RMSE measure, at 95% confidence level, the best performing VaR model is HS 50 model and the worst ranked model is HHS model. At 99% confidence level the best ranking VaR model is HS 50 and the worst ranked model is the HS 500. According to MAPE measure, at 95% confidence level, the best performing VaR model is the BRW model with $\lambda = 0.97$, and the worst ranked models are GARCH-RiskMetrics and HHS models. At 99% confidence level the best ranking VaR model is the EWMA Monte Carlo model and the worst ranked model is the HS 50 model. In the analysed period, at 95% confidence level, VaR model with the lowest average VaR was the HS 50 model (1,204%), HHS model reported the highest average VaR of 1,793%. The difference between the lowest and the highest average VaR at 95% confidence level is 48,92%. At 99% confidence level, VaR model with the lowest average VaR was the HS 50 model (1,814%), HS 500 model reported the highest average VaR of 2,974%. The difference between the lowest and the highest average VaR at 99% confidence level is 63,95%.

Table 144 - Backtesting results and diagnostics of 500 VaR forecasts for CYSMGENL index daily log returns, 95% confidence level, period 13.01.2004 -31.12.2005

	HS 50	HS 100	HS 250	HS 500	BRW λ=0,97	BRW λ=0,99	Normal VCV	Risk Metrics	Normal MC	EWMA MC	GARCH RM	HHS
Number of failures	32	29	25	17	27	19	16	15	17	17	10	10
Frequency of failures	0.064	0.058	0.05	0.034	0.054	0.038	0.032	0.03	0.034	0.034	0.02	0.02
Kupiec test (p value)	0.066371	0.17647	0.44706	0.94408	0.29612	0.87277	0.96571	0.98014	0.94408	0.94408	0.99954	0.99954
Christoffersen UC test (p value)	0.16777	0.42294	1	0.082169	0.6852	0.19939	0.048624	0.027102	0.082169	0.082169	0.000493	0.000493
Christoffersen IND test (p value)	0.056742	0.0238	0.15562	0.12343	0.060759	0.032264	0.096153	0.33489	0.12343	0.60145	0.18573	0.18573
Christoffersen CC test (p value)	0.062886	0.05638	0.36489	0.067383	0.15875	0.04435	0.035856	0.054634	0.067383	0.1926	0.000961	0.000961
Lopez test	7.1875	4.2028	0.16105	-7.8844	2.1416	-5.853	-8.8818	-9.9302	-7.8798	-7.925	-14.962	-14.97
Blanco-Ihle test	19.628	19.854	13.161	7.8048	11.947	11.905	8.1436	4.4086	8.3577	4.7865	2.0546	1.5497
RMSE	0.012454	0.012428	0.012518	0.014993	0.013395	0.012975	0.014343	0.014538	0.01434	0.014289	0.016829	0.017437
MAPE	1.8279	2.7805	2.818	3.3392	1.5162	2.4688	2.9875	2.0274	2.8429	1.7955	3.3815	3.3815
Average VaR	-0.012044	-0.012238	-0.012894	-0.015673	-0.013193	-0.013344	-0.015142	-0.014903	-0.015088	-0.01461	-0.017354	-0.017929
Acceptance (Kupiec test)	NO	YES	YES	YES	YES	YES	YES	YES	YES	YES	YES	YES
Christoffersen IND test	NO	NO	YES	YES	NO	NO	NO	YES	YES	YES	YES	YES

Table 145 - Backtesting results and diagnostics of 500 VaR forecasts for CYSMGENL index daily log returns, 99% confidence level, period 13.01.2004 -31.12.2005

	HS 50	HS 100	HS 250	HS 500	BRW λ=0,97	BRW λ=0,99	Normal VCV	Risk Metrics	Normal MC	EWMA MC	GARCH RM	HHS
Number of failures	14	13	5	4	9	6	8	3	8	5	3	2
Frequency of failures	0.028	0.026	0.01	0.008	0.018	0.012	0.016	0.006	0.016	0.01	0.006	0.004
Kupiec test (p value)	0.000206	0.000646	0.38404	0.56039	0.031102	0.23708	0.06711	0.73638	0.06711	0.38404	0.99019	0.99741
Christoffersen UC test (p value)	0.000914	0.00274	1	0.64143	0.10602	0.66302	0.21487	0.33148	0.21487	1	0.008738	0.001851
Christoffersen IND test (p value)	0.054505	0.039413	0.75037	0.7993	0.007289	0.05405	0.60964	0.84892	0.60964	0.75037	0.84892	0.89904
Christoffersen CC test (p value)	0.000645	0.001349	0.95065	0.8687	0.007399	0.1422	0.40678	0.61281	0.40678	0.95065	0.031556	0.007796
Lopez test	9.0806	8.0807	0.052169	-0.98404	4.0558	1.0302	3.0502	-1.9843	3.052	0.020338	-6.9917	-7.9963
Blanco-Ihle test	5.963	5.5848	2.6515	0.68855	3.8444	1.5693	2.3528	0.75319	2.4803	0.98375	0.34632	0.12772
RMSE	0.019067	0.021875	0.021501	0.029459	0.021912	0.025138	0.020238	0.020776	0.020039	0.020548	0.021321	0.022937
MAPE	2.0524	1.6259	0.85786	0.7182	1.2244	1.202	1.2344	0.73815	1.2344	0.48379	1.4564	1.5985
Average VaR	-0.018143	-0.021179	-0.022584	-0.029743	-0.021239	-0.02554	-0.021454	-0.021023	-0.021225	-0.020692	-0.021668	-0.023171
Acceptance (Kupiec test)	NO	NO	YES	YES	NO	YES	NO	YES	NO	YES	YES	YES
Christoffersen IND test	NO	NO	YES	YES	NO	NO	YES	YES	YES	YES	YES	YES

MALTEX index

Performance of tested VaR models for Maltan MALTEX index at 95 and 99% confidence level is given in tables 146 and 147. According to Kupiec test at 95% confidence level all of the tested VaR models passed the test, except the historical simulation models with 50 and 100 day rolling window, which reported the observed frequency of failures of 7,6% and 6,4% respectively. With frequency of failure of 7,6% (52% more than expected) HS 50 is the model with highest reported frequency of failures. At 99% confidence level historical simulation models with 50, 100 and 250 day rolling window failed the test and reported the observed frequency of failures of 2,8% for HS 50 and HS 100 and 2,2% for HS 250. Both BRW models with λ = 0.97 and 0.99 failed the Kupiec test at 99% confidence level with reported frequency of failures of 2,2% and 1,6% respectively. Normal variance-covariance and Normal Monte Carlo model also failed the Kupiec test at 99% confidence level with reported frequency of failures of 2,2% and 2,4% respectively. Other models successfully passed the Kupiec test at 99% confidence level. With frequency of failure of 2,8% (almost three times more than expected) HS 50 and HS 100 are model with the highest reported frequency of failures. According to Christoffersen independence test at 95% confidence level all tested VaR model failed the test at 10% significance level. At 99% confidence level HS 50, HS 100, HS 250, HS 500, both BRW models with λ = 0.97 and 0.99, Normal variance-covariance and Normal Monte Carlo model all failed the Christoffersen independence test. Based on Lopez test at 95% confidence level VaR model with the worst ranking based on underestimation of risk is the HS 50 model, and the worst ranking model based on overestimation of risk is the RiskMetrics model. The best ranked VaR model is the BRW model with λ = 0.99. At 99% confidence level VaR model with the worst ranking based on underestimation of risk is again the HS 50 model, and the worst ranking model based on overestimation of risk is the HHS model. The best ranked VaR model is the GARCH-RiskMetrics model. Based on Blanco-Ihle test at 95% confidence level the best ranking VaR model is the HHS model and the worst is the HS 50 model, meaning that it experienced the highest losses in excess of forecasted VaR. At 99% confidence level the best ranking VaR model is again the HHS model and the worst is again the HS 50 model. According to RMSE measure, at 95% confidence level, the best performing VaR model is HS 500 model and the worst ranked model is HHS model. At 99% confidence level the best ranking VaR model is Normal Monte Carlo and the worst ranked model is the HHS model. According to MAPE measure, at 95% confidence level, the best performing model is the BRW model with λ = 0.97 and the worst ranked model is HS 50. At 99% confidence level the best ranking VaR models are RiskMetrics and EWMA Monte Carlo model and the worst ranked model is HS 50 model. In the analysed period, at 95% confidence level, VaR model with the lowest average VaR was the HS 50 model (0,836%), HHS model reported the highest average VaR of 1,172%. The difference between the lowest and the highest average VaR at 95% confidence level is 40,19%. At 99% confidence level, VaR model with the lowest average VaR was the HS 100 model (1,463%), HHS model reported the highest average VaR of 1,949%. The difference between the lowest and the highest average VaR at 99% confidence level is 33,22%.

Table 146 - Backtesting results and diagnostics of 500 VaR forecasts for MALTEX index daily log returns, 95% confidence level, period 19.12.2003 -31.12.2005

	HS 50	HS 100	HS 250	HS 500	BRW λ=0,97	BRW λ=0,99	Normal VCV	Risk Metrics	Normal MC	EWMA MC	GARCH RM	HHS
Number of failures	38	32	29	29	29	25	23	15	23	17	22	18
Frequency of failures	0.076	0.064	0.058	0.058	0.058	0.05	0.046	0.03	0.046	0.034	0.044	0.036
Kupiec test (p value)	0.004606	0.066371	0.17647	0.17647	0.17647	0.44706	0.61007	0.98014	0.61007	0.94408	0.6879	0.91354
Christoffersen UC test (p value)	0.012912	0.16777	0.42294	0.42294	0.42294	1	0.67759	0.027102	0.67759	0.082169	0.53008	0.13135
Christoffersen IND test (p value)	0.000923	0.000409	0.000664	0.004448	0.0238	0.000737	0.000253	0.073289	0.000253	0.016105	0.012682	0.023097
Christoffersen CC test (p value)	0.000188	0.000749	0.002211	0.012694	0.055638	0.003357	0.001136	0.017492	0.001136	0.012199	0.036752	0.024262
Lopez test	13.185	7.1658	4.1659	4.1589	4.1476	0.14955	-1.8724	-9.9247	-1.8704	-7.9197	-2.912	-6.9333
Blanco-Ihle test	28.751	21.818	21.739	19.101	18.747	17.613	13.924	6.5804	14.502	7.1809	7.4822	5.0329
RMSE	0.009685	0.009608	0.009283	0.009086	0.010274	0.009652	0.010206	0.011404	0.010194	0.011111	0.010616	0.011426
MAPE	2.8653	2.3317	2.596	2.606	1.3591	2.3815	2.611	1.7082	2.4414	1.5262	2.0549	1.8279
Average VaR	-0.008362	-0.00873	-0.008615	-0.008573	-0.009389	-0.009157	-0.0101	-0.01132	-0.010046	-0.010852	-0.010786	-0.011724
Acceptance (Kupiec test)	NO	NO	YES	YES	YES	YES	YES	YES	YES	YES	YES	YES
Christoffersen IND test	NO	NO	NO	NO	NO	NO	NO	NO	NO	NO	NO	NO

Table 147 - Backtesting results and diagnostics of 500 VaR forecasts for MALTEX index daily log returns, 99% confidence level, period 19.12.2003 -31.12.2005

	HS 50	HS 100	HS 250	HS 500	BRW λ=0,97	BRW λ=0,99	Normal VCV	Risk Metrics	Normal MC	EWMA MC	GARCH RM	HHS
Number of failures	14	14	11	7	11	8	11	7	12	7	5	1
Frequency of failures	0.028	0.028	0.022	0.014	0.022	0.016	0.022	0.014	0.024	0.014	0.01	0.002
Kupiec test (p value)	0.000206	0.000206	0.005208	0.13232	0.005208	0.06711	0.005208	0.13232	0.001901	0.13232	0.38404	0.96025
Christoffersen UC test (p value)	0.000914	0.000914	0.019918	0.39657	0.019918	0.21487	0.019918	0.39657	0.007663	0.39657	1	0.02824
Christoffersen IND test (p value)	0.00024	0.00024	0.01859	2.71E-05	2.28E-05	7.84E-05	0.01859	0.65537	0.00156	0.65537	0.75037	0.94947
Christoffersen CC test (p value)	4.83E-06	4.83E-06	0.004172	0.000105	8.47E-06	0.00019	0.004172	0.63195	0.000192	0.63195	0.95065	0.089933
Lopez test	9.0861	9.0755	6.0651	2.0506	6.0593	3.0523	6.0608	2.0311	7.0661	2.0311	0.021748	-3.9981
Blanco-Ihle test	8.0993	6.621	5.1271	3.2902	4.9743	3.9556	4.6325	1.8141	5.1692	1.8882	1.1596	0.054165
RMSE	0.015232	0.014296	0.014546	0.01483	0.016758	0.017363	0.014151	0.016222	0.014057	0.015662	0.014758	0.019224
MAPE	2.0449	1.9676	1.2519	0.98254	1.5162	0.92519	1.2519	0.5187	1.4963	0.5187	0.73815	0.75062
Average VaR	-0.014756	-0.014632	-0.015081	-0.015721	-0.016748	-0.017866	-0.0148	-0.016349	-0.014652	-0.015733	-0.015254	-0.019489
Acceptance (Kupiec test)	NO	NO	NO	YES	NO	NO	NO	YES	NO	YES	YES	YES
Christoffersen IND test	NO	NO	NO	NO	NO	NO	NO	YES	NO	YES	YES	YES

Summary of findings

After reviewing the performance of individual VaR models, at 95% and 99% confidence level for every analysed stock index from transition countries, compliance with the regulatory framework of VaR models for the entire market is analysed. Overall summary results are very useful to see how tested VaR models fare with regulatory backtesting framework based on the complete testing sample. Kupiec test and Christoffersen independence test are used to identifying VaR models that are acceptable to the regulator, and actually provide the desired level of safety to individual banks and, due to contagion effect, to the entire banking sector. The results of the overall acceptance, according to Kupiec and Christoffersen independence test, of tested VaR models on the stock markets of transition countries, at 95% confidence level are presented in table 148.

Table 148 - Number of VaR model failures according to Kupiec and Christoffersen independence test, tested on 12 selected stock indexes, 500 observations, at 95% confidence level

Model	HS 50	HS 100	HS 250	HS 500	BRW λ=0,97	BRW λ=0,99
Kupiec test	9	4	2	1	0	0
Christoffersen IND test	7	5	7	6	5	6

Model	Normal VCV	Risk Metrics	Normal MC	EWMA MC	GARCH RM	HHS
Kupiec test	1	1	1	1	0	0
Christoffersen IND test	6	4	5	4	2	2

From the data in table 148 it is clear that at 95% confidence level, tested VaR models perform very differently with a majority of VaR models failing Kupiec test for at least one stock index. The results of Christoffersen independence test cause even greater concern because all of the tested VaR models failed the test for more than one stock index.

The only VaR models that passed the Kupiec test across all the analysed stock indexes are the HHS model, GARCH-RiskMetrics model and both BRW models with λ = 0.97 and 0.99. The worst performer according to Kupiec test, out of the tested VaR model was the HS 50 model, which failed the Kupiec test for nine out of twelve stock indexes. HS 50 model is followed by HS 100 (four failures) and HS 250 (two failures) models. It is surprising that even RiskMetrics model that is famous for its good track record at 95% confidence level failed the Kupiec test for one stock index (SBI20 index).

None of the twelve tested VaR models satisfied the Christoffersen independence test across all the analysed stock indexes, but the two models with the best performance are the HHS model and GARCH-RiskMetrics model that failed the test for two out of twelve indexes. Both models failed the Christoffersen independence test for MALTEX and VILSE index. The worst performers are HS 50 and HS 250 models (seven failures), followed by HS 500 and BRW model with $\lambda = 0.99$ (six failures).

Overall, the best performers according to Kupiec and Christoffersen independence test at 95% confidence level across stock indexes of transition countries are the HHS model and the GARCH-RiskMetrics model. The worst performers are the HS 50 an HS 100 models.

Although it is informative to look at VaR model performance at different confidence levels, the true test of VaR model acceptability to the regulators is its performance at 99% confidence level, as prescribed by the Basel Committee. The results of the overall acceptance, according to Kupiec and Christoffersen independence test, of tested VaR models on the stock markets of transition countries, at 99% confidence level are presented in table 149.

Table 149 - Number of VaR model failures according to Kupiec and Christoffersen independence test, tested on 12 selected stock indexes, 500 observations, at 99% confidence level

Model	HS 50	HS 100	HS 250	HS 500	BRW $\lambda=0,97$	BRW $\lambda=0,99$
Kupiec test	12	12	4	1	11	1
Christoffersen IND test	3	3	4	2	3	3

Model	Normal VCV	Risk Metrics	Normal MC	EWMA MC	GARCH RM	HHS
Kupiec test	8	4	8	6	3	0
Christoffersen IND test	2	2	2	2	0	0

The data from table 149 reveals a very distributing finding that should serve as a great warning to both regulators and market participants. At 99% confidence level, almost all of tested VaR models perform very poorly. In the analysed period, only one tested VaR model – the HHS model satisfied the Kupiec test at 99% confidence level across all of the analysed stock indexes from transition countries. The results of Christoffersen independence test are equally alarming because only two VaR models (HHS model and GARCH-RiskMetrics model) passed the test for all of the tested stock indexes.

The HHS model is the only VaR model that passed the Kupiec test for all of the analysed stock indexes at 99% confidence level. HHS model is followed by HS 500 model and BRW model with $\lambda = 0.99$, which failed the Kupiec test for one index. HS 500 model failed the Kupiec test for BUX index, and BRW model with $\lambda = 0.99$ failed the Kupiec test for MALTEX index. The GARCH-RiskMetrics models that shared the first place with HHS model at 95% confidence level failed the Kupiec test at 99% confidence level for three out of twelve analysed stock indexes (SBI20 index, PX50 index and SKSM index).

The worst performers according to Kupiec test, out of the twelve tested VaR model, at 99% confidence level, were the HS 50 and HS 100 models, which failed the Kupiec test for all of the twelve tested stock indexes. HS 50 and HS 100 models are followed by BRW model with $\lambda = 0.97$ (eleven failures), Normal variance-covariance and Normal Monte Carlo model (eight failures). The drastic difference in the performance of the two BRW models at 99% confidence level can be attributed to the fact that volatility in the capital markets of transition countries is very persistent and in such circumstances fast decaying volatility models perform very poorly. Two out of twelve tested VaR models satisfied the Christoffersen independence test at 99% confidence level across all the analysed stock indexes. Equally to the results obtained for 95% confidence level HHS model and GARCH-RiskMetrics are the best performers even at 99% confidence level. The worst performer according to Christoffersen independence test is the HS 250 models (four failures), followed by HS 50, HS 100, BRW models with $\lambda = 0.97$ and 0.99, which all recorded three failures. Overall, the best performer according to both the Kupiec and Christoffersen independence test at 99% confidence level across stock indexes of transition countries is the HHS model. The worst performers are the HS 50 and HS 100 models. Performed backtests at both 95% and 99% confidence level clearly point to the conclusion that the widespread models of calculating Value at Risk, such as Historical simulation, Normal variance-covariance model and RiskMetrics system do not capture the dynamics of the data generating processes of transition countries' stock indexes.

6.5   Discussion

From obtained results for the stock indexes from most of the transition countries it is clear that these markets are experiencing a common, strong positive trend, which clearly violates the stationarity assumption of the time series. On the other hand, logarithmic differences of these time series can be treated as stationary. As could be expected, the financial markets of the transition countries are experiencing a boom due to the catching up of these economies to the European standards and strong inflow of foreign direct and portfolio investments. Furthermore, securities from these markets are trading at a discount compared to securities from old EU member states. The only indexes that diverge from a strong positive trend present in CEE countries, Baltic states and Croatia, in the analysed period, are CYSMGENL, WIG20 and MALTEX index. The CYSMGENL index shows no common features with any of the other analysed indexes, which may indicate that investors did not perceive this stock market as potentially prosperous and benefiting from joining into EU. MALTEX and WIG20 index do not show a positive trend throughout the entire analysed period, from 2000 to 2006, but after a sharp decline in the value of their indexes they also experienced a strong positive trend in the second half of the observation period. As was stated earlier, volatility clustering and occurrence of extreme positive and negative returns characterises the returns of stock indexes from transition countries. From table 123 and individual statistical analyses of stock indexes from transition countries performed in previous chapters, it was determined that all of the indexes are characterised by fat tails and asymmetry, with seven indexes having negative skewness and five indexes having positive skewness. Lilliefors and Jarque-Bera tests of normality for the tested stock indexes of transition countries confirm the conclusion drawn from findings of skewness and kurtosis, that there is close to zero probability of empirical distributions of these returns being normally distributed.

The stock index with the highest daily mean return in the analysed period is the VIN index (0,13%), and the index with the lowest mean value is the CYSMGENL index (- 0,12%). CYSMGENL index is also the only index that has negative mean value in the analysed period. Investing long-term in VIN index yielded the highest gains, and investing in CYSMGENL yielded the highest losses. The most volatile index in the analysed period is the RIGSE index with standard deviation of 1,63%. The least volatile index in the same period is SBI20 index with standard deviation of 0,69%. In the analysed period the largest daily gain of 14,98% is recorded for CROBEX index. In the same period, the highest daily loss of 15,67% is recorded for VIN index.

In the analysed period RIGSE index has the highest value of negative asymmetry (- 1,278), and SBI20 index has the highest value of positive asymmetry (1,119). This means, that among the tested stock indexes, SBI20 index has the highest probability of experiencing positive returns, and RIGSE index has the highest probability of experiencing negative returns. Highest value of excess kurtosis is found for VIN index (23,7), and lowest value is found for PX50 index (4,36). Consequently, investing in VIN index means that investors have to be prepared for extreme positive and negative returns. Average excess kurtosis across the stock indexes of transition countries equals 12,8, which is a very high value compared to stock indexes from developed countries or FX markets.

According to Lilliefors test of normality among the tested stock indexes, BUX index is closest to being normally distributed. According to Jarque-Bera test of normality WIG20 index can be considered as being closest to normality. It is worth noting that both of these indexes have an insignificant probability of being normally distributed. Both normality tests identify the RIGSE index as being the farthest from normality.

These characteristics of analysed stock indexes of transition countries have serious consequences for the performance of tested VaR models in these markets. It means that VaR models that are based on assumption of normally distributed returns, such as Normal variance-covariance model, RiskMetrics model and Normal and EWMA Monte Carlo cannot properly account for the risk present in these indexes and will, as a consequence, underestimate the true level of risk. Even more troubling for the VaR models based on normality assumption, as well as for the nonparametric and semi-parametric approaches that are based on the assumption of independently and identically distributed observations, such as historical simulation and BRW approach is the fact that the daily log returns of stock indexes in the transition markets exhibit a significant degree of autocorrelation and heteroskedasticity, is one of the most common obstacles to proper implementation of many VaR models. This finding is very indicative for risk managers, because it proves that the elementary assumption of many VaR models is not satisfied, and that the VaR figures obtained from such models cannot be trusted and at best, provide only unconditional coverage.

Since autocorrelation and heteroskedasticity automatically exclude the possibility of observations being independently and identically distributed, it is necessary to capture the structure of the analysed data and obtain independently and identically distributed observations. To render the observations independently and identically distributed the transformation of original return data is performed by fitting an ARMA-GARCH model. As was proven in the empirical study, ARMA-GARCH model successfully captured the dynamics of stock indexes from transition countries, and produced standardised innovations that under a number of tests proved to be independently and identically distributed. In modelling conditional volatility basic GARCH (1,1) model was sufficient for all but one stock index. In modelling conditional volatility for RIGSE index it was necessary to include a leverage term in the conditional volatility equation. The most parsimonious asymmetric GARCH model that captured the leverage effect in the RIGSE index returns was the GJR-GARCH (1,1) model. Finding that the ARMA-GARCH model successfully captures the dynamics of analysed stock indexes is important for both regulators and risk professionals in the transition countries, indicating that it is necessary to implement a more sophisticated conditional volatility models to adequately capture the dynamics of these markets. VaR models that assume constant volatility or VaR models that take a more simplictic view of volailtity modelling, such as equally weighted and exponentially weighted (e.g. RiskMetrics) models will not perform satisfactory in these conditions. Estimated ARMA-GARCH parameters for stock indexes of transition countries are presented in table 150.

Table 150 - Estimated ARMA-GARCH parameters for stock indexes of transition countries

	Mean			Volatility			
	C	AR	MA	K	GARCH	ARCH	Leverage
CROBEX	0			1.06E-05	0.8323	0.11082	
VIN	0	0.14457		1.25E-05	0.78932	0.1405	
SBI20	0.000514	0.42607 / -0.14067		6.69E-06	0.50069	0.39003	
BUX	0			8.59E-06	0.89067	0.066215	
WIG20	0			5.6E-06	0.93292	0.047987	
PX50	0.000755			4.69E-06	0.90381	0.069603	
SKSM	0.000689		-0.05749	1.27E-05	0.85016	0.07733	
TALSE	0.00096		0.21580 / 0.09233	6.76E-06	0.84035	0.10469	
VILSE	0	1.08050 / -0.08366	-0.96844	1.31E-05	0.55848	0.25825	
RIGSE	0.000755		-0.13221	4.69E-06	0.90381	0.069603	-0.39327
CYSMGENL	-0.00135	0.13036		6.04E-06	0.79835	0.19802	
MALTEX	-0.00054	0.27526		6.71E-06	0.64587	0.18561	

As can be seen from table 150 some of the tested indexes like SBI20, VILSE, MALTEX, VIN and CYSMGENL show unusually low persistence in volatility but are very reactive to previous period's residuals, which will make VaR forecasts based on GARCH volatility very spiky. Majority of tested stock indexes is not even closely integrated as is presumed by EWMA volatility modelling that is underlying the RiskMetrics system. VILSE index is farthest from being integrated with $\alpha + \beta$ being only 0,8167. All of the indexes from transition countries, except CYSMGENL index, mean revert, i.e. there is convergence in term structure forecasts to the long-term average volatility level. CYSMGENL index distinctly differs from other tested stock indexes and could be modelled by an IGARCH model or a simple EWMA model since it is close to being fully integrated. Being integrated means that the volatility of CYSMGENL index is itself a random walk process that has undefined unconditional variance and term structure. Estimated GARCH parameters of stock indexes from transition countries point to the conclusion that VaR models based on simpler conditional volatility models, such as MA or EWMA will be underestimating or overestimating the true level of risk. Due to different assumptions and volatility prediction techniques, different VaR models provided forecasts for tested stock indexes that differed significantly. For example, at 95% confidence level TALSE index recorded the greatest difference between the highest average VaR forecasted by GARCH-RiskMetrics model and lowest average VaR forecasted by HS 50 model, which was 77,94%. TALSE index, at 99% confidence level also recorder the greatest difference between the highest average VaR forecasted by HHS model and lowest average VaR forecasted by HS 50 model, which was 77,89%. The highest frequency of failures at 95% confidence level was recorder in VILSE index by HS 50 model and it amounted to 8,6%, which is 72% more than the expected frequency of failures. At 99% confidence level the highest frequencies of failure were recorded also in VILSE index, again by HS50 model (3,6%) and in SBI20 index by RiskMetrics model (3,6%) which is 3,6 times more than the expected frequency of failures.

In order to come to some general conclusion about the performance of VaR models in emerging European markets it is necessary to evaluate the performance of each tested VaR model across all of the analysed stock indexes. To accomplish this it is necessary to rank the competing VaR models by their ability to provide satisfactory market risk conditional coverage for the analysed stock indexes. Ranking of the analysed VaR models is primarily performed by distinguishing between VaR models that satisfy the Kupiec test and those that fail the test. VaR models that satisfy the Kupiec test are tested by Christoffersen independence test. Models that pass the Christoffersen independence test are than ranked according to their Blanco-Ihle score and by their MAPE and RMSE measures. VaR models that fail the Kupiec test are ranked by their frequency of failures, giving better ranking to models with lower frequency. Further ranking for VaR models that failed the Kupiec test follows the same procedure that applies to VaR models that satisfied the Kupiec test. Based on their performance, VaR models are given points from 1 to 12, giving the best VaR model for a particular stock index one point, and giving the worst performing VaR model twelve points. Rankings obtained by following the outlined procedure are presented in table 151.

Table 151 - Ranking of VaR models across analysed stock indexes by their backtesting performance at 99% confidence level

	SBI20	BUX	WIG20	PX50	SKSM	CROBEX
HS 50	10	12	12	12	12	12
HS 100	6	11	11	9	9	11
HS 250	4	6	5	5	4	9
HS 500	3	9	3	2	2	3
BRW λ=0,97	8	10	7	8	6	10
BRW λ=0,99	1	5	4	3	3	4
Normal VCV	7	8	6	10	7	7
Risk Metrics	12	3	9	6	10	5
Normal MC	9	7	8	11	8	8
EWMA MC	11	4	10	7	11	6
GARCH RM	5	2	1	4	5	2
HHS	2	1	2	1	1	1
	VIN	TALSE	RIGSE	VILSE	CYSMGENL	MALTEX
HS 50	12	12	12	12	12	12
HS 100	10	11	10	11	11	11
HS 250	8	7	4	9	6	9
HS 500	4	3	3	3	5	5
BRW λ=0,97	11	9	11	10	10	8
BRW λ=0,99	5	4	5	6	7	6
Normal VCV	7	5	9	4	8	7
Risk Metrics	3	8	7	7	3	4
Normal MC	9	6	6	5	9	10
EWMA MC	6	10	8	8	4	3
GARCH RM	2	2	1	1	2	2
HHS	1	1	2	2	1	1

From the scoring in table 151 it can be concluded that for SBI20 index the best performer is the BRW model with λ = 0.99, followed by the HHS model. The worst performers for SBI20 index are the RiskMetrics model and EWMA Monte Carlo model. Such results for RiskMetrics and EWMA Monte Carlo model come as no surprise knowing that the volatility process of SBI20 index is not close to being integrated and has very different volatility parameters than assumed under EWMA volatility model used by RiskMetrics and EWMA Monte Carlo. Historical simulation models had mixed results, with HS models with longer rolling windows being far superior to models with shorter rolling windows. GARCH-RiskMetrics model although far better than the basic RiskMetrics model is ranked fifth, which can be explained by low volatility persistence in SBI20 index which clearly creates problems for purely parametric approaches of measuring market risk. The best performer for the BUX index is the HHS model followed by the GARCH-RiskMetrics model. RiskMetrics model placed also very high at third place. The worst performers for BUX index are the HS50 and HS100 models. BRW models are not ranked high, but are far better ranked than most of historical simulation models. Historical simulation models with longer rolling windows performed better than models with shorter rolling windows. The best performer for the WIG20 index is the GARCH-RiskMetrics model followed by the HHS model. The worst performers for WIG20 index are the HS50 and HS100 models. Historical simulation models with longer rolling windows performed very good with HS 500 model taking the third place. Surprisingly RiskMetrics model was ranked very low as well as both Monte Carlo models. RiskMetrics was ranked even lower than the Normal variance-covariance model. BRW models gave mixed results, with BRW model with $\lambda = 0.99$ being ranked better than most of the historical simulation models. The best performer for the PX50 index is the HHS model followed by the HS 500 model. The worst performers for PX50 index are the HS50 and Normal Monte Carlo model. BRW model with $\lambda = 0.99$ took the third place. GARCH-RiskMetrics and RiskMetrics models did not perform very well, with GARCH-RiskMetrics model being again significantly better than RiskMetrics model. The best performer for the SKSM index is the HHS model followed by the HS 500 model. The worst performers for SKSM index are the HS50 and EWMA Monte Carlo model. BRW model with $\lambda = 0.99$ took the third place. GARCH-RiskMetrics and RiskMetrics models did not perform very well, with RiskMetrics model being among the worst performers for this index, even worse than the Normal variance-covariance model. The best performer for the CROBEX index is the HHS model followed by the GARCH-RiskMetrics model. The worst performers for CROBEX index are the HS50 and HS100 models. HS 500 model was ranked third. Historical simulation models with longer rolling windows performed far better than models with shorter rolling windows. BRW models are not ranked high, but are far better ranked than most of historical simulation models. The best performer for the VIN index is the HHS model followed by the GARCH-RiskMetrics model. RiskMetrics model placed also very high at third place. The worst performers for VIN index are the HS50 model and BRW model with $\lambda = 0.97$. Historical simulation models with longer rolling windows performed far better than BRW models. The best performer for the TALSE index is the HHS model followed by the GARCH-RiskMetrics model. The worst performers for TALSE index are the HS50 and HS100 models. HS 500 model was ranked third. BRW models are not ranked high, but are far better ranked than historical simulation models, with the exception of HS 500 model. RiskMetrics is among the worst performers for this index, being even worse than the Normal variance-covariance model. The best performer for the RIGSE index is the GARCH-RiskMetrics model followed by the HHS model. HS 500 model was ranked third. BRW models are not ranked high, but are far better ranked than historical simulation models, with the exception of HS 500 model. The worst performers for RIGSE index are the HS50 model and BRW model with $\lambda = 0.97$. RiskMetrics is not among the best ranked VaR models for this index but it is better than Normal variance-covariance model and EWMA Monte Carlo model. The best performer for the VILSE index is the GARCH-RiskMetrics model followed by the HHS model. HS 500 model was ranked third. BRW models are not ranked high, but BRW model with $\lambda = 0.99$ is far better ranked than majority of historical simulation models. The worst performers for VILSE index are the HS50 model and BRW model with $\lambda = 0.97$. RiskMetrics is not among the worst performers for this index, but is worse than the Normal variance-covariance model. The best performer for the CYSMGENL index is the HHS model followed by the GARCH-RiskMetrics model. RiskMetrics model is placed also very high at third place. The worst performers for CYSMGENL index are the HS50 and HS100 models. BRW models did not perform very well with HS 250 and HS 500 models being better ranked. The best performer for the MALTEX index is the HHS model followed by the GARCH-RiskMetrics model. EWMA Monte Carlo model placed very high at third place. The worst performers for MALTEX index are the HS50 and HS100 models. RiskMetrics is not among the best performers for this index, but is better than the Normal variance-covariance and Normal Monte Carlo model. BRW models are not ranked high, but are far better ranked than historical simulation models, with the exception of HS 500 model.

According to the performed tests and rankings, the HHS VaR model performed extremely well. HHS model is ranked as the best performer for eight out of twelve indexes and for the remaining four indexes it is ranked as second. GARCH-RiskMetrics model as the closest competitor to HHS model, was ranked as the best VaR model only for three indexes, but on two occasions was ranked as low as fifth (SBI20 and SKSM index). Overall ranking results for analysed VaR models by their backtesting performance are given in table 152.

Table 152 - Overall ranking scores of VaR models by their backtesting performance at 99% confidence level

Model	Score	Place
HHS	16	1
GARCH RM	29	2
HS 500	45	3
BRW λ=0,99	53	4
HS 250	76	5
Risk Metrics	77	6
Normal VCV	85	7
EWMA MC	88	8
Normal MC	96	9
BRW λ=0,97	108	10
HS 100	121	11
HS 50	142	12

Source: Table 151

Overall the HHS model is the best performing tested VaR model across the stock indexes from transition countries. In the second places lagging behind the HHS model by almost double the points is a modification of RiskMetrics model, the GARCH-RiskMetrics model. HS 500 model performed surprisingly well on the tested sample of stock indexes and although it is very simple, proved to be an acceptably good VaR estimator. The worst performing VaR models are the HS 50 and HS 100 models. Classical parametric VaR models, the RiskMetrics model and Normal variance-covariance model are not placed very high in the overall ranking (sixth and seventh place) indicating that they are not very well suited for forecasting VaR in the transition countries.

The obtained results, summarised in tables 151 and 152 confirm that the widespread models of calculating Value at Risk, such as Historical simulation, Normal variance-covariance model and RiskMetrics system do not capture the dynamics of the data generating processes of stock indexes in transition countries.

Based on the obtained results, this conclusion can be accepted, but with an important notice that the HS 500 model performed surprisingly well although the basic prerequisites for its proper implementation, such as IID of returns, are not satisfied in the testing sample. This interesting phenomenon has a very simple explanation. Due to the extreme losses that occurred prior to and during the testing period HS 500 VaR model set its forecasts very high and automatically achieved unconditional risk coverage without taking into consideration the actual level of risk. Because it reacts very slowly to changes in volatility its average VaR is among the highest of all the tested VaR models. Although HS 500 model provides correct unconditional coverage for all but one tested stock index, it would prove very costly for a bank implementing it, because in times of low volatility it signals the need for high provisions, which creates high opportunity costs. On the other hand, due to its very low reactivity and high persistence, HS 500 model hides a very serious danger of underestimating the true level of risk for longer periods of time if the market enters a volatile period after a longer period of low volatility. BRW model with $\lambda = 0.99$ is placed fourth in the overall ranking, being superior to all historical simulation models except the historical simulation model with the longest rolling window – HS 500. RiskMetrics is ranked sixth making it superior to other basic parametric approaches, such as Normal variance-covariance model, and Normal and EWMA Monte Carlo models.

Results from tables 149, 150, 151 and 152 give enough evidence to safely say that extensions of basic Value at Risk models, such as age-weighted Historical simulation and RiskMetrics system show improvements in measuring market risk, over the basic models.

Although the difference in ranking and total score of BRW model with $\lambda = 0.99$ and HS 500 is minor, the HS 500 model again stand out and partially defies this hypothesis but characteristic reasons for such behaviour are already explained. Based on the performed analysis it is safe to say that in the capital markets of transition countries, BRW model is extremely sensitive to the choice of decay factor. The proof of this can be seen from ranking of the same model but with a slightly different decay factor. BRW model with decay factor of 0.99 is ranked as fourth, but BRW model with decay factor of 0.97 is among the worst ranked VaR models. Since it is obvious that ad hoc setting of decay factor does not function in the capital markets of transition countries some formal procedure should be developed to estimate the optimal value of decay factor. With the optimal decay factor for each market it is very possible that the BRW model would perform much better.

Tables 149, 150, 151 and 152 show that modifying the RiskMetrics model with GARCH based volatility forecasting brought significant improvements to basic RiskMetrics model, making it a very good risk measure for tested stock indexes second only to HHS VaR model. These finding clearly indicate that modifying the RiskMetrics model with GARCH based volatility forecasting yields significant improvement over the standard RiskMetrics model when applied to stock indexes of transition countries. Along with the analysis of backtesting results the qualitative characteristics of tested VaR models should also be taken into consideration to provide their complete picture. Qualitative characteristics for each of the tested VaR models are presented in table 153.

Table 153 - Characteristics of tested VaR models

Characteristics	Normal VCV	RiskMetrics	GARCH-RiskMetrics	Historical simulation	BRW	Monte Carlo	EWMA Monte Carlo	HHS
Distribution	normal	normal	normal	actual	quasi-actual	assumed	assumed	quasi-actual
Tails	normal	normal	fat	actual	quasi-actual	assumed	assumed	quasi-actual
Reaction speed	slow	fast	fast	slow	medium	medium	fast	fast
Intellectual effort	low	moderate	moderate	very low	moderate	high	high	high
Model risk	huge	huge	moderate	moderate	low	high	high	low
Computation time	low	low	moderate	low	moderate	high	high	high
Communicability	easy	easy	moderate	easy	moderate	moderate	difficult	moderate

Table 153 shows that the HHS model developed by the author has a number of advantages over most of the other tested VaR models. HHS model uses a quasi-actual distribution of empirical returns, since GARCH volatility updating modifies the empirical distribution of the data. The same applies to the treatment of tails. Reaction speed of the HHS model is fast, reacting through GARCH volatility estimation to every change in the level of volatility regardless of the sign of the returns. Model risk associated with HHS model is quite low because the only parameters that have to be estimated for the model are GARCH model parameters, besides which no other assumptions are made. Unfortunately, intellectual effort in implementing HHS model is quite high as well as the computational time, but with the development of faster computer processors and greater investment in education, this should present a minor problem. The main characteristics, underlying logic and main advantages of HHS model are validated by all of the performed tests, individual as well as the overall ranking results. All of the tests and rankings clearly show that HHS model managed to incorporate the best characteristics of parametric and nonparametric approaches to calculating VaR and produced superior VaR estimates to all the other tested VaR models.

This finding indicates that the Hybrid Historical simulation overcomes serious drawbacks of parametric and nonparametric approaches and provides superior Value at Risk forecasts than adequately capture market risk present in the capital markets of transition countries.

Presented findings bear very important implications that have to be addressed by regulators and risk practitioners operating in transition countries. Risk managers have to start thinking outside the frames set by their parent companies or else their banks investing in these markets may find themselves in serious trouble, dealing with losses that they were not expecting. Contrary to the widespread opinion it is not enough to blindly implement the VaR models that are being offered by various software companies and financial institutions. Every VaR software package that a bank is thinking about implementing should be rigorously tested and analysed to see if it really provides a correct estimate of the true level of risk a bank is exposed to. National regulators have to take into consideration that simplistic VaR models that are widely used in some developed countries are not well suited for these illiquid and developing financial markets. Before allowance is given to banks on using internal VaR models that are either purchased or developed in-house, national regulators should rigorously checks and analyse the backtesting performance as well as the theoretical framework of such models for any inconsistencies and unwanted simplifications.   As the obtained results show, returns on stock indexes from transition countries are characterised by fat tails, asymmetry, autocorrelation and heteroskedasticity, all of which considerably complicate VaR estimation and require more complex, computationally and intellectually demanding VaR models, such as the HHS model. The obtained results from this research also indicate that it may be highly misleading to compare VaR numbers across financial institutions if the reported VaR figures are based on different VaR models. As was shown, VaR estimates for the same stock index according to two different VaR models differed by more than 77%. However, it has to be pointed out that while acknowledging all the flaws and inconsistencies of VaR concept as a risk measure, VaR is an extremely useful tool for financial institutions with regard to their in-house risk management.

INDEX

A
ARMA Models, 100
Ask price, 102

B
Backtest / Backtesting, 39-46, 179-183
Bank for International Settlements, 23-41
Barings Bank, 2
Basle Accord, 24-26, 44
BDS Test, 189
Benchmark, 7, 45, 192-194, 367
Berkowitz, 189-191, 359
Beta, 8,11, 67, 110, 116,124
Big Bang, 25
Bins, 162
Black-Scholes option pricing model, 18
Blanco-Ihle test, 194, 318-326
Bloomberg, 74, 158, 202
Bonds, 11, 88, 147, 159, 181, 201
Bootstrap, 157, 162-169, 175-180, 362-371
Box-Cox transformation, 118

C
Capital allocation, 56, 79, 118
Capital at risk, 71
CAPM, 25, 72
Cautchy (Lorentzian) distribution, 138, 144
Central limit theorem, 130, 134,142, 184
Characteristic function, 142, 144
Characteristics of stock market indexes of EU:
  Cyprus-CYSMGENL index, 296-311, 346-349, 353
  Czech Republic-PX50 index, 233-243, 251, 326 ,346-352
  Estonia- TALSE index, 268-278, 334, 350-352
  Hungary-BUX index, 217-226, 234-242, 322, 346-352
  Latvia-RIGSE index, 277-288
  Lithuania-VILSE index, 286-295, 338, 350-353
  Malta-MALTEX index, 306-314, 342, 346, 353
  Poland-WIG20 index, 225-234, 324, 347, 352
  Slovakia-SKSM index, 203, 241-252, 292-311, 346-353
  Slovenia-SBI20 index, 207-216, 247-252, 319, 344-352
Chi-squared distribution, 135
Christoffersen test, 185, 201
Closed-form solutions, 142, 145

Clustering, 102-124, 200-226, 242-269
Confidence intervals, 161
Confidence regions, 184
Convexity, 8, 73, 85
Correlation, 36-41, 95-115, 201-224, 261-282, 291-314, 356-371
Covariance, 12, 67-76, 91-103, 147-158, 319-354
Credit derivatives, 9
Credit risk, 4-14, 22-37, 42-53, 181,357
Crnkovic-Drachman test, 189-191, 319

D
Daily earnings at Risk, 71
Data, 5-10, 60-70, 99-113, 129-139, 174-192, 229-239, 291-303, 354-373
Default, 3-7, 16-21, 43, 63, 70
Default Risk, 4, 17-18
Delta, 8, 19, 34, 73-78
Domains of attraction, 143
Duration, 8, 33, 73, 81, 159, 319

E
Elliptical distribution, 141-145
Empirical distribution, 190, 347
ERM crisis, 46
Exotic derivatives, 8
Expected shortfall, 85, 357, 372-373
Extreme Value Theory, 59, 138, 175-175, 363-369
EWMA, 113, 147-156, 198-206, 319-354

F
Fast fourier transform, 176
Fat tails, 134, 141-144, 151-158, 347, 356-366
Formula, 85, 112, 126, 130-139, 145, 168

G
Gamma, 8, 19, 39, 73-78
Gamma function, 135
GARCH, 100-128, 199-216, 282-304, 322-346, 351-355
Generalised hyperbolic distribution, 145
Geometric Brownian motio, 141-143, 156
Geometric Distributions, 169
Ghost effect, 147-148, 159, 179
Gibbs simpling tool, 146
Greeks, 69

H
Hedge ratios, 18-19
Histograms, 162-163, 317
Hybrid historical simulation 175-181

LITERATURE AND SOURCES

Literature:

1. Acerbi C., Nordio C., Sirtori C.: Expected Shortfall as a Tool for Financial Risk Management. Abaxbank, Feb 2001. 10 p.
    [URL: http://www.gloriamundi.org/picsresources/ncs.pdf], (28.01.2006.)

2. Acerbi C., Tasche D.: Expected Shortfall: a natural coherent alternative to Value at Risk. May 2001. 9 p.
    [URL: http://www.gloriamundi.org/picsresources/expshortfall.pdf], (28.01.2006.)

3. Acerbi C., Tasche D.: On the Coherence of Expected Shortfall. Apr 2002. 19 p.
    [URL: http://www.gloriamundi.org/picsresources/cadt.pdf], (28.01.2006.)

4. Alexander C.: Risk Management and Analysis, Volume 1: Measuring and Modeling Financial Risk. New York: John Wiley & Sons, 2000. 281 p.

5. Alexander C.: Market Models: A Guide to Financial Data Analysis. New York: John Wiley & Sons, 2001. 494 p.

6. Alexander J. G., Baptista M. A.: CVaR as a Measure of Risk: Implications for the Portfolio Selection. Feb 2003. 34 p.
    [URL: http://www.gloriamundi.org/picsresources/gjaamb.pdf], (18.12.2006.)

7. Allen S.: Financial Risk Management: A Practitioner's Guide to Managing Market and Credit Risk. New York: John Wiley & Sons, 2003. 393 p.

8. Allen L., Saunders A.: Understanding Market, Credit, and Operational Risk: The Value at Risk Approach. Oxford: Blackwell Publishing, 2004. 284 p.

9. Andersen G. T., Bollerslev T.: Answering the critics: Yes, ARCH models do provide good volatility forecasts. NBER Working paper series, Apr 1997. 37 p.

10. Andersen G. T., Bollerslev T., Diebold X. F.: Parametric and nonparametric volatility measurement. NBER Working paper series, Aug 2002. 68 p.

11. Andersen G. T., Bollerslev T., Diebold X. F.: Some like it Smooth, and some like it Rough: Untangling continuous and jump components in measuring, modelling and forecasting asset return volatility. CFS Working paper, Sep 2003. 42 p.

12. Andersen G. T., Bollerslev T., Diebold X. F., Ebens H.: The distribution of stock return volatility. NBER Working paper series, Oct 2000. 30 p.

13. Andersen G. T., Bollerslev T., Diebold X. F., Labys P.: The distribution of Exchange Rate Volatility. NBER Working paper series, Aug. 1999a. 49 p.

14. Andersen G. T., Bollerslev T., Diebold X. F., Labys P.: Realized volatility and correlation. New York: Stern School of Business Working Paper Series, Oct 1999b. 22 p.

15. Andersen G. T., Bollerslev T., Diebold X. F., Labys P.: Modelling and forecasting realized volatility. The Wharton School, University of Pennsylvania, Jan 2001. 45 p.

16. Andersen G. T., Bollerslev T., Meddahi N.: Correcting the errors: A note on Volatility forecast evaluation based on High-frequency data and realized volatilities. CIREQ, Working paper No. 21., 2002. 15 p.
17. Artzner P., Delbaen F., Eber J.M., Heath D.: Thinking coherently. Risk 10, 1997. p. 68-71.
18. Artzner P., Delbaen F., Eber J.M., Heath D.: Coherent measures of risk, Mathematical Finance 9, Nov 1999. p. 203-228.
19. Baillie T. R., Bollerslev T.: The Message in Daily Exchange Rates: A Conditional Variance Tale. Journal of Business and Economic Statistics 7, 1989. p. 297-305.
20. Baillie T. R., Bollerslev T.: Common Stochastic Trends in a System of Exchange Rates. Journal of Finance, Vol. 44., No. 1., Mar 1989. p. 167-181.
21. Baillie T. R., DeGennaro P. R.: Stock Returns and Volatility. The Journal of Financial and Quantitytive Analysis, Vol. 25., No. 2., Jun 1990. p. 203-214.
22. Baillie T. R., Bollerslev T.: Exchange rate volatility. Review of Economic studies, 2001. p. 566-585.
23. Balaban E., Bayar A., Faff R.: Forecasting stock market volatility: Evidence from fourteen countries. Edinburgh: University of Edinburgh, Center for financial markets research, Working paper 02.04, 2002. 29 p.
24. Balaban E.: Comparative forecasting performance of symmetric and asymmetric conditional volatility models of an exchange rate. University of Edinburgh, Center for financial markets research, Working paper 02.06, 2003. 14 p.
25. Bams D., Wielhouwer L. J.: Empirical Issues in Value-at-Risk Time Varying Volatility, Fat Tails and Parameter Uncertainty, Dec 2000. 21 p. [URL: http://www.gloriamundi.org/picsresources/dbjw.pdf], (09.02.2006.)
26. Bao Y., Lee T.H., Saltoglu B.: Evaluating Predictive performance of Value at Risk models in emerging markets: A Reality Check. Draft, Nov 2004. 33 p. [URL: http://www.gloriamundi.org/picsresources/thlbs.pdf], (28.04.2006.)
27. Barnett A. W., Powell J., Tauchen G.: Nonparametric and Semiparametric Methods in Economics and Statistics. Proceedings of the Fifth International Symposium in Economic Theory and Econometrics, Cambridge: Cambridge University Press, 1991. 493 p.
28. Basak S., Shapiro A.: Value-at-Risk-Based Risk Management: Optimal Policies and Asset Prices. The Review of Financial Studies, Vol. 14., No. 2., 2001, p. 371-405.
29. Bauer C.: Value at risk using hyperbolic distributions. Journal of Economics and Business 52, 2000. p. 455-467.
30. Beder S. T.: VaR: Seductive but dangerous. Financial Analysts Journal, Vol. 51., No. 5., Sep/Oct 1995. p.12-23.
31. Bensalah Y.: Asset Allocation using Extreme Value Theory. Bank of Canada Working Paper, 2002. 20 p.
32. Benson P., Zangari P.: A general approach to calculating VaR without volatilities and correlations. RiskMetrics Monitor, 1997. p. 19-23.

33. Bera K. A., Lee S.: On the formulation of a general structure for conditional heteroskedasticity. University of Illinois at Urbana-Champaign, Working Paper, 1990. 38 p.

34. Bera K. A., Higgins L. M.: ARCH models: Properties, estimation and testing. Journal of Economic Survey, Vol.7., No.4., 1993. p. 305-366.

35. Berenson L. M., Levine M. D.: Basic Business Statistics – Concepts and Applications. 6th edition, New Jersey: Prentice Hall, 1996. 943 p.

36. Berger N. A., Herring J. R., Szegö P. G.: The Role of Capital in Financial Institutions. Journal of Banking and Finance 19, 1995. p. 393-430.

37. Berkowitz J.: Testing density forecasts, with applications to risk management. Journal of Business and Economic Statistics 19, 2001. p. 465-474.

38. Berkowitz J., O'Brien J.: How accurate are VaR models at commercial banks?. Journal of Finance, 2002, 34 p.
[URL: http://www.gloriamundi.org/picsresources/jbjo.pdf], (20.05.2006.)

39. Bessis J.: Risk Management in Banking. 2nd edition, New York: John Wiley & Sons, 2002. 792 p.

40. Billio M., Pelizzon L.: Value at Risk: a multivariate switching regime approach. Journal of empirical finance 7, 2001. p. 531-554.

41. Black F.: Studies of Stock Price Volatility Changes. Proceedings from the American Statistical Association, Business and Economic Statistics Section, 1976. p. 177-181.

42. Black F., Scholes M.: The pricing of options and corporate liabilities. Journal of Political Economy 81, 1973. p. 637-657.

43. Blanco C., Ihle G.: How Good is Your VaR Using Backtesting to Assess System Performance. Financial Engineering News, Aug 1998. p. 1-2.

44. Blattberg C. R., Gonedes J. N.: A Comparison of the Stable and Student Distribution of Statistical Models for Stock Prices. Journal of Business 47, 1974. p. 244-280.

45. Bollerslev T.: Generalized autoregressive conditional heteroscedasticity. Journal of Econometrics 31, 1986. p. 307-327.

46. Bollerslev T., Chou F. R., Kroner F. K.: ARCH Modeling in Finance: A Review of the Theory and Empirical evidence. Journal of Econometrics 52, 1992. p. 5-59.

47. Bollerslev T., Ghysels E.: On Periodic Autoregressive Conditional Heteroskedasticity. Montreal: CIRANO, Sep 1994. 16 p.

48. Bollerslev T., Engle F. R., Nelson B. D.: ARCH Models. in Handbook of Econometrics, Vol. 4., Engle R.F., McFadden D.L. (ed.); Amsterdam: Elsevier Science, 1994. p. 2961-3040.

49. Bollerslev T., Mikkelsen O. H.: Long-term equity anticipation securities and stock market volatility dynamics. Journal of Econometrics, 92, 1999. p. 75-99.

50. Bouchaud J.P., Potters M.: Theory of financial risk: Basic notions in probability. Chapter 1 of Theory of Financial Risks, Apr 2001. 51 p.
[URL: http://www.science-finance.fr], (09.01.2006.)

51. Boudoukh J., Richardson M., Whitelaw F. R.: The Best of Both Worlds: A hybrid Approach to Calculating Value at Risk. Risk, Vol. 11., No. 5., May 1998. p. 64-67.

52. Box E.P. G., Jenkins M. G., Reinsel C. G.: Time Series Analysis: Forecasting and Control. 3rd edition, New Jersey: Prentice Hall, 1994. 598 p.

53. Brockwell J. P., Davis A. R.: Time Series: Theory and Methods. 2nd edition, New York: Springer, 1991. 577 p.

54. Brockwell J. P., Davis A. R.: Introduction to Time Series and Forecasting. 2nd edition, New York: Springer, 2002. 434 p.

55. Broda S., Paolella M. S.: Saddlepoint Approximations for the Doubly Noncentral t Distribution. Zurich: University of Zurich, NCCR Finrisk Working Paper 304, 2006. 18 p.

56. Brodie M., Glasserman P.: Simulation for option pricing and risk management. in Risk Management and Analysis, Vol. 1, Alexander C. (ed.); New York: John Wiley, 1998. p. 174-207.

57. Brooks C., Clare A.D., Persand G.: A word of caution on calculating market based minimum capital risk requirements. Journal of Banking and Finance 24., 2000. p. 1557-1574.

58. Brooks C., Persand G.: Value at Risk and Market Crashes. ISMA Centre, Discussion Papers in Finance, 2000. 30 p.

59. Brooks C., Burke P. S., Persand G.: Benchmarks and the accuracy of GARCH model estimation. International Journal of Forecasting 17., 2001. p. 45-56.

60. Brooks C., Persand G.: Model Choice and Value-at-Risk Performance. Financial Analysts Journal, Vol. 58., No. 5., Sep/Oct 2002. p. 87-97.

61. Brooks C., Persand G.: Volatility forecasting for Risk Management. Journal of forecasting, 22, 2003. p. 1-22.

62. Buser S., Chen A., Kane E.: Federal Deposit Insurance, Regulatory Policy, and Optimal Bank Capital. The Journal of Finance, Vol. 35., No. 1., Mar 1981. p. 51-60.
[URL:http://links.jstor.org/sici?sici=0022-1082%28198103%2936%3A1%3C51%3AFDIRPA%3E2.0.CO%3B2-C&origin=repec], (20.05.2006.)

63. Butler J.S., Schachter B.: Estimating Value-at-Risk with a Precision Measure by Combining Kernel Estimation with Historical Simulation. Review of Derivatives Research 1, 1998. p. 371-390.

64. Campbell Y. J., Lo W. A., MacKinlay A. C.: The Econometrics of Financial Markets. Princeton, New Jersey: Princeton University Press, 1997. 611 p.

65. Campbell R., Koedijk K., Kofman P.: Increased Correlation in Bear Markets. Financial Analysts Journal, Vol. 58., No. 1., Jan/Feb 2002. p. 87-94.

66. Campbell R. H., Siddique A.: Autoregressive Conditional Skewness. The Journal of Financial and Quantitative Analysis, Vol. 34., No. 4., Dec 1999. p. 465-487.

67. Caporin M.: Evaluating Value-at-Risk Measures in Presence of Long Memory Conditional Volatility. GRETA, Working paper series n.05.03, 2003a. p. 34.

68. Caporin M.: The Effects of Misspecification and Aggregation on Value-at-Risk Measures with Long Memory Conditional Variances. GRETA, Working paper series n.02.11, 2003b. p. 135.

69. Caporin M.: The Trade Off Between Complexity and Efficiency of VaR Measures: A Comparison of RiskMetric and GARCH-Type Models, 2003c. p. 30.
[URL: http://www.gloriamundi.org/picsresources/mcga.pdf], (11.07.2006.)

70. Carlstein E.: The use of subseries values for estimating the variance of a general statistic from a stationary sequence. Annals of Statistics 14, 1986. p. 1171-1179.

71. Cayon E., Sarmiento A. J.: Is Historical VaR a Reliable Tool for Relative Risk Measurement in the Colombian Stock Market?: An Empirical Analysis Using the Coefficient of Variation, Pontificia Universidad Javeriana, Working paper series, Mar 2004. 17 p.
[URL:http://gloriamundi.org/ShowTracking.asp?ResourceID=453056898], (03.11.2005.)

72. Cheng S., Liu Y., Wang S.: Progress in Risk Measurement. Advanced Modelling and Optimization, Vol. 6., No. 1., 2004. 20 p.

73. Chou Y. R.: Volatility Peristence and Stock Valuations: Some Empirical Evidence Using Garch. Journal of Applied Econometrics, Vol. 3., No. 4., Oct/Dec 1988. p. 279-294.

74. Christie A. A.: The Stochastic Behavior of Common Stock Variance: Value, Leverage and Interest Rate Effects. Journal of Financial Economics 10, 1982. p. 407-432.

75. Christoffersen P.: Evaluating Interval Forecasts. International Economic Review, 1998. 28 p.
[URL: http://www.gloriamundi.org/picsresources/peterc.pdf], (25.02.2006.)

76. Christoffersen P., Hahn J., Inoue A.: Testing and Comparing Value-at-Risk Measures, Montreal: CIRANO, Paper 2001s-03, 2001. 22 p.

77. Clark K. P.: A Subordinated Stochastic Process Model with Finite Variance for Speculative Prices. Econometrica 41, 1973. p. 135-156.

78. Connor G.: A structured GARCH model of daily equity return volatility. May 2001. 22 p. [URL: http://fmg.lse.ac.uk/pdfs/dp370.pdf], (11.07.2006.)

79. Cont R., Potters M., Bouchaud J.P.: Scaling in stock market data: Stable laws and beyond. Mimeo, Centre d'Etudes de Saclay and Universite de Nice, 1997. 11 p.

80. Constantinos S.: Regulating Market Risk in Banks: A Comparison of Alternative Regulatory Regimes. The World Bank, Financial Sector Development Department, Policy Research Working Paper 1692, Dec 1996. 48 p.

81. Crnkovic C., Drachman J.: Quality control. Risk, Vol. 9., No. 9., 1996. p. 139-143.

82. Crouhy M., Galai D., Mark R.: Risk Management. New York: McGraw Hill, 2001. 717 p.

83. Culp C., Miller M.H., Neves A.M.P.: Value at risk: uses and abuses. Journal of Applied Corporate Finance 10, 1997. p. 26-38.

84. Danielsson J.: The emperor has no clothes: Limits to risk modelling. Mimeo, London School of Economics, Sep. 2001. 30 p.

85. Danielsson J., de Haan L., Peng L., de Vries G. C.: Using a Bootstrap Method to Choose the Sample Fraction in Tail Index Estimation. Journal of Mathematical Analysis and its Applications, Jan 1999. 24 p.

86. Danielsson J., de Vries G. C.: Beyond the Sample: Extreme Quantile and Probability Estimation. London: London school of Economics, Discussion Paper 298, Jul 1998. 39 p.

87. Davidson R., MacKinnon G. J.: Econometric Theory and Methods. Oxford: Oxford University Press, 2004. 750 p.

88. Day E. T., Lewis M. C.: Stock Market Volatility and the Information Content of Stock Index Options. Journal of Econometrics 52, 1992. p. 267-287.

89. De Raaji G., Raunig B.: A Comparison of Value at Risk Approaches and Their Implications for Regulators. Oesterreichische Nationalbank, Focus on Austria, No. 4., 1998. p. 57-71.

90. Deans J.: Backtesting. in Lore M. and Borodovsky L. (editors): The Professional's Handbook of Financial Risk Management. Oxford: Butterworth-Heinemann, 2000. p. 261-289.

91. Diebold X. F., Hickman A., Inoue A., Schuermann T.: Converting 1-Day Volatility to h-Day Volatility: Scaling by $\sqrt{h}$ is Worse than You Think. Wharton, Working paper series 97-34, Jul 1997. 18 p.

92. Diebold X. F., Hahn J., Tay S. A.: Multivariate Density Forecast Evaluation and Calibration in Financial Risk Management: High-Frequency Returns on Foreign Exchange. The Review of Economics and Statistics, Vol. 81., No. 4., Nov 1999. p. 661-673.

93. Dimson E., Marsh R. P.: Capital Requirements for Securities Firms. The Journal of Finance, Vol. 50., No. 3., 1995. p. 821-851.

94. Dimson E., Marsh R. P.: Stress Tests of Capital Requirements. Journal of Banking and Finance, 21, 1997. p. 1515-1546.

95. Ding Z., Engle F. R., Granger C.: A long memory property of stock markets returns and a new model. Journal of Empirical Finance 1, 1993. p. 83-106.

96. Dowd K.: A VaR approach to risk-return analysis. Journal of Portfolio Management 25, 1999. p. 60-67.

97. Dowd K.: Accounting for value at risk. Journal of Risk Finance 2, 2000. p. 51-58.

98. Dowd K.: Measuring market risk. New York, John Wiley & Sons, 2002. 370 p.

99. Drost C. F., Nijman E. T.: Temporal Aggregation of Garch Processes. Econometrica, Vol. 61., No. 4., Jul 1993. p. 909-927.

100. Duan J.C.: Augmented GARCH (p,q) process and its diffusion limit. Journal of Econometrics, 79, 1997. p. 97-127.

101. Eberlein E., Keller U., Prause K.: New insights into smile, mispricing and value at risk: the hyperbolic model. Journal of Business 71, 1998. p. 371-406.

102. Efron B.: Bootstrap Methods: Another Look at the Jackknife. Annals of Statistics, 7, 1979. p. 1-26.

103. Embrechts P., Resnick I. S., Samorodnitsky G.: Extreme value theory as a risk management tool. „Extremes and Insurance" XXVIII-th International ASTIN Colloquium, Cairns, 1997. 22 p.

104. Embrechts P.: Extreme Value Theory: Potential and Limitations as an integrated risk management tool. ETH Zurich, Jan 2000. 12 p.
[URL: http://www.gloriamundi.org/picsresources/peevtpot.pdf], (12.09.2005.)

105. Enders W.: Applied Econometric Time Series. 2nd edition, New York, John Wiley & Sons, 2004. 460 p.

106. Engle F. R.: Autoregressive conditional heteroscedasticity with estimates of the variance of United Kingdom inflation. Econometrica, 50, 1982. p. 987-1008.

107. Engle F. R.: ARCH selected readings. Oxford, Oxford University Press, 2004. 403 p.

108. Engle F. R.: Wald, Likelihood ratio, and Lagrange multiplier tests in Econometrics. Chapter 13, in Handbook of Econometrics, Vol 2, Edited by Z. Griliches and M.D. Intriligator, Elsevier Science Publishers, 1984. p. 776-826.

109. Engle F. R., Lilien M. D., Robins P. R.: Estimating Time-varying Risk Premia in the Term Structure: The ARCH-M Model. Econometrica, 55, 1987. p. 391-407.

110. Engle F. R., Takatoshi I., Lin W.L.: Meteor Showers or Heat Waves? Heteroskedastic Intra-Daily Volatility in the Foreign Exchange Market. Econometrica, 58/3, 1990. p. 525-542.

111. Engle F. R., Lee G.J. G.: Long run volatility forecasting for individual stocks in a one factor model. University of California at San Diego, Economics Working Paper Series, Jul 1993a. 23 p.

112. Engle F. R., Lee G.J. G.: A permanent and transitory component model of stock return volatility. University of California at San Diego, Economics Working Paper Series, Nov 1993b. 29 p.

113. Engle F. R., Ng K. V.: Measuring and testing the impact of news on volatility. Journal of Finance, Vol. 48., No.5., Dec 1993. p. 1749-1778.

114. Engle F. R., Mezrich J.: Grappling with GARCH. Risk, Vol. 8., No. 9., Sep 1995. p. 112-117.

115. Evans M., Hastings N., Peacock B.: Statistical Distributions. Third Edition, John Wiley & Sons, New York, 2000. 221 p.

116. Fallon C. E., Sabogal S. J.: Is historical VaR a reliable tool for relative risk measurement in the Columbian stock market?: An empirical analysis using the coefficient of variation. Ponificia Universidad Javeriana, 2004. 18 p.
[URL:http://cuadernosadministracion.javeriana.edu.co/pdfs/6_27.pdf](12.03.2006.)

117. Fallon W.: Calculating Value-at-Risk. Wharton, Working paper series 96-49, Jan 1996. 37 p.

118. Fama F. E.: The Behavior of Stock Market Prices. Journal of Business, 38, 1965. p. 34-105.

119. Finger C. C.: Testing RiskMetrics volatility forecasts on emerging markets data. RiskMetrics Monitor, 1996. p. 3-19.

120. Finger C. C.: A methodology to stress correlations. RiskMetrics Monitor, 1997. p. 3-11.

121. Fornari F., Mele A.: Recovering the probability density function of asset prices using GARCH as diffusion approximations. Journal of empirical finance, 8, 2001. p. 83-110.

122. Frachot A.: Factor Models of Domestic and Foreign Interest Rates with Stochastic Volatilities. Mathematical Finance, 5, 1995. p. 167-185.

123. Franses P. H., van Dijk D.: Forecasting Stock Market Volatility Using (Non-Linear) GARCH Models. Journal of Forecasting, 15, 1996. p. 229-235.

124. Freedman D.A., Peters S.C.: Bootstrapping a regression equation: Some empirical results. Journal of American Statistical Association, 79, 1984. p. 97-106.

125. French R. K., Roll R.: Stock Return Variances: The Arrival of Information and the Reaction of Traders. Journal of Financial Economics, 17, 1986. p. 5-26.

126. Galac T., Dukić L.: Rezultati četvrtog HNB-ova anketiranja banaka, Croatian National Bank, Aug 2005. 64 p.

127. Gallo M. G., Pacini B.: The effects of trading activity on market volatility. The European Journal of Finance, 6, 2000. p. 163-175.

128. Galluccio S., Bouchaud J.P., Potters M.: Rational decisions, random matrices and spin glasses. Physica A, No. 259., 1998. p. 449-456.

129. Gibson S. M., Pritsker M.: Improving Grid-based Methods for Estimating Value at Risk of Fixed-Income Portfolios. Board of Governors of the Federal Reserve System Working Paper Series, 2000. 29 p. [URL:http://www.federalreserve.gov/pubs/feds/2000/200025/200025pap.pdf], (28.11.2004.)

130. Gilli M., Këllezi E.: An Application of Extreme Value Theory for Measuring Risk. 2003. 24 p. [URL: http://www.gloriamundi.org/picsresources/mgek.pdf], (28.06.2005.)

131. Giot P., Laurent S.: Market Risk in Commodity Markets: A VaR Approach. Nov 2002. 25 p.

132. Giot P., Laurent S.: Value-at-Risk for Long and Short Trading Positions. Journal of Applied Econometrics, Vol. 18., 2003. p. 641-664

133. Giot P., Laurent S.: Modelling Daily Value-at-Risk Using Realized Volatility and ARCH Type Models. Journal of Empirical Finance, 11, 2004. p. 379-398.

134. Glosten R. L., Jagannathan R., Runkle E. D.: On the Relation between the Expected Value and the Volatility of the Nominal Excess return on Stocks.

Federal Reserve Bank of Minneapolis, Research Department Staff Report No. 157, Aug 1993. p. 1-36.

135. Gołajewska M., Wyczański P. (Editors): Stability and Structure of Financial Systems in CEC5. National Bank of Poland, Warsaw, May 2002. 64 p.

136. Gourieroux C.: ARCH Models and Financial Applications. New York, Springer, 1997. 228 p.

137. Gourieroux C., Laurent J.P., Scaillet O.: Sensitivity analysis of Value at Risk. Journal of Empirical Finance, 7, 2000. p. 225-245.

138. Gourieroux C., Jasiak J.: Financial Econometrics: Problems, Models and Methods. New Jersey, Princeton University Press, 2001. 513 p.

139. Green H. W.: Econometric Analysis. 5th edition, New Jersey, Prentice Hall, 2003. 1026 p.

140. Guermat C., Harris D.F. R.: Forecasting value at risk allowing for time variation in the variance and kurtosis of portfolio returns. International Journal of Forecasting, 18, Elsevier, 2002. p. 409-419.

141. Gujarati N. D.: Basic Econometrics. 4th edition, New York, McGraw Hill, 2003. 1002 p.

142. Haas M., Mittnik S., Paolella S. M.: Modelling and Predicting Market Risk with Laplace-Gaussian Mixture Distributions. CFS Working paper, No. 2005/11, Mar 2005. 36 p.

143. Hagerud E. G.: A Smooth Transition ARCH model for Asset returns, Working Paper Series in Economics and Finance, No.162, Nov 1996. p. 1-26.

144. Hagerud E. G.: Specification Test for Asymmetric GARCH, Working Paper Series in Economics and Finance, No.163, Jan 1997a. p. 1-32.

145. Hagerud E. G.: Modelling Nordic Stock Returns with Asymmetric GARCH Models. Working Paper Series in Economics and Finance, No.164., 1997b. p. 1-26.

146. Hall M.: The Measurement and Assessment of Market Risk: A Comparison of the European Commission and Basic Committee Approach. Banca Nationale Del Lavoro, Quarterly Review No. 194., Sep 1995. 7 p.

147. Hall P.: Methodology and Theory for the Bootstrap. in Handbook of Econometrics, Vol. 4., Engle R.F., McFadden D.L. (ed.); Amsterdam, Elsevier Science, 1994. p. 2342-2381.

148. Hamilton D. J.: Time Series Analysis. New Jersey, Princeton University Press, 1994. 799 p.

149. Hamilton D. J., Susmel R.: Autoregressive conditional heteroskedasticity and changes in the regime. Journal of Econometrics, 64, 1994. p. 307-333.

150. Härdle W., Hlavka Z., Stahl G.: On the Appropriateness of Inappropriate VaR Models. SFB Discussion Paper 2006-003, 2006. 26 p.

151. Hartz C., Mittnik S., Paolella S. M.: Accurate Value-at-Risk Forecasting Based on the (good old) Normal-GARCH Model. National Centre of Competence in Research Financial Valuation and Risk Management Working Paper No. 333, Jul 2006. 28 p.

152. Harvey R. C., Whaley E. R.: Market volatility predictions and the efficiency of the S&P 100 index option market. Journal of financial economics, 31, 1992. p. 43-73.

153. Hendricks D.: Evaluation of Value-at-Risk Models using Historical data. FRBNY Economic Policy Review, Apr 1996. p. 39-69.

154. Hendricks D., Hirtle B.: Bank Capital Requirements for Market Risk: The Internal Models Approach. FRBNY Economic Policy Review, Dec 1997. p. 1-12.

155. Hentschel L.: All in the family: Nesting symmetric and asymmetric GARCH models. Journal of Financial Economics 39, Vol. 39., No. 1., Sep 1995. p. 71-104.

156. Heynen R., Kemna A., Vorst T.: Analysis of the term structure of implied volatilities. Journal of Financial Quantitative Analysis, Vol. 29., No. 1., 1994. p. 31-56.

157. Higgins L. M., Bera K. A.: A class of nonlinear ARCH models. International Econom. Review Vol. 33, No. 1., 1992. p. 137-158.

158. Holton A. G.: Simulating Value-at-Risk with Weighted Scenarios. Risk, Vol. 11., No. 5., May 1998. p. 60-63.

159. Holton A. G.: History of Value-at-Risk: 1922-1998. Contingency Analysis, Working paper, Jul 2002. 27 p.

160. Holton A. G.: Value-at-Risk: Theory and Practice. San Diego, Academic Press, 2003. 405 p.

161. Hongwei T., Wei Z.: A New Method to compute Value-at-Risk: Extreme Value Theory. School of Management, Tianjin University, 1999. 11 p.

162. Hoppe R.: VaR and the unreal world. Risk 11, 1998. p. 45-50.

163. Hoppe R.: Finance is not physics. Risk Professional, Vol. 1., No. 7., Oct 1999. 5 p.
[URL: http://www.gloriamundi.org/picsresources/rbh3.pdf], (11.07.2005.)

164. Hsieh A. D.: Modeling Heteroscedasticity in Daily Foreign Exchange Rates. Journal of Business & Economic Statistics. Vol. 7., No. 3., Jul 1989. p. 307-317.

165. Hsieh A. D.: Chaos and Nonlinear Dynamics: Application to Financial Markets. Journal of Finance, 46, 1991. p. 1839-1877.

166. Hsieh A. D.: Implications of Nonlinear Dynamics for Financial Risk Management. Journal of Finance and Quantitative Analysis, 28, 1993. p. 41-64.

167. Huisman R., Koedjik K.G., Pownall R.A.J.: VaR-x: fat tails in financial risk management. Journal of Risk 1, 1998. p. 47-61.

168. Hull J., White A.: Incorporating volatility updating into the Historical Simulation method for Value at Risk. Journal of Risk, 1998a. 19 p.

169. Hull J., White A.: Value at Risk when daily changes in market variables are not normally distributed. Journal of Derivatives, 1998b. p. 9-19.

170. Ibragimov R.: Portfolio Diversification and Value at Risk under Thick-Tailedness. Yale ICF Working Paper No. 05-10, May 2005. 23 p.

171. Jackson P.: Risk Measurement and Capital Requirementsfor Banks. Bank of England Quarterly Bulletin, May 1995. p. 177-184.

172. Jackson P.: Bank Capital Standards: New Basel Accord. Bank of England Quaterly Bulletin, Spring 2001. p. 55-63.

173. Jackson P., Maude J. D., Perraudin W.: Bank Capital and Value at Risk. Bank of England, 1998. 37 p. [URL:http://www.bankofengland.co.uk/publications/workingpapers/wp79.pdf], (11.07.2005.)

174. Jackson P., Perraudin W.: Introduction: Banks and systemic risk. Journal of Banking and Finance, 26, 2002. p. 819-823.

175. Jackson P., Perraudin W., Saporta V.: Regulatory and economic solvency standards for internationally active banks. Journal of Banking and Finance, 26, 2002. p. 953-976.

176. Jia J., Dyer J.S.: A standard measure of risk and risk-value models. Management Science 42, 1996. p. 1691-1705.

177. Johnston J., DiNardo J.: Econometric methods. 4th edition, New York, McGraw-Hill, 1997. 531 p.

178. Jorion P.: In defense of VaR. Derivatives Strategy 2, 1997. p. 20-23.

179. Jorion P.: Value at Risk, The New Benchmark for Managing Financial Risk. 2nd edition, New York, McGraw Hill, 2001. 544 p.

180. Ju X., Pearson D. N.: Using value-at-risk to control risk taking: how wrong can you be?. Journal of Risk, Vol.1., No. 2., 1999. p. 5-36.

181. Karanasos M., Kim J.: Moments of the ARMA-EGARCH model. Econometrics Journal, Vol. 6, 2003. p. 146–166.

182. Kendall M.G., Stuart A.: The Advanced Theory of Statistics. Vol 2: Inference and Relationship. Third Edition, London, Griffin, 1973. 496 p.

183. Kennedy P.: A guide to econometrics. 5th edition, Cambridge, MIT Press, 2003. 623 p.

184. Kim J., Finger C. C.: A stress test to incorporate correlation breakdown. RiskMetrics Journal, 2000. p. 61-75.

185. Kohler H.: Statistics for Business and Economics. Third Edition, HarperCollins College Publishers, 1994. 1043 p.

186. Kolb W. R.: Futures, options and swaps. 4th edition, Cornwall, Blackwell Publishing, 2003. 887 p.

187. Koponen I.: Analytic approach to the problem of convergence of truncated Lévy flights towards the Gaussian stochastic process, Physical Review E, Vol. 52., No. 1., 1995. p. 1197-1199.

188. Kritzman M., Rich D.: The Mismeasurement of Risk. Financial Analysts Journal, Vol. 58., No. 3., May/Jun 2002. p. 91-99.

189. Kroner F. K., Kneafsey P. D., Claessens S.: Forecasting Volatility in Commodity Markets. The World Bank, International Economics Department, Debt and International Finance Division, Policy Research Working Paper 1226, Nov 1993. 28 p.

190. Künsch H.R.: The Jackknife and the Bootstrap for General Stationary Observations. Annals of Statistics 17, 1989. p. 1217-1241.

191. Kupiec P.: Techniques for verifying the accuracy of risk management models. Journal of Derivatives, 3, 1995. p. 73-84.

192. Kupiec P., O'Brien J.: A Pre-commitment Approach to Capital requirements for Market risk. Federal Reserve Bank of Chicago, Journal Proceedings, May 1995. p. 552-562.

193. Kupiec P., O'Brien J.: The Pre-commitment Approach: Using Incentives to set Market risk Capital requirements. Federal Reserve Board, FEDS Working paper, 1997. 52 p.

194. Lagnado R., Delianedis G., Tikhonov S.: Monte Carlo simulation of non-normal processes. MKIRisk Discussion Paper, MKIRisk, London, 2000. 11 p.

195. Laloux L., Cizeau P., Bouchaud J.P., Potters M.: Noise Dressing of Financial Correlation Matrices. Physical Review letters, Vol. 83., No. 7., Aug 1999. p. 1467-1470.

196. Lamoureux G. C., Lastrapes D. W.: Heteroskedasticity in Stock Return Data: Volume versus GARCH Effects. The Journal of Finance, Vol. 45., No. 1., Mar 1990. p. 221-229.

197. Laubsch A.: Estimating index tracking error for equity portfolios. RiskMetrics Monitor, 1996. p. 34-41.

198. Lehar A., Scheicher M., Schittenkopf C.: GARCH vs. stochastic volatility: Option pricing and risk management. Journal of Banking Finance 26, 2002. [URL: http://www.gloriamundi.org/picsresources/lamscs.pdf], (10.01.2006.)

199. Lehnert T., Wolff C.P. C.: Modeling Scale-Consistent VaR with the Truncated Levy Flight. LIFE Working Paper 01-001, Dec 2001. 21 p.

200. LeSage P. J.: The Theory and Practice of Spatial Econometrics. 1999. 296 p. [URL: http://www.econ.utoledo.edu], (11.01.2005.)

201. LeSage P. J.: Applied Econometrics using MATLAB. 1999. 333 p. [URL: http://www.econ. utoledo.edu], (11.01.2005.)

202. Lewis E. E.: Methods of Statistical analysis in Economics and business. Boston, Houghton Miflin Company, 1973. 686 p.

203. Li W.K., Ling S., McAleer M.: A survey of recent Theoretical results for time series models with GARCH errors. The Institute of Social and Economic Research, Osaka University, Discussion paper No. 545, Jun 2001. 36 p.

204. Lillo F., Mantegna N. R.: Variety and volatility in financial markets. Physical review, Vol. 62., No. 5., Nov 2000. p. 6126-6134.

205. Linsmeier J. T., Pearson D. N.: Value at Risk. Financial Analysts Journal, Vol. 56., No. 2., Mar/Apr 2000. p. 47-67.

206. Lintner J.: The valuation of risk assets and the selection of risky investments in stock portfolios and capital budgets. Review of Economics and Statistics, 47, 1965. p. 13-37.

207. Lopez A. J.: Methods for evaluating value-at-risk estimates. Federal Reserve Bank of New York, Economic Policy Review, 2, Oct 1998. p. 3-17.

208. Lopez A. J.: Regulatory evaluation of value-at-risk models. Journal of Risk 1, 1999. p. 37-64.

209. Lucas A.: A note on optimal estimation from a risk management perspective under possibly misspecified tail behavior. Journal of Business and Economic Statistics 18, 2000. p. 31-39.

210. Lucchetti R., Rossi E.: Artificial regression testing in the GARCH-in-mean model. Econometrics Journal 8, 2005. p. 306-322.

211. Lumsdaine R.L.: Finite sample properties of the maximum likelihood estimation in GARCH(1,1) and IGARCH(1,1) models: A Monte Carlo investigation. Journal of Business Economics and Statistics, Vol. 13., No. 1., 1995. p. 1-10.

212. Maddala G.S., Li H.: Bootstrap based tests in financial models. in Handbook of Statistics, Vol. 14., Maddala G.S., Rao C.R. (ed.); Amsterdam, Elsevier Science, 1996. p. 463-488.

213. Madhavan A., Yang J.: Practical Risk Analysis. The Journal of Portfolio Management, Vol. 30., No. 1., 2003. p. 73-86.

214. Magnusson G., Andonov S.: Basel Capital adequacy ratio and the Icelandic banking sector. IOES working paper series, May 2002. 51 p.

215. Mandelbrot B.: The Variation of Certain Speculative Prices. Journal of Business, 36, 1963. p. 394-419.

216. Mandelbrot B.: Fractals and Scaling in Finance: Discontinuity, Concentration, Risk. New York, Springer, 1997. 551 p.

217. Manganelli S., Engle F. R.: Value at Risk models in Finance. ECB working paper series, No. 75., Aug 2001. 40 p.

218. Mantegna R.N., Stanley H.E.: An Introduction to Econophysics: Correlations and Complexity in Finance. Cambridge: Cambridge University Press, 2000. 145 p.

219. Markowitz M. H.: Portfolio Selection, Journal of Finance, Vol. 7., No. 1., 1952. p. 77-91.

220. Markowitz M. H.: The early history of portfolio theory: 1600-1960, Financial Analysts Journal, Vol. 55., No. 4., 1999. p. 5-16.

221. Marrison C.: The Fundamentals of Risk measurement. New York, McGraw Hill, 2002. 415 p.

222. Marshall C., Siegel M.: Value at risk: Implementing a risk measurement standard. Journal of Derivatives 4, 1997. p. 91-110.

223. Masry E., Mielniczuk J.: Local linear regression estimation for time series with long range dependence. Stochastic Processes and their Applications, 82, 1999. p. 173-193.

224. Mausser H., Rosen D.: Beyond VaR: From measuring Risk to managing Risk. Algo Research Quaterly, Vol. 1., No.2., Dec 1998. p. 5-20.

225. McCullough B., Renfro C.: Benchmarks and software standards: a case study of GARCH procedures. Journal of Economic and Social Measurement 25, 1998. p.59-71.

226. McDonald B. J.: Probability Distributions for Financial Models. in G.S. Maddala and C.R. Rao, Handbook of Statistics, Vol. 14., Elsevier Science, 1996. p. 427-461.

227. McNeil J. A.: Extreme Value Theory for Risk Managers. ETH Zurich, May 1999. 22 p.
[URL: http://www.gloriamundi.org/picsresources/maevt.pdf], (01.05.2005.)

228. McNeil J. A., Frey R.: Estimation of tail-related risk for heteroskedastic financial time series: an extreme value approach. Journal of Empirical Finance 7, 2000. p. 271-300.

229. McNeil J. A., Frey R., Embrechts P.: Quantitative Risk Management; Concepts, Techniques and Tools. New Jersey, Princeton University Press, 2005. 538 p.

230. Merton R.C.: On the pricing of corporate debt: the risk structure of interest rates. Journal of Finance 42, 1974. p. 463-470.

231. Meyfredi J.C.: History of the Risk Concept and Risk Modeling. EDHEC Risk and Asset Management Research Centre. 2004. 9 p.

232. Meyfredi J.C.: History of the Risk Concept and Risk Modeling. EDHEC Risk and Asset Management Research Centre. Oct 2004. 9 p.

233. Mills C. T.: The Econometric Modelling of Financial Time Series. 2nd edition, Cambridge, Cambridge University Press, 2004. 372 p.

234. Mittnik S., Paolella M. S.: Conditional Density and Value-at-Risk Prediction of Asian Currency Exchange Rates. Journal of Forecasting, 19, 2000. p. 313-333.

235. Mittnik S., Paolella M. S., Rachev S.T.: Diagnosis and treating the fat tails in financial returns data. Journal of Empirical Finance 7, 2000. p. 389-416.

236. Moreno R.: The changing nature of risks facing banks. in "The banking system in emerging economies: how much progress has been made?", BIS papers No. 28, Aug 2006. p. 67-98.

237. Mossin J.: Equilibrium in a capital asset market. Econometrica, 34, 1966. p. 768-783.

238. Taleb N.: Dynamic Hedging: Managing Vanilla and Exotic Options. New York, John Wiley & Sons, 1997a. 506 p.

239. Taleb N.: Against VaR. Derivatives Strategy 2, 1997b. p. 21-26.

240. Nelson B. D.: Conditional Heteroskedasticity in Asset Returns: A New Approach. Econometrica, Vol. 59., No. 2., Mar 1991. p. 347-370.

241. Nelson B. D.: Filtering and Forecasting with Misspecified ARCH Models: Getting the Right Variance with the Wrong Model. Journal of Econometrics, 52, 1992. p. 61-90.

242. Nelson B. D., Cao Q. C.: Inequality Constraints in the Univariate GARCH Model. Journal of Business & Economic Statistics. Vol. 10., No. 2., Apr 1992. p. 229-235.

243. Nelson B. D., Foster P. D.: Filtering and Forecasting with Misspecified ARCH models II: Making the Right Forecast with the Wrong Model. NBER Technical Working Paper Series, No. 132., Dec 1992. 50 p.

244. Pafka S., Kondor I.: Evaluating the RiskMetrics Methodology in Measuring Volatility and Value-at-Risk in Financial Markets. Mar 2001. 7 p. [URL: http://www.gloriamundi.org/picsresources/evalrm.pdf], (11.02.2005.)

245. Pagan R A., Schwert G. W.: Alternative Models for Conditional Stock Volatility. Journal of Econometrics, 45, 1990. p. 267-290.

246. Pallotta M., Zenti R.: Risk analysis for asset managers: Historical Simulation, the Bootstrap approach and Value at Risk calculation. RAS Asset Management, 2000. 44 p.

[URL: http://www.gloriamundi.org/picsresources/rzmp.pdf], (12.11.2004.)

247. Palm F.C.: GARCH Models of Volatility. in Handbook of Statistics, Vol. 14., Maddala G.S., Rao C.R. (ed.); Amsterdam, Elsevier Science, 1996. p. 209-240.

248. Papageorgiou A., Traub J.: Beating Monte Carlo. Risk, Vol 9., No. 6., Jun 1996. p. 63-65.

249. Parrondo M.R. J.: Calculation of the Value at Risk in emerging markets. Santander Investments report, Feb 1997. 38 p.

250. Phelan J. M.: Probability and Statistics Applied to the Practice of Financial Risk Management: The Case of JP Morgan's RiskMetrics. Wharton, Working paper series 95-19, 1995. 56 p.

251. Pindyck S. R., Rubinfeld L. D.: Econometric models and economic forecasts. 4th edition, Singapore, Irwin/McGraw Hill, 1998. 634 p.

252. Plerou V., Gopikrishnan P., Rosenow B., Nunes Amaral A. L., Stanley H. E.: Universal and Nonuniversal Properties of Cross Correlations in Financial Time Series. Physical Review letters, Vol. 83., No. 7., Aug 1999. p. 1471-1474.

253. Ploegmakers H., Schweitzer M., Rad T. A.: Risk Adjusted Performance Measurement and Capital Allocation for Trading Desks within Banks. Managerial Finance, Vol. 3., No. 3., 2000. p. 39-50.

254. Politis D.N., Romano J.P.: The stationary bootstrap. Journal of American Statistical Association, 89, 1994. p. 1303-1313.

255. Potter M. S.: Nonlinear Time Series Modelling: An Introduction. Journal of Economic Surveys, Vol. 13., No. 5.,1999. 30 p.

256. Pritsker M.: The Hidden Dangers of Historical Simulation. Board of Governors of the Federal Reserve System Working Paper Series, 2001. 61 p. [URL: http://www.gloriamundi.org/picsresources/mphd.pdf], (18.10.2004.)

257. Pyle H. D.: Bank Risk Management: Theory. Conference on Risk management and regulation in banking, Jerusalem, May 17-19 1997. 15 p.

258. Robinson M. P.: Testing for strong serial correlation and dynamic conditional heteroskedasticity in multiple regression. Journal of Econometrics 47, 1991. p. 67-84.

259. Rockafellar R. T., Uryasev S.: Optimization of Conditional Value-at-Risk. Center for Applied Optimization, Research Report #99-4, Sep 1999. 26 p.

260. Rockafellar R. T., Uryasev S.: Conditional Value-at-Risk for General loss distribution. University of Florida, Gainesville, Center for Applied Optimization Research Report #2001-5, Jul 2001. 34 p.

261. Roy D. A.: Safety first and the holding of assets, Econometrica 20, 1952. p. 431-449.

262. Santoso W.: Value at Risk: An Approach to Calculating Market Risk. Banking Research and Regulation Directorate, Bank Indonesia, Dec 2000. 43 p.

263. Saunders A., Cornett M. M.: Financial Institutions Management: A Risk Management Approach. New York, McGraw Hill Irwin, 2003. 778 p.

264. Schwert G. W.: Why Does Stock Market Volatility Change Over Time. Journal of Finance, 44, 1989a. p. 1115-1153.

265. Schwert G. W.: Business Cycles, Financial Crises, and Stock Volatility. Carnegie-Rochester Conference Series on Public Policy, 39, 1989b. p. 83-126.
266. Schwert G. W.: Stock Market Volatility. Financial Analysts Journal, May/Jun 1990. p. 23-34.
267. Schwert G. W., Seguin J. P.: Heteroskedasticity in Stock Returns. Journal of Finance, Vol. 45., No. 4., Sep 1990. p. 1129-1155.
268. Sentana E.: Quadratic ARCH models. Review of Economic Studies, Vol. 62., No. 4., 1995. p. 639–661.
269. Sharpe F. W.: A simplified model for portfolio analysis. Management Science, 9, 1963, p. 277-293.
270. Sharpe F. W.: Capital asset prices: A theory of market equilibrium under conditions of risk. Journal of Finance, Vol. 19., No. 3., 1964. p. 425-442.
271. Shaw T. W.: Sampling Student's T distribution – use of the inverse cumulative distribution function. The Journal of Computational Finance, Vol. 9., No. 4., 2006. p. 37-73.
272. Shiller J. R.: The Volatility of Stock Market Prices. Science, Vol. 235., No. 4784., Jan 1987. p. 33-37.
273. Shirreff D.: Swap and think, Risk, Vol. 5., No. 3., 1992. p. 29-35.
274. Silverman B.W.: Density Estimation for Statistics and Data Analysis. London, Chapman and Hall, 1986. 176 p.
275. Sinha T., Chamu F.: Comparing Different Methods of Calculating Value at Risk. Instituto Tecnologico Autonomo de Mexico, Jan 2000. 16 p. [URL: http://www.gloriamundi.org/picsresources/tapens.pdf], (11.07.2005.)
276. Soczo C.: Comparison of Capital Requirements Defined by Internal (VaR) Model and Standardized Method. Periodica polytechnica ser. soc. man. sci. Vol. 10., No. 1., 2001. p. 53-66.
277. Šošić I., Serdar V.: Uvod u statistiku. Zagreb, Školska knjiga-Zagreb,1997. 363 p.
278. Tasche D.: Expected Shortfall and Beyond. Technische Universität München, Mar 2002. 18 p. [URL: http://www.gloriamundi.org/picsresources/dt0302.pdf], (28.07.2006.)
279. Taylor S.J.: Modeling stochastic volatility: A review and comparative study. Mathematical Finance, Vol. 4., No. 2., 1994. p. 183-204.
280. Tilman M. L., Brusolilovskiy P.: Measuring predictive accuracy of value-at-risk models: issues, paradigms, and directions. Journal of Risk Finance Vol. 2., No. 3., 2001. p. 83-91.
281. Tobin J.: Liquidity preference as behavior towards risk. The Review of Economic Studies, 25, 1958. p. 65-86.
282. Tompkins G. R., D'Ecclesia L. R.: Unconditional Return Disturbances: A Non Parametric Simulation Approach. Feb 2004. 31 p. [URL: http://www.gloriamundi.org/picsresources/rtrd.pdf], (20.11.2004.)
283. Tsay S. R.: Analysis of Financial Time Series. New York: John Wiley & Sons, 2002. 448 p.
284. Valentinyi-Endrész M.: Structural breaks and financial risk management. Magyar Nemzeti Bank, MNB Working paper 2004/11, 2004. 60 p.

285. Vasicek O.A.: An Equilibrium Characterization of the Term Structure. Journal of Financial Economics 5, Nov 1977. p. 177-188.

286. Venkataraman S.: Value at risk for a mixture of normal distributions: The use of quasi-Bayesian estimation techniques. Federal Reserve Bank of Chicago, Economic perspectives, Mar/Apr 1997. p. 3-13.

287. Vitas D.: The Impact of Regulation on Financial Intermediation. The World Bank, Financial Sector Development Department, Policy Research Working Paper 746 Aug 1991. 40 p.

288. Vose D.: Risk analysis: A quantitative guide. 2nd edition, New York, John Wiley & Sons, 2000. 418 p.

289. Watson J. C., Billingsley P., Croft D. J., Huntsberger V. D.: Statistics for Management and Economics. 4th edition, Boston, Allyn and Bacon, 1990. 992 p.

290. Weston S., Gray B.: The Supervisory Treatment of Banks' Market Risk. Reserve Bank of Australia, Research Discussion Paper 9408, Dec 1994. 38 p.

291. Wilson T.: Infinite Wisdom, Risk, Vol. 6., No. 6., 1993. p. 37-45.

292. Wilson B. H., Turcotte H. L., Halpern D.: Advanced Mathematics and Mechanics Applications using Matlab. 3rd edition, New York, Chapman & Hall/CRC, 2003. 616 p.

293. Wong, C.S. M., Cheng, Y.W., Wong, Y.P. C.: Market risk management of banks: Implications from the accuracy of VaR forecasts, Journal of Forecasting, 22, 2002. 19 p.
    [URL: http://www.gloriamundi.org/picsresources/mwwccw.pdf], (17.04.2005.)

294. Wright H. J., Bollerslev T.: High frequency data, frequency domain inference and volatility forecasting. Board of Governors of the Federal Reserve System Working Paper Series, Oct 1999. 27 p.

295. Yamai Y., Yoshiba T.: On the Validity of Value-at-Risk: Comparative Analyses with Expected-Shortfall. Bank of Japan, Institute of Monetary and Economic studies, Jan 2002a. p. 57-86.

296. Yamai Y., Yoshiba T.: Comparative Analyses of Expected Shortfall and Value-at-Risk under Market Stress. CGFS conference, Vol. 2., Part 14., Oct 2002b. 70 p.

297. Yang Y. W. et al.: Applied Numerical Methods using Matlab. New York: John Wiley & Sons, 2005. 509 p.

298. Yu L.H. P., So K.P. M.: Estimating value at risk with using GARCH models: Can we do better if long memory exists?. 2002. 8 p.
    [URL: http://www.gloriamundi.org/picsresources/mkps3.pdf], (17.04.2005.)

299. Zakoian J. M.: Threshold heteroskedastic models. Journal of Economic Dynamics and Control, 18, 1994. p. 931–955.

300. Zangari P.: A Value-at-Risk analysis of currency exposures. RiskMetrics Monitor, 1996a. p. 26-33.

301. Zangari P.: An improved methodology for measuring VaR. RiskMetrics Monitor, 1996b. p. 7-25.

302. Zangari P.: When is non-normality a problem? The case of 15 time series from emerging markets. RiskMetrics Monitor, 1996c. p. 20-32.

303. Zangari P.: Streamlining the market risk measurement process. RiskMetrics Monitor, 1997a. p. 29-35.

304. Zangari P.: What risk managers should know about mean reversion and jumps in prices. RiskMetrics Monitor, 1997b. p. 12-41.

305. Žiković S.: Implications of Actively Managing Market Risk via Value at Risk Methodology in Commercial banks. 24th International scientific conference on organizational science development "Synergy of Methodologies", Portorož, Republic of Slovenia, 2005a. p. 1446-1454.

306. Žiković S.: Structuring of an optimal portfolio composed of Croatian stocks and measuring the market risk using VaR methodology, Ljubljana, Faculty of Economics, 2005b. 132 p.

307. Žiković S.: Implications of Measuring VaR using Historical simulation; an Example of Zagreb Stock Exchange index – CROBEX. Chapter in the book: Resource Allocation and Institutions: Explorations in Economics, Finance and Law, edited by John Roufagalas, Athens, Athens Institute for Education and Research, 2006a. p. 367-389.

308. Žiković S.: Applying hybrid approach to calculating VaR in Croatia. International Conference of the Faculty of Economics in Sarajevo – "From Transition to Sustainable Development: The Path to European Integration", Sarajevo, Bosnia and Herzegovina, 12. – 13. Aug 2006b. 21 p.

309. Žiković S., Bezić H.: Is historical simulation appropriate for measuring market risk? : A case of countries candidates for EU accession. CEDIMES conference, Ohrid, Macedonia, 23-27. Mar 2006. 20 p.

Sources:

310. Bank of Latvia: Annual reports 2000 – 2005.

311. Bank of Lithuania: Annual reports 2000 – 2005.

312. Bank of Slovenia: Annual reports 2000 – 2005.

313. Banque de France: Annual reports 2000 – 2005.

314. Basel Committee on Banking Supervision: Amendment to the Capital Accord to incorporate Market Risks. Bank for International settlements, Jan 1996a. 54 p.

315. Basel Committee on Banking Supervision: Supervisory framework for the use of "backtesting" in conjunction with the internal models approach to market risk capital requirements. Bank for International settlements, Jan 1996b. 15 p.

316. Basel Committee on Banking Supervision: Sound Practices for Managing Liquidity in Banking Organisations. Feb 2000. 27 p.

317. Basel Committee on Banking Supervision: Working Paper on the treatment of Operational Risk. Bank for International settlements, Sep 2001. 35 p.

318. Basel Committee on Banking Supervision: Quantitative Impact Study 3 Instructions. Bank for International settlements, Oct 2002a. 44 p.

319. Basel Committee on Banking Supervision: Quantitative Impact Study 3 Technical Document. Bank for International settlements, Oct 2002b. 174 p.

320. Basel Committee on Banking Supervision: Sound Practices for the Management and Supervision of Operational Risk. Bank for International settlements, Feb 2003. 14 p.

321. Basel Committee on Banking Supervision: International Convergence of Capital Measurement and Capital Standards – A revised framework. Bank for International settlements, Jun 2004a. 238 p.

322. Basel Committee on Banking Supervision: Bank failures in Mature Economies. Bank for International settlements, Working paper No. 13, Apr 2004b. 66 p.

323. Basel Committee on Banking Supervision: Amendments to the Capital Accord to incorporate market risks. Bank for International settlements, Nov 2005. p. 63.

324. Basel Committee on Banking Supervision: The banking system in emerging economies: how much progress has been made?. BIS papers No. 28, Aug 2006. 382 p.

325. Committee of Chief Risk Officers: Valuation and Risk Metrics. CCRO, 2002. 60 p.

326. Croatian National Bank: Annual reports 2000 – 2005.

327. Czech National Bank: Annual reports 2000 – 2005.

328. Deloitte: 2002 Global Risk Management survey. Deloitte Development LLC, 2002. 17 p.
[URL:http://www.dtti.com/dtt/cda/doc/content/GlobalRiskManagementDP_040303.pdf], (17.11.2006.)

329. Deloitte: 2004 Global Risk Management survey. Deloitte Development LLC, 2004. 46 p.
[URL:http://www.deloitte.com/dtt/cda/doc/content/dtt_financialservices_GlobalRiskManagementSurvey2005_061204-v2.pdf], (17.11.2006.)

330. Deutsche Bundesbank: Annual reports 2000 – 2005.

331. Estonian National Bank: Annual reports 2000 – 2005.

332. Fitch P. Thomas: Dictionary of Banking Terms. 4th edition, New York, Barron's, 2000. 529 p.

333. Hungarian National Bank: Annual reports 2000 – 2005.

334. National Bank of Poland: Annual reports 2000 – 2005.

335. National Bank of Slovakia: Annual reports 2000 – 2005.

336. Oesterreichische Nationalbank: Annual reports 2000 – 2005.

337. PricewaterhouseCoopers: Risk management survey. PricewaterhouseCoopers, 2002. 16 p.
[URL: http://www.pwc.com/images/gx/eng/fs/111802rm.pdf], (17.11.2006.)

338. RiskMetrics: Technical Document. 4th edition, J.P. Morgan/Reuters, 1996. 279 p.

339. http://www.bank.lv/lat/main/all/ (11.11.2008)

340. http://www.banque-france.fr/ (07.06.2008)

341. http://www.bis.org/ (11.01.2009)

342. http://www.bsi.si/ (17.12.2008)

343. http://www.bundesbank.de/ (04.10.2008)
344. http://www.centralbank.gov.cy/nqcontent.cfm?a_id=1 (22.02.2008)
345. http://www.centralbankmalta.com/ (18.03.2008)
346. http://www.cnb.cz/cz/index.html (21.04.2008)
347. http://www.ecb.int/ecb/html/index.en.html (02.11.2008)
348. http://www.eestipank.info/frontpage/et/ (04.11.2008)
349. http://www.hnb.hr/ (03.06.2009)
350. http://www.lb.lt/home/default.asp (07.05.2008)
351. http://www.mnb.hu/Engine.aspx (12.06.2008)
352. http://www.nbp.pl/ (07.09.2008)
353. http://www.nbs.sk/ (07.09.2008)
354. http://www.oenb.at/ (15.09.2008)

www.ingramcontent.com/pod-product-compliance
Lightning Source LLC
Chambersburg PA
CBHW082129210326
41599CB00031B/5919